FIFTH EDITION

CANADIAN CRIMINAL JUSTICE

A PRIMER

FIFTH EDITION

CANADIAN CRIMINAL JUSTICE

A PRIMER

CURT T. GRIFFITHS
SIMON FRASER UNIVERSITY

NELSON EDUCATION
CELEBRATE LIFELONG LEARNING

1914–2014: Nelson Education celebrates 100 years of Canadian publishing

NELSON / EDUCATION

Canadian Criminal Justice: A Primer, Fifth Edition

by Curt T. Griffiths

Vice President, Editorial Higher Education:
Anne Williams

Executive Editor:
Maya Castle

Marketing Manager:
Terry Fedorkiw

Developmental Editor:
Suzanne Simpson Millar

Photo Researcher:
Jessie Coffey

Permissions Coordinator:
Jessie Coffey

Production Service:
MPS Limited

Copy Editor:
Dawn Hunter

Proofreader:
MPS Limited

Indexer:
Edwin Durbin

Design Director:
Ken Phipps

Managing Designer:
Franca Amore

Interior Design:
Carianne Sherriff and Courtney Hellam

Cover Design:
Martyn Schmoll

Cover Image:
"Blue Sky" by Pierre Bellemare

Part Opener/Chapter Opener Image:
Dr.G/Shutterstock.com

Compositor:
MPS Limited

Library and Archives Canada Cataloguing in Publication Data

Griffiths, Curt T. (Curt Taylor), author Canadian criminal justice : a primer / Curt T. Griffiths, Simon Fraser University.—Fifth edition.

First edition written by Alison J. Cunningham.Revision of: Canadian criminal justice : a primer / Curt T. Griffiths. – 4th ed.—Toronto : Nelson Education, c2010.Includes bibliographical references and index.ISBN 978-0-17-652920-8 (pbk.)

1. Criminal justice, Administration of—Canada—Textbooks. I. Title.

HV9960.C2G75 2014
364.971   C2014-900846-5

ISBN-13: 978-0-17-652920-8
ISBN-10: 0-17-652920-9

To Sandra, my partner on the journey of radical amazement

and

To the Bradys and their adventures

past, present, and future

Brief **Contents**

Table of **Contents**

ix

ix

Table of Contents

xii

Acknowledgments

I would like to acknowledge the many people throughout the criminal justice system who have contributed to the ideas and information that have been incorporated into this book. Special thanks to my students in the School of Criminology, whose questions and insights have contributed to the evolution of my thinking about criminal justice. As always, my love and thanks to my life partner, Sandra Snow, for her unwavering support and encouragement.

I would also like to thank the reviewers of the previous edition of the text for their invaluable comments, criticisms, and suggestions:

Dawn Anderson, University of Regina

Marilyn Belle-McQuillan, University of Calgary

Beth De Beer, Douglas College

Alison Dunwoody, University of Alberta

Phil Goodman, University of Toronto at Mississauga

Roland LaHaye, Mount Royal University

John Legault, Fanshawe College

Add a special thanks to Dawn Hunter for her outstanding editing work on the manuscript.

As always, it has been a pleasure to work with the professionals at Nelson: Maya Castle, Susan Calvert, and Suzanne Simpson Millar.

A FINAL WORD

Any attempt to capture the dynamics of the criminal justice system can give no more than a snapshot of a shifting landscape. New legislation, court decisions, and critical events ensure that the criminal justice system will remain in the headlines. The challenge is to be informed on these changes and consider their implications for Canadian society, communities, and individuals.

As always, I encourage feedback on the book generally and on any specific materials in it, errors of fact, and omissions. Feel free to contact me at griffith@sfu.ca with any comments, questions, or suggestions for future editions of the book.

Thanks.

Curt Taylor Griffiths, Ph.D.

Vancouver, British Columbia

February 2014

Introduction

THE GOAL OF THIS BOOK

The Canadian criminal justice system is a complex, dynamic, and ever-changing enterprise. How the various components of the system operate and the extent to which they succeed in preventing and responding to crime and criminal offenders affects not only the general public but criminal justice personnel and offenders as well. This edition of *Canadian Criminal Justice: A Primer*, the fifth, is designed with the same basic objectives as the previous editions: to present in a clear and concise fashion materials on the criminal justice system in Canada and to highlight the key issues surrounding this country's responses to crime and offenders. This book is not an exhaustive examination of all facets of the criminal justice process. Rather, its intent is to present, with broad brushstrokes, information on the structure and operations of the criminal justice system, at the same time identifying some of the more significant challenges and controversies that arise at each stage of the justice process.

In the years since the fourth edition of this book was published, much has changed not only in Canadian society generally but in the arena of crime and criminal justice as well. The criminal justice system in the early 21st century operates in a changing world. The advent of a number of technologies and the emergence of the global community are creating opportunities to develop more effective responses to crime and social disorder, but they are also presenting the justice system with significant challenges. There is little doubt that the 9/11 terrorist attacks on the United States ushered in a new era in which security and safety have assumed even more importance. These attacks, and the responses of Canada and other Western governments to what has become a pervasive threat of terrorism, have also brought to the fore the inherent tension between the rights of citizens and the requirements of due process on the one hand and the need to protect and safeguard communities and their residents on the other. In the face of increasing global uncertainty, these types of issues will likely continue to present Canadians, their politicians, and the criminal justice system with difficult challenges and choices. The increasing diversity of Canadian society is also challenging the criminal law and the criminal justice process.

There has also been a discernible shift toward a "get tough" approach to crime and criminal offenders, including legislation setting out more mandatory minimum sentences and restrictions on conditional release. Whether this change will have the intended effect remains to be determined, although the experience from the United States, which adopted a similar approach over a decade ago, suggests this approach may not.

Another key feature of criminal justice in the early 21st century are discussions about the economics of criminal justice, that is, whether the system is sustainable in a time of the fiscal crises of governments. Reductions in resources may provide the catalyst for innovation and reforms in the justice system.

Increasing concerns about public safety and security have often overshadowed other developments in the justice system. Recent years have witnessed a continued expansion of restorative and community justice programs, a continuing evolution of community policing, increasing protections and rights for the victims of crime, and innovative correctional programs for female offenders. Problem-solving courts are providing an alternative way to address the needs of specialized populations. On the less positive side, there continues to be considerable disparity in the sentences meted out in the criminal courts; public confidence in the criminal justice system (with the exception of the police) remains rather low; Aboriginal people continue to be greatly over-represented at all stages of the justice system; and inmate populations continue to face high rates of infectious diseases, including HIV/AIDS and hepatitis C. The provincial, territorial, and federal governments continue to confront fiscal crises that have resulted in significant reductions in monies available for criminal justice programs and services.

CHANGES TO THE FIFTH EDITION

This edition of the book is divided into five parts, which provide students with a clear and logical learning path: Part I, Canadian Criminal Justice: Setting the Framework Part II, The Police; Part III, The Criminal Courts; Part IV, Corrections; and Part V, Reconsidering Criminal Justice.

This edition has a number of new chapters. **Chapter 1, The Foundations of Criminal Justice,** was designed to provide students with a foundation for their study of the Canadian criminal justice system. The intent is to ensure that students understand that the foundation of the criminal justice system has historical antecedents, and the operation of the system has been and is significantly impacted by the *Charter of Rights and Freedoms*. The chapter includes a discussion of the key principles of the rule of law, selected excerpts from the *Charter*, a discussion of the functions of the criminal law in Canadian society, the classification of offences in Canada, perspectives on the origins and application of the criminal law, and how what is against the law changes over time. The latter part of the chapter presents cases illustrating the dynamic and often confusing application or non-application of the criminal law, such as in the case of polygamous families in British Columbia (non-application of the criminal law) and the case of marijuana (sort-of application, sometimes).

Chapter 2, The Structure and Process of Criminal Justice, outlines the framework of Canadian criminal justice. A new box section provides the students with a discussion of the differences between criminology and criminal justice, two notions that are often confused with each other. The two models of criminal justice administration are presented: the due process model and the criminal control model, each providing different explanations for the objectives of the criminal justice system. This discussion sensitizes the students to the fact that the criminal justice system may have a number of different agendas and that a critical view of how the system operates is required. Similarly, there is a discussion of the influences on the justice system, again highlighting to students the dynamic nature of criminal justice and that it is not only the legislative framework that impacts how the system operates and the decisions that are made but also a variety of other factors. Students are informed that the justice system in Canada operates in environments that may have a significant impact on the demands that are made on it and its response. The chapter ends with a look at several current trends in Canadian criminal justice, including the escalating costs of criminal justice and the emergence of a conservative penal populism.

Chapter 3, Crime, Victims, and the Community, was in previous editions of *Canadian Criminal Justice: A Primer*, but had been discontinued in recent editions. It has returned. It includes a discussion of crime patterns and trends, with the caveat that there is a dark figure of crime caused by under-reporting to the police. This dark figure

XV

includes crimes of violence. The discussion of crime victims highlights the continuing plight of victims in the justice system and instances in which victims are revictimized by the actions of criminal justice decision makers. In recent years, the federal Conservative government has taken steps to increase the role of victims in the justice system. Several of these are controversial and include giving victims a role in the plea bargaining process. While the history of the criminal justice system is one of increasing centralization and professionalization, the emergence and spread of social media has injected the community back into the criminal justice equation. This change has led to the rise of community surveillance in which any person with a cellphone can record the actions of police officers on the street, as well as persons involved in law-breaking (including hockey riots). The consequences of this rapid turn of events are discussed.

Chapter 13, Restorative Justice: An Alternative Approach to Crime, Victims, and Offenders, is now presented as a full chapter. Restorative justice (RJ) has become a key feature of the Canadian criminal justice system, and various programs are operating both within the justice system and in conjunction with it. The literature in this area has become so expansive as to require a separate chapter in which students can learn about the basic principles of RJ, the various programs that exist across the country, the issues that surround the use of RJ, and its effectiveness. Rather than having these materials scattered throughout the text, as in previous editions, this chapter brings all the materials on restorative justice together in one place, allowing students to focus on the issues.

Chapter 14, Going Forward: Challenges to and Opportunities for Criminal Justice Reform, was conceived to provide a wrap-up for the text and ideas for moving forward. It sets out a number of challenges for the criminal justice system, including the difficulties the system has had in developing evidence-based practices (policies and programs grounded in research findings), the difficulties in holding many criminal justice system decision makers accountable for their actions, the challenges of doing justice in a diverse society, and a reiteration of the key issues of ethics and accountability in criminal justice. The chapter provides a number of opportunities for criminal justice reform, including the potential for expanding effective criminal justice interventions, mobilizing communities, and using the fiscal crises of governments to develop new models of justice administration. The chapter concludes with some core questions that students should ask in any discussions of the criminal justice system and its various components. This list is designed to send students forward with a critical eye and an informed perspective.

In addition to these new chapters, there have been significant changes throughout the text, including the following.

Chapter 4, The Structure and Roles of the Police, has an updated discussion of the role and activities of the police, a new section on downloading and its impact on police services, and a discussion of the challenges of police work.

Chapter 5, Police Powers and Decision Making, discusses new court cases defining police powers, an At Issue discussion about whether the police should be allowed to collect DNA samples from persons who have not been convicted of a crime and whether the police should adopt body-worn videos, an expanded discussion of the police use of force with persons with mental illnesses, a discussion of the shooting death of Sammy Yatim on a Toronto streetcar in 2013, an expanded discussion of biased policing and racial profiling, and a new section on police ethics and accountability.

Chapter 6, Police Strategies and Operations, includes an updated discussion of community policing and its evolution, new research files summarizing findings on the effectiveness of primary and secondary crime prevention programs, new research files summarizing the findings on the effectiveness of crime attack and crime response strategies, a new section discussing the increasing use of high technology by police and the issues raised by this development, and an updated discussion of the issues surrounding the police and at-risk and vulnerable groups, including marginalized women.

Chapter 7, The Structure and Operation of the Criminal Courts, has an expanded discussion of problem-solving courts and their effectiveness, new materials on judicial ethics and accountability, an extended discussion of the courtroom workgroup, a new discussion of the issues surrounding the appointment of judges and diversity in the judiciary, and new materials on judicial ethics and accountability and on the issue of independent oversight of the judiciary.

Chapter 8, The Prosecution of Criminal Cases, offers an expanded discussion of judicial interim release (bail), new materials on plea bargaining, a revised discussion of fitness to stand trial and excuse-based defences and procedural defences, an expanded discussion of the criminal jury and jury decision making, and updated discussions on case delay and wrongful convictions.

Chapter 9, Sentencing, includes an expanded discussion of the sentencing of Aboriginal offenders and a new research file summarizing the findings on the effectiveness of sentencing.

Chapter 10, Corrections in the Community: Alternatives to Confinement, has a new table comparing probation and parole; an expanded discussion of the role and activities of probation officers; a discussion of the principles of risk, need, and responsivity in probation practice; a new discussion of the pains of probation for offenders; and a new research file summarizing what is known about the effectiveness of alternatives to confinement.

Chapter 11, Correctional Institutions, includes updated materials on special populations in correctional institutions, including female offenders; an updated discussion of the case of Ashley Smith; and a new research file on the effectiveness of correctional treatment interventions.

Chapter 12, Release and Reentry, offers updated and revised materials on conditional release, a new research file on the effectiveness of conditional release, and a new research file on the effectiveness of selected supervision and control strategies.

The entire format of the text has been altered to make it more user-friendly and inviting to the reader.

ANCILLARIES

ABOUT THE NELSON EDUCATION TEACHING ADVANTAGE (NETA)

The **Nelson Education Teaching Advantage (NETA)** program delivers research-based instructor resources that promote student engagement and higher-order thinking to enable the success of Canadian students and educators. To ensure the high quality of these materials, all Nelson ancillaries have been professionally copy edited.

Be sure to visit Nelson Education's **Inspired Instruction** website at www.nelson.com/ inspired/ to find out more about NETA. Don't miss the testimonials of instructors who have used NETA supplements and seen student engagement increase!

- **Planning Your Course:** *NETA Engagement* presents materials that help instructors deliver engaging content and activities to their classes. **NETA Instructor's Manuals** not only identify the topics that cause students the most difficulty but also describe techniques and resources to help students master these concepts. Dr. Roger Fisher's *Instructor's Guide to Classroom Engagement* accompanies every Instructor's Manual.

- **Assessing Your Students:** *NETA Assessment* relates to testing materials. **NETA Test Bank** authors create multiple-choice questions that reflect research-based best practices for constructing effective questions and testing not just recall but also higher-order thinking. Our guidelines were developed by David DiBattista, psychology professor at Brock University and 3M National Teaching Fellow, whose research has focused on multiple-choice testing. All Test Bank authors receive training at workshops conducted by Prof. DiBattista, as do the copy editors assigned to each Test Bank. A copy of *Multiple Choice Tests: Getting Beyond Remembering*, Prof. DiBattista's guide to writing effective tests, is included with every Nelson Test Bank.

- **Teaching Your Students:** *NETA Presentation* has been developed to help instructors make the best use of Microsoft® PowerPoint® in their classrooms. With a clean and uncluttered design developed by Maureen Stone of StoneSoup Consulting, **NETA PowerPoints** features slides with improved readability, more multimedia and graphic materials, activities to use in class, and tips for instructors on the Notes page. A copy of *NETA Guidelines for Classroom Presentations* by Maureen Stone is included with each set of PowerPoint slides.

INSTRUCTOR RESOURCES

All NETA and other key instructor ancillaries are provided on the Instructor Companion Site at www.nelson.com/crimjusticeprimer5e.com, giving instructors the ultimate tool for customizing lectures and presentations.

- **NETA Test Bank:** This resource was written by Sheri Fabian and Aynsley Pescitelli, Simon Fraser University. It includes more than 350 multiple-choice questions written according to NETA guidelines for effective construction and development of higher-order questions. The Test Bank was copyedited by a NETA-trained editor for adherence to NETA best practices. Also included are more than 280 true/false questions, 150 short-answer questions, and 140 essay questions.

  The NETA Test Bank is available in a new, cloud-based platform. **Testing Powered by Cognero®** is a secure online testing system that allows you to author, edit, and manage test bank content from any place you have Internet access. No special installations or downloads are needed, and the desktop-inspired interface, with its drop-down menus and familiar, intuitive tools, allows you to create and manage tests with ease. You can create multiple test versions in an instant, and import or export content into other systems. Tests can be delivered from your learning management system, your classroom, or wherever you want.

- **NETA PowerPoint:** Microsoft® PowerPoint® lecture slides for every chapter have been created by Nathan Innocente, University of Toronto. There is an average of 30 slides per chapter, many featuring key figures, tables, and photographs from *Canadian Criminal Justice: A Primer*, Fifth Edition. NETA principles of clear design and engaging content have been incorporated throughout, making it simple for instructors to customize the deck for their courses.

- **Image Library:** This resource consists of digital copies of figures, short tables, and photographs used in the book. Instructors may use these jpegs to customize the NETA PowerPoint or create their own PowerPoint presentations.

- **NETA Instructor's Manual:** This resource was written by Sheri Fabian, Simon Fraser University. It is organized according to the textbook chapters and addresses key educational concerns, such as typical stumbling blocks student face and how to address them. Other features include common student misconceptions, in-class activities, online activities, and links to video clips with questions for discussion or homework submission.

- **DayOne:** Day One—Prof InClass is a PowerPoint presentation that instructors can customize to orient students to the class and their text at the beginning of the course.

STUDENT ANCILLARIES

Nelson Education's **Companion Website** for *Canadian Criminal Justice: A Primer*, Fifth Edition, brings course concepts to life with interactive learning and exam preparation tools that integrate with the printed textbook. Students activate their knowledge through quizzes, games, and flashcards, among many other tools.

The **Companion Website,** at www.nelson.com/crimjusticeprimer5e.com, provides students with interactive learning tools, including

- quizzes
- flashcards
- critical thinking questions
- online glossary

PART I

CANADIAN CRIMINAL JUSTICE:

SETTING THE FRAMEWORK

The following items, all of which appeared in the news in the past few years, are snapshots that reveal the dynamic nature of the Canadian criminal justice system in the early 21st century.

- On April 4, 2013, Rehtaeh Parsons, a young woman in Nova Scotia, attempted to commit suicide after images of her being gang-raped are posted on the Internet. She died three days later. The renowned "hacktivist" group, Anonymous, then posted videos chastising the justice system and threatening to name the young men involved in the attack. **At issue**: should there be legislation to stop groups, such as Anonymous, from posting statements on the Internet and disclosing the names of alleged suspects who are under age? (See Chapter 3.)

- On June 13, 1991, Royal Canadian Mounted Police (RCMP) officers arrested Kyle Unger for the murder of Brigitte Grenier at a rock concert the previous year. Unger had confessed to the murder to undercover police officers posing as members of an organized crime gang who required him to admit any prior criminal activity before being accepted into the group. Unger stated that he had committed the murder. He was arrested, tried, and convicted. After serving 14 years in prison, he was found to have been wrongfully convicted. **At issue**: To what extent should the police be able to engage in trickery as part of a criminal investigation? (See Chapter 6.)

- In 2012, a Muslim woman living in Ontario (known only as N.S. because of a publication ban) wanted to wear her niqab (full-face veil) while testifying in a preliminary hearing involving charges against her uncle and cousin for sexual assault. **At issue**: should the woman be allowed to testify against her alleged perpetrators while wearing clothing that obscures all of her face except her eyes? (See Chapter 8.)

The chapters in Part 1 of the text provide the foundation for examining the various facets of the criminal justice system. Chapter 1 sets out the foundations of the legal system and discusses the origins and application of the criminal law. The discussion notes that who and what are defined as criminal is ever changing and that, in a democratic society, tensions often exist between the criminal law and the rights of individuals. Chapter 2 explores the structure and process of criminal justice, examining the models of criminal justice administration, the flow of cases through the justice system, and how the Canadian criminal justice system is structured. Ethics, which is a key feature in the criminal justice system, is introduced and will be examined throughout the text. Chapter 3 concludes Part I by examining the issues surrounding crime, victims, and the general public.

CHAPTER 1

THE FOUNDATIONS OF CRIMINAL JUSTICE

LEARNING OBJECTIVES

After reading this chapter, you should be able to
- discuss the key principles of the rule of law
- describe the main provisions of the *Charter of Rights and Freedoms*
- discuss the functions of the criminal law
- identify and discuss the principles of Canadian law
- describe the categories of criminal offences
- describe and contrast the two models of the origins and application of the criminal law
- discuss the criminal law as dynamic rather than static

THE RULE OF LAW

Rule of law

The requirement that governments, as well as individuals, be subjected to and abide by the law.

A fundamental component of the criminal justice system is the **rule of law**. The key principles of the rule of law are set out in Box 1.1.

BOX 1.1 KEY PRINCIPLES OF THE RULE OF LAW

- The government and its officials and agents as well as individuals and private entities are accountable under the law.
- The laws are clear, publicized, stable and just, are applied evenly, and protect fundamental rights, including the security of persons and property.
- The process by which the laws are enacted, administered and enforced is accessible, fair and efficient.
- Justice is delivered timely by competent, ethical, and independent representatives and neutrals who are of sufficient number, have adequate resources, and reflect the makeup of the communities they serve.

Source: Excerpted from The World Justice Project, "What is the Rule of Law?", http://www.worldjusticeproject/org/what-rule-law. Reprinted with permission of The World Justice Project.

The essence of the rule of law is that no one person is above the law; all persons are bound by the law and are entitled to protection by the law; and the law should be observed and enforced equally. While they are admirable principles, the issue becomes complex in a diverse society.

The rule of law can be traced back to the English *Magna Carta*, which was originally issued by King John near Windsor Castle in England in June 1215. A number of passages in the document spoke to judicial procedure, including the creation of a permanent court at Westminster, the imposition of fines on commoners and peers alike "only according to the degree of the offense." Perhaps the most famous, and

King John signs the *Magna Carta* at ▶ Runnymede, near London, in June 1215.

enduring, was the statement: "No Free-man shall be taken, or imprisoned, or dispossessed, of his free tenement, or liberties, or free customs, or be outlawed, or exiled, or in any way destroyed; nor will we condemn him, nor will we commit him to prison, excepting by the legal judgment of his peers, or by the law of the land. To none will we sell, to none will we deny, to none will we delay right or justice".[1]

The *Magna Carta* and other documents provided the basis for the emergence of the rule of law, which became the foundation of English law and, subsequently, of the Canadian (English-speaking) legal system.

The principles of the rule of law and the influence of the *Magna Carta* can be seen in the **Canadian Charter of Rights and Freedoms,** which is the primary law of the land and guarantees fundamental freedoms, legal rights, and quality rights for all citizens of Canada, including those accused of crimes. See Box 1.2.

The *Charter of Rights and Freedoms* provides protection for individuals and ensures fairness during legal proceedings. All the components of the criminal justice system must operate in a way that does not violate the rights guaranteed to Canadians in the *Charter*. Canadian courts have restricted, extended, or better defined the *Charter* rights of citizens. Unfortunately, as we'll see throughout the text, the criminal justice system does not always act in a manner that respects and protects the *Charter* rights of Canadian citizens.

Canadian Charter of Rights and Freedoms

The primary law of the land and guarantees fundamental freedoms, legal rights, and quality rights for all citizens of Canada, including those accused of crimes.

THE CRIMINAL LAW

The criminal law is one of the types of public law, the others being constitutional law, administrative law, and taxation law. **Criminal law** can be defined as "that body of law that deals with conduct considered so harmful to society as a whole that it is prohibited by statute, prosecuted and punished by the government".[2] The criminal law defines those acts, which (or omissions) are against the law and sets out the available penalties. It also sets out the rules that police and judges must follow in criminal matters, including procedures for making arrests, gathering evidence, and presenting evidence in court. Private law, by contrast, regulates relationships between individuals other than the state and is used to resolve disputes between private citizens.

The functions of the criminal law are given in Box 1.3.

Criminal law

That body of law that deals with conduct considered so harmful to society as a whole that it is prohibited by statute and prosecuted and punished by the government.

PRINCIPLES OF CANADIAN LAW

A number of principles provide the foundation for Canadian law, including the following:

- *Actus non facit reum nisi mens sit rea:* An act does not make a person guilty unless he or she has a guilty mind. Each crime has two components. The first is *actus reus* or the act of doing something. The second is *mens rea* or the guilty intent. To be convicted of most crimes (but not all), a person must have done something criminal and usually (but not always) must have intended to do it. A few offences impose strict or absolute liability and the Crown need not prove *mens rea*. Possession of burglary instruments (s. 351 of the *Criminal Code*) is one example. Children under 12 and people with some severe mental disorders are deemed unable to form *mens rea* and therefore will not be held criminally responsible for their actions. There are provisions that apply to the criminal conduct of children, but these provisions are found in child protection statutes rather than in the *Criminal Code*.

BOX 1.2   EXCERPTS FROM THE *CANADIAN CHARTER OF RIGHTS AND FREEDOMS*

1. The *Canadian Charter of Rights and Freedoms* guarantees the rights and freedoms set out in it subject only to such reasonable limits prescribed by law as can be demonstrably justified in a free and democratic society.

FUNDAMENTAL FREEDOMS

2. Everyone has the following fundamental freedoms:
   (a) freedom of conscience and religion;
   (b) freedom of thought, belief, opinion and expression, including freedom of the press and other media of communication;
   (c) freedom of peaceful assembly; and
   (d) freedom of association.

LEGAL RIGHTS

7. Everyone has the right to life, liberty and security of the person and the right not to be deprived thereof except in accordance with the principles of fundamental justice.

8. Everyone has the right to be secure against unreasonable search or seizure.

9. Everyone has the right not to be arbitrarily detained or imprisoned.

10. Everyone has the right on arrest or detention
    (a) to be informed promptly of the reasons therefore;
    (b) to retain and instruct counsel without delay and to be informed of that right; and
    (c) to have the validity of the detention determined by way of *habeas corpus* and to be released if the detention is not lawful.

11. Any person charged with an offence has the right
    (a) to be informed without unreasonable delay of the specific offence;
    (b) to be tried within a reasonable time;
    (c) not to be compelled to be a witness in proceedings against that person in respect of the offence;
    (d) to be presumed innocent until proven guilty according to law in a fair and public hearing by an independent and impartial tribunal;
    (e) not to be denied reasonable bail without cause;
    (f) except in the case of an offence under military law tried before a military tribunal, to the benefit of trial by jury where the maximum punishment for the offence is imprisonment for five years or a more severe punishment;
    (g) not to be found guilty on account of any act or omission unless, at the time of the act or omission, it constituted an offence under Canadian or international law or was criminal according to the general principles of law recognized by the community of nations;
    (h) if finally acquitted of the offence, not to be tried for it again and, if finally found guilty and punished for the offence, not to be tried or punished for it again; and
    (i) if found guilty of the offence and if the punishment for the offence has been varied between the time of the commission and the time of sentencing, to the benefit of the lesser punishment.

12. Everyone has the right not to be subjected to any cruel and unusual treatment or punishment.

13. A witness who testified in any proceedings has the right not to have any incriminating evidence so given used to incriminate that witness in any other proceedings, except in a prosecution for perjury or for the giving of contradictory evidence.

14. A party or witness in any proceedings who does not understand or speak the language in which the proceedings are conducted or who is deaf has the right to the assistance of an interpreter.

EQUALITY RIGHTS

15. (1) Every individual is equal before and under the law and has the right to the equal protection and equal benefit of the law without discrimination and, in particular, without discrimination based on race, national or ethnic origin, colour, religion, sex, age or mental or physical disability.
    (2) Subsection (1) does not preclude any law, program or activity that has its object the amelioration of conditions of disadvantaged individuals or groups including those that are disadvantaged because of race, national or ethnic origin, colour, religion, sex, age or mental or physical disability.

ENFORCEMENT

24. (1) Anyone whose rights or freedoms, as guaranteed by this Charter, have been infringed or denied may apply to a court of competent jurisdiction to obtain such remedy as the court considers appropriate and just in the circumstances.
    (2) Where, in proceedings under subsection (1), a court concludes that evidence was obtained in a manner that infringed or denied any rights or freedoms guaranteed by this Charter, the evidence shall be excluded if it is established that, having regard to all the circumstances, the admission of it in the proceedings would bring the administration of justice into disrepute.

Source: *The Canadian Charter of Rights and Freedoms*, Sections 1, 2, 7-15, 24, http://laws-lois.justice.gc.ca/eng/Const/page-15.html.

> ### BOX 1.3   THE FUNCTIONS OF THE CRIMINAL LAW
>
> In Canadian society, the criminal law
>
> - acts as a mechanism of social control
> - maintains order
> - defines the parameters of acceptable behaviour
> - reduces the risk of personal retaliation (vigilantism, or people taking the law into their own hands)
> - assists in general and specific deterrence
> - criminalizes behaviour
> - protects group interests
>
> Some observers also say that the criminal law marginalizes the most vulnerable groups in society. One research study examined the legislation passed in Ontario and in British Columbia—the *Safe Streets Act*—that was designed to reduce the "disorder" created in public spaces by homeless persons. The criminalization and penalization of the homeless resulted in 21,742 tickets being issued in Toronto and Ottawa between 2000 and 2006 under the *Safe Streets Act* to individuals who listed as their address a homeless shelter or a community organization.[3]
>
> #### QUESTION
>
> Can you think of a law that might result in more persons in poverty being charged with an offence?
>
> Source: Chesnay, C.T., C. Bellot, and M.-E. Sylvestre. 2013. "Taming Disorderly People One Ticket at a Time: The Penalization of Homelessness in Ontario and British Columbia," *Canadian Journal of Criminology and Criminal Justice* 55 No. 2, 161-85.

- *Nullum crimen sine lege, nulla poena sine lege:* No crime without a law, no punishment without a law. This principle means that the rules cannot be changed in the middle of the game. Laws cannot be applied retroactively.

- *Ignorantia juris non excusat:* Ignorance of the law is no excuse. The expectation is that every citizen should be familiar with all the laws and therefore able to distinguish between legal and illegal behaviour. This expectation is a fiction because the law is constantly changing and, at any point, is subject to debate and differing interpretations. However, the legal system would grind to a halt if defendants were able to claim that they had no idea their alleged offences were illegal.

- *Nemo tenetur seipsum accusare:* No one is compelled to incriminate himself or herself. Criminal suspects and defendants have the right to remain silent during the police investigation. If they are threatened or forced to make a confession, that statement will be inadmissible in court. In addition, criminal defendants may choose not to testify in their defence. This principle is enshrined in the *Charter*.

- *Nemo debet bis vexari pro eadem causa:* No one should be twice troubled by the same cause. This principle is more commonly known as *double jeopardy*. An alleged offender cannot, under most circumstances, be tried twice for the same offence. In contrast to the American criminal justice system, however, an alleged offender in Canada can be retried after being acquitted if the Crown successfully appeals the decision by claiming problems with the correct application of the law at the trial.

THE SYSTEM OF CRIMINAL LAW

The Canadian legal system is a common law system. This system originated in Europe and was imported to Canada in the 17th and 18th centuries. The common law emerged from decisions made by judges in the royal courts and is based on the notion of **precedent**: "whenever a judge makes a decision that is said to be legally enforced,

Precedent

A judicial decision that may be used as a standard in subsequent similar cases.

this decision becomes a precedent: a rule that will guide judges in making subsequent decisions in similar cases".[4] A unique feature of the common law is that is exists in past decisions of judges rather than being embodied in legal codes or legislation.

The legal system operates under precise albeit not always logical rules. Canada inherited the British system of **common law**; as a consequence, our **statute law**—both civil (except in Quebec) and criminal—is found both in statutes and in judicial precedents (the latter referred to as **case law**). In other words, many laws—such as those in the *Criminal Code*—are written down or codified. But through their decisions in cases, judges can interpret, modify, extend, restrict, or strike down statutory laws.

The courts are organized in a hierarchy, with the Supreme Court of Canada at the top. The principle whereby higher courts set precedents that lower courts must follow is known as **stare decisis** (Latin for "to stand by what was decided"). Underlying this principle is the idea that like cases should be treated alike. Especially when the law is not precise, judicial interpretation can add clarification so that all courts are playing by the same rules, so to speak. Once the Supreme Court of Canada rules on a thorny legal issue, all courts below it are bound to apply that ruling in subsequent cases.

WHAT IS A CRIME?

A **crime** is generally defined as an act or omission that is prohibited by criminal law. Every jurisdiction sets out a limited series of acts (crimes) that are prohibited and punishes the commission of these acts by a fine or imprisonment or some other type of sanction. In exceptional cases, an omission to act can constitute a crime. Examples are failing to give assistance to a person in peril or failing to report a case of child abuse.

As noted earlier, the two critical ingredients of a crime are the commission of an act (*actus reus*) and the mental intent to commit the act (*mens rea*). A crime occurs when a person

- commits an act or fails to commit an act when under a legal responsibility to do so
- has the intent, or *mens rea*, to commit the act
- does not have a legal defence or justification for committing the act
- violates a provision in criminal law

THE CLASSIFICATION OF OFFENCES

The *Criminal Code* has three categories of criminal offences: **summary conviction offences**, **indictable offences**, and **hybrid** (or **elective**) **offences**. See Box 1.4.

CRIMINAL LAW VERSUS CIVIL (TORT) LAW

As one among several legal systems that exist in Canada, the criminal justice system concerns itself only with offenders who are criminally liable for wrongdoing. The government assumes the responsibility for prosecuting the alleged offender who, on conviction, is placed under the supervision of corrections authorities. In contrast, civil law cases are disputes between individuals. The person who feels wronged brings the legal action, and the "loser" may be required to pay damages.

A key difference between criminal law and civil law relates to the standard of proof required to convict a person of wrongdoing. In a criminal trial, the prosecutor

Common law

Law that is based on custom, tradition, and practice and is generally unwritten.

Statute law

Written laws that have been enacted by a legislative body, such as the Parliament of Canada.

Case law

Law that is established by previous court decisions and based on the rule of precedent.

Stare decisis

The principle by which the higher courts set precedents that the lower courts must follow.

Crime

An act or omission that is prohibited by criminal law.

Summary conviction offences

Generally less serious offences that are triable before a magistrate or judge and, on conviction, carry a maximum penalty of a fine (not to exceed $5000) or six months in a provincial correctional facility or both.

Indictable offences

Generally more serious criminal offences that may carry maximum prison sentences of 14 years to life; examples include murder, robbery, and aggravated sexual assault.

Hybrid (or elective) offences

Offences that can be proceeded summarily or by indictment—a decision that is always made by the Crown.

BOX 1.4   THE CATEGORIES OF CRIMINAL OFFENCES

Summary Conviction Offences	Indictable Offences	Hybrid Offences
Less serious (e.g., trespassing at night, causing a disturbance)	More serious (e.g., sexual assault, robbery)	Most *Criminal Code* offences (e.g., assault, sexual assault, assault with a weapon)
Triable before a magistrate or judge in lower courts; cases remain in lower courts	Accused can be tried in a number of courts (e.g., Provincial Court, Superior Court), depending on such factors as the seriousness of the alleged offence and the court chosen by the accused; in many cases, a preliminary hearing is held to determine where there is sufficient evidence to proceed; they may begin in lower courts but be heard in a higher court.	Once a charge is laid, the Crown may choose to proceed by either indictment or summarily (a discretionary decision not generally reviewable by any court); factors influencing the decision may include the severity of the offence, the prior record of the accused, and the impact of the alleged offence on the community.
Proceedings must commence within six months after the alleged offence.	No time limit for proceedings to commence (no statute of limitations)	Time limit if the Crown proceeds summarily; no time limit if by indictment; the time factor may influence the decision of the Crown to proceed by indictment.
Maximum penalty of a fine (not to exceed $5000) or (generally) six months in jail or both	Maximum penalty can be life imprisonment	Maximum penalty depends on whether the Crown proceeds summarily or by indictment

must prove that the defendant is guilty "beyond a reasonable doubt." In a civil trial, liability is determined by using the standard of "the balance of probabilities." The standard is one of reasonable probability or reasonable belief rather than proof beyond a reasonable doubt. Because this reasonable probability is a much lower standard of proof, a defendant might be found not guilty in criminal court but liable in a civil suit. This outcome occurred in the case of OJ Simpson, a former NFL football player who was found not guilty in 1995 by a criminal jury in the deaths of his ex-wife, Nicole Brown Simpson, and her boyfriend, Ronald Goldman. In the view of the jury, the evidence presented by the prosecution did not establish Simpson's guilt beyond a reasonable doubt. In a subsequent civil trial in 1997, a jury found that there was a preponderance of the evidence that his conduct resulted in the deaths of the two victims. A $33.5 million penalty was imposed on the court, to be paid to the victim's families. As of 2014, only a small portion of the money had been paid.

THE ORIGINS AND APPLICATION OF THE CRIMINAL LAW

The origins and application of criminal law have two main explanations. The first, the **value consensus model**, views crime and punishment as reflecting society's commonly held values and its limits of tolerance. This view assumes that a consensus exists on what should be against the law. Through the application of laws, a society reaffirms the acceptable boundaries of behaviour and maintains social cohesion. Indeed, consensus probably *does* exist that murder should be against the law. Incest is another act that is widely condemned. Such offences, called *mala in se* (wrong in themselves), are perceived as so inherently evil as to constitute a violation of "natural law."

The **conflict model**, the second theory of the origins and application of criminal law, draws our attention to the fact that some groups are better able than others to influence

Value consensus model
The view that the behaviours are defined as criminal and the punishment imposed on offenders reflects commonly held opinions and limits of tolerance.

Conflict model
The view that crime and punishment reflect the power some groups have to influence the formulation and application of criminal law.

which behaviours and persons are criminalized. In particular, conflict theorists see the rich and privileged as having an advantage in influencing law reform.

Scholars who conduct research by using a conflict perspective might ask the following questions:

- Why does a person who steals less than $100 from a convenience store often receive a much more severe sentence than a stockbroker who runs a Ponzi scheme that results in the loss of millions of dollars of investor's money? (See Box 2.4 about the case of the pizza thief in Chapter 2.)

- Why are crimes committed by corporations (such as overpricing goods, failing to create and maintain healthy and safe working environments, and illegally disposing of hazardous wastes) most often dealt with through civil suits and the imposition of fines rather than under criminal law?

- Why are Canadian correctional institutions populated by large numbers of Aboriginal people and by those with low education and skill levels, high rates of alcohol and drug addiction, and dysfunctional family backgrounds? Are these groups actually more criminal than other groups in society? (See Chapter 11.)

- With crime rates generally on the decline, why did the federal government pass legislation increasing the number of mandatory minimum sentences? (See Chapter 2.)

- What role do interest groups play in influencing the enactment of criminal legislation or in decriminalizing certain behaviour?

Conflict theorists highlight some of the inequities and paradoxes in the system. If someone takes money from a bank at gunpoint, it is called robbery. A business decision that causes a company to collapse, thus depriving thousands of shareholders of their money, is called a bad day on the stock market. Conflict theorists believe that our attention is wrongly focused on street crime when the greater risk to most people lies in the actions of elites, including corporations that dump toxic waste, fix prices, condone unsafe workplaces, and evade taxes.

SOURCES OF CRIMINAL LAW IN CANADA

Canada has two primary sources of the criminal law: legislation and judicial decisions. Merely denoting the sources of the criminal law, however, tells us very little about the *process* of lawmaking or the factors that influence the creation of the criminal law. A variety of explanations have been used by scholars studying the phenomena of crime and the societal response to it. Historically, researchers focused on the individual offender and attempted to determine what factors distinguish criminals from non-criminals. The nearly exclusive focus on the criminal offender overshadowed the process through which behaviours and individuals came to be defined as criminal. In recent years, however, attention has increasingly focused on the process by which laws are formulated and applied and to the activities of legislations, special-interest groups, and criminal justice decision makers. Throughout the text, the activities of criminal justice decision makers, including police officers, judges, and parole board members, will be discussed.

WHAT'S AGAINST THE LAW?

Have you ever thought about why marijuana use in most instances is illegal but drinking alcohol is not? To say the least, people do not always agree about what should be against the law. Murder? Yes. Impaired driving? Yes. Bank robbery? Sure.

Polygamy? Well . . . yes in law, no in terms of enforcement (at least as of 2014; see below).

Most of Canada's criminal law was inherited from Victorian England, and many of those offences can be traced even further back, some to biblical times or earlier. Some of our laws seem archaic, and a perusal of the *Criminal Code* reveals laws that are no longer enforced: alarming the Queen (s. 49), inciting to mutiny (s. 53), duelling (s. 71), obstructing a clergyman from performing any function in connection with his calling (s. 176), setting man traps (s. 247)—wherein a homeowner sets a trap in an attempt to prevent a break and enter—and feigning marriage (s. 292), among others.

In Canadian society, a wide range of behaviours are, although deviant, nevertheless not against the law. While *crime* is behaviour that breaks the law, *deviance* is behaviour that is contrary to the norms and values of the larger society. Dressing Goth is not against the law but may be viewed as deviant by the average person as may be cross-dressing. Deviance includes criminal behaviour and a wide range of other behaviours. What is viewed as deviant changes over time: in the 1960s hippies, distinguished by long hair and ponytails on males, were viewed as deviant; today, they are not viewed as unusual.

The criminal law is not static, however, and, almost overnight, legislative enactments or judicial decisions can render behaviours that were previously illegal merely defiant. In 2013, for example, the Supreme Court of Canada (SCC) struck down Canada's prostitution laws as unconstitutional (*Canada (Attorney General) v. Bedford* (2013), SCC 72).

Criminologists often conduct historical analyses in an attempt to understand (1) the factors involved in the defining of behaviours as criminal, (2) an increase or a decrease in the severity of the criminal law, (3) the response of the criminal justice system, and (4) the factors that influence the repeal of a criminal law, resulting in the decriminalization of certain behaviours. Canadian criminologist Neil Boyd has pointed out that "law can be fully comprehended only by documenting and analyzing the social, political, and economic contexts that give it life and continue to influence its existence".[5]

Researchers have conducted historical studies of criminal law reform in an attempt to understand how the social, economic, and political environment may influence legislation. For example, laws against opium use first passed in the early 20th century have been linked to anti-Asian prejudice among Euro-Canadians of the day. Similarly, a review of how marijuana came to be illegal in Canada reveals the prominent role of Emily Murphy, an Alberta magistrate who was also an anti-drug crusader. Writing under the pen name of Janey Canuck, she wrote a series of articles that were later made into a book titled *The Black Candle*. In the book, Murphy "raged against 'Negro' drug dealers and Chinese opium peddlers 'of fishy blood' out to control and debase the white race".[6]

The shifts in the definition of behaviours as illegal or deviant provide fascinating insights into the dynamic nature of criminal law. For example, a serious violation of the criminal law can occur, and yet the behaviour of the individuals involved may not be viewed as criminal. A historical example is the violation of the prohibition laws against drinking alcoholic beverages by Canadians during and after World War I. Erosion of public support for anti-drinking laws, however, ultimately resulted in the repeal of prohibition. More recently, the widespread recreational use of marijuana by many Canadians has led to calls for its legalization. See At Issue 1.1.

As society changes, certain behaviours can be also be criminalized. The pervasiveness of computer technology led to a number of additions to the *Criminal Code*, including destroying or altering computer data (s. 430[1.1]) and using the Internet to distribute child pornography (s. 163.1) and to communicate with a child for the

Surveys indicate that 9 percent of all Canadians have used cannabis (marijuana) at least once in the past year, and nearly 25 percent of those persons indicated that they used the drug daily.[7] A report by the United Nations Office on Drugs and Crime puts the figure of persons ages 15 to 64 who have smoked marijuana or used another cannabis product during the past year at 16.8 percent. This number places Canadians as the leaders in cannabis consumption in the industrialized world.[8] It is estimated that the annual police and court costs of enforcing marijuana laws are at least $500 million. The majority of arrests are for simple possession. Polls indicate that the majority (57 percent) of Canadians want to legalize marijuana. In 2013, an organization called Sensible BC began a petition drive to gather 400,000 signatures, the number required to hold a marijuana referendum that would call on the BC government to pass the *Sensible Policing Act*. The Act would "stop police from searching or arresting otherwise law-abiding citizens for possession of marijuana" and also "demands that the federal government repeal marijuana prohibition".[9]

In 2012, the leader of the federal Liberal Party, Justin Trudeau, stated that he believed that marijuana should be decriminalized, regulated, and taxed.[10] A 2012 study estimated that the recreational market for marijuana in B.C. was more than $350 million, which if taxed would be a valuable source of revenue for the government.[11] In 2013, the Canadian Association of Chiefs of Police voted overwhelmingly to reform the nation's drug laws to allow police officers to issue a ticket to any person found with 30 grams or less of marijuana. As of 2013, officers have only the option of issuing a caution or laying or recommending (depending on the jurisdiction) criminal charges.[12]

In 2012, citizens in the states of Colorado and Washington voted to legalize marijuana for personal use, which brought the law in these states in direct conflict with federal drug laws, which make drug possession, including marijuana, an offence. Residents in these states ages 21 and older are allowed to possess one ounce (30 grams) of marijuana, although it cannot be smoked in public.

QUESTIONS

What is your view on the legalization of marijuana? Would you sign the Sensible BC petition? Would you vote to legalize marijuana? Is there a tipping point at which prohibition and enforcement are no longer effective as deterrents? How is this tipping point to be determined for any type of behaviour, such as widespread violation of the law, as with marijuana use? Should public polls be used to find it?

purposes of facilitating the commission of certain sexual offences (s. 172.1). The pervasiveness of cellphones has led to new legislation related to distracted driving.

Conversely, some activities have been decriminalized over the years; that is, the laws against them have been repealed or struck down. Laws that were applied against gay and lesbian people and Chinese immigrants no longer exist. The Supreme Court of Canada has used the *Charter of Rights and Freedoms* to strike down laws that are inconsistent with the *Charter*'s provisions and protections.

Sometimes, it appears that certain persons or groups are in violation of the criminal law, yet legal action has not been taken or has not been successful. A good example is the ongoing controversy surrounding the religious community of Bountiful, B.C., where polygamy (having more than one spouse at the same time; also called *plural marriages*) is still practised. In the case of Bountiful, the men are married to more than one woman.

THE POLYGAMOUS FAMILIES OF BOUNTIFUL, B.C.: *CHARTER* RIGHTS VERSUS THE CRIMINAL LAW

Polygamy, the practice of having more than one spouse at one time, is prohibited under the *Criminal Code of Canada*:

Section 293. (1): Every one who

(a) practises or enters into or in any manner agrees or consents to practise or enter into

(i) any form of polygamy, or

(ii) any kind of conjugal union with more than one person at the same time, whether or not it is by long recognized as a binding form of marriage, or

(b) celebrates, assist or is a party to a right, ceremony, contract or consent that purports to sanction a relationship mentioned in subparagraph (a)(i) or (ii),

is guilty of an indictable offense and liable to imprisonment for a term not exceeding five years.

Despite this *Criminal Code* prohibition, the small religious community of Bountiful, B.C. has openly practised polygamy for many years. The following timeline of events surrounding the community and the response of the justice system is instructive and provides key insights into the actual dynamics that may surround the application of the law. In addition to the issue of polygamy, there have been ongoing concerns about under-age marriages and child sexual exploitation in the community.

1990: the RCMP begin an investigation of Bountiful and recommend that criminal charges be laid (in B.C., it is up to Crown counsel to lay charges); no charges are laid as the provincial Criminal Justice Branch receives reports from experts that the law banning polygamy is unconstitutional (see section 2(a) of the *Charter of Rights and Freedoms* in Box 1.1)

2004: the RCMP launch a second investigation based on reports of child brides as young as 12 in the community. A senior Vancouver lawyer is hired to review the police file and recommends that charges not be laid; the Attorney General appoints another special prosecutor who recommends that charges be laid against two of the community leaders. These charges are later stayed by a B.C. Supreme Court judge who holds that the second prosecutor was improperly hired.

2011: The B.C. Supreme Court rules to uphold the *Criminal Code* provision making polygamy illegal, noting that while the law does infringe on the constitutional right of religious freedom, it is necessary to counter the harms done by polygamy to women, children, and society.

2012: Another special prosecutor is appointed, prompted by media reports that girls as young as eight years old have been sent to a religious community in the United States to marry older men.

2013: The special prosecutor continues to consider whether criminal charges can be laid against those practising polygamy in Bountiful.

Considerable debate has surrounded the Bountiful case. See At Issue 1.2.

THE CANADIAN PRESS/Jonathan Hayward

◀ Winston Blackmore, the religious leader of the polygamous community of Bountiful, B.C., shares a laugh with six of his daughters and some of his grandchildren, in this 2008 photo.

Many legal scholars have argued that the polygamy law does not pass the constitutional "smell test," particularly in view of the legalization of same-sex marriages, and that polygamy should be accepted as another reflection of the diversity in Canadian society.[13] Others counter that the prohibition is constitutional, that it reflects sounds social policy, and that "unlike the recognition of same-sex marriage, which promoted equality and saved government resources, the recognition of polygamy is often exploitative of women and harmful to children, and its practice is contrary to fundamental Canadian values".[14] This case has been ongoing for more than two decades, suggesting that the government is in no hurry to prosecute.

QUESTION

In your view, how should this issue be resolved? Which arguments in this debate to you find most persuasive?

Moral entrepreneurs

Individuals, groups, or organizations that seek action against certain groups of people or certain behaviours and bring pressure on legislators to enact criminal statutes.

A key role in criminalizing certain activities is often played by **moral entrepreneurs**—individuals, groups, or organizations that seek action against certain groups of people or certain behaviours and bring pressure on legislators to enact criminal statutes. Historically, and recently, moral entrepreneurs have tended to be most active in the area of victimless crimes, such as drug and alcohol use and prostitution. Examples of moral entrepreneurs include Mothers Against Drunk Driving (MADD) and pro-choice and anti-abortion groups.

In 2009, Johnson Aziga, an HIV-positive man, was convicted of first-degree murder in the deaths of two of his sex partners (he infected 11 woman in total) and given an automatic life sentence. The defendant was aware of his HIV status and, at the time of his sexual relations, was under a public health order that required him to inform his sexual partners of his medical condition. This case was the first time a person in Canada was convicted of murder through the spread of HIV. In 2011, an Ontario court judge granted the Crown's request that Mr. Aziga be declared a dangerous offender, which means that he will be incarcerated for an indefinite time.[15]

In recent years, the criminal law has been applied to incidents on sports playing fields. On-ice violence among hockey players has been scrutinized by the criminal justice system.[16] In 2004, Vancouver Canuck player Todd Bertuzzi pled guilty in court to assault causing bodily harm. The incident occurred during a hockey game between the Canucks and the Colorado Avalanche and involved Bertuzzi attacking Avalanche player Steve Moore from behind with several blows to the back of his head. The attack effectively ended Moore's hockey career.

The court imposed a conditional discharge, placed Bertuzzi on probation, and ordered him to perform 80 hours of community service. In another case in 2009, a high school rugby player in Ontario was convicted of manslaughter in the death of a rival player, Manny Castillo, during a rugby game. The victim suffered severe head injuries after being picked up by the accused and slammed headfirst into the ground. The accused was sentenced to one year of probation, including community service and a requirement to attend anger management counselling.[17] The debate about whether the criminal courts should be involved in cases involving violence in sports continues. See At Issue 1.3.

15

SHOULD THE CRIMINAL LAW BE APPLIED TO CASES OF VIOLENCE IN SPORTS?

In sentencing the defendant in the Manny Castillo case (discussed above), the presiding judge stated that sports playing fields were not a "criminal law–free zone" and that "the laws of Canada apply equally, on and off the playing field".[18] Lawyers who oppose this view argue that there is an element of consent when players step onto the playing field or rink. From this perspective, using the legal system is not the most appropriate way to respond to incidents that occur during games: "The bottom line is that athletes, just like those in the military should be subject to different rules of conduct. Even if a player crosses over the line of what is acceptable conduct, the place to deal with this is within the league".[19] An additional argument is that the relatively light sentences handed down by criminal courts in the cases of in-game violence dilute the impact of the criminal law as a deterrent.

QUESTION

In your view, should the criminal law be applied to cases of in-game violence where injuries have occurred?

THE CRIMINAL LAW IN A DIVERSE SOCIETY

The application of the criminal law is challenging in a diverse society, such as Canada, where visible and cultural minority groups are a growing portion of the population. The tension between cultural practices in countries of origin and accepted behaviour

BOX 1.5 **THE SHAFIA HONOUR KILLINGS**

In January 2012, a father, mother, and brother were convicted in the deaths of three female family members in what were described as "honour killings." Tooba Mohammad Yahya, Mohammed Shafia, and their son, Hamed, had pled not guilty in the deaths of four family members who were found in the family's vehicle submerged in a lock on the Rideau canal in Ottawa in June 2009. The victims were Hamed's three sisters and their father's other wife from a polygamous marriage. The three were subsequently convicted of first-degree murder and given automatic life sentences with no chance of parole for 25 years. The Shafias had moved to Canada from Afghanistan 15 years earlier, and there was evidence of abuse in the family as the father attempted to control his daughter's social lives and exercise his patriarchal authority. He was particularly upset that one of the daughters was dating and wanted to move out of the family home.

Tooba Mohammad Yahya; her husband, Mohammad Shafia; and their son, Hamed Mohammad Shafia, are escorted by police officers into the Frontenac County Court courthouse on the first day of trial in Kingston, Ontario, on October 20, 2011.

A research study found that honour killings are on the rise in Canada, with 12 victims since 1999.[20] This case ignited an ongoing debate as to whether there should be a separate section in the *Criminal Code* for honour killings to highlight the inappropriateness and to deter this practice in Canada. Opponents to a new section contend that existing provisions in the *Criminal Code* are sufficient and that persons perpetuating honour killings have always received the maximum allowable sentence under law.[21] As of 2014, the federal government had no plan to amend the *Criminal Code*. (See the Media Link "The House of Shafia" at the end of the chapter.)

THE CANADIAN PRESS/Sean Kilpatrick

in Canadian society are often acute. A key issue is the extent to which the criminal law can be effective in modifying cultural practices that contravene the values of Canadian society. This issue emerged in the Shafia honour killings in Ontario in 2011. See Box 1.5.

The Shafia case raises the larger issue of whether there are limits on the ability of the criminal law to change behaviour.

SUMMARY

This chapter has set out the foundations of the legal system, including the rule of law and the principles contained in the *Canadian Charter of Rights and Freedoms*. The role, principles, origins, and application of the criminal law were examined, and a number of case studies were presented to illustrate the dynamic nature of the criminal law and the challenges of applying the criminal law in a diverse society.

KEY POINTS REVIEW

1. A key component of the criminal justice system is the rule of law, which was first established in the *Magna Carta* in England in 1215.

2. The criminal law has a number of functions, including maintaining order, defining the parameters of acceptable behaviour, and assisting in general and specific deterrence, among others.

3. A number of principles provide the foundation for Canadian law, including the two components of a crime: *actus reus* (the act of doing something) and *mens rea* (guilty intent).

4. The Canadian legal system is a common law system.

5. Significant differences exist between criminal law and civil law.

6. There are differing views on the origins and application of the criminal law.

7. The two primary sources of criminal law in Canada are legislation and judicial decisions.

8. In Canadian society, a wide range of behaviours are deviant but are not against the law.

9. A key notion is that the law can only be fully understood by examining the social, political, and economic contexts within which it exists.

10. The areas in which the criminal law is applied are ever changing, as are the challenges in imposing the law in a diverse society.

KEY TERM QUESTIONS

1. What are the origins and principles of the **rule of law**?

2. Describe the fundamental freedoms, equality rights, and enforcement provisions of the ***Canadian Charter of Rights and Freedoms***.

3. What is the **criminal law**?

4. Define and describe the role of **precedent** and **stare decisis** in the legal system.

5. Describe and compare **common law**, **case law**, and **statute law**.

6. What is a **crime**?

7. Describe the key features of **summary conviction offences**, **indictable offences**, and **hybrid offences**.

8. Contrast the **value consensus model** and the **conflict model** as explanations for the origins and application of criminal law.

9. Who are **moral entrepreneurs** and what role do they play in the creation of criminal laws?

MEDIA LINK

 "The House of Shafia"
CBC Fifth Estate
or go to the book's website at
www.nelson.com/
crimjusticeprimer5e.com

CHAPTER 2

THE STRUCTURE AND PROCESS OF CRIMINAL JUSTICE

LEARNING OBJECTIVES

After reading this chapter, you should be able to

- define and contrast criminology and criminal justice
- discuss the key differences between the fields of criminology and criminal justice
- compare and contrast the two models of criminal justice administration
- discuss the various influences on the criminal justice system
- discuss the roles and responsibilities of the provincial and territorial governments, and the federal governments as related to criminal justice
- discuss the deterrent value of the criminal justice system
- describe the importance of accountability, legitimacy, and evidence-based practice in the criminal justice system
- discuss several trends in Canadian criminal justice in the early 21st century

CRIMINOLOGY VERSUS CRIMINAL JUSTICE: WHAT IS THE DIFFERENCE?

The terms **criminology** and **criminal justice** are often used interchangeably, and the two fields of study do share some commonalities: the study of law and legislation, the study of crime trends and patterns, and the formulation and application of the criminal law, among others. There are differences, however, and some of these are set out in Box 2.1.

Scholars have argued that criminal justice is not a sub-field of criminology, although they are related: how persons who violate the law are viewed and the explanations of their behaviour are related to the response of the justice system.[1]

Scholars have also noted that in the study of the criminal justice system, researchers have tended to focus on the decision making of personnel at the various stages of the criminal justice process (e.g., police officers, judges, parole board members). Less

Criminology

The scientific study of crime and criminal behaviour.

Criminal justice

The study of social control and the agencies that are involved in the apprehension, prosecution, defence, sentencing, incarceration, and supervision of those suspected or charged with or convicted of criminal offences.

BOX 2.1 KEY DIFFERENCES BETWEEN THE FIELDS OF CRIMINOLOGY AND CRIMINAL JUSTICE

Note that the entries aligned in each column are not meant to be *directly* comparable.

Criminology's Focuses	Criminal Justice's Focuses
crime and criminal behaviour (law breaking)	law making
the causes of crime	social control and punishment
the explanations of crime (e.g., rational choice, biological explanations of criminal activity)	the mandate and activities of the police, courts, corrections
specific types of criminal activity (e.g., violence, white-collar crime, organized crime)	decision makers in the justice system (e.g., police officers, Crown counsel, judges)
crime patterns and crime trends	non-governmental organizations involved in responding to and assisting offenders
the nature and extent of victimization	at-risk and vulnerable populations (e.g., Aboriginal persons) in the criminal justice system
how certain groups (e.g., persons in poverty, women) become criminalized	the role and activities of the community in responding to crime, disorder, and offenders
the formulation and application of the criminal law; law as an instrument of social control	the formulation and application of the criminal law; law as an instrument of social control
public perceptions of the law, crime, and offenders	ethics and accountability in the justice system
comparative studies of crime among jurisdictions and nations	misbehaviour and corruption of criminal justice personnel
specific groups of offenders (e.g., chronic offenders)	racism and sexism in the criminal justice system
the legislation of morality (e.g., studies of prostitution laws, drug laws)	comparative studies of criminal justice systems
methods for conducting research on crime and criminal offenders	methods for conducting research on the criminal justice system
	structures of governance of criminal justice agencies
	the effectiveness of criminal justice strategies, interventions, and decision making

attention has been given to criminal justice agencies as organizations and the factors that facilitate or hinder effective criminal justice practice.[2] Throughout the text, we'll examine these issues and set out what is known about what works (and what doesn't) in the criminal justice system

THE CRIMINAL JUSTICE SYSTEM

Some debate continues as to whether the criminal justice system really is a "system." (Yes, some scholars spend sunny days in July thinking about these things.) A number of observers have argued that the criminal justice system is best described as a "loosely coupled system" within which there are checks and balances.[3]

A number of factors work against the criminal justice system being a system in the true sense of the word: (1) the different mandates of criminal justice agencies and (2) a lack of interoperability, that is, the inability of the hardware and software from multiple databases from multiple agencies to communicate with one another. The failure of agencies to share information can have significant consequences for victims, offenders, and the community. Incomplete materials in an offender's file, such as risk assessments and in-depth examinations of release plans, can hinder the ability of a parole board to make an informed decision on an inmate's application for conditional release. Similarly, the failure of a halfway house to notify parole supervision authorities in a timely manner of an offender being missing can jeopardize the safety of crime victims and the community. With these caveats in mind, the discussion in the text will refer often to the criminal justice system.

WHAT IS THE CRIMINAL JUSTICE SYSTEM?

Criminal justice system

All the agencies, organizations, and personnel that are involved in the prevention of, and response to, crime and to persons charged with criminal offences and persons convicted of crimes.

The **criminal justice system** is generally considered to contain all the agencies, organizations, and personnel that are involved in the prevention of, and response to, crime and to persons charged with criminal offences and persons convicted of crimes. It not only includes criminal justice professionals but also thousands of volunteers who work in criminal justice agencies, NGOs (non-governmental organizations), and other not-for-profit groups who deliver programs and services on a contract basis. For example, these groups supervise offenders on bail, assist victims, provide community-based and institutional programming, and supervise parolees.

The criminal justice system includes crime prevention and crime reduction, the arrest and prosecution of suspects, the hearing of criminal cases by the courts, sentencing and the administration and enforcement of court orders, parole and other forms of conditional release, and supervision and assistance for ex-offenders released into the community. These groups include, among others, the John Howard Society of Canada, the Elizabeth Fry Society, the St. Leonard's Society of Canada, and various Aboriginal organizations. Provincial and territorial governments often contract organizations like these to deliver such services. In recent years, restorative justice approaches have become part of the criminal justice process as well.

Crime control (model of criminal justice)

An orientation to criminal justice in which the protection of the community and the apprehension of offenders are paramount.

Due process model (of criminal justice)

An orientation to criminal justice in which the legal rights of individual citizens, including crime suspects, are paramount.

MODELS OF CRIMINAL JUSTICE ADMINISTRATION: DUE PROCESS VERSUS CRIME CONTROL

Two competing value systems underlying the administration of criminal justice have been identified: the **crime control model** and the **due process model**. These were first set out by the late Herbert L. Packer, a law professor at Stanford University.[4]

BOX 2.2 THE CRIME CONTROL AND DUE PROCESS MODELS OF CRIMINAL JUSTICE ADMINISTRATION

Crime Control Model	Due Process Model
The primary purpose of the criminal justice system is protection of the public through deterrence and incapacitation of offenders.	The primary purpose of the criminal justice system is to ensure that there is equal justice for all citizens, regardless of wealth, social status, or political connections.
Criminal offenders responsible for their behaviour.	Criminal offenders are responsible for their behaviour.
The administration of justice should be swift, certain, and efficient.	The administration of justice must be deliberate and ensure procedural fairness.
The criminal justice system should focus on the rights of victims rather than on protecting the rights of criminal defendants.	The criminal justice system should focus on ensuring that the rights of criminal defendants are protected and that the powers and discretion of criminal justice decision makers are structured and confined.
There is a strong presumption of guilt.	There is a presumption of innocence and the onus is on the criminal justice system to prove guilt; it is possible for a defendant to be factually guilty but legally innocent if proper procedures and rights of the accused have been violated.
It reflects conservative values.	It reflects liberal values.

In their pure form, the models conflict with each other. In practice, the criminal justice system reflects elements of both models. And which model is emphasized at any time will depend on a variety of factors, not the least of which is the perspective of the government of the day. See Box 2.2.

There is a fundamental and ever-shifting balance to be struck between (1) giving criminal justice agencies, such as the police and prosecutors, the unfettered power to apprehend and prosecute offenders (crime control); and (2) protecting citizens from the potential abuses of that power (due process).

The political climate of a jurisdiction may determine which model is predominant. In the early 21st century, the Canadian federal government has emphasized a crime control approach, passing legislation that increased the number of mandatory minimum sentences and limited the use of conditional sentences (house arrest) for offenders convicted of serious and violent crimes.

THE DYNAMICS OF CRIMINAL JUSTICE

A key feature of criminal justice research is documenting the *dynamics* of the criminal justice process and exploring the disconnect between the formally stated objectives of the various components of the justice system and actual practice. The materials in this text are designed to highlight the activities of individual justice personnel and how justice system organizations and agencies carry out their mandates. In a democratic society, tension will always exist between the efforts of the state to maintain order and to ensure the rights of citizens. The actions and decisions of individual criminal justice personnel and of their agencies are discussed in later chapters.

FIGURE 2.1 ▶

The Influences on the Criminal Justice System

Discuss how each of the identified influences might impact the criminal justice system. Can you think of other influences on the criminal justice system?

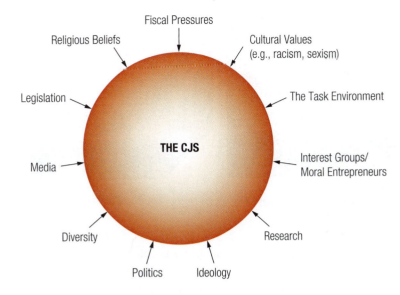

To understand the criminal justice system requires a perspective that extends beyond organizational charts and legislative frameworks. A number of observers have pointed out that there has been little progress in developing theories of criminal justice in part because of the complexity, diversity, and scope of the criminal justice system.[5] Traditionally, scholars have studied the three components of the justice system—the police, courts, and corrections—and have not focused on the development of unifying theories.

In considering the operation of the criminal justice system, a number of different facets can be examined, including (1) the behaviour of criminal justice personnel (e.g., police officers), (2) the activities of criminal justice organizations (e.g., correctional institutions), and (3) the aggregate characteristics of the criminal justice system and its components in the context of larger societal issues, such as racism and inequality.[6]

In addition, many influences are external to the justice system yet may have a significant impact on its operations. These assist us in understanding the how and why of the decisions that are made in the criminal justice system. See Figure 2.1.

THE TASK ENVIRONMENTS OF CRIMINAL JUSTICE

Task environment

The cultural, geographic, and community setting in which the criminal justice system operates and justice personnel make decisions.

A **task environment** in the context of the criminal justice system is the cultural, geographic, and community setting in which the criminal justice system operates and in which criminal justice personnel make decisions. These environments range from small Inuit villages in Nunavut to inner-city neighbourhoods in major urban centres, such as Toronto.

The characteristics of a particular task environment influence the types of crime and social disorder that justice system personnel are confronted with, the decision-making options that are available, the effectiveness of justice policies and programs, and the potential for developing community-based programs and services. In addition, the same urban area may contain a variety of task environments, ranging from neighbourhoods with a high concentration of shelters for the homeless, to neighbourhoods with large populations of recently arrived immigrants, to exclusive high-income neighbourhoods. Unique challenges are faced by criminal justice personnel in remote and northern areas of the country, where there are few resources and community-based programs for victims and offenders.

23

Vancouver's poverty-ridden Downtown Eastside   Chinatown in Montréal   Qikiqtarjuaq, Nunavut, population 520

▲ What do each of the photos suggest to you about the task environment and the demands on and challenges for the criminal justice system?

Crime manifests itself differently in remote Arctic villages than on Vancouver's skid row or in a wealthy suburban Montréal neighbourhood (the highest rates of violent crime are in Canada's North). City police may be faced with gang activity and traffic management; rural police may have to deal more with marijuana cultivation. In short, the demographics of the area, the local economic conditions, and the ethnic mix combine to influence decisions. As these factors vary, so too will the types of crime or social disorder, community expectations regarding enforcement, the community's capacity to address local issues, and relations between the justice system and the citizens it serves.

THE ROLE AND RESPONSIBILITIES OF GOVERNMENTS IN CRIMINAL JUSTICE

Each level of government in Canada—federal, provincial, and municipal—plays a role in the justice system. The division of responsibilities between the federal and provincial or territorial governments was spelled out in the *Constitution Act, 1867*.

The basic division is that the federal government decides which behaviours are criminal offences, while the provincial or territorial governments are responsible for law enforcement and for administering the justice system. See Table 2.1.

Note that a number of unique features of the criminal justice system would not be apparent in the *Constitution Act*. The RCMP, for example, are involved as a federal, provincial and territorial, and municipal police service. In the territories and in provinces other than Ontario, Québec, and Newfoundland and Labrador, the RCMP is the contracted provincial police service. And in provinces other than Québec and Ontario, the RCMP in involved in policing municipalities under contract. In Ontario, the Ontario Provincial Police (OPP) also polices some municipalities under contract.[7]

The federal government is responsible for the *Criminal Code*. This federal legislation sets out criminal laws, procedures for prosecuting federal offences, and sentences and procedures for the administration of justice. The original version of the *Criminal Code* dates from 1869. It was initially consolidated in 1892 and since that time has been amended and revised. The most recent version is three times as long as the original version.

There is also federal legislation that targets specific types of criminal behaviour and offenders. The *Anti-terrorism Act* (2001, c. 41),[8] for example, gives the justice system broad powers to identify, prosecute, convict, and punish terrorist groups and individuals, while the *Sex Offender Information Registration Act* (2004, c. 10)[9] established a national sex offender database containing information on convicted sex offenders.

Constitution Act, 1867

The legislation setting out the division of responsibilities between the federal and provincial or territorial governments.

Criminal Code

Federal legislation that sets out criminal laws, procedures for prosecuting federal offences, and sentences and procedures for the administration of justice.

24

TABLE 2.1   DIVISION OF GOVERNMENT RESPONSIBILITIES IN CRIMINAL JUSTICE

Federal	Provincial or Territorial	Municipal
Department of Justice	Ministry of Attorney General	enact bylaws valid within the city limits; collect fines; control police budgets (except where policed under contract with the RCMP/OPP/SQ)
Public Safety Canada	Ministry of Public Safety, etc.	
absolute power to create, amend, and repeal criminal law for the entire country (Criminal Code)	enact laws for areas under provincial jurisdiction (e.g., impaired driving, distracted driving); oversee; operate provincial police services in Ontario, Québec, Newfoundland and Labrador; manage courthouses; employ Crown attorneys; prosecute offences; employ some judges; operate problem-solving courts; operate probation services; operate correctional institutions and community-based corrections programs and services; operate parole boards and parole services in Québec and Ontario	
federal police (RCMP)		
federal prosecutors		
set procedures for prosecution; prosecute some federal offences, including drug offences		
Supreme Court of Canada		
operate correctional institutions (Correctional Service Canada)		
operate the Parole Board of Canada		
Canadian Security Intelligence Service (CSIS)		
Canada Border Services Agency (CBSA)		

THE FLOW OF CASES THROUGH THE CRIMINAL JUSTICE SYSTEM

A flow chart illustrating how cases proceed through the criminal justice system is presented in Figure 2.2.

You will want to refer to this figure often as you read the rest of the chapters. The figure is useful for showing where a person is in the system at any point in the process; however, it provides little insight into the actual *dynamics* of criminal justice—that is, how decisions are made by justice personnel, the challenges they face in preventing and responding to crime, the role of crime victims, and the new initiatives that are being undertaken in an effort to make the justice system more effective. These and other issues will be addressed in later chapters.

The criminal justice system responds to law breaking with investigation, prosecution, and (when appropriate) punishment. It does not, however, respond to every breach of the law. Only a portion of the criminal acts committed come to the attention of the police, and a much smaller percentage of these are heard in the courts or lead to a sentence of incarceration. In reality, most cases are resolved with a guilty plea (often through plea negotiation) and few cases go to trial. So dramatic is the attrition of cases in Canadian criminal justice that it is often represented graphically by a funnel. See Figure 2.3.

Figure 2.4 presents statistics illustrating the attrition of spousal assault cases that are reported by victims.

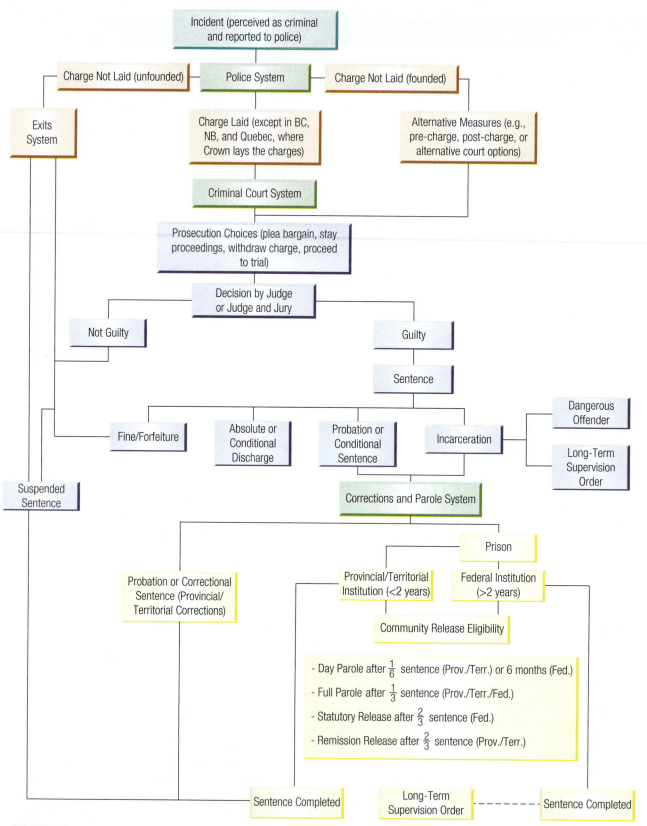

▲ **FIGURE 2.2**

Flow of Cases through the Criminal Justice System

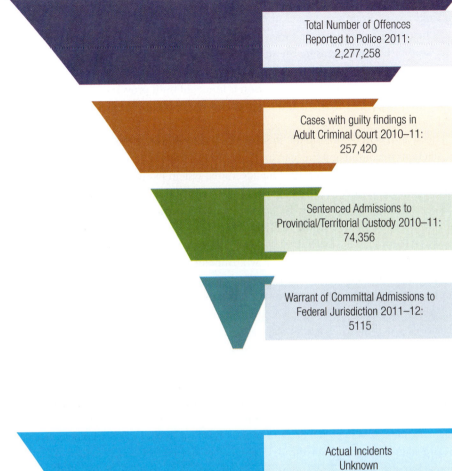

FIGURE 2.3 ▶

The Criminal Justice Funnel

Source: Criminal Justice Funnel, *Corrections and Conditional Release: Statistical Overview*, page 13. Public Safety Canada, http://www.publicsafety. gc.ca/cnt/rsrcs/pblctns/2012-ccrs/2012-ccrs-eng.pdf. Reproduced with the permission of the Minister of Public Safety and Emergency Preparedness Canada, 2013.

Total Number of Offences Reported to Police 2011: 2,277,258

Cases with guilty findings in Adult Criminal Court 2010–11: 257,420

Sentenced Admissions to Provincial/Territorial Custody 2010–11: 74,356

Warrant of Committal Admissions to Federal Jurisdiction 2011–12: 5115

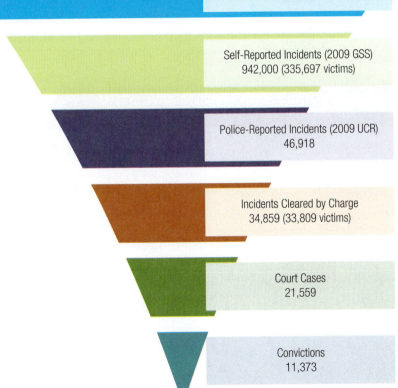

FIGURE 2.4 ▶

The Attrition of Reported Spousal Assault Incidents, 2009

Notes: GSS stands for the General Social Survey. UCR stands for Uniform Crime Reporting Survey.

Source: *An Estimation of the Economic Impact of Spousal Violence in Canada, 2009*, Figure 3.1. Spousal Violence Attrition Pyramid, http://www.justice.gc.ca/eng/rp-pr/cj-jp/fv-vf/rr12_7/rr12_7.pdf, Department of Justice Canada, 2012. Reproduced with the permission of the Department of Justice Canada, 2014.

Actual Incidents Unknown

Self-Reported Incidents (2009 GSS) 942,000 (335,697 victims)

Police-Reported Incidents (2009 UCR) 46,918

Incidents Cleared by Charge 34,859 (33,809 victims)

Court Cases 21,559

Convictions 11,373

27

The Canadian criminal justice system is an **adversarial system**. The advocates for each party—in criminal cases, the defence lawyer and prosecutor—present their cases before a neutral judge or a jury. The standard that must be met by the prosecution is proof **beyond a reasonable doubt**; that is, "no other logical explanation can be derived from the facts except that the defendant committed the crime, thereby overcoming the presumption that a person is innocent until proven guilty."[10] You will recall from Chapter 1 that this is a much higher burden of proof than is required in civil cases.

This system is in contrast to the inquisitorial system of justice that operates in many jurisdictions in continental Europe. In this system, a judge, or panel of judges, assumes the role of investigating the crime. Our adversarial system has many rules of procedure and evidence governing criminal prosecutions. Some of these common law rules have been enshrined in the *Charter of Rights and Freedoms*. Several of the basic principles of the adversarial system are set out in Box 2.3.

A basic premise of the adversarial system is that the truth will emerge from the materials presented by the defence and Crown. Another premise is that the judge or jury will be a neutral third party and will make decisions solely on the evidence, not subject to any other influence. The over-representation of people from marginal groups and Aboriginal peoples in sentenced populations raises questions as to whether the adversarial system provides a level playing field and suggests that defendants with more resources (i.e., can hire the best defence lawyers) may be able to tip the scales of justice in their favour.

Critics of the adversarial system contend that the process encourages the parties to present a distorted version of events. There are also concerns with the quality of legal representation for many defendants and the ability of the criminal justice system to solve problems rather than merely reacting to them. This latter concern has provided the impetus for the development of specialized courts, which use the approach of therapeutic jurisprudence in a problem-solving framework in which court personnel collaborate with the police, social services, and mental health professionals (see Chapter 7). The attempt to improve the problem solving of the justice system has also led to the development of various restorative justice approaches.

Adversarial system

A system of justice that is based on two opposing sides—the prosecution and the defence—arguing the guilt or innocence of a person before a judge or jury.

Beyond a reasonable doubt

The standard that must be met to convict a defendant in a criminal case, which requires that the facts presented provide the only logical explanation for the crime.

BOX 2.3   BASIC PRINCIPLES OF THE ADVERSARIAL SYSTEM OF CRIMINAL JUSTICE

Presumption of innocence	A defendant is deemed innocent of the charge(s) until convicted by evidence proving beyond a reasonable doubt that the act was committed.
The Crown bears the burden of proof	It is the task of the Crown to prove guilt, not the responsibility of the accused to prove his or her innocence.
Doli incapax (Latin for "too young for evil")	A child under 12 cannot be held criminally responsible or prosecuted for criminal acts.
Severe mental disorders (insanity)	No one is criminally responsible and liable to punishment if incapable of knowing the act was wrong owing to a mental disorder.
Attempts are crimes	Those who attempt crimes (going beyond merely the planning stage) commit an offence and are generally subject to half the penalty that the completed act would draw.

THE ROLE OF DISCRETION IN THE CRIMINAL JUSTICE SYSTEM

Discretion

The freedom to choose among different options when confronted with the need to make a decision.

Criminal justice personnel respond to a wide variety of events in a wide variety of settings in conditions that often are not ideal. They carry out their tasks within the framework of written laws and policies; but they also exercise considerable **discretion** when making decisions. This flexibility can lead to inconsistencies in how laws are applied, how cases are processed in the courts, and what decisions are made about offenders by correctional officers, parole boards, and parole officers. In fact, historically, the justice process has been structured so as to provide criminal justice professionals with a considerable amount of discretion. However, this appears to be changing. The increasing focus on risk management and risk assessment in corrections, for example, has diminished the discretion exercised by probation officers.[11]

Many factors influence criminal justice personnel when they make discretionary decisions. At the centre of all these influences is the decision maker, a human being who brings to his or her work a unique combination of education, training, personal experiences, and perhaps religious beliefs. It would be naive to think that life experiences and community pressure do not sometimes influence the decisions made by criminal justice personnel. For example, the decision making of parole boards has come under intense scrutiny in recent years, in large part because of several high-profile cases in which offenders released by parole boards committed heinous crimes.

Even if discretion were not a factor, different justice system personnel would often make different decisions in a given situation. This difference is referred to as *disparity* in decision making and is due, in large measure, to the considerable professional autonomy of criminal justice personnel. For example, a sentencing judge may order probation, even though another judge would have sent the same offender to prison. Similarly, a parole applicant's chances for release may depend on the composition of the parole board panel that particular day.

ETHICS IN CRIMINAL JUSTICE

Ethics

"The foundation of knowledge that describes right/wrong or better/worse ... and applies to harm/care and fairness/reciprocity."

Ethics is an important issue in the criminal justice system. Ethics can be defined as "the foundation of knowledge that describes right/wrong or better/worse . . . and applies to issues of harm/care and fairness/reciprocity."[12] Many factors enter into judging ethical acts, as events and situations rarely present a right/wrong scenario. Most situations fall into a "grey" area—"the space between black and white."[13]

The focus on ethics highlights the presence of moral issues in the criminal justice system. The foundation of the system is the criminal law, enacted by legislators; criminal justice agencies are staffed by personnel with a range of professional qualifications, and persons who become involved in the justice system present with a broad range of issues, including mental illness and addiction.

Combined with the discretion that is given to criminal justice personnel, including police officers, judges, probation and parole officers, and others who work in the justice system, it is not surprising that ethical considerations are ever-present.[14]

Ethical issues

"Broad social questions, often concerning the government's social control mechanisms and the impact on those governed, for example, what laws to pass, what sentences to attach to certain crimes."

Criminologist Jocelyn Pollock has described several dimensions of ethics in criminal justice, including **ethical issues**, which are "broad social questions, often concerning the government's social control mechanisms and the impact on those

29

governed, for example, what laws to pass, what sentences to attach to certain crimes" and **ethical dilemmas**, which are situations in which criminal justice personnel must decide what do to.[15] Pollock notes that "the ethical issues that arise in relation to criminal justice are serious, difficult, and affect people's lives in fundamental ways."[16,17]

Police officers are faced with ethical dilemmas. For example, considerable controversy surrounds the use of police informants and paying known offenders for information.[18] See At Issue 2.1.

Hopefully, criminal justice personnel who have had ethics training are aware of the ethical issues that surround the exercise of discretion and are able to recognize the consequences of their actions.[19]

Canadian courts have also become more active in addressing the rights of inmates, including the right to serve time in a safe and secure environment. In an increasing number of cases, the federal government has been sued civilly by inmates who were victimized while serving time. Examining the ethical dilemmas that arise in the criminal justice system reveals that there is often a disconnect between what is legal and what is ethical. This difference will be illustrated again in our examination of police powers and decision making in Chapter 5 and in treatment interventions with inmates in correctional institutions in Chapter 11.

Ethical dilemmas

Situations in which criminal justice personnel must decide what do to.

IS THE CRIMINAL JUSTICE SYSTEM A DETERRENT?

Studies of the deterrent effect of the criminal law suggest that the law can serve as a deterrent only when certain conditions are present: (1) people must be aware that legal sanctions will be applied if they engage in certain behaviours; (2) there must be certainty of punishment; and (3) the sanction must be applied swiftly when a crime

AT ISSUE 2.1 SHOULD THE POLICE PAY OFFENDERS FOR INFORMATION ON KILLINGS?

Clifford Robert Olson was a serial child killer who terrorized the Greater Vancouver region during 1980–1981. He stalked and killed at least 11 children and sexually abused many others. Once apprehended, he blackmailed authorities in a cash-for-corpses agreement whereby his family was paid $100,000 in exchange for him leading police to the bodies of his victims. The decision on the part of the police was highly controversial and the ethics of the police decision were debated for many years.[20]

A similar case occurred recently in Winnipeg, wherein the Winnipeg Police Service paid a serial killer $1500 for information on missing and murdered women in Manitoba. Arrested on a sexual assault charge unrelated to homicides, Shawn Lamb subsequently made a deal with the police to provide information on two women he confessed to killing if money were deposited into his canteen account in the jail. He subsequently agreed to a plea bargain and was sentenced to 20 years in prison with no possibility of parole for 10 years.[21]

QUESTIONS

In your view, what ethical issues are raised by the practice of paying offenders for information? Do you agree with the decisions of the police in the Olson case and the Lamb case to pay for information? Should there be guidelines on when and how much offenders should be paid for information?

is committed.[22] Most Canadians are not involved in criminal offending, but people choose not to violate the law for a variety of reasons. These include pressures to conformity (e.g., family, employment, peers). The criminal law would not be ranked in the top reasons, if it were ranked at all.

For those persons who do become involved in conflict with the law, the criminal law may not be much of a deterrent either. Many offenders have a mental illness, an addictions, or fetal alcohol syndrome (a brain impairment). Still others are caught in situations of poverty and are on the margins of mainstream society. A smaller percentage are driven by the prospect of financial gain (i.e., persons involved in organized crime).

For those intent on committing crime, it is likely that the criminal law and the criminal justice system offer little in the way of deterrence. Punishment is neither certain nor swift. The clearance catch rate for many types of crime is quite low. The criminal justice system is based on an adversarial model that incorporates many elements of due process. The response of the system is often slow and deliberate, and defence lawyers may delay proceeding in an attempt to improve the position of their clients. Months and even years can pass before a determination of guilt or innocence is made and the appeal process exhausted. In the early 21st century, case delay has become a major issue in the criminal courts (see Chapter 8). Restorative justice approaches offer the prospect of a more timely, and effective, response to criminal offenders. These options are discussed in Chapter 13.

Summing up a review of the research on deterrence, one scholar concluded: "The empirical evidence leads to the conclusion that there is a marginal deterrent effect for legal sanctions . . . it is very difficult to state with any precision how strong a deterrent effect the criminal justice system provides."[23]

THE CRIMINAL JUSTICE SYSTEM AND AT-RISK AND MARGINALIZED PERSONS

ABORIGINAL PEOPLE IN THE CRIMINAL JUSTICE SYSTEM

Many Aboriginal people live on the margins of Canadian society. This fact is reflected in pervasive poverty, high rates of unemployment, low levels of formal education, and high death rates from accidents and violence. More than half of Aboriginal students fail to graduate from high school, and the unemployment rate among Aboriginal people is twice that of non-Aboriginals. Aboriginal youth may be prime targets for gang recruitment, which may result in involvement in the criminal justice and corrections systems.[24]

The subordinate political and economic condition of Aboriginal peoples is a consequence of their colonization by Europeans and of Canadian government policies that have exerted control over virtually every aspect of Aboriginal life. Racism and discrimination toward Aboriginal people have increased their marginality and vulnerability. Poverty, poor healthcare, and inadequate housing are pervasive in First Nations across Canada where deplorable conditions prevail. Significant challenges are faced by the increasing number of Aboriginal people residing in urban areas. These struggles include finding adequate housing and accessing programs and services.[25]

The residential school system, wherein Aboriginal children were forcibly removed from their families often for many years, contributed to the destruction of traditional culture and values, fractured Aboriginal families, resulted in widespread sexual victimization, and destroyed the fabric of many First Nations.[26]

One legacy of the colonization of Aboriginal peoples is their over-representation in the criminal justice system. Aboriginal people are over-represented in proportion to their numbers in the general population at all stages of the criminal justice system, from arrest to incarceration. An investigation into the Ontario justice system in 2013 found a "state of crisis," concluding that conflict exists between the adversarial system of justice and traditional Aboriginal approaches and that systemic discrimination against Aboriginals occurs in the criminal justice system.[27] Examples of cases in which the criminal justice system has discriminated against Aboriginal persons are discussed throughout the text. Of particular concern is the plight of Aboriginal women, among whom are high numbers of missing and murdered women. This issue is discussed in Chapter 6.

KEY CONCEPTS IN CRIMINAL JUSTICE

LEGITIMACY

Key to the effectiveness of the criminal justice system is that it be perceived as legitimate by citizens. The discussion in Chapter 3 will reveal that, with the exception of the police, the public holds a generally dim view of the criminal justice system (and the levels of support for the police have been dropping). Police initiatives are more effective when community residents view their efforts as legitimate (see Chapter 6). There are significant consequences when the public does not have confidence in the criminal justice system (see Chapter 3). Similarly, research studies show that offenders who participate in drug courts as an alternative to the traditional justice system are more likely to be successful if they view the judge as legitimate, that is, if there is procedural fairness in the court and the judge is attentive and respectful.[28]

One manifestation of the shift toward crime control is the focus on risk management and surveillance. This change has been accompanied by an increasing application of high technology, particularly in policing and in community-based and institutional corrections. This use has potentially significant consequences for the rights and privacy of citizens and offenders that are only now being raised.

ACCOUNTABILITY AND OVERSIGHT

Closely related to establishing the legitimacy of the criminal justice system is the creation of structures of accountability and oversight. In recent years, steps have been taken to increase the accountability of the criminal justice system. This change has coincided with the increasing involvement of the courts and the Canadian Human Rights Tribunal, which are now imposing on justice personnel a **duty to act fairly** in managing offenders. This duty means that decisions must be fair and equitable. Justice system personnel may be subject to criminal or civil prosecution, as well as to both internal and external review bodies. For example, police officers can be held accountable for their actions under civil law, the *Criminal Code*, provincial or territorial statutes, and freedom of information acts. Civilian oversight of the police has expanded to address the concerns surrounding police investigating police. Police boards, complaint commissions, and investigative units, both civilian and from other

Duty to act fairly

The obligation of corrections to ensure that that offenders are treated fairly by corrections personnel.

police services, have the authority to oversee and review the actions and decisions of police officers.

The policies and decisions made by systems of corrections are examined by the courts in view of the provisions of the *Charter of Rights and Freedoms and the Corrections and Conditional Release Act.* In corrections, offenders must have the opportunity to respond to any assessments made by correctional personnel about their conduct and performance. In 2012, for example, a federal judge ordered a review of the inmate grievance system in federal correctional facilities. This order was based on a finding that delays in resolving official grievances was contributing to increasing tensions and violence.[29] Reviews can be conducted by the federal Office of the Correctional Investigator, and coroner's inquests and commissions of inquiry and task forces also take place. Note that, unlike the decisions of the courts, the recommendations from these bodies are not binding on criminal justice agencies. Table 2.2 sets out a comparison of the accountability of criminal justice personnel.

Also note that the most extensive oversight is of the police. The multiple layers of oversight of the police are a consequence of the broad powers that police officers exercise, including the authority to use lethal force. However, other criminal justice personnel can make decisions that can have lethal consequences: a judge or jury wrongfully convicting a person who is subsequently attacked and killed inside a correctional institution; the parole board releasing a dangerous offender who subsequently causes the death of someone in the community; the decision of a Crown counsel to stay the proceedings against a person charged with a serious criminal offence who subsequently offends in a violent, lethal manner (as happened when a BC Crown counsel decided to stay proceedings against Robert Pickton in 1989; Pickton went on to murder dozens of women); the failure of corrections personnel to intervene to prevent a prisoner from committing suicide (as happened in the case of Ashley Smith, see Chapter 11); or the failure of a parole officer to adequately supervise

TABLE 2.2 ACCOUNTABILITY OF CRIMINAL JUSTICE PERSONNEL. A COMPARISON

Position	Internal and External Oversight
police officer	internal and external accountability; civilian oversight; subject to criminal charges and civil suits
Crown counsel	subject to internal review; no independent oversight; generally immune from prosecution and being required to testify in court
defence lawyer	subject to review and sanction by professional association; no independent oversight
judge	provincial and territorial judges subject to internal review; federal judges subject to review, sanctioning, or dismissal by the Canadian Judicial Council; eight public inquiries into the behaviour of judges from 1971 to 2009; removal is rare; no external independent oversight for any judges
probation officer	subject to internal review; generally immune from prosecution; no external independent oversight
parole board member	subject to internal review; generally immune from prosecution; no external independent oversight
parole officer	subject to internal review; generally immune from prosecution; no external independent oversight

TABLE 2.3   EVIDENCE-BASED PRACTICES VERSUS TRADITION-BASED PRACTICES

	Evidence-Based Practices	Emotion-Based Practices
Purpose	Provide efficient and effective responses to problems	Respond to individual beliefs and desire for revenge
Assumption	Policies and practices should be based on evidence.	Policies should be responsive to emotions.
Relationship to the Goals of the Criminal Justice System	Practices are developed with a focus given to all goals of the criminal justice system.	The focus is primarily on retribution and just desserts.
Focus on Cost	Cost effectiveness is central to decision making.	Limited focus
The Role of the Community	The community plays an active role by providing information that can be used to determine effectiveness.	The community plays a passive role, with opinions serving as the public's input.
The Role of Leaders	Leaders promote cultural change in the organization.	Leaders manage and maintain traditional strategies.
Role of Line Officers	Implement and set new practices	Maintain status quo
Time Orientation	Focus on present and future	Focus on the past
Focus on Evaluation	Extensive	Limited
The Role of Researchers	Researchers evaluate programs to determine effectiveness and recommend changes.	Researchers study public attitudes and provide little input to program effectiveness.
Definition of Success	Quality of program	Quantity of offenders

Source: Adapted from M. DeMichele and B. Payne. 2009. *Offender Supervision with Electronic Technology. Community Corrections Resource.* Washington, D.C.: U.S. Department of Justice. p. 50. http://www.appa-net.org/eweb/docs/APPA/pubs/OSET_2.pdf

a high-risk offender in the community, resulting in harm (or death) to a person in the community.

EVIDENCE-BASED POLICIES AND PROGRAMS

Throughout the text, the term **evidence-based practice** is used in discussions of policies and programs at various stages of the criminal justice system. Evidence-based practices are those policies, strategies, and programs that have been shown by evaluation research to be effective in achieving specified objectives.

These can be contrasted with tradition-based practices that are the result of established routines, politics, the philosophies of agencies, organizations, individuals, and emotion. See Table 2.3.

Attempts to implement evidence-based practices have been uneven and many agencies do not have the capacity to become knowledgeable about effective approaches or do not have the organizational capacity to alter their approach.

Evidence-based practice

Policies, strategies, and programs that have been shown by evaluation research to be effective in achieving specified objectives.

SELECTED TRENDS IN CANADIAN CRIMINAL JUSTICE

A number of very distinct trends in the criminal justice system in the early 21st century are having an impact on criminal justice agencies and the response to criminal offenders. These trends include, but are certainly not limited to, the following: higher costs, the increased centralization of authority, a conservative penal populism and punitive penology, the changing boundaries of criminal justice agencies, the increased use of surveillance, the downloading of responsibilities onto the justice system, and the challenges of diversity.

THE ESCALATING COSTS OF THE CRIMINAL JUSTICE SYSTEM

The criminal justice system is a very expensive enterprise. Over the past decade, criminal justice expenditures have increased both in real terms and as a percentage of GDP (gross domestic product). See Figure 2.5. A breakdown of expenditures is presented in Figure 2.6.

The estimated annual cost for policing in Canada is more than $13 billion, and expenditures have increased for the past 13 years.[30] Corrections expenditures have also increased, reaching $2.4 billion in 2010–2011, a 30 percent increase over the previous five years.[31] The cost of housing a male inmate in a maximum-security institution is more than $100,000 a year, and the costs for female inmates are even higher. In contrast, the average annual cost per offender for community supervision is about one-quarter that of an inmate in a minimum-security institution ($113,974 for an offender in an institution; $29,537 for an offender in the community).[32] An analysis of data for one federal female offender currently serving a 21.5-year sentence estimated the total cost at $7.4 million.[33]

The Parliamentary Budget Officer has estimated that the provisions of Bill C-10 and other legislation passed by the federal government will result in significant increases in criminal justice expenditures for case prosecution, incarceration, parole reviews, and supervision in the community—the majority of these costs to be downloaded onto the provincial and territorial governments.[34] These cost

FIGURE 2.5 ▶

Canadian Crime Rate and Criminal Justice Expenditure as a Percentage of GDP

Source: R. Story and T.K. Yalkin. 2013. *Expenditure Analysis of Criminal Justice in Canada.* Ottawa: Office of the Parliamentary Budget Officer, p. 2; http://www.pbo-dpb.gc.ca/files/files/Crime_Cost_EN.pdf. Reproduced with the permission of the Parliamentary Budget Officer, 2013.

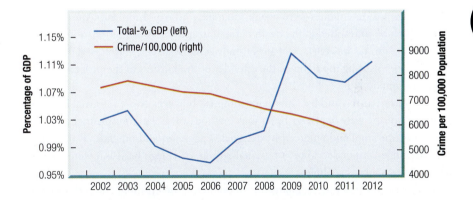

FIGURE 2.6 ▶

Criminal Justice Expenditure Proportion, 2012

Source: R. Story and T.K. Yalkin. 2013. *Expenditure Analysis of Criminal Justice in Canada.* Ottawa: Office of the Parliamentary Budget Officer, p. 18; http://www.pbo-dpb.gc.ca/files/files/Crime_Cost_EN.pdf. Reproduced with the permission of the Parliamentary Budget Officer, 2013.

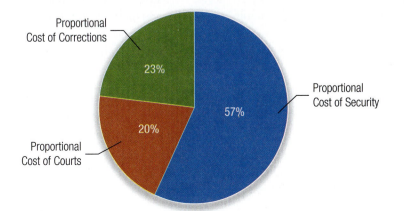

increases are occurring at a time when the police-reported crime rate continues to decline.[35]

A key question that is being raised is whether the Canadian public is getting value for money; that is, do the expenditures on the police, the courts, and corrections and related programs and services make communities safe from crime, address the needs of crime victims, and intervene to reduce the likelihood that offenders will continue their criminal behaviour? Unfortunately, the answer to these questions is often "We're not certain." Too often, criminal justice agencies have not had the capacity to assess their performance and to determine the outcomes of their strategies and decisions. This situation is slowly changing because of the fiscal crises of governments: the criminal justice system is under increasing pressure to adopt evidence-based practices (often referred to as *best practices*), to develop performance measures, and to document outcomes.

THE INCREASING CENTRALIZATION OF AUTHORITY

A major contributor to the rising expenditures in the criminal justice system has been the historical trend toward an expanding criminal justice system. This expansion mirrors the trend toward the centralization of authority, the increased professionalization of criminal justice, and a concurrent reduction in substantive community participation in the justice system.

Before the rise of complex societies, order was maintained through informal social controls. Behaviour was regulated by norms, folkways, and mores, and there were strong in-group pressures to conform. The response to harmful acts generally took the form of personal and group retaliation and was based on the notion of revenge. Other informal control techniques were gossip, ridicule, and expulsion from the group, the last of which often resulted in the death of the transgressor. A primary attribute of these societies and groups was the lack of any formal agents of social control. And they had no provision for ensuring the rights of the offender or the fairness of the process by which they were sanctioned.

As societies evolved and became more complex, however, these informal social control mechanisms were replaced by formal methods of social control, including laws, enacted by the state and enforced by designated agencies and officials. Transgressions were no longer responded to on a personal, group, or village basis but were viewed as acts against society as a whole.

Systems of criminal justice, charged with enforcing the criminal law and responding to offenders, emerged and expanded. Criminal justice professionals assumed control of the prevention of and response to crime. The long-standing assumption has been that highly trained professionals, such as judges, are required to ensure that the criminal justice system is effective. As a result, communities and their residents became less and less involved in the process of social control. The increasing centralization of the social control function resulted in the transfer of power and authorities to governments and criminal justice agencies.

Despite the continued growth and proliferation of criminal laws and criminal justice agencies and personnel, evidence suggests that formal social control mechanisms may, in many instances, be less effective than are informal mechanisms in controlling behaviour and maintaining order in society. In fact, as discussed in Chapter 1, the effectiveness of the criminal law may be limited. This reality has contributed to the trend of exploring alternative approaches to justice, including restorative justice, which provides for the involvement of community residents and which is premised on a different set of principles than the traditional, adversarial system of justice (see Chapter 13).

THE EMERGENCE OF CONSERVATIVE PENAL POPULISM AND PUNITIVE PENOLOGY

Penal populism

Corrections policies that are formulated in pursuit of political objectives, often in the absence of an informed public or in spite of public opinion.

The political climate of a jurisdiction may determine the response to criminal offenders. In the United States, **penal populism** has been manifested by the three-strikes-and-you're-out legislation and mandatory minimum sentences, among other policies. In penal populism, government policies that appeal to the public are used to promote the electoral popularity of the government of the day but are ineffective in ensuring justice and reducing crime rates. These policies are often not reflective of public opinion or are formulated in the absence of an informed public.[36] This model, in turn, has resulted in *tough on crime* legislation and policies.[37] An increase in the number of mandatory minimum sentences and legislating restrictions on the conditional release of offenders from incarceration are just two of the ways in which governments move forward this agenda. See Box 2.4.

These policies resulted in significant increases in prison populations and in the number of minorities who are incarcerated. In 2011, one in nine Black men between 20 and 34 years of age was confined in prison, and one in four Blacks men were either confined or had been in prison at some point in their lives.[38]

In 2009, the California state auditor estimated that the three strikes legislation was going to cost taxpayers an extra $19.1 billion.[39] In response to these excessive costs, California and other states have begun to roll back three strikes

---

BOX 2.4 "THREE STRIKES AND YOU'RE OUT!" THE CASE OF THE PIZZA THIEF

In March, 2005, Jerry Dewayne Williams was sentenced to 25 years to life under California's "three strikes" law for stealing a slice of pizza from a group of youths who were dining on an extra-large pie at Redondo Beach Pier near Los Angeles. Williams had five previous felony convictions, and the original charge of petty theft (a summary-type offence in the United States) was upgraded to a felony because of his previous convictions. Following the sentencing, the prosecutor noted that Williams was being sentenced not for the theft but for his history of offending: "The people of California are sick and tired of revolving-door justice, they're sick of judges who are soft on crime. It is wrong to focus on the last offence."[40] The case of the pizza thief became the focal point of the debate over California's tough on crime approach. William's attorney subsequently successfully pleaded with the sentencing judge to reduce the sentence, and William was released after serving five years.

This case reflects an extreme example of the get tough approach to crime and offenders that has been operating in the United States for many years. Although Canada does not have three strikes legislation, a significant shift has occurred in Canada that includes an expansion of the number of mandatory minimum sentences. In this chapter, we've explored the structure and process of criminal justice and can see that the response to crime and criminal offenders has become more imitative of the United States, while that jurisdiction has begun to back away from a focus on severe punishments. In 2013, the U.S. Attorney General called mandatory minimum jail sentences "counterproductive" and indicated that the federal government would move toward eliminating these and other harsh sentencing guidelines for non-violent drug offenders.[41] The focus instead would shift to addressing poverty and community conditions that spawned drug use.

legislation. Increasingly, authorities are turning their attention to reintegration and community-based treatment programs, including treatment for drug addiction.

◀ Protestors against Bill C-10

Concurrent with these developments were a number of court decisions, including one from the U.S. Supreme Court, that held that prison overcrowding violated the constitutional rights of inmates and directed states to reduce prison populations. Thousands of inmates were released early, overwhelming community corrections staff and programs. In 2009, the prison population in California fell to its lowest level in 38 years.[42]

In Canada in the early 21st century, there has been a discernible shift toward punitive penology. Federal legislation has increased the severity of criminal sanctions and expanded the control that is exercised over offenders.

This shift away from a liberal model of criminal justice policy and practice that prevailed for decades is reflected in the provisions of Bill C-10 and other legislation enacted during 2010–2012: new and increased mandatory minimum sentences, constraints on the use of conditional sentences, and new criminal offences.[43] Other legislation passed during 2010–2012 abolished the two-for-one credit for time served before sentencing and eliminated accelerated parole review, under which non-violent, first-time offenders were eligible for parole after serving one-sixth of their sentence rather than the standard one-third.

There has been judicial push-back against the restrictions imposed on sentencing. In a number of cases, criminal court judges have held that mandatory minimum sentences violated *Charter of Rights and Freedom* provisions against cruel and unusual punishment. In 2013, the Ontario Court of Appeal struck down as unconstitutional and as "cruel and unusual punishment" the three-year mandatory minimum for possessing a loaded prohibited gun and for five years on the second offence. Given the broad range of activities that would be subject to the legislation, from a gun licence violation to possession of a gun for purposes of criminal activity, the Court noted that there could be a "cavernous disconnect" between the severity of the offence and the severity of the sentence.[44] The effectiveness of mandatory minimum sentences is discussed in Chapter 9.

In 2013, the federal government proposed a Victim Bill of Rights that would require that crime victims be more extensively involved in the criminal justice process. One provision, for example, would require Crown prosecutors to secure the approval of victims before signing off on plea bargains with the defendant's legal counsel (see Chapter 3).

Criminal justice agencies are also the target of civil suits launched by crime victims and inmates. Prisoners have taken systems of corrections to court over such issues as living conditions inside correctional institutions, prison disciplinary actions, and various regulations. In 2013, it was revealed that Public Safety Canada does not document the costs of legal fees for the five agencies that fall under its mandate: the RCMP, the Correctional Service Canada (CSC), CSIS, the Parole Board of Canada, and CBSA, or Public Safety itself.[45] In a response to a written question posed by an MP, the public safety minister responded that no answer could be provided because of "inconsistent filing systems, insufficiently detailed records, overly tight timelines, and, in the case of CSIS, the need to protect 'operational security'."[46]

CHANGING BOUNDARIES OF CRIMINAL JUSTICE AGENCIES

Historically, clear boundaries have existed between the various components of the criminal justice system. This division often resulted in agencies operating in silos, focused only on their specific mandate and not considering the larger context of a problem of crime and disorder, specific patterns of criminal behaviour, or the needs of offenders, which are often multifaceted (such as those with addictions or mental health issues).

Recent years have witnessed the development of integrated multi-agency teams. These teams may be focused on a specific neighbourhood or on a group of offenders and bring together police officers, social workers, mental health workers, and other community resources. This approach to problem solving is more holistic and has the potential to effectively address the underlying issues that contribute to crime and disorder, rather than merely responding to the symptoms of these issues.

Although agencies can benefit by moving out of their silos, there are concerns that these teams blur the mandates of individual components of the justice system; for example, when parole officers work in teams with police officers, it may create an inordinate focus on surveillance and control to the detriment of the helping and assistance role of parole officers.[47] These changing boundaries are also illustrated by the rise of tiered policing, wherein private security and para-police are assuming functions traditional performed by sworn police officers.

THE RISE OF THE SURVEILLANCE SOCIETY

A key feature of life in the early 21st century is the pervasiveness of technology and, more specifically, surveillance technology. Most citizens do not realize that, everyday, their activities are recorded by video cameras, while shopping, standing at a bus stop, or driving. Ostensibly, surveillance technology ensures the safety and security of the general public. A major challenge is defining the parameters within which technology can be used and how the privacy and other rights of citizens can be protected. Since the 9/11 terrorist attacks, there has been an increasing focus on security.

In studying the levels of trust and support for government surveillance policies, researchers have found that persons with higher levels of education are more supportive of security and surveillance legislation that restricts civil liberties and that there is less support among persons of lower socio-economic status.[48] This finding is contrary to what we might expect until we consider that more highly educated persons have a great stake in the system than marginalized persons. Persons of lower socio-economic status may also be more likely to have had direct contact with the criminal justice system and to experience violations of their constitutional rights.

The use of high technology in the criminal justice system is in its infancy although concerns are already being raised. In some instances, technology has obvious benefits, such as allowing prison inmates to use Skype with their loved ones who may be unable to travel to the

Chris Slane (www.slane.co.nz)

39

institution for visits or reducing re-offending by sex offenders by monitoring them with GPS.[49] However, privacy laws have not kept pace with these developments, leaving it to citizens to voice their concerns about and, in some instance, opposition, to specific surveillance strategies. This occurred in 2012 in Seattle, when a public outcry forced the Seattle Police Department to terminate an unmanned drone pilot project (see Chapter 6). As of 2013, several Canadian police services were using unmanned drones in the absence of any legislative restrictions. The impact of technology on criminal justice will be considered throughout the text.

Ironically, a key feature of the surveillance society is the use of technology by citizens. In Chapter 3, we'll see that images taken of rioters involved in the post-game-seven hockey riot in Vancouver in 2011 produced a form of vigilante justice while also providing the Vancouver Police Department with unprecedented video evidence that was subsequently used to identify, charge, and convict persons involved in the riot. As of late 2013, 258 persons had been formally charged and 126 had received sentences ranging from a conditional discharge to more than a year in jail.[50] Chapter 5 includes a discussion of how cellphone cameras have impacted the decision making of police officers on the street.

DOWNLOADING ONTO THE JUSTICE SYSTEM

The discussion in the chapters that follow will reveal that the criminal justice system is populated by a disproportionate number of persons with mental illness, addictions, and other challenges. These persons present challenges for the police, courts, and corrections. A feature of policing in the early 21st century, for example is the downloading of responsibilities by governments; that is, the police are being required to fill gaps in service that are the mandated responsibility of other agencies and organizations.

Police services across the country are spending an increasing portion of their time responding to high-risk and vulnerable populations, including those with mental illnesses. The chief of the London, Ontario, police service estimates that the police response to people with mental illnesses cost $12 million in 2012, monies that the chief acknowledges would be better spent developing programs and services for this high-needs population.[51] We'll explore this issue further in Chapter 4.

THE CHALLENGES OF DIVERSITY

Any study of the criminal justice system must consider the diversity that exists in Canadian society. This diversity extends to Aboriginal peoples, gender, LGBT, visible and cultural minorities, and other groups. Although Canada prides itself on being a multicultural society, this concept has been challenged in recent years. The issue has been heightened by Bill C-60 that was proposed in Québec in 2013. While the chances of the bill being passed into law were reduced with the defeat of the Parti Québécois in early 2014, that it was proposed and had widespread support among Québeckers raises important issues. See At Issue 2.2.

The criminal justice system has often struggled with accommodating diversity, and examples of this are cited throughout the text. It was only in the 1980s, for example, that the RCMP changed its policy to allow Sikh members to wear a turban as part of the uniform, a practice that would be banned under the aforementioned Bill C-60 in Québec.

AT ISSUE 2.2 SHOULD BILL C-60, THE QUÉBEC CHARTER OF VALUES, BE ALLOWED TO STAND IN CANADA?

In 2013 in Québec, the Parti Québécois introduced Bill C-60, "Charter Affirming the Values of Securlarism and the Religious Neutrality of the State, as Well as the Equity of Men and Women, and the Framing of Accommodation Requests," most commonly referred to as the Charter of Values. Key provisions of the bill include the following:

Protesters in Québec demonstrate against Bill C-60.

- Amend the *Québec Charter of Rights and Freedoms.*
- Establish a duty of neutrality for all personnel employed by the state.
- Limit the wearing of "conspicuous" religious symbols by state personnel.
- Make it mandatory for state personnel to have their face uncovered when providing or receiving a state service.

Included is the following wording: "In the exercise of their functions, personnel members of public bodies must not wear objects such as headgear, clothing, jewelry or other adornments which, by their conspicuous nature, overtly indicate a religious affiliation." Many observers contend that the legislation is aimed primarily at Muslim women who wear the hajib (headscarf) and niqab (veil).

Québec's Privacy Commission has determined that the proposed charter violates the fundamental rights of citizens.[52] The issue whether the legislation is moral has also been raised.[53] Polls indicate that most Canadians oppose the notion of a person working for the state being fired for not adhering to the requirements of the new charter.[54] (See the Media Links "Quebec's Charter of Values" and "Quebec Charter of Values Reduced to Absurdity in Fake Ads" at the end of the chapter.)

The proposed bill likely died with the defeat of the Parti Québécois in early 2014. However, the fact that it was ever introduced makes it an important topic for discussion.

QUESTIONS

What is your view of this proposed legislation? Do you accept the arguments put forth by the Parti Québécois?

SUMMARY

This chapter has focused on the structure and process of criminal justice. The key differences between the fields of criminology and criminal justice were identified, and the two competing models for the administration of justice—the crime control model and the due process model—were discussed. The roles and responsibilities of the federal, provincial or territorial, and municipal governments in criminal justice were set out, and the flow of cases through the justice system, exemplified by a crime funnel, was depicted. The importance of considering the ethical dimensions of criminal justice and the exercise of discretion were examined. Many of the issues that arise in the justice system are related to the exercise of discretion by criminal justice personnel. The accountability of criminal justice personnel, the role of legitimacy, and the importance of evidence-based practice were discussed. Several trends in criminal justice in the early 21st century were identified.

KEY POINTS REVIEW

1. The criminal justice system is a human enterprise as it involves people (criminal justice personnel) making decisions about other people (suspects and offenders).

2. There are key differences between the fields of criminology and criminal justice.

3. The criminal justice system is generally considered to contain all the agencies, organizations, and personnel that are involved in the prevention of, and response to, crime and to persons charged with criminal offences and persons convicted of crimes.

4. The criminal justice system includes the police, courts, and corrections, as well as other agencies and organizations.

5. The two competing models of criminal justice administration are the due process model and the conflict model.

6. Responsibility for criminal justice is shared among the federal, provincial or territorial, and municipal governments.

7. The flow and attrition of cases through the criminal justice system can be represented graphically by means of a funnel.

8. The basic principles of the adversarial system of criminal justice includes the presumption of innocence, the Crown bearing the burden of proof, and that age and mental capacity may limit criminal responsibility.

9. There are a number of external influences on the criminal justice system, including fiscal pressures, politics, and legislation.

10. Discretion and ethics play important roles in the criminal justice system.

11. Important concepts in the study of criminal justice include accountability, legitimacy, and the use of evidence-based practice.

12. There are a number of trends in criminal justice in the early 21st century, including escalating costs, the increased centralization of authority, the emergence of a conservative penal populism, and the rise of surveillance, among others.

KEY TERM QUESTIONS

1. Define and contrast the fields of **criminology** and **criminal justice**.

2. Identify the components of the **criminal justice system**.

3. Compare and contrast the **crime control** and **due process models** of criminal justice administration.

4. What is a **task environment** in criminal justice, and why is this concept important in the study of criminal justice?

5. Why is the *Constitution Act, 1867* important in the study of Canadian criminal justice, and what responsibilities does it assign for criminal justice?

6. What is the *Criminal Code*?

7. Define what is meant by the **adversarial system**, note its key principles, and then identify advantages and disadvantages of this system of criminal justice.

8. What does **beyond a reasonable doubt** mean in the adversarial system of criminal justice?

9. What roles do **discretion**, **ethics**, and the **duty to act fairly** play in the criminal justice system?

10. Describe and contrast **ethical issues** and **ethical dilemmas**.

11. What is **penal populism**, and how is it manifested in the criminal justice system?

12. What is **evidence-based practice**, and why is it important in any study of the criminal justice system?

MEDIA LINKS

"Quebec's Charter of Values," *The Agenda* with Steve Paikin or go to the book's website at www.nelson.com/ crimjusticeprimer5e.com

"Quebec Charter of Values Reduced to Absurdity in Fake Ads" or go to the book's website at www.nelson.com/ crimjusticeprimer5e.com

"UK Addiction to Surveillance: The Big Brother Society" or go to the book's website at www.nelson.com/ crimjusticeprimer5e.com

43

CHAPTER 3

CRIME, VICTIMS, AND THE COMMUNITY

LEARNING OBJECTIVES

After reading this chapter, you should be able to

- discuss Canadian crime rates and trends
- identify the factors related to crime reporting
- identify and discuss the factors related to the risk of becoming a crime victim
- describe programs and services for crime victims
- discuss public perceptions of crime and the criminal justice system
- discuss the role of the media in creating public images of crime and criminal justice
- discuss the impact of social media on the criminal justice system and the community
- discuss the activities of groups such as Anonymous

CRIME RATES

Crime rate

The number of incidents known to the police expressed in terms of the number of people in the population.

The **crime rate** is the number of criminal incidents known to the police expressed in terms of the number of people in the population. It is generally spoken of in terms of the number of incidents for each 100,000 people (adults and children). Most discussions rely on official statistics, which can provide a *general* picture of crime rates and trends. Some observers have argued that the method by which the federal government compiles crime statistics results in an inaccurate view and that, in fact, the rates of certain categories of crime may not be declining. This method includes counting only the most serious crimes among multiple offences committed by the same person, reporting the rates rather than the volume of crime, and dealing with variations in police reporting practices.[1]

Another problem with using the official crime rate is that many crimes are not reported by victims, while other crimes go undetected. This difference results in a **dark figure of crime**.

Dark figure of crime

The difference between how much crime occurs and how much crime is reported to or discovered by the police.

Findings from research studies have revealed the following:

- The rate of reporting to the police has declined in recent years. As much as half of the estimated incidents involving victims are never brought to the attention of the police. Fewer than 4 in 10 incidents involving sexual assault, robbery, assault, break and enter, theft of motor vehicles and motor vehicle parts, and vandalism are reported to police.

- The likelihood of victims calling the police is not related to the seriousness of the offence; even violent offences often go unreported.

- Reporting practices vary across different regions of the country.

- There are age and gender differences in reporting by crime victims.

- Crime is underreported in many Aboriginal communities. One study found that even though 52 percent of the incidents of victimization involved a violent crime, 74 percent of the victims did not report the crime to the police.[2]

- A utilitarian factor appears to be at work in victims' decisions to call the police. Crime victims know that, for many types of crimes, there is little the police can do.[3]

A number of strategies are used in an attempt to gain a more accurate view of the incidence of crime. These include self-report surveys, which ask respondents whether they have committed a criminal offence, and victimization surveys, which ask respondents whether they have been victimized and whether they reported it to the police (and why not, if they didn't). These methods have shortcomings that often make it difficult to accurately determine the amount of crime.

The majority of crimes known to the police are brought to their attention by the victims of crime or witnesses to crime. Less than 5 percent of crimes are discovered by the police without the assistance of the public or a crime victim.

CRIME TRENDS

Official statistics on crime indicate the following:[4]

- The police-reported crime rate has declined and is at its lowest level since 1972.

- The crime severity index, which includes the volume and seriousness of police-reported crime, has declined over the past decade.

- The rates of crime are highest in the territories and in the Western regions of the country (see Figure 3.1).

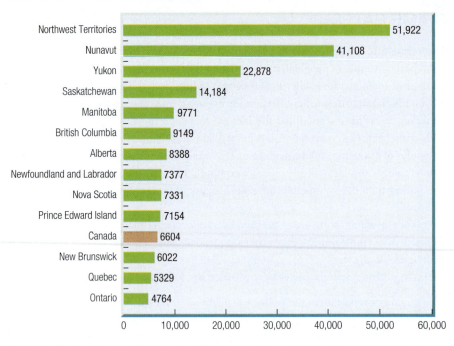

Source: Canadian Crime Rates, per 100,00 population, 2011, from *Corrections and Conditional Release: Statistical Overview*, http://www.publicsafety.gc.ca/cnt/rsrcs/pblctns/2012-ccrs/2012-ccrs-eng.pdf. Reproduced with the permission of the Minister of Public Safety and Emergency Preparedness Canada, 2013.

- Violent crime continues to decline, although the rates remain high in the territories and in selected Western cities, including Winnipeg and Saskatoon, and in Thunder Bay.
- Property crimes have generally declined over the past decade.
- Police-reported youth crime has declined in recent years.

Figures 3.2 and 3.3 illustrate the downward trends in violent and non-violent crimes in Calgary from 2002 to 2011.

It's unlikely that the declining crime rates are a result of the "get tough" approach of the federal government, including the expansion of the number of mandatory minimum sentences (see Chapter 2). Crime rates were decreasing long before the government began implementing its legislative agenda, and the decline is most likely due to a number of factors, including a decline in the number of males in the crime-prone 18–24 age range and the increasing use of technology for crime prevention. The use of effective strategies by the police, discussed in Chapter 6, has also contributed to crime prevention.[5]

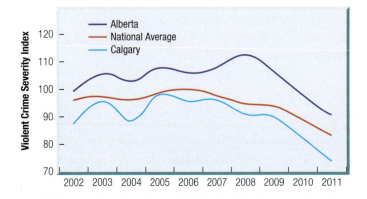

◄ FIGURE 3.2

Violent Crime Severity Index, Calgary 2002–2011

Source: Calgary Police Service. 2012. *Annual Statistical Report 2007-2011. Statistical Survey*, p. 7. http://www.calgary.ca/cps/Documents/statistical-reports/2007-2011-annual-statistical-report.pdf?noredirect=1. Reprinted by permission of the Calgary Police Service.

FIGURE 3.3 ►

Non-violent Crime Severity Index, Calgary 2002–2011

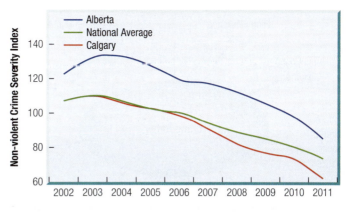

Source: Calgary Police Service. 2012. *Annual Statistical Report 2007-2011. Statistical Survey*, p. 10. http://www.calgary.ca/cps/Documents/statistical-reports/2007-2011-annual-statistical-report.pdf?noredirect=1. Reprinted by permission of the Calgary Police Service.

CRIME IN FIRST NATIONS AND INUIT COMMUNITIES

Two of the biggest challenges facing the criminal justice system are the high rates of crime and victimization in many Aboriginal communities and the overrepresentation of Aboriginal people at all stages of the justice process. The situation is particularly acute in communities north of 60: Yukon, the Northwest Territories, and Nunavut, where the crime rates are as much as five times higher than for Canada as a whole.

First Nations women are particularly vulnerable to violence, and too often, few programs and resources are available to assist them. These women typically must leave their own community to seek safety in a women's shelter, often hundreds of kilometres from home. The remote location and small population of northern communities means that the police are most often the only nearby representatives of the justice system. Court services are delivered via fly-in or drive-in circuit courts composed of a judge, a Crown attorney, a defence lawyer, and court officials (see Chapter 7). Corrections services are often non-existent, and correctional institutions are usually hundreds or thousands of kilometres away.

There are also high rates in crime and victimization among Aboriginal peoples in urban centres. These rates are often an extension of on-reserve conditions of violence, poverty, and addiction, the unfortunate legacy of the colonization of Aboriginal peoples and their marginal status in Canadian society. In Winnipeg, for example, the north end area of the city is afflicted by high levels of crime, including violence associated with Aboriginal gangs.

THE COSTS OF CRIME

The estimated annual cost of the criminal justice system was around $31 billion. If the other costs of crime are factored in, including the pain and suffering experienced by victims, the reduction in quality of life, and lost income, the figure balloons to nearly $100 billion a year.[6] This expense is highlighted in the justice system costs and collateral costs for specific types of crime.

For spousal violence (for women and men), the annual cost is estimated to be $7.4 billion. This amount includes costs associated with the criminal justice and civil justice system; the intangible costs to victims, including pain and suffering and loss of life; healthcare costs; and third-party costs (i.e., the impact on families and employers); among others.[7] The cybercrime of hacking is estimated to cost

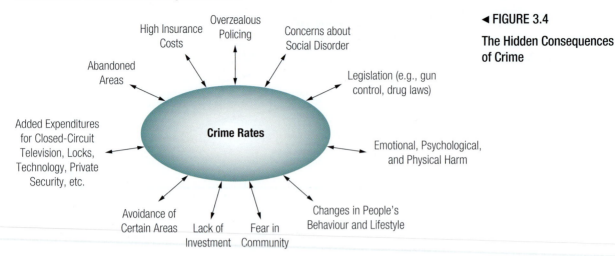

What are the implications for each of the consequences in the figure?

Source: C.G. Nicholl. *Community Policing, Community Justice, and Restorative Justice: Exploring the Links for the Delivery of a Balanced Approach to Public Safety.* (Washington, DC: Office of Community-Oriented Policing Programs, 1999).

Canadians $1.4 billion a year (and $110 billion globally; see the PowerPoint slide set from the 2012 Norton Cybercrime Report at www.slideshare.net/NortonOnline/2012-norton-cybercrime-report-14207489).

Recall the discussion in Chapter 1 about the potential decriminalization of marijuana possession. Figures from 2011 indicate that Canada spends $500 million annually on the enforcement and court processing of cannabis offenders, the majority of whom were charged and convicted of simple possession. In 2011, the cost to taxpayers in B.C. was about $8750 to convict a person on a simple possession charge.[8,9]

A number of costs or consequences of crime are not easily assigned a dollar value but are important to consider. These are depicted in Figure 3.4.

THE VICTIMS OF CRIME

Studies of victimization, most often involving self-report surveys, indicate the following:[10–13]

- Just over one-quarter of Canadians report being the victim of a crime. The majority of these incidents are non-violent and involve the theft of property.
- The rates of victimization are higher in Western Canada.
- Break and enter is more likely to be reported to the police than physical assaults.
- The majority of victims of violent crime are under age 30.
- Males between the ages of 18 and 24 are the most likely to be the victims of violent offences.
- The rates of victimization of Aboriginal peoples are higher than for non-Aboriginal people, and Aboriginal women are three times as likely as non-Aboriginal women to report that they have been the victim of spousal abuse.

In 2007, the federal Conservative government created the office of Ombudsman for Victims of Crime. A number of observers have expressed concerns that crime victims have been used for political purposes to further the *get tough on crime* agenda of the federal government.

THE FEAR OF CRIME AND THE RISKS OF VICTIMIZATION

Surveys indicate that the large majority (more than 90 percent) of Canadians are satisfied with their personal safety and are not concerned about becoming the victim of a crime.[14] This figure, however, may mask specific hot spots where community residents may be fearful of crime.

A variety of individual and neighbourhood factors contribute to the perceptions of crime and the fear of crime among community residents:[15]

- The fear of crime is greater in areas with a high proportion of low-income families, residents who are members of visible minority groups, and lone-parent families.
- Residents who identify social disorder in their neighbourhood also report higher levels of fear of crime.
- Citizens 65 and older tend to be more fearful of crime, as are those persons who have been previously victimized.

Several factors (many of which are interrelated) are linked to the risk of becoming a victim, including age (highest rates are among ages 15–24), gender (women are more likely to be the victims of sexual assault), and marital status (single men and women have highest rates of being violently victimized, with women who are separated from their partners being five times as likely to be killed by their ex-partners as are other women).

In many regions of the country, Aboriginal persons are at a high risk of being victimized. Aboriginal communities have rates of violent death three times as high as those of non-Aboriginal communities, and these rates are even higher in Inuit communities. Compounding the problem is the lack of resources and access to assistance for victims of crime in Northern and remote regions of the country.

VICTIMS OF CRIME AND THE CRIMINAL JUSTICE SYSTEM

Federal and provincial or territorial legislation sets out the rights of victims and defines their role in the justice process. Procedures have been established to provide victims with information on the status of cases and to notify victims if the offender is being released from custody or has escaped from custody. In addition, in several jurisdictions the definition of *victim* has been expanded to include the immediate family members of murder victims. These developments have been driven at least in part by the recognition that the criminal justice system has for too long focused more on the rights of offenders than on the rights of crime victims.

Evidence also shows that the psychological harm criminal offenders inflict on victims and communities has not been adequately addressed by the criminal justice system.

The role of crime victims in the criminal justice process will be highlighted throughout this book. Victims often initiate the criminal justice process by reporting the incident to the police (Chapter 4).

49

THE CHALLENGES FOR CRIME VICTIMS

Crime affects victims physically, psychologically, emotionally, financially, and socially. After the initial trauma of the crime, victims can be made to feel worse by the actions of criminal justice officials, resulting in **revictimization**.

Many crime victims find the justice system to be complex and confusing, and they have difficulty understanding the decisions that are made and the sanctions that are imposed on their perpetrators. One study found that crime victims often confused probation with conditional sentences, and others did not understand how the presiding judge weighed the various factors involved in the crime in deciding on the sentence.[16] Historically, this uncertainty has been compounded by criminal justice system personnel who were not trained to be sensitive to the needs of crime victims.

Although victims are a heterogeneous group with diverse needs and perceptions, their complaints and concerns have common themes. Historically, crime victims have been an afterthought in the criminal justice system. Criticisms that may be voiced by victims include not receiving sufficient information about developments in the case and being excluded from key decisions that are made throughout the criminal justice process.

Efforts to involve victims in the criminal justice process have increased, primarily through the presentation of victim-impact statements in court and through attendance at parole board hearings. But research studies have found that only a small percentage of crime victims submit impact statements in court and even fewer do in parole hearings. Victim impact statements are more likely to be submitted in cases involving serious offences.[17] Some observers have argued that empowering crime victims by involving them in the criminal justice system introduces undue emotionalism and increases the punitiveness of the system. See At Issue 3.1.

Revictimization

The negative impact on victims of crime caused by the decisions and actions of criminal justice personnel.

AT ISSUE 3.1 WHAT ROLE SHOULD VICTIMS PLAY IN THE CRIMINAL JUSTICE PROCESS?

In 2013, the Office of the Federal Ombudsman for Victims of Crime issued a report supporting the creation of a Victims Bill of Rights and passage of legislation to empower victims and provide a more active role for crime victims in the criminal justice process. Among the recommendations were that crime victims be informed of their rights when contacted by the police (similar to an accused person being read their rights on arrest), that victims automatically be kept informed of the progress of an offender's case through the justice system, that victims be notified of parole and review board decisions, that they be consulted by Crown counsel, and that they be given the right to access to free legal counsel in cases where the victim feels that these rights have been denied.

Bill C-479, which was being discussed as of early 2014, contains these and other provisions, including the right of offenders to review a decision of Crown counsel not to prosecute the accused and the right of victims to have input into plea negotiations. There is also a provision giving crime victims the rights to review the pre-sentence report (see Chapter 9) that is prepared on the offender. Offenders convicted of serious crimes who are rejected for parole release would have to wait five years for another hearing, rather than the current two-year waiting period.

QUESTIONS

What is your view about the proposed rights for crime victims? In what way would passage of Bill C-479 strengthen the justice system? In what ways might it undermine the administration of justice and due process?

BOX 3.1 STIGMATIZING AND BLAMING CRIME VICTIMS: MANITOBA JUSTICE ROBERT DEWAR

In February 2011, Manitoba Justice Robert Dewar sentenced Kenneth Rhodes to a two-year conditional sentence after finding him guilty of the rape of a 26-year-old woman. Crown counsel had asked for a sentence of three years in confinement. In giving his reasons for not sending the defendant to prison, Justice Dewar noted that the victim was wearing provocative clothing, including a tube top with no bra, stiletto heels, and lots of make-up. This outfit, the judge concluded, was an invitation to Mr. Rhodes, whom the judge described as a "clumsy Don Juan" who was insensitive to the victim's wishes not to have sexual relations. The judge indicated that the victim and her friend had "made it publicly known that they wanted to party" and that "sex was in the air."

The case sparked outrage across the country, including organized SlutWalks and calls for Justice Dewar to resign.

A complaint was filed with the Canadian Judicial Council, which reviewed the case. Its decision was to require Justice Dewar to meet with a gender-equality expert. Justice Dewar received no further sanction and resumed his judicial duties, including presiding over cases involving sexual assault.

QUESTION

In your view, should Justice Dewar have been forced to resign from the bench? Why? Why not?

Manitoba Justice Robert Dewar

Participants in the Toronto SlutWalk protesting the decision and comments of Manitoba Justice Robert Dewar.

Attitudes that victims are responsible for their plight still exist in the criminal justice system, as illustrated by the case presented in Box 3.1.

PROGRAMS AND SERVICES FOR VICTIMS OF CRIME

Over the past two decades, a wide range of programs and services have been developed to address the physical, emotional, and financial consequences of victimization, as well as to provide victims with information about the justice process and the progress of cases through the justice system. Most areas have victim services programs, many of which are operated by police services. These programs are often staffed by trained volunteers who work under the direction of a supervisor who is employed by the police service.

One initiative is the Regina Children's Justice Centre, profiled in Box 3.2.

A number of services that are not part of the justice system assist crime victims with their medical, therapeutic, spiritual, and housing needs. These include crisis lines,

> **BOX 3.2   THE REGINA CHILDREN'S JUSTICE CENTRE**
>
> The Regina Children's Justice Centre (RCJC) is a collaborative effort of the Regina Police Service, child protection workers, the Regina Qu'Appelle Heath Agency, and Crown counsel. It is designed to provide an integrated approach to the investigation of cases of alleged physical and sexual abuse of children and to cases involving child exploitation, Internet exploitation of children, and child pornography. The RCJC manages approximately 250 cases a year and uses a child-centred approach that is designed to prevent the revictimization of child victims.[18]

sexual assault crisis centres, hospitals, mental health agencies, translation and cultural interpretation services, child protection agencies, shelters for battered women and children, and second-stage housing programs. Self-help groups have been created by groups of former victims in all areas of the country, and several of these organizations both assist victims and lobby for victim-oriented reforms. These include the Canadian Resource Centre for the Victims of Crime and (as noted in Chapter 1) Mothers Against Drunk Driving (MADD).

Despite the proliferation of programs and services for crime victims in recent decades, few victims take advantage of these resources. A survey in Alberta, for example, found that only 3 percent of the victims surveyed ($N = 540$) accessed any programs or services for victims.[19] This low rate is due, in part, to the failure of the police to provide information to crime victims. In the same survey in Alberta, of those respondents ($N = 277$) who reported a crime to the police, only a small number were provided information on victims programs (17 percent) or were referred to other agencies for help (15 percent).

Immigrant and women and those who are members of visible minority groups may experience particular difficulties in accessing victim programs and services. These difficulties centre on an inability to speak or understand either English or French, a lack of knowledge about the legal and social service system and the resources that are available, a fear of deportation, and pressure from extended family members to remain silent.[20]

COMPENSATION FOR CRIME VICTIMS

Crime victims have several ways to seek financial redress for the harm caused by the victimization, including compensation for property offences by **restitution** paid by the offender upon an order by the court and through private insurance. Victims of personal injury offences can apply for financial compensation from the provincial government to cover expenses and damages directly related to the crime.

Criminal injury compensation programs operate in all provinces except Newfoundland and Labrador but not in the territories. Given the high rates of crime and victimization in these jurisdictions, this is of concern. Victims may be compensated for out-of-pocket expenses, such as lost wages and, in some provinces, for pain and suffering caused by the offence.

Criminal justice agencies may also be held accountable by crime victims and offenders through the civil courts. Crime victims may sue to recover damages from justice agencies that did not fulfill their mandate to protect, and offenders and suspects may sue to recover damages for actions taken by criminal justice personnel. Examples of such actions include excessive force by police, wrongful convictions by the criminal

Restitution
A court-ordered payment that the offender makes to the victim to compensate for loss of or damage to property.

Criminal injury compensation
Financial remuneration paid to crime victims.

courts, and the failure of systems of corrections to manage the risk posed by offenders in the community who subsequently inflicted harm on victims.

A landmark case with respect to the civil liability of a criminal justice agency was the case of *Jane Doe v. Toronto (Metropolitan) Commissioners of Police* (1998). In this case, Ms. Doe sued the Police Services Board, arguing that her victimization by a serial rapist was due to the negligence of the police in informing her that a rapist was active in her neighbourhood. The presiding judge in the Ontario Court (General Division) agreed that the police were negligent in failing to warn Jane Doe and other women in the area. The Toronto Police were ordered to pay $220,000 to Ms. Doe for pain and suffering and medical interventions.[21]

THE COMMUNITY AND THE CRIMINAL JUSTICE SYSTEM

In Chapter 2, it was noted that a key trend has been the increasing centralization of social control into what has become the criminal justice system. This trend resulted in the transfer of power and authorities to governments and criminal justice agencies. A significant outcome of this process was the marginalization of the community. For many years, the last vestige of significant community participation in the justice system was the jury, composed of ordinary citizens from the community. In the past two decades, two major developments have altered the criminal justice landscape and provided an opportunity for direct community involvement in the criminal justice system: the rise of social media and the pervasive cellphone camera (discussed below) and the emergence of various restorative justice approaches (discussed in Chapter 13).

This diminished role for the community is unfortunate, as it has been shown that strong social supports can contribute to pro-social behaviour and reduce the levels of criminality.[22]

PUBLIC CONFIDENCE IN THE CRIMINAL JUSTICE SYSTEM

As discussed in Chapter 1, a key requirement for an effective criminal justice system is that it be viewed as legitimate by the general public. The justice system must be viewed as ensuring the security of the community while at the same time protecting the rights of citizens.

Research studies indicate, however, that the following are true:

- Canadians generally express low levels of confidence in the criminal justice system.
- The Canadian public seems to have less confidence in the justice system than in other public sector institutions, such as education.[23,24]
- Although police services have typically recorded levels of support in the 80+ percent range, public trust in the police has declined in recent years, in large measure because of a number of high-profile incidents (discussed in Chapter 5): one national poll found that between 2003 and 2011, police officers' ratings on the trust survey had declined from 73 percent to 57 percent.[25]
- Despite the continuing decline in official crime rates, the Canadian public feels that the criminal justice system is too lenient on offenders.[26,27]
- While survey respondents have a fairly high level of trust in physicians (48 percent) and police officers (48 percent), the levels of trust of judges (27 percent) and lawyers (11 percent) are much lower.[28]

Source: C.G. Nicholl, *Community Policing, Community Justice, and Restorative Justice: Exploring the Links for the Delivery of a Balanced Approach to Public Safety* (Washington, NC: U.S. Department of Justice, Office of Community Oriented Policing Services, 1999).

- Canadians consistently overestimate the levels of crime and the rates of recidivism, underestimate the severity of punishment given to offenders, tend to believe that the criminal justice system is biased in favour of defendants, and overestimate both the rates of parole release and the reoffending rates of parolees.

A report of the Canadian Bar Association found widespread distrust of the justice system, which was viewed as being only "for people with money, arbitrary, difficult to navigate and inaccessible to ordinary people...and even unfair."[29]

Figure 3.5 identifies some of the negative consequences when communities depend on the justice system to respond to and solve a variety of problems. The vicious circle that results from unmet expectations is depicted in Figure 3.6.

In the words of one observer, the hidden message in Figure 3.6 is that "paid professionals are seen as care providers and problem solvers, inferring that community groups do not need to bother.... [P]rofessionals compound this sense by operating on assumptions about their own capacity for defining problems and coming up with remedies, rejecting citizens as problem definers and solvers."[30]

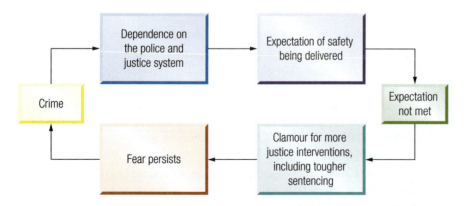

Source: C.G. Nicholl, *Community Policing, Community Justice, and Restorative Justice: Exploring the Links for the Delivery of a Balanced Approach to Public Safety* (Washington, NC: U.S. Department of Justice, Office of Community Oriented Policing Services, 1999).

Community residents protest against a sex ▶ offender released from prison taking up residence in their neighbourhood.

Red Deer Advocate/Randy Fiedler

Community sentiment about offenders and the justice system are often expressed through interest groups that lobby for more severe sanctions for criminal offenders, longer periods of incarceration, and more stringent requirements for release. Community residents, for example, are often very vocal in opposing offenders who have been released from prison taking up residence in their neighbourhood.

This opposition is often referred to under the acronym **NIMBY** (not in my backyard). This term refers to the resistance that communities display in response to correctional systems' efforts to locate programs and residences for offenders in a specific area. Citizen protests against the release of violent offenders and their relocation in the community are not unusual. In extreme cases, vigilantism may occur when community residents take the law into their own hands or, as has happened in the United States, citizens arm themselves. The Armed Citizen Project, for example, dispenses free guns to residents in high-crime areas so they can protect themselves.[31]

Research studies suggest that the levels of public confidence in the criminal justice system are not related to either the crime rate or victimization. Similarly, there appears to be no relationship between the severity of sanctions imposed on offenders in the criminal courts and public confidence in the criminal justice system.[32] These facts suggest that public confidence is a complex, multifaceted concept and that the use of the notion of a lack of public confidence in the criminal justice system as a rationale for punitive practices is not grounded in empirical research.

NIMBY (not in my backyard)

The resistance that communities display in response to correctional systems' efforts to locate programs and residences for offenders in a specific area.

THE MEDIA AND PUBLIC ATTITUDES TOWARD THE CRIMINAL JUSTICE SYSTEM

The media plays a significant role in shaping public attitudes toward the criminal justice system. For most Canadians, television, the Internet, and newspapers are the primary sources of information about crime and the criminal justice system.[33] The public seems to have an insatiable appetite for crime and chaos; witness the success of the television drama *CSI* and its various spinoffs. Crime and police shows produced in Canada and the United States consistently attract the largest viewing audiences. These shows, however, may oversimplify complex issues of crime and criminal justice. The media tend to be biased toward sensational crimes and to simplify crime and justice issues, and the public for its part tends to generalize from specific events.

The incidents that are reported and featured in the media tend to be those with negative outcomes. Think about the last time you heard a good-news story about offenders released from prison on parole (e.g., "As is our custom on the final Friday of each month on this newscast, we congratulate all of the offenders who successfully completed parole this month!"), as opposed to the more commonly heard comment by a newsreader on the nightly news: "Smith, on parole from Collins Bay penitentiary, was arrested for a series of armed robberies in the Kingston area."

The tendency of the media to focus on sensational cases, combined with the failure of criminal justice agencies to educate the populace, contributes to an uninformed and misinformed public. For example, with respect to conditional release, the public over-estimates the number of offenders who are released on parole, their revocation rates, and the recidivism rate generally.[34]

A research study (N = 4245) of California residents found that those persons who watched more television news and crime-focused reality shows were more likely to feel that punishment and incapacitation rather than rehabilitation should be the goals of the criminal justice system.[35]

OTHER FACTORS AFFECTING PUBLIC CONFIDENCE IN THE CRIMINAL JUSTICE SYSTEM

In addition to the impact of the media, research findings suggest that attitudes toward, and trust in, the criminal justice system are influenced by several other factors, including whether the person had a positive experience with the justice system, his or her personal feelings of safety, and the age of the person. Individuals who are most satisfied with their personal safety tend to have more positive attitudes toward the police, while those who have been arrested by the police or had contact with the police as a crime victim tend to have less positive views of the police. There is some evidence that community residents have more negative views of the police if residents perceive that there is a high level of disorder in the community. Neighbourhood disorder may be viewed as the responsibility of the police, a perception that highlights the often unrealistic expectations of the public.[36]

Findings from studies that have examined efforts to involve and educate the public about the criminal justice system have been mixed. An evaluation of the effectiveness of the federal government initiatives designed to engage and educate the general public on issues related to corrections was unable to determine whether these initiatives improved public confidence in the criminal justice system.[37] Other studies have found that programs and materials designed to provide community residents with factual information in crime and the criminal justice system resulted in higher levels of confidence in the system.[38]

SOCIAL MEDIA, THE COMMUNITY, AND CRIMINAL JUSTICE

As noted earlier, one of the key trends in Canadian criminal justice is the increasing centralization and professionalization of the criminal justice system. This trend has largely excluded the community, with the exception of persons involved in community organizations and in volunteer work. That is, until the emergence of **social media**.

Technology now allows any citizen with a cellphone or tablet to record, photo, transmit, and receive information instantaneously, without filters and outside mainstream media, which has traditionally dominated the production and dissemination of news. Citizens are involved in creating news rather than being passive consumers of information. The speed at which photos and videos of events travel has transcended traditional media and the justice system itself. This speed is having an impact on communities, persons who are engaged in disruptive activities, and criminal justice personnel, particularly the police (discussed in Chapter 5).

Note that not all criminal justice personnel are subject to the eye of cellphones and tablets: probation officers, judges, Crown counsel, corrections officers, parole board members, and parole officers conduct their business away from public (and camera)

Social media

Forms of electronic communication that allow users to post and share ideas, information, videos, and photographs.

view. Social media has had the greatest impact on the police, which is discussed in Chapter 5.

While it is not possible to determine the role that technology will play in re-inserting the community into the criminal justice equation, some hints are provided by a number of recent events.

THE RISE OF COMMUNITY SURVEILLANCE: THE VANCOUVER HOCKEY RIOT OF 2011

Following the Vancouver Canucks' loss to Boston in game seven of the Stanley Cup playoffs in June 2011, a riot ensued in Vancouver that resulted in millions of dollars in property damage. The riot erupted after as many as 100,000 people crowded into the downtown area, many of whom were watching the game on big screens that had been erected. Fights broke out, cars (including two police cruisers) were set on fire, and stores were looted. It took police more than three hours to restore order.

During the melee, thousands of photos and videos were taken on cellphones and in media-shot footage. In the days following the riot, a grassroots campaign of "name and shame" emerged. This plan involved posting online images of rioters taken by cellphones or tablets. These images were often accompanied by names and home or work addresses or requests for identification. Citizens turned in so many cellphone images of rioters to the police that the computer system crashed; they also outed many of the rioters, sharing information on Facebook and other social media outlets about the identify of rioters and again, in many instances, their home address and place of employment.

The consequences for persons in the photos and videos were swift, often harsh, and public. Rioters going to work the next day found themselves out of a job. One rioter who was a professional mountain biker and who wore a T-shirt with the name of his sponsor on it lost that sponsorship deal and several others. A student at the University of British Columbia who was photographed looting a men's clothing shop lost her job the next day, and one donor to the university threatened to withdraw support if she wasn't expelled.[39]

The images were also used by police investigators to identify and arrest persons who had committed criminal offences, many of whom were subsequently convicted.

A number of observers expressed concern with these events, describing the response as representing an online lynch-mob mentality and that persons captured on social media were "judged in the court of Facebook."[40] In this court, there were no due process or Charter rights but rather guilt by association. Concerns were raised about vigilante justice and the violation of individual civil liberties.

Community "justice" raced ahead of the criminal justice system. On the basis of footage from news organizations, police sources, and the thousands of images submitted to the police by citizens, several hundred rioters were charged and most were found guilty. Many of the identified persons issued apologies and admitted their criminal actions in online postings or in public statements to the media.

One of the rioters who was outed and subsequently convicted of riot-related charges stated that the online backlash had gone too far: "The whole social media thing ... it's great that people are trying to help catch and identify people, but it has become a problem in that people are actually ruining people's lives. The consequences are far greater than they need to be."[41] Observers offered that the intensity of the backlash against the rioters was fuelled by a widely held view that the rioters had soiled the international image of Vancouver that had been so carefully constructed during the 2010 Winter Olympic Games.

The massive online reaction to the riot and the rioters was unprecedented and raises serious questions about whether, and how, the more damaging elements of this phenomenon can be monitored and controlled. As of early 2014, nearly three years after the riot, charges were still being laid by Crown counsel and sentences meted out in Vancouver provincial court.

The impact of social media on one participant who became the poster boy of the riot is described in Box 3.3.

The Vancouver hockey riot demonstrated how social media can, on the one hand, be used to reinforce safety and security and a sense of community and, on the other, that social media has the potential to undermine community by being completely unregulated. With social media, every citizen is a potential watchdog, and notions of due process and the presumption of innocence are irrelevant. Similarly, it is without the protection of the *Charter of Rights and Freedoms*. A key issue is what happens when a person is alleged to have committed a crime and his or her identification is posted on the Internet, but it is subsequently determined that this person did not commit the act. The original allegations are not removed from the Internet and may follow the individual for the remainder of his or her life. (See the Media Link "Vancouver Riot, June 2011: Canucks Lose to Bruins in Stanley Cup" at the end of the chapter.)

BOX 3.3   A VANCOUVER HOCKEY RIOTER PAYS THE PRICE

One of the most widely circulated images from the riot was that of a rioter who was photographed attempting (unsuccessfully as it turned out) to light a police car on fire. This image was immediately uploaded to the Internet, and the rioter was subsequently identified as Nathan Kotylak, a 17-year-old high school student who was a member of the Canadian national under-18 water polo team with an athletic scholarship offer to the University of Calgary.

The consequences of his actions were significant. Once identified, his family's address was posted on the Internet, as was the address and phone number of his father's medical practice. Threats toward their personal safety forced the family to flee their home and his father to temporarily close his medical office. Nathan was subsequently suspended from the national water polo team and did not attend his high school convocation ceremonies. These consequences were in addition to criminal charges. A Facebook group, calling itself "100,000 strong to ban Nathan Kotylak from the Canada Olympic team" emerged, describing itself as "A group dedicated to supporting Canadian values and to denounce the actions of Nathan Kotylak."[42] Nathan's ex-girlfriend chimed in online, describing him as a "pathological narcissistic" who "deserves everything he gets."[43] Interestingly, this person subsequently created a Support Nathan Kotylak Facebook group.

Through legal counsel, the family obtained a court order allowing him to be identified (as a minor, his identity was protected by law under the *Youth Criminal Justice Act*) and he subsequently made a public apology.

For many on social media, the apology was not accepted. Comments posted included the following:

> this guy has balls? What, r u fricken kidding me . . . he read a statement prepared by a lawyer . . . his family should be ashamed of him . . . as a Canadian, this guy doesn't deserve to be representing my country anytime soon . . . he took that away

Nathan Kotylak and his parents

Stuart Davis/Vancouver Sun

from himself . . . I don't f'n buy a word he says. (see the comments section at www.youtube.com/watch?v=VFw2n4VntU)

As of 2013, Nathan was attending Harvard University and playing on the varsity water polo team. No criminal charges had been laid, although Internet postings continued to call for his extradition back to Canada to face charges.

QUESTIONS

What is your view of the response to Nathan's behaviour? Do you agree with him being banned from the national water polo team? Do you think that this case illustrates the need for government regulation of the Internet? If you had been at the riot and taken photos of persons involved in the riot (e.g., looting, setting vehicles on fire), would you have submitted them to the police? Would you submit the digital images or identify a photo of a family member? a close friend? a neighbour? a fellow employee? a person you knew but didn't like?

There is little doubt that *cyber citizens* have rapidly become an important feature of the societal landscape. The question is how this newfound power will be used and what, if any, monitoring mechanisms will be put in place.

"ANONYMOUS" AND THE HACKTIVISTS: GUARDIANS OF JUSTICE OR VIGILANTES?

A new feature of the criminal justice landscape has been the rise of hacktivist groups, such as Anonymous. In addition to engaging in various hacking activities, Anonymous has used the Internet as a platform in an attempt to hold alleged offenders and the criminal justice system accountable. The group, of unknown size, is distinguished by the Guy Fawkes masks that members wear to protect their identity. The group has been involved in a number of high-profile crime cases in Canada and the United States. It identifies persons through a process called *doxing*—searching for clues in online sources, including Facebook and comment boards. Information on one site is linked to information from other sites.[44]

THE DEATH OF AMANDA TODD

On October 10, 2012, 16-year old Amanda Todd committed suicide by hanging at her home in British Columbia. Before her death, she had posted a video on YouTube that described, via flash cards, her experience of being blackmailed, bullied, and physically assaulted.

In Grade 7, Amanda had been convinced by a stranger on the Internet to bare her breasts. The image was subsequently posted online and resulted in her being teased and bullied in school. A new term was coined to describe this action: *sextortion*.

She turned to drugs and alcohol and, at one point, attempted suicide, and this information was posted by others on line as well. Anonymous became involved in the case and alleged in a recorded statement on YouTube that they had identified the man who had blackmailed her.

The group published his name and address and he subsequently received death threats on Facebook and in emails. The police investigated and found that Anonymous had identified the wrong person. Another person, this time in the United States, was subsequently identified as being responsible. As for its error in publishing the identity of the first person online, Anonymous did not issue an apology, stating that "it didn't care" if it was a case of mistaken identity since the man has been accused of similar crimes.[45] In January 2014, Dutch police arrested a man who is suspected of encouraging young women, including Amanda Todd, to perform sex acts in front of a web camera. He then used the images to extort and harass his victims. (See the Media Link "Amanda Todd's Story: Struggling, Bullying, Suicide, Self-Harm" at the end of the chapter.)

▼ Rehtaeh Parsons, December 9, 1995–April 7, 2013

THE DEATH OF REHTAEH PARSONS

Rehtaeh Parsons, a 17-year-old Nova Scotia woman, committed suicide in 2013. Her death occurred after she had been gang raped two years earlier at a party. The images of the rape had been posted online, and for the next two years, she was subjected to bullying online, at school, and in the community.

The RCMP investigated the case, but there were no arrests or charges. Two years after the incident, Anonymous posted a message on YouTube threatening to disclose the identities of the four boys involved in the rape.

59

The RCMP and the minister of justice in Nova Scotia publicly condemned the threat, with the minister stating, "We don't want another child taking her life because some vigilante group thinks it's OK...maybe it's a wrong name—then what would [that] do to someone?."[46]

In April 2013, Anonymous issued a press release containing additional information on the boys who they allege were involved in the rape.[47] In August 2013, police arrested two men in connection with the case.

In late 2013, the federal government introduced legislation that would make the distribution of sexually explicit images without a person's consent a criminal offence. The legislation covers intimate images of a sexual nature, and both adults and youth can be charged for the offence. (See the Media Link "17yr Old Girl Rehtaeh Parsons Commits Suicide After Being Raped" at the end of the chapter.)

◀ Members of Anonymous join a protest in Steubenville, Ohio

AP Photo/Steubenville Herald-Star, Michael D. McElwain

A CASE OF RAPE IN STEUBENVILLE, OHIO

Anonymous has also been active in cases in the United States. The group leaked a video showing members of a small town Ohio high school football team mocking a 16-year-old girl who had been raped at a summer party in August 2012.

The activism of Anonymous included participating in local protests and contributed to deep divisions in the community.[48] Two of the high school football players were subsequently convicted of rape and sentenced to custody.[49]

OTHER ACTIVIST AND DIRECT ACTION GROUPS

Another example of direct action by community members was a group known as the "The Justice Trolls," high school students in Chilliwack, B.C., who conducted stings of suspected sexual predators. Posing online as 15-year-old girls, the group then confronted the men in person, dressed as Batman, Robin, the Flash, and other superheroes. The encounters were then posted on a YouTube site called "To Troll a Predator".[50] Their actions led to charges being filed against several men (one a school teacher) for child luring via the Internet.

The activities of these groups continue to be controversial. See At Issue 3.2.

AT ISSUE 3.2 ANONYMOUS: SHOULD IT BE REGULATED?

Considerable debate has surrounded the activities of Anonymous. Critics are concerned that the group's activities border on vigilantism and that the organization is not accountable. Others applaud the group's efforts in the area of criminal justice to ensure justice and to hold the criminal justice system accountable. A common view, expressed by one observer, is "that it is a force for both good and bad."[51]

QUESTIONS

What are your views on the activities of Anonymous in the cases of Amanda Todd and Rehtaeh Parsons? Should Anonymous be banned? regulated?

SUMMARY

The discussion in this chapter has centred on crime, victims, and the community. The challenges of determining how much crime there is was discussed, and it was noted that a dark figure of crime exists primarily because of non-reporting of crimes to the police. This figure includes many serious offences. A review of crime trends indicated that police-reported crime continues to decline, although crime rates remain high in the territories and in many First Nations communities. The costs of crime are extensive, and many consequences of crime affect the victims and the community.

The discussion noted that although the majority of Canadians are satisfied with their personal safety, young males, persons who are single, and women may be at a higher risk of being victimized. Crime victims often experience challenges in the criminal justice system, including revictimization by personnel who are insensitive to their needs. Until recently, the community was largely excluded from participation in the justice system, although that has changed with the advent of social media. It was noted that the rise of community surveillance has significant implications for persons whose actions are recorded and, potentially, for the community at large.

KEY POINTS REVIEW

1. For a variety of reasons, it is difficult to determine how much crime there is.

2. The police-reported crime rate continues to decline but remains high in the territories, many First Nations communities, and in some urban areas.

3. The costs of crime are substantial, not only in terms of dollars but also with respect to the hidden consequences of crime.

4. Young adults, women, and single persons may be at a high risk of victimization.

5. Crime victims often find the criminal justice system to be complex and confusing and have often been an afterthought.

6. Crime victims may be subjected to revictimization by insensitive and poorly trained criminal justice personnel.

7. There is an ongoing debate on the role of victims in the criminal justice process.

8. The media plays a role in the perceptions that the general public has of the criminal justice system, although the precise impact of television and various electronic messaging systems is difficult to determine.

9. Until recently, the community was marginalized by the criminal justice system, although this has changed with the growth of social media.

10. The use of social media to document events and persons involved in incidents raises questions about due process and *Charter* rights.

11. The activities of groups that use social media and the Internet in an attempt to ensure justice for victims and hold the justice system accountable are a new feature of the criminal justice landscape.

KEY TERM QUESTIONS

1. What is the **crime rate** and how is it calculated?

2. What is meant by the **dark figure of crime**?

3. Describe the phenomenon of **revictimization** in the criminal justice system.

4. Discuss **criminal injury compensation** programs and **restitution** as remedies for crime victims.

5. What is meant by the term **NIMBY**, and how is it related to discussions of the community and the criminal justice system?

6. Describe how **social media** is changing the role of the community vis-à-vis the criminal justice system.

MEDIA LINKS

 "One Victim's Story"
or go to the book's website at
www.nelson.com/
crimjusticeprimer5e.com

"Christopher's Journey"
or go to the book's website at
www.nelson.com/
crimjusticeprimer5e.com

 "Prince George Victim Services"
or go to the book's website at
www.nelson.com/
crimjusticeprimer5e.com

 "Vancouver Riot, June 2011:
Canucks Lose to Bruins in
Stanley Cup"
or go to the book's website at
www.nelson.com/
crimjusticeprimer5e.com

"Amanda Todd's Story:
Struggling, Bullying, Suicide,
Self-Harm"
or go to the book's website at
www.nelson.com/
crimjusticeprimer5e.com

"17yr Old Girl Rehteah Parsons
Commits Suicide After Being
Raped"
or go to the book's website at
www.nelson.com/
crimjusticeprimer5e.com

PART II
THE
POLICE

Chapter 4: The Structure and Roles of the Police
Chapter 5: Police Powers and Decision Making
Chapter 6: Police Strategies and Operations

• •

Policing is perhaps the most high-profile, dynamic, and oftentimes controversial component of the Canadian criminal justice system. It is police officers who respond to criminal offences, disorder, and conflict in the community. How police services and police officers respond to the multifaceted demands that are placed on them affects individual citizens and their neighbourhoods and communities, as well as officers and the police services within which they work. Police are the only agents of the criminal justice system with whom most Canadians ever have contact.

In contrast to personnel in other components of the justice system, police officers work in environments that are always changing. Technological developments, most notably the prevalence of mobile phone cameras; Internet-based platforms, such as YouTube; and social networking sites, like Facebook, have significantly increased the visibility of police actions.[1]

The chapters in this part focus on the various facets of Canadian policing. Chapter 4 describes the structure and operation of police services. A brief history of policing is presented and how the role of the police has evolved is examined. The four levels of policing—federal, provincial or territorial, municipal, and First Nations are discussed, as is the recruitment and training of police officers. The chapter concludes with an examination of the features of the police occupation.

Chapter 5 focuses on police powers and decision making. The powers of the police with respect to detention and arrest, seizure, and the use of force are discussed, as are the issues surrounding the abuse of these powers. Discretion is considered as a core element in police work, and the factors impacting police decision making are identified. Specific attention is given to the challenges of policing a diverse society and the issues that arise when police officers abuse their discretion and engage in biased policing and racial profiling. The provisions for holding the police accountable for their decisions are also discussed.

Chapter 6 examines the strategies that the police employ to prevent and respond to crime. Models of police practice are considered, and particular attention is given to the effectiveness of police interventions.

65

CHAPTER 4

THE STRUCTURE AND ROLES OF THE POLICE

LEARNING OBJECTIVES

After reading this chapter, you should be able to

- discuss the evolution and the current structure of policing in Canada
- define police work and describe the issues that surround police work in a democratic society
- discuss the various roles of the police, and what is meant by *political policing*
- describe the structures of police governance
- discuss several of the common misconceptions about policing
- describe the recruitment and training of police officers
- describe what is meant by the *working personality of police officers* and the issues that surround this concept
- discuss the challenges of police work

A BRIEF HISTORY OF POLICING

THE EMERGENCE OF MODERN POLICING

The first full-time police force was created in London in 1829 by Sir Robert Peel in response to increasing fear of crime and disorder associated with the Industrial Revolution. Before this, policing was a community responsibility based on the notion that every individual was responsible to his or her neighbours. Peel faced opposition from the public and politicians who were concerned about the power that would be vested in a formal police force, and when Peel finally won acceptance of his police plan for London, he was denounced as a potential dictator.

Peel attempted to legitimize the new police force by arguing that the police would serve the interests of all citizens, that the police would include the prevention of crime as part of their mandate, and that the force's officers would be recruited from the working class. In a determined effort to create a professional police force and to reduce public suspicion and distrust of the police, he established high standards of recruitment and training and selected constables from the community. He also introduced the concept of community police stations. In contrast to the local watchmen who preceded them, the new police were to be proactive rather than reactive and were to engage in crime prevention activities.

Peel formulated several principles for law enforcement, which even today are viewed as the basis for policing.[2] See Box 4.1.

BOX 4.1   THE PRINCIPLES OF SIR ROBERT PEEL

1. The basic mission of the police is to prevent crime and disorder.

2. The ability of the police to perform their duties depends on public approval of their actions.

3. Police must secure the cooperation of the public in voluntary observance of the law to secure and maintain the respect of the public.

4. The degree of public cooperation with police diminishes proportionately to the necessity of the use of physical force.

5. Police maintain public favour by constantly demonstrating absolute impartial service, not by catering to public opinion.

6. Police should use physical force only to the extent necessary to ensure compliance with the law or to restore order only after persuasion, advice, and warnings are insufficient.

Sir Robert Peel (1788–1850), creator of the first modern police force and author of Peel's principles.

7. Police should maintain a relationship with the public that is based on the fact that the police are the public and the public are the police.

8. Police should direct their actions toward their functions and not appear to usurp the powers of the judiciary.

9. The test of police efficiency is the absence of crime and disorder.

Source: Reith, C. 1956. *A New Study of Police History.* London: Oliver and Boyd.

THE EVOLUTION OF POLICING IN CANADA

In the early days, before Canada existed as the country it is today, laws were enforced on an informal basis by community residents. In Halifax, for example, tavern owners were charged with maintaining order. For many years, policing remained closely tied to local communities. As settlements grew and the demands of law and order increased, however, this arrangement lost its effectiveness. The first police constables appeared on the streets of Québec City in the mid-1600s and in Upper Canada (now Ontario) in the early 1800s.

The early municipal police forces generally had a three-part mandate: (1) to police conflicts between ethnic groups, and between labourers and their employers; (2) to maintain moral standards by enforcing laws against drunkenness, prostitution, and gambling; and (3) to apprehend criminals.[3] The historical record indicates that early municipal police forces were heavily influenced by politics and patronage.

Many of the jurisdictions that ultimately became provinces after Confederation in 1867 originally had their own police forces. Most often, these were established in response to the disorder associated with gold strikes (e.g., in British Columbia and Ontario). The earliest police force of this type was founded in 1858 in British Columbia (then a colony); that force continued to police the province until 1950, when policing services were contracted out to the Royal Canadian Mounted Police (RCMP). The police forces that had been established in Alberta, Saskatchewan, and Manitoba suffered from poor leadership and a lack of qualified officers. Between 1917 and 1950, the RCMP assumed provincial policing responsibilities in all provinces except Ontario, Québec, and parts of Newfoundland and Labrador. To this day, those are the only three provinces with provincial police forces.

The North-West Mounted Police (now the RCMP) was founded in 1873 to maintain law and order in, and to ensure the orderly settlement of, the previously unpoliced and

Courtesy of Glenbow Museum and Archives

◄ North-West Mounted Police officers, Fort Walsh, Saskatchewan (c. 1874–1880).

sparsely settled North-West Territories (then, in rough terms, present-day Alberta and Saskatchewan). During its early years, the force was beset by internal difficulties and resented by both settlers and federal legislators. The historical record points to high rates of desertion, resignation, and improper conduct, in part because of the harsh conditions of the frontier.

Attempts during the 1920s to phase out the force were driven by resistance in many regions to its expansion into provincial policing. It was anticipated that as these areas became more populated, the responsibility for policing would shift to local communities; for a variety of reasons, this did not happen. The emergence of the RCMP as a national police force involved in policing provinces and municipalities was, in fact, more an accident of history than part of a master plan.[4]

Today, there are about 70,000 police officers in Canada, or 199 police officers per 100,000 population. This number is considerably lower than other jurisdictions, including Scotland (337), England and Wales (244), and the United States (238).[5] The number of police offenders in Canada has gradually increased over the past decade, even though the official rates of crime have decreased. The number of female police officers has also increased, with one in five officers being women. Policing is the largest component of the justice system and receives the biggest slice of the funding pie (approximately 60 percent).

CONTEMPORARY CANADIAN POLICING

The police respond to a wide variety of demands and situations—many unrelated to crime and to the maintenance of public order—and carry out their duties in settings ranging from megacities (such as Montréal, Toronto, and Vancouver) to rural communities and hamlets in the remote North.

Being on the front lines, the police have more contact with the general public than other criminal justice personnel. Many police are highly visible; by contrast, other professionals in the criminal justice system (judges, probation officers, correctional officers) operate in relative obscurity. Criminal court judges, for example, make decisions within the safe confines of a courthouse and have the luxury of considering the case facts and carefully weighing the interests of the community, the victim, and the offender before issuing a judgment; although their decisions may be controversial, they are in large measure immune from the scrutiny that police officers receive in carrying out their day-to-day tasks.

THE LEVELS OF POLICING

Policing in Canada is carried out at several levels: federal, provincial and territorial, municipal, and First Nations. One might also add private security officers, who are assuming a greater role in areas that were traditionally in the domain of the public police. Other police services include the Canadian Pacific Police Service (which fulfills policing roles for its organization) and in major urban centres, such as Montréal, Toronto, and Vancouver, transit police forces provide security and protection for property and passengers on public transportation systems. The officers of the South Coast British Columbia Transportation Authority Police Service have full powers as peace officers and are the only transit officers in Canada that carry handguns.

The arrangements for delivering police services across Canada are quite complex. In Ontario, for example, London Police—an independent municipal police service—is responsible for policing within the city boundaries, while the London detachment of the Ontario Provincial Police (OPP) has jurisdiction in the rural areas outside the city. The RCMP has its provincial headquarters in London and operates as a federal police force in the areas policed by the London Police and the OPP.

The Royal Newfoundland Constabulary—a provincial police force—is responsible for providing policing services to three areas of Newfoundland and Labrador: St. John's, Mount Pearl, and the surrounding communities referred to as Northeast Avalon; Corner Brook; and Labrador West, which includes Labrador City, Wabush, and Churchill Falls. The rest of the province is policed, under contract, by the RCMP.

In the Greater Vancouver Region, some municipalities are policed by municipal police services, while others are policed under contract by the RCMP. Concerns about the extent to which the municipal and RCMP detachments in the area effectively communicate with one another and address the challenges of organized crime and gang violence, among other issues, have led to calls for a regional police service.

FEDERAL POLICE: THE ROYAL CANADIAN MOUNTED POLICE

The RCMP is organized into 15 divisions, plus the RCMP federal headquarters in Ottawa. Each division is headed by a commanding officer.

The ***Royal Canadian Mounted Police Act*** (RS 1985, c. R-10) provides the framework for the force's operations. As the federal police force in all provinces and territories, the RCMP enforces most federal statutes and the provisions of various legislative Acts. A number of features distinguish the RCMP from other Canadian police services. These include training all of its recruits at a central location in Regina, Saskatchewan, and then deploying them across the country in detachments from sea to sea to sea. Also, unlike their municipal and provincial police counterparts, RCMP officers are not unionized. The RCMP is involved in a broad range of policing activities, including federal policing, contract policing at the provincial, territorial, and municipal levels, and international peacekeeping. One result is that the resources and capacities of the Mounties are often overextended, and observers have questioned whether the RCMP has sufficient resources to deliver policing services effectively on all of these fronts.[6]

The RCMP is a federal police force, yet about 60 percent of its personnel are involved in **contract policing**—that is, they serve as provincial, territorial, and municipal police officers under agreements between the RCMP and the provinces or territories. (Note again that Ontario and Québec have their own provincial police forces and that the Royal Newfoundland Constabulary serves parts of Newfoundland and Labrador.) The RCMP's involvement in policing at the municipal level (under contract with municipalities), the provincial and territorial level (under contract with provinces and territories), and the federal level makes it a truly national police force.

There are, however, increasing concerns in municipalities policed under contract by the RCMP about fiscal accountability: while municipal police services are subject to local police boards and municipal councils, in those municipalities that the RCMP polices under contract, there are no police boards, and the local mayor and council have no mandate to oversee their work. Some observers thus argue that the RCMP is *in* but not *of* the communities it polices and that it is often difficult to ensure that RCMP detachments are responsive to the community's priorities and requirements.

Royal Canadian Mounted Police Act
Federal legislation that provides the framework for the operation of the RCMP.

Contract policing
An arrangement whereby the RCMP and provincial or territorial police forces provide provincial and municipal policing services.

PROVINCIAL POLICE

There are three provincial police forces in Canada: the Ontario Provincial Police (OPP; www.opp.ca), the Sûreté du Québec (SQ; www.suretequebec .gouv.qc.ca), and the Royal Newfoundland Constabulary (RNC; www.rnc .gov.nl.ca). Provincial police forces are responsible for policing rural areas and the areas outside municipalities and cities. They enforce provincial laws and the *Criminal Code*. Some municipalities in Ontario are policed under contract by the OPP. Outside Ontario and Québec and certain parts of Newfoundland, the RCMP provides provincial policing under contract with provincial governments. When the RCMP acts as a provincial police force, it has full jurisdiction over the *Criminal Code* and provincial laws.

REGIONAL POLICE SERVICES

A notable trend in Canada has been the creation of regional police services. This generally involves amalgamating several independent police departments to form one large organization. Regional police services have been a feature of policing in Ontario for many years.

Today, a number of regional police services, including the Peel Regional Police (the largest regional police force in Canada) and the Halton Regional Police, are providing policing services to more than 50 percent of Ontarians. In Québec, the Montréal Police Service provides policing services to the City of Montréal and several surrounding municipalities. There are only two regional police forces west of Ontario: the Dakota Ojibway Police Service in Manitoba and the Lakeshore Regional Police Service, an Aboriginal police force that provides services to five First Nations in northern Alberta.

Proponents of regional policing contend that it is more effective at providing a full range of policing services to communities and is less expensive than having a number of independent municipal departments. Critics of regional policing argue that a regional police service is too centralized and does not offer the opportunity for effective community policing. The trend toward regionalization will continue to be driven by fiscal considerations and by the growing need for police services to maintain interoperability.

MUNICIPAL POLICE

As the name suggests, municipal police services have jurisdiction within a city's boundaries. Municipal police officers enforce the *Criminal Code*, provincial or territorial statutes, and municipal bylaws, as well as certain federal statutes, such as the *Controlled Drugs and Substances Act*. Most police work is performed by services operating at this level.

A municipality can provide police services in one of three ways: by creating its own independent police service; by joining with another municipality's existing police force, which often means involving itself with a regional police force; or by contracting with a provincial police force—the OPP in Ontario, the RCMP in the rest of Canada (except Québec).

Municipal police officers constitute the largest body of police personnel in the country, if you include both police employed by municipal departments and those who have been contracted through the RCMP or the OPP. There is no provision under Québec provincial law for the Sûreté du Québec to contract out municipal policing services. The Toronto Police Service has more than 5000 officers; at the other end of the spectrum, some remote communities are policed by detachments of only one or two officers.

▲ OPP officers.

© Queen's Printer for Ontario, 2014. Reproduced with permission.

▼ Toronto Police Service officers.

THE CANADIAN PRESS/Chris Young

71

Municipalities with their own policing services generally assume the costs of those services, which are sometimes underwritten by the provincial government. A notable trend in Ontario has been a decline in the number of independent municipal police services in favour of contracting with the OPP, although in recent years, a number of municipalities have explored the potential of re-establishing municipal police services to reduce costs.

FIRST NATIONS POLICE

Aboriginal peoples are becoming increasingly involved in the creation and control of justice programs. It is in the area of policing that they have assumed the greatest control over the delivery of justice services. This control is perhaps appropriate, given the conflicts that have arisen between the police and Aboriginal peoples both in the past and in the present day.

Within the framework of the federal First Nations Policing Policy, the federal government, the provincial and territorial governments, and First Nations communities can negotiate agreements for police services that best meet the needs of First Nations communities. These communities have the option of developing an autonomous, reserve-based police force or using First Nations officers from the RCMP or the OPP in Ontario. Funding for Aboriginal police forces is split between the province or territory and the federal government.

Among the larger Aboriginal police forces—which are involved in policing multiple reserve communities—are the Six Nations Police Service in Ontario, the Amerindian Police in Québec, and the Dakota Ojibway Police Service in Manitoba. There are smaller Aboriginal police forces in other provinces. Aboriginal police officers generally have full powers to enforce, on reserve lands, the *Criminal Code*, federal and provincial statutes, and band bylaws. The Supreme Court has held that First Nations police constables in Ontario have "territorial jurisdiction" that is not confined to the territorial boundaries of the reserve (*R. v. DeCorte*, [2005]1 SCR 133).

The activities of First Nations police forces are overseen by reserve-based police commissions or by the local band council. Aboriginal police forces often work closely with the OPP, the SQ, and the RCMP.

POLICE PEACEKEEPING

RCMP officers, along with their provincial and municipal counterparts, are involved in a variety of international peacekeeping activities, including assignments in Sierra Leone, Afghanistan, Sudan, and Haiti. The officers function mainly as technical advisers and instruct local police forces in new policing strategies.

There has been considerable debate around the effectiveness of these deployments, with some observers arguing that the impact of the officers is minimal and that the missions are mounted to "show the flag," that is, to raise the profile of the Canadian government overseas. Among the difficulties that have been identified are the lack of pre-deployment training for officers being sent on peacekeeping missions and the fact that Canadian officers are often part of a multinational force of police officers, among whom there is wide disparity in both skills and level of professionalism.[7–9] The deployment of police officers overseas is one example where police officers may be being used for political purposes.

PRIVATE SECURITY SERVICES

Recent years have seen exponential growth in private security, which is now providing services previously performed by provincial and municipal police services. There are two main types of private security: security firms that sell their services to businesses, industries, private residences, and neighbourhoods; and companies that employ their own in-house security officers. Across Canada, a number of communities have hired private security firms to provide 24-hour security patrols.

Private security officers outnumber police officers by four to one in Canada and are engaged in a wide range of activities, including crowd control, protecting businesses and property (including shopping malls and college and university campuses), and conducting investigations for individuals and businesses. In some venues, such as sporting events and concerts, private security officers and police officers may work in collaboration.

The expansion of the activities of private security firms into areas traditionally serviced by public police organizations has often resulted in uncertainty about the powers and authority of private security officers. Generally, private security personnel have no more legal authority than ordinary citizens to enforce the law or protect property. However, private security officers can arrest and detain people who commit crimes on private property. Recent court cases suggest that private security personnel must adhere to the provisions in the *Charter of Rights and Freedoms* only when making an arrest.

The rapid growth of the private security industry has led to concerns with the transformation of private security officers into *parapolice* through the extension of their activities beyond loss prevention and the protection of property to encompass order maintenance and enforcement.[10,11] Other observers have expressed the concern that although public police are accountable to oversight commissions and—in the case of municipal and provincial or territorial police forces—to elected community officials, no similar systems of governance are in place for private security officers.[12]

DEFINING POLICE WORK

Policing

"The activities of any individual or organization acting legally on behalf of public or private organizations or persons to maintain security or social order."

Canadian police scholars Curtis Clarke and Chris Murphy have offered a broad definition of **policing** that includes public and private police. They define policing as "activities of any individual or organization acting legally on behalf of public or private organizations or persons to maintain security or social order while empowered by either public or private contract, regulations or policies, written or verbal."[13]

This definition is an acknowledgement that the public police no longer have a monopoly on policing, although, with a few exceptions, they retain a monopoly on the use of force. An increasing role in safety and security in the community is being played by private security services and parapolice officers (i.e., community constables that have limited powers of enforcement). Police scholars David Bayley and Clifford Shearing have labelled this phenomenon the **pluralization of policing**.[14]

Pluralization of policing

The sharing of responsibility for safety and security in the community between public and private police.

POLICE WORK IN A DEMOCRATIC SOCIETY

No other pubic organization can directly impact the rights and freedoms of individual citizens to the extent of the police.

—Paul McKenna[15]

The Law Reform Commission of Canada has identified four key values that form the framework within which to understand police work in Canadian society:[16]

- *Justice*: the requirement that the police maintain peace and security in the community while ensuring that individuals are treated fairly and human rights are respected.
- *Equality*: all citizens are entitled to policing services that contribute to their feelings of safety and security.
- *Accountability*: the actions of police services, and police officers, are subject to review.
- *Efficiency*: policing services must be cost-effective.

It is in attempting to reconcile these values that the inherent tensions of policing in a democratic society are revealed. The police mandate entails mutually contradictory ends: protecting both public order and individual rights. There is a natural tension between the requirement that the police enforce and legitimize the decisions of government while at the same time serving the public interest.[17] It is not surprising that police officers often experience conflict in carrying out their duties.

These tensions may also result in conflicts between the police and other components of the criminal justice system, notably the courts. Police officers often complain that the rights of offenders are given more attention than those of victims and law-abiding citizens, and officers are often frustrated when offenders are released on technicalities or receive court sentences that they deem to be lenient. There is little doubt that the *Charter* and court decisions have had a major impact on the powers and procedures of the police, as is discussed in Chapter 5. The increasing use of technology in police work has also raised concerns, in particular about the privacy of citizens (this topic is also addressed in Chapter 5).

GOVERNANCE OF THE POLICE

While it is important that the police be free from political interference, there must be governmental and judicial oversight of police activities.

> No other criminal justice professional comes under as much constant and public scrutiny—but no other criminal justice professional wields so much discretion in so many circumstances. The scrutiny is understandable when one realizes that the police are power personified.[18]

A key issue in any discussion of police work is how the police are to be governed. On the one hand, the police require a degree of operational autonomy to effectively and efficiently carry out their mandated tasks. Given the nature of their mandated role, the police need to be free from government interference and influence. It is important that the police not become an instrument for implementing government policy or to support specific political agendas. Historically, this has been unavoidable.

On the other hand, the principles of due process and of a democratic society require that there be mechanisms in place to govern the police, to ensure that police services do not exceed their mandate and compromise the rights of citizens. However, as several observers have noted, the precise nature and extent of the independence required by the police has remained unclear.[19]

Figure 4.1 sets out the structures of police governance. Note that there are differences in how federal, provincial or territorial, regional, and municipal police services are governed. Important to the discussion are the explanations of **police acts, policing standards,** and **police boards and police commissions.**

Police acts
The legislative framework for police service.

Policing standards
Provisions that set out how police services are to be maintained and delivered.

Police boards and police commissions
Bodies that provide oversight of police.

FIGURE 4.1 ▶

Structures of Police Governance

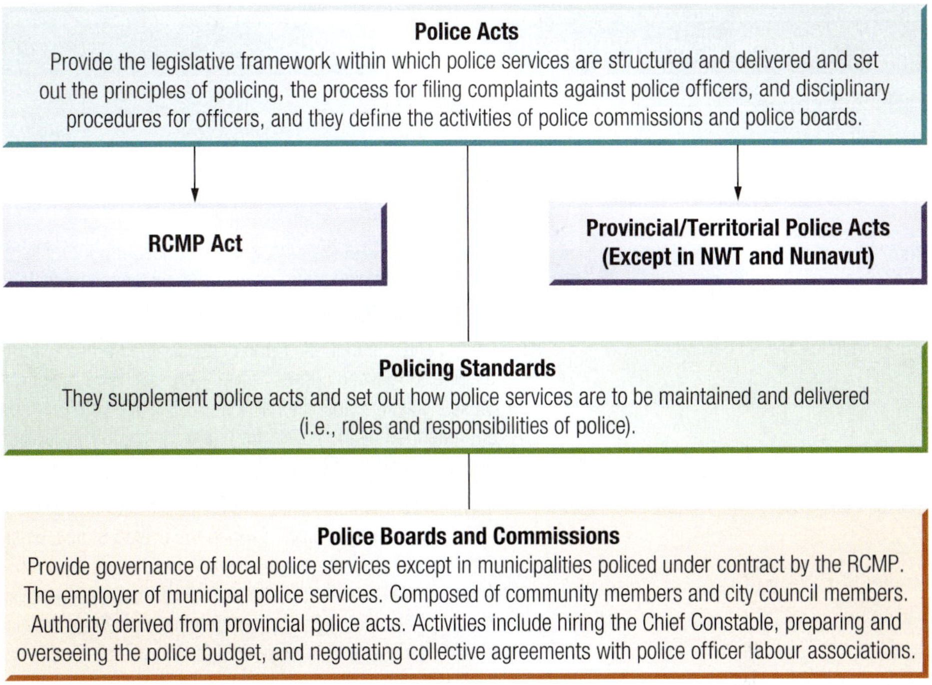

Police Acts
Provide the legislative framework within which police services are structured and delivered and set out the principles of policing, the process for filing complaints against police officers, and disciplinary procedures for officers, and they define the activities of police commissions and police boards.

RCMP Act

Provincial/Territorial Police Acts (Except in NWT and Nunavut)

Policing Standards
They supplement police acts and set out how police services are to be maintained and delivered (i.e., roles and responsibilities of police).

Police Boards and Commissions
Provide governance of local police services except in municipalities policed under contract by the RCMP. The employer of municipal police services. Composed of community members and city council members. Authority derived from provincial police acts. Activities include hiring the Chief Constable, preparing and overseeing the police budget, and negotiating collective agreements with police officer labour associations.

THE ROLES AND ACTIVITIES OF THE POLICE

Part of understanding the roles and activities of the police in contemporary society separates fact from fiction. Some of the more common misconceptions of police work are presented in Box 4.2.

Traditionally, the police role was classified into three major categories:

- *Crime control.* Responding to and investigating crimes, and patrolling the streets to prevent offences from occurring.
- *Order maintenance.* Preventing and controlling behaviour that disturbs the public peace, including quieting loud parties, policing protests, responding to (and often mediating) domestic and neighbourhood disputes, and intervening in conflicts that arise between citizens. It is this role of the police that is most often the subject of criticism and investigation.
- *Crime prevention and service.* Collaborating with community partners to prevent crime and providing a wide range of services to the community, often as a consequence of the 24-hour availability of the police.

These distinctions, however, may not accurately capture the diversity and complexity of the police role in a highly technological, global society. Increasingly, police officers are being viewed as knowledge workers who spend a considerable amount of time gathering and processing information. Police work also extends far beyond the street level and cuts across jurisdictional and international boundaries. As well, many police observers have argued that this new era in policing is one in which the traditional distinction between public and private police has become blurred and that the networks of policing are now much more complex than in the past.

Police scholar Peter Manning pointed out three decades ago that many of the difficulties experienced by the police in fulfilling their mandate are the result of having staked out a "vast and unmanageable social domain."[20] This directive has led to unrealistic expectations on the part of the general public as to what the police can realistically

75

BOX 4.2 COMMON MISCONCEPTIONS OF MODERN POLICE WORK

Misconception	Fact
Police work in itself prevents crime.	The specific causes of criminal behaviour and disorder in a community are generally beyond the capacity of the police to address on their own. However, adoption of the principles and practice of community policing, with its emphasis on partnerships with neighbourhoods, the private sector, not-for-profit organizations, and other government ministries and agencies, may increase the preventive capacity of the police. And evidence suggests that specific police strategies, such as *target hardening*, can impact specific types of crime in a defined area (see Chapter 6).
The Mounties always get their man.	It's not only the Mounties who don't get their man or woman: police services generally struggle to solve the myriad crimes they are presented with. For many categories of offences, particularly those involving transnational crime and white collar crime, the chances of being detected and apprehended by the police are relatively small. This low rate is due, in part, to a lack of police resources and the fact that, in the past, police resources were not effectively allocated.
Police work involves the frequent use of force.	If TV shows and films about the police were to be believed, police officers are involved in shootouts on a daily basis. Even in the United States, where guns are far more prevalent than in Canada, officers are generally reluctant to use deadly force or physical force. In 97 percent of all police incidents, mere presence and communication skills are used to diffuse and resolve crises. Many police officers go their entire careers without drawing or discharging their weapons except in training. However, the potential for the use of force is present in every encounter.
Police work is dangerous.	Statistically, police work is a less hazardous occupation than underground mining and refuse collection. Police work has often been described as long hours of boredom punctuated by brief periods of fear and sheer terror. Officer complacency is one of the biggest dangers in police work.
Police work primarily involves pursuing criminals.	Contrary to popular images, and most fictional accounts, the majority of a police officer's time is on order maintenance and service-type activities, including attending traffic accidents and mediating disputes between citizens and among family members. While the specific breakdown of service, order maintenance, and crime control varies across different task environments, pursuing and apprehending criminals generally accounts for less than 20 percent of an officer's time and tasks.
When you call the police, they come.	With the exception of smaller communities that may receive *Cadillac service* under a "no call too small" policy, police patrol units may not be dispatched. Statistics from Toronto, for example, indicate that fewer than one-half (47 percent) of the calls for service resulted in the dispatch of a patrol unit.[21] Sometimes, even 9-1-1 calls may be screened out (with, in some instances, tragic consequences). See Chapter 5.

accomplish in terms of crime prevention and response. And it has challenged police services to document the effectiveness and efficiencies of their operations.

Over the years, the responsibility for maintaining order, preventing crime, and responding to crime has become increasingly centralized in the agencies of the criminal justice system, including the police. The consequences of this were discussed in Chapter 3. This centralization of authority has been accompanied by a reduction in community involvement to the point where the Canadian public has come to rely—some would say rely too heavily—on the police to respond to and solve a wide variety of problems and situations. Often, the police on their own lack the capacity to address these problems and situations effectively.

In considering the myriad roles of the police in Canadian society, the following questions can be posed: What does the community expect of the police? How do the police view their role? How are the police used by governments to monitor and control groups that are deemed to be threats to social stability?

▼ Vancouver police officers in Chinatown.

Courtesy of the Vancouver Police Department.

> ### BOX 4.3   POLICE RESPONSE TO INCIDENTS IN THE UNITED KINGDOM
>
> An analysis of 4.7 million recorded incidents in six police services in the United Kingdom found that a high percentage of the incidents to which police officers respond included either a crime having been committed or the risk of a crime being committed. In contrast to the widely held view that only about 20 percent of police officers time is spent on crime, the study found that if responding to incidents where there was a *risk* of crime, it was at least 80 percent.
>
> Additional findings of the study included the following:
>
> 1. An overwhelming portion of the police officers' time was spent on crime or stopping things that the public felt are dangerous or wrong or should cease immediately.
>
> 2. In 28 percent of the 4.7 million recorded incidents, a crime had actually taken place and in 17 percent of the 4.7million incidents some form of anti-social behaviour had occurred.
>
> 3. In the bulk of the remaining incidents (a further 55 percent), there was the *potential* for crime that the police could not discount without a closer examination of the circumstances.
>
> 4. In almost 90 percent of incidents recorded in the six police services, there was a crime or the potential for a crime to happen. Across the 36 shifts observed, officers spent about 80 percent of their time on activity that related directly or indirectly to crime.
>
> Overall, the significance of this study was that preventive and enforcement role of police officers may consume most of police officers' time. These findings suggest that there may be some limitations in the extent to which parapolice and private security can assume responsibility for areas currently addressed by sworn police officers.
>
> Source: Her Majesty's Inspectorate of Constabulary. 2012. *Taking Time for Crime: A Study of How Police Officers Prevent Crime in the Field*, London. http://www.hmic.gov.uk/media/taking-time-for-crime.pdf.

For most police officers, the primary role is that of peacekeeper rather than law enforcer: depending on the specific area being policed, officers may spend the majority of their time attending to order maintenance types of activities and less than 25 percent of their time in law enforcement activities. For most officers, this figure is considerably lower. Most of the calls made to the police are for information, order maintenance, and other service-related activities. A large portion of police work involves police officers restoring order in situations of conflict without the use of the criminal law.[22] Much depends, however, on the specific environment in which police officers carry out their work. Some communities present more demands and challenges than others.

A recent research study from the United Kingdom, however, suggests that it is necessary to take a closer look at the types of incidents to which police officers respond. See Box 4.3.

FACTORS INFLUENCING THE ROLE AND ACTIVITIES OF THE POLICE

A number of factors influence the role and activities of the police, and the ability of the police to effectively respond to community expectations and to crime and disorder in any one jurisdiction. Some of these are depicted in Figure 4.2.

GEOGRAPHY

Canada is a huge but sparsely populated country. A unique feature of Canadian police work is that OPP, SQ, and RCMP officers are posted to small Aboriginal communities in the northern regions of the provinces and territories. RCMP officers, often working in detachments as small as three members, are responsible for policing Aboriginal and

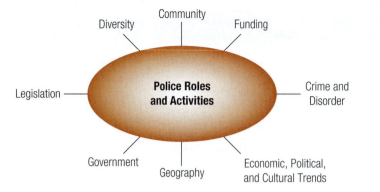

Inuit communities in Yukon, the Northwest Territories, and Nunavut. The challenges of policing in remote communities, many of which are afflicted by high rates of crime and social disorder, have remained largely unexplored by Canadian police scholars.[23] Officers in these communities must be highly adaptable and, in the absence of the supportive infrastructure found in larger police services, self-sufficient.

LEGISLATION

New laws and amendments to the existing legislation can have a sharp impact on police powers, on the demands placed on police services, and on how police services set (and try to achieve) their operational priorities. Literally overnight, behaviour that was once criminal can become legal, and behaviour that was once legal can become criminal. *The Anti-terrorism Act*, for example, gives police expanded powers to deal with individuals identified as posing a threat to safety and security; it has also established a new crime—*terrorist activity*.

The police are also spending an increasing amount of time documenting their activities and fulfilling procedural requirements. The decision of the Supreme Court of Canada in *R v Stinchcombe* (1991) held that accused persons had a constitutional right to full disclosure of materials related to the police investigation. This judgment requires the police to prepare detailed reports, and case investigators may spend as much time on this disclosure as on the initial investigation. The *Freedom of Information and Protection of Privacy Act* (1994) allows the public to request information from the police on a variety of matters, and the police must meet extensive requirements to obtain search warrants and DNA warrants. The expectation is that police services have the capacity to fulfill these requirements. Although crime rates have declined, the workload of the police has increased: a study of workload of the RCMP found that over a 30-year period (1975–2005), the time required to complete all the procedural elements had increased dramatically. For example, for break and enter it now takes between 5 and 10 hours (up from 1 hour), domestic assault takes 10 to 12 hours (up from 1 hour), and driving under the influence take 5 hours (up from 1 hour).[24]

DIVERSITY

As noted in Chapter 2, a key feature of Canada is its diversity, which includes visible minority groups, newcomers, Indigenous peoples, religious beliefs, and sexual orientation, among others. Canada is fast becoming even more diverse. In Toronto, for example, the visible minority population increased by 32 percent between 1996 and 2006 and now represents almost half the population.[25] See Figure 4.3.

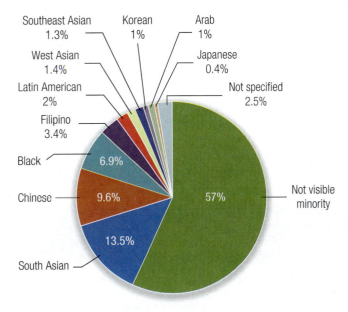

FIGURE 4.3 ►

Population Composition in Toronto, 2006 Census

Sources: Statistics Canada. 2007. *Canada's Ethnocultural Mosaic, 2006 Census: Canada's major census metropolitan areas.* http://www12.statcan.ca/census-recensement/ 2006/as-sa/97-562/p21-eng.cfm

For example, 15 percent of the country's population was born outside Canada, and that percentage is expected to rise in the coming years. Two-thirds of arriving immigrants settle in the megacities of Vancouver, Toronto, and Montréal, and many of them have had negative experiences with, or hold less than favourable attitudes toward, the police in their countries of origin. Urban centres are also attracting increasing numbers of Aboriginal people from rural and remote areas.

This diversity has significant implications for police work. Section 15(1) of the *Charter of Rights and Freedoms* guarantees equality rights: "Every individual is equal before and under the law and has the right to the equal protection and equal benefit of the law without discrimination and, in particular, without discrimination based on race, national or ethnic origin, colour, religion, sex, age or mental or physical disability." Section 3(e) of the *Canadian Multicultural Act* (RS, 1985, c. 24 (4th Supp.)) states that it is the policy of the Government of Canada to "ensure that all individuals receive equal treatment and equal protection under the law, while respecting and valuing their diversity."

The *Canadian Human Rights Act* prohibits discrimination on the grounds of race, national or ethnic origin, colour, religion, age, sex, sexual orientation, marital status, family status, disability and conviction for which a pardon has been granted.[26] Many provinces, including Ontario, B.C., Alberta, and Manitoba, have human rights codes that mirror the federal human rights code and contain sections creating human rights tribunals and proclaiming the right of residents to be free from discrimination.

The debate over racial profiling by the police, discussed in Chapter 5, is illustrative of the human rights issues that come with policing a diverse community.

CRIME AND SOCIAL DISORDER

Police officers are confronted by various levels of criminal activity and social disorder. Although crime rates in Canada generally have declined, some urban, rural, and remote areas of the country have high rates of serious crime. Recall from Chapter 3 that the rates of violent crime in Canada are highest in remote, northern Aboriginal and Inuit communities, areas with the fewest resources. Similarly, the city of Winnipeg is the violent crime capital of Canada, and certain areas of the city, including the north end, have high crime rates.

Considerable differences may exist in the calls for service to the police even in urban centres. See Box 4.4.

More serious calls for service may require patrol officers to remain at the scene for longer periods. For example, priority 1 calls (the most serious) were 9 percent of the

BOX 4.4   COMPARISON OF TOP FIVE CALLS FOR SERVICES RECEIVED BY THE WATERLOO REGIONAL POLICE SERVICE AND THE WINNIPEG POLICE SERVICE, 2011

Waterloo Regional Police Service

1. bylaw complaint
2. injured/sick person
3. compassionate to locate
4. motor vehicle collision/property damage
5. domestic dispute

Winnipeg Police Service

1. domestic disturbance
2. check well-being
3. disturbance
4. suspicious person
5. traffic complaints

QUESTION

What do these two lists suggest about the role and activities of the police in the Waterloo Region and in Winnipeg?

Now, compare these two police services with the types of calls received by the Lethbridge Regional Police Service (Alberta), a less highly urbanized area:

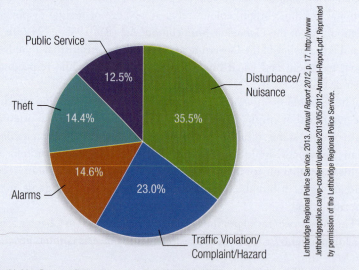

Lethbridge Regional Police Service Top Five Call Types, 2012.

Lethbridge Regional Police Service. 2013. *Annual Report 2012*, p. 17. http://www.lethbridgepolice.ca/wp-content/uploads/2013/05/2012-Annual-Report.pdf. Reprinted by permission of the Lethbridge Regional Police Service.

Sources: Waterloo Regional Police Service. 2011-2012. At Your Service Magazine, p. 17; Winnipeg Police Service, 2011. Annual Report, 2011, p 25; Lethbridge Regional Police Service, 2012. Annual Report 2012, p. 17.

calls received by the Toronto Police Service in 2011, yet these calls took up 23 percent of the total service time for calls.[27] In jurisdictions with high numbers of priority 1 calls, officers may experience heavy workloads.

The complexity of crime has also continued to increase. Many forms of criminal activity are highly sophisticated and involve international criminal syndicates that require costly and time-consuming investigations. These syndicates engage in such transnational criminal activities as human trafficking, money laundering, and drug smuggling.

FUNDING

Policing is an expensive proposition and eats up a substantial portion of municipal budgets: Vancouver (22.4 percent); Peel Regional, Ontario (28.7 percent); and Calgary (23.8 percent) head the list, with other cities (Toronto, 9.7 percent) taking a lower percentage of the overall city budget. A major contributor to these costs are the salaries of police officers, which have risen steadily, often in excess of the cost of living.[28] The other factors driving police costs include technology and the considerable resources required to investigate more sophisticated types of criminal activity.

At the same time, many municipal councils are under pressure to hold the line on budgets and tax levies. A key debate that has emerged in the early 21st century surrounds what is called the *economics and sustainability of policing*. Are the ever-increasing costs of policing sustainable, particularly when official crime rates continue to decline? Municipal councils may have to decide between additional funding for the police service and maintaining hours for libraries and community centres. Many police services across Canada are operating below their authorized sworn officer strength because of budget cutbacks. The issue is addressed further in Chapter 6.

GOVERNMENT

Ideally, policing in a democratic society is focused on the safety and security of citizens while ensuring that the rights of citizens (and suspects) are protected. The police are to be apolitical, fair, and impartial. However, all police services operate in a political environment since the police are mandated to enforce the criminal law, which reflects political values and political ends.[29] The historical record indicates that governments have used the police to quell protests and other movements that were viewed as a threat to social order.

The reasons for the founding of the RCMP, for example, have long been debated. Some have suggested that the force was established mainly to preserve peace in the West and to protect Aboriginal people from whisky traders and overaggressive settlers. Others contend that the North-West Mounted Police played much the same role as the Canadian Pacific Railway—that is, to establish political and economic sovereignty over the farthest reaches of the country. This included settling Indigenous lands in an orderly manner (i.e., with white settlers) and guarding against perceived threats of American annexation.

At various times in Canadian history, the police, particularly the federal RCMP, have been used as an instrument of surveillance and control by the federal government. This action has been referred to as **political policing**. Canadian scholar Reg Whitaker and his colleagues note that, traditionally, Canada was unique among Western countries in

Political policing

The use of the police by governments as an instrument of surveillance and control.

focusing its intelligence-gathering on Canadian citizens rather than other countries.[30] This included spying on groups during the Great Depression in the 1930s who were viewed as having Communist leaning and on university faculty and students during protests in the 1960s.

In the early 1900s, the federal government used the Mounted Police to quell labour unrest and to counter what it perceived as the growing influence of left-wing activists.[31] The breaking of the Winnipeg General Strike in 1919 is an example of how the federal police were used to suppress the activities of labour unions. See Box 4.5.

BOX 4.5 BLOODY SATURDAY: THE BREAKING OF THE WINNIPEG GENERAL STRIKE BY THE RCMP, JUNE 21, 1919

Library and Archives Canada, C-37275

RCMP on horseback charge striking workers in downtown Winnipeg.

The Winnipeg General Strike of 1919 is perhaps Canada's most famous work stoppage. The strike was part of the labour unrest that arose after World War I and was fuelled by massive unemployment and inflation of the Great Depression, as well as by the success of the Russian Revolution in 1917. The strike was called after negotiations broke down between labour and management in the building and metal trades; workers were demanding the right to bargain collectively, as well as improved wages and working conditions. The strike spread across the city until nearly 30,000 workers had left their jobs. Other public sector employees, including police officers, firefighters, and utilities workers, soon joined the strike in support of the workers and coordinated the provision of essential services. Anxious to prevent the spread of labour unrest to other cities, the federal government intervened.

On June 17, the government arrested 10 leaders of the Central Strike Committee and 2 propagandists from the newly formed One Big Union (their convictions were later overturned). On June 21, in what came to be known as Bloody Saturday, Mounted Police officers charged into a crowd of protesters, injuring 30 and killing 1. Federal troops later occupied the city. Faced with the combined forces of the government and the employers, the strikers returned to return to work on June 25. It would take another three decades for Canadian workers to gain the right to union recognition and collective bargaining.

Throughout the 20th century the RCMP carried out extensive surveillance of politicians, university students, and faculty; and it maintained confidential files on hundreds of thousands of Canadians. Covert surveillance on university campuses began during World War I and continued into the late 1990s.[32,33] The RCMP was especially interested in left-wing student organizations and faculty during the 1960s, and it used student informants and undercover police to gather information. In the 1980s, a Royal Commission that was investigating alleged illegal activities of the RCMP reported that the RCMP Security Service (since disbanded and replaced by the civilian Canadian Security Intelligence Service) maintained hundreds of thousands of files on Canadians.[34]

More recently in 2010, the use of the police to quell protests at the G20 meeting of world leaders in Toronto generated considerable controversy. The Toronto police arrested more than 1000 persons during the protests, the largest mass arrest in Canadian history. Most were later released without being charged. There were hundreds of citizen complaints about the excessive use of force by police, and in 2013, one officer was convicted of assault of a protestor. Canadian police scholar Chris Murphy has observed that "this event was a post-9/11 example of both the politicization and securitization of Canadian public policing and public safety."[35] For Murphy, "securitization" means that the police are a major component of a security strategy. Murphy notes that the federal government spent $1 billion on public safety to ensure that the G20 meetings would take place in a safe and secure environment. Yet the images of riot police making mass arrests and responding aggressively to a largely passive public protest placed the police in the role of "protecting the security priorities of government."[36]

COMMUNITY

The adoption of a community policing model in the 1980s (discussed in Chapter 6) precipitated the expansion of the role and activities of the police. Police services began to develop collaborative partnerships with agencies and neighbourhoods to develop strategies to prevent and respond to crime and social disorder. Police officers were given the autonomy to engage in problem-solving activities to proactively address the underlying causes of crime and social problems, moving out of a reactive approach. Concurrently, the demands and expectations of the police among community residents increased. Today, depending on the particular community or neighbourhood being policed, the police may find themselves over-subscribed and unable to meet the needs of the community. As the discussion in Chapter 6 will reveal, this shortfall has been compounded by downloading onto the police of responsibilities more appropriately held by other agencies.

DOWNLOADING

A feature of policing in the early 21st century is downloading; that is, the police being required to fill gaps in service that are the mandated responsibility of other agencies and organizations. Throughout North America, massive downloading onto police services has been carried out by municipal and provincial or territorial governments. For example, when governments cut the numbers of social workers and mental health workers, funding for shelter beds and for specialized facilities for the those with mental illness, it has a direct impact on the demands placed on police resources. As a consequence, police services across the country are spending an increasing portion of their time responding to high-risk and vulnerable populations, including those with mental illnesses. In a report titled *Lost in Transition*, the Vancouver Police Department (VPD) documented the extensive, and time-consuming, contacts with persons with mental illnesses in the Downtown Eastside area of the city. The study found that 31 percent of calls for service received by the VPD had a mental health component. Some individuals had almost daily contact with the police.[37] Also, in many cities, the police are confronted with the needs of various newcomer groups, in the absence of provincially or territorially funded programs and services.

THE RECRUITMENT AND TRAINING OF POLICE OFFICERS

POLICE RECRUITMENT

The high-visibility and high-demand role of police officers requires that only highly qualified persons are recruited and trained. Even with the cutbacks in policing budgets, police services are competing for qualified candidates.

People who are interested in a career in policing must have both **basic qualifications** and **preferred qualifications**. The basic qualifications include Canadian citizenship (although some departments consider landed immigrants), a minimum age of 19 (the average age of police recruits in many departments is more than 25), physical fitness, and a Grade 12 education. Also, the applicant cannot have any prior criminal convictions or pending charges and must exhibit common sense and good judgment.

Preferred qualifications—which are highly prized by police services—include any (or, ideally, a combination of) knowledge of a second language or culture, related volunteer experience, a postsecondary education, and work or life experience. Ontario has standardized the criteria for assessing prospective applicants through the Constable Selection System, which is used by most of the province's police services. Prospective recruits file one application, which is then vetted through this system. This arrangement has done away with multiple applications to different police services and consequent duplication of the assessment effort.

A challenge is to develop measures to assess the validity of the criteria used to select and train police recruits, and to determine whether the attributes of police recruits have an impact on their performance during their policing careers.[38] It has been noted that police recruits are not blank slates when they arrive at the training academy and bring with them attitudes and beliefs that may influence their views as police officers of persons and situations. A key issue is how these are either enhanced or modified by their experience in the training academy.[39] While all the major police services in Canada administer psychological tests to applicants, in Québec, this includes testing designed to measure the applicant's emotional intelligence and determine whether the person will encounter problems if hired in the police service.

Over the past decade, police recruiting has undergone significant changes because of the increasing pressure on police services to reflect the gender and cultural and ethnic diversity of the communities they police. Police services are actively seeking female and visible minority group applicants. Of the 3267 police officers in the Montréal police in 2013, 1117 were women (34 percent), 12 (0.37 percent) were First Nations, and 402 (12.31 percent) were members of ethnic and visible minorities.[40]

Many police services have developed special initiatives and programs to attract qualified visible minority and Aboriginal recruits. The OPP, for example, operates PEACE (Police Ethnic and Cultural Exchange), wherein student members of

Basic qualifications (for police candidates)
The minimum requirements for candidates applying for employment in policing.

Preferred qualifications (for police candidates)
Requirements that increase the competitiveness of applicants seeking employment in policing.

84

visible minorities participate in a police-sponsored summer employment program, and OPPBound, in which potential recruits (specifically, women and people from visible minorities) participate in a variety of activities with in-service officers and at the Provincial Police Academy. Among the recruiting initiatives of the Toronto Police Service is an attempt to increase the number of applicants from the Somali community. While an estimated 80,000 Somalis live in Toronto, only two full-time members and one auxiliary member of the 5400-member police service are Somali. Similarly, the RCMP has set targets for increasing the number of women, people from visible minorities, and Aboriginal peoples and has several initiatives designed to increase the number of successful applicants.

In 2013, the Edmonton Police Service announced that had approved a new design for the police uniform that includes a hajib (a scarf that covers the head and chest) that would be worn by female Muslim police officers. This change is part of an effort to attract Muslim women into the police service.

Although the number of female police officers and officers from visible minority groups in Canadian police services has gradually increased, both groups are under-represented in police services and, particularly, at the higher ranks. These facts are illustrated in Table 4.1.

POLICE TRAINING

Just as important as recruiting qualified people to become police officers is training them well. Several different models of police training are used in Canada. Municipal police recruits may be trained in-house, at a residential or non-residential training academy, or a combination of both. Recruits in the Calgary Police Service (CPS) are trained at the Chief Crowfoot Learning Centre, which is operated by the CPS, while municipal officers in Ontario receive a portion of their training in-house before being sent to the Ontario Police College in Alymer, Ontario. In British Columbia, recruits in municipal police services are sent to the Justice Institute of British Columbia, a non-residential facility, where they complete a three-block training course. Blocks I and III are in the academy and block II is completed in the field under the supervision of a field training officer in their home department.

In contrast, RCMP cadets are sent to the RCMP training depot in Regina for six months of training before being sent to a detachment for six months of field training.

TABLE 4.1 COMPOSITION PROFILE BY UNIFORM RANK, 2010, TORONTO POLICE SERVICE

Senior Officers	racial minorities: 12% Aboriginal: 0% females: 14%
Staff Sergeants and Sergeants	racial minorities: 12% Aboriginal: 0.6% females: 17%
Constables	racial minorities: 20% Aboriginal: 1% females: 18%

Source: Adapted from Toronto Police Service. 2011. *Planning for the Future…Scanning the Toronto Environment*, p. 207. Toronto. http://www.torontopolice.on.ca/publications/files/reports/2011envscan.pdf.

Unlike their provincial and municipal counterparts, the cadets are not hired by the RCMP before being sent to training and may be offered employment as a regular member after successfully completing training at the depot.

Police recruits generally receive instruction in the law, community relations, methods of patrol and investigation, and firearms handling. They are also provided with driver training and physical training. Having completed this training, the recruits are usually assigned to general patrol duties for three to five years. Thereafter, they are eligible to apply to specialty units.

Besides providing knowledge and skills, training academies provide a mechanism for socializing new recruits into the occupation of policing. Far too little attention has been paid by police scholars to the experiences of police recruits in training programs as they are transformed into police constables and to how these experiences shape their attitudes, expectations, and behaviour. This process of socialization into the police occupation may have an impact on the recruit's self-image, values, perceptions, and behaviour. Most police recruits are motivated, at least initially, by a desire to help people and serve the community. The training experience can have a strong influence on this, however. Research studies have found that, for many recruits, the police academy experience makes them more cynical, more suspicious of people, and, generally, more vigilant.[41] The extent to which recruits exhibit these attitudinal and behavioural traits, however, depends on the personalities and values of the individual. Some attributes of the police academy do not fit well with the principles of community policing, including a hierarchical, paramilitary structure that encourages an "us versus them" mentality, deference to authority, and the development of strong bonds and in-group loyalty among recruits. The extent to which these features of the police academy experience have hindered the implementation of community policing has yet to be researched in Canada.[42]

Despite the critical role that recruit training plays in policing careers, very little is known about how new recruits feel about the training they receive. As well, little is known about the relevance and impact of academy training once recruits are assigned to operational patrol. It does appear that the occupational culture of front-line policing exerts an equal if not greater influence on the attitudes and behaviour of the new police officer than does the formal instruction received at the police academy.[43]

THE FIELD TRAINING EXPERIENCE

During the second component of the training and learning process, known as **operational field training**, the recruit learns to apply the basic principles taught at the training centre. Under the guidance and assistance of a senior officer, the recruit is exposed to a wide variety of general police work.

Operational field training
Instructing the recruit in how to apply principles from the training academy in the community.

During this critical phase, the specially trained senior officer (often referred to as the field trainer or mentor) makes sure that the recruit is able to meet the demands and challenges of police work.

The length, and structure, of field training varies among police services. For example, Vancouver police recruits spend up to 17 weeks under the supervision of a field training officer (FTO), whereas new RCMP officers work with a field coach for 24 weeks after graduating from the RCMP Training Academy and being sworn in as peace officers. And while municipal police recruits in B.C. complete their field training during block II, before returning to the police academy for block III, new RCMP officers receive their field training *after* completing the program at the training academy.

Police services are paying increasing attention to ensuring continuity between the training a recruit receives in the academy and the supervision provided once the new recruit is involved in operational policing. FTOs play a significant role in the training process and have a strong influence on the attitude and policing style that the new recruit develops. A key objective of the FTO is to enhance the skills and knowledge the recruit has gained at the academy in a way that lessens the disconnect between the training academy and the street. Meeting this goal will reduce the likelihood that the new officer will become cynical and discard the skill sets and attitudes learned in recruit training.

There is some evidence, though, that field training may negate the recruit's positive attitudes toward various aspects of policing, including community policing and problem solving.[44] Given the importance of FTOs in moulding the attitudes and perceptions of new recruits, it is important for police services to select FTOs carefully and to monitor their approach to that role. New recruits need to be matched with competent and motivated trainers who represent the best skill sets the organization has to offer.

THE POLICE OCCUPATION

Clearly, police officers are required to play a multifaceted role: counsellor, psychologist, enforcer, mediator, and listener. They must be able to understand and empathize with the feelings and frustrations of crime victims; at the same time, they must develop strategies to cope with the dark side of human behaviour, which they encounter every day. Officers must walk a fine line between carrying out their enforcement role and ensuring that the rights of law-abiding citizens and suspects are protected.

THE WORKING PERSONALITY OF POLICE OFFICERS

Working personality of the police

A set of attitudinal and behavioural attributes that develops as a consequence of the unique role and activities of police officers.

The various pressures and demands placed on police officers contribute to what researchers have called the **working personality of the police.** This concept is used to explain how the police view their role and the world around them. It was first identified and defined by the criminologist Jerome Skolnick: "The police, as a result of the combined features of their social situation, tend to develop ways of looking at the world distinctive to themselves, cognitive lenses through which to see situations and events."[45]

Among the features of the working personality are a preoccupation with danger, excessive suspiciousness of people and activities, a protective cynicism, and difficulties exercising authority in a manner that balances the rights of citizens with the need to maintain order. It is argued that as a consequence of these personality attributes, many police officers tend to view policing as a career and a way of life, rather than merely a nine-to-five job; value secrecy and practise a code of silence to protect fellow officers; and exhibit strong in-group solidarity—often referred to as *the blue wall*—owing to job-related stresses, shift work, and an us versus them division between police and civilians. As well, police officers tend to hold conservative political and moral views and to exhibit attitudes, often referred to as *the blue light syndrome*, that emphasize the high-risk, high-action component of police work.[46]

In the nearly 50 years since Skolnick first proposed the notion of a working personality, there have been many changes in the activities and strategies of police officers, as well as in the diversity of police officers themselves. One of the most significant developments has been the emergence of community policing, a model of policing centred on police–community partnerships that bring officers into close contact with community residents in a wide range of crime prevention and response activities. Various community policing strategies can succeed in reducing the distance (and distrust) between the police and the communities they serve. (See Chapter 6.)

These and other changes in the activities of the police have led to the suggestion that the us versus them dichotomy is much too general and that it fails to account for the wide variety of relationships that exist between the public and the police, as well as the differences among police officers themselves with respect to how the police role is carried out.[47,48]

That a police subculture exists has many positive implications. For example, it encourages camaraderie and trust among police officers, helps individual officers cope with the more stressful aspects of police work, and is a source of general support. A more negative view of the police subculture is warranted, however, if and when the group solidarity it generates comes at the expense of positive police–community relations, an openness to new strategies and models of policing, or a cover-up of police wrongdoing.

THE CHALLENGES OF POLICE WORK

Although police work can be satisfying and challenging, it can also be stressful. The effects of stress experienced by police officers range from minor annoyances (which can be managed) to alcohol or drug addiction and suicide.[49,50] A sample of officers ($N = 225$) in the United States who were surveyed five months after leaving the training academy identified a number of stressors on the job. The highest rated items were "danger on the streets" (49 percent), following by work schedule (40 percent), report writing (37 percent), and the challenges of maintaining a work-life balance (35 percent).[51]

A study of work-life and employee well-being among a large sample ($N = 4500$) of Canadian police officers found that[52]

> Police officers devote long hours to work. Three quarters of the officers in our sample (78%) work more than 45 hours per week. Two thirds (64%) cannot get everything done during work hours and take home work to complete outside of their regular hours on evenings and weekends.

Research studies in the United States have found that officers working in smaller police services experience higher levels of stress than their colleagues in larger police services.[53] In Canada, police officers in remote areas, assigned to small detachments, may experience high stress levels because of the challenging environments in which they work. Remote and rural communities often have much higher rates of crime — especially violent crime — than urban centres. Policing in these high-demand environments, where back-up may not be readily available, can take a toll on officers. In recognition of this, officers are generally posted to these isolated locations for no more than two or three years. Traumatic events, such as homicides, suicides, the deaths of children, and multi-victim accidents, can take a toll on officers and lead to burnout.[54] Officers who are involved in critical incidents, such as a shooting or who are exposed to extreme violence, individual suffering, and death may develop **post-traumatic stress disorder (PTSD)**, an extreme form of critical-incident stress that includes nightmares, hypervigilance, intrusive thoughts, and other forms of psychological distress.[55]

These experiences may be compounded by shift work, which results in officers working all hours of the day and night, with a significant impact on sleep patterns. A

Post-traumatic stress disorder (PTSD)

An extreme form of critical-incident stress that includes nightmares, hypervigilance, intrusive thoughts, and other forms of psychological distress.

study (N = 4957) of a sample of police officers in Canada and the United States found that just over 40 percent of the officers suffered from at least one sleep disorder.[56]

Some observers contend that the police organization itself may be a greater source of stress than police operations.[57] Female officers, for example, may experience higher levels of stress than their male counterparts because of harassment and more subtle forms of discrimination.[58] A national survey of RCMP officers (N = 12,129) found that 19 percent of the respondents indicated that they had been harassed on the job by a superior, supervisor, or co-worker during the previous year (although there was no gender breakdown indicated).[59] A review by the Commission for Public Complaints Against the RCMP of more than 700 harassment complaints filed between 2005 and 2011 found the that 90 percent of the complaints related to bullying, including psychological abuse, belittling, and demeaning behaviour; 6 percent concerned discrimination associated with ethnicity, a disability, or some other factor; and 4 percent of the complaints related to sexual harassment.[60] The Commission also found that in some provinces, male members of the RCMP accounted for an equal share of the complaints against the RCMP.

These findings suggest that workplace conflicts in the RCMP extend beyond sexual harassment. Among the recommendations of the report were that the RCMP develop a timely and transparent process for responding to complaints (some were found to have taken up to four years to investigate and complete), develop a mandatory training program for harassment investigators, and send employees for training on issues related to harassment in the workplace. Of some concern were the findings from an internal survey (N = 426) conducted in one RCMP division that found that female officers did not trust the RCMP to deal appropriately with complaints of harassment.[61]

In late 2013, a class action harassment suit brought by nearly 300 women who are current or former RCMP officers was working its way through the courts. The suit alleges that the women experience or experienced gender-based discrimination and harassment, including name-calling, sexist pranks, and verbal propositions for sexual favours.[62] See the Media Link "Behind the Line" at the end of the chapter.

Research studies in the Unites States suggest that, in general, the suicide rates of police officers are not significantly different from those of the general population, nor do police officers seem to consume alcohol in greater amounts than the general population.[63,64] Studies have also found that the divorce rate for police officers is lower than that of the general population.[65] Of course, it may be that the police occupation is more stressful but that officers have developed more effective coping mechanisms than their counterparts in other federal agencies. And lower rates do not detract from the importance of considering the impact of policing on the personal lives of officers.

Research does suggest that high stress levels may make officers more susceptible to misconduct and that constant exposure to stressors may also lead to burnout, a general term used to describe physical, emotional, and mental exhaustion.[66,67]

SUMMARY

The discussion in this chapter has examined the structure and roles of the police in Canada. Modern policing developed in England in the early 1800s, and a number of key principles of policing were identified that provide the basis for policing in contemporary times. Community self-policing in early Canada gradually gave way to organized police services, and today policing is carried out at the federal, provincial or territorial, municipal and First Nations levels. It was noted that there has been a pluralization of policing, wherein the public and private police share responsibility for the safety and security of communities. A challenge of policing is to balance the natural tensions that exist between maintaining order while ensuring individual rights, and the various structures of police governance are designed to help maintain the balance.

A number of factors that influence the role and activities of the police were identified and discussed. Of particular concern is the use of the police by governments to quell protests and maintain security at the cost of individual rights.

The chapter concluded with a discussion of the recruitment and training of police officers and the various features of the police occupation that may have a significant impact on their personal lives.

KEY POINTS REVIEW

1. The first full-time police force was created in London in 1829 by Sir Robert Peel who set out a number of principles that still apply to policing.

2. Early municipal police forces in Canada had a mandate to police conflicts between groups, to maintain moral standards, and to apprehend criminals.

3. It is by historical accident that the RCMP is today involved in federal, provincial and territorial, and municipal policing.

4. The four levels of policing in Canada are federal, provincial or territorial, municipal, and First Nations.

5. The RCMP has a number of distinct features, including training all its recruits in a central location before their deployment across the country and, unlike their municipal and provincial counterparts, not being unionized.

6. There has been a rapid growth in private security services.

7. In a democratic society, natural tensions exist between the power and authority of the police and the values and processes that exist in a democratic society.

8. The structures of police governance include police acts, policing standards, and police boards and commissions.

9. A number of misconceptions surround police work.

10. Traditionally, the police role was categorized into crime control, order maintenance, and service, although today these may not capture the complexity of the police role.

11. Most activities of the police do not involve crime control.

12. There are a variety of influences on the roles and activities of the police.

13. Recruiting qualified people is a challenge for police services.

14. Police services have developed a number of programs to increase the number of applicants from visible and cultural minority groups.

15. There are a variety of models for training police recruits across the country.

16. The various pressures and demands placed on police officers contribute to what researchers have called the working personality of the police, although some evidence suggests that there has been some erosion in the us versus them mentality of the police.

17. Police officers experience numerous challenges in carrying out their mandate.

KEY TERM QUESTIONS

1. What does the *Royal Canadian Mounted Police Act* do?

2. What is **contract policing**?

3. Define **policing**.

4. What is meant by the **pluralization of policing**?

5. What role do **police acts**, **policing standards**, and **police boards and commissions** play in the governance of the police?

6. Identify the **basic** and **preferred qualifications** for police candidates required by police services in the recruitment process.

7. Define **political policing** and provide examples.

8. What is meant by the **working personality of the police**?

9. Describe the role of **operational field training** in policing.

10. What is **post-traumatic stress disorder (PTSD)**, and what aspects of police work may contribute to it?

MEDIA LINK

"Behind the Line," *CBC Fifth Estate* or go to the book's website at www.nelson.com/crimjusticeprimer5e.com

CHAPTER 5

POLICE POWERS AND DECISION MAKING

LEARNING OBJECTIVES

After reading this chapter, you should be able to

- describe the powers of the police with respect to detention and arrest, search and seizure, use of force, and interrogation of crime suspects
- discuss the impact of the *Charter of Rights and Freedoms* on police powers
- describe several high-profile Supreme Court of Canada decisions relating to search and seizure
- discuss the issues surrounding entrapment by the police
- discuss what is meant by the one plus one use of force standard
- describe the issues that surround the use of the Taser as a less-lethal force option
- describe the factors that appear to be associated with the use of various force options
- describe the provisions for police accountability

▲ A protest poster depicting the police as instruments of oppression

Courtesy of Paul Kambulow.

Tension will always exist between the need to maintain order and the rights of citizens. This tension is evident in the discussion of the powers of the police. How can society extend the police sufficient authority to ensure order and pursue criminals, while at the same time protecting the rights of citizens? To imagine what life would be like in a police state, you need only look to countries where the police have no limits on their powers. A police force with unlimited power might not only be more effective, but it would also interfere with the freedoms Canadians enjoy.

Some in Canada feel that the police have too much power. Defining the limits of police power is an ongoing process.

One of the difficulties is that persons who have contact with the police may not know what powers the police have and their own individual rights. This lack of knowledge may be particularly problematic for persons newly arrived in Canada and may also be the case for many Canadian citizens, including seniors and persons with mental illnesses. The situation is made even more complex by the fact that the powers of the police, and the limitations placed on the police by legislation and court decisions, are constantly evolving. The Lexum Collection online at http://scc.lexum.org is a good resource for following Supreme Court of Canada (SCC) decisions related to police powers.

Historically, Canadians have been willing to trust that the police would do the right thing in exercising their powers and were prepared to give the police more powers to detect and arrest criminals, even if this meant that the civil rights of some individuals would be violated. In recent years, however, because of a number of high-profile incidents and the increased visibility of the police, these views seem to be shifting.

THE *CHARTER OF RIGHTS AND FREEDOMS* AND POLICE POWERS

The police derive their powers from a number of sources, including statute law, case law, common law, and municipal bylaws (see Chapter 1).[1] The *Criminal Code*, for example, provides the authority to arrest (section 495), to use force (section 25), to search (with a warrant; section 487), and to obtain DNA samples (section 487.05), among others.

But perhaps no other single piece of legislation has had a greater impact on the powers and activities of the police than the *Charter of Rights and Freedoms*.[2] Besides entrenching constitutional rights for persons accused of crimes, the *Charter* gave those accused the right to challenge the actions of the police in situations where those rights might have been violated. *Charter* rights combine with the existing legal rules to prevent the unlimited use of police power. These safeguards include the following:

- The police cannot use certain investigative techniques (such as electronic surveillance) without prior judicial authorization.
- If the police gather evidence illegally, it may be excluded from a trial if its use would bring the administration of justice into disrepute.
- A defendant who feels that police officers or prosecutors have used unfair tactics can plead not guilty and cite *abuse of process* as a defence.
- Severe restrictions have been placed on the investigative strategy of placing an undercover officer in a jail cell to elicit evidence from a criminal suspect.

93

- All relevant information gathered during a case investigation must be disclosed to the defence attorney.

- Warrantless searches have been deemed to be unreasonable. Police officers must now clearly articulate why they have a conducted a search without a warrant.

The police have also retained significant powers through the Supreme Court of Canada:

- It has ruled in favour of the police practice of using thermal-imaging technology deployed for aircraft to detect high levels of heat from homes, a key indicator of marijuana grow-ops (*R. v. Tessling*, [2004]3 SCR 432).

- It has established the legality of "Mr. Big" stings, wherein suspects are placed in a position where they "confess" to have committed a crime (*R. v. Grandinetti*, [2005]1 SCR 27).

- The court has reaffirmed the principle that the police can continue to question a suspect at length, even if the suspect repeatedly tries to invoke his right to silence (*R. v. Singh*, [2007]3 SCR 405).

- It has held that the *Charter* does not require the presence, on request, of defence counsel during a custodial interrogation (*R. v. McCrimmon*, [2010]2 SCR 402; *R. v. Sinclair*, [2010]2 SCR 310).

Also, as a result of judicial decisions, police officers now have the authority to use a warrant to obtain DNA from a suspect, by force if necessary; to obtain a variety of warrants to intercept private audio and video communications; to run *reverse stings* (e.g., sell drugs as part of an undercover operation and then seize both the money and the drugs); and to obtain foot, palm, and teeth impressions from a suspect.

In recent years, the powers of the police have been extended in an attempt to better prevent and respond to organized crime and terrorist activity. Under the *Anti-terrorism Act*, for example, a peace officer may arrest a person without a warrant and have that person detained in custody if the officer suspects, on reasonable grounds, that the person's detention is necessary to prevent a specific terrorist activity.

To enhance the capacity of the justice system to respond to organized crime, federal legislation has been enacted that gives the police who are working undercover the authority to break most criminal laws (exceptions: those relating to murder, assault causing bodily harm, sexual offences, and obstruction of justice) and that reduces the burden of proof for prosecutors attempting to convict members of criminal organizations. Legislative enactments have also criminalized mere involvement with a criminal organization, whether or not the individual actually breaks the law.

The following police powers are discussed below: the power to detain and arrest, search and seizure, entrapment, the right to remain silent, and the Mr. Big strategy.

THE POWER TO DETAIN AND ARREST

When most people think of police powers, they think automatically of arrest. Over the years, considerable confusion has surrounded the arrest process. Many citizens do not know when the police have the right to make an arrest; nor do they know what their rights are in an arrest situation.

The power to arrest is provided by the *Criminal Code* and other federal statutes, as well as by provincial legislation, such as motor vehicle statutes. An arrest can be made to prevent a crime from being committed, to terminate a breach of the peace, or to compel an accused person to attend trial.

94

A formal arrest triggers certain requirements on the part of the police (e.g., to advise the suspect of the reason for the arrest, of the right to counsel, of the right to remain silent). That said, most persons are released shortly thereafter on an appearance notice, an undertaking to appear, or a summons to appear in court at a future date. These notices are issued because the person meets the "public interest" requirements of the *Bail Reform Act* (i.e., the seriousness of the offence; identify is established; there is no concern of a continuation of the offence, of a failure to appear in court, or for destruction of evidence; see below). A criminal suspect who is placed in custody will generally be released as soon as possible, on the authority of the arresting officer, the officer in charge of the police lockup, or a justice of the peace (JP).

If an arrest is warranted, and if there is time to do so, a police officer can seek an **arrest warrant** by swearing an **information** in front of a JP. If the JP agrees that there are "reasonable grounds to believe that it is necessary in the public interest," a warrant will be issued directing the local police to arrest the person. Accessing a JP may be difficult in rural areas. Several provinces (including British Columbia, Ontario, Manitoba, and Alberta) have developed telewarrant programs that provide 24-hour access to JPs. Police officers can apply for and receive warrants by fax or telephone instead of having to appear in person before a JP.

Sometimes the police must act quickly and have no time to secure a warrant from a JP. Police officers can arrest a suspect *without* an arrest warrant in the following circumstances:

- They have caught a person in the act of committing an offence.
- They believe, on reasonable grounds, that a person has committed an indictable offence (see Chapter 1).
- They believe, on reasonable grounds, that a person is about to commit an indictable offence.

Two additional conditions apply to making an arrest. First, the officer must not make an arrest if he or she has no reasonable grounds to believe that the person will fail to appear in court. Second, the officer must believe on reasonable grounds that an arrest is necessary in the public interest. An arrest is in public interest is defined specifically as the need to

- establish the identity of the person
- secure or preserve evidence of or relating to the offence
- prevent the continuation or repetition of the offence or the commission of another offence

However, provisions in the *Anti-terrorism Act* give the police the power of preventive arrest. This power allows them to arrest persons without a warrant on reasonable *suspicion* (rather than the standard of reasonable grounds), if it is believed that the arrest will prevent a terrorist activity. The person need not have committed any crime and can be detained for up to 72 hours.

In practice, arrests are usually made only in the case of indictable offences. For minor crimes (summary conviction offences), an arrest is legal only if the police find someone actually committing the offence or if there is an outstanding arrest warrant or *warrant of committal* (a document issued by a judge directing prison authorities to accept a person into custody upon his or her sentencing), a *bench warrant* for failure to appear at a court process, or a document issued by a parole board to revoke an offender's conditional release.

In some circumstances, an arrest can be unlawful. An officer who makes an arrest without reasonable grounds risks being sued civilly for assault or false imprisonment.

Arrest warrant

A document that permits a police officer to arrest a specific person for a specified reason.

Information

A written statement sworn by an informant alleging that a person has committed a specific criminal offence.

95

Moreover, a person who resists an unlawful arrest is not guilty of resisting a police officer in the execution of his or her duty. To make a *lawful* arrest, "a police officer should identify himself or herself, tell the suspect that he or she is being arrested, inform the suspect of the reason for the arrest or show the suspect the warrant if there is one, and, where feasible, touch the suspect on the shoulder as a physical indication of the confinement."[3]

What is the difference between arrest and detention? An officer can detain a person without arrest. The Supreme Court of Canada has held that a detention occurs when a police officer "assumes control over the movement of a person by a demand or direction that may have significant legal consequence and that prevents or impedes access to [legal] counsel" (*R. v. Schmautz*, [1990]1 SCR 398). In contrast, the primary purpose of an arrest is to compel an accused to appear at trial.

Whether the person has been arrested or detained, an important threshold in the criminal process has been crossed. According to section 10 of the *Charter*, anyone who has been arrested or detained has the right to be informed promptly of the reason for the arrest or detention. That person also has the right to retain and instruct counsel without delay, and, furthermore, must be told about that right without delay. However, the suspect can choose to exercise that right or not. Also, a suspect who is interviewed by Canadian police officers in the United States must be informed of the right to counsel (*R. v. Cook*, [1998]2 SCR 597). The *Charter*-based warning read by police officers in independent municipal police services in British Columbia is reproduced in Box 5.1. The wording of this communication of *Charter* rights may vary across police services.

Suspects have a right to retain counsel but do not have an absolute right to have that counsel paid for by the state. Moreover, section 10 of the *Charter* does not impose a duty on provincial or territorial governments to provide free legal representation to everyone who cannot afford it. In many provinces, free preliminary legal advice is available 24 hours a day through a toll-free number. When an arrested or a detained person does not have or know a lawyer, police must inform that person of this number and hold off on further questioning to give the suspect an opportunity to access this advice. After that, however, to get free legal representation the suspect must qualify for legal aid (see Chapter 8).

Failure to advise a person in a timely manner of the right to counsel on arrest is an infringement of his or her *Charter* rights. In addition, the Supreme Court of Canada has held that a person's *Charter* rights are violated when the police (1) refuse to hold off and continue to question an arrested person despite repeated statements that he or she will say nothing without consulting a lawyer, (2) belittle the person's lawyer with the express goal or intent of undermining the person's relationship with that lawyer, or (3) pressure the person to accept a deal without first affording the person the option to consult with a lawyer.

SEARCH AND SEIZURE

The power of the police to search people and places and to seize evidence also illustrates the fine balance that must be maintained between crime control and due process. Historically, under the common law, the manner in which evidence was gathered did not affect its admissibility in a criminal trial. That all changed with the *Charter*, section 8 of which protects all citizens against unreasonable search or seizure. Evidence obtained during an illegal search may be excluded from trial if, as indicated in section 24 of the *Charter*, its use would bring the justice system into disrepute.

BOX 5.1 COMMUNICATING *CHARTER* RIGHTS UPON ARREST OR DETENTION

1. **Sec. 10(a)** I am arresting/detaining you for _____ (State reason for arrest/detention, including the offence and provide known information about the offence, including date and place.)

2. **Sec. 10(b)** It is my duty to inform you that you have the right to retain and instruct counsel in private without delay. You may call any lawyer you want.

3. There is a 24-hour telephone service available which provides a legal aid duty lawyer who can give you legal advice in private. This advice is given without charge and the lawyer can explain the legal aid plan to you.

4. If you wish to contact a legal aid lawyer I can provide you with a telephone number.

5. Do you understand?

6. Do you want to call a lawyer?

Supplementary *Charter* Warning: (If an arrested or detained person initially indicated that he or she wished to contact legal counsel and then subsequently indicates that he or she no longer wishes to exercise the right to counsel, read the following additional charter warning.)

You have the right to a reasonable opportunity to contact counsel. I am not obliged to take a statement from you or ask you to participate in any process which could provide incriminating evidence until you are certain about whether you want to exercise this right.

Do you understand?

What do you wish to do?

Secondary Warning: (Name), you are detained with respect to (reason for detainment). If you have spoken to any police officer (including myself) with respect to this matter, who has offered to you any hope of advantage or suggested any fear of prejudice should you speak or refuse to speak with me (us) at this time, it is my duty to warn you that no such offer or suggestion can be of any effect and must not influence you or make you feel compelled to say anything to me (us) for any reason, but anything you do say may be used in evidence.

Written Statement Caution: I have been advised by (investigating officer) that I am not obliged to say anything, but anything I do say may be given in evidence. I understand the meaning of the foregoing and I choose to make the following statement.

Approved Screening Device (ASD) Demand: In accordance with the provisions of the *Criminal Code*, I hereby demand that you provide a sample of your breath, forthwith, suitable for analysis using an approved screening device.

Breath Demand: I have reasonable and probable grounds to believe that you are committing, or within the preceding three hours have, as a result of the consumption of alcohol, committed an offence under Section 253 of the *Criminal Code*, and I hereby demand that you provide now, or as soon as is practicable, such samples of your breath as are necessary to enable a proper analysis to be made to determine the concentration, if any, of alcohol in

your blood and to accompany me for the purpose of enabling such samples to be taken.

Blood Demand: I have reasonable and probable grounds to believe that you are committing, or within the preceding three hours have, as a result of the consumption of alcohol, committed an offence under Section 253 of the *Criminal Code*, and I hereby demand that you provide now, or as soon as is practicable, such samples of your blood as are necessary to enable a proper analysis to be made to determine the concentration, if any, of alcohol in your blood.

Samples of your blood will be taken by, or under the direction of, a qualified medical practitioner who is satisfied that the taking of those samples will not endanger you or your health.

7. **MVA Section 90.3—12-Hour Licence Suspension:** I have reasonable and probable grounds to believe

   (1) you have alcohol in your body

   or

   (2) you have failed or refused to comply with the demand to provide a sample of your breath that is necessary to enable a proper analysis of your breath to be made by means of an approved screening device.

8. I therefore direct you to surrender your driver's licence. Your licence to drive is now suspended for a period of 12 hours from this time and date.

9. If you produce, to a Peace Officer having charge of this matter, a certificate of a medical practitioner signed after this suspension is issued stating that your blood alcohol level does not exceed 3 milligrams of alcohol in 100 millilitres of blood at the time the certificate was signed, the suspension is terminated.

10. **MVA Section 215—24-Hour Roadside Prohibition:** I have reasonable and probable grounds to believe that your ability to drive a motor vehicle is affected by alcohol (or by drug), and I therefore direct you to surrender your driver's licence.

11. You are now prohibited from driving a motor vehicle for a period of 24 hours from this time and date.

12. **(for alcohol)** However, if you do not accept this prohibition, you have a right to either request a breath test or obtain a certificate from a medical practitioner. In the event that your blood alcohol level is shown not to exceed 50 milligrams of alcohol in 100 millilitres of blood by the test or certificate, this prohibition from driving is terminated.

13. **(for drug)** However, if you do not accept this prohibition, you have a right to attempt to satisfy a peace officer having charge of this matter that your ability to drive a motor vehicle is not affected by a drug other than alcohol, and if the peace officer is so satisfied this prohibition from driving is terminated.

OFFICIAL WARNING: You are not obliged to say anything, but anything you do say may be given in evidence.

Source: Copyright © Province of British Columbia. All rights reserved. Reprinted with the permission of the Province of British Columbia.

BOX 5.2 *R. V. MANN*—A CASE OF DETAINMENT, SEARCH, AND SEIZURE

As two police officers approached the scene of a reported break and enter, they observed M., who matched the description of the suspect, walking casually along the sidewalk. They stopped him. M. identified himself and complied with a pat-down search of his person for concealed weapons. During the search, one officer felt a soft object in M.'s pocket. He reached into the pocket and found a small plastic bag containing marijuana. He also found a number of small plastic baggies in another pocket. M. was arrested and charged with possession of marijuana for the purpose of trafficking. The trial judge found that the search of M.'s pocket contravened section 8 of the Canadian *Charter of Rights and Freedoms*. He held that the police officer was justified in his search of M. for security reasons but that there was no basis to infer that it was reasonable to look inside M.'s pocket for security reasons. The evidence was excluded under s. 24(2) of the Charter, as its admission would interfere with the fairness of the trial, and the accused was acquitted. The Court of Appeal set aside the acquittal and ordered a new trial, finding that the detention and the pat-down search were authorized by law and were reasonable in the circumstances.

The Supreme Court subsequently decided that the acquittal should be restored. The majority of the justices found that the police were entitled to detain M. for investigative purposes and to conduct a pat-down search to ensure their safety, but that the search of M.'s pockets was unjustified and that the evidence discovered in them must be excluded. The court found that the police officers had reasonable grounds to detain M. and to conduct a protective search, but no reasonable basis for reaching into M.'s pocket. This more intrusive part of the search was an unreasonable violation of M.'s reasonable expectation of privacy with respect to the contents of his pockets.

QUESTIONS

Do you agree with the decision of the Supreme Court in this case? Explain. Does this decision place too many restrictions on the powers of the police? What if the officers had found a handgun rather than marijuana?

Source: *R. v. Mann, 2004 SCC 52, [2004] 3 S.C.R. 59*. Canadian Legal Information Institute. http://www.canlii.org/ca/cas/scc/2004/2004scc52.html

The Supreme Court of Canada has held *R. v. S.A.B.*, [2003]2 SCR 678, that for a search to be reasonable, (1) it must be authorized by law, (2) the law itself must be reasonable, and (3) the manner in which the search was carried out must be reasonable. These requirements are illustrated in the case of *R. v. Mann*, [2004]3 SCR, presented in Box 5.2.

The courts have considerable room for interpretation as to what constitutes an unreasonable search in any particular case and when admission of evidence would bring the administration of justice into disrepute. Since the passage of the *Charter* in 1982, there have been hundreds of court cases and numerous books and legal articles dealing with this issue; the same three decades have seen an ongoing debate about what constitutes a reasonable search. As a result, conditions and requirements have emerged regarding prior authorization for a search. Generally, a **search warrant** must be issued. The Supreme Court of Canada has decided that warrants are required in the following situations:

Search warrant

A document that permits the police to search a specific location and take items that might be evidence of a crime.

- where there is to be secret recording of conversations by state agents
- in cases involving video surveillance
- for perimeter searches of residential premises
- before the installation of tracking devices to monitor people's movements

Search warrants are generally issued by JPs. Before a warrant can be issued, an information must be sworn under oath before a JP to convince him or her that there are reasonable and probable grounds that there is, in a building or place, (1) evidence relating to an act in violation of the *Criminal Code* or other federal statute, (2) evidence that might exist in relation to such a violation, or (3) evidence intended to be used to commit an offence against a person for which an individual may be arrested without a warrant.

The following scenario illustrates the principle of reasonable and probable grounds. Your neighbours feel that you match the description of a crime suspect in a bank robbery reenacted on a televised *Crime Stopper* program. They telephone the police and anonymously provide your name and address. Can this tip be used to establish reasonable and probable grounds for a search of your home? The answer is no. Although a possible starting point for a police investigation, anonymous tips do not provide reasonable and probable grounds. A concern in establishing reasonable and probable grounds is the source of the information, the credibility of which is likely to be questioned if it is anonymous.

A search without a warrant will generally be illegal, except in two types of situations:

1. While arresting a person, the officer may search the person and the immediate surroundings for self-protection (that is, to seize weapons), to prevent the destruction of evidence (for example, to stop the person from swallowing drugs), or for means of escape.

2. In an emergency situation where an officer believes that an offence is being, or is likely to be, committed or that someone in the premises is in danger of injury, a premise may be entered. In *R. v. Godoy*, [1999]1 SCR 311, for example, the Supreme Court of Canada held that the forced entry of police officers into a residence from which a disconnected 9-1-1 call had been made, and the subsequent arrest of a suspect who had physically abused his common law partner, was justifiable.

The passage in 2001 of Bill C-36, the *Anti-terrorism Act*, expanded the authority of the police to search property associated with terrorist groups or activity. One of the more significant decisions on searches was made by the Supreme Court in *R. v. Feeney*, [1997]3 SCR 1008. See Box 5.3.

BOX 5.3   *R. V. FEENEY*: AN ILLEGAL SEARCH AND SEIZURE

As part of a murder investigation, the police knocked on the door of the accused's home. Receiving no answer, they entered the home, woke the accused, and arrested him after seeing blood on his shirt. The officers informed the accused of his right to counsel, but not of the immediate right to counsel, and seized evidence from his home that was subsequently used to obtain a search warrant to retrieve additional evidence. At trial, the accused was convicted of second-degree murder. His appeal was unanimously dismissed by the B.C. Court of Appeal. The issue for the Supreme Court was whether the police had violated the accused's right under the *Charter* to be free from unreasonable search or seizure and his right, on being arrested, to have access to legal counsel without delay and—either being so—what evidence, if any, should be excluded under section 24(2) of the *Criminal Code*. From an examination of the facts in the case, the court concluded that the legal requirements for a warrantless arrest following a forced entry into a person's private premises had not been met. More specifically, the arresting officer had not believed he had reasonable grounds to arrest before the forcible entry.

The court held that to protect the privacy rights of Canadians under the *Charter of Rights and Freedoms*, the police must obtain a search warrant before entering a dwelling to arrest or apprehend a suspect. In response to this decision, Parliament amended the *Criminal Code* to require that as a general rule, peace officers must obtain a warrant before entering a dwelling to apprehend or arrest someone, but police may enter dwellings and arrest or apprehend without a warrant in those circumstances where entry is required to prevent bodily harm or death or to prevent the loss or destruction of evidence in the case.

Source: *R. v. Feeney, [1997] 3 S.C.R. 1008*. Canadian Legal Information Institute. http://www.canlii.org/en/ca/scc/doc/1997/1997canlii301/1997canlii301.html

In another case, *R. v. AM*, [2008]1 SCR 569, (2008), SCC 19), the Supreme Court held that the use of police drug sniffer dogs to conduct random searches for drugs in schools and other public places violated the rights of citizens under the *Charter* not to be subject to unreasonable search and seizure. The principal of an Ontario high school had issued a standing invitation for the police to bring sniffer dogs into the school to enforce the school's zero tolerance policy for drugs and alcohol.

During the search, the drug dog zeroed in on a student's backpack, which was found to contain 10 bags of marijuana, 10 magic mushrooms, and various types of drug paraphernalia. The student, A.M., was charged with criminal offences. However, Ontario youth courts subsequently cleared the youth, deciding that his *Charter* rights had been violated. The primary issue for the Supreme Court was whether the use of the sniffer dog was an unreasonable invasion of privacy that amounted to unreasonable search and seizure under the *Charter*. (The *Charter* states that everyone has the right to be secure against unreasonable search or seizure). In its decision, the Supreme Court held that the sniffer dog's activities constituted a search under the provisions of the *Charter* and that the dog's search of the backpack as part of a general "sniff search" violated the student's *Charter* rights.[1] However, in 2013, in a case that suggested the Supreme Court was adopting the federal government's tough on crime approach, the court held that a drug sniffer dog could be used in a case where the police officer had reasonable suspicion that the suspect was involved in a drug-related offence (*R. v. MacKenzie* (2013), SCC 50). This decision expanded the situations in which the police could use dogs to search premises, in this case a vehicle that had been stopped for erratic driving. Writing for the majority, one of the justices stated that every police move should not be "placed under a scanning electron-microscope."[5] Critics lambasted the decision, one law professor stating that the ruling "has the effect of giving an enormous amount of deference to the instincts and subjective views of police officers, at the expense of some of the liberties we assumed were in place since the Charter [of Rights and Freedoms] came" into effect in 1982.[6]

While the Feeney case and the *R. v. AM* cases constrained police practice with respect to searches, the Supreme Court appeared to expand police powers of search in the case of Wendell Clayton and Troy Farmer (*R. v. Clayton*, [2007]2 SCR 725). See Box 5.4.

Ultimately, it is the courts that decide whether a search warrant has been properly obtained and executed or whether a warrantless search was legal.

BOX 5.4 A 9-1-1 CALL, POLICE ROADBLOCK, AND SEARCH

A caller to 9-1-1 stated that several young men outside a Toronto-area strip club were brandishing weapons. The police responded and set up a roadblock, stopping vehicles leaving the club. Clayton and Farmer, who were in a vehicle not specified by the 9-1-1 caller, were stopped and searched by police officers, who found a pair of loaded, semi-automatic handguns in their vehicle. In 2005, the Ontario Court of Appeal, in acquitting the two accused, had ruled that the gun evidence should be excluded as it was obtained by the use of a blockade that was unlawful since there was no evidence that anyone was in danger, and the police did not limit their search to vehicles described by the 9-1-1 caller. In a 9–0 ruling, however, the Supreme Court of Canada overturned the decision of the Ontario Court of Appeal, deciding that the search was justified. In the decision, one justice wrote that stropping any vehicles that were leaving the parking lot of the club was an "eminently reasonable response," particularly in light of the seriousness of gun-related crime. To critics, the decision of the Supreme Court was a further indication that the court has adopted more of a law-and-order stance in recent years.[7]

BOX 5.5 THE SEARCH OF A COMPUTER

In an investigation of a suspected marijuana grow-op, the police obtained a warrant to search the home of Thanh Long Vu for evidence of the theft of electricity and documentation identifying the owners or occupants of the residence. Entering the residence, the police found marijuana, two computers, and a cellular phone. The police searched the computers as part of their investigation to determine who lived in the home. Vu was subsequently charged with production of marijuana, possession of marijuana for the purpose of trafficking, and theft of electricity.

At trial, Vu's defence lawyer argued that the search of the computers violated his s. 8 *Charter* rights ("everyone has the right to be secure against unreasonable search or seizure"). The trial judge agreed, noting that the search warrant did not mention access to computers as a source of information regarding the identity of the owners/occupants of the residence and therefore did not allow a search of the computers. The judge excluded most of the evidence found in the computers and acquitted Mr. Vu of the drug charges. The B.C. Court of Appeal subsequently set aside the acquittals and ordered a new trial. Mr. Vu appealed to the SCC.

The SCC dismissed Mr. Vu's appeal. In its decision, the court reiterated the importance of the police obtaining prior authorization before a state incursion occurs to ensure that the privacy rights of the individuals are balanced against the interests of the state. In the words of one justice, "It is difficult to imagine a more intrusive invasion of privacy than the search of a personal or home computer."[8] If, as part of a search, the police find computers that may hold important information for the investigation, they must obtain a separate search warrant. The court found that, although the evidence in this case was illegally obtained, it should be admitted at trial since it did not bring the administration of justice into disrepute, the violation was not serious, and "the state of the law with respect to computer searches was uncertain when the police carried out their investigation" (*R. v. Vu* (2013), SCC 60).

A recent decision of the SCC highlighted how the powers of the police need to be clearly defined in the Age of the Internet. In late 2013, the federal government introduced legislation that would expand police powers to allow the police to take steps to prevent Internet and cellular phone companies from removing potentially incriminating evidence before a warrant is secured. See Box 5.5.

The Vu case illustrates the complexities that surround privacy and police access to computers and cellphones and the emerging case law in this area. In 2013, the SCC held that the police are required to have a special wiretap warrant to access a suspect's text messages from their wireless provider (*R. v. TELUS* (2013), SCC 16), and the Court of Appeal for Ontario held that the police could look through a suspect's cellphone on arrest if the content was not password protected. In this instance, no warrant was required; had the cellphone been password protected, the police would require a warrant to access the contents (*R. v. Fearon* (2013), ONCA 106).

ENTRAPMENT: A MISUSE OF POLICE POWERS

Entrapment means just what it sounds like: a person ends up committing an offence that he or she would not otherwise have committed, largely as a result of pressure or cunning on the part of the police. In these situations, the police are most often operating undercover. The following are controversial examples of police practice:

- An expensive car is left with the keys in the ignition, observed by concealed officers waiting to arrest anyone who steals it.
- A police officer poses as a young girl while trolling websites frequented by pedophiles.
- An undercover officer poses as an intoxicated subway passenger, wearing expensive jewellery and a Rolex watch. Anyone who mugs him is arrested.

- An undercover officer poses as a potential client to arrest a prostitute who offers his or her sexual services.

Proactive techniques like these can be an effective and cost-efficient use of personnel. They can help prevent crime in "victimless" offences (such as prostitution and drug possession) of the sort that are unlikely to generate citizen complaints. The controversy stems from the fact that there is a line between catching those habitually involved in lawbreaking and creating situational criminals. The concern is that in some situations, typically law-abiding people could be enticed into committing a crime.

The courts have determined that the line is crossed when a person is persistently harassed into committing an offence that he or she would not have committed had it not been for the actions of the police. People cannot be targeted at random. Rather, reasonable suspicion should exist that the person is already engaged in criminal activity. For example, in the prostitution example above, the actions of the police do not constitute entrapment because such a reasonable suspicion exists. One of the more important cases on entrapment is *R. v. Mack*, [1988]2 SCR 903, presented in Box 5.6.

Canadian courts have generally not allowed the defence of entrapment, which requires there to have been a clear abuse of process. In *R. v. Pearson*, [1998]3 SCR 620, the court made a clear distinction between the issue of entrapment and innocence: "Entrapment is completely separate from the issue of guilt or innocence. It is concerned with the conduct of the police and is dealt with at a separate proceeding from the trial on the merits" (see also *R. v. Campbell*, [1998]3 SCR 533).

The discussion surrounding the need to balance the powers of the police with the rights of citizens is ongoing and is likely to intensify. An example is the debate that ensued in 2013 when several Canadian police chiefs advocated for allowing the police to collect DNA samples from persons who are arrested (but not yet convicted). See At Issue 5.1.

BOX 5.6 THE CASE OF THE RELUCTANT DRUG TRAFFICKER

The defendant was charged with drug trafficking. At the close of his defence, he brought an application for a stay of proceedings on the basis of entrapment. His testimony indicated that he had persistently refused the approaches of a police informer over six months and that he was persuaded to sell him drugs only because of the informer's persistence, his use of threats, and the inducement of a large amount of money. He also testified that he had previously been addicted to drugs but that he had given up his use of narcotics. The application for a stay of proceedings was refused, and he was convicted of drug trafficking. The Court of Appeal dismissed an appeal from that conviction.

The central issue for the Supreme Court of Canada was whether the defendant had been entrapped into committing the offence of drug trafficking. The court held that the police in this case were not interrupting an ongoing criminal enterprise; the offence was clearly brought about by their conduct and would not have occurred without their involvement. The court stated that the persistence of the police requests, the equally persistent refusals, and the length of time needed to secure the defendant's participation in the offence indicated that the police had tried to make the appellant take up his former lifestyle and had gone further than merely providing him with the opportunity. For the court, the most important and determining factor was that the defendant had been threatened and had been told to get his act together when he did not provide the requested drugs. This conduct was unacceptable and went beyond providing the appellant with an opportunity. The court found that the average person in the appellant's position might also have committed the offence, if only to finally satisfy this threatening informer and end all further contact. The court ruled that the trial judge should have entered a stay of proceedings.

Source: *R. v. Mack, [1988] 2 S.C.R. 903*. Canadian Legal Information Institute. http://www.canlii.org/ca/cas/scc/1988/1988scc100.html

SHOULD THE POLICE BE ALLOWED TO COLLECT DNA SAMPLES FROM ARRESTED PERSONS WHO HAVE NOT BEEN CONVICTED?

In 2013, several Canadian police chiefs advocated for the powers of the police to be expanded to collect DNA evidence from arrested persons. At the time, the police were only allowed to gather DNA from certain convicted offenders (i.e., sex offenders). In the words of the chief of the Ottawa Police Services, "I think if we're expected to solve crimes and to do a better job at solving more crimes, this is using science to our advantage to ensure that those individuals who are responsible for committing these types of crimes are brought to justice."[9] The federal government indicated that it was considering expanding the use of DNA, the justice minister stating, "I maintain that, you know, a genetic fingerprint is not different (from traditional fingerprinting) and could be used in my view as an investigative tool."[10]

This news item generated considerable controversy and debate. The online comments to the justice minister's statement trended heavily toward opposing the idea and a reiteration that in the Canadian criminal justice system, a person is innocent until proven guilty.

QUESTIONS

What is your position on whether the police should be allowed to take DNA samples from persons who have been arrested? What is the most persuasive argument in favour of, or opposed, to this proposal?

Source: Bell, D. 2013. "Ottawa Police Chief Supports Taking DNA from Anyone Arrested." *Ottawa Sun*, October 4. Accessed February 25, 2014. http://www.ottawasun.com/2013/10/04/ottawa-police-chief-supports-taking-dna-records-from-anyone-arrested; "Chief Rich Hanson's Call for DNA Sample Collection at Arrests Gains Traction in Ottawa." 2013. *Huffington Post Alberta,* October 4. Accessed February 25, 2014. http://www.huffingtonpost.ca/2013/10/04/dna-sample-police-chief-rick-hanson_n_4045157.html.

103

THE RIGHT OF SUSPECTS TO REMAIN SILENT

Under Canadian law, police officers have no formal powers to compel crime suspects to answer their questions. Suspects have a right to remain silent, and police officers must inform them of that right. They must also inform suspects that any statements they do make may be used against them in a criminal trial.

There are some exceptions to this. The right to remain silent does not extend to situations where it would permit a citizen to obstruct a police officer from carrying out his or her duties. For example, if you ride your bike through a red light and a police officer wants to issue you a traffic citation, you must produce identification. (And, in practice, remaining silent may only make things worse: a person who refuses to answer some general questions asked by the officer may raise suspicions that result in an arrest.) Police officers must also inform suspects that any statements they do make may be used against them in a criminal trial.

Other issues concern the rights of citizens in interrogation situations. In the case of confessions, for example, the rule of law is that statements made by crime suspects to persons in positions of authority outside of the court are not admissible unless it can be proven to the court that the statements were made freely and voluntarily.

The courts have also taken a dim view of the use of trickery by police to obtain confessions. The classic case is when an undercover police officer is placed in a cell with a crime suspect and then attempts to encourage the suspect to make incriminating statements. The Supreme Court of Canada has held that there are strict limits on the extent to which police can use this tactic to obtain a confession from a suspect who has refused to make a formal statement to the police. Voluntary statements made by a suspect to a cellmate (who may be an undercover police officer) may not violate the suspect's right to remain silent and may be admissible at trial, if such admission does not bring the administration of justice into disrepute. Suspects who have low levels of intelligence or other impairment may not understand their right to silence and its implications.

False confessions may also be made by persons who have a mental illness or who are stressed, fatigued, or experiencing withdrawal symptoms from drugs or alcohol.[11] A false confession, in turn, may lead to a person being wrongfully convicted.

THE MR. BIG STRATEGY

A particularly controversial police investigation technique is known as the "Mr. Big" strategy. This involves police undercover officers making contact with crime suspects who are subsequently introduced to Mr. Big, a purported organized crime boss. The targets are then invited to join the crime group, but only if they admit to having committed a major crime. The strategy is prohibited in the United States and Europe, where it is considered to be entrapment, although Canadian courts have ruled that the police may engage in deception to catch criminals. Critics argue that the practice raises legal, moral, and ethical issues. Suspects who are questioned about crimes in a Mr. Big scenario enjoy none of the legal safeguards of those who are interrogated in a "custodial" setting.[12] There are also concerns that the strategy leads to false confessions and the conviction of innocent persons.[13] In some cases, suspects who have confessed to police in a Mr. Big operation were later exonerated by DNA evidence.[14] In early 2014, a case (*R. v. Hart*) before the SCC was an appeal from a lower court ruling upholding the conviction of Nelson Hart, who was found guilty of first-degree murder in the deaths of his twin three-year-old daughters. Mr. Hart was convicted on the basis of a "confession" obtained during a Mr. Big scenario.[15] The outcome of this case may determine the future use of, and limitations on, the Mr. Big investigative strategy.

THE POLICE USE OF FORCE

The legal authority for the police to use force is found in the *Criminal Code*, which sets out the following principles: (1) officers exercising force must be performing a duty they are required or authorized to do; (2) they must act on reasonable grounds; (3) they may use only so much force as is necessary under the circumstances; and (4) they are responsible for any excessive use of force. Provisions governing the use of force are also contained in provincial police statutes.

The use of force is intended to gain control and compliance—for example, during an arrest or while breaking up an altercation. Degrees of force can be placed on a continuum from officer presence and verbal commands through to lethal force. Police are trained to match the degree of force to the immediate requirements of the situation. The generally accepted use-of-force standard is **one plus one**, meaning that police officers have the authority to use one higher level of force than that with which they are confronted. The use of force in excess of what is necessary can leave the officer criminally or civilly liable for assault or, in rare cases, murder.

In 2012, a Toronto police officer was charged with second-degree murder for the death of a suspect during a police drug raid. The officer's weapon discharged during an altercation with the suspect. At the end of a preliminary hearing, the presiding judge determined that there was not sufficient evidence to proceed and ordered a discharge. The Crown appealed and another judge ruled that the shooting was "totally accidental." In October 2013, the Crown filed an appeal. In early 2014, the Ontario Court of Appeal dismissed the Crown appeal and the officer was exonerated.

One plus one (use of force)

The generally accepted use-of-force standard that police officers have the authority to use one higher level of force than that with which they are confronted.

▼ Police officers use force to make an arrest.

Simon Hayter/Getty Images

In 2013, the police officer who shot Sammy Yatim on a Toronto streetcar (see Box 5.9 later in the chapter) was charged with second-degree murder and trial was pending in early 2014. This charge will require the Crown to prove that the officer intended to kill Yatim.

In Ontario, 22 officers were criminally charged in relation to 19 deaths between 1993 and 2013. While there were convictions for impaired driving-related deaths, dangerous driving, and criminal negligence causing death, all the officers charged with manslaughter and murder were acquitted. It appears that juries are very reluctant to convict police officers who are charged with manslaughter or murder.[16]

A CONCEPTUAL FORCE OPTIONS FRAMEWORK

The *force options* approach to the use of force by police is the foundation of most police training in Canada. The approach is positive and professional in explaining how and why police use force in their day-to-day activities. It also provides police administrators and judicial review personnel with an objective framework in which to analyze use-of-force situations. It also allows police officers to explain, within an accepted format, how and why force was applied at the time of the altercation.

The force options framework serves as a guideline and all police personnel are provided with a working model that clearly outlines the course of action to take in use-of-force situations. Although police officers often have no control over the types of encounter situations they become involved in, they can achieve a measure of control by exercising an appropriate level of response. These responses include five distinct force options that are available to police officers:

1. *Officer presence.* The mere presence of a police officer may alter the behaviour of the participants at an altercation, thereby enabling control of the situation.

2. *Dialogue.* Verbal and nonverbal communication skills may resolve the conflict and result in voluntary compliance.

3. *Empty hands.* Physical force is used to gain control.

4. *Compliance tools.* Equipment or weapons are used to gain control.

5. *Lethal force.* The situation requires complete incapacitation of the subject in order to gain control, and lethal force is the only option available to reduce the lethal threat.

LESS-LETHAL FORCE OPTIONS

A less-lethal force option can be described as a force option that is *highly unlikely* to cause death or serious injury to an individual when *properly applied* by a police officer. However, it is possible that death or serious injury may occur, hence the term *less-lethal*. Less-lethal weapons include pepper spray, tear gas, and conducted energy weapons (CEWs; most commonly referred to as Tasers).

The possibility of serious harm is especially great if the force option is improperly applied by the police officer. In these instances, the less-lethal options may contribute to or even cause serious injury or death, which is illustrated by the ongoing controversy surrounding the use of Tasers by police officers.

THE TASER: LESS-LETHAL OR LETHAL WEAPON?

Tasers were adopted by Canadian police services as a force option beginning in the late 1990s. The Taser fires two metal darts that are attached to wires and enter the subject's skin, providing a shock of up to 50,000 volts of electricity.

The expanded use of the Taser by police services is credited with reducing both the number of deaths of persons as a result of the police use of lethal force and the number of officers injured in the course of carrying out their duties.[17]

105

Widespread concern has developed about the use of the Taser on persons who are in a state of *excited delirium*, which may be the result of severe drug use (often cocaine or crystal meth), mental illness, or other causes, and which results in the person being incoherent, violent, and non-compliant. The concern is that the use of electric shocks on these persons can cause a heart attack, although the most recent research has been unable to establish a causal relationship between the use of Tasers and sudden in-custody deaths.[18]

The issues surrounding the use of Tasers and the extent to which their use may cause death are highlighted in the case of Robert Dziekanski, a Polish immigrant who died after being Tasered at Vancouver International Airport. See Box 5.7.

Research on Tasers, including concerns with police over-reliance on them and high-profile incidents in which Taser use was associated with death, has led to the

BOX 5.7   THE DEATH OF ROBERT DZIEKANSKI

The most high-profile incident involving the police use of Tasers to date was the death of Robert Dziekanski at the Vancouver International Airport. At 2:50 p.m. on October 13, 2007, Mr. Dziekanski, an immigrant from Poland, arrived at the airport following a long flight from Poland. He was fatigued from the flight and spoke no English. For reasons that have still not been adequately explained, Mr. Dziekanski spent nearly 12 hours wandering around the international arrivals area without securing the assistance that

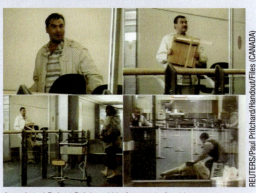

An agitated Robert Dziekanski before and after his encounter with four police officers at Vancouver International Airport.

REUTERS/Paul Pritchard/Handout/Files (CANADA)

would have led him to his waiting mother. At 1:20 a.m., he became agitated and confused, his situation made more difficult by his limited English. The airport operations centre received calls that a man was acting strangely, and security personnel and RCMP officers were called. Four RCMP officers arrived on the scene and, within minutes, had Tasered Mr. Dziekanski five times. He was restrained by the officers and died shortly thereafter of a heart attack. An autopsy revealed that there were no drugs or alcohol in Mr. Dziekanski's system.

The encounter was captured on a cellphone camera by a passenger in the terminal (see the Media Link at the end of the chapter). The RCMP originally stated that Mr. Dziekanski had been Tasered twice, although the video indicated that he had been Tasered five times. The provincial government subsequently launched a public inquiry headed by a retired judge, Thomas Braidwood, which focused on how police use Tasers and, in the second phase of the inquiry, examining all the circumstances surrounding the death of Mr. Dziekanski. On numerous occasions during the hearing, the four RCMP officers involved in the incident, and their superior officers, provided conflicting testimony.

Among the findings of the inquiry were that the responding officers had not made any reasonable attempt to de-escalate the situation, that the use of the Taser against Mr. Dziekanski had been premature and inappropriate, and that the four officers involved in the incident had given conflicting testimony to the inquiry that was not credible. The officers were subsequently charged with perjury for lying to the commission. In 2013, one of the officers was found not guilty of perjury.[19] The other cases remain before the courts. Also in 2013, a report from the B.C. Coroner's office determined that Mr. Dziekanski's death was a homicide but did not make any determination as to who was responsible for the death. The mandate of the coroner's office does not include assigning blame.

development of more stringent policies on Taser use. In British Columbia, the police can deploy a Taser only when a subject is causing bodily harm or about to cause bodily harm. RCMP officers are allowed to use the Taser only in instances where there is a threat to the officer or the general public. Previously, officers could deploy the Taser on *actively resistant* persons, such as persons who did not comply with the direction of a police officer. In the five years following Mr. Dziekanski's death, Taser use by police officers in British Columbia decreased by 87 percent.[20]

DEADLY ENCOUNTERS: THE POLICE USE OF LETHAL FORCE

The decision to use lethal force is the most critical one any police officer can take. The decision is often made in a split second in circumstances involving fear, confusion, and cognitive distortion.[21] Generally, officers are permitted to use guns only to protect themselves or others from serious injury or to stop a fleeing felon whose escape is likely to result in serious injury or death. The police use of lethal force is a rare occurrence in Canada, averaging fewer than 10 cases per year nationwide, as compared with the approximately 300 persons who are shot and killed by U.S. police officers every year.[22]

In the majority of police shootings that result in fatalities, the deceased had just committed a serious criminal offence. In some incidents, the deceased was wanted by the police for a serious criminal offence, such as murder, attempted murder, robbery, aggravated assault, or drug trafficking.

There also shooting incidents that are victim-precipitated homicides, sometimes called **suicide by cop**. Often, these incidents involve despondent individuals who are suffering from suicidal tendencies, mental illness, or extreme substance abuse, and who act in a manner calculated to force police to use lethal force.[23] Victim-precipitated incidents account for roughly 30 to 45 percent of all fatal police shootings that occur in Canada.[24] A case of suicide by cop is presented in Box 5.8.

Police officers involved in a fatal shooting may experience physiological, psychological, physical, and emotional reactions, including depression, guilt, and nightmares.[25]

DECISION MAKING AND FORCE OPTIONS

Standard police procedures require that officers responding to an incident engage in a continual risk assessment of the situation in determining the appropriate level of intervention. In conducting this assessment, the responding officers must gather as much

Suicide by cop

Instances in which despondent individuals act in a manner calculated to force police to use lethal force.

BOX 5.8 SUICIDE BY COP

A male subject, emotionally upset because of marital difficulties, had talked with his family about dying. The subject then went to a convenience store and purchased a quantity of beer and wine, advising the clerk that it would be his last. The subject then became involved in a lengthy police pursuit that ended when his vehicle was stopped by deployment of a spike belt by police. On exiting his vehicle, the subject produced a shotgun and placed it under his chin. He then told police personnel that if they did not kill him he would kill an officer. The subject then turned and pointed his shotgun at two police officers and began to approach them. In response, both officers discharged their weapons killing the subject. It was later learned that the shotgun was unloaded.

Source: Parent, R.B. 2006. "The Police Use of Deadly Force: International Comparisons." *The Police Journal*, 79, 230–37.

information as possible when the call is first received, while en route, during entry into the immediate area where the subject is located, and as the incident unfolds.

From an analysis of all the available information surrounding an incident, the officer will attempt to select the most appropriate use of force response. The goal is to use the least violent option available that will safely gain control of the situation. The generally accepted use-of-force standard, as discussed earlier, is one plus one. The use of force in excess of what is necessary can leave the officer criminally or civilly liable for assault.

Each encounter situation in which a police officer becomes involved has a unique set of circumstances, and each has the potential to escalate rapidly, requiring the officer to make a split-second decision. Incidents involving persons who have mental illness or are drug impaired are often characterized by a high level of unpredictability. This volatility may make it difficult for police officers to develop, and effect, a prescribed plan of action.

The absence of national use-of-force statistics in Canada precludes a determination of the frequency with which the various force options are used. Research and statistical information from the United States indicate that police officers use force infrequently, with less than 1 percent of people who had face-to-face contacts with the police indicating that officers used or threatened force.

Research studies have found that young, inexperienced male officers are more likely to use force improperly and that officers with four-year university degrees and with more years of policing experience are less likely to use physical force.[26,27] This has particular implications in contemporary police services, as an increasing number of officers have fewer years on the job. Research also suggests that male officers are more likely to shoot than female officers, and officers with a college education were less likely to be involved in shootings than officers with lower levels of education. Police officers with a history of involvement in shootings appear to be more likely to be involved in additional shooting incidents.[28]

THE USE OF FORCE AND PERSONS WITH MENTAL ILLNESSES (PWMI)

Chapter 4 looked at a key issue confronting Canadian police services: downloading. Police are being required to deal with persons who are more appropriately helped within the mandate of other agencies. The strategies that police services use in an attempt to respond to the challenges of persons with mental illnesses (PwMI) are discussed in depth in Chapter 6.

The increasing number of encounters between police officers and PwMI have led to several high-profile incidents involving the use of lethal force. These include the shooting of Sammy Yatim on a Toronto streetcar in 2013 (see Box 5.9). In 2013, a coroner's inquest examined the deaths of three PwMI in Toronto: Reyal Jardine-Douglas, Sylvia Klibingaitis, and Michael Eglinton, who were killed by police officers. See the Media Links at the end of the chapter for more information and for accounts of the impact on his relatives of the Mr. Yatim's death. The shooting of Sammy Yatim accelerated the discussion as to whether police officers in Canada should be required to wear body-worn video (BWV). See At Issue 5.2.

Despite tragedies, such as the shooting death of Sammy Yatim, in the overwhelming number of cases, police officers successfully resolve incidents involving PwMI. And it does not appear that PwMI are subject to any higher levels of force than those without mental illnesses.[29]

BOX 5.9   THE TORONTO STREETCAR SHOOTING: THE DEATH OF SAMMY YATIM

On July 27, 2013, Toronto Police responded to a call about a disruptive passenger on a streetcar. The man had wielded a knife and ordered everyone off of the streetcar. Witnesses would later say that he appeared to be unstable. Police officers surrounded the streetcar. Sammy Yatim, an 18-year-old with a history of mental illness, was subsequently shot nine times by Constable James Forcillo, a six-year member of the Toronto Police Service. A total of 22 police officers were present at the scene. Mr. Yatim was then Tasered before being taken to hospital, where he was pronounced dead. The Ontario Special Investigations Unit assumed control of the investigation and subsequently charged Constable Forcillo with murder.[30] The trial was pending as of early 2014.

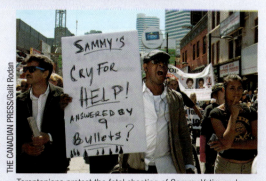

THE CANADIAN PRESS/Galit Rodan

Torontonians protest the fatal shooting of Sammy Yatim and set up a memorial on the spot where he was killed in a streetcar.

The shooting sparked outrage in the community and a review of police use of force practice. This incident prompted an external review of the police use of force in the Toronto Police Service, with a specific focus on police encounters with PwMI.

AT ISSUE 5.2   SHOULD ALL POLICE OFFICERS BE EQUIPPED WITH BODY-WORN VIDEOS?

Body-worn videos (BMVs) can capture what the police officer is seeing, doing, and saying during an encounter. Among the potential benefits of BMVs is increasing the transparency of police operations and the accountability of police officers; providing accurate evidence of police-citizen encounters, which can reduce complaints against the police (and associated civil suits) and reduce false accusations; and providing a more complete recording of police–citizen encounters than those recorded on cellphones cameras by citizens

TOM BRAID/EDMONTON SUN/QMI AGENCY

Edmonton Police Service officer with body-worn video

and the officer's court notebook.[31,32] In this way, BWVs may serve to counter the selective recordings by citizens.

However, a number of issues surround the deployment of BWVs, including privacy issues for the officer and the general public and concerns that an omnipresent camera will discourage officers from engaging in certain encounter situations and affect, in a negative manner, how they exercise discretion. There are also concerns that the presence of BMVs will make victims, witnesses, and suspects reluctant to speak with the police, diminish the value of an officer's word in court, and undermine public confidence in the police. As well, this technology does not record how the officer perceives what he or she is seeing and how this information is being cognitively processed.

Several Canadian police services have begun equipping their officers with BWVs.

QUESTIONS

In your view, should all police officers be equipped with BWVs? What arguments in support of, and what concerns, do you find most persuasive?

POLICE DISCRETION AND DECISION MAKING

Police officers make many decisions in carrying out their tasks in the community, the majority of which are routine. Some decisions, however, are high in risk and in consequences.

THE EXERCISE OF DISCRETION

A patrol officer who is faced with a decision and who chooses an option is exercising **discretion**. Discretion is an essential component of policing because no set of laws or regulations can prescribe what a police officer must do in each and every circumstance. Because it is impossible for officers to enforce all laws all the time, they practise *selective* or *situational enforcement*. As the seriousness of the incident increases, however, the amount of discretion an officer can exercise decreases.

Discretion

The freedom to choose among different options when confronted with the need to make a decision.

For police personnel, the authority to use discretion is set out in statutes, such as the *Criminal Code*. For example, if an individual is found committing an offence, he or she *may be* arrested; arrest, then, is not a strict obligation on the part of the police. The decisions a police officer makes may ultimately be scrutinized by the courts or the public, particularly when it is alleged that the officer abused his or her discretionary powers and in doing so violated a person's legal rights. In the case of *R. v. Beaudry*, [2007] 1 SCR 190, the SCC held that a police officer's discretion is not absolute, and its use must be justified on both subjective and objective grounds. Officer Beaudry was convicted of obstruction of justice for having failed to gather evidence in an incident involving another police officer who was suspected of impaired driving.

In cases of domestic violence, some jurisdictions have *mandatory charge* or *zero tolerance* policies that curtail police discretion. These policies require police officers to arrest the suspect when it appears that an assault has occurred, even if the alleged victim does not want an arrest to be made. Until the early 1980s, a woman who had been assaulted by an intimate partner (usually with no witnesses) had to initiate the prosecution herself by laying an information with a justice of the peace. This requirement made the victim vulnerable to intimidation by the offender, and it was not uncommon for victim-complainants to refuse to cooperate with the police and the Crown attorney (in some cases, women were jailed for refusing to testify at trials).

Even under today's zero tolerance policies, it is difficult for the Crown to proceed without the victim's testimony. Ironically, zero tolerance policies have resulted in cases where the victims of domestic violence have been charged with obstruction of justice for failing to cooperate with prosecutors. And there is concern that, for a variety of reasons, female victims of domestic violence will not call the police if there is a zero tolerance policy in place; this hesitation may place them at a higher risk of revictimization.

Patrol officers bring to their work a set of cognitive lenses through which they make determinations about the people and events they encounter. They use a conceptual shorthand consisting of **typifications** and **recipes for action** to tailor their decision making to the particular area and population being policed.[33] A visual cue, such as a poorly dressed individual in an upscale neighbourhood, would attract the attention of officers on patrol, as would a behaviour or activity considered out of place in a particular area. The risk is that racial or economic profiling may result. Officers who are assigned to one geographical area for an extended time develop an intimate knowledge of its persons and places, and extensive contacts with community groups, agencies, and organizations that facilitate police–community partnerships and the identification of and response to problems. How a situation or a person is typified may play a significant

Typifications

Constructs based on a patrol officer's experience that denote what is typical about people and events routinely encountered.

Recipes for action

The actions typically taken by patrol officers in various kinds of encounter situations.

role in the recipes for action. This determination may involve judgments by police officers as to who they regard as "good" and "bad" people,[34] which may, in turn, affect how the officers exercise their discretion.

FACTORS INFLUENCING PATROL OFFICERS' DECISION MAKING

Field research studies indicate that several factors may influence the decision making of police officers in encounter situations. Some of these are internal to the police service (i.e., departmental policies), while others are in the environment in which the police service carries out its tasks. A number of these are depicted in Figure 5.1.

The policing task environment. Across Canada, a wide variety of policing or task environments exist, ranging from small Inuit villages in the Arctic to large urban centres. All these present different challenges. Particular urban areas may also have different environments. Toronto, for example, has numerous distinct districts, including the old Chinatown, which is centred on the corner of Dundas Street and Spadina Avenue; Rosedale, a wealthy enclave just north of the central business district; and Jane–Finch in the northwest, which is home to mixed ethnic and cultural groups living in high-density public housing, has a young and transient population, and suffers from a high crime rate.

The person of interest. Suspects who are uncooperative or disrespectful are more likely to be charged or arrested than those who behave in a deferential and civil manner. The encounter may be more challenging if the person of interest has recently arrived in Canada and has limited English- or French-language skills. The inability of police officers to speak a second language can hinder the development of police–community partnerships and contribute to misunderstandings that can have serious consequences.

Police officers are now more frequently in contact with PwMIs, as noted earlier. In some Canadian cities, up to 30 percent of the calls to which officers respond involve a PwMI. The concerns surrounding the disproportionate number of police encounters with PwMIs was a primary catalyst for the development of mental health courts in several jurisdictions.

Some research evidence suggests that, in some jurisdictions, persons of interest who are not white and are male and of lower socio-economic status are more likely to be checked by patrol officers through CPIC (Canadian Police Information Centre); they are also more likely to be searched by officers.[35]

FIGURE 5.1 ▶

Major Influences on the Decision Making of Police Officers in Encounter Situations

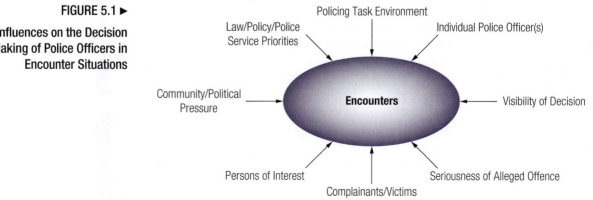

Can you think of other factors that might influence the actions taken by police officers in encounters?

The individual police officer. The policing style of individual patrol officers may influence how they exercise discretion in encounter situations. Research studies have shown that the age, gender, length of service, ethnicity, and level of education of patrol officers can influence the decisions they make. For example, as a group, female patrol officers are less likely than male officers to provoke violence in encounter situations, make fewer arrests than their male counterparts, are less likely to be involved in serious misconduct, and may be more effective in their interactions with the general public than male officers.[36]

Complainant preferences. A consistent finding in the studies of police decision making is that the wishes of the complainant have a significant impact on the decision making of police officers in encounter situations.

Seriousness of the alleged offence. As would be expected, the seriousness of the alleged offence is strongly related to the action taken by police officers in encounter situations. Those suspects alleged to have committed serious crimes are more likely to be arrested than those alleged to have committed minor offences. As the seriousness of the alleged crime increases, the amount of discretion available to officers is diminished, as is the influence of complainant preference and other extralegal factors, such as the suspect's ethnicity and demeanour. This affect may be mitigated if the police service is pursuing a zero tolerance approach wherein even small infractions of the law are responded to aggressively (see Chapter 6).

Law, policy, or police service priorities. Laws, policies, and the priorities of the police service may affect officer decision making. If a police service is engaged in policing designed to clean up crime hot spots or is pursing a policy of zero tolerance (see Chapter 6), it will influence the actions that officers take in encounter situations. In these circumstances, the police make arrest persons for even minor violations.[37]

Visibility of the decision. A key feature of policing is the increasing visibility of police decision making, in large measure because of the proliferation of cellphone cameras. Police officers are aware that their actions in encounters are often recorded and portions may be posted on YouTube before the officer completes the required paperwork, particularly in encounters where some level of force is used. This visibility may result in officers being hesitant to make certain decisions or to use justifiable levels of force. See the Media Links at the end of the chapter for a unique situation in which two Hamilton, Ontario, police officers made an arrest and then one officer turned to bystanders who are recording the incident and explained the reasons for their actions.

DISCRIMINATION AND RACIAL PROFILING

In carrying out their tasks, police officers must be aware of the legislative provisions that require the equal treatment of citizens. As noted in Chapter 4, Section 15(1) of the *Charter of Rights and Freedoms* guarantees equality rights: "Every individual is equal before and under the law and has the right to the equal protection and equal benefit of the law without discrimination and, in particular, without discrimination based on race, national or ethnic origin, colour, religion, sex, age or mental or physical disability." Section 3(e)of the *Canadian Multicultural Act* (RSC, 1985, c. 24 (4th Supp.)) states that it is the policy of the Government of Canada to "ensure that all individuals receive equal treatment and equal protection under the law, while respecting and valuing their diversity."

The *Canadian Human Rights Act* prohibits discrimination on the grounds of "race, national or ethnic origin, colour, religion, age, sex, sexual orientation, marital status, family status, disability and conviction for which a pardon has been granted."[38] Many provinces, including Ontario, B.C., Alberta, and Manitoba, have human rights codes that mirror the federal human rights code and contain sections proclaiming the right of residents to freedom from discrimination and creating human rights tribunals.

Although police officers require the ability to exercise discretion in carrying out their tasks, there are concerns that, in some instances, this results in **discrimination**. Discrimination can be described as "making a distinction in favor of or against, a person or thing based on the group, class, or category to which that person or thing belongs rather than on individual merit."[39]

Bias-free policing requires police officers to make decisions "based on reasonable suspicion or probable grounds rather than stereotypes about race, religion, ethnicity, gender or other prohibited grounds".[40]

Note that bias-free policing applies to a wide range of persons and groups in society. In recent years, a flashpoint between the police and visible minority communities has been **racial profiling**. Police officers discriminate against persons and groups when they engage in racial profiling. The Ontario Court of Appeal, in *R. v. Brown*, [2003] OJ No. 1251, defined racial profiling as involving "the targeting of individual members of a particular racial group, on the basis of the supposed criminal propensity of the entire group."

Concerns have been heightened in the years since the 9/11 terrorist attacks on the United States; Muslims and people who seem to be of Middle Eastern origin have been singled out for discriminatory treatment by security personnel at airports, by customs officers, and by the police.[41] And concerns have been expressed that the use of profiling in enforcement efforts against drug couriers then results in racial profiling.[42]

There are documented cases of individual police officers engaging in behaviour that has been found to be racist and discriminatory. See the Media Links for an on-the-street recording of an encounter between an Black male and two Caucasian police officers in Philadelphia.

In 2011, the Montreal police chief admitted that racial profiling was widespread in the police force and the department implemented a number of training initiatives designed to alter the organizational culture and the attitudes and behaviours of officers. Despite this, the number of racial profiling complaints filed with the Québec Human Rights Commission rose by 52 percent between 2011–2012 and 2012–2013.[43]

RACIAL PROFILING VERSUS CRIMINAL PROFILING

Part of the difficulty in determining whether a police service and its officers engage in racial profiling is distinguishing between racial profiling and criminal profiling. As discussed in Chapter 4, a defining attribute of the police culture is suspiciousness of people and circumstances. While critics of the police argue that racial profiling is endemic to police work, police officers contend that they profile criminals, with particular attention to "signals and 'unusual fits.'" This is the process of *typification* discussed earlier in the chapter.[44]

An officer in the Hamilton Police Service who is a member of a visible minority group offered the following perspectives on racial profiling, criminal profiling, and the importance of the context in which a person is identified for a police stop:

> When we're out on the street, we rely on our instincts. We are trained investigators in the sense that we need to do profiling. And what kind of profiling is that? Criminal profiling. It has nothing to do with racial profiling.... We profile criminals.[45]

Discrimination

"Making a distinction in favour of or against a person or thing based on the group, class or category to which that person or thing belongs rather than on individual merit."

Bias-free policing

The requirement that police officers make decisions "based on reasonable suspicion or probable grounds rather than stereotypes about race, religion, ethnicity, gender or other prohibited grounds."

Racial profiling

"The targeting of individual members of a particular racial group, on the basis of the supposed criminal propensity of the entire group" (*R. v. Brown*, [2003] OJ No. 1251).

113

In November 2005, Mr. Rawle Maynard, who is Black, was driving home from work when he was followed by a police car driven by Toronto Police Service officer Ryan Baker. The trailing police officer had received a report of an incident at the Malvern Town Centre that involved a Black man with a gun. Mr. Maynard's car was stopped by the police officer. There was a verbal confrontation between the officer and Mr. Maynard, centering on Mr. Maynard's refusal to identify himself to the officer. The confrontation escalated and the officer drew his weapon. Following the arrival of back-up patrol units, Mr. Maynard was put into the back of a patrol car. He was subsequently released when additional information on the original incident was provided to the patrol officer.

Mr. Maynard filed a complaint with the Ontario Human Rights Commission (OHRC), alleging that he had been the victim of a racial profiling. In June 2012, Mr. Maynard was awarded $40,000 by the Human Rights Tribunal of Ontario. In issuing her decision, the Vice-Chair of the Human Rights Tribunal of Ontario stated that Mr. Maynard had been "stereotyped as a person with some probability of being involved in a gun-related incident" because he was a young Black man and that "I do not believe that if the suspect had been a Caucasian man in the same circumstance, with no other defining characteristics, particularly age ... [that the officer] ... would have chosen to investigate the first Caucasian man who was driving the same car at the same intersection. It is consistent with a finding of racial profiling that all black men, or all black men of a certain age, driving along in the area in a black car were possible suspects at the moment that Officer Baker decided to commence his investigation of Mr. Maynard" [at 177].

Source: Human Rights Tribunal of Ontario. 2012. *Between Rawle Maynard and Ontario Human Rights Commission and Toronto Police Services Board, Ryan Baker, Brendan Stevenson, Michael Limsiaco, David Russell. Maynard v. Toronto Police Services Board, 2012.* HRTO 1220. Reprinted by permission of the Human Rights Tribunal of Ontario.

How can it be determined whether a police officer is engaged in racial profiling or criminal profiling? A case of racial profiling heard by the Ontario Human Rights Commission is presented in Box 5.10.

Critics of racial profiling argue that there is no evidence that this strategy increases the apprehension rate of offenders or results in reductions in the crime rate. Canadian courts have generally accepted the position of police services that criminal profiling, rather than racial profiling, is used in enforcement efforts and, in cases where racial profiling is alleged to have occurred, seek direct evidence of profiling rather than circumstantial evidence.[46]

Field research experiments have also shown that racial profiling exists in the wider society and is not limited to some police officers. See the Media Link "What Would You Do . . . ." and consider the implications of what transpires.

THE POLICE AND ABORIGINAL PEOPLES

A key feature of Canadian criminal justice is the overrepresentation of Aboriginal people at all stages of the justice system. The high rates of Aboriginal arrests in many regions of the country have raised the question as to whether police officers discriminate against Aboriginal people. Although there is no evidence that Aboriginal people are systemically discriminated against by the police, serious incidents in several jurisdictions have subsequently been found to be the result of discriminatory actions on the part of police officers. On example is the incidents that occurred in Saskatoon, Saskatchewan, where observers eventually coined the term *starlight tour* to describe the police practice of picking up impaired Aboriginal people in the city, transporting them to outlying areas, and dumping them. In at least one case, these actions were directly responsible for the unlawful confinement of an Aboriginal person (see Box 5.11).

BOX 5.11   "STARLIGHT TOURS" IN SASKATCHEWAN

In January 2000, two Saskatoon police officers picked up an Aboriginal man, Darrell Night, drove him to an industrial park on the outskirts of the city, and abandoned him in extreme winter weather. Luckily, Night was assisted by a security guard. He made his way back to the city, where he subsequently filed a complaint with the police. On the basis of his testimony, two city police officers were convicted at trial of unlawful confinement, fired from their positions, and sentenced to eight months in jail. The court rejected a request by the two officers that they be sentenced by an Aboriginal sentencing circle. In 2003, the Saskatchewan Court of Appeal upheld the convictions and the officers began serving their sentences.

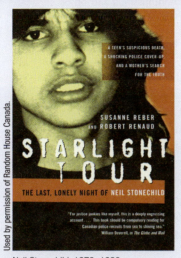

Neil Stonechild, 1973–1990

Used by permission of Random House Canada.

The Night case raised suspicions that the Saskatoon police had transported and dumped other Aboriginal people outside the city, some of whom had frozen to death. Similar incidents included the discovery of the frozen bodies of Rodney Naistus on January 29, 2000 (a day after Night had been dumped), in the same industrial area, and of Lawrence Wegner, found frozen to death on February 3, 2000, in a field outside the city. Naistus was naked from the waist up; Wegner was not wearing shoes and had no jacket, even though it was winter. Subsequent investigations by the RCMP were not able to determine the circumstances surrounding the deaths of the two men.

The cases, however, focused attention on the death of an Aboriginal teenager, Neil Stonechild, whose frozen body had been found in a field on the outskirts of Saskatoon ten years earlier, on November 29, 1990. Stonechild was last seen alive by his friend Jason Roy; at the time, Stonechild was struggling with two Saskatoon police officers, who forced him into the back of a police cruiser. The temperature on the night Stonechild disappeared was −28°C. In February 2003, the province's justice minister announced a commission of inquiry into Stonechild's death. In its final report[47] (available online at www.stonechild-inquiry.ca/finalreport/default.shtml), the commissioner, the Hon. Mr. Justice D.H. Wright, found that Stonechild was in the custody of the police on the night he disappeared and that the injuries that were on his body were caused by handcuffs. However, there was no evidence presented that the two police constables actually dropped Stonechild outside the city, and, therefore, the circumstances surrounding his death remain undetermined. Wright, however, was severely critical of the initial investigation conducted by the Saskatoon police and rejected the version of events offered by the police. Despite this, the absence of evidence precluded criminal charges being laid against the officers who were last seen with Stonechild. For an account of the Stonechild case, see *Starlight Tour: The Last, Lonely Night of Neil Stonechild*.[48] The two officers were subsequently dismissed by the police service, and in 2008, the Supreme Court denied an appeal by the two officers to have the findings of the Wright inquiry quashed.

These cases heightened tensions between Aboriginal people (particularly Aboriginal youths) and the police and seriously undermined earlier efforts by the Saskatoon police to improve relations between the police and Aboriginal peoples.

Sources: CBC News Online. 2003. "Cold Case: The Lawrence Wegner Story"; G. Smith. 2004. "The Death of Neil Stonechild," *The Globe and Mail*, A1, A13; Hon. Mr. Justice D.H. Wright, (Commissioner). 2004. *Commission of Inquiry into Matters Relating to the Death of Neil Stonechild*, Regina: Department of Justice, Province of Saskatchewan, http://www.stonechildinquiry.ca.

POLICE ACCOUNTABILITY

The considerable powers of the police, including the authority to use lethal force and the ability to exercise discretion, requires that there be structures of accountability and oversight. For Canadian criminologists Curtis Clarke and Chris Murphy the **principle of accountability** means that "the actions of policing individuals/agencies are subject to review [and] there are formal channels that individuals can use to lodge complaints against policing bodies."[49]

Canadian police services are held accountable through several means:[50]

Principle of accountability

"The actions of police officers and police services are subject to review [and] there are formal channels that individuals can use to lodge complaints against the police."

- *political accountability* to governing authorities
- *legal accountability* to the law through the courts and judiciary
- *accountability to administrative agencies*, including complaints commissions, human rights commissions, provincial police commissions, auditor generals, and ombudsmen

- *direct public accountability* through such mechanisms as freedom of information legislation
- *special ad hoc accountability* through such processes as royal commissions and other public inquiries

To these one might add *accountability to the public*, given the rise of community surveillance in the age of the cellphone camera.

Historically, the police investigated themselves. However, the increasing visibility of the police and a number of high-profile incidents have increased media and public scrutiny of the police. This watchfulness provided the catalyst for the rise of civilian oversight and the emergence of models of accountability that include civilian involvement in investigations and, in several jurisdictions, independent civilian investigations and oversight.[51]

Police officers can be held accountable for their actions under the *Criminal Code*, as well as under civil law, provincial and territorial statutes, and freedom of information acts. As well, various police boards, complaint commissions, and investigative units both within and outside police services have the authority to oversee and review the actions and decisions of police officers.

Two external boards of review oversee the activities of RCMP officers: the External Review Committee and the Commission for Public Complaints against the RCMP. The former hears appeals from RCMP members who have been disciplined for an infraction of force regulations. The latter is an independent federal agency that receives and reviews complaints made by citizens about the conduct of RCMP officers who are policing under contract (that is, who are serving as provincial, territorial, or municipal police officers; see www.cpc-cpp.gc.ca).

Governments may call commissions of inquiry or appoint task forces to enquire into specific incidents involving the police. In certain cases of a police-involved death, a coroner's inquest will be held. The objective of the inquest is to determine the identify of the deceased, the medical cause of the death, and when, where, and how the death occurred. The inquest will also issue a number of (non-binding) recommendations designed to prevent deaths of a similar nature in the future.[52]

POLICE ETHICS

In carrying out their tasks, Canadian police officers are required to adhere to codes of conduct and ethics. These are contained the various provincial police acts across the country, in provincial policy documents, and in the manuals of individual police services. The British Columbia Police Code of Ethics, for example, contains the statement of fundamental principles of policing, guiding values (i.e., citizenship, fairness, integrity, and respect), a statement of the primary responsibilities of police officers, and questions that should guide the ethical decision making of officers.[53] Among the questions that are designed to assist police officers in avoiding ethical difficulties are the following: "Is the activity or decision consistent with organizational or agency policy and the law?" "Do the outcomes or consequences generate more harm than good?" "What are the outcomes or consequences resulting from the activity or decision and whom do they affect?" "Can the activity or decision be justified legally and ethically?" The Code of Conduct for Ontario police officers is set out in the Ontario *Police Services Act* (2010).

FIGURE 5.2 ▶

Alleged Misconduct among Toronto Police Officers, 2012

A review of the figures indicates that "discreditable conduct" is the most frequent complaint, with the most common behaviour being "acts in a disorderly manner." Complaints are most often made against officers with less than one to five years' experience. Note that only 1.5 percent of the complaints were for "discrimination."

Note: PSA stands for the Ontario *Police Services Act.* TPS stands for Toronto Police Services.

Sources: Adapted from Toronto Police Services. 2012. *Professional Standards Annual Report, 2012,* p. 14. http://www.torontopolice.on.ca/publications/files/reports/prs2012annualreport.pdf.

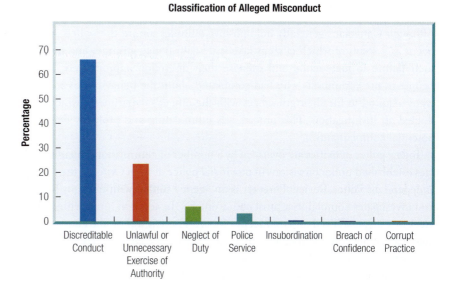

Classification of Alleged Misconduct

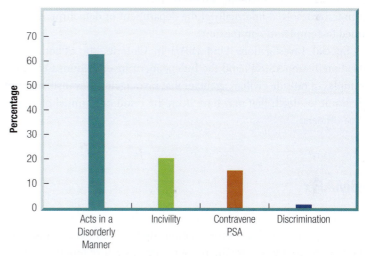

Discreditable Conduct Allegations

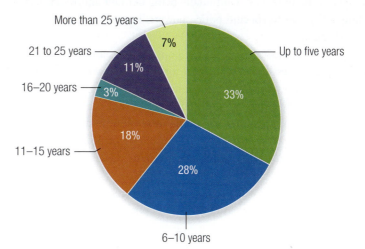

117

COMPLAINTS AGAINST THE POLICE

Although Canadians generally hold positive attitudes toward the police, incidents do occur as a result of which citizens take issue with police attitudes and behaviours or their failure to take action and exercise their discretion appropriately. Historically, people in the community who had complaints about the behaviour of police officers were required to file their grievances with the officer's department, which then conducted an investigation. This process was intimidating and probably deterred many potential complainants.

Today, police activities are overseen by a number of commissions, boards, and agencies established under provisions in provincial police acts. In Ontario, the Office of the Independent Police Review Director is an agency staffed with civilians that receives and investigates complaints against police officers. In addition, units within police services investigate alleged misconduct by officers. There is still public concern about the adequacy of the complaint process. In a 2012 survey of Canadians (N = 1869), only 71 percent of respondents agreed with the statement that "the RCMP investigates public complaints appropriately and with transparency."[54]

The most frequent complaints against police officers involve abuses of authority, the attitudes of officers, and the quality of service provided. Less frequent are complaints for very serious charges, including excessive use of force and death. The vast majority of complaints are resolved informally at the department or detachment level and are not forwarded to complaints commissions.

The Special Investigations Unit (SIU) in Ontario, the Alberta Serious Crime Investigation Team (ASIRT) and the Independent Investigations Office (IIO) in B.C. are examples of outside civilian agencies that investigate cases involving serious injury, sexual assault, or death that may have been the result of criminal offences committed by police officers.

SUMMARY

The discussion in this chapter has focused on police powers and decision making. At the outset of the chapter, the tense relationship between the need to maintain order and the requirement to ensure the rights of citizens was reiterated. The impact of the *Charter of Rights and Freedoms* on police powers was examined, and it was noted that the powers of the police are continually being defined and redefined by the courts. Attention was given to specific police powers, including arrest and detention, and search and seizure.

There was an extensive discussion of police powers and the use of force, and the use and impact of less-lethal and lethal force options were examined. A number of case studies were presented, including incidents involving PwMI. The role of discretion in policing was discussed and many factors that may influence the decisions of police officers in encounter situations were identified. It was noted that while the exercise of discretion can enhance the efforts of police officers, the potential for discrimination and racial profiling also exists. Case studies were presented to illustrate.

The chapter concluded with a discussion of the structures of accountability for police and the role of ethics and codes of conduct in policing.

KEY POINTS REVIEW

1. The police derive their powers from statute law, case law, the common law, and municipal bylaws.

2. The *Charter of Rights and Freedoms* has had a significant impact on police powers.

3. Suspects who are detained or arrested must be informed of their rights under the *Charter*.

4. The power of the police to search people and places and to seize evidence illustrates the fine balance that must be maintained between crime control and due process.

5. Canadian courts have generally not allowed the defence of entrapment, which requires there to have been a clear abuse of process.

6. The legal authority for the police to use force is found in the *Criminal Code*.

7. The force options framework serves as a guideline for police officers in use-of-force situations.

8. Considerable controversy has surrounded the use of Tasers as a less-lethal force option.

9. Standard police procedures require that officers responding to an incident engage in a continual risk assessment of the situations in determining the appropriate level of force to be used.

10. A number of high-profile incidents have heightened awareness of the issues surrounding the use of force and PwMI.

11. The exercise of discretion is a key feature of policing.

12. A variety of factors may influence the exercise of discretion by police officers in encounter situations.

13. There are ongoing concerns as to whether police officers are biased in their treatment of visible and cultural minorities.

14. The "Starlight Tours" in Saskatchewan are an example of police discrimination toward Aboriginal peoples.

15. In carrying out their tasks, Canadian police offices are required to adhere to codes of conduct and to principles of ethics.

16. Police activities are overseen by a variety of commissions, boards, and agencies established under provincial police acts.

KEY TERM QUESTIONS

1. What role do an **arrest warrant** and an **information** play in police response to accused persons?

2. What is **discretion,** and how does it affect the exercise of police powers?

3. What are **search warrants,** and how have the courts viewed the use of search warrants by police?

4. Describe the phenomenon of **suicide by cop.**

5. What is meant by the **one plus one** use-of-force standard?

6. What are **typifications** and **recipes for action**? How do these concepts contribute to our understanding of the decision making of the police?

7. Define **discrimination**, **bias-free policing**, and **racial profiling**, and then discuss why these concepts are important in the study of policing.

8. What is the **principle of accountability**?

MEDIA LINKS

"Robert Dziekanski Taser Death a Homicide: Coroner"
or go to the book's website at
www.nelson.com/
crimjusticeprimer5e.com

"SIU Called in After Man Shot Dead by Police Outside Scarborough Bank"
or go to the book's website at
www.nelson.com/
crimjusticeprimer5e.com

"Enhanced Video of Shooting of Sammy Yatim by Toronto Police"
or go to the book's website at
www.nelson.com/
crimjusticeprimer5e.com

"Honest Cops"
or go to the book's website at
www.nelson.com/
crimjusticeprimer5e.com

"Police Unlawful Harassment and Racial Profiling 9/27/13 Philly, PA"
or go to the book's website at
www.nelson.com/
crimjusticeprimer5e.com

"What Would You Do? Bike Theft (White Guy, Black Guy, Pretty Girl)"
or go to the book's website at
www.nelson.com/
crimjusticeprimer5e.com

CHAPTER 6
POLICE STRATEGIES AND OPERATIONS

LEARNING OBJECTIVES

After reading this chapter, you should be able to
- compare and contrast the professional model of policing, community policing, and community-based strategic policing
- discuss the various techniques that are used in community-based strategic policing
- discuss the challenges of developing and sustaining police–community partnerships
- describe the various approaches to crime prevention and their effectiveness
- discuss crime response strategies and crime attack strategies and their effectiveness
- discuss the issues that surround the increasing use of high technology in responding to and attacking crime
- describe the issues that surround measuring the effectiveness of police strategies and operations
- discuss the police and vulnerable and at-risk groups, including persons with mental illness and marginalized women

Canadian police carry out their tasks in social, cultural, and political environments considerably more complex than those faced by their predecessors. Over the past two decades, police services have developed a wide range of strategies for preventing and responding to crime. There have also been major shifts in police practice, from more traditional approaches to multifaceted strategies that rely on sophisticated analyses. In this chapter, we'll trace this evolution and explore the strategies that police services are using to prevent and respond to crime and social disorder.

THE PROFESSIONAL MODEL OF POLICING

Even after the creation of formal police services in Canada, policing remained closely tied to communities; police officers patrolled communities on foot and were responsible for a variety of tasks. With the introduction of mobile patrol cars in the 1920s and 1930s, a **professional model of policing** emerged that was based on the three Rs: random patrol, rapid response, and reactive investigation.

Professional model of policing
A model of police work that is reactive, incident driven, and centred on random patrol.

The central premise of random patrol, also known as the *watch system*, is that the mere presence and visibility of patrol cars serve as a deterrent to crime and at the same time make citizens feel safer. During a typical shift, patrol officers respond to calls and spend the rest of their time patrolling randomly, waiting for the next call for service. In this model of policing, any information that is gathered by the police is limited to specific situations and does not include an analysis of the problems that precipitate crime and social disorder. Little attention is given to proactive police interventions designed to prevent crime and to address the underlying causes of crime in communities. In this model of policing, there is no, or limited use, of analytics to inform police policy and operations.

Research studies have found, however, that, with the exception of specific targeted strategies, levels of crime are generally unaffected by increases in the number of patrol cars, quicker response times by patrol officers, or the number of arrests made by patrol officers.[1] This lack of impact is due, in part, to the fact that many of the incidents to which the police respond are only symptoms of larger problems in the community. In fact, it is *how* police resources are allocated and deployed that makes a difference. If the police respond only when they are called and deal only with the incident at hand, the reasons *why* the incident occurred in the first place remain unaddressed, and this missed opportunity increases the likelihood that similar incidents will happen again.

The emergence of community policing was precipitated in part by the recognition that the police cannot prevent and respond to crime on their own; they require the assistance of a variety of agencies and organizations, as well as community residents.

COMMUNITY POLICING

The 1980s witnessed the reemergence of an approach to policing that focused on the community. In a back-to-the-future move, the tenets of community reflect Peel's principles, which were set out in the early 1800s (see Box 4.1 in Chapter 4). These beliefs highlighted the importance of the police being connected to, rather than apart from, the community and accountable to the community.

DEFINING COMMUNITY POLICING

Community policing is based on the idea that the police and the community must work together as equal partners to identify, prioritize, and solve problems, such as

Community policing
A philosophy of policing centred on police–community partnerships and problem solving.

crime, drugs, fear of crime, social and physical disorder, and general neighbourhood decay, with the goal of improving the overall quality of life in the area. Community policing is based on the three Ps: prevention, problem solving, and partnership with the community.

The police assume a proactive role in addressing issues in the community. This task requires that patrol officers be given the autonomy and opportunity to identify and address issues in their areas.

The adoption of the community policing model resulted in the expansion of the police mandate and activities. No longer were police officers solely focused on law enforcement but were required to become involved in a variety of activities related to the quality of life in the community and to working proactively with community residents to reduce victimization and the fear of crime, as well as to identify and address community problems. As community policing has evolved, it has also come to include a variety of operational strategies that are focused on crime control and suppression, although the fundamental premise that the police must work closely with the community has not changed.

Community policing is about much more than the introduction of new programs to a community: it involves substantial changes in the organization and delivery of police services, as well as an expansion of the roles and responsibilities of line-level police officers. Organizationally, patrol officers are given the autonomy and resources to identify issues in the areas they police and develop problem-solving strategies, often in partnership with the community or neighbourhood.

Some evidence suggests that community policing approaches have an impact on crime rates, including violent crimes and property crimes, when used with a targeted approach.[2]

COMMUNITY-BASED STRATEGIC POLICING

Beginning in the late 1990s and accelerating with the 9/11 terrorist attacks on the United States on September 11, 2001, police services have been facing increasing pressure to focus on public safety and security and to be more proactive in addressing specific threats. At the same time, they are expected to continue strengthening ties with other agencies and with the communities they serve. It appears that a new model of policing is emerging in the early 21st century—a post-community policing model that incorporates the principles of community policing while at the same time including crime response and crime attack strategies and a continuing emphasis on crime prevention. All of these approaches are discussed in this chapter. This model has been labelled **community-based strategic policing**, the title capturing the importance of community engagement and of police services being strategic in their policies and operations.[3]

A number of techniques are used by police services to drive community-based strategic policing. Many of these are known as best practices, that is, operational strategies that have proven to be successful in preventing and responding to crime in other jurisdictions. These include Compstat, environmental scans, and analytics and intelligence-led policing.

Community-based strategic policing

A model of police work that incorporates the key principles of community policing with crime prevention, crime response, and crime attack approaches.

COMPSTAT

Derived from the words *computer statistics*, **Compstat** is designed to increase the effectiveness and efficiency of police services while also holding supervisors accountable for achieving objectives in crime reduction. Crime data are analyzed to provide

Compstat

A strategy designed to increase the effectiveness and efficiency of police services while holding police personnel accountable for achieving crime reduction objectives.

intelligence to officers on where crimes are being committed and who is committing the crimes. Supervisors are made accountable for addressing the identified crime and disorder issues in their areas, often in a general meeting of senior police leadership and supervisors.[4]

Some version of Compstat is being used in most major police services. As one staff sergeant stated, "Whether it's giving an area special attention, deploying undercover surveillance teams; or having teams develop their own projects, it's almost always driven by Compstat" (personal communication to author, June 2013).

Considerable debate continues as to the effectiveness of Compstat and how it interfaces with the principles of community policing. There is concern that Compstat places too heavy an emphasis on crime fighting and generally does not include measures of other strategies within the community policing model.[5] Compstat is a good example of how community policing has transformed with the increasing use of analytics.

ENVIRONMENTAL SCANS

Environmental scans are studies designed to identify community, legislative, policy, and other forces in the community (here referred to as *the environment*) that will result in demands on the police. A typical environmental scan involves gathering information on a number of factors external to the police service, including demographic, social, and economic trends; crime trends; calls for police service; and the impact of legislative and policy changes. Many police services conduct scans annually to ensure a constant flow of information. On the basis of these data, changes in policies and operational practice can be made.

ANALYTICS AND INTELLIGENCE-LED POLICING

Intelligence-led policing is policing that is guided by the collection and analysis of information that is used to inform police decision making at both the tactical and the strategic level.

Intelligence-led policing is one example of how police services use technology to generate information and to use departmental resources more effectively. Key to intelligence-led policing are *crime maps*—computer-generated maps of specific geographic areas that illustrate the incidence and patterns of specific types of criminal activity. This information can then be used to identify crime hot spots to which patrol and investigative units can then be sent.

Some police observers have cautioned that although intelligence-led policing has potential, translating it from concept into actual practice involves several challenges, including resistance within the police organization itself and the need to develop working relationships between crime analysts and police operations personnel.[6] There is an absence of published research studies on the effectiveness of this strategy, although it has considerable potential to be a component of crime reduction efforts.

Despite the importance of intelligence-led policing, many police service limited analytical capacity and, as a consequence, patrol operations are not led by it. In 2013, for example, the Vancouver Police Department (1700 sworn and civilian members) employed 32 crime analysts, while the Winnipeg Police Service (1811 sworn and civilian members) had 2 crime analysts. Similarly, in many police services, the shifting and deployment of officers is not driven by crime analysis, the identification of hot spots and chronic offenders, or the variations in demands for service.

The next generation of intelligence-led policing will involve predictive policing: using analytics to determine a priori when and

Intelligence-led policing

Policing that is guided by the collection and analysis of information that is used to inform police decision making at both the tactical and the strategic level.

▼ A crime map of Vancouver showing crime hot spots.

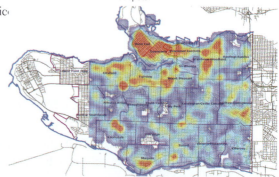

TABLE 6.1 COMPARISON OF THE PROFESSIONAL AND COMMUNITY–BASED STRATEGIC MODELS OF POLICE WORK

	Professional Model	Community-Based Strategic Model
Administrative Approach (Locus of Control)	centralized/hierarchical	decentralized with strong management and organizational support
Authority	statute	community/statute
Community Role	report violations of the law; passive; no involvement in identification and response to crime and disorder	strategic partnerships, formalized by protocols and agreements, which integrate into police operations
Operational Focus	crime and disorder	crime and disorder; national security; quality of life; fear of crime and disorder
Operational Strategies	random patrol; reactive investigations; rapid response	targeted/directed patrol focused on hot spots; strategic partnerships: integrated service delivery; intelligence-led policing; ongoing evaluation; problem-based deployment of personnel

Source: From GRIFFITHS. *Canadian Police Work*, 3E. © 2013 Nelson Education Ltd. Reproduced by permission. www.cengage.com/permissions.

where crimes will be committed and, in some instances, which offenders will be committing them.[7] A police member in the Los Angeles Police Department who is involved in the development of predictive policing stated, "The predictive vision moves law enforcement from focusing on what happened to focusing on what will happen and how to effectively deploy resources in front of crime, thereby changing outcomes."[8]

See Table 6.1 for a comparison of the professional and the community-based strategic models of police work.

THE COMMUNITY AND THE POLICE

A key attribute of policing in the early 21st century is community consultation and collaboration, the notion being that for the police to be effective, residents must be involved in identifying problems of crime and disorder and in generating solutions to those problems. This partnership requires police services to develop strategies for community engagement, including outreach efforts to address the suspicion and distrust that may exist among vulnerable groups, such as Aboriginal peoples, visible or cultural minority groups, and newcomer groups.

The strategies used by police services to achieve these objectives include recruitment and use of volunteers in community police stations and storefronts, foot and bike patrols, community police stations and storefronts, and team policing. Team policing—also referred to as zone or turf policing—involves permanently assigning teams of police to small neighbourhoods in an effort to maximize interaction and communication with the community. Note that the assignment of patrol officers to a fixed geographic area is part of the organizational component of community policing.

The Ottawa Police Service, for example, sponsors a Somali youth basketball league, which is a volunteer, not-for-profit basketball league that provides a safe environment for Somali youth. It develops life and leadership skills among the participants and provides positive role model.

Police services and officers across the country involve themselves in many types of charitable events that not only raise money for important causes but also provide opportunities for officers to contribute to the community and to encounter community residents in a non-law-enforcement capacity. One high-profile initiative is Cops for Cancer, which involves a wide range of fundraising activities—for example, officers shave their heads to raise money; others cycle cross-country, raising awareness and collecting donations.

THE CHALLENGES IN DEVELOPING AND SUSTAINING POLICE-COMMUNITY PARTNERSHIPS

Efforts of the police to develop collaborative partnerships with the community may face challenges. Community surveys have consistently found high (albeit declining) levels of public support for the police (though they remain much higher than for any other component of the criminal justice system) and an expectation that police services will engage in proactive, preventive policing and reactive, enforcement-related activities. Police services often struggle to meet the expectations of the public.

In addition, certain segments of the community may hold less positive views of the police, in part because of unrealistic expectations. Research studies show that citizens and communities that are in disorder tend to express lower levels of confidence in the police, reflecting the perception that the police are at least partially responsible for the disorder and crime.[9] Of all the agencies in the criminal justice system, community residents tend to hold the police most responsible for neighbourhood disorder.[10] Across Canada are certain hot spots of police–community conflict, much of it in Aboriginal and visible or cultural minority communities.

Research studies indicate that police strategies that are most effective in improving public confidence in the police are those that increase community engagement.[11] Canadian police services have applied a number of strategies to connect with community organizations and residents. The Edmonton Police Service, for example, has neighbourhood empowerment teams (NETs) that focus on developing community partnerships and community capacities. The goals are to prevent and respond to crime and social disorder and to improve social development in the community. A key component of the NETs is storefront offices to provide a police presence in the community. An evaluation of the program found strong support among community residents and improved attitudes toward the police, particularly among minority groups.[12] The impact on crime rates has been less clear, although the NETs have achieved significant progress toward the overall objective of improving community wellness.

CRIME PREVENTION

Crime prevention programs are generally aimed at reducing crime, generating community involvement in addressing general and specific crime problems, and heightening citizens' perceptions of safety. The three main approaches to crime prevention are primary, secondary, and tertiary prevention. Police departments are most extensively involved in primary crime prevention programs, although they do participate in secondary and (to a lesser extent) tertiary crime prevention as well.

▼ Edmonton Police Service officers play hockey with neighbourhood kids.

David Bloom/Edmonton Sun/QMI Agency

"We're from the Neighborhood Watch committee. We've heard you're wearing a fake Rolex."

Primary crime prevention programs

Programs that identify opportunities for criminal offences and alter those conditions to reduce the likelihood that a crime will be committed.

Most crime prevention programs operated by Canadian police services have not been evaluated, and, in some cases, programs that have been determined by evaluative studies to be ineffective are still being sponsored by police.

PRIMARY CRIME PREVENTION PROGRAMS

Primary crime prevention programs identify opportunities for criminal offences and alter those conditions to reduce the likelihood that a crime will be committed. They are most often aimed at property offences. The effectiveness of several of the more common primary police crime prevention are set out in Research File 6.1.

Closed circuit televisions (CCTVs) are perhaps the most controversial of the primary crime prevention programs. Although CCTV has been used extensively in Britain and the United States for many years, it is only recently that cameras have been installed in some Canadian municipalities. While concerns over privacy have been expressed, Canadian society is well on the way to becoming a surveillance society. The movements and behaviour of citizens are recorded tens or perhaps hundreds of times per day as they move around the community. There are cameras on buses, in taxis, and in most private businesses, not to mention in every smartphone.

RESEARCH FILE 6.1	THE EFFECTIVENESS OF SELECTED PRIMARY CRIME PREVENTION STRATEGIES

Program	Strategy	Effectiveness
Crime Prevention Through Environmental Design (CPTED)	Altering the physical environment of structures and places to reduce criminal opportunities (e.g., improved lighting)	In some jurisdictions, altering the designs of buildings and pedestrian routes has helped to reduce levels of robberies, assaults, and residential break and enters.
Closed circuit television (CCTV)	Placing cameras in business or residential areas to provide live images 24/7	Pilot projects in Calgary and Toronto and cities in the United States and the United Kingdom found that CCTVs are most effective when targeted at specific locales (e.g., drug-dealing spots, parking garages) and can assist in investigations.[13–15] They may be most effective in reducing levels of disorder and in providing evidence to assist police in apprehending perpetrators after a crime has been committed.[16,17]
Operation Identification/ Operation Provident	Citizens and businesses mark their property with ID numbers to make it difficult to fence stolen goods and to assist in recovery by the police	The impact on property crimes uncertain. ID programs do increase police–public interaction and citizens' awareness of police crime prevention activities. They may displace crime.
Neighbourhood Watch	Organizes residents to make them aware of strangers and criminal activities in their neighbourhood	It is effective in reducing crime in some communities, although little is known about the factors that influence its effectiveness. Implementation is most successful in low crime, middle-class neighbourhoods.[18]
Citizen patrols	Citizen foot and vehicle patrols under supervision of the police	American and European studies have found some reduction in crime levels and in citizen fear of crime. No Canadian evaluations.
Media-based programs	Educate the public about crime and solicit public assistance in locating offenders (e.g. tip lines, Crime Stoppers), often for a monetary reward	These programs can increase arrest rates, although little impact on the overall crime rate. They do stimulate community involvement.[19]

SECONDARY CRIME PREVENTION PROGRAMS

Secondary crime prevention programs focus on areas that produce crime and other types of disorder. Some initiatives focus on identifying high-risk offenders and include analyses that target high-crime areas. Others are designed to help vulnerable groups avoid becoming the victims of crime. See Research File 6.2 for a summary of selected secondary crime prevention programs.

> **Secondary crime prevention programs**
>
> Programs that focus on areas that produce crime and disorder.

CRIME PREVENTION IN ABORIGINAL COMMUNITIES

Developing and implementing effective crime prevention programs in Aboriginal communities has proven to be a challenge both for police services (Aboriginal and non-Aboriginal) and communities themselves. The crime prevention initiatives that have been developed to date fall into one of two categories: (1) programs that are part of an overall crime prevention strategy, developed by senior police administrators and implemented in both Aboriginal and non-Aboriginal communities; and (2) programs that are developed by police officers at the local level in collaboration with chiefs, band councils, and community residents. Needless to say, these latter programs have been the most effective. The effectiveness of programs increases when community residents have a significant role in the design and delivery of the interventions.

The Six Nations Police (Ontario) operate Police Athletic League for Students (PALS). PALS is directed at high-risk youth from ages 6 to 12. Youths from participating schools spend one afternoon per week with police officers in a variety of athletic activities.

POLICE LEGITIMACY AND CRIME PREVENTION

An important issue in any discussion of the effectiveness of crime prevention programs is whether specific initiatives are effective in preventing crime, or whether the specific strategy or program is being used to increase police legitimacy.

Two examples that illustrate this are police gun buyback programs and the DARE (Drug Abuse Resistance Education) program for high school students (mentioned in Research File 6.2). Many urban police services sponsor gun buyback programs, paying cash or giving grocery gift cards or other rewards in exchange for weapons in an attempt to reduce the numbers of firearms and crime in the community.

There is no evidence that these programs reduce the levels of gun-related violence, particularly in the United States, where there are more than 310 million guns, one for every man, woman, and child in the country.[20] Yet the programs provide police services with a high-profile initiative that gives the impression that serious and violent crime is being addressed.

DARE is a drug-prevention program. Originally directed toward substance abuse—alcohol, tobacco, and drugs—the DARE program has been expanded in many jurisdictions to include conflict resolution, gang prevention, parent education, and after-school learning and recreation.

Research studies conducted on DARE programs over a decade ago found that while strong support exists for the program among parents, educators, the police, and youth, the program has very little impact on student attitudes and beliefs about drugs or drug use. The extent to which the program is effective in the other areas has not been examined.

▼ Toronto Police Chief Bill Blair highlights a gun buyback program that awards a free camera for every gun turned in to police.

Jack Boland, Toronto Sun/QMI Agency

RESEARCH FILE 6.2   THE EFFECTIVENESS OF SELECTED SECONDARY CRIME PREVENTION PROGRAMS

Program	Strategy	Effectiveness
Drug Abuse Resistance Education (DARE) for youth	School-based program that provides information to youth about the perils of drug use	While the program generally has high levels of support among educators, parents, and youth, the program has no impact on student attitudes and beliefs about drugs or drug use;[21] some evidence suggests that the program may improve youth attitudes toward the police, particularly among youth from minority groups.[22]
Crime Prevention Through Social Development (CPSD)	Collaborative efforts to reduce the risks faced by individuals, families, and communities (e.g., early intervention programs, programs to strengthen families, and to increase community capacities to prevent crime)	There is some evidence of effectiveness; the Better Beginning, Better Futures program in Ontario reduced youth arrests and decreased grade repetitions, among other positive findings.[23] To be effective, the police, social agencies, and community groups must collaborate.[24]
Programs for at-risk youth (e.g., summer camps, wilderness experience programs)	Developing leadership and life skills in at-risk youth and increasing positive police–youth interactions	Few evaluations have been done. Programs may have a positive impact on youth attitudes and behaviour, but follow-up is required or results fade over time.
Police school liaison officer programs	Police officers are assigned to schools on a residential (full-time, in school) or non-residential (periodic officer visits) basis. Officers make class presentations and participate in school activities. Objectives are primary and secondary crime prevention.	Few evaluations have been done. Programs may increase the legitimacy of the police with students and have indirect benefits (e.g., identifying at risk youth, providing intelligence to patrol and investigative units); no impact on school safety or crime rates.[25] They may result in criminalization of disciplinary situations.
Positive Youth Development program	A holistic strategy based on Crime Prevention Through Social Development designed to build capacity in communities and in youth, to improve the quality of life and decision making among youth, and to facilitate the development of positive attitudes and behaviour; multi-agency (including the police) initiatives may be directed toward individual youth, families, and communities.	They have the potential to significantly impact youth with low levels of competencies and to improve community capacities to assist at-risk youth.[26]
Crime reduction	A holistic, multi-agency approach designed to prevent and deter crime; apprehend and prosecute or treat offenders; and address citizens' fear of crime	It is effective in facilitating the development of police–community–agency partnerships. The absence of evaluations makes it difficult to determine program success and the factors that contribute to positive, and sustainable, outcomes.
Community mobilization	A strategy designed to reduce crime and victimization, strengthen at-risk communities and families, and increase community wellness; involves government agencies (health, education, social services, etc.), community groups, the police, and others working collaboratively to address larger social issues and the needs of at-risk families and individuals.	A program in Prince Albert, SK, the first in Canada, resulted in fewer calls for police service, reduced rates of violent and property crime, and a decline in emergency room visits;[27] it is being implemented in other Canadian cities.

129

The DARE program is a good example of a widely used program whose effectiveness is more often assumed than demonstrated and a program that many police services continue to promote because it increases their legitimacy in the community.[28] This use of an ineffective program has led a number of observers to call for the implementation of evidence-based crime prevention.[29]

CHALLENGES IN CRIME PREVENTION

There are several possible reasons that crime prevention strategies have not been as successful as the police and public had hoped. First, the public often are not aware of police crime prevention initiatives. An environmental scan conducted by the Ottawa Police Service (OPS), for example, found that, with the exception of Neighbourhood Watch and Crime Stoppers (both of which receive considerable media attention), most residents did not know much about the OPS's crime prevention programs.[30]

Second, and closely related to the lack of public knowledge of crime prevention programs, is a low level of community participation. Only about 10 percent of households participate in crime prevention programs. Ironically, citizens who do participate in community crime prevention initiatives tend to live in neighbourhoods with few problems; in other words, they are among those *least* at risk of victimization. For the full potential of crime prevention initiatives to be realized, it is essential that there be participation by residents in those neighbourhoods affected by high rates of crime and trouble.

CRIME RESPONSE STRATEGIES

Police services use a variety of crime response strategies. Among the more common are the following: the broken windows approach, zero tolerance policing and quality-of-life policing, and problem-oriented policing (POP).

CONFRONTING CRIME AND DISORDER IN THE BIG APPLE: THE "BROKEN WINDOWS" APPROACH

In the early 1980s, two U.S. criminologists, James Q. Wilson and George L. Kelling wrote an article entitled "Broken Windows: The Police and Neighborhood Safety."[31] Broken windows was a metaphor for neighbourhood deterioration and was based on the observations of patrol officers that if a window was broken in a building and not replaced, in very short order all of the windows would be broken. According to this approach, a broken window that remains in place is a statement that no one cares enough about the quality of life in the neighbourhood to bother fixing the little things that go wrong. While a broken window is a small thing, it triggers further neglect and results in the progressive deterioration of the entire neighbourhood. Wilson and Kelling argued that police services had neglected little things—the law enforcement equivalent of broken windows—and that a need had arisen to reorient the efforts of police work. The central thesis of the broken windows theory, then, is that "the existence of unchecked and uncontrolled minor incivilities in a neighbourhood—for example, panhandling, public drunkenness, vandalism and graffiti—produces an atmosphere conducive to more serious crime".[32]

To address this, NYPD patrol officers concentrated on quality-of-life crimes and were tasked with ridding the streets of nuisance crime—panhandlers, noise, vandals, and "squeegee merchants," groups of youths who approach drivers to wash their windshields—which made people fearful. The model of policing emphasized rapid deployment of officers and relentless follow-up. Twice-weekly Compstat meetings took place, and a number of organizational changes took place in the NYPD, including a move to informed decision making; a decentralization of resources, including a closer match between problems and resources; greater command accountability; and an emphasis on performance. The implementation of the broken windows approach was associated with a significant reduction in crime levels in New York City.

Considerable controversy has surrounded the broken windows theory, and questions have been raised as to the effectiveness of the various policing strategies that are based on its tenets: Are policing initiatives targeting disorder effective in reducing the levels of crime? If they are, then at what cost? What about the potential for over-policing and increased public concern with safety?[33,34]

Research conducted in a crime-ridden Chicago neighbourhood found that it was criminal opportunity—the presence of potential victims who had cash or contraband—rather than the cues of broken windows—that was most associated with criminal activity in an area. These opportunities were enhanced by the presence of liquor stores, fast food restaurants, and cheque-cashing stores.[35] There is a growing recognition, however, that an order-maintenance approach centred on preventing disorder in the community can result in a reduction in the levels of fear among citizens and a corresponding increase in their quality of life.[36]

ZERO TOLERANCE POLICING AND QUALITY-OF-LIFE POLICING

Zero tolerance policing

A police strategy that focuses on disorder and minor infractions; most often associated with the broken windows approach to policing a community.

A policing strategy that has gained popularity in the past decade or so is **zero tolerance policing**, also referred to as *confident policing*, *proactive policing*, or *community policing with the gloves off*. The key principle here is that a strict order-maintenance approach by the police in a specific area, coupled with high police visibility and presence, with a focus on disorder and minor infractions, will reduce more serious criminal activity. This aggressive policing strategy has often resulted in charges that the police are over-policing in certain communities and neighbourhoods and are conducting racial profiling.

In New York City, the police used "stop and frisk" in an attempt to reduce the levels of violent crime. Persons were stopped and frisked for weapons and other contraband. Police officers were required to have only reasonable suspicion that a crime was about to occur. Critics pointed to data indicating that a disproportionate number of Black and Latino people were targeted, and a report by the state Attorney General found that only 3 percent of 2.4 million stops resulted in a conviction.[37] A federal court ruled in 2013 that the practice violated the constitutional rights of minority groups in the city.[38]

Similar criticism has surrounded the practice of *carding* used by the Toronto Police Service. Patrol officers gather personal data from persons in encounters that are usually non-criminal. This information is then entered into a database to be used by the police in future investigations. Between 2008 and 2012, police officers filled out 1.8 million cards and a disproportionate number were for Black people, in particular young, Black males.[39] This imbalance led to calls for the Toronto Police Service to modify or eliminate its carding program.

Increased police visibility is a core component of **quality-of-life policing**, which involves efforts to improve conditions in an area by targeting disruptive and annoying behaviour, such as panhandling, loitering, and public drug and alcohol use.

A highly visible police presence may deter and alter criminal behaviour, increase residents' sense of security, and increase the legitimacy of the police. These strategies are often applied in conjunction with police crackdowns, which are designed to instill in the criminal population the perception that they are more likely to be apprehended or intervened against.

PROBLEM-ORIENTED POLICING (POP)

Problem-oriented policing (POP) is based on the idea that policing should address the root causes of recurring problems of crime and disorder and then fashion solutions to those problems, often in collaboration with community residents.

A central tenet of POP is the iceberg (or 80/20) rule, the view that crime (20 percent of the iceberg) is only a visible symptom of invisible, much larger problems (the 80 percent of the iceberg that lies below the water's surface).

The SARA (scanning, analysis, response, and assessment) problem-solving model helps officers identify and respond to problems, with the assistance of various agencies, organizations, and community groups. It involves identifying the problem; determining the cause, scope, and effect of the problem; developing a plan to address and solve the problem; and determining whether the intervention was successful.

Problem solving is central to the RCMP's CAPRA model. The letters stand for focusing on *clients*, *acquiring* and *analyzing* information, developing and maintaining *partnerships*, generating an appropriate *response*, and *assessing* the intervention.

The particular problem to be addressed may be community wide and require a long-term plan, or it may involve a single individual and a situation that can be addressed relatively quickly. A good example is what are known as *problem premises*, which consume considerable police resources. In Vancouver, for example, one relatively small rooming house was flagged as a problem premise: police were called to the address 259 times in 18 months. A total of 413 officers were on-scene for more than 320 hours, and the overall cost to the taxpayers was $25,000. The Vancouver Police Department targeted specific individuals living in the rooming house and the number of calls for service was reduced.[40]

Research File 6.3 presents research findings on the effectiveness of selected crime response strategies.

CRIME ATTACK STRATEGIES

Crime attack strategies are proactive operations used by the police to target and apprehend criminal offenders, especially those deemed likely to reoffend, and specific areas or neighbourhoods. These approaches include increased patrol visibility, including foot patrols; proactive policing by patrol officers; and rapid patrol response.

TACTICAL OR DIRECTED PATROL

One widely used strategy is the tactical or directed patrol, which involves saturating high-crime areas (or hot spots) with police officers, or targeting individuals engaged in specific types of criminal activity. This plan may include areas that generate frequent hard crime calls (for holdup alarms, shootings, stabbings, auto thefts, thefts from autos, assaults, sexual assaults) or (for audible break-in alarms, disturbances, drunks, noise,

Quality-of-life policing
Police efforts to improve conditions in an area by targeting disruptive and annoying behaviour.

Problem-oriented policing (POP)
A tactical strategy based on the idea that the police should address the causes of recurrent crime and disorder.

Crime attack strategies
Proactive operations by the police to target and apprehend criminal offenders.

132

RESEARCH FILE 6.3 THE EFFECTIVENESS OF SELECTED CRIME RESPONSE STRATEGIES

Strategy	Technique	Effectiveness
Problem-oriented policing (POP)	Police attempt to address the root causes of crime and disorder, and fashion solutions to those problems in collaboration with community residents. SARA is used.[41]	It has the potential to reduce crime and disorder and to reduce the fear of crime. It can improve police–community relations and develop skills in patrol officers.[43]
Broken windows	The existence of unchecked and uncontrolled minor infractions and incivilities in a neighbourhood produces an environment conducive to serious crime.[42]	Studies on the impact of broken windows have produced mixed results. Some studies have found no impact on crime rates; others have found a reduction in property crime rates.[44,45] It is likely that the broken windows approach may work in some types of neighbourhoods and that its impact may be increased if it is combined with community policing initiatives. There is concern that in adopting the broken windows approach, the increased police activity may result in elevated levels of fear in the community. The legitimacy of the police may be compromised if certain segments of the community perceive they are being targeted.[46]
Zero tolerance and quality-of-life policing	Influenced by broken windows theory. Strict order maintenance approach in a specific area, including high police visibility and a focus on disorder and minor infractions. Often involve police crackdowns on specific criminal activities, such as drug dealing.	Police presence may alter offenders' behaviour. Increased police visibility increases citizens' sense of security, may deter criminal behaviour, and increases police legitimacy.[47]

unwanted individuals, vandalism, prowlers, fights). These hot spots, which are often identified through intelligence-led policing, are plotted on crime maps.

Directed forms of patrol are usually either location- or person-oriented. Tactical patrol strategies give police managers greater control over their most valuable resource—the time and activities of patrol officers. Foot and bicycle patrols may also be used in hot spot areas. The Vancouver Police Department, for example, uses dedicated foot patrol officers in beat enforcement teams in the troubled Downtown Eastside area of the city.

TARGETING HIGH-RISK OFFENDERS

Many police services have developed initiatives designed to target high-risk offenders, including the following examples.

▼ Vancouver Police Department Beat Enforcement Team members in the troubled Downtown Eastside area of the city.

Wikipedia Commons

The Calgary Police Service Serious Habitual Offender Program (SHOP) and Multi-Disciplinary Resource Team (MDRT). SHOP is a multi-agency (police, probation, Crown, social services agencies, and corrections) information and case management program for youths and adults designated as serious habitual offenders. SHOP monitors the activities of offenders both during custody and after release in an attempt to reduce serious crime. The MDRT initiative is designed for early intervention and support for high-risk youths in the city.

Repeat Offender Program Enforcement Squad (ROPE). The ROPE squad, with officers from a number of municipal, provincial, regional, and federal police services, locates and apprehends criminal offenders who are unlawfully at large because they have violated the conditions of their release from custody, have failed to return to custody, or have escaped from correctional authorities.

The Integrated Police-Parole Initiative (IPPI). This program places police officers in the parole offices of the Correctional Service of Canada (CSC). These officers work alongside patrol officers to monitor the activities of high-risk offenders released into the community. A preliminary evaluation of the program found a reduction in technical violations of condition release by offenders in those CSC offices participating in the IPPI program, suggesting that this approach may assist with reintegration of offenders.[48] IPPI is a good example of a **tertiary crime prevention** program, as the efforts of the police and their partners are directed toward preventing reoffending. But these types of police strategies have not been without controversy.

Tertiary crime prevention
Programs that focus on intervening in the lives of known offenders to reduce the likelihood of reoffending.

The Toronto Police Service Anti-Violence Intervention Strategy (TAVIS). TAVIS was created by the Toronto Police Service to reduce the high levels of gun violence and to enhance public safety in high-crime neighbourhoods in Toronto. Its strategies include intervention, prevention, and community support and mobilization. A key strategy is building relationships with the residents in at-risk neighbourhoods. Community meetings, high-profile police patrols, and the identification of crime hot spots and individuals involved in gun violence are all components of TAVIS (www.torontopolice.on.ca/tavis/).

In recent years, criticism has been directed toward TAVIS for allegedly engaging in over-policing of Black neighbourhoods. This censure includes concerns that officers arbitrarily stop and search Black people and the perception that Black youth are harassed and criminalized. Support for this view is provided by an analysis of police records indicating that Black males are stopped disproportionately in comparison to white males.[49]

TAVIS provides a good example of how police initiatives may not only reduce levels of crime and violence but also undermine the legitimacy of the police among community residents.

TARGETING SPECIFIC TYPES OF CRIME

Police services may also develop strategies to address specific types of crime. The *bait car* program is designed to reduce auto thefts and to apprehend offenders involved in committing this crime.

The program involves rigging police-owned vehicles with audio and visual equipment and GPS, as well as with technology that allows the vehicle to be stopped remotely. The bait car program has resulted in significant decreases in the rates of auto theft in the jurisdictions where it is used.

Police services have also been very proactive in attempts to suppress gang activity and its associated violence. This work has included targeted investigations, the development of integrated gang task forces, and other initiatives.

Many police services participate in Bar Watch and Restaurant Watch in an attempt to reduce gang violence. Bars that are approved by the police install metal detectors and identification scanners and agree to allow the police to enter the bar and remove patrons without permission. The program, however, has not been without controversy, centring on issues related to civil liberties and personal privacy. This problem raises, again, the tensions that exist in a democratic society between safety and security and individual rights.

COMMUNITY NOTIFICATION

Another proactive strategy that many Canadian police services use to manage high-risk offenders is community notification. This practice involves advising the media, crime victims, and the public when certain offenders are released (generally from federal

RESEARCH FILE 6.4   THE EFFECTIVENESS OF SELECTED CRIME ATTACK STRATEGIES

Strategy	Technique	Effectiveness
Tactical or directed patrol	Proactive, aggressive patrol in high-crime areas. Patrol officers use unallocated time to engage in purposeful activities directed by analysis of crime data. May be location-focused or person (offender)-oriented. Often applied in conjunction with crackdowns, focusing on specific types of criminal activities (e.g., drug dealing).	Increasing the number of uniformed police officers in patrol cars in hot spots and during hot times (crime peaks) may significantly reduce levels of criminal activity. Proactive police arrests, including zero tolerance arrest policies that focus on high-risk people and offences, can reduce the levels of serious violent crime. The impact of crackdowns may depend on the community. They are resource intensive, and it is difficult to sustain positive results over the long term. May undermine the legitimacy of the police, particularly among young men and other groups who are more likely to be the targets of police attention.[51]
Hot spots policing	Police focus on areas that have a high concentration of crime or disorder and a high risk of criminal victimization.[50]	It can reduce crime and disorder without displacing crime to surrounding areas; long-term effectiveness is enhanced by the use of POP.[52]
Focusing on high-risk offenders	Special police units to monitor chronic and violent offenders. Often involves collaboration of multiple police services and other agencies.	It can result in high levels of arrest and incarceration, and reduction in violent crime incidents.
Bike patrols	Officers on bikes are often deployed to areas of high crime and disorder. Provide excellent mobility in the urban environment.	They can be an effective component of community policing. Bike patrol officers can have much more personal contact with citizens than patrol car officers.[53]
Foot patrols	Officers walk a beat in a neighbourhood or district. Some police services have dedicated foot patrols, while others encourage officers to park their patrol cars and walk when they have the opportunity.	Evidence is emerging that strategically directed foot patrols can reduce the levels of crime and disorder in neighbourhoods;[54] they reduce citizens' fear of crime and calls for service. They improve officer's familiarity with neighbourhoods. To be effective, they must be deployed as part of a comprehensive community policing strategy rather than as an add-on.
Community notification	Advising the media, crime victims, and the general public when certain offenders are released from confinement. Used most frequently with sex offenders.	There is no evidence that it reduces reoffending. It may increase citizens' fear of crime and further marginalize offenders released from confinement. Raises issues of public security versus individual privacy.

correctional facilities). It does not appear that this strategy increases public safety (see Chapter 12).

The strategy, technique, and effectiveness of selected crime response and crime attack strategies are set out in Research File 6.4.

THE INCREASING USE OF HIGH TECHNOLOGY IN CRIME RESPONSE AND CRIME ATTACK

Police services are increasingly adopting new technologies to improve their effectiveness and efficiency. Crime analysts use sophisticated statistical programs to create crime maps and to provide intelligence to police officers in patrol and investigative units. A key issue is how this technology will be managed to ensure that the rights of citizens are protected, another balancing of the efforts to ensure public safety and security while protecting citizens' rights. This tension was illustrated in the issues surrounding police body-worn videos discussed in Chapter 5. A new challenge is being posed by the availability of unmanned aerial vehicles (more commonly referred to as *drones*). See At Issue 6.1.

MEASURING THE EFFECTIVENESS OF POLICE STRATEGIES AND OPERATIONS

Most police services in Canada remain wedded to two traditional measures of police performance that are holdovers from the professional model of policing: crime rates and clearance rates. Even in those police services that have adopted a community policing approach, the performance assessments of individual police officers are still heavily oriented toward enforcement activities.[55]

AT ISSUE 6.1 "LOOK, UP IN THE SKY! IT'S A BIRD! IT'S A PLANE! IT'S A DRONE!"

Since the terrorist attacks of 9/11, unmanned aerial vehicles (UVAs) or drones have been used by the U.S. military to track and attack persons identified as terrorists. This technology has been adapted to develop small drones that can be used by police services. These drones can be fitted with cameras, licence-plate readers, radar, and thermal-imaging devices.[56] Some models in the U.S. are equipped with Tasers, automatic shotguns, and grenade launchers (see the Media Links at the end of the chapter).

A police officer operates a drone.

Among the potential uses of drones in policing are surveying accident scenes, photographing crime scenes, monitoring crowds, searching for lost persons and, of course, surveilling people and suspected criminals. Many of the drones are small enough to fit in a backpack and can be deployed by patrol officers. For cash-strapped police services, drones are viewed as a cost-effective alternative to helicopters and even police personnel.[57]

Drones are now being used by Canadian and U.S. police services. The Halton Regional Police are using drones to locate marijuana grow-ops. That model of drone fits into a backpack, although officials have been quick to state that the drones will not be used for surveillance. Transport Canada has issued flight certificates for drones used by police, which require them to be flown within eyesight of the operator and only during daylight hours. However, there are no regulations or legislation in Canada limiting how drones can be used by police services. There have been calls for policies for drone use that would address privacy concerns.[58–60] In 2013, the Seattle Police Department was forced to return two drones to the manufacturer following a public outcry.[61]

QUESTIONS

Assume that your municipality is holding a referendum on whether or not the local police service should be allowed to use drones in police operations. Would you vote in favour of or against allowing the police to use drones? If you would vote in favour, what restrictions, if any, would you place on how drones were used? What oversight structures would you put in place? If you voted against the police being able to use drones, what are the primary reasons for your position?

136

John Giles/PA Wire via AP Images

CRIME RATES AND CLEARANCE RATES

Strategic plans of police services generally contain percentage targets for crime reduction, and annual reports highlight achievements in reducing specific types of criminal activity in the community. **Clearance rates** are the proportion of the actual incidents known to the police that result in the identification of a suspect, whether or not that suspect is ultimately charged and convicted. Using these measures is problematic on a number of counts.

Crime rates suffer from problems of interpretation. For example, does an increase in official crime rates mean the police are ineffective? Or does it mean they are catching more criminals? Another problem with using official crime rates to assess police effectiveness is that the focus is on crime fighting to the exclusion of other measures of police performance. In addition, much of what the police are asked to do by governments and communities and, in some instances, are required by legislation and policy to do has little to do with crime rates. In most jurisdictions, police officers do not spend most of their time pursuing criminals (although as noted in Chapter 4, they may be responding to incidents that have the *potential* to include a violation of the law). It is also important to note that the police may have little impact on the reasons crime occurs; those factors include poverty, social issues, addiction, and family dysfunction.[62]

Further, not all police officers work in the same types of communities: some communities are more crime ridden than others. Research in Québec has found, for example, that police services in small communities are more likely to clear crimes than in large urban areas and in areas with high poverty levels;[63] and police officers do not all engage in the same type of police work: some are involved in patrol, others in investigative units, and so on.

With respect to the effectiveness of specialized law enforcement initiatives, Canadian criminologist Thomas Gabor has noted that there have been few Canadian evaluations of law enforcement efforts to target organized crime and white-collar criminals.[64] Gabor argues that it is important to gather information on other factors, including enforcement costs, the number of investigations that lead to convictions, and the degree to which specific policing initiatives are effective in disrupting organized crime.

CRIME DISPLACEMENT

In attempting to determine the effectiveness of police strategies, there is the slippery issue of **crime displacement**—"the relocation of crime from one place, time, target, offense, or tactic to another as a result of some form of crime initiative."[65] The implementation of a crime prevention program in one neighbourhood, for example, may cause criminals to move to an area that does not have the program. Instead of reducing crime, the program has just moved it. One way to reduce crime displacement is to implement crime prevention programs on a community-wide basis rather than only in specific areas. Also, it may be necessary to target a wide range of criminal activity instead of focusing only on specific types of crime.

ADDITIONAL MEASURES OF POLICE EFFECTIVENESS

Reducing social disorder and providing reassurance to the community are equally important roles of the police, yet these activities are generally not measured. A number of additional measures of performance capture the multifaceted role of the police, including levels of community and victim satisfaction with the police and feelings of safety, as measured by surveys; the success of the police in achieving effective target hardening and problem solving with respect to specific types of crime in identified problem areas in the community; and the extent to which the police are involved in

Clearance rates

The proportion of the actual incidents known to the police that result in the identification of a suspect, whether or not that suspect is ultimately charged and convicted.

Crime displacement

The relocation—because of effective crime prevention and crime response initiatives—of criminal activity from one locale to another.

137

developing innovative programs to address issues related to community diversity (for example, issues relating to the lesbian, bisexual, gay, and transgender communities; to visible minority groups; and to Aboriginal peoples).

THE ECONOMICS OF POLICE STRATEGIES AND OPERATIONS: ARE THE POLICE WORTH THE MONEY?

A critical issue in Canadian policing is the debate over the economics of policing, that is, whether governments can afford the increasing costs of police services. This discussion is occurring against the backdrop of declining crime rates (see Chapter 3). The argument is made that policing as it is currently constituted is not sustainable.

The cost–benefits of policing are only now beginning to be documented by empirical research studies. Research studies in the United States (there are no Canadian studies) have found that investing in street-level policing and strategies, such as hot spots policing, can reduce prison populations and curb the increasing costs of corrections.[66,67] U.S. researchers have calculated that, in the United States, money diverted from correctional institutions to policing would buy at least four times as much reduction in crime. Shrinking the prison population by one-quarter would result in sufficient savings to hire an additional 100,000 police officers.

The former commissioner of corrections for the state of New York has stated, "If you had a dollar to spend on reducing crime, and you looked at the science instead of the politics, you would never spend it on the prison system."[68] Conversely, all else being equal, a 10 percent reduction in the size of a typical police service has been found to lead to a 6 percent increase in robberies, a 3 percent increase in serious assaults, and a 4 percent increase in vehicle theft.[69]

The implications of this finding are potentially significant in Canada, where as discussed in Chapter 2, the federal government has embarked on an ambitious legislative agenda that will most likely result in additional persons being processed through the criminal justice system and more persons incarcerated in correctional institutions.[70]

THE POLICE AND VULNERABLE OR AT-RISK GROUPS

It is police officers who have the most contact with persons who are vulnerable or members of at-risk groups, and many of the controversies that surround policing in the early 21st century revolve around this issue: "To what extent do police services respond appropriately to the needs of these groups, which may include persons with mental illnesses, sex trade workers, Aboriginal peoples, especially Aboriginal women, and others?"

THE POLICE AND PWMI

It was noted in Chapter 5 that patrol officers are encountering more and more persons with mental illnesses (PwMI). A number of these encounters have ended tragically. In contrast to the portrayal of the police in the popular media, officers are as likely to be called to a mental illness crisis as to a robbery. In Vancouver, a study found that 31 percent of the calls for service received by the department had some mental health component, and there were individuals who had near daily contact with the police.[71] Police officers may spend significant amounts of time waiting with PwMI to be admitted to hospitals. A study in Edmonton found that during a three-month period in 2013, officers spent 1500 hours in hospitals, costing the police service approximately $100,000 and taking them away from patrol duties. Fifty-four percent of the hours were related to PwMI.[72]

The number of incidents involving PwMI increased significantly when provincial governments failed to provide enough community-based treatment programs and facilities following the massive deinstitutionalization of PwMI during the 1960s and 1970s. This lack has resulted in massive downloading onto the police, who have become de facto community mental health workers and are the first responders to PwMI on the streets and in neighbourhoods. Police services have been strong advocates for adequate funding for community mental health programs and services that will address the needs of this vulnerable population.[73]

Patrol officers often determine whether PwMI will be put into the criminal justice system or diverted to the mental health system. However, officers face numerous difficulties in dealing with PwMI on the street, including a lack of referral resources and the fact that many of the PwMI cannot be apprehended under mental health acts, as they do not meet the criteria of being a danger to themselves or others.

Concerns have been raised that the police inappropriately use arrest to resolve encounters with PwMI; this is most commonly referred to as the criminalization of PwMI. Research studies, however, have not supported this assertion.[74] Rather, Canadian police officers generally demonstrate high levels of benevolence and empathy toward PwMI, as well as a strong interest in linking them with appropriate services.[75]

Over the past decade, police agencies have been developing specialized approaches for managing encounters with PwMI.[76,77] Most major police services ensure that officers receive crisis intervention training (CIT) where they learn about mental illness and various strategies for managing encounters with PwMI. Positive outcomes have been reported by police services that have adopted the CIT model, including lower rates of arrest of PwMI.[78] The Edmonton Police Service has developed a training program to improve interaction and communication between PwMI and the police. (See the Media Links at the end of the chapter.) The training has resulted in less use of force with PwMI.[79]

Police services have also developed innovative initiatives with mental health agencies. The Durham Regional Police Service, Toronto Police Service, and Vancouver Police Department, among others, operate patrol units staffed by a police officer and a mental health worker. A study of an integrated mobile crisis service in Halifax, involving clinicians and police officers, found that there were improved response times despite an increase in the use of this service by patients, families, and service partners and an increase in the use of follow-up services by patients, as compared with a control group.[80]

There are, however, limits on what the police can accomplish without effective partnerships with other agencies and organizations. A key challenge is the lack of operability between the police and other agencies and non-governmental organizations. This deficiency has hindered the development of multifaceted interventions that may be effective in addressing the needs of this population. As one officer who has policed the troubled Downtown Eastside in Vancouver stated, "The police are not the appropriate resource for dealing with the mentally ill" (personal communication to author, November 2013).

THE POLICE AND MARGINALIZED WOMEN

A number of high-profile events in recent years have focused attention on the issues surrounding the police and marginalized women. More specifically, there are concerns and accusations that police services have not acted to protect these women or taken proactive measures to investigate the cases of missing and murdered women. The particular vulnerabilities of Aboriginal women have been highlighted.

While the number of missing and murdered women has not been established, it may be in the hundreds. Among the challenges of investigating these cases are a lack of investigative capacities in police service, a lack of coordination among police services, the mobility of the victims, and delays in reporting.[81]

THE TRAGEDY OF MISSING AND MURDERED WOMEN

The Native Women's Association of Canada estimates that, as of 2010, there were 582 cases of missing and murdered Aboriginal women and girls.[82] This figure is disputed by the RCMP, which places the number at less than 100. From its investigation, Human Rights Watch concluded that "The failure of law enforcement authorities to deal effectively with the problem of missing and murdered indigenous women and girls in Canada is just one element of the dysfunctional relationship between the Canadian police and indigenous people."[83] The report, based on 87 interviews that included 42 Indigenous women and 8 Indigenous girls, documented their experiences of abuse at the hands of the police and the absence of police action to investigate cases of domestic abuse and of missing and murdered women.

A focus of concern is Highway 16, which runs across the northern part of B.C., christened the Highway of Tears. Since 1969, 32 women have been murdered or gone missing on this stretch of highway, most while hitchhiking. An RCMP special unit is conducting an ongoing review of the cases, although the majority remain unsolved. In Manitoba, a joint RCMP–Winnipeg Police Service task force was, in late 2013, examining a number of missing persons and homicide cases dating back to 1961.

Missing and murdered women are viewed by many as one of Canada's top human rights issues. Although a United Nations Human Rights investigator and Aboriginal leaders and organizations have called for a national inquiry into missing and murdered women, as of early 2014, the federal government had not acted on this.

▼ A billboard on the Highway of Tears in northern British Columbia.

Steve Bosch/Vancouver Sun

THE MISSING WOMEN IN BRITISH COLUMBIA: MASS MURDER AND A FAILURE OF POLICE INVESTIGATION?

During the mid to late 1990s, several sex trade workers from Vancouver's Downtown Eastside began to go missing. These women, many of who had addiction problems, disappeared and did not make contact with family or friends. One suspect who emerged was a pig farmer, Robert "Willie" Pickton, whose property was in the rapidly developing suburban municipality of Coquitlam, a few kilometres from Vancouver. Coquitlam is policed under contract by the RCMP. Both the Vancouver Police Department and the Coquitlam RCMP were slow to initiate investigations, and there were ongoing issues between the two police services, including a lack of communication and information sharing. Pickton was finally arrested in 2002, and the search for evidence on his property over the next several years became the largest and most expensive police investigation in Canadian history. Over two years, 235,000 pieces of DNA evidence were gathered and the remains of 30 women were identified. It is estimated that Pickton killed 65 women over 15 years on his farm. In 2007, Pickton was convicted of second-degree murder of six women and given a life sentence with no possibility of parole for 25 years.

▼ The pig farm of Robert "Willie" Pickton in the Vancouver-area suburb of Coquitlam (note the adjacent subdivision of new houses).

Copy photo by John Lehmann/Globe and Mail

The Vancouver Police Department conducted an extensive internal review of its handling of the Pickton investigation and identified a number of organizational factors that hindered the investigation.[84] The provincial government subsequently appointed a retired judge to conduct an examination of the missing women's investigation. Among the findings of the final report were that the police had failed to act to protect marginalized women and that there were systematic failures in the investigative process that delayed the apprehension of Pickton.[85] More specifically, the police were criticized for a failure of leadership, a failure to consider and pursue all investigative strategies, and inadequate staffing and resources. Compounding these were the lack of a regional police service that would have facilitated communication and the sharing of information among police investigators.

SUMMARY

This chapter has examined the various strategies that the police use to prevent and respond to crime, with particular emphasis on the efforts of police services to build sustainable partnerships with communities and to use the latest technologies for detecting crimes and investigating cases. The traditional professional model of policing has evolved into community-focused strategic policing, which incorporates elements of community policing with crime prevention, crime response, and crime attack strategies. This model of police work makes extensive use of data analysis, which allows police policies and operations to be intelligence led. A number of policies and operations have been found to be effective in preventing and reducing levels of crime and social disorder, although some of the more aggressive police tactics have been criticized for being disproportionately focused on minorities, in particular, Black people. The increasing use of high technology in policing, including the use of unmanned drones, has raised privacy issues and is another example of the tensions that exist between the need to maintain order while ensuring the rights of citizens.

Canadian police services have encountered challenges in policing vulnerable and at-risk groups, including PwMI and marginalized women. Some of these are a consequence of downloading (see Chapter 5), while others are a result of poor leadership and a failure of police investigations. These issues are highlighted by the numbers of missing and murdered women in Canada.

KEY POINTS REVIEW

1. The traditional (or professional) model of police work is based on random patrol, rapid response, and reactive investigation.

2. The community policing model is premised on the three Ps: prevention, problem solving, and partnership.

3. Community-focused strategic policing is the predominant model in Canadian policing in the early 21st century.

4. Compstat, environmental scans, and analytics and intelligence-led policing are several techniques that are used in community-focused strategic policing.

5. Police services are involved in a wide range of programs and partnerships with the community, although there are often challenges in developing and sustaining partnerships.

6. There are a variety of primary and secondary crime prevention programs, some of which have proven successful.

141

7. Many of the crime response and crime attack strategies used by the police have been shown to reduce crime and social disorder.

8. Police services are increasingly adopting new technologies to improve their effectiveness and efficiency, although some innovations, including drones, have stirred controversy.

9. Developing measures of police performance that capture the variety of activities of the police have proven to be a challenge.

10. Police services have encountered challenges in addressing the needs of vulnerable and at-risk groups, including persons with mental illnesses and marginalized women.

KEY TERM QUESTIONS

1. Compare and contrast the **professional model of policing**, **community policing**, and **community-based strategic policing**.

2. What role do **Compstat**, and **intelligence-led policing** play in community-focused strategic policing?

3. Define and discuss **primary** and **secondary crime prevention programs** and note the effectiveness of these initiatives.

4. Describe **problem-oriented policing (POP)**, **zero tolerance policing**, and **quality-of-life policing**, and discuss their effectiveness in reducing crime and disorder.

5. Describe the **crime attack strategies** used by police and the effectiveness of these approaches.

6. What role do **clearance rates** and **crime displacement** play in discussions of measuring police performance?

MEDIA LINKS

"TAVIS: Police Unit Faces Criticism as It Tries to Bridge Gaps in Toronto Neighbourhoods" or go to the book's website at www.nelson.com/crimjusticeprimer5e.com

"Toronto Police TAVIS Stop of Four Teens Ends in Arrests, Captured on Video" or go to the book's website at www.nelson.com/crimjusticeprimer5e.com

"Bait Car—Censored Montage" or go to the book's website at www.nelson.com/crimjusticeprimer5e.com

"'ShawdowHawk' Police Drone Armed with Tasers, Automatic Shotguns, Grenade Launchers" or go to the book's website at www.nelson.com/crimjusticeprimer5e.com

"Edmonton Police Using Less Force with Mentally Ill after University of Alberta Course" or go to the book's website at www.nelson.com/crimjusticeprimer5e.com

"Highway of Tears," *CBS 48 Hours* or go to the book's website at www.nelson.com/crimjusticeprimer5e.com

PART III
THE CRIMINAL COURTS

Chapter 7:   The Structure and Operation of the Criminal Courts
Chapter 8:   The Prosecution of Criminal Cases
Chapter 9:   Sentencing

• •

The criminal courts occupy a strategic position in the Canadian criminal justice system. Important decisions are made at all stages of the court process: the decision of Crown counsel to take a case forward; plea negotiations between the Crown and defence lawyers that may result in a guilty plea in exchange for certain considerations, including dropping some charges; the decisions of judges and juries; and perhaps the most important decision in the entire justice system: whether the charged person is guilty.

In this section, we'll consider the structure and operation of the criminal courts, as well as how cases are processed through the criminal courts. Chapter 7 sets out the structure of the criminal courts in Canada, including the specialized problem-solving courts that have been created in recent years. The flow of cases through the criminal courts is examined, and the issues surrounding the oversight and accountability of the judiciary are considered.

Chapter 8 examines the prosecution of criminal cases, beginning with the pre-trial process. Among the topics discussed are the role of Crown counsel, the laying of an information and laying of a charge, the ways in which an accused can be compelled to appear in court, plea negotiations, the trial, and others.

Chapter 9 considers sentencing in the criminal courts, including the purpose and principles of sentencing, the discretion exercised by judges, and Aboriginal peoples and sentencing.

CHAPTER 7

THE STRUCTURE AND OPERATION OF THE CRIMINAL COURTS

After reading this chapter, you should be able to

- discuss the structure and operation of the criminal courts
- describe the process by which judges are appointed in Canada and discuss the issues surrounding this process
- describe specialized courts and their effectiveness in addressing the needs of vulnerable accused persons
- describe the challenges that surround providing judicial services in remote areas of the country by the circuit courts
- describe the flow of cases through the court system
- identify and discuss the issues surrounding judicial ethics and accountability
- describe the work of the Supreme Court of Canada and the issue of balancing security and the rights of the accused
- discuss the provisions for accountability and review of judicial conduct

▲ A provincial courtroom.

The criminal courts play an important, multifaceted role in Canada's criminal justice system, yet for many Canadians, the courts remain something of a mystery. This vagueness is due, in some measure, to the fact that the deliberations of judges and the activities of Crown counsel and defence lawyers are much less visible than the activities of the police.

Although the process for disposing of cases has changed little over the past two centuries, the cases coming into the courts are more complex than they once were, the legal issues are more challenging, and workloads are heavier. Many observers attribute these increased workloads and the resulting strains to the impact of the *Charter of Rights and Freedoms.*

The courts are responsible for determining the guilt or innocence of accused persons and for imposing an appropriate sentence on those who are convicted. They are also responsible for ensuring that the rights of accused persons are protected; this often involves monitoring the activities of the various agents of the criminal justice system (including the police and systems of corrections). The decisions of the courts reflect ongoing efforts to balance the rights of the accused with the need to protect society. The principle of *judicial independence* is viewed as essential to the proper functioning of the courts. This principle holds that citizens have the right to have their cases tried by tribunals that are fair, impartial, and immune from political interference (more on judicial independence later in the chapter).

Canada does not have a uniform court system. This often leads to considerable confusion when the various provincial and federal courts are discussed. This chapter will attempt to clearly and concisely describe the system of courts; that said, students are well advised to familiarize themselves with the structure and names of the various courts in their own jurisdiction. Each province and territory maintains a website that provides detailed information on its court system.

With the exception of Nunavut, Canadian jurisdictions have four levels of courts that deal with criminal cases: provincial and territorial courts, provincial and territorial superior courts, provincial and territorial appellate courts, and the Supreme Court of Canada (SCC). Nunavut has a unified or single-level court, the Nunavut Court of Justice. The powers of the lower courts have been combined into one superior court in which all judges can hear all types of cases. The SCC remains the highest court for all jurisdictions. Figure 7.1 provides an outline of the Canadian criminal court system.

Statistics from 2011–2012 indicate that the number of criminal court cases completed declined from the previous year, the majority of cases involved a non-violent offence, and 80 percent of cases involved a young male accused.[1]

Figure 7.2 presents an overview of the cases completed in adult criminal court in 2011–2012.

The cases most frequently heard in criminal court are impaired driving (11 percent), theft (10 percent) (over $5000, under $5000, and motor vehicle theft), and common assault (10 percent).[2] Approximately two-thirds of the completed cases in criminal court result in a finding of guilt. Of those cases that go to trial, the acquittal rate is 3 percent.[3]

THE PROVINCIAL AND TERRITORIAL COURT SYSTEM

There is some variation in the names given to the provincial and territorial courts across the country; even so, the system is much the same in all jurisdictions. In every province and territory, except Nunavut, as noted earlier, the court system has two levels: provincial and superior.

147

Supreme Court of Canada
- established by Parliament
- became the final court of appeal for criminal cases in 1933 and for civil cases in 1949
- has judges who are federally appointed by the prime minister
- operates under the *Supreme Court* Act
- is the final court of appeal for criminal and civil law

Provincial and Territorial Courts of Appeal
- are administered by the provinces and territories
- have judges who are federally appointed
- hears appeals from decisions in superior courts and provincial and territorial courts
- some jurisdictions have a single court with a trial division and an appellate rather than a court of appeal and superior court

Provincial and Territorial Superior Courts
- administered by the provinces
- have judges who are federally appointed
- try the most serious cases
- are the court of first appeal for the provincial and territorial courts

Federal Court of Appeal
- established by Parliament
- hears appeal from the federal courts
- has judges who are federally appointed
- has some limited criminal jurisdiction

Provincial and Territorial Courts
- are administered by the provinces and territories
- have judges who are provincially or territorially appointed
- hear cases involving federal or provincial and territorial laws (exception is Nunavut where the Court of Justice deals with both territorial and superior court cases)
- have jurisdiction over most criminal offences, traffic violations, and provincial or territorial regulatory offences (i.e., fish and wildlife)
- hear preliminary hearings in serious cases to determine whether there is sufficient evidence to proceed to trial

Federal Court
- established by Parliament
- has judges who are federally appointed
- hears matters subject to federal statutes
- has some limited criminal jurisdiction

The provincial and territorial courts are the lowest level of courts; nearly all criminal cases begin and end in them. Their judges are appointed by the provinces and territories, which also fund these courts and have jurisdiction over them. Provincial and territorial court judges sit without juries. These courts also hear cases under the *Youth Criminal Justice Act* and cases involving alleged offences against provincial or territorial statutes. Provincial and territorial courts may also include family courts and small claims courts. Provincial and territorial court judges (along with justices of the peace) may preside over preliminary inquiries, which are held to determine whether there is sufficient evidence to warrant a trial.

Historically, the provincial and territorial courts dealt with less serious cases. This limit has changed in recent years, however; the judges in these courts now hear increasingly serious offences. Provincial and territorial court judges are confronted with specialized populations that may strain court resources and challenge judges to apply

FIGURE 7.2 ▶

Cases Completed in Adult Criminal Court, 2011/2012

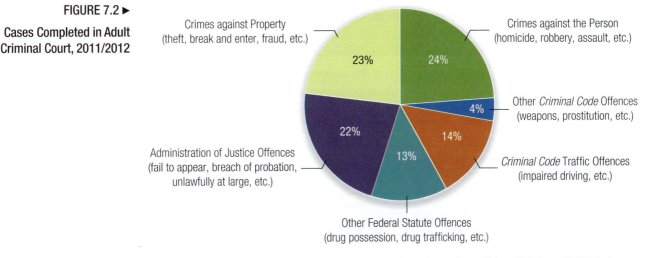

Source: J. Boyce. 2013. "Adult Criminal Court Statistics in Canada, 2011/2013," *Juristat*. Ottawa: Minister of Industry, pp. 27-28; http://www.statcan.gc.ca/pub/85-002-X/2013001/article/11804-eng.pdf

more appropriate sentences. Some observers now argue that the traditional distinction between the provincial and territorial courts and the higher-level superior courts has blurred somewhat in recent years. For example, research has found that although the superior courts hear proportionately more serious offences and more cases involving multiple offences, provincial and territorial courts hear more of these cases in terms of absolute numbers.[4]

PROVINCIAL AND TERRITORIAL SPECIALIZED PROBLEM-SOLVING COURTS

Problem-solving courts

Specialized courts that are designed to divert offenders with special needs from the criminal justice system.

In recent years, a number of specialized, **problem-solving courts** have been developed that attempt to divert offenders with special needs from the criminal justice system. These specialized courts include community courts, drug courts, and mental health courts, among others.

Drug treatment courts (DTCs) target the needs of persons with addictions who are in conflict with the law; mental health courts attempt to address the needs of persons with mental illnesses (PwMI) who come into conflict with the law; a Downtown Community Court in Vancouver focuses on offenders in the highly troubled Downtown Eastside area of the city; in Toronto, the Integrated Violence Court handles both criminal and family law cases. In these courts, offenders may avoid incarceration by agreeing to abide by specified conditions. In DTCs, for example, the offender may agree to participate in a drug-abuse treatment program and to submit to regular drug testing.[5]

The three defining attributes of problem-solving courts are (1) a focus on addressing the underlying problems of offenders, victims, and communities; (2) interagency and interdisciplinary collaboration; and (3) accountability to the community.[6] These principles are complementary to those of restorative justice (see Chapters 2 and 13). Unlike traditional courts, these community-based courts have the potential to improve the quality of life in communities, increase resident familiarity with the court process, and increase community satisfaction with the response to persons in conflict.[7]

TABLE 7.1	COMPARISON OF TRADITIONAL COURTS AND PROBLEM-SOLVING COURTS
Traditional Courts	**Problem-Solving Courts**
adversarial and legalistic	therapeutic and restorative
anonymous and impersonal	personalized
little collaboration among criminal justice, social service, and other agencies and community organizations	collaborative
offence focused	offender focused
sanction focused	problem focused
generic supervision	individualized supervision
minimal community involvement	community involvement (e.g., personal mentors)

The intent of these problem-solving courts is to shift from an adversarial or legalistic approach to one centred on treatment and rehabilitation. The focus is on addressing the underlying issues that contributed to criminal offending and developing an intervention plan to address the behaviour and the circumstances that contributed to it.[8] All are designed to address the revolving door syndrome that affects many offenders, facilitate a collaboration among justice and social service agencies, and formulate and implement problem-solving interventions. Many of the principles of restorative justice are reflected in the practice of problem-solving courts. Table 7.1 provides a comparison of traditional courts with problem-solving courts.

Specialized problem-solving courts incorporate the concept of **therapeutic justice**, which involves the use of the law and the authority of the court as change agents in promoting the health and well-being of offenders while ensuring that their legal rights are protected and that justice is done.

Offender participation in problem-solving courts is voluntary, but there is considerable variation among the courts in the types of cases that are handled, eligibility criteria, the sanctions that are imposed, the length and type of supervision, and the involvement of justice, social service, and community agencies.[9] Some take only offenders who have committed less serious crimes; while others will accept more serious offenders. The DTCs in Canada accept only those offenders who have committed non-violent, drug-related offences.[10] Some courts operate at the pre-plea level, while others require an admission of guilt and acceptance of responsibility.

Critics of therapeutic justice argue that it blurs the line between treatment and enforcement and that there are coercive aspects of problem-solving courts (e.g., drug-treatment courts requiring abstinence by drug users rather than taking a harm-reduction approach).[11]

Two examples of problem-solving courts are drug treatment courts and mental health courts.

DRUG TREATMENT COURTS

Drug treatment courts provide an alternative forum for responding to offenders who have been convicted of drug-related offences. Offenders avoid incarceration by agreeing to abide by specified conditions, including participation in a drug abuse treatment program and regular drug testing. Cases are diverted to the DTC by Crown counsel, who

Therapeutic justice

The use of the law and the authority of the court as change agents in promoting the health and well-being of offenders while ensuring that their legal rights are protected and that justice is done.

determines whether the accused is eligible. As noted, persons charged with violent offences are not eligible. The approach of DTCs is non-adversarial, and there is an attempt to link offenders with treatment programs and services.

The traditional roles of the judge, prosecution, and defence lawyers are altered in the DTCs. Judges become active in treatment planning and in monitoring, rewarding, and, where required, sanctioning offenders, while defence lawyers and prosecutors work as a team in an attempt to address the addiction needs of offenders.[12]

The Edmonton Drug Treatment Court program, for example, involves a team of professionals, including the presiding judge, Crown counsel, duty counsel, individual defence counsel, and program staff, including case managers for treatment and probation.[13]

Total abstinence from drugs is not mandatory; however, to remain in the program, offenders must report relapses to program staff and demonstrate a reduction in their level of drug dependency. On completing the program, those who have been charged with less serious offences may have the charges stayed or withdrawn, while those charged with more serious offences may receive probation. Those offenders who fail to abide by the conditions of the program are processed through the regular courts. Note that although offenders who are sent to a DTC are being diverted from the traditional court system, the drug treatment court is still a court of law.

DIVERSION OF PERSONS WITH MENTAL ILLNESSES: THE MENTAL HEALTH COURT (MHC)

Many persons who come into conflict with the law have some form of mental illness. The importance of addressing the needs of this population became more urgent with the closing of psychiatric hospitals as part of the philosophy of deinstitutionalization that began in the 1970s. One concern is that, in the absence of community-based resources, persons with mental illnesses will be criminalized. The challenges faced by the police in responding to persons with mental illnesses persons was discussed in Chapter 5.

One example of a problem-solving court that focuses on PwMI is the Yukon Community Wellness Court (CWC), which was established to address the needs of offenders with alcohol and drug problems, mental health issues, and other underlying issues that may be related to their offending. Participation is voluntary and offenders must admit guilt. Persons committing sex crimes and serious and violent offences are excluded. The CWC incorporates the principles of therapeutic justice and restorative justice and offers a multifaceted approach, including supervision that is culturally relevant, to reduce reoffending, while still addressing the needs of the victim and the community. A key feature of the CWC is providing offenders with a support network during and after the program and sentencing.

An evaluation of the CWC concluded that the court provided a valuable alternative to the traditional criminal court and was effective in meeting its objectives. Offenders who completed the program felt that the program was generally very helpful to them and had provided an opportunity for them to change their lives. However, only 10 of the 63 offenders who were initially admitted to the CWC successfully completed the program. Many of the offenders had previous criminal records and a long history of alcohol or drug abuse or mental illness. This challenge is one faced by all the specialized courts.[14]

THE EFFECTIVENESS OF SPECIALIZED COURTS

Assessing the effectiveness of various types of specialty courts is difficult because of the wide variations in admissions criteria, services provided, and how success is measured.[15]

151

Ongoing issues with many of the courts are high rates of non-compliance with the conditions imposed by the court and non-completion of programs (84 percent in one study of the Toronto Drug Treatment program.[16] Many of the courts have had difficulty attracting Aboriginal men and women.[17] The use of specialized courts by visible minority groups is also unknown, as are the factors that may facilitate or hinder the effectiveness of these courts in a diverse community. Canadian and U.S. research studies suggest that persons who do not have a stable residence, have substance abuse issues, and who have a severe mental illness were less likely to complete or partially complete a program.[18] The relationship between gender and ethnicity and program completion has not been examined in Canada.

Despite this, some evidence suggests that these courts may be an effective alternative to the traditional criminal justice system. The courts appear to be most effective in reducing reoffending when the principles of risk, needs, and responsivity (discussed in Chapter 10) are followed, that is, when attention is given to selecting offenders who are most suited for the program in terms of their level of risk, their needs, and their motivation or ability to complete the requirements imposed by the court.[19,20] (See the Media Links at the end of the chapter.)

ABORIGINAL COURTS

Section 718.2(e) of the *Criminal Code* requires judges to consider sentencing options other than incarceration, particularly for Aboriginal offenders. The principle that the judiciary should make efforts to explore alternative sentencing options— including the use of restorative justice—was affirmed by the Supreme Court of Canada in *R. v. Gladue*, [1999]1 SCR 688. To address the needs of Aboriginal offenders more effectively, several provinces have created courts specifically for Aboriginal people.

The Gladue Courts (Toronto). The Gladue Courts are a component of the Ontario Court of Justice. These courts deal with the cases of Aboriginal people who have been charged in Toronto and handle bail hearings, remands, trials, and sentencing. The judge, the Crown, and the defence lawyers, court clerks, and court workers are all Aboriginal persons. When the cases are processed, every attempt is made to explore all possible sentencing options and alternatives to imprisonment.

Tsuu T'ina Nation Peacemaker Court (Alberta). This initiative on the Tsuu T'ina Nation near Calgary involves a Peacemaker working with the Crown counsel to identify cases that could appropriately be diverted to the community's peacemaking program. The cases so identified are adjourned by the court so that a Peacemaker can open a restorative justice process involving the victim, the accused, elders, and community residents. A plan of action is designed, the purpose of which is to facilitate healing and address the issues associated with the harm done. Interventions include apologies, restitution payments, alcohol or drug treatment programs, and the requirement that the offender hold a traditional feast. Once this process is completed, the case returns to court, where the presiding judge considers outcomes of the peacemaking process in passing sentence. (See Chapter 13.)

Table 7.2 provides a brief summary of the objectives, processes, and effectiveness of specialized courts. Note that much of the research has been conducted in the United States and that studies vary considerably in their design and in the data sets used for the analysis. Exercise caution in generalizing these findings.

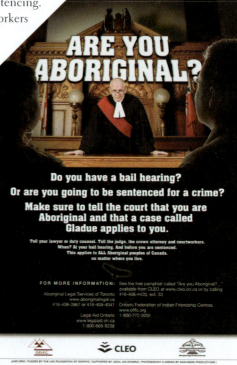

▼ This poster was produced to raise awareness of Gladue rights and the importance of ensuring that the court is aware that the defendant is Aboriginal.

Courtesy Community Legal Education Ontario/ Éducation juridique communautaire Ontario.

TABLE 7.2 THE OBJECTIVES, PROCESS, AND EFFECTIVENESS OF SPECIALIZED COURTS

Type of Court	Objective or Process	Outcomes
Mental health court (MHC)	reduce the criminalization of persons with mental illnesses; operate at pre-and post-charge stage	reduce reoffending by 10 to 75 percent; can reduce the amount of time offenders spend in custody, increase access to treatment services, and change life circumstances (e.g., homelessness), particularly for persons who complete the program;[22,23] court personnel perceive that MHCs improve clients' lives, reducing reoffending and reducing criminal court workloads, and hold offenders accountable;[24] evaluation of the Calgary Diversion Service for offenders with mental illnesses found high rates of client satisfaction and a significant reduction in charges, court appearances, and the need for acute care services;[25] potentially significant reductions in reoffending
Drug treatment court (DTC)	address alcohol or drug addiction of offenders and reduce reoffending; treatment-oriented approach with specified conditions (e.g., abstinence)	even helps offenders with lengthy criminal records;[26] offenders who do not complete the program tend to lack family support, have unstable housing, and lack motivation;[27] per-client costs less than in traditional courts;[28] high rates of non-completion; women and Aboriginal peoples less likely to participate and to complete[29]
Vancouver Downtown Community Court (DCC)	address the needs of residents in the Downtown Eastside area; reduce crime and recidivism; improve public safety and justice efficiencies[21]	interim evaluation revealed that case processing times were longer than in regular provincial court; shorter stays in pre-trial detention; higher use of alternative measure sentencing options; high rates of completion of community service hours; low rates of attendance at recommended information sessions and other referrals (e.g., housing assistance); a higher rate of return to the DCC than occurs in the provincial court;[30] significant reductions in re-offending, particularly for property offences;[31] no impact on case backlogs in the provincial courts[32]
Aboriginal courts	address the special circumstances of Aboriginal offenders; ensure culturally appropriate sentencing; reduce the numbers of Aboriginal persons in confinement	evidence that Aboriginal courts result in more detailed documentation on offenders, but absence of evaluations preclude a determination of their effectiveness;[33] increasing rates of incarceration of Aboriginal offenders are cause for concern

PROVINCIAL AND TERRITORIAL CIRCUIT COURTS

In many northern and remote areas, judicial services are often provided via circuit courts. Circuit court parties, composed of a judge, a court clerk, a defence lawyer, a Crown counsel, and perhaps a translator, travel to communities (generally by air) to hold court. Many communities are served every month; others are visited quarterly or even less often if there are no cases to be heard or if the weather or mechanical problems with the court plane prevent a scheduled visit. The most extensive provincial and territorial circuit court systems are in the Northwest Territories, northwestern Ontario, northern Québec, and Nunavut.

Concerns about the circuit court system include the lengthy court dockets resulting from the backlog of cases; time constraints on the court party, which often preclude effective Crown and defence preparation and result in marathon court sessions that frequently last up to 12 hours; the shortage of interpreters as the Aboriginal accused may understand little English or French and even less of the legal terminology spoken in court; and the general difficulties arising from the cultural differences between Canadian law and its practitioners and Aboriginal offenders, victims, and communities.[34]

Circuit court judges often face a difficult decision: should they remove the convicted person from the community and place him or her in confinement hundreds or even thousands of kilometres away? To address this concern, the circuit courts are encouraging community Elders to participate in the court process and are supporting the development of community forums for dispute resolution and for alternatives to incarceration. Restorative justice strategies are often applied in this environment. However, circuit court judges must balance the need to develop culturally and community-relevant approaches to conflict

Courtesy of Lyn Hancock.

▲ A circuit court sitting in the community of Paulatuk, Northwest Territories.

BOX 7.1 CIRCUIT COURT DAY, NORTHERN SASKATCHEWAN

August 15, 2002: It's a nice day, so people amble about outside, waiting for the judge to arrive. A big fellow wears a black shirt which taunts: "I DID NOT ESCAPE. THEY GAVE ME A DAY PASS." On one side of the building is located the community hall, which serves as both bingo parlour and courtroom—when a trial runs too long, the bingo players bang on the door to be let in—and on the other side is the village office. All the windows have bars or are covered with wire mesh, which is why it seems such a dismal place. The railing on the stairs has mostly fallen away, and the floor of the entryway has a gaping hole in it. How someone hasn't broken their leg is a wonder. On the outside wall of the village office, in bright blue paint, is scribbled "FUCK" in huge letters; on the community-hall side, there's a smaller "Fuck" painted in the same painful blue. Piles of garbage and rubble are scattered around.

The interior is not much better. The walls are streaked and need a paint job, the grey-white floor has tiles missing. An old, faded red Christmas decoration hangs from the Exit sign, which has not lit up in years. The smell of cigarettes, smoked during frantic rounds of bingo, hangs in the air. A steel door right near the judge's chair opens onto the "executive washroom," a small space with toilet, sink, and one chair. This is the defence lawyer's consultation room, where he or she discusses a client's case—often for the first time. The lawyer sits on the toilet, the client on the chair, or the other way around.

The first group of accused file in. Since they are being held in custody, all are handcuffed and shackled, looking haggard from lack of sleep.... The captives sit in chairs directly behind the prosecutor, which, he admits, makes him very nervous. Quietly, a toddler escapes from his stroller and runs toward his father. Despite his fetters, he lifts the child to his knee and kisses him. Another young prisoner, wearing a red Indian Posse bandana, sits and smooches with his girl, who is about seven months pregnant. She is oblivious to his chains. Another shackled captive explains that he is trying to get back into school: the judge listens as he munches on an apple. An attractive young woman is called to the witness stand, which consists of a rickety chair. She wobbles, obviously inexperienced at walking with her legs chained. The court is told that, under the influence of alcohol, she stabbed her husband twice. The wounds were not life-threatening. She has a history of depression—twice she has tried seriously to commit suicide—and no previous record. She is given a suspended sentence, and ordered to attend an alcohol treatment centre. The RCMP officer undoes her handcuffs and shackles and she joins the crowd in the back of the room.

Source: *Bitter Embrace: White Society's Assault on the Woodland Cree* by Maggie Siggins © 2005. Published by McClelland & Stewart. Used with the permission of the author.

resolution and case processing with the need to ensure that the rights and safety of crime victims are protected. This balance is especially important in cases involving women and young girls who have been the victims of domestic violence or sexual assault.

In an attempt to make the justice system more relevant to Aboriginal people, Saskatchewan has established a Cree Court in Prince Albert. This court travels to remote communities to hear cases. Its judges and lawyers are Cree speakers, and it is often attended by a Cree-speaking probation officer. Translators are provided when necessary. This court makes it possible for crime victims, witnesses, and defendants to speak in their own language.

The Cree Court and similar initiatives are designed to address the serious issues that surround the delivery of justice services in many rural and remote Aboriginal communities (see Box 7.1).

THE PROVINCIAL AND TERRITORIAL SUPERIOR COURTS

The superior courts are the highest level of courts in a province or territory and are administered by the provincial and territorial government; however, superior court judges are appointed and paid by the federal government. The name of the superior court generally identifies its location (e.g., the Court of Queen's Bench of Manitoba). About 10 percent of criminal cases are heard in the superior courts.

Superior courts generally have two levels: trial and appeal. These two levels may be included in the same court, with two divisions (trial and appeal), or they may be two separate courts. In Ontario, the Court of Appeal is independent and separate from the Superior Court of Justice and the Ontario Court of Justice, which are the main two trial courts in the province.

The trial-level superior court hears cases involving serious criminal offences; the appeal-level superior court hears criminal appeals (and civil appeals as well) from the superior trial court. The trial court may be known as the Supreme Court or the Court of Queen's Bench; the appeal court is usually called the Court of Appeal. These courts hear cases involving the most serious offences, such as murder. Trials at this level may involve juries. After a case has been decided at the trial level, the accused has the right to appeal the verdict or the sentence, or both, to a higher court. Appeals of provincial court decisions may have to be heard first in a superior court. Appeals from the trial divisions of the superior courts go directly to the provincial or territorial court of appeal. There is one court of appeal in each province and territory, except in Québec and Alberta, where there are two. In all provinces, these courts are called the Court of Appeal (e.g., the Court of Appeal for British Columbia or the Québec Court of Appeal).

The primary activities of appeal courts centre on reviewing decisions of the lower courts. The focus is on how the law was applied to the facts in the case.[35] While many preliminary matters are dealt with by a single judge, certain final hearings require at least three judges to hear the appeal, and the final decision rests with the majority. Oral arguments are made to a three-judge panel by lawyers for both parties. However, it has been pointed out that appeal court judges are much more isolated than trial court judges, spending most of their time "researching and writing their opinions in their own chambers, enjoying only limited contact with others (primarily their own law clerks)."[36]

THE SUPREME COURT OF CANADA

If at least one appellate judge dissents (that is, does not agree with the majority), the unsuccessful party may pursue another appeal at the federal level. The "court of last resort"—the Supreme Court of Canada—is located in Ottawa but hears cases from all provinces and territories. The Supreme Court was established under the *Constitution Act* (1867), which authorized Parliament to establish a general court of appeal for Canada, although the bill creating the Court was not passed until 1875. The governor in council appoints the nine judges of the Supreme Court; those chosen must be superior court judges or lawyers with at least 10 years' standing at the bar in a province or territory. The appointees are selected from the major regions of the country; however, three of the judges on the court must be from Québec. The decisions of the Supreme Court are final and cannot be appealed. However, in some instances Parliament has passed legislation in response to a decision of the Supreme Court that has effectively changed the result of the decision. This change occurred in the case of *R. v. Feeney*, [1997]3 SCR 1008 (see Box 5.3).

Two other federal courts are the Federal Court and the Tax Court of Canada. The Federal Court has a Trial Court and a Court of Appeal, and hears all cases that concern matters of federal law, including copyright law, maritime law, the *Human Rights Act*, the *Immigration Act*, and appeals from the Parole Board of Canada.

SUPREME COURT DECISIONS: BALANCING THE NEED FOR SAFETY AND SECURITY AND THE RIGHTS OF THE ACCUSED

While the Supreme Court receives hundreds of applications for leave to appeal, it generally grants only about 10 percent of requests. Cases are heard by an odd number of judges—five, seven, or nine—to avoid ties. The cases that are decided by the Supreme Court of Canada often involve interpretations of the *Charter of Rights and Freedoms* or complicated issues in private and public law. In many cases that come before the Supreme Court, either the defendant or the Crown asks for permission, or *leave*, to appeal the decision of a lower court. In some instances, the federal government asks the Supreme Court for a legal opinion on an important legal question, a process that is referred to as a *reference*. In 1998, the federal government asked the Court to decide whether Québec could secede unilaterally from Canada under the Constitution and whether international law gives the Province of Québec the right to secede unilaterally from Canada (*Reference re Secession of Quebec*, [1998]2 SCR 217). The federal government asked the Supreme Court for a non-binding opinion as to whether the government could redefine marriage to allow for same-sex marriages. The court ruled (*Reference re Same-Sex Marriage* (2004), 3 SCC 698) that the federal government could do so, which resulted in legislation giving gays and lesbians the right to marry.

There is an inherent tension between individual rights as set out in the *Charter of Rights and Freedoms* and the need to protect the general public. This tension is illustrated in *R. v. Sharpe*, [2001]2 SCR 45. In *Sharpe*, the Supreme Court upheld the law relating to the possession of child pornography (with certain exceptions; see Box 7.2). In other cases, laws have been struck down. In *Morgentaler v. R.*, [1988]1 SCR 30, for example, the Court held that the procedures for obtaining a therapeutic abortion as defined in section 287 of the *Criminal Code* infringed on the right to security of the person because of the uneven availability of services across the country. And in *R. v. Zundel*, [1992]2 SCR 731, the Court held that the offence of spreading false news (s. 181) and even hate literature is constitutionally invalid because it infringes the

> ### BOX 7.2 *R. V. SHARPE*: A CASE OF COMPETING RIGHTS
>
> In *R. v. Sharpe*, [2001]2 SCR 45, the accused was charged with two counts of possession of child pornography under section 163.1(4) of the *Criminal Code* and two counts of possession of child pornography for the purposes of distribution or sale under section 163.1(3). Among other materials, Sharpe had in his possession pictures of young boys engaged in sexual activities and a collection of child pornography stories (titled *Kiddie Kink Classics*) that he had written.
>
> At trial, the B.C. Supreme Court acquitted Sharpe of the charge of possession of child pornography. The acquittal was later upheld by the B.C. Court of Appeal, which stated that the *Criminal Code* section on possession of child pornography was "one step removed from criminalizing simply having objectionable thoughts."
>
> The case was appealed to the Supreme Court of Canada by the Province of British Columbia. The federal government, most provincial governments and police associations, and a variety of child advocate and child protection organizations argued that the need to protect children from sexual exploitation outweighed any protections that might be offered to Sharpe under the *Canadian Charter of Rights and Freedoms*. In a unanimous ruling, the Supreme Court upheld the law that makes it a crime to possess child pornography. Sharpe was convicted of possessing more than 400 photographs that met the legal definition of child pornography. "Freedom of expression," the chief justice stated, "is not absolute," given the constitutional limitations provided under sec. 1 of the *Charter*, which expressly permit the court to consider "reasonable limits in a free and democratic society."
>
> The controversial part of the Supreme Court's decision was its creation of two exceptions. The first of these asserted the right to protect private works of the imagination or photographic depictions of one's own body; the second permitted the possession of child pornography by those who create sexually explicit depictions of children for their own personal pleasure. The Supreme Court of Canada directed that Sharpe be retried on the charge of possessing child pornography and be required to prove that his case met the requirements of one of the two exceptions. Some critics asserted that the SCC's decision was tantamount to a legalization of child pornography. In March 2002, a B.C. Supreme Court justice ruled that Sharpe's written work, which contained descriptions of child sex and violence, had "artistic value," and Sharpe was acquitted (*R. v. Sharpe*, [2002]BCSC 423).

fundamental freedoms of thought, belief, opinion, and expression and is not a reasonable limit in a democratic society. Although the laws referred to in these cases are still part of the *Criminal Code*, they cannot be used to prosecute anyone.

The decisions of the Supreme Court in *Charter*-related cases can also affect legal procedures. In *R. v. Stinchcombe*, [1991]3 SCR 326, for example, the Court held that the prosecution must give all relevant evidence gathered by the police to the defence to permit a defendant to make a full answer and defence to the charges.

The SCC has been criticized on the one hand for engaging in social activism in its decision making and, on the other hand, for being too deferential to law enforcement, particularly in the area of interrogation of suspects.[37] The federal conservative government has increased its criticism of the court, including court decisions that it perceives have undermined anti-terrorism efforts by striking down certain provisions in the legislation on security certificates (see Chapter 8).[38] In 2013, a retiring justice of the SCC lamented the fact that "gun-shy politicians were routinely foisting 'hot potato' political issues onto judges who have no choice but to take them," noting, "the message is clear. Let the judges do it."[39]

An example is the ongoing battle over drug policy in Canada. In 2011, the SCC ruled in favour of PHS Community Services Society, a nonprofit organization that operates the Insite supervised injection site for drug users in Vancouver. In the case of *Canada (Attorney General) v. PHS Community*

Courtesy of J.J. McCullough/Filibuster Cartoons.

Services Society, [2011]3 SCR 134 The court held that efforts of the federal government to close the facility violated the rights of life and security of the person under sec. 7 of the *Charter of Rights and Freedoms*.[40]

Recall from Chapter 2 that interest groups often play a role in the formulation and application of the criminal law. The Supreme Court frequently permits intervenors (persons or parties not directly involved in the case) to file written materials and in some instances to make oral arguments in support of their position. The extent to which these intervenors affect the final outcome of a case is uncertain.

THE COURTROOM WORKGROUP

The professionals who populate the criminal court courtroom can be described as the **courtroom workgroup**.[41] Its permanent members have traditionally been the presiding judge, Crown counsel, and defence lawyer. Other professionals may appear on occasion (e.g., expert witnesses). The advent of problem-solving courts (discussed earlier in the chapter) has resulted in an expansion of the courtroom workgroup to include representatives from agencies and community organizations; various restorative justice approaches include members of the community as well (see Chapter 13).

Courtroom workgroup
The criminal justice professionals, including the judge, Crown counsel, and defence lawyer, who are present in the criminal courtroom.

THE JUDGE

The presiding judge in a criminal case is a trier of fact and plays a variety of roles. These include interpreting the law, assessing whether evidence can be admitted, ruling on motions made by the Crown counsel and defence lawyer, and determining the truthfulness of evidence. In most cases, the role also includes making a decision on the guilt or innocence of the accused and passing sentence. A key role of the judge is serving as a gatekeeper of evidence presented during the trial, including expert testimony, one legal scholar noting, "As gate-keepers, judges serve to balance the utility of [expert testimony] against its possible prejudicial effects."[42]

In cases involving a jury, the jury is the trier of fact, and the judge assumes the role of explaining legal procedures and specifics about the law, as well as giving the jury instructions on how to apply the law in reaching its decision on the guilt or innocence of the accused.[43] In all cases, the judge determines the sentence. For each sentence, judges are expected to provide oral and written reasons for their decision. Lawyers use these reasons to help predict outcomes in future cases with similar facts. Juries do not give reasons with their verdicts.

DEFENCE LAWYERS

Defence lawyers represent persons who are charged with criminal offences. The primary responsibility of the defence lawyer is to ensure that the rights of the accused person are protected throughout the criminal justice process. Defence lawyers are often actively involved in attempting to negotiate a plea for their client outside of the formal court process (see Chapter 8). At trial, the defence lawyer presents evidence and questions witnesses, experts, and others (and less often the accused) to build a case showing the innocence of the accused. The defence lawyer is also involved in cross-examining witnesses for the prosecution and challenging the evidence that is presented by the Crown. Some accused persons are represented by legal aid lawyers (see Chapter 8).

CROWN COUNSEL

Crown counsel have been described as a "cornerstone of the criminal justice system."[44] Crown counsel carry out tasks on behalf of the community rather than the victims of crime. These lawyers are responsible for laying charges against accused in some provinces and are also involved in the prosecution of accused persons.[45]

The role, duties, and responsibilities of provincial and territorial Crown counsel are set out in legislation. Federal prosecutors are employed by the Public Prosecution Service of Canada and operate within the framework of the *Director of Public Prosecutions Act* (SC 2006, c. 9, s. 121). These Crown prosecute cases under federal statutes, including drugs, organized crime, and terrorism.[46] In recent years, Crown counsel have experienced increasing workloads because of the complexity of criminal cases, budget reductions, and legislation enacted by the federal government, including mandatory minimum sentences, that may encourage accused persons to take their case to trial.[47] The role of Crown counsel in prosecuting cases is discussed in more detail in Chapter 8.

OTHER COURTROOM PERSONNEL

Besides lawyers and judges, other court personnel play important roles in the processing and disposition of cases. Court administrators—also known as court registrars or court clerks—perform a variety of administrative tasks. For example, they appoint staff, manage court finances, sign orders and judgments, receive and record documents filed in the court, and certify copies of court proceedings. On request, the court reporter can make a verbatim (word for word) transcript of everything that is said during the trial. This transcription is possible because the proceedings are recorded.

Sheriffs support the court by assisting in jury management, escorting accused and convicted persons, and providing security in the courtroom. In some provinces they serve legal documents, seize goods, and collect fines.

FEATURES OF THE COURTROOM WORKGROUP

The members of the courtroom workgroup—the judge, Crown counsel, and defence lawyer—are permanent fixtures in the court, have professional and often personal relationships, and, it is argued, share a common commitment to the adversarial system of criminal justice.[48] Most accused persons play little or no role in the court process, are merely visitors (albeit for some accused, frequent visitors) to the court, and have no relationships with the others. The diversity of Canadian society is not reflected in the courtroom workgroup.

The power differential between the decision makers and the persons who become involved in the criminal justice system has been extensively documented and is often cited as a reason for the failures of the criminal justice system. Nearly two-thirds of defendants plead guilty and many of these pleas are a result of plea negotiations (see Chapter 8). Accused who appear in criminal courts, who are disproportionately Aboriginal, Black, and disenfranchised persons from lower socio-economic levels of the community. Many have mental illnesses. Two key issues for many accused persons are the access to legal representation and access to legal aid (discussed in Chapter 8).

Concerns with the vulnerabilities of accused persons and the inability of the criminal courts to address the needs of persons with special challenges have been major catalysts for the development of several types of specialized courts, discussed earlier. As well, it is argued that restorative justice approaches (examined in Chapter 13) hold considerably

159

more promise to address the needs of the community, the victim, and the offender. A key feature of restorative justice is the involvement of the community and a reduced role for criminal justice professionals.

WHERE DO JUDGES COME FROM?

Judges at the provincial and territorial court level are appointed by provincial or territorial governments, while judges of the superior courts are appointed by the federal government. Appointments are for life so that once on the bench, judges need not consider the career implications of making controversial decisions. The appointment of judges is a historical legacy from England: "The courts were the King's courts and the judges were the King's judges."[49]

Each province and territory has in place a judicial advisory committee composed of lawyers and laypersons generally appointed by the Attorney General. These screening committees forward nominations to the justice minister, who makes the final appointments. Most provinces have a parallel process for provincially appointed judges, and these referrals are made to the Attorney General. The majority of the members of judicial screening committees are drawn from the legal profession, with only a small representation from the community. Noticeably absent from screening committees are persons from the communities who are most vulnerable and at-risk and members from other diverse groups. At the federal level, regional committees composed largely of members of the legal profession and community members appointed by Ottawa create lists of candidates that are forwarded to the Department of Justice and debated in cabinet. It is argued that this process mitigates diversity in the judiciary.

Under the Canadian Constitution, SCC judges are to be appointed by the Governor General of Canada. In practice, however, it is the prime minister and his or her cabinet who make the selections, and approval by the governor general is a formality. The prime minister is not required to seek approval of the selection via a vote in Parliament nor required to consult with provincial and territorial leaders as to who should be recommended for appointment. The *Supreme Court Act* (1985) does require that the potential appointee be a judge in a provincial or territorial superior court or have at least 10 years experience as a lawyer. As noted earlier, the Act stipulates that at least three of the judges on the nine-judge court must be from Québec.

Concerns about the lack of consultation led to the creation in 2004 of an ad hoc Parliamentary committee that reviews a list of seven candidates and shortlists three from which the prime minister will select one. However, the final decision rests with the prime minister in the executive branch of government. The prime minister's selection cannot be blocked by either the committee or Parliament. This process is in contrast to the procedure in the United States, where presidential appointments to the U.S. Supreme Court must be confirmed by the U.S. Senate, which is a part of the legislative branch.[50]

Observers have noted that the federal Conservative Party has made appointments to the SCC that have shifted the court to the right, that is, to a more conservative stance; compare to the decision of the SCC in *R. v. MacKenzie* in support of the expansion in the use of drug sniffer dogs (Chapter 5). The SCC judge appointed in 2013 was considered a leader in maritime law, leaving some observers to wonder about his views of the *Charter of Rights and Freedoms*, with a law professor at York University's Osgoode Hall Law School commenting, "I think an expert in admiralty law is an odd choice, because it's not a very strong match with the court's core jurisdiction in public law, the *Charter [of Rights and Freedoms]* and criminal law."[51] In March 2014, the SCC nullified the appointment, holding that it did not meet the eligibility criteria set out in the Supreme Court Act. More specifically, the appointed judge had not served the requisite ten years on the bench in Quebec and had been appointed while serving on the Federal Court of Appeals (Reference re *Supreme Court Act*, ss. 5 and 6, 2014 SCC 21). In 2012, the federal government announced that federal cabinet ministers would not be ruled out for judicial appointments.[52]

A study of federal, non-Supreme Court appointments found that more than half of appointees were supporters of the federal Liberal Party.[53] The authors cross-referenced the records of donations to political parties between 1997 and 2003 and found that 53 percent of the appointees were probable or possible supporters of the Liberal Party. Only 4 percent were probable supporters of an opposition party. These findings raise concerns about the part played by political affiliation when federal judges are selected and the possible influence of patronage in the process for selecting judges.

Similar concerns have been raised about the appointment of provincial and territorial court judges. In Alberta, the president of the Criminal Trial Lawyers' Association in 2013 stated, "You can find judicial appointments of people who aren't specifically qualified, and no more so than anyone else, who obviously received an appointment because of their political connections."[54]

The record indicates that, as of 2013, two of the three most recently appointed judges had ties to the provincial Conservative Party. One of the lawyers appointed to the provincial court was the president of a local Conservative riding association; another donated to the campaign of the provincial justice minister. The chair of the provincial court nominating committee is a Calgary lawyer who is a frequent donor to the provincial Conservative Party. Another member of the nominating committee was president of the provincial Conservative Party for four years.[55] For a closer look at the members of the provincial judge nominating committee (as of 2013), see "Who Picks Alberta's Provincial Court Judges?" at www.cbc.ca/edmonton/interactive/judicial-appointments/.

DIVERSITY IN THE JUDICIARY

An ongoing issue is the absence of diversity in the judiciary, where older, Caucasian males are most common. Judges are often drawn from the ranks of Crown prosecutors or the defence bar, and all are required to be law school graduates. Of the 100 new federally appointed judges between 2009 and 2012, 98 were white, the exception being two Métis judges appointed in B.C. and Nova Scotia.[56] In B.C., 6 of 104 provincial court judges were members of visible minority communities; no judges from a minority group were appointed between 2001 and 2008.[57] This demographic is not often reflective of the larger community, nor of the accused persons who appear before the courts.

Concerns with the selection process and the lack of diversity on the bench are reflected in the comments of an Aboriginal lawyer in Halifax: "While the law is objective, a person's assessment of the facts, including another's behavior, motives and justifications, is inevitably coloured by who we are and where we come from."[58] Commenting on the lack of diversity in the judiciary, a high-level member in the federally appointed court expressed concerns with the lack of transparency in the selection and an understanding of who is appointed and on what basis: "The key stage of the federal process is so invisible that it is virtually impossible to determine if the objective of increased diversity is being given weight as a guiding principle, apart from occasional, general statements from Ministers of Justice."[59] In 2013, a retiring female Supreme Court of Canada justice lamented the absence of women on the high court. Her replacement was a male, leaving three women on the nine-member bench.[60]

AT ISSUE 7.1   SHOULD CANADIAN JUDGES BE ELECTED?

In contrast to our neighbours to the south, Canada has no elected judges. Among the arguments offered in support of electing judges are the following:

- A poll of 1000 Canadians in 2007 found that 63 percent were in favour of elected judges.
- Judges are being asked to make decisions that rightfully should be made by elected politicians, that is, highly politicized issues, such as polygamy and the decriminalization of marijuana (see Chapter 2).
- An elected judiciary would be more accountable to the public "and less likely to cling to the ideology of their elite educations."[61]
- The process of selecting judges would be public and transparent, unlike the current arrangements.

Opponents to the election of judges counter with the following arguments:

- The election of judges would compromise judicial independence.
- Judicial candidates would be forced to pander to public opinion in their decision making.
- The selection of judges would become politicized.
- The chronically low voter turnout rate would ensure that the sentiment of the general public about a judicial candidate would not be expressed.

The limited amount of research that has been conducted on elected judges versus appointed judges is inconclusive, although one U.S. study found that appointed judges wrote higher quality opinions, but elected judges wrote more opinions. This suggests that the elected judges in the study were more focused on service to the public (i.e., behaving like politicians), whereas appointed judges were more focused on establishing case precedent (i.e., behaving like professionals).[62] Another U.S. study found that appointed judges were more effective than their elected counterparts, as measured by the number of mistakes made, and exhibited a better ability to change preconceived notions about a case.[63]

QUESTIONS

What arguments do you find most persuasive? If you were given a vote as to whether judges should be elected, how would you vote, and why?

Concerns over the decisions of judges, the perceived inadequacy of the complaint process, and the lack of independent oversight of the judiciary have prompted some to argue that the process of selecting judges should be more transparent and that members of the judiciary should be more accountable to the community. These concerns raise the spectre of electing judges, rather than appointing them. See At Issue 7.1.

THE FLOW OF CASES THROUGH THE COURT SYSTEM

Figure 7.3 sets out the procedure for criminal cases. Note that summary conviction offences and indictable offences have different procedures. A criminal trial that involves a jury moves through some additional stages. These are set out in Figure 7.4.

MODE OF TRIAL

As discussed earlier, the key roles in criminal courts are played by the judge, the prosecutor or Crown counsel, the defence counsel, the witnesses, and the jury. The trier of fact in a criminal case—usually a judge—decides whether the guilt of the accused

FIGURE 7.3 ▶

Procedure in Criminal Cases

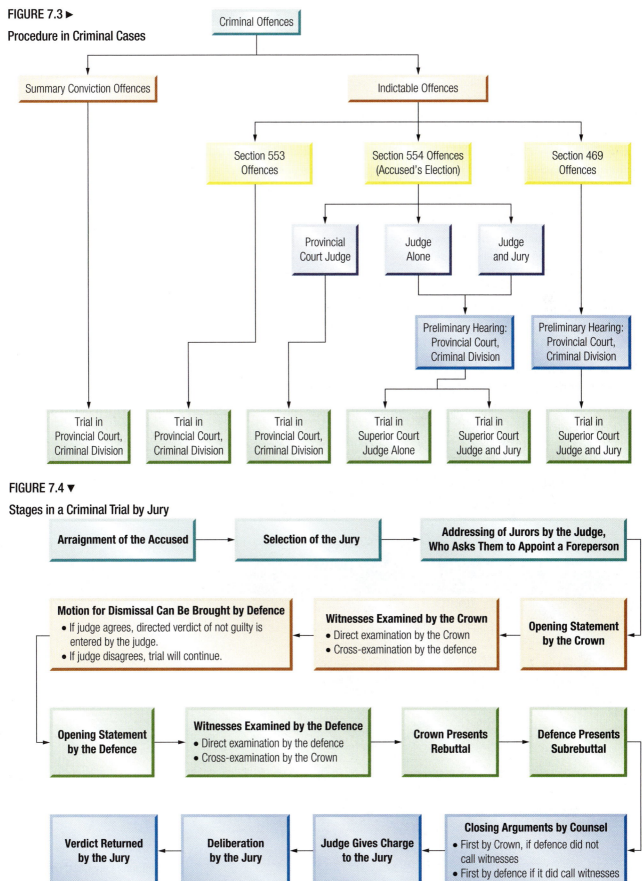

FIGURE 7.4 ▼

Stages in a Criminal Trial by Jury

person has been proven beyond a reasonable doubt. In a small number of cases, a jury of citizens makes this decision. Jury trials are virtually mandatory in some types of cases, an available option in many, and prohibited in others. Jury trials are not available for summary conviction offences; nor, with a handful of exceptions, are they available in youth court. There are key differences in the prosecution of summary conviction offences, indictable offences, and charges heard.

In cases involving trial by jury, the presiding judge must order a pre-hearing conference, which is attended by the Crown, the defence counsel, and the judge. They can discuss any matters to promote a fair and expeditious trial. In non-jury cases, pre-trial conferences are optional. Informal pre-trials are becoming increasingly common. They take place in a judge's chambers and involve an off-the-record discussion of issues surrounding the case. These discussions provide an opportunity for plea bargaining, since the presence of a judge can promote a fair resolution between the two parties (which is preferable to eleventh-hour bargaining on the courthouse steps).

The accused person is generally present throughout the proceedings and may testify but is not required to do so. To avoid media scrutiny, a famous person being charged may be represented by counsel, negotiate a guilty plea through a plea bargain, or not appear at all.

Figure 7.5 illustrates the traditional common law court setting. To take a virtual tour of several provincial courts in Alberta, visit www.albertacourts.ab.ca/Home/Contact/VirtualCourtTours/tabid/111/Default.aspx.

SUMMARY OFFENCES OR PROCEEDING SUMMARILY

When the case involves a summary conviction offence, or when the Crown proceeds summarily, it is resolved in a provincial court. Summary trials do not involve juries, and the sentences are usually less severe.

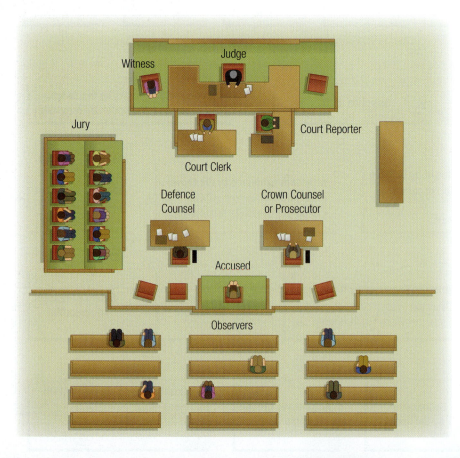

◀ **FIGURE 7.5**

The Common Law Court Setting

INDICTABLE OFFENCES

When the accused is charged with an indictable offence, or the Crown proceeds by indictment on a **hybrid (elective) offence**, a different sequence of events unfolds. The *Criminal Code* defines three categories of indictable offences: (1) offences under the absolute jurisdiction of provincial or territorial courts, (2) offences under the absolute jurisdiction of superior courts, and (3) electable offences.

The key difference is *election*—that is, the right of the accused to choose to be tried by a judge instead of a jury.

ABSOLUTE JURISDICTION OF PROVINCIAL AND TERRITORIAL COURTS

Section 553 of the *Criminal Code* lists the less serious indictable and hybrid (elective) offences wherein the accused person has no choice but to be tried in a provincial and territorial court, even if the Crown proceeds by indictment. The offences include theft (other than cattle theft), obtaining money on false pretences, fraud, and mischief (where the subject matter of the offence is not a testamentary instrument and its value does not exceed $5000). The list also includes keeping a gaming or betting house and driving while disqualified. There are no jury trials in provincial or territorial court.

ABSOLUTE JURISDICTION OF PROVINCIAL AND TERRITORIAL SUPERIOR COURTS

Section 469 of the *Criminal Code* is a list of serious offences that are also non-electable offences. The list includes murder, treason, and piracy. These cases must be tried in a superior court before a jury unless both the accused and the provincial Attorney General agree to waive this right.

The processing of non-electable offences begins with a preliminary hearing, sometimes called a **preliminary hearing**. This (usually) short hearing is held to determine whether there is a prima facie case—that is, sufficient evidence to justify the time and expense of a criminal trial. A magistrate or provincial or territorial court judge listens to some (or all) of the Crown witnesses. The court may order a publication ban to protect the identity of any victim or witness and is required to order a publication ban to protect the identity of all victims of sexual offences and witnesses of sexual offenders who are less than 18 years old.[64]

The judge does not rule on the guilt of the accused at the preliminary hearing but must decide if the Crown has evidence that could be used to prove guilt. If the judge believes the Crown does, there is a prima facie case. If there is not a prima facie case, the judge will dismiss the case or at least dismiss the problematic charges against the accused. Usually, the matter is committed to trial, and a trial date is set. The accused person can waive the right to a preliminary hearing and go directly to trial. In rare cases, which generally involve more serious allegations, the provincial or territorial Attorney General can skip the preliminary hearing and go straight to trial. This course of action is called *preferring the indictment*.

ELECTABLE OFFENCES

Most indictable offences fall into neither of the two categories just described. These are the electable offences, and the accused person has three modes of trial from which to choose: (1) trial by a provincial or territorial court judge, (2) trial by a superior court judge sitting alone, or (3) trial by a superior court judge and a jury.

Hybrid (elective) offences
Offences that can be proceeded summarily or by indictment, a decision that is always made by the Crown.

Preliminary hearing
A hearing to determine if there is sufficient evidence to warrant a criminal trial.

The *Charter* guarantees the right to a jury trial if the alleged offence carries a maximum sentence of more than five years' imprisonment. However, not every accused person wants a jury trial.

Once an accused person has elected, he or she can reelect another option or enter a guilty plea, in which case there will not be a trial. It is also possible (although this happens rarely) that the provincial or territorial Attorney General may intervene and require a jury trial if the offence is punishable by more than five years' imprisonment and if the accused has chosen one of the first two options. Accused persons who choose option 1 do not have a preliminary hearing and waive their right to trial by jury. Accused persons who choose option 2 or 3 are entitled to a preliminary hearing unless they waive that right. Accused persons who abscond and who fail to appear for trial by jury on the appointed court date may lose their right to a jury trial.

TRIAL BY JURY

Jury decisions must be unanimous. Unlike their American counterparts, Canadian jurors are prohibited from discussing their deliberations afterward with the media. Each province and territory has legislation that sets out the qualifications for jurors and that provides other directives for selecting juries and guiding their activities. Jury duty is still regarded as a civic duty; with a few exceptions, a person called for jury duty will be required to serve. The role of the jury in the criminal court process is examined in Chapter 8.

JUDICIAL ETHICS AND ACCOUNTABILITY

A key theme in this text are ethics and accountability in the criminal justice system. Accountability is an often-contentious issue with respect to the legal profession generally and, more specifically, the judiciary.

ETHICAL PRINCIPLES FOR JUDGES

Provincial, territorial, and federal court judges are guided by ethical principles that are set out in various provincial and territorial documents and, for federally appointed judges, by the Canadian Judicial Council. In Ontario, the Principles of Judicial Office encompass standards of integrity in personal and professional conduct and highlight impartiality and objectivity, a duty to follow the law, and the importance of appropriate personal conduct.[65]

The ethical principles for federally appointed judges include judicial independence, integrity, impartiality, and diligence and equality.[66] The principle of integrity is set forth as "judges should strive to conduct themselves with integrity so as to sustain and enhance public confidence in the judiciary."[67] This requires that a judge's conduct be "beyond reproach."[68]

STRUCTURES AND PROCESSES OF ACCOUNTABILITY

Historically, the focus in Canada has been on judicial independence rather than on judicial accountability. Provincial and territorial court judges are held accountable to various bodies. In Ontario, for example, the Ontario Judicial Council (OJC) operates under the *Courts of Justice Act* (RSO 1990, ch. c. 43) and investigates complaints made by the general public about provincial courts judges (www.ontariocourts.ca/ocj/). See the annual report of the OJC for case summaries of complaints.[69]

In jurisdictions that do not have stand-alone judicial councils, procedures have been established for receiving, assessing, and responding to complaints. In Manitoba, for example, public complaints about provincial court judges are reviewed by the chief judge of the provincial court, who will notify the affected judge and make one of several decisions: (1) determine there is no basis for the complaint, (2) resolve the complaint with the complainant, (3) advise the complainant that the complaint should be dealt with in another manner, or (4) refer the complaint to a judicial board of inquiry for further investigation. The board is composed of a lawyer, a judge from the Court of Queen's Bench (the highest trial court in the province; the judge is federally appointed), and a person who is neither a lawyer nor a judge.[70] In this scheme, the powers of the chief judge of the provincial court are extensive.

The primary structure of accountability for federally appointed judges is the Canadian Judicial Council (www.cjc-ccm.gc.ca), created under the *Judges Act*, chaired by the chief justice of Canada, and composed of judges. In keeping with its mandate—which is set out in the *Judges Act*—this council provides continuing education for judges, addresses issues concerning the administration of justice, and makes recommendations on judicial salaries and benefits. To exercise judicial accountability, the council investigates complaints made about federally appointed judges, be they from litigants, lawyers, complainants, accused persons, interest groups, or even other judges. Most complaints are made by the general public. An alleged inability to execute the functions of a judge because of mental infirmity is also grounds for complaint.

Sanctions range from removal from the bench (an extremely rare occurrence) to a leave of absence with pay or a letter of reprimand. Alternatives to these include counselling, educational workshops, or an apology from the judge to the complainant. In more serious cases, judges often choose to resign before the council completes its inquiry.

PUBLIC COMPLAINTS ABOUT JUDGES

Recall in Chapter 5 the discussion of public complaints against the police and the initiatives that have been taken in recent years to make the complaint process more transparent and to include civilian oversight of the handling of complaints. These developments stand in contrast to the complaint process for judges.

Complaints about judges arise from intemperate remarks or inappropriate conduct, either on or off the bench. Displays of gender bias, racial bias, religious bias, conflict of interest, and cultural insensitivity are grounds for complaint, as is undue delay in rendering a decision (which should usually take no more than six months). Recall the case of Manitoba Justice Robert Dewar in Chapter 3 (Box 3.1) and the protests that were ignited when his comments in a sexual assault case seemed to blame the victim for the attack. Noting that the Justice Dewar acknowledged that he "made a poor choice of words and offered his full apology," the council required him to take gender sensitivity training.[71]

Judges who have been sanctioned by the Council can appeal to the Supreme Court of Canada. In 2002, for example, the SCC upheld the decision of the New Brunswick Judicial Council to remove a provincial court judge from the bench (*Moreau-Berube v. New Brunswick (Judicial Council,* [2002]1 SCR 249). After hearing a number of break-and-enter cases in court, the judge had stated: "If a survey were taken in the Acadian Peninsula, the honest people against the dishonest people, I have the impression the dishonest people would win.... The honest people in the Peninsula, they are very few and far between."[72] This was the first time a Canadian judge had ever been removed for comments made from the bench, although some investigations have resulted in several judges "being allowed" to resign.

Some observers have questioned the adequacy and impartiality of the structures for judicial accountability, especially in view of the fact that judges are generally appointed for life.

THE ISSUE OF INDEPENDENT OVERSIGHT OF THE JUDICIARY

In Chapters 2 and 4, it was noted that the police are the only criminal justice agency that is subjected to binding outside civilian oversight. The legal profession, including the judiciary, is self-regulated; that is, the only structures of accountability exist within the legal profession. Concerns have been raised about the ability of provincial law societies to both represent and regulate the profession and about the effectiveness of the Canadian Judicial Council as an oversight body.[73] However, it is noted that most complaints that are made to the Canadian Judicial Council are not made public and are kept private between the complainant, the council, and the judge.

A key argument that is made against outside oversight of judges is that of **judicial independence**, which means that "judges are not subject to pressure and influence, and are free to make impartial decisions based solely on fact and law."[74] Judicial independence has been cited as a primary reason that most Canadian judges do not allow cameras in their courtrooms.[75]

One question is whether this extends to independence from oversight. Arguments in support of ensuring judicial independence distinguish between judges and the police and prosecutors, noting that the latter "are in the employ and within the authority of the executive branch of government and ... are agents of the Crown," whereas judges "are not subject to the direction or control of the executive branch of government."[76]

A review of the record indicates that few complaints ultimately result in the removal of a judge from the bench. As well, since the disciplinary procedure was established in 1971, there have been very few public inquiries by the council into the behaviour of a federal judge. Most complaints, (which average fewer than 200 per year) are handled by the chairperson of the council and are not publicized. It might be argued that this practice limits the transparency of the council's work.

The case of a judge who was investigated by the council is presented in Box 7.3.

Judicial independence
The notion that "judges are not subject to pressure and influence, and are free to make impartial decisions based solely on fact and law."

BOX 7.3 THE CONDUCT OF NOVA SCOTIA JUSTICE J.E. SCANLAN

In 2008, a complaint was filed against Nova Scotia Justice J.E. Scanlan alleging certain improprieties in his personal life. The complaint did not relate to any decisions or activities in the courtroom. Rather the complaint was filed by the ex-husband of Scanlan's current wife. A five-judge panel with the Canadian Judicial Council (all from outside Nova Scotia) reviewed all of the evidence and found that Scanlan had accompanied Karen Quigley (who was then his girlfriend) to two meetings with the RCMP in relation to laying a complaint against her ex-husband. Following the laying of the complaint, Justice Scanlan was taken off the bench while the complaint was investigated.

The review panel took three years to complete its investigation. In its decision on the complaint in November 2011, the panel concluded that while Justice Scanlan's presence at the meetings with the RCMP "could be seen as an attempt by a judge to use the prestige of judicial office to influence officials or seek a certain outcome," the judge "did not wilfully try to influence the RCMP officers and did not act in bad faith."[77] However, the panel did express its concerns that it might be perceived that he was attempting to influence the course of events and in a letter instructed him to avoid such situations in the future. No further sanctions were imposed, and Justice Scanlan returned to the bench. In 2013, Justice Scanlan was appointed to the Supreme Court of Nova Scotia by the federal minister of justice.[78]

QUESTIONS

What are your views on the process and outcome of the Scanlan case? In your view, was the response of the review panel appropriate? Do you think that Judge Scanlan should have been promoted to the Supreme Court of Nova Scotia?

BOX 7.4   THE CASE OF JUDGE DAVID RAMSAY

On June 1, 2004, former B.C. provincial court judge David Ramsay was sentenced to seven years in prison for sexually assaulting several teenage Aboriginal girls in Prince George. He pleaded guilty to one count of sexual assault causing bodily harm, three counts of buying sex from minors, and one count of breach of trust. The sentence was two years longer than Crown counsel had asked for. During the sentencing hearing, Ramsay apologized to four of his victims, who were in court.

Evidence presented to the court indicated that Ramsay had sexually abused the young women, who were involved in the sex trade, over a 10-year period, intimidating them into remaining silent about his violent attacks on them. The girls, some as young as 12, had appeared in court before Judge Ramsay, who was aware of their life circumstances and their vulnerabilities. Ramsay was found guilty and sentenced to seven years in prison. His application for day parole was denied in 2007, and, in 2008, he died of an illness in a New Brunswick jail.

The RCMP authorities in Prince George were criticized for their slow response to the allegations against Ramsay; reports of his abuses had been circulating in the city for several years. After Ramsay was sentenced, two RCMP officers who had at one time been stationed in Prince George were themselves investigated for misconduct amid allegations that they had covered up Ramsay's exploits. It was alleged that one of these officers had had sex with underage prostitutes in Prince George as well; he was suspended with pay while his case was investigated by the RCMP major crime section. Because of delays in the RCMP investigating the case, no further action was taken against the officer.

The Assembly of First Nations and the Native Women's Association of Canada called for an inquiry into the administration of justice in cases involving sexual assault against Aboriginal women and young women. The government did not act on this suggestion.

Some instances of judicial misconduct never come to the attention of the federal and provincial or territorial councils, owing to potential complainants feeling intimidated by the judge in question, the justice system, and the complaint process. This fear may be felt particularly by people in vulnerable and at-risk groups and even members of visible minorities, where a lack of knowledge of the complaint process, suspicion of the justice system, and language barriers may deter complaints.

It is likely that this occurred in the case of Judge David Ramsay, a provincial court judge in British Columbia (see Box 7.4). This case highlights the power that judges wield in the community, as well as the vulnerability of women, especially young women—in this case, Aboriginal young women.

SUMMARY

The discussion in this chapter has centered on the structure and operation of the Canadian criminal courts. The four levels of courts that deal with criminal cases were discussed, as well as the role and activities of judges, defence counsel, and Crown counsel. Problem-solving courts, focused on therapeutic justice, have emerged as an alternative to the traditional adversarial model of justice for vulnerable persons accused of criminal offences. Unique challenges surround the delivery of court services in remote and northern communities.

The decisions of the Supreme Court illustrate the ongoing tension between balancing the rights of citizens as enshrined in the *Charter of Rights and Freedoms* with the need to protect the general public. The issues surrounding the appointment of judges were examined, including the role of politics in the selection process. Increasing attention is being given to judicial ethics and accountability, and concerns have been expressed that the current structures and processes are not sufficiently independent and transparent.

KEY POINTS REVIEW

1. The criminal courts play an important, multifaceted role in the criminal justice system.

2. Four levels of courts deal with criminal cases: provincial and territorial courts, provincial and territorial superior courts, provincial and territorial appellate courts, and the Supreme Court of Canada.

3. In recent years, a number of problem-solving courts have been created that attempt to divert offenders with special needs from the criminal justice system.

4. Unique challenges are confronted by provincial and territorial circuit courts that provide court services to northern and remote communities.

5. There is an inherent tension between individual rights as set out in the *Charter of Rights and Freedoms* and the need to protect the general public, and this tension is often evident in the cases heard by the Supreme Court of Canada.

6. The courtroom workgroup is composed of the professionals who work in the criminal courts and includes the judges, defence lawyers, and Crown counsel.

7. Defendants in the criminal courts are disproportionately Aboriginal, Black, and disenfranchised persons from the lower socio-economic levels of the community.

8. Judges at the provincial and territorial court level are appointed by their respective governments, while judges of the superior courts are appointed by the federal government.

9. There are concerns about the process by which judges are nominated and appointed.

10. An ongoing issue is the absence of diversity in the judiciary.

11. There are arguments in favour of and opposed to the election of judges.

12. Judicial ethics and the structures of judicial accountability have come under increased scrutiny in recent years.

13. In contrast to the police, the judiciary has no civilian oversight, and the complaint process is far less transparent than in policing.

KEY TERM QUESTIONS

1. What is meant by the **courtroom workgroup**, and why is this notion important in understanding the operation of the criminal courts?

2. Describe the approach of **problem-solving courts**, provide an example, and discuss the effectiveness of these courts.

3. What is **therapeutic justice**, and how does it differ from the traditional approaches of the criminal court?

4. Describe **hybrid (or) elective offences**.

5. What is a **preliminary hearing**, and what role does it play in the criminal court process?

6. Define **judicial independence**, and discuss how it assists in understanding the role of the judiciary.

MEDIA LINKS

 "Three videos on the operation of the Vancouver Downtown Community Court"
or go to the book's website at
www.nelson.com/
crimjusticeprimer5e.com

"King County (Seattle, WA) therapeutic court for offenders with mental illnesses"
or go to the book's website at
www.nelson.com/
crimjusticeprimer5e.com

"Drug Courts: Personal Stories—Narratives from across New York State"
or go to the book's website at
www.nelson.com/
crimjusticeprimer5e.com

171

CHAPTER 8

THE PROSECUTION OF CRIMINAL CASES

LEARNING OBJECTIVES

After reading this chapter, you should be able to

- describe the pre-trial process in the criminal courts
- discuss judicial interim release (bail) and the issues that surround its use
- describe security certificates and discuss the controversy that surrounds their use
- discuss legal representation for defendants, the provisions for legal aid, and the issues surrounding remand
- describe the practices for determining fitness to stand trial
- identify the issues surrounding plea bargaining
- discuss the role of juries in criminal trials and the research on jury decision making
- identify the various defences that are used by persons charged with a crime
- discuss the issues surrounding wrongful convictions

THE PRE-TRIAL PROCESS

A number of steps are involved in bringing a case to criminal court, and a major role is played by Crown counsel.

THE ROLE OF CROWN COUNSEL

Crown attorneys are lawyers who represent the Crown (or government) in court and who are responsible for prosecuting criminal cases. The responsibility for prosecuting cases is shared between the provinces and the federal government, with provincially appointed Crown attorneys prosecuting *Criminal Code* offences and federally appointed Crown attorneys prosecuting persons charged with violating other federal statutes, such as the *Controlled Drugs and Substances Act*. In Yukon, the Northwest Territories, and Nunavut, federally appointed Crown attorneys are responsible for prosecuting all cases.

Crown attorneys are involved in a range of activities. They provide advice to police officers at the pre-charge stage; they prepare for trial (e.g., they collect evidence from the police and other sources, research case precedents, and interview victims, witnesses, and experts who may be called to testify); and they prepare for post-trial appeals. Crown counsel are also involved in negotiating pleas, developing trial strategies, managing witnesses, arguing conditions of bail, recommending sentences to the court, and appealing sentences deemed too lenient. Crown attorneys must also remain up-to-date on changes in the law and in judicial precedent, including decisions in *Charter* cases.

Crown prosecutors exercise a considerable amount of discretion in case processing, and this power has been reaffirmed by the Supreme Court of Canada (*R. v. Jolivet*, [2000]1 SCR 751).

At trial, the Crown presents the state's case in an attempt to prove beyond a reasonable doubt that the accused is guilty of the offence with which he or she has been charged. Historically, the role of Crown counsel was viewed as one of being a representative of justice rather than that of partisan advocate: "Their role is not to win convictions at any cost but to put before the court all available, relevant, and admissible evidence necessary to enable the court to determine the guilt or innocence of the accused."[1]

This principle was established nearly 60 years ago by the Supreme Court of Canada (SCC) in *Boucher v. The Queen*, [1955] SCR 16: "It cannot be overemphasized that the purpose of a criminal prosecution is not to obtain a conviction. . . . The role of prosecutor excludes any notion of winning or losing; his function is a matter of public duty".[2]

How this view of the Crown's role is reconciled with the demands of an adversarial system remains to be explored.

The challenge of increasing workloads in the criminal justice system is reflected in the work of Crown counsel, many of whom process up to 50 cases a day and work 90 hours a week. In the words of one Crown counsel,

> You know I've winged many cases. I've seen me do trials when the first time I ever read the file was when I was calling my first witness 'cause I never had time. Just didn't have time to prepare for it. I'll call my witness, and while he's walking up to the stand I'll read his statement, and then I'll find out what he's got to say and then I'll question him. I did that many times.[3]

Increasingly, prosecutors must deal with sensitive cases involving sexual offences, family violence, and the victimization of children. New technologies, such as DNA evidence, require prosecutors to have specialized knowledge (or access to it). As discussed in Chapter 7, in some regions of the country, prosecutors travel with circuit courts or to satellite court locations and thus often have little time for case preparation. Other challenges are the cultural and language barriers that are encountered in northern and remote Aboriginal communities, as well as in some urban centres.

In considering the prosecution process, it is important to note that considerable case attrition occurs, and many cases do not progress very far into the system (see Figure 2.3). The police or the Crown send many offenders to alternative measures programs—a process known as diversion (discussed in Chapter 10).

LAYING AN INFORMATION AND LAYING A CHARGE

The police are usually responsible for laying an information, which is then ratified or rejected by the Crown. An information is a document that briefly outlines an allegation that a person has contravened a criminal law in a certain location during a specified period. Multiple offences are divided into separate counts.

Not all cases must be brought before a justice of the peace (JP). For certain offences, police officers are authorized to issue summons, traffic offence notices, appearance notices, and promise-to-appear notices. In such cases, accused persons are released *on their own recognizance*, which means they are responsible for ensuring that they appear in court on the designated date.

The information may be laid either after the suspect has been informed (as in the case of an arrest without a warrant or the use of an appearance notice) or before (see Figure 8.1). Remember from Chapter 5 that there are a limited number of circumstances in which the police can arrest without a warrant; there is a presumption that an appearance notice will be used for most cases. On receiving the information, the JP may not agree that the informant has made out a case; in practice, however, this rarely happens. If the JP determines there is sufficient reason to believe that a crime has been committed, he or she will issue either a warrant for the arrest of the person named in the information or a summons that directs the named person to appear in provincial court on a specified date.

The police and the Crown exercise a considerable amount of discretion in deciding whether to lay a charge.[4] Charges are not laid in one-third of all violent crimes and property crimes that are cleared by the police, and, across the country, 30 percent of all criminal cases are stayed, dismissed, or withdrawn by prosecutors and judges.[5] Reasons for not charging include the victim or complainant being reluctant to cooperate, the suspect or an essential witness dying, or the suspect being committed to a psychiatric facility or being under 12. The judiciary, including the SCC, have been reluctant to review prosecutorial decision making; however, the Supreme Court has held that provincial law societies are permitted to review such decisions to ensure adherence to professional standards (*Krieger v. Law Society of Alberta*, [2002]3 SCR 372).

Legal, administrative, and political factors may also influence the decision to lay a charge. Legal considerations include the reliability and likely admissibility of available evidence and the credibility of potential witnesses. Administrative factors include the workload and case volume of the Crown counsel's office, as well as the time and cost of prosecution relative to the seriousness of the crime. Political considerations include the need to maintain the public's confidence in the justice system.

In New Brunswick, Québec, and British Columbia, the Crown must give approval before the police can lay a charge. Once the decision has been made to lay a charge, a police officer can initiate the process by laying an information before a JP. When doing so, the officer is called an *informant*. In practice, most informants are police officers, but any person can lay an information if he or she, on reasonable grounds, believes that a person has committed an offence.

Not all crime victims support charges being filed. Victims of domestic violence or spousal assault, for example, may refuse to cooperate with the Crown for a variety of reasons, including fear of retaliation, economic insecurity, and family pressures. Victims who are also involved in criminal activities (such as gang members) may be understandably reluctant to appear in court and to provide testimony against accused persons. In these circumstances, crime victims may not make use of the specialized services that are available.

COMPELLING THE APPEARANCE OF THE ACCUSED IN COURT

After a prosecution has been initiated, the next step is to ensure that the accused appears in court to answer the charge. This appearance can be accomplished in a number of ways—for example, by arresting and placing the accused person in remand custody until the court appearance or by allowing the accused person to remain at liberty in the community with a promise to appear on the court date. If the accused person does not appear, the judge can issue an arrest warrant. Figure 8.1 illustrates the various ways for compelling an accused person to appear in court.

APPEARANCE NOTICE

If the alleged offence is not serious and the police have no reason to believe that the accused will fail to appear in court, an appearance notice can be issued, followed by the laying of an information. The appearance notice sets out the details of the allegation against the accused person, provides the court date, and warns the accused

FIGURE 8.1 ►

Compelling the Appearance of the Accused

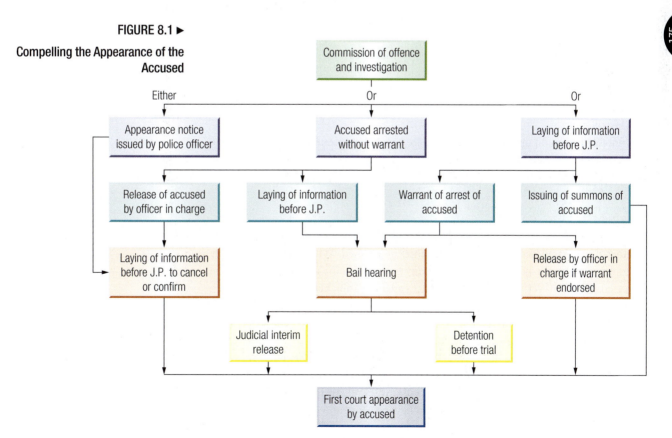

Source: Mewett, Alan W., and Mr. Justice Shaun Nakatsuru. 2001. *An Introduction to the Criminal Process in Canada,* 4e. (Toronto: Carswell), p. 72. Reproduced by permission of Carswell, a division of Thomson Reuters Canada Limited.

that failure to appear in court is a criminal offence. If the charge is an indictable or elective offence, the appearance notice directs the person to appear at a specific location to be fingerprinted, pursuant to the *Identification of Criminals Act*. If the suspect is a young person, the appearance notice emphasizes the right of accused youths to legal representation.

SUMMONS

Another option is for the police to lay the information first, in which case the JP will likely issue a summons, which briefly states the allegation and directs the person to appear in court on a certain day. The fingerprint demand is also made, where applicable, as is the statement about youths' right to counsel under the *Youth Criminal Justice Act*. The summons is then served on the accused, usually by a police officer. If the accused does not appear in court, and if there is proof that he received the summons, the judge may issue a bench warrant for his arrest; in addition, the accused may be charged criminally with failing to appear in court.

ARREST

If the situation dictates, the police can arrest without a warrant (see Chapter 5) and *then* lay the information. Or, if there is time, an officer may seek an arrest warrant from a JP. Following the arrest, the next decision to be made is whether to release the accused from police custody or keep him or her in custody. Remember that the *Charter* protects people from arbitrary detention. The presumption is that everyone will be released from police custody after arrest.

There are only three circumstances in which immediate release might *not* occur: (1) the charge pertains to a serious indictable offence carrying a maximum sentence of more than five years in prison, (2) the police have reasonable grounds to believe the person will not appear in court, or (3) the police have reasonable grounds to believe it is necessary, in the public interest, to detain the accused. The public interest is defined as the need to establish the person's identity, to secure or preserve evidence, or to prevent the continuation or repetition of the offence or the commission of another offence.

A notable exception involves situations where a person is arrested pursuant to a security certificate (discussed below).

RELEASE BY THE POLICE

When issuing an arrest warrant, the JP usually gives the police some direction as to whether the accused person should be detained or released. When an arrest is made without a warrant, the police have the authority to release some accused persons from police custody; however, in some circumstances a bail hearing before a JP or a judge is required. When the offence is summary or elective (or one of a specified list of less serious indictable offences, including theft under $5000), the arresting officer can simply issue an appearance notice or explain that a summons will be sought. In these circumstances, even those persons who have been arrested need not be placed in police custody.

For indictable offences carrying a maximum prison sentence of five years or less, the officer in charge of the police lockup has the authority to release the person from police custody. Several means are available to the officer in charge to compel the accused's later appearance in court. Beginning with the least consequential, they are a promise to appear, an undertaking to appear, and a recognizance not exceeding $500 (with or without deposit).

JUDICIAL INTERIM RELEASE (BAIL)

Judicial interim release (or bail)
The release by a judge or JP of a person who has been charged with a criminal offence pending a court appearance.

Judicial interim release (or bail) is the release of a person who has been charged with a criminal offence. It is overseen by a judicial functionary—usually a JP—but by a superior court judge if the offence is a serious one, such as murder. A person in police custody who is not released by the officer in charge must be brought to court within 24 hours or as soon as is reasonably possible. In addition, if the arrest warrant was issued by a JP, the police must bring the arrested person before a JP, unless release was authorized when the warrant was issued.

Persons can be detained by the court only in situations where it is necessary to ensure attendance in court, in order to protect the public, and to maintain confidence in the administration of justice. The JP or judge must determine whether the accused will be released or will remain in custody until the case is disposed of. Section 11(e) of the *Charter* stipulates that any person charged with an offence has the right "not to be denied reasonable bail without just cause." Section 515 of the *Criminal Code*, entitled "Judicial Interim Release," requires judges to release accused persons on bail unless the Crown can show why bail should be denied.

If the Crown chooses to oppose the release of the accused, the Crown must demonstrate, at a *show cause hearing*, that detention of the accused until the trial date is necessary. In support of the recommendation that the accused be held in custody, the Crown can produce evidence of prior criminal convictions, other charges currently before the courts, or previous instances of failing to appear in court. In some cases, *reverse onus* applies; in other words, the accused must show cause why a release is justified. These situations include when the alleged indictable offence occurred while the person was on bail for another charge. Detained persons seeking pre-trial release are often required to make multiple appearances in court before a ruling is made; overcrowded court dockets and a lack of personnel to participate in bail hearings are among the probable reasons for the delays.

Accused persons may also be asked to enter into a recognizance in which they agree to forfeit a set amount of money if they fail to appear in court. Generally, there is no requirement that the money be produced before the accused is released. However, a monetary deposit may be required if the accused is not normally a resident of the province or territory or lives more than 200 kilometres away.

Another option is to release the accused on a recognizance in which a *surety* promises to forfeit a set amount of money if the accused fails to appear in court. A surety is a friend or relative who agrees to ensure the accused person's appearance for trial. In most cases involving a surety, a deposit is not required. However, if a large sum of money is involved, the existence of collateral to guarantee the payment may have to be demonstrated. If a surety withdraws support, the accused will be placed in custody unless another surety is immediately available.

Research studies have found that the decision to grant bail is influenced by a number of factors, including the number of criminal charges pending, whether the accused has a fixed address, and any concerns raised by background information on the accused provided by the police, including prior criminal activity. Men appear to be denied bail more often than women. Some evidence suggests that when accused persons who are denied bail and are remanded into custody, it increases the likelihood that the accused will accept a plea bargain.[6,7]

Note that bail in Canada is different from the bail often seen on American television. In the United States, a deposit of money is required to guarantee a person's appearance in court; this practice is followed only in exceptional cases in Canada. In the United States, bounty hunters, on behalf of bail companies, will track persons who have skipped bail. Canadian courts are generally sensitive to the possibility that cash bail requirements could leave accused persons of modest means to languish in custody while their more affluent counterparts remain free while awaiting trial.

THE CONDITIONS OF BAIL

If the JP or judge decides to release the accused, the conditions under which that release will take place must be determined. Again, the Crown must show cause why conditions should be attached to the release. Bail has statutory and other conditions. Statutory conditions include reporting to a bail supervisor, while other conditions may include abstaining from alcohol or drugs, being under house arrest, or not having contact with certain persons. Young offenders may be required to live with a responsible person who agrees to guarantee that the youths will appear in court.

In some regions of the country, accused persons who are released on bail may be subject to bail supervision by probation officers or electronic monitoring (see Chapter 10). Accused persons who violate the conditions of release or who fail to appear in court at the designated time may have new charges filed against them for failing to comply. This offence carries a sentence of two years in jail if it is processed as an indictable offence.

There has been a trend toward increasing the number of bail conditions and the length of bail supervision, in part because of increasing concerns with risk aversion in the criminal justice system. This trend has led some observers to argue that persons on bail are being set up for failure and are at high risk of being charged for failing to comply.[8,9] There are specific concerns about persons on bail who have addiction or mental health challenges. A study by the John Howard Society of Ontario found that 70 percent of the persons on bail had substance abuse issues, and 40 percent had mental health issues, while 30 percent had concurrent challenges with both. The study found that abstaining from drugs and abstaining from alcohol were often imposed as conditions of bail and were closely related to failing to comply. As one lawyer commented: "The minute they don't comply, that's another offence. It's not a crime to drink alcohol but once it gets put into your bail conditions, drinking alcohol is an offence. It's an enormous pressure on people when they're on a long list of conditions."[10] In addition, considerable time and expense may be incurred by police services in re-arresting offenders who have violated the conditions of their bail release.

ASSESSING RISK

It important that decisions to grant bail be carefully considered to ensure that the accused will abide by the conditions of the release and does not present a risk to the community. The decision of prosecutors to release an accused person on bail can have devastating consequences. In 2007, Peter Lee went on a killing spree in Oak Bay, British Columbia, killing his wife, his six-year-old son, his in-laws, and, finally himself. Lee had previously attempted to kill his wife by driving his car, in which his wife was a passenger, into a pole. Over the express opposition of the police, Crown prosecutors allowed Lee to be released on $5000 bail, with the condition that he have no contact with his wife. Even though Lee began stalking his wife and violated other bail conditions, prosecutors did not have him arrested and he remained free to commit the murders.

In a subsequent corner's inquiry into the incident, it was requested that the prosecutors who did not oppose the decision to release Lee from police custody attend and speak to the inquiry. The provincial government refused to make the prosecutors available to testify. The decision was upheld by the B.C. Supreme Court, which held that forcing the prosecutors to testify would infringe on their professional independence. This case generated considerable controversy. It has been suggested that risk assessments be conducted on certain accused persons, particularly in cases involving domestic violence.[11]

THE CHANGING NATURE OF JUDICIAL INTERIM RELEASE

A number of legal scholars have argued that, as currently practised, judicial interim release is not being used as intended under the *Bail Reform Act* (1972). More specifically, critics contend rather than being the exception as envisioned by the *Bail Reform Act* (1972), the grounds for detention have been expanded. The has resulted in increasing number of accused persons being held in **remand**, despite falling crime rates (see Chapter 11). A concern is that the presumption of innocence, a cornerstone of the legal system, is being undermined and that the number of "legally innocent" persons in jail has been increasing.[12] The changes in how bail is used in the criminal courts has been ascribed, in part, to a punitive penology and to an increasing aversion to risk among criminal justice decision makers.[13]

The report on bail produced by the John Howard Society of Ontario found that "less people are being released on bail, less quickly, and with more conditions, during a time of historically low and still-declining crime rates."[14]

PRE-TRIAL REMAND

Persons are remanded into custody through the issuance of a warrant of committal by a JP or judge. Other accused are placed in custody after violating their release conditions. Remand admissions to provincial or territorial institutions, then, include accused persons who have been charged with an offence and ordered by the court to be held in custody until their court appearance. These individuals have not been sentenced to custody or to a community sanction; they are being held because it is feared they will not appear for court, may reoffend before their court date, or have not arranged bail. The challenges presented by offenders on remand are discussed in Chapter 11.

Accused persons who are remanded in custody still have the option of reapplying to the court for release before trial. In fact, all detention orders must be reviewed by a judge (after 90 days in the case of indictable offences) to determine whether continued detention is necessary. One of the options available to the judge is to order that the case be expedited (heard as soon as possible). More adults are now being held in custody awaiting trial or sentencing than there are adults in provincial or territorial sentenced custody (see Chapter 11). Up to 80 percent of some provincial jail populations are composed of persons on remand. This number increasingly includes women who are not serving sentences.[15]

SECURITY CERTIFICATES

Under the *Immigration and Refugee Protection Act*, **security certificates** can be issued against non-citizens (visitors, refugees, or permanent residents) in Canada who are deemed to pose a threat to national security. These persons can then be held in detention, without charge, for an indefinite time. The certificates must be signed by both the minister of citizenship and immigration and the minister of public safety and emergency preparedness. Note that security certificates are not a criminal proceeding but a process within the *Immigration and Refugee Protection Act*.

Foreign nationals who have a security certificate issued against them are automatically detained; permanent residents may also be detained if it is determined that they

Remand

The status of accused persons in custody awaiting trial or sentencing.

Security certificates

A process whereby non-Canadian citizens who are deemed to be a threat to the security of the country can be held without charge for an indefinite time.

are a danger to society or are likely not to appear for court proceedings. Otherwise, permanent residents can be released under strict bail conditions. A security certificate allows indefinite detention without charge or trial. The government is required only to provide a summary of the case against the person who is subjected to a security certificate. Case proceedings are usually conducted in secret. The reasonableness of the security certificate is reviewed by a judge of the Federal Court. If the court upholds the security certificate, it becomes a removal order from Canada, and the person is deported to his or her home country. The Federal Court's decision in cases involving security certificates is final and cannot be reviewed.

Security certificates have been part of the *Immigration and Refugee Protection Act* since 1978, but it is only since the terrorist attacks on the United States on September 11, 2001, that this process has generated controversy. Since that date, 27 security certificates been issued for individuals who were deemed to pose a security threat to Canada. Among the cases were the following:

- Adil Charkaoui, from Morocco, was identified as an al-Qaeda sleeper agent by the Canadian Security Intelligence Service (CSIS) and determined to be a threat to the security of Canada. He was arrested in 2003 and held in detention until 2005, when he was released under bail conditions that included electronic monitoring. The Federal Court of Appeal dismissed his challenges to the security certificate process; however, in 2005, the Supreme Court of Canada agreed to hear his appeal, which centred on the constitutionality of security certificates. In 2007, the Court determined that the security certificate law was unconstitutional and directed the federal government to rewrite the legislation to ensure that citizen's rights under the charter of rights and freedoms were protected. In 2009, a Federal Court judge dismissed the case against Charkaoui and halted efforts to deport him after the federal government refused to disclose intelligence information on the case.

- Mohamed Mahjoub arrived in Canada in 1996 using a forged passport. He was arrested as a security threat in the year 2000 and placed under a security certificate. Security officials produced evidence that he had contact with individuals and organizations involved in terrorist activities but did not present detailed information. In 2013, the Federal Court upheld the security certificate against Mahjoub, even though it found that the government had violated his constitutional rights. The federal government is attempting to deport him to Egypt.

- Mohamed Harkat, an Algerian refugee, was arrested on a security certificate in 2002. In 2013, his lawyers appeared before the SCC to argue that the process violates the *Charter* because it requires very little evidence about the allegations that a person poses a security threat to Canada. The SCC heard the case behind closed doors and a ruling is pending as of early 2014.

Amnesty International and other human rights groups have argued that the security certificate process violates fundamental human rights, including the right to a fair trial and the right to protection against arbitrary detention. Of concern is that much of the evidence in security certificate cases is heard *in camera* (behind closed doors), with only the Federal Court judge and government lawyers and witnesses present. Although persons who have been detained receive a summary of a portion of the evidence, the specific allegations against them and the sources of the allegations are not disclosed to them. As well, evidence against the detainee may be presented in court without the detainee and his or her lawyer being present, which precludes a cross-examination of witnesses.

The ongoing controversy surrounding security certificates highlights the continual challenge of balancing individual rights with those of society. The debate is likely to continue.

DEFENDANTS' ACCESS TO LEGAL REPRESENTATION

All adults accused of crimes have the right to retain legal counsel. The *Charter of Rights and Freedoms* stipulates that persons who are arrested and detained must be informed of this fact; and they must be permitted to contact a lawyer before giving a statement, if they so choose. The right to retain legal counsel levels the playing field, so to speak, between the accused and the police and Crown attorney. Most Canadians are unaware of their rights or the intricacies of this country's complex legal system. In our adversarial system, the police and prosecution enjoy the home field advantage, and the lawyer is on the defendant's team.

Most accused persons require legal representation, yet not all of them can afford a lawyer. There is no blanket right to state-paid legal representation. At arrest, the police officer recites this *Charter* warning: "It is my duty to inform you that you have the right to retain and instruct counsel without delay" (see Box 5.1). The right to *retain* counsel, however, does not impose an absolute duty on provincial or territorial governments to provide all accused persons with *free* counsel (see the discussion of legal aid below). However, all persons who are arrested or detained must have the opportunity to access preliminary advice from duty counsel through a toll-free telephone line, where such services exist. According to the Supreme Court of Canada (*R. v. Prosper*, [1994] 3 SCR 236), detainees must be told they may qualify for free counsel if they meet the financial criteria of the local legal aid plan. However, the Supreme Court has also ruled that impoverished persons do not have a blanket right to legal counsel and that it was within the authority of the provincial and territorial governments to determine guidelines and criteria (*British Columbia (Attorney General) v. Christie*, [2007] 1 SCR 873).

A major challenge in the territories is ensuring that accused persons have representation before their first appearance. Representation is often done over the telephone and is often of poor quality.[16]

LEGAL AID FOR THE ACCUSED

Clearly, it would be unacceptable for wealthy criminal defendants to have lawyers while poor defendants go unrepresented. At the same time, the universal provision of free legal representation would be expensive. There are also concerns about whether free representation can be as good as representation paid for by the accused.

Although every province and territory has a legal aid plan, they vary greatly with respect to which types of cases qualify for assistance and which income levels are sufficiently low that an applicant is entitled to full or partial coverage. In recent years, several provinces have lowered the qualifying income levels as one means of stemming the dramatic rise in legal aid costs. Also, some types of cases no longer qualify for legal aid. It is not uncommon, for example, for applicants to be required to demonstrate that they face the very real prospect of being incarcerated for the offence. The stringent requirements to qualify for legal aid have been identified as a major impediment to access to justice.[17]

Across the country, legal aid services are delivered by lawyers in private practice who are paid through a legal aid plan, by legal aid staff lawyers, and by lawyers working in legal aid. These services include duty counsel services in provincial courthouses. Note that lawyers are not required to take legal aid cases.

The three models for the delivery of legal aid services by the provinces and territories are set out in Table 8.1.

TABLE 8.1	MODELS OF LEGAL AID SERVICES
Model	**Features**
Judicare	Historically the most common; accused persons who qualify for a legal aid certificate retain a private lawyer who bills the legal aid plan for services rendered.
Legal aid clinic	Salaried lawyers provide services through a clinic; generally less expensive than the judicare model; becoming more common in an attempt to reduce costs; used in Ontario; may be geographically centred (e.g., Westend Legal Services in Ottawa), culturally centred (e.g., Aboriginal Peoples Legal Clinic in Toronto), and problem based (e.g., family law clinic).
Mixed	Both private and legal aid staff lawyers provide legal services.

Source: Adapted from Attorney General of Ontario. 2010. "The Choice of Delivery Models for Legal Aid." Accessed March 2, 2014. http://www.attorneygeneral.jus.gov.on.ca/english/about/pubs/olar/ch7.asp.

A widely documented crisis in legal aid is occurring in Canada, including underfunding, disparities in coverage, fragmentation wherein a client may only qualify for legal aid for a portion of their legal problem, and a lack of access to legal aid services among marginalized groups, including Aboriginal peoples, newcomers, the poor, and others.[18] In the words of a prominent Toronto defence lawyer: "Most poor people never get anywhere near legal aid."[19] This lack of aid is a major issue in the larger debate over access to justice and the concern over the increasing number of persons in criminal courts who are self-represented.

FITNESS TO STAND TRIAL

A fundamental principle of the common law is that the accused person must be fit to stand trial. During the early stages of the court process, a lawyer may suspect that his or her client is suffering from some degree of mental illness. The existence of a mental disorder at the time of the offence may be integral to the defence strategy. However, mental disorder is a concern for another reason: accused persons who cannot understand the objective and consequences of the proceedings because of mental disorder are unfit to stand trial. In other words, they are unable to instruct their counsel or even fully appreciate that they are on trial.

At the request of the defence counsel or on its own initiative, the court may order that the accused person be assessed to determine fitness. That order is normally in force for no more than five working days, but a longer period can be ordered in "compelling circumstances." Section 2 of the *Criminal Code* states that an offender is unfit to stand trial when it is determined by the court that he or she is

> Unable on account of mental disorder to conduct a defence at any stage of proceedings before a verdict is rendered or to instruct counsel to do so, and, in particular, unable on account of mental disorder to (a) understand the nature or object of the proceedings, (b) understand the possible consequences of the proceedings, or (c) communicate with counsel.

Almost always, the fitness of an accused person to stand trial is assessed by a psychiatrist while the accused is either remanded in custody or at a hospital or psychiatric facility. Those found unfit to stand trial may be detained in a mental health facility until deemed fit to stand trial by a body, such as the Ontario Review Board. Once the accused is found fit, the trial can resume. If a person never achieves a state of fitness, the Crown may conclude that it is no longer prudent to continue the criminal prosecution.

In cases where the alleged offence is not serious, an accused who is found to be unfit to stand trial may simply be diverted into the provincial or territorial mental health system.

Persons who are found fit to stand trial may still use the defence of not criminally responsible on account of mental disorder (NCRMD; discussed below). As Canadian criminologist Simon Verdun-Jones has noted, "the mere fact that an accused person was mentally disordered at the time of the alleged offence does not automatically excuse him or her from criminal responsibility."[20]

ASSIGNMENT AND PLEA

The arraignment of the accused takes place early in the process, if not at first appearance. The charges are read in open court, and the accused can enter a plea. The two most common pleas are guilty and not guilty. If a plea of guilty is entered, the case goes directly to sentencing (see Chapter 9); a plea of not guilty results in the case being bound over for trial. Technically, every accused person—even those who are guilty—can plead not guilty. Remember that in our adversarial system of justice, all accused persons are presumed innocent and the onus is on the Crown to prove guilt. Pleading not guilty, therefore, is not the same as claiming innocence.

Accused persons may plead not guilty because they are, in fact, innocent; because they have a plausible defence and want to exercise their right to a trial; or because their lawyer has advised them to do so. Although most cases end with a guilty plea, they do not always begin that way. Accused persons often plead not guilty at the outset of the process, in part to strengthen their position in any plea bargaining that may take place. Accused who pleads not guilty can change their plea to guilty at any point before the verdict.

PLEA BARGAINING

"In the halls of justice, the only justice is in the halls."

—Lenny Bruce, comedian

Logically, it would seem to be to a defendant's advantage to take a chance and go to trial, in the hope that incriminating evidence will be declared inadmissible or a key witness will become unavailable. However, the court system would be overwhelmed if the majority of cases went to trial. This overload is one justification for plea bargaining—a controversial but pervasive practice that is not written in law or policy.

Plea bargaining

An agreement whereby an accused pleads guilty in exchange for the promise of a benefit.

What is **plea bargaining**? Simply put, it is an agreement in which an accused gives up the right to make the Crown prove the case at trial in exchange for the promise of a benefit. For example, the Crown can promise the possibility of a lower sentence by withdrawing some charges, by reducing a charge to a *lesser but included offence* (that is, an offence that is similar but not as serious), by proceeding summarily rather than with an indictment, by asking the judge that multiple prison sentences run concurrently rather than consecutively, or by agreeing to a joint submission to the judge about sentencing. In addition (see Chapter 9), there is a pervasive belief—which may well be true—in the existence of a guilty plea "discount": that is, a defendant who pleads guilty can expect a lower sentence than if convicted after trial.

Historically, plea bargaining was felt not to have a role in the criminal justice process. The Law Reform Commission concluded that plea bargaining was "contrary to the whole notion of justice" and should be eliminated.[21] However, 20 years later, in *R. v. Burlingham*, [1995]2 SCR 206, the Supreme Court of Canada endorsed plea bargaining as an indispensable, integral part of the criminal justice process, stating, "To the extent that the plea bargain is an integral element of the Canadian criminal process, the Crown and its officers engaged in the plea bargaining process must act honourably and forthrightly."[22] The reasons that plea bargaining changed from pariah to accepted practice remain to be explored by Canadian scholars.

What follows is a description of the Cave—a cramped, windowless room in a Scarborough, Ontario, courthouse and the site of plea negotiations:

> The Cave exists for one purpose—for prosecutors to cut deals with defence lawyers and generally hasten cases. A circus-like atmosphere prevails in the main corridor directly outside the Cave. Police, lawyers, defendants and their families compete for standing space and wait for these cases to be called. The Cave door is almost always open, revealing two prosecutors who sit like expectant shopkeepers. Periodically, a defence lawyer or duty counsel ventures in to sound out a prosecutor about a particular case. The prosecutor may or may not end up having carriage of the case, but he or she can offer an informal view of what a fair plea bargain might involve.[23]

CRIME VICTIMS AND PLEA NEGOTIATION

Although crime victims are increasingly involved in sentencing hearings and parole hearings, less attention has been given to the potential role of crime victims in the plea negotiation process. Canadian criminologists Verdun-Jones and Tijerino argue that giving crime victims the right to participate in plea negotiations has a number of benefits.[24] For example, victims can provide the Crown with information about the incident; they may emerge more satisfied with the criminal justice process; and the opportunity to participate in the plea negotiation process may help them heal.

Plea negotiations do have a number of potential benefits for crime victims. A guilty plea by the accused spares the victim the trauma of testifying in court, ensures that the case does not drag on for months or years, and eliminates the uncertainty over the final verdict of the judge or jury. The existing guidelines, policies, and laws encourage prosecutors to ascertain the views of victims and to inform them of the outcome of plea negotiations. The final responsibility for assessing the appropriateness of a plea agreement rests with Crown counsel, although ultimate jurisdiction for the outcome of the case still resides in the court. In Manitoba, crime victim legislation requires Crown counsel to consult with crime victims regarding any plea negotiation. Legislation introduced by the federal government in 2013 would give crime victims a role in the plea negotiation process (see Chapter 3).

JUDGES AND PLEA BARGAINING

Judge may experience frustration with the plea bargaining process. One Ontario provincial court judge stated: "Pre-trial negotiations are fine when they are properly conducted. But my problem is that I question how many of them are properly conducted. And even if they are properly conducted, half the time I'm not told on the record why the lawyers came to the agreement they did. Justice is becoming less and less visible."[25] Among the provisions of section 606 of the *Criminal Code* are that the trial judge must determine that the guilty plea has been entered into voluntarily and that the accused understands the nature and consequences of the plea.

In one case, the Nova Scotia Supreme Court overturned the decision of a provincial court trial judge not to accept a joint recommendation (plea bargain) for the sentencing of a sex offender submitted by Crown and defence counsel (R. v. Hamm, [2005]230 NSR (2nd) 41). The trial judge declined to accept the proposed sentence

184

of house arrest (conditional sentence) for nine months, followed by three years' probation, noting the premeditated nature of the offence and the fact that the assaults on the 13-year-old victim occurred over several months. The trial judge instead sentenced the offender to seven months in jail, to be followed by three years' probation. The Supreme Court judge, in reversing the trial judge's decision and imposing the sentence recommended by the Crown and defence, stated that the judge had erred in not giving counsel notice that he was not going to accept the proposed sentence and that he had not provided sufficient reasons for not accepting the joint recommendation. While not common, it is possible for the provincial attorney generals to revoke a plea bargain if the agreement was not in the best interests of the administration of justice.

In the case of *R. v. Nixon*, [2011] SCR 566, the SCC has held that plea bargain agreements between Crown and defence are not binding. Olga Nixon had driven her motor home through an intersection and struck another vehicle, killing a husband and wife and injuring their young son. Among the charges laid against her by Crown were dangerous driving causing death. The Crown and the defence lawyer reached a plea bargain under which Nixon would plead guilty to a charge of careless driving under the provincial *Traffic Safety Act* and be fined $1800. On further consideration, the Crown repudiated the agreement and proceeded to trial on the original charges. Nixon appealed, alleging abuse of process under sec. 7 of the *Charter*. In its ruling, the SCC stated that "the repudiation of a plea agreement was a matter of prosecutorial discretion not review by the courts, subject to the doctrine of abuse of process." Abuse of process would occur in instances in which the conduct of the Crown compromised the fairness of the trial or undermined the integrity of the judicial process. Neither was found to have occurred in the Nixon case.

The majority of cases that come to the criminal court are resolved not in a courtroom but in behind-the-scenes negotiations between Crown counsel and defence lawyers. Plea bargaining (or negotiations) is a fixture in the Canadian criminal justice system even though there is no mention of plea bargaining in the *Criminal Code* and no federal or provincial/territorial legislation or guidelines exist to regulate this practice. See At Issue 8.1.

AT ISSUE 8.1 SHOULD PLEA BARGAINING BE ABOLISHED OR AT LEAST REGULATED?

Supporters of plea bargaining argue that it has the following important functions:

- Plea bargaining saves time and taxpayers' money by encouraging guilty pleas.
- It reduces the backlog of cases.
- It spares complainants the difficult task of testifying.
- It helps offenders take responsibility for their crimes by admitting guilt.
- It does not compromise the administration of justice.
- It provides an opportunity to get evidence against co-defendants or others that might not otherwise be available to the police or Crown.

Detractors counter that plea bargaining has it downsides:

- Plea bargaining brings the administration of justice into disrepute.

- It does not follow any policy or guidelines and is therefore subject to abuse.
- It places pressure on innocent defendants to "cop a plea" to avoid being found guilty at trial and receiving a more severe sentence.
- It places pressure on persons who committed the offence to plead guilty.
- It is a closed process that is not subject to public scrutiny and threatens the rights of accused persons.

QUESTIONS

What arguments do you find most persuasive? What is your view on the practice of plea bargaining?

185

DISCLOSURE OF EVIDENCE

Understanding the strength of the Crown's case helps an accused person and his or her lawyer decide on a plea. Early in the process, the Crown must give the defence lawyer access to all evidence that might be presented by the prosecution in a trial, especially any potentially *exculpatory evidence* (evidence that might indicate the accused did not commit the crime). This process is called *disclosure of evidence* or *discovery* and includes, among other materials, the names and addresses of persons the Crown intends to call as witnesses, the results of any examinations or tests on the accused, materials from wiretaps and surveillance, and the names of expert witnesses that the Crown intends to call. The failure to disclose evidence can trigger a *Charter* remedy because it impairs an accused person's right to make full answer and defence to the charges. However, the disclosure requirement does not work in reverse: the defence is not obliged to disclose material to the prosecution. The increasing requirements of disclosure have placed an added resource burden on police services, who may spend as much time preparing documents related to the investigation as in the investigation itself (see Chapter 4).

THE TRIAL

As discussed in Chapter 7, the trier of fact in a criminal case—usually a judge—decides whether the guilt of the accused person has been proven beyond a reasonable doubt. In a small number of cases, a jury of citizens makes this decision. Jury trials are not available for summary conviction offences; nor, with a handful of exceptions, are they available in youth court. The flow of cases through the court system is depicted in Figure 8.2.

A trial takes place if the accused person who pleads not guilty does not change that plea and the Crown does not withdraw the charges or terminate the matter with a **stay of proceedings**. Especially in provinces or territories where the police have sole responsibility for laying charges, a Crown attorney may review cases early in the process and screen out those that might not succeed, as well as those for which there is insufficient evidence to secure a conviction. Because of this practice of case screening, and guilty pleas on the part of accused persons, most cases do not go to trial. Trials are actually quite rare, occurring in only about 10 percent of criminal cases.[26] The majority of cases are resolved via plea bargaining or by the Crown council staying the proceedings or withdrawing the charges.

Stay of proceedings
An act by the Crown to terminate or suspend court proceedings after they have commenced.

CLOSED COURTROOMS

It is a fundamental principle of justice that trials must be public. Only rarely will a judge agree to exclude all or any members of the public from the courtroom for all or part of the proceedings. To eliminate or reduce the number of observers, the judge must be convinced that it is in the interests of public morals, the maintenance of order, or the proper administration of justice.

There are no limitations as to the types of cases from which the public may be excluded. However, the issue usually arises when a crime victim or witness is apprehensive about testifying in front of people—a common occurrence with sexual crimes. Potential embarrassment on the part of the victim is insufficient reason to clear a

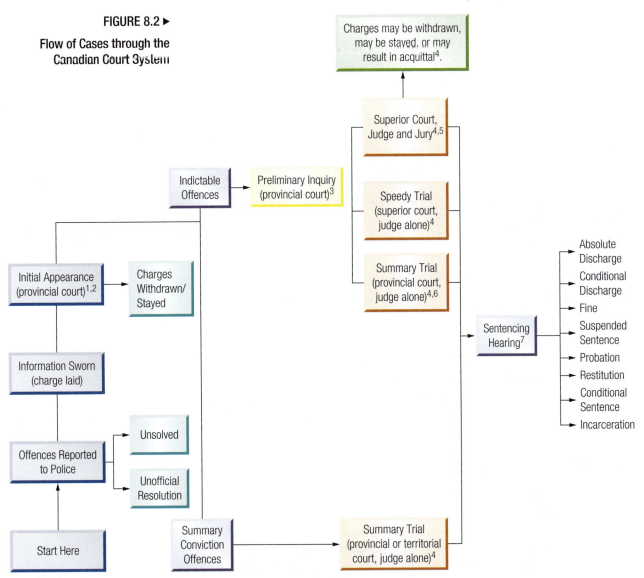

FIGURE 8.2 ▶

Flow of Cases through the Canadian Court System

[1] Appearance compelled by summons, arrest, or appearance notice.

[2] Initial sorting and judicial interim release (bail) are dealt with; election as to mode of trial may occur here or at a later hearing.

[3] Bypassed redirect indictment by the Crown, for offences within the absolute jurisdiction of the provincial or territorial court (s.483), and where accused elects a summary trial.

[4] Charges may be withdrawn, may be stayed, or may result in an acquittal in any mode of trial.

[5] This is the only mode of trial for more serious offences (s.427).

[6] This is the only mode of trial for less serious offences (s.483).

[7] Not all dispositions are available regarding all offences.

courtroom. It must be demonstrated that the witness could not relate the full details of the offence, perhaps because of extreme fear or the stress of a crowded courtroom. The primary concern is not with protecting the emotional well-being of the witness but rather with ensuring that justice is done. If fear or stress on the part of the victim were to result in incomplete testimony, the proper administration of justice would be compromised. The applicant—usually the prosecutor—must prove that public exclusion is necessary.

PUBLICATION BANS

In trials involving certain offences, the judge can order that the identity of the complainant or of a witness and any information that could disclose the identity of the complainant or of a witness will not be published in any document or broadcast in any way. This rule applies when the case involves incest, extortion, a sexual assault, a sexual offence involving children, or what is commonly called loan sharking. The name of the accused may be included in the ban if release of the name would identify the victim. If requested by the prosecutor, the ban is mandatory. If the prosecutor has forgotten to ask, the judge must inform the victim, or any witness under 18, of the right to make such a request. It is a summary conviction offence to contravene a publication ban.

"**Your Honor, the relevance of this line of questioning will become apparent in a moment.**"

"RAPE SHIELD" PROVISIONS

The term *rape shield* (an ill-chosen label) refers to the admissibility of evidence about a sexual assault victim's sexual history (with people other than the accused). Since their enactment in 1976, these contentious provisions have received intense judicial scrutiny and have been modified several times. In 2000, the SCC in *R. v. Darrach*, [2000]2 SCR 443, upheld the constitutionality of the *Criminal Code*'s rape shield provisions. Generally, these provisions make the sexual history of the victim inadmissible as evidence in court when defendants want to show that the complainant was more likely to have consented to the alleged offence or is less worthy of belief. The restriction is not absolute, and defendants can argue that the information is necessary for their defence.

188

THE CASE FOR THE CROWN

The trial begins with the prosecution calling witnesses and presenting evidence in support of the position that the accused is guilty. For interpersonal offences, the testimony of the complainant may well be the Crown's key evidence. At the very least, the Crown attorney must produce evidence covering all the major elements of the offence. For example, in a murder case the Crown must show that someone died and that the death was culpable homicide (that is, not an accident or death by natural causes). There should be evidence linking the accused to that death (e.g., eyewitnesses, fingerprints, DNA evidence, or circumstantial evidence, such as a strong motive on the part of the accused). Expert witnesses may be called to interpret evidence or to present findings from the police investigation.

It is the task of the Crown to prove the guilt of an accused person beyond a reasonable doubt; if the Crown fails to do this, there can be no conviction.

THE CASE FOR THE DEFENCE

The defence attorney can cross-examine Crown witnesses and challenge the admissibility of Crown evidence. At the close of the Crown's case, the defence may enter either an insufficient-evidence motion or a no-evidence motion, suggesting to the judge that the state has not made its case and that there is no point to continuing the trial. If the judge agrees, the case is dismissed. If not, the defence presents its case.

As part of the case for the defence, the accused person may testify (give evidence) on his or her own behalf but is not obliged to do so. For accused persons who testify in court, there are advantages and disadvantages. On the one hand, testifying gives defendants an opportunity to present their side of the story and establish credibility. On the other hand, a defendant who testifies opens the door to cross-examination by the Crown prosecutor, who will attempt to point out weaknesses and inconsistencies in the testimony. In addition, if the defendant presents good character or reputation as a reason why he or she could not have committed the offence, the prosecution is free to enter into evidence any previous convictions. Otherwise, the jury or judge cannot learn if the accused has a prior criminal record (at least until the sentencing phase, if the defendant is found guilty).

An accused acting as his or her own counsel is not usually permitted to cross-examine a witness under 14 in cases involving sexual offences or violent crimes. The court will appoint a lawyer to undertake that task. The judge has discretion and can permit an unrepresented defendant to conduct the cross-examination if the proper administration of justice requires it.

An in-depth discussion of the myriad defences available to accused persons is beyond the scope of this text. We can, however, highlight several of the more common defences that are used in the criminal court process. These can be generally grouped into (1) "you've got the wrong person," (2) the mental state of the accused at the time the alleged offence occurred, (3) justifications (or excuses) for having committed a criminal act, and (4) procedural defences.

THE "YOU'VE GOT THE WRONG PERSON" DEFENCE

This defence strategy centres on one of two possibilities: that the police arrested the wrong person or that the complainant fabricated the allegation, thus no crime was committed. To support a claim of false accusation, the defence may present evidence verifying the defendant's alibi. One example of a verified alibi is establishing that the defendant was in jail when the offence was committed.

THE MENTAL STATE OF THE ACCUSED AT THE TIME OF THE ALLEGED OFFENCE

The three most common defences focusing on the mental state of the accused at the time of the alleged offence are (1) mental disorder (NCRMD), (2) intoxication, and (3) automatism.

NOT CRIMINALLY RESPONSIBLE ON ACCOUNT OF MENTAL DISORDER (NCRMD)

Not criminally responsible on account of mental disorder (NCRMD)

A defence that the accused person is not responsible for an act because of his or her mental state at the time.

Accused persons who are found fit to stand trial may use the defence of **not criminally responsible on account of mental disorder (NCRMD)**. This defence is contained in section 16 of the *Criminal Code*.

An assessment ordered by the court is used to determine this verdict, which is not a finding of guilt or a conviction for the offence. The accused person is determined not to have been responsible for his or her behaviour at the time the offence was committed. The court has a number of option for persons determined to be NCRMD: detention in a hospital, a conditional discharge, or an absolute discharge.[27] Verdun-Jones cautions that NCRMD is not a true defence, as a verdict of NCRMD is not that the accused didn't commit the offence but that the defendant is not criminally responsible for the act because of his or her mental state at the time.[28] This defence was used in a case that involved the death of a Toronto Police officer.

On January 12, 2011, Toronto Police Service Sgt. Ryan Russell responded to a call of a stolen snowplow careening through the streets, smashing cars and causing property damage. Sgt. Russell was the first officer to arrive on the scene. As he approached the snowplow, it suddenly turned and headed straight toward him. Russell fired three shots from his service revolver, but the snowplow continued and ran over the officer, who later died in hospital. The driver of the snowplow was 45-year-old Richard Kachkar, a man with a history of mental illness. His lawyer used the defence of NCRMD, and after a seven-week trial, the jury found him NCRMD. Accepting a joint submission of the Crown and defence, Kachkar was ordered detained at a secure forensic unit. His case will be subject to an annual review.

▲ Toronto Police Service Sgt. Ryan Russell

The NCRMD defence was also used in a high-profile case involving a gruesome crime committed on a Greyhound bus. In July 2008, Vincent Li, a passenger on a Greyhound bus travelling through Manitoba, attacked a fellow passenger, stabbing him to death, decapitating him, and cannibalizing part of the victim's body. Li was charged with second-degree murder and pled not guilty. The defence counsel argued that Li was not criminally responsible for his actions because of mental illness. At trial, evidence was presented by a forensic psychiatrist that Li was a schizophrenic and suffered a major psychotic episode that led to the killing. Li had told the psychiatrist that God had told him that the victim was a force of evil who was about to stab Li unless he took action to protect himself. Testimony from the psychiatrist was that Li was not capable of understanding that his actions were wrong.

▲ Richard Kachkar

Both Crown and defence argued that Li was not criminally responsible because of his mental illness, and the presiding judge agreed. Li was sent to a provincial psychiatric facility and placed under the authority of a provincial review board, which will determine how long he remains in the facility. The case stirred considerable controversy when, in 2013, the Manitoba Review Board accepted the recommendation from Li's mental health treatment team that he be allowed to have supervised excursions into Winnipeg and surrounding areas.[29] In early 2014, the review board granted Li unescorted trips from the mental hospital into the community of Selkirk, Manitoba.[30] A federal cabinet minister from Manitoba criticized the provincial Crown attorney for not appealing the decision of the board, although the Crown does not have the authority to intervene in the decisions of the review board.[31]

Another high-profile case was that of Allan Schoenborn who killed his three children in 2008 in British Columbia, was found NCRMD, and sent to a forensic facility.

Persons who are found NCRMD are subjected to annual reviews by provincial review boards and may qualify for escorted and unescorted passes into the community. Historically, the victim's families were not notified of decisions made by the review boards. The outcry from the victim's families in these and other cases, along with high exposure in the media, prompted the federal government in 2013 to propose Bill C-54. This legislation would have designated persons found NCRMD as high risk, allowed them to be held for longer periods without review, and made it difficult for them to leave a secure forensic facility even under escort. But the bill did not become law.

AUTOMATISM

In what is considered the landmark ruling on the defence of automatism in *R. v. Stone*, [1999] 2 SCR 290, a justice of the SCC defined automatism as "a state of impaired consciousness . . . in which an individual, though capable of action, has no voluntary control over that action."

In 1987 a Toronto-area man drove across town, fatally stabbed his mother-in-law, and promptly turned himself in to the police, confessing repeatedly to the crime. Despite overwhelming evidence that he had killed the woman, he was acquitted at trial. The jury accepted the defence evidence that the man had been sleepwalking and therefore could not have formed the requisite *mens rea*.

The defence of automatism does not always result in an outright acquittal. In 1996, Calgary socialite Dorothy Joudrie was tried for the attempted murder of her estranged husband to whom she had been married for 39 years. The evidence was clear that she had shot him six times (he survived to testify as a Crown witness). Her defence was non-insane automatism. She claimed that she had no memory of the offence and that she had been in a dissociative or automatonic state brought about by years of mental and physical abuse at the hands of her husband, as well as by his leaving her for another woman. Had Joudrie's defence succeeded (like that of the sleepwalker), she would have walked out of the court a free woman. However, the jury—possibly believing that she was suffering from the so-called insane automatism—handed down a finding of NCRMD. See *R. v. Fontaine*, [2004]1 SCR 702, for a more recent case involving mental disorder automatism.

INTOXICATION

Some of the most controversial defences relate to the argument that the accused is not criminally liable because he or she could not have formed *mens rea*. This mental state could have been temporary and situational or the result of a long-term mental disorder. To convict in most cases, the judge or jury must believe that the action under scrutiny—the *actus reus*—was a voluntary exercise of the person's will. In a 1994 decision, the Supreme Court of Canada found a man not guilty of raping a woman because he had been so intoxicated that his actions were not voluntary (*R. v. Daviault*, [1994]3 SCR 63). This decision triggered a public outcry, and the federal government responded by amending the *Criminal Code* to specify that self-induced intoxication cannot be used to excuse certain types of interpersonal offences, including assault and sexual assault, even if *mens rea* is absent.

JUSTIFICATIONS: EXCUSE-BASED DEFENCES

The second set of defence strategies can be categorized as excuse-based defences. These are set out in Figure 8.3.

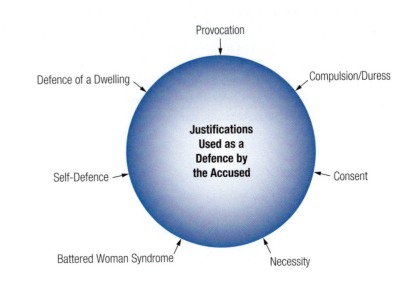

FIGURE 8.3 ▶

Justifications Used as a Defence by the Accused

A full discussion of each of these defences could consume an entire text ,[32] so here only a limited comment is made. For SCC cases involving excuse-based defences, see *R. v. Ryan* (2013), SCC 3.

PROVOCATION

The defence of provocation is often associated with claims of self-defence. Persons charged with murder can claim provocation to justify a reduction to the charge of man-slaughter (here, provocation is a partial defence). In recent years, the courts have heard a number of these cases, and the decisions seem to turn on the specific events. Critics claim that the SCC has placed restrictions on the right of accused to use provocation as a defence. In *R. v. Cairney*, (2013) SCC 55, the SCC rejected Mr. Cairney's defence that he was provoked into killing Stephen Ferguson, who was extremely abusive toward Mr. Cariney's cousin over a long period. On one occasion, Mr. Cariney had witnessed Mr. Ferguson kneel on his cousin's throat and threaten to kill her. Mr. Cairney argued at trial that knowing and witnessing the abuse for over decade had caused him to lose control and shoot Mr. Ferguson.

CONSENT

The defence of consent is based on the argument that the complainant voluntarily agreed to engage in the activity in question. A common example: two individuals can consent to a fistfight if both parties appreciate the risks and neither is seriously injured. However, lack of resistance to an assault or a sexual assault does not con-stitute consent if the submission of the complainant was achieved by force, threats, fraud, or the exercise of authority. An example of this last is where there is a clear power imbalance, as in the case of teacher–student, doctor–patient, or parent–child relationships.

Consent can be real, or it can be apprehended if the accused mistakenly believed that a non-consenting complainant consented. In the past, some accused persons were able to argue successfully that they honestly believed the complainant was consenting to sexual activity—that no meant yes. Parliament has responded by restricting the use of consent as a defence for sexual offences. Since 1988, for example, consent has not been available as a defence if the complainant was under 14 at the time of the offence.

In 1992, the "no means no" law (amendments to the *Criminal Code*) was enacted. If a sexual assault complainant expresses "by words or conduct, a lack of agreement to engage in the activity," consent to the activity is deemed not to have been obtained. Neither can consent be used as a defence if "the complainant, having consented to the sexual activity, expresses, by words or conduct, a lack of agreement to continue to engage in the activity." Also, consent cannot be voluntarily given by someone who is induced to engage in the activity with a person who is abusing a position of trust, power, or authority. Nor is apprehended consent a defence to a sexual assault if the accused person's belief in consent arose from self-induced intoxication or reckless or willful disregard, or if the accused did not take reasonable steps to ascertain whether the com-plainant was, in fact, consenting.

BATTERED WOMAN SYNDROME

Experienced by women who have suffered chronic and severe abuse, battered woman syndrome (BWS) is a condition characterized by feelings of social isolation, worth-lessness, anxiety, depression, and low self-esteem. In the landmark case *R. v. Lavallee*, [1990]1 SCR 852, the Supreme Court of Canada accepted BWS as a defence, and it has since been used successfully in subsequent cases.[33]

In *R. v. Malott*, [1998]1 SCR 123, the Supreme Court of Canada dismissed the appeal of a woman who had been convicted of killing her abusive husband and who had used BWS as a defence at her trial. In its judgment, the SCC stated that the trial judge had properly informed the jury with respect to the evidence on BWS and how such evidence related to the law of self-defence. The court further noted, "'Battered woman syndrome' is not a legal defence in itself, but rather is a psychiatric explanation of the mental state of an abused woman which can be relevant to understanding a battered woman's state of mind."

PROCEDURAL DEFENCES

This category of defence strategies focuses not on the guilt or innocence of the accused but rather on the conduct of the police or prosecution or perhaps the validity of the law itself. In common parlance, this is known as *getting off on a technicality*. The judge can rule on most of these issues before the trial even starts, but *Charter* arguments can sidetrack a trial until the issue is resolved.

Procedural defences fall roughly into four categories:

- *Challenging the validity of the applicable law.* Some successful procedural defences have attacked the constitutionality of the law used to charge the accused.

- *Challenging the validity of the prosecution.* Another strategy is to claim that the police or prosecutors acted unfairly in the investigation or charging of the accused. Entrapment and abuse of process (discussed in Chapter 5) are two examples of unfair conduct.

- *Contesting the admissibility of evidence gathered by the police.* If key evidence is excluded, not enough evidence may remain to prove guilt beyond a reasonable doubt. As noted in Chapter 5, a confession gained after an unlawful arrest may be ruled inadmissible if its use would bring the system of justice into disrepute.

- *Seeking a remedy for violation of a* Charter *right.* In extreme circumstances, the violation of an accused person's *Charter* rights can be remedied by the termination of the prosecution. There have been cases in which the *Charter* right to trial within a reasonable time was violated and a stay of proceedings was ordered by the presiding judge.

THE JURY

The right of an accused to have a trial by jury is set out in section 11(f) of the *Charter of Rights and Freedoms* and states, "Any person charged with an offence has the right except in the case of an offence under military law tried before a military tribunal, to the benefit of trial by jury where the maximum punishment for the offence is imprisonment for five years or a more severe punishment."

Until the reemergence of restorative justice approaches to criminal justice two decades ago (see Chapter 13), the criminal jury was the last vestige of significant community involvement in the administration of justice. Juries are involved in determining the guilt or innocence of accused persons, deciding parole eligibility for some convicted offenders, and choosing whether the eligibility for parole is reduced. Jury trials are actually quite rare in the justice system and most criminal matters are tried by judge alone.

The responsibility for setting the qualifications for jurors falls under provincial jurisdiction. Juries are composed of citizens between the ages of 18 and 65 or 69 who do not have a criminal record or physical or mental impairment. Potential jurors are identified from tax assessment lists or voter's list. Persons in certain professions, including lawyers, physicians, and law enforcement officials, are excluded from jury duty. With the exception of Yukon, the Northwest Territories, and Nunavut, where juries are composed of 6 persons, all juries in criminal cases have 12 jurors. Juries are finders of fact, while the role of the judge is to interpret the law and instruct the jurors. It is the jury that will determine the guilt or innocence of the accused person. Jury decisions must be unanimous.

The three essential attributes of a criminal jury are (1) impartiality, (2) competence, and (3) representativeness (*R. v. Bain*, [1992]1 SCR 91). The SCC has assigned to Crown counsel the role of ensuring that the jury meets these requirements and has stated that "the Crown Attorney should use the means at his or her disposal to exclude prospective jurors that could be biased in favour of the prosecution, even if the defence is not aware of this fact" (*R. v. Bain*, [1992]1 SCR 910).

One high-profile issue with respect to juries is the lack of Aboriginal representation on juries hearing cases involving an Aboriginal accused. In 2011, a judge in Thunder Bay, Ontario, postponed a murder trial because the jury pool did not include Aboriginals. The Nishnawbe Aski Nation, which represents 49 communities, had pointed out that the Kenora, Ontario, judicial district jury rolls included names of residents from only 14 of the communities.[34]

A subsequent inquiry, conducted for the province by a retired SCC judge, found that the criminal justice system as applied to Aboriginals persons in the province, and particularly in the northern regions of the province, was in crisis and that the status quo was not sustainable.[35] The inquiry team met with 32 First Nations and 4 Ontario Aboriginal organizations. Among their findings were that many Aboriginal peoples had experienced systemic discrimination by the criminal justice system and that the lack of representation of Aboriginal peoples on jury rolls was symptomatic of a larger problem of Aboriginal distrust of and lack of knowledge about the criminal justice system and, more specifically, juries. Among the barriers that were identified as hindering Aboriginal peoples participating on juries were the cost of transportation and language barriers experienced by Aboriginal peoples who speak neither English nor French.

In 2013, Clifford Kokopenace's manslaughter conviction was overturned by the Ontario Court of Appeal on the basis that his rights were violated by the provincial government, which failed to ensure there was proper representation of Aboriginal peoples on jury rolls, even though the problem had been widely documented.[36] The appeal court upheld Kokopenace's conviction for the stabbing death of his friend on the Grassy Narrows reserve as reasonable but sent the case back for a new trial.

JURY DECISION MAKING

Since jury deliberations are secret, research on jury deliberations and decision making is based on mock (pretend) juries, as no recording devices or observers are allowed into jury rooms. In contrast to the United States, in Canada, it is not permissible to interview jurors about the deliberations when the case is concluded.

There are concerns about the generalizability of findings from mock jury studies to actual juries. Many mock juries are composed of university students who participate in faculty-sponsored research, and their deliberations and decisions may differ from those of both mock and real juries, which have broader community representation.[37] University students, for example, may generally be more liberal than members from the community and this "town versus gown" effect may have an impact on how the jury processes information from the trial, the deliberations, and final decision. Research in the United States has produced conflicting findings: in one study, the students' sentence recommendations were more punitive than those of a mock jury composed of community residents, while another found that students were more lenient in assigning guilt in homicide cases than were community members.[38,39] An unexplored area is the impact of diversity on the deliberations and decisions of juries. As noted. in Canada, a high-profile issue is that Aboriginal persons are under-represented on juries (see below), although it is unknown how an increase in Aboriginal jurors will affect case outcomes for both Aboriginal and non-Aboriginal accused.

Among the concerns that surround the use of juries is that jurors may not understand evidence that is presented at trial because of its complexity or the manner in which it is presented by the defence and prosecutor.[40] In the words of one legal scholar, "one cannot ignore the limits of juries' abilities to accurately determine the facts from the hodgepodge of truths, errors, biases, and lies presented at trial."[41] Evidence suggests that jurors often have difficulty understanding the law and, in some instances, are uncertain of the definition of "beyond a reasonable doubt," a core concept in the determination of guilt or innocence of an accused person.[42]

It has also been suggested a "CSI effect" (of the popular television show *Crime Scene Investigation*) may exist, wherein jurors expect that there will be clear and unequivocal scientific evidence presented by the prosecutor that can support a conviction. Research, however, has failed to support the CSI effect, although jurors appear to have high expectations that prosecutors will present scientific evidence in support of an argument that the accused person is guilty.[43]

One area of concern is the instructions that are given to jurors following the trial and before deliberations. These instructions generally relate to the charges facing the defendant and the standard of proof that the jurors must use in weighing the evidence that has been presented at trial. From 30 to 50 percent of jury instructions that are reviewed on appeal result in orders for new trials because of errors made by the judge in giving instructions to the jury. Jury instructions are not mentioned in the *Criminal Code*, and this has resulted in considerable disparity in how this most important component of the judicial process is managed by judges.

In rare cases, juries have engaged in nullification, failing to convict an obviously guilty accused because the laws do not represent the will of the community. This has occurred in marijuana cases and in a series of jury decisions relating to abortion (*R. v. Krieger*, [2006]2 SCR 501, 2006 SCC 47; *R. v. Morgentaler*, [1988] SCR 30).

It does not appear that personal characteristics of jurors play a significant role in decision making, and non-evidentiary factors tend to play a role when the evidence presented to the jury is not clearly in favour of the prosecution or defence.[44] Individual jurors do participate differentially in deliberations, and jurors also appear to experience considerable pressure to reach a unanimous verdict, making efforts to avoid a *hung jury*, a situation in which consensus cannot be reached on the guilt or innocence of an accused.

Note that there has been very little research on Canadian juries, and it is, therefore, difficult to determine the applicability of these findings to the Canadian context.

APPEALS

After a case has been concluded in court, the possibility of appeal exists. Not every case can be appealed; in fact, in the majority of cases an appeal is *not* filed. The right to appeal exists only in certain situations; in others, the Court of Appeal can grant leave (permission) to appeal. Unlike in the United States, where only the defence can appeal, in Canada either the Crown prosecutor or the defence lawyer can file an appeal. A distinction is made between grounds for appeal that involve questions of law, those that involve questions of fact, and those that involve both. Also, note that summary conviction and indictable offences have different appeal procedures.

Once an appeal has been launched, the incarcerated appellant may be released on bail until the appeal is heard. The judge who hears this request considers, among other things, the *prima facie* merits of the appeal itself to ensure that frivolous appeals cannot routinely be used to defer the serving of a prison sentence.

An appeal may be directed at the verdict, the sentence, or both. However, most appeals are directed at the sentence: the incarcerated appellant thinks it is too severe, or the prosecutor thinks it is too lenient. The appellate court assesses the sentence against the prevailing norms found in reported case law. In deciding the case, the court may raise the sentence, lower it, or refuse to interfere with what the trial judge ordered.

An appeal of the verdict usually requires some demonstration that a legal error was made at the trial or that new, exculpatory evidence has been discovered. Verdict appeals have five possible outcomes. The court can (1) decide not to hear the appeal, (2) hear the appeal and dismiss it, (3) substitute a conviction on a lesser but included offence (and probably reduce the sentence), (4) direct that the offender be acquitted, or (5) order a new trial.

CRIME VICTIMS AND THE COURT PROCESS

In Chapter 3, it was noted that there has been a growing emphasis on the rights and needs of crime victims. This section examines those needs and rights in the context of the criminal court process.

ENSURING THE SAFETY OF VICTIMS

Between arrest and sentencing, the crime victim may be concerned about retaliation and intimidation by the offender. The legal mechanisms for protecting victims from pre-trial intimidation include non-association conditions of pre-trial release, which require the defendant agree not to communicate with any witnesses in the case, including victims, and peace bonds designed to ensure the safety of victims.

VICTIMS AS WITNESSES

At trial, victims may be called to testify. They are summoned to court (by subpoena) and are paid a small fee just like any other witness. Testifying in a public courtroom, in the presence of the alleged perpetrator, is an emotionally arduous task for victims. The *Criminal Code* contains concessions for crime victims who testify in court; most of these, however, are offered at the discretion of the trial judge. These provisions (see below) were developed in response to concerns that the victims of sexual offences were often victimized a second time by the experience of testimony and cross-examination.

A high-profile issue that has arisen recently, and which is illustrative of the challenges that the criminal justice system faces in accommodating diversity, is whether a victim who is a Muslim and wears the niqab (a full face veil revealing only the eyes) should be permitted to testify against the person who allegedly committed an offence against her. See At Issue 8.2.

In 2008, a preliminary hearing was held in an Ontario provincial court involving a case in which the cousin and uncle of a woman known as N.S., the alleged victim, were charged with sexual assault. When called by the prosecution as a witness, N.S., a Muslim, indicated that she wanted to testify wearing her niqab. She stated that her religious belief required her to wear a niqab in public where men and other close family members might see her. N.S. indicated that she had removed her niqab for her driver's licence photo (taken by a woman) and would remove it if required to clear customs. The presiding judge held that N.S.'s religious beliefs were not that strong and ordered her to remove her niqab. N.S. objected and applied to the Superior Court of Justice to quash the provincial court order and to permit her to testify wearing the niqab.

The case moved on to Superior Court of Justice and then to the Ontario Court of Appeal, and ultimately to the SCC. In 2012, in *R. v N.S.* (2012), SCC 72, the SCC ruled that a Muslim witness may be required to remove her niqab to testify in court, depending on the seriousness of the case and the sincerity of her religious beliefs. Included in its ruling was the statement, "Always permitting a witness to wear the niqab would offer no protection for the accused's fair trial interest and the state's interest in maintaining public confidence in the administration of justice. However, never permitting a witness to testify wearing a niqab would not comport with the fundamental premised under the Charter that rights should be limited only to the extent that the limits are shown to be justifiable. The need to accommodate and balance sincerely held religious beliefs against other interests is deeply entrenched in Canadian law" (2012: 5). If wearing the niqab did not pose a risk to a fair trial, then it would be permitted. The case was returned to the provincial judge to make the final determination, which was to require N.S. to remove her niqab to testify.[45,46]

Other common law jurisdictions are confronting a similar challenge. In 2013, a judge in the United Kingdom held that a Muslim woman who was a defendant in a criminal case could wear the niqab during all parts of the trial, except when giving evidence, at which point it would have to be removed. However, the judge also ruled that the defendant would not have to testify in open court with her face uncovered and could choose to give evidence via a video link or from behind a screen in the courtroom as long as the judge, jurors, and her defence counsel could see her. The woman ultimately decided not to testify in her defence.[47] In a previous case, a British judge had rule that a Muslim woman would not be allowed to sit as a juror in an attempted murder trial unless she uncovered her face veil.[48]

QUESTIONS

What is your perspective on this issue? Do you think that the SCC struck the right balance? Why or why not?

Muslim women wearing their niqab.

THE CANADIAN PRESS/Chris Young

THE CHALLENGE OF MEGA-TRIALS

The criminal courts may be overwhelmed in certain cases that result from a major tragedy or police enforcement initiative. Stronger enforcement efforts against outlaw motorcycle gangs and criminal syndicates have resulted in criminal trials involving multiple defendants, lengthy witness lists, and thousands of pages (and in many instances thousands of pieces) of evidence.[49] Also, these types of cases are expensive. It is estimated, for example, that the convictions of four associates of the Rock Machine motorcycle gang in Québec in 2001 for drug trafficking under the anti-gang legislation cost taxpayers $5.5 million. And in 2003, four Hells Angels pleaded guilty to similar charges in Montreal after the province constructed a special, high-tech courtroom at the cost of $16.5 million.

The most costly trial to date in Canada was the case involving Air India Flight 182, which exploded and crashed into the Atlantic Ocean off the west coast of Ireland in 1985 while on a flight from Montréal to London. All 329 passengers on board, most of whom were Canadian citizens, were killed. The investigation into the bombings centred on certain individuals in British Columbia's Sikh community, who were involved in the struggle for an independent Khalistan in India. An Air India Task Force, led by the RCMP and working alongside police agencies in Europe, India, the United States, and Asia, spent 15 years investigating the case, at one point offering a $1 million reward for evidence that would help convict the perpetrators.

In 2000, two B.C. residents were charged with multiple offences under the *Criminal Code* relating to the deaths of the passengers and crew on Air India 182. The charges included first-degree murder, conspiracy to commit murder, and attempted murder. In 2001, a third defendant was charged with the same offences; two years later, he pled guilty to manslaughter for his part in the bombing and received a sentence of five years.

The Crown proceeded by direct indictment against the remaining two defendants. The trial began in April 2003 and went on for 19 months and 232 court days until December 2004. It was held in the B.C. Supreme Court in Courtroom 20, which had been built at an estimated cost of $7.2 million, specifically for the Air India trial and for future mega-trials. In March 2005, the presiding judge found the two defendants not guilty on all charges. By that time, the Air India case had cost the federal government and the Government of British Columbia nearly $60 million. More than 300 RCMP officers have worked on the case over the past 20 years; more than 1000 witnesses and experts have been interviewed, some of them multiple times. Before and during the trial, more than 30 lawyers worked on the case on the defence and prosecution sides and more than one million documents of evidence were produced.

CASE DELAY AND BACKLOG IN THE CRIMINAL COURTS

Case delay and backlog are endemic in the Canadian criminal justice system and appear to be immune from reform efforts designed to improve the case process. The staying (that is, suspension or discontinuance) of nearly 100,000 criminal cases a year in Canada is due, in part, to failures to get the cases to court within a reasonable period. Although the median time taken to complete adult criminal court cases (117 days) declined in 2011–2012, it is still longer than 10 years ago (median time 105 days in 2001–2002).[50] In an investigation into the "culture of delay" in the criminal justice system found that "the culture of delay is resistant to change because there are several benefits to those working within the system that are gained from delay and no accepted means of enforcing timeliness as a priority."[51]

In Ontario, the Justice on Target initiative is designed to improve case flow in the criminal courts and has set benchmarks for processing various types of cases. However, the information presented in Table 8.2 suggests that case delay continues to be a major issue. Indeed, in 2013, the president of the Ontario Crown Attorneys' Association stated that Crown offices were forced to use a triage system to prioritize cases: "We are forced to deal away less serious cases in order to handle more serious ones. So, we focus on crimes against the person and that means that crimes against property get deal away. We're forced to make a decision. We don't have the resources to prosecute everything."[52]

Case backlog and case delay are due to a number of factors, including a lack of judicial resources, ineffective use of resources, too few judges, the complexity of criminal

TABLE 8.2	CASE TYPE, BENCHMARKS, AND ACTUAL PROCESSING TIME IN ONTARIO CRIMINAL COURTS, 2013	
Case Type	**Benchmark**	**Benchmark Met**
less complex (break and enter, theft, mischief, etc.)	5 appearances 90 days	63.1% of the time 61.4% of the time
more complex (violent offences, including homicide and sexual assault, gang-related charges, etc.)	10 appearances 240 days	66.6% of the time 67.0% of the time
provincial and federal (one or more federal charges, i.e., drug possession, in combination with provincial offences)	9 appearances 180 days	63.5% of the time 63.5% of the time

Source: Ontario Ministry of the Attorney General. 2013. "Benchmarks for Effective Criminal Courts." Accessed March 1, 2014. http://www.attorneygeneral.jus.gov.on.ca/english/jot/benchmarks.asp. © Queen's Printer for Ontario, 2013. Reproduced with permission.

cases (multi-charge cases compose a majority of the cases in criminal court), and, historically, attempts by legal counsel and inmates to lengthen the period of remand, driven in part by two-for-one credit for jail time served before sentencing. The use of alternative dispute measures and restorative justice approaches hold considerable promise in assisting court systems to reduce the case delays and backlogs (see Chapter 13). However, an attempt to reduce the long processing times in bail cases through the use of video remand court, wherein the accused appears in the hearing from detention via video link, resulted in longer case processing times in large measure because of repeated adjournments.[53]

There is little doubt that case delay is having a significant impact on the administration of justice. In 2011, 31 alleged members and associates of the Hells Angels motorcycle gang had their case thrown out of court by a Québec judge because of what the judge determined was unreasonable delays before trial. The judge determined that the delays prevented the accused from receiving fair trials. In the case, 156 suspects had been apprehended two years earlier as result of a major police initiative. The judge acknowledged that the criminal justice system did not have the capacity to hold trials for all the accused in a timely manner. The case would have involved 2200 witnesses and the submission of millions of pages of documents from the investigation, including wire taps and surveillance. The lawyers had estimated that it would take 10 years before the last accused would have been tried.[54]

In a similar case, in 2013, a B.C. Supreme Court judge stayed charges against a high-ranking member of the Hells Angels on the grounds that his *Charter* rights had been violated by the two-and-a-half-year delay in the case coming to trial.[55] Also, in British Columbia, it took four years after two people were killed when a B.C. ferry sank in 2006 for charges of criminal negligence causing death to be laid by Crown counsel, another three years for the trial to begin, and another six months before a verdict was rendered (guilty) and sentence passed. As of early 2014, two years after the Stanley Cup post–game seven hockey riot in Vancouver (see Chapter 3), persons were still being charged and brought to trial, most of them for mischief and assault.

WRONGFUL CONVICTIONS

The criminal justice system operates within a legal and procedural framework that is designed to ensure that the rights of those accused of criminal offences are protected and that their guilt must be proved beyond a reasonable doubt. Despite this, there has emerged in recent years an increasing concern about wrongful convictions (also referred to as miscarriages of justice)—cases in which individuals were convicted who were later found to be innocent. In many instances, these people served time in prison for crimes they did not commit.[56] See the Media Link "A Question of Innocence" at the end of the chapter.

Settlements in cases of wrongful conviction can be millions of dollars, as in the case of Réjean Hinse who was wrongfully convicted and spent five years in prison and another ten years on parole. In 2012, A Québec judge awarded him $8.6 million in damages from the federal government. In conjunction with a $4.5 million settle with the Province of Québec, these awards amounted to the largest amount paid for a wrongful conviction, as of early 2014.

THE REVIEW OF WRONGFUL CONVICTIONS

Over the past decade, a number of government-sponsored inquiries into wrongful convictions have taken place. Wrongful convictions rarely occur as the result of a single mistake or event; they are almost always a consequence of a series of events. These include tunnel vision on the part of police and the Crown (that is, the focus of the investigation was too narrow); mistaken eyewitness identification and testimony; false confessions; the testimony of in-custody informers; and defective, unreliable, and unsubstantiated expert testimony.[57,58]

Research studies have consistently found that eyewitness testimony is notoriously unreliable and caution should be exercised by justice system personnel in using eyewitness testimony to establish the facts in a criminal case.[59]

In other cases, accused persons have been wrongfully convicted on the basis of testimony from experts and suspect scientific evidence (see below). This occurred in cases involving deaths that were attributed to shaken baby syndrome and, most recently, in a case involving child homicide in Canada. See the Media Link "Diagnosis Murder."

Sections 696.1 to 696.6 of the *Criminal Code*—"Applications for Ministerial Review—Miscarriages of Justice"—give the federal minister of justice the power to review criminal cases to determine whether there has been a miscarriage of justice. These regulations set out the requirements for an application for a criminal conviction review. Completed applications are forwarded to the Criminal Conviction Review Group; lawyers on that body review and investigate the applications and make recommendations to the minister.[60] The Association in Defence of the Wrongfully Convicted (www.aidwyc.org) has been instrumental in having the convictions of a number of persons overturned.

Two of the earliest high-profile cases of wrongful conviction were those of David Milgaard and Donald Marshall. David Milgaard was convicted and given a life sentence in 1970 for the murder of a Saskatoon nursing aide. He spent 23 years in prison before the Supreme Court of Canada set aside his conviction in 1992. Five years later, he was exonerated by DNA evidence. In 1999, Larry Fisher was found guilty of the murder. Milgaard received a $10 million settlement for his wrongful imprisonment.

Donald Marshall, a Mi'kmaq, was sentenced to life imprisonment in 1971 and spent 11 years in prison before being acquitted by the Nova Scotia Court of Appeal in 1983. A Royal Commission of Inquiry concluded that incompetence on the part of the police and the judiciary contributed to his wrongful conviction; so did the fact that he was an Aboriginal person.[61]

"He'll do."

THE ROLE OF THE POLICE IN WRONGFUL CONVICTIONS

The police role in wrongful convictions is often associated with the interrogation of a suspect and a confession (later found to be false) to having committed the crime. Although false confessions are rare, investigating officers must always carefully assess the reliability of a suspect's statement or confession against all other known facts. Innocent people often waive their right to legal assistance, and certain interview techniques can elicit false confessions. It has been stated that "innocence puts innocents at risk."[62] False confessions may also be made by persons who have a mental illness, who are stressed and fatigued, and who are experiencing withdrawal symptoms from drugs or alcohol.[63] This, in turn, may lead to a person being wrongfully convicted.

Officers must be aware that the way in which questions are asked may induce a suspect to falsely confess. In the words of a man who (along with two others) falsely confessed to the rape and murder of a 14-year-old girl in Regina (and was later exonerated when DNA evidence convicted another man),

> I'm not even sure how to explain it because I'm not sure how it happened to me. . . . All I know is for hours on end I said 'No, I had nothing to do with it.' Next thing you know I'm sitting there going 'Sure, why not. I did it.' More or less it's like they kill your spirit or something.[64]

Observers have questioned whether the *Charter of Rights and Freedoms* has assisted in reducing the number of wrongfully convicted.[65] Few constraints, for example, have been placed on police interrogation, even with a suspect's right to silence, potentially resulting in false confessions. The use of Mr. Big stings in police investigations, discussed in Chapter 6, may also lead to false confessions.[66]

For an excellent case study of false confessions, see the documentary film "The Confessions," produced for the program *Frontline* by the Public Broadcasting System in the United States. The film tells the story of the false confessions of four U.S. Navy sailors to a crime they did not commit. It can be viewed at www.pbs.org/wgbh/pages/frontline/the-confessions/. The website also includes an interview with a retired New York Police Department detective, an expert on false confessions, and two of the defence lawyers involved in the case, and contains links to research on interrogation and false confessions.

THE ROLE OF CROWN COUNSEL

Crown counsel exercise considerable control over how cases are processed in the justice system, from participating in plea bargaining with defence lawyers to the selecting jurors and how evidence against the accused is presented. In extreme cases, Crown counsel do not abide by the law or professional ethics, and this can lead to wrongful convictions. In Manitoba, Crown prosecutor George Dangerfield presided over at least four cases in which accused persons were subsequently found to have been wrongfully convicted. Subsequent investigations discovered that Dangerfield failed to disclose exculpatory evidence, that is "evidence that may justify or excuse an accused defendants actions, and which will tend to show the defendant is not guilty or has no criminal intent."[67] In addition to the shattered lives of the persons prosecuted by Dangerfield, the Province of Manitoba has paid out millions of dollars to the wrongfully convicted. See the Media Link "The Wrong Man" at the end of the chapter.

▲ Former Manitoba Crown prosecutor George Dangerfield (right)

▲ Frank Ostrowski, Sr. was wrongfully convicted in a case prosecuted by George Dangerfield.

▲ James Driskell was wrongfully convicted in a case prosecuted by George Dangerfield.

Three of the persons who were wrongfully convicted in cases prosecuted by George Dangerfield were Thomas Sophonow, James Driskell, and Frank Ostrowski, Sr.:

- In 2000, DNA evidence cleared Thomas Sophonow of the killing of a shop clerk in Winnipeg in 1981. Tried three times before being convicted, Sophonow spent nearly four years behind bars before the Manitoba Court of Appeal acquitted him in 1985. As compensation for his wrongful conviction, the City of Winnipeg, the Government of Manitoba, and the federal government contributed to a $2.6 million settlement.

- James Driskell was convicted of first degree murder in 1991 on the basis of perjured testimony from two witnesses and poor forensic work. He spent 12 years in prison before being exonerated by DNA evidence. It was later revealed that the police and Dangerfield concealed evidence for a decade that indicated that the two witnesses had been paid to testify and had also been granted immunity. Driskell sued the government of Manitoba and, in 2011, he settled out of court for $970,000.

- Frank Ostrowski, Sr. spent 23 years in prison before a federal investigation determined that a likely miscarriage of justice occurred. Among the findings of the investigation were that the police and Crown counsel Dangerfield had concealed the fact that a key prosecution witness had perjured himself and been given a deal for testifying against Ostrowski.[68]

THE ROLE OF EXPERT WITNESSES

Expert witnesses can have a significant impact on the criminal court process. Conflicting testimony may be given by experts on behalf of the Crown and the defence. Scholars have noted that historically the judiciary has been reluctant to examine the independence, validity, and reliability of expert witnesses.[69] Traditionally, experts testifying in court were generally from the hard sciences, including forensics. In recent years, experts from the soft sciences, including criminology, psychology, and anthropology, are involved as expert witnesses, and this has raised concerns of the reliability and validity of the testimony.[70]

Louie Palu/The Globe and Mail

▲ Discredited and disbarred forensic pathologist Charles Smith

A recent high-profile case in Ontario, however, involved Dr. Charles Smith, a forensic pathologist whose expert testimony in several cases of child death contributed to the wrongful conviction of several persons. An inquiry conducted by Mr. Justice Stephen Goudge found that Smith made false and misleading statements to the court in his testimony and that Smith was an unqualified pathologist who did not acknowledge the limits of his professional expertise.[71] A report of the Ontario coroner concluded that 20 of 44 autopsies carried out by Smith on deceased children had significant problems. His testimony in court may have resulted in the wrongful conviction of 13 persons and an additional number who were initially wrongfully charged with killing children.[72]

Among the victims of Dr. Smith's false, unqualified, misleading evidence were the following:

- William Mullins-Johnson was found guilty of first-degree murder of his niece by a jury in 1994. Mullins-Johnson spent 12 years in prison before his conviction was overturned. In 2010, Mullins-Johnson was awarded $4.25 million in compensation for his wrongful conviction. As Mullins-Johnson stated, "I was held accountable for things that didn't even happen."[73]

- Tammy Marquardt was convicted and sentenced to life in prison in 1995 for killing her two-year-old son. Her other two children were taken from her and put up for adoption. She served 13 years in prison before her conviction was set aside in 2011. Prosecutors agreed that the trial had been faulty because of Smith's testimony.

Smith had presented evidence on causes of death even though his formal training was in pediatric pathology, which is the study of disease in children and youth. Smith was subsequently stripped of his medical licence by Ontario College of Physicians and Surgeons, which made a finding of professional misconduct and incompetence. The board noted that Dr. Smith "expressed opinions ... that were either contrary to, or not supported by, the evidence" and that "these failures compromised the administration of justice."[74]

SUMMARY

The discussion in this chapter has focused on the prosecution of criminal cases. There are a number of events that occur before trial that affect the outcome of cases. Judicial interim release (bail) is available for many offenders and often has conditions attached that, in the view of some observers, set the accused person up to fail. While all accused persons have the right to legal representation, there is no obligation on the provinces or territories to pay for it, and many people without means do not quality. Another controversial practice in the criminal courts is plea bargaining which is not subject to any legislative provisions or guidelines. Defence lawyers can employ a number of defences at trial, including not criminally responsible on account of mental disorder (NCRMD), which has stirred controversy. Although jury trials are rare in the criminal justice system, little is known about the challenges that juries face in understanding testimony and reaching a verdict. Despite various reform efforts, the criminal court process remains challenged by case delays and backlogs, as well as by dynamics that lead to wrongful convictions.

KEY POINTS REVIEW

1. Crown counsel are responsible for prosecuting cases and are involved in a wide range of activities, including screening cases, negotiating pleas, and recommending sentences to the court.

2. Many factors influence the decision of the police or the Crown as to whether to lay a charge.

3. There are a variety of ways to ensure that an accused person will appear in court, including issuing an appearance notice, issuing a summons, and remanding the person into custody.

4. The decision to grant judicial interim release (bail) is influenced by a number of factors and conditions may be attached to the release.

5. Security certificates are processes whereby non-citizens of Canada who are deemed a threat to the country can be held, without charge, for an indefinite time with the objective of deportation.

6. There is no blanket right to state-paid legal representation, and funding cuts in legal aid have made it difficult for many accused to access legal assistance.

7. There are three models of legal aid services: judicare, which involves the use of private lawyers; legal aid clinics; and a model that provides a combination of private and legal aid staff lawyers.

8. The arrangements for the provision of legal aid vary across the country, and qualifying is often difficult.

9. A fundamental principle of the common law is that the accused person must be fit to stand trial.

10. Plea bargaining is a widely used, yet controversial, practice in the criminal justice process.

11. The most common defences for accused can be generally grouped into (1) "you've got the wrong person," (2) the mental state of the accused at the time the alleged offence occurred, (3) justifications (or excuses) for having committed a criminal act, and (4) procedural defences.

12. A number of issues surround juries, including the lack of representation of Aboriginal peoples on juries, the validity of using mock juries in an attempt to understand jury decision making, and questions as to whether jury members can understand complex evidence.

13. Emphasis is increasingly being placed on the rights of crime victims in the court process.

14. Mega-trials and case delay or backlogs present major challenges to the courts.

15. Increasing attention is being given to the wrongfully convicted and to the activities and decisions of the police, prosecutors, and judges that contribute to miscarriages of justice.

KEY TERM QUESTIONS

1. What is **judicial interim release (bail)**, and what are the issues that surround its use?

2. What role does **remand** play in the pre-trial process?

3. Why are **security certificates** the focus of controversy?

4. What are the issues that surround **plea bargaining**?

5. In what situations would a Crown counsel enter a **stay of proceedings**?

6. Describe the defence of **not criminally responsible on account of mental disorder**, and note why is it controversial.

MEDIA LINKS

 "NCR: Not Criminally Responsible," *CBC Doc Zone* or go to the book's website at www.nelson.com/ crimjusticeprimer5e.com

"Diagnosis Murder: Exploring the Suspect Science Behind Shaken Baby Accusations," *CBC Fifth Estate* or go to the book's website at www.nelson.com/ crimjusticeprimer5e.com

"A Question of Innocence," *CBC Fifth Estate* or go to the book's website at www.nelson.com/ crimjusticeprimer5e.com

"The Wrong Man," *CBC Fifth Estate* or go to the book's website at www.nelson.com/ crimjusticeprimer5e.com

205

CHAPTER 9

SENTENCING

LEARNING OBJECTIVES

After reading this chapter, you should be able to
- identify the purpose and principles of sentencing
- identify and discuss the goals of sentencing
- discuss the sentencing options available to judges
- discuss the judicial options of judicial determination and judicial restraint order, and the dangerous offender and long-term offender designations
- identify and describe the considerations judges make in sentencing
- discuss the issues surrounding the sentencing of Aboriginal offenders
- discuss the issues surrounding sentencing and crime victims
- discuss the effectiveness of various sentencing options

Sentencing is a complicated human process that is handled best when that complexity is recognized and accepted. Individual judges, prosecutors, defence lawyers and correctional professionals, influenced inevitably by prevailing local cultural norms and constrained by general rules and criteria, should be allowed, case-by-case to do what they believe to be just and appropriate.[*]

— Tonry[1]

THE PURPOSE AND PRINCIPLES OF SENTENCING

Section 718 of the *Criminal Code* sets out the purpose and principles of sentencing:

> The fundamental purpose of sentencing is to contribute, along with crime prevention activities, to respect for the law and the maintenance of a just, peaceful and safe society by imposing just sanctions that have one or more of the following objectives:
>
> **(a)** to denounce the unlawful conduct;
>
> **(b)** to deter the offender and other persons from committing offences;
>
> **(c)** to separate offenders from society, where necessary;
>
> **(d)** to assist in rehabilitating offenders;
>
> **(e)** to provide reparations for harm done to victims or to the community; and
>
> **(f)** to promote a sense of responsibility in offenders, and acknowledgement of the harm done to victims and to the community.

Section 718.1 states that a sentence must be proportionate to the gravity of the offence and to the degree of responsibility of the offender. Section 718.2 states that a court that imposes a sentence must also take into consideration the following principles:[**]

> **(a)** a sentence should be increased or reduced to account for any relevant aggravating or mitigating circumstances relating to the offence or the offender, and, without limiting the generality of the foregoing,
>
> **(i)** evidence that the offence was motivated by bias, prejudice or hate based on race, national or ethnic origin, language, colour, religion, sex, age, mental or physical disability, sexual orientation, or any other factor, or
>
> **(ii)** evidence that the offender, in committing the offence, abused the offender's spouse or child, or
>
> **(iii)** evidence that the offender, in committing the offence, abused a position of trust or authority in relation to a victim shall be deemed to be aggravating circumstances;
>
> **(iv)** evidence that the offence was committed for the benefit of, at the direction of or in association with a criminal organization.
>
> **(b)** a sentence should be similar to sentences imposed on similar offenders for similar offences committed in similar circumstances;
>
> **(c)** where consecutive sentences are imposed, the combined sentence should not be unduly long or harsh;
>
> **(d)** an offender should not be deprived of liberty, if less restrictive sanctions may be appropriate in the circumstances; and
>
> **(e)** all available sanctions other than imprisonment that are reasonable in the circumstances should be considered for all offenders, with particular attention to the circumstances of Aboriginal offenders.

"You're going to do time, but I'm trying to get it in dog years."

© Leo Cullum/The New Yorker Collection/The Cartoon Bank

[*]Tonry, M. 2013. "'Nothing' Works: Sentencing 'Reform' in Canada and the United States", *Canadian Journal of Criminology and Criminal Justice*, 55(4), 465-79.

[**]*The Canadian Charter of Rights and Freedoms*, Sections 718.1 and 718.2, http://laws-lois.justice.gc.ca/eng/const/page-15.html

THE GOALS OF SENTENCING: THE CASES OF MR. SMITH AND MR. JONES

Sentencing goals in the criminal courts fall into three main groups: utilitarian, retributive, and restorative. The real cases of "Mr. Smith" and "Mr. Jones" (not their real names) will be used to illustrate how these sentencing goals are applied. Mr. Smith was a Québec-based police chief and swimming coach who was convicted of four counts of sexual assault for fondling two girls, ages 12 and 13. Mr. Jones, a computer engineer based in British Columbia, was convicted of sexual assault for fondling his young stepdaughter over a two-year period. The cases of Mr. Smith and Mr. Jones—neither of whom had a prior criminal record—were heavily publicized in their respective communities, and both men eventually lost their jobs.

UTILITARIAN GOALS

Utilitarian sentencing goals focus on the *future* conduct of Mr. Smith, Mr. Jones, and others who might commit similar offences. The sentence is designed to protect the public from future crimes in the following ways:

- By discouraging potential Mr. Smiths and Mr. Joneses from crime. This is *general* deterrence.

- By discouraging Mr. Smith and Mr. Jones from doing it again. This is *specific* deterrence.

- By curing Mr. Smith and Mr. Jones of what made them do it. This is *rehabilitation*.

- By keeping Mr. Smith and Mr. Jones in jail to protect society. This is *incapacitation*.

RETRIBUTIVE GOALS

The past, rather than the future, is the focus of retributive sentencing goals, which include the following:

- *denunciation*—that is, expressing society's disapproval of the behaviour of Mr. Smith and Mr. Jones

- *retribution*—that is, making the two men "pay" for their offences, based on the philosophy "an eye for an eye"

A key concept in retributive sentencing is *proportionality*—that is, the sentence handed down should be proportionate to the gravity of the offence and to the convicted person's degree of responsibility.

RESTORATIVE GOALS

The most widely used restorative approaches are victim–offender reconciliation, circle sentencing, and family group conferencing. (See Chapter 13.) As noted in Chapter 2, restorative justice is based on the principle that criminal behaviour injures not only the victim but communities and offenders as well. It follows that efforts to resolve the problems that the criminal behaviour has created should involve all three parties.

Regarding Mr. Smith and Mr. Jones, their victims were children, who because of their age would be excluded from any restorative justice forum. However, the victims' families would have the opportunity to discuss the impact of the crimes, and Mr. Smith and Mr. Jones would be held accountable for their criminal behaviour.

WHAT SENTENCES DID MR. SMITH AND MR. JONES RECEIVE?

The offence of sexual assault carries a maximum penalty of 10 years' imprisonment. Neither Mr. Smith nor Mr. Jones had a prior criminal record, and both had a good job history; on the other hand, their offences were serious and had a significant impact on the victims. One of Mr. Smith's victims suffered long-term emotional and academic problems; Mr. Jones's former spouse and children experienced considerable emotional difficulties. In both cases, the children had been young and vulnerable. Mr. Smith had been an authority figure in the community, and parents had trusted him to supervise their children—a trust he violated. Similarly, Mr. Jones had violated the trust of his stepdaughter and most likely would have continued sexually abusing her had she not told her mother about his improper behaviour.

Mr. Smith was sentenced to three years' probation (the maximum) and 180 hours of community service. The Crown appealed the sentence on the grounds that it was too lenient. However, the Québec Court of Appeal upheld the sentence, in part because Mr. Smith had been fired from his job as police chief and so had already experienced a severe sanction. The appeal court acknowledged that child abuse typically demands a denunciatory sentence for the protection of society but noted that each case must be judged on its merits.

Mr. Jones was not so fortunate. He was sentenced to 18 months' confinement in a provincial correctional facility and three years' probation (the maximum). In explaining the sentence, the presiding judge cited the objectives of denunciation and general and specific deterrence.

SENTENCING OPTIONS

The sentencing options from which Canadian judges may select are set out in Table 9.1.

Note that some of these options may be mixed and matched; for example, judges may impose a period of probation in conjunction with a sentence of two years less a day

Suspended sentence

A sentencing option whereby the judge convicts the accused but places the offender on probation; successful completion results in no sentence being given.

Conditional sentence of imprisonment

Offenders who receive a sentence or sentences totalling less than two years serve their time in the community under the supervision of a probation officer.

TABLE 9.1 SENTENCING OPTIONS

Absolute discharge	The offender is found guilty but is technically not convicted and is set free with no criminal record.
Conditional discharge	The offender is found guilty and released on the condition that he or she comply with the conditions of a probation order. If the offender fails to meet the conditions, he or she may be returned to court to be sentenced on the original charge.
Suspended sentence	The offender is convicted of the offence, but the imposition of the sentence is suspended pending successful completion of probation.
Fine	The offender must pay a specific amount of money within a specified time or face the prospect of imprisonment for fine default; the offender may be able to work off the fine in a fine option program.
Intermittent sentence	The offender is sentenced to jail, generally served on weekends and when not in custody, subject to a probation order with specific conditions. It is available only for sentences that do not exceed 90 days.
Probation	The offender is placed under supervision in the community for a specified time (maximum three years), must fulfill general conditions, and may be required to adhere to or complete specific conditions (e.g., attend alcohol or drug counselling; see Chapter 10).
Conditional sentence	The offender receives a term of confinement (less than two years) and is allowed to serve it in the community under the supervision of a probation officer, provided he or she meets certain specified conditions (although the offender is *not* on probation and may be imprisoned for violation of conditions; see Chapter 10).
Imprisonment	The offender is sentenced to a period of confinement (see Chapter 10).

for offenders in provincial or territorial systems, or they may impose fines along with probation or a period of confinement. Most people convicted of criminal offences are not sent to prison but rather are placed under some form of supervision in the community.

Convicted persons may also be required to pay compensation to the victim, commonly known as *restitution.* These are typically cash payments in compensation for stolen or damaged property and may also include expenses associated with offences that caused bodily harm (e.g., repairing teeth damaged in an assault). The main problem with restitution orders is that they are difficult to enforce. Very little can be done if the offender does not pay. Embedding restitution orders in probation orders is one option such that non-payment becomes a breach of probation.

U.S. judges have also used public shaming as part of sentences. This often requires the offender to stand in a public place with a sign indicating their offence. In Texas in 2010, for example, Daniel Mireles and his wife stole $250,000.00 from the crime victim's fund and, as part of his sentence, he will be required to stand outside a mall in Houston for six years holding a sign that reads "I am a thief. I stole $250,000 from the Harris County crime victim's fund. Daniel Mireles."[2] Online comments in response to this story were both supportive and critical of this sentencing strategy, with some arguing that it would make people think twice about committing offences, and others fearing it signalled a return to the early days of punishment, when offenders were humiliated in the public square.

What are your thoughts on the public shaming? Do you think it could be used as a condition of probation or as an alternative to incarceration?

▲ Serving a sentence that includes public shaming.

TYPES OF SENTENCES

Sentences imposed in court can be concurrent, consecutive, or intermittent. In **concurrent sentences**, the sentences received by the offender are merged into one sentence and served simultaneously. For example, an offender sentenced to two terms of 9 months each will serve a 9-month sentence (not an 18-month sentence).

In the case of **consecutive sentences**, the sentences are served in sequence: one begins after the other has ended. For example, an offender sentenced to two terms of 9 months each will serve 18 months.

Intermittent sentences are served on a part-time basis (generally weekends, from Friday evening until Monday morning) and are generally no more than 90 days long. Intermittent sentences may pose challenges for provincial and territorial systems of corrections. Many facilities are over capacity and overcrowded, and it may be difficult to find appropriate accommodations for these individuals.

Provisions in the *Criminal Code* state that all sentences are to be concurrent unless the trial judge specifies that the sentences are to be consecutive. However, sentences under the *Provincial Offences Act* are to be consecutive unless the sentencing judge specifies that the sentences are to run concurrently.

Concurrent sentences
Sentences that are amalgamated and served simultaneously.

Consecutive sentences
Sentences that run separately and are completed one after the other.

Intermittent sentence
A sentence that is served on a part-time basis, generally on weekends.

JUDICIAL DETERMINATION

Federal inmates typically can apply for release on full parole after serving one-third of their sentence. Section 743.6 of the *Criminal Code* gives sentencing judges the authority to impose on some offenders receiving a sentence of imprisonment of two years or more the requirement that the offender serve one-half of the sentence before being eligible for parole, instead of the typical one-third. The primary objectives of this provision are protection of the public and specific and general deterrence.

Judicial determination is used in less than 5 percent of federal cases, but Aboriginal offenders are over-represented in the group of offenders receiving judicial determination. Offenders receiving judicial determination are more likely than other offenders to serve their entire sentence in confinement.

Judicial determination

An order by the sentencing judge that the offender serve one-half of the sentence before being eligible to apply for parole.

JUDICIAL RESTRAINT ORDER

Under section 810 of the *Criminal Code*, Crown Counsel may lay an information before a justice of the peace if they have reasonable grounds to believe that another person will injure you, your spouse, your children, or your property. The person need not have a criminal history at the time of the application. Other sections—810.01(1), fear of a criminal organization offence; 810.1(1), fear of a sexual offence; and 810.2, fear of serious personal injury—require an information to be laid before a provincial court judge. Section 810 has withstood *Charter* challenges.

If the JP or the judge is satisfied that there are reasonable grounds for the threat, the defendant is required to enter into a recognizance to keep the peace and be of good behaviour for a period not to exceed 12 months. The court may also impose conditions on the defendant—for example, to abstain from possessing a firearm, to avoid contact with persons under 14, or to stay away from places frequented by children (such as school or daycare grounds). Violation of the conditions of an 810 order is an offence and can result in imprisonment. A defendant can also be imprisoned for refusing to agree to an 810 order. Critics of section 810 argue that the conditions are too broad in their application in that no crime need have been committed for them to be imposed.

Section 810 orders can also be imposed by judges when an offender is released from custody following the completion of his or her sentence (see Chapter 12).

LIFE IMPRISONMENT

Under the *Criminal Code*, persons convicted of murder are subject to life imprisonment. This means that the offender is under sentence for life, although he or she may serve this sentence both in prison and on release on parole in the community. The *Criminal Code* sets out the minimum number of years that an offender must serve in prison before being eligible to apply for release on parole. The key word is *apply*—there is no guarantee that the parole board will grant a release.

As part of its crime policy legislative agenda, the federal government in 2011 passed the *Protecting Canadians by Ending Sentence Discounts for Multiple Murders Act*, which permits a judge, in cases involving more than one murder, to add up parole eligibility periods within a life sentence consecutively, rather than concurrently, as had been past practice. In 2013, Travis Baumgartner, an armoured car guard who killed four of his colleagues in an on-the-job robbery, made a plea deal that would give him a life sentence with no chance of parole for 40 years. Prior to the legislation, Baumgartner would have had to serve a maximum of 25 years before being eligible for parole.[3]

The death penalty was abolished by Parliament in 1976 and replaced with a mandatory life sentence without possibility of parole for 25 years in cases of first-degree murder (although it was retained for a number of military offences, including treason and mutiny). The debate over the death penalty continues, however. See At Issue 9.1.

211

EXTRAORDINARY MEASURES: DANGEROUS AND LONG-TERM OFFENDERS

Two other dispositions are quite different from the sentences discussed so far in that they are not time limited and are used only in the most serious and unusual cases. These dispositions involve declaring offenders either dangerous offenders or long-term offenders.

DANGEROUS OFFENDER (DO) DESIGNATION

Section 752 of the *Criminal Code* contains procedures and criteria for declaring someone a dangerous offender. That section defines a **dangerous offender** (DO) as a person who is given an indeterminate sentence on conviction for a particularly violent crime and who has demonstrated a pattern of committing serious violent offences. In the judgment of the court, the offender's behaviour is unlikely to be controlled or prevented by normal approaches to behavioural restraint. The purpose of the section is to identify those persons with unacceptable propensities for violence and to incapacitate them to protect the public interest.

A person can be declared a DO by a sentencing judge only if the Crown makes a formal application after conviction but before sentencing. The provincial Attorney General must approve such an application beforehand.

If the Crown proves the case, the judge *may* order detention for an indeterminate period. If this happens, the offender is detained in a federal prison, but there is no set length on the sentence. The offender can be released by the National Parole Board the following year, the following decade, or never (see Chapter 12). These applications are rare, and a high burden of proof is on the Crown. Two elements are considered in making this determination: *past* offence history and the likelihood of serious offences in the *future*.

The first threshold is that the current offences of conviction must involve at least one serious personal injury offence—that is, an indictable offence for which the possible sentence is at least 10 years and that involved the use or attempted use of violence against another person, or conduct endangering or likely to endanger the life or safety of another person, or conduct inflicting or likely to inflict severe psychological damage on another person.

Dangerous offender

A designation made by the judge after conviction that results in an indeterminate term of imprisonment in a federal correctional institution.

The second threshold involves past behaviour of the offender that reflects a pattern of persistent, aggressive behaviour; a failure to control sexual impulses; and other behaviour that indicates that the offender has difficulty controlling his or her behaviour.

This indeterminate sentencing option is unique in that judges are explicitly called on to predict, based on patterns of past behaviour, the likelihood of serious offences in the future. Specifically, the Crown must prove (beyond a reasonable doubt) that the offender "constitutes a threat to the life, safety or physical or mental well-being of other persons."[7]

Expert witnesses are often called to help the court make these determinations. At least two psychiatrists—one nominated by the defence, the other by the prosecution—must testify. Other experts may be called, and the offender can call witnesses to testify to his or her character and reputation.

▲ Dangerous offender Albert Muckle.

There has been a general increase in the number of DO designations (32 in 2010–2011) largely because of an increase in proactive efforts of Crown counsel and public concerns about violent offenders.[8] Aboriginal offenders are disproportionately designated as DOs. DOs generally have lengthy criminal records involving violence. Albert Muckle, for example, was found to be a DO and given an indeterminate sentence in 2006 after being convicted of a brutal attack that nearly killed a pregnant woman in Banff, Alberta. Muckle was born in prison to his incarcerated mother and had a criminal history dating back to his youth. At the court hearing, a report prepared by psychiatrists concluded that he was a psychopath. In 2013, the Alberta Court of Appeal denied his leave to appeal his sentence and his designation as a DO.[9]

LONG-TERM OFFENDER (LTO) DESIGNATION

Long-term offender

A designation under section 752 or 753 of the *Criminal Code* that requires the offender to spend up to 10 years under supervision following the expiry of his or her sentence.

Section 753 of the *Criminal Code* contains provisions for declaring someone a **long-term offender** (LTO). Crown counsel may use this option when the case falls short of the stringent criteria for filing a DO application. As with dangerous offenders, evidence must be presented to indicate that there is substantial risk that the offender will commit a serious personal offence after release from prison. However, there must also be risk assessment evidence demonstrating that the offender may be effectively managed in the community with appropriate supervision and treatment.[10]

The designation is available only for those offenders who have received a sentence of more than two years. At sentencing, the judge sets the length of the long-term supervision order. This means that after the sentence ends (which includes confinement and post-release supervision), the long-term supervision order comes into effect. This order requires that the offender be supervised by a parole officer for the remaining period of the order, which may be up to 10 years. The Parole Board of Canada sets the conditions under which the offender will be supervised following the expiration of his or her sentence.

LONG-TERM OFFENDERS AND LONG-TERM SUPERVISION ORDERS: WHAT'S THE DIFFERENCE?

The LTO designation is imposed by the sentencing judge and is the actual sentence of the court under section 753.1 of the *Criminal Code*. A long-term supervision order refers to the administration of the sentence and is the responsibility of the Parole Board of Canada under the *Corrections and Conditional Release Act*.

ADDITIONAL SENTENCING OPTIONS

When handing down a sentence, the judge can attach to it one or more other dispositions contained in the *Criminal Code*, including specified prohibitions and forfeitures. Prohibitions can include prohibition from driving, from attending places frequented by children, and from possessing firearms.

Convicted offenders may be required to forfeit goods to the Crown. For example, those found in possession of counterfeit money, narcotics, illegal pornography, hate propaganda, or some types of explosives and weapons may be required to hand the items over to the government. Forfeited items are either destroyed or sold with the proceeds going to the government. A *proceeds of crime* provision in the *Criminal Code* also allows the government to seize money, property, or goods accumulated as a result of crimes.

THE DECISION MAKING OF JUDGES

The decision making of trial judges has three important steps: identifying the relevant factors in the case, identifying the relevant law, and combining the relevant facts and the law to produce the correct outcome.[11] Judges may experience difficulties in carrying out these activities: expert witnesses may provide conflicting testimony; defence lawyers may attempt to obscure the facts to try to gain advantage for their clients, and witnesses may be unable to recollect the events that occurred, particularly if the incident occurred years ago.

"As a mitigating circumstance, may I say that my client's getaway car was a hybrid."

© Leo Cullum/The New Yorker Collection/The Cartoon Bank

SENTENCING CONSIDERATIONS

Criminal court judges consider a wide range of factors in determining the sentence to be imposed on a convicted offender. The purposes of sentencing and the various sentencing options available to judges were presented earlier in the chapter. The additional information that judges may consider in any case are set out in Box 9.1.

BOX 9.1   SENTENCING CONSIDERATIONS

Aggravating circumstances	Facts about an offender and the offence that are considered negative and tend to increase the severity of a sentence (e.g., violence).
Mitigating circumstances	More positive facts about the offender and the offence that may decrease the severity of a sentence (e.g., being Aboriginal, having an addiction).
Case law precedent	Judges will consider sentencing decisions in previous similar cases. A general principle is that there should be similar sentences in similar cases.
Pre-sentence reports (PSR)	The PSR, prepared by probation officers, presents information on the offender's background, present situation, and risk or needs. It also sets out options for sentencing that the judge will consider.
Victim impact statements	These contain information on the harm done to the victim (psychological and physical) and the consequences of the victimization.
Psychological assessments	These are completed on offenders and addresses their mental state and treatment needs.
Aboriginal offenders	Section 718.2(e) requires judges to consider alternatives to incarceration for Aboriginal offenders.

For most offences, judges have wide latitude in deciding on a sentence, which results in variability in sentencing decisions across the country. There is, for example, considerable variation with respect to the use of imprisonment. For example, in PEI, nearly 70 percent of convictions resulted in a sentence of imprisonment (the majority for impaired driving), compared with 30 percent in Saskatchewan and just under 40 percent in British Columbia.[12] While a number of factors that contribute to this variability (e.g., the specific mix of offences that are presented to judges), there do appear to be different approaches to the use of imprisonment across the country.

What is generally not considered by Crown, defence lawyers, and judges are the **collateral consequences of sentencing**. These are the sanctions and disqualifications that are placed on persons who have been convicted of a criminal offence and on the families of offenders who have been incarcerated.[13]

In many U.S. states, convicted felons are prohibited from accessing student loan programs and being employed in certain types of businesses. They may have their criminal record uploaded to the Internet and may not be eligible to apply for government contracts. Collateral consequences also include the impact of a conviction or a particular sentence on the offender's family (see Chapters 11 and 12). All of these may hinder the offender's efforts at rehabilitation and, for those offenders in confinement, reentry into the community.

The failure of the criminal justice system to consider collateral consequences may undermine its effectiveness. Many restorative justice approaches, on the other hand, consider these types of consequences and may be more effective in fashioning sanctions that produce positive outcomes (see Chapter 13).

SENTENCING ABORIGINAL OFFENDERS

The *Criminal Code* has a special provision (section 718.2(e)) for the sentencing of Aboriginal offenders. It is designed to reduce the over-representation of Aboriginal people in correctional institutions. It was reaffirmed by the Supreme Court of Canada in *R. v. Gladue*, [1999]1 SCR 688. In that landmark case, the court held that when a term of incarceration would normally be imposed, judges must consider the unique circumstances of Aboriginal people.

Specifically, Section 718.2(e) requires judges to consider (1) the unique systemic or background factors that may have contributed to the criminal behaviour of the Aboriginal person before the court, and (2) specific sentencing procedures and sanctions (including restorative justice and traditional healing practices) that may be more appropriate for the individual Aboriginal offender. These guidelines include taking into consideration colonialism, residential schools, and the marginality of Aboriginals in Canadian society.

The *Gladue* decision was confirmed by the Supreme Court of Canada in *R. v. Ipeelee* (2012), SCC 13, [2012]1 SCR 433. See Box 9.2. In 2012, the Ontario Appeal Court ruled that two Aboriginal men arrested for drug smuggling at the U.S. border should not be extradited to the United States because their Aboriginal heritage would not be considered at sentencing, as required in Canada (*United States v. Leonard (2012), ONCA 622*).

Section 718.2(e) continues to be the subject of debate. See At Issue 9.2.

Collateral consequences (of sentencing)
The sanctions and prohibitions that are placed on persons convicted of criminal offences (and their families), particularly those offenders who have been incarcerated.

The *Gladue* decision
A decision by the SCC that held that when a term of incarceration would normally be imposed, judges must consider the unique circumstances of Aboriginal people.

BOX 9.2 *R. V. IPEELEE*

Manasie Ipeelee is an Aboriginal offender with a lengthy record of convictions for violent offences and a history of alcohol and drug abuse. Ipeelee was designated a long-term offender and sentenced to six years in prison to be followed by a long-term supervision order (LTSO; he was to be supervised for 10 years following the expiry of his sentence).

Following his release from confinement, Ipeelee committed a new offence while under the influence of alcohol, breaching a condition of his LTSO. He was then sentenced to three years in prison, less six months time served in remand. Ipeelee appealed this sentence, but it was dismissed by the Appeal Court. In a subsequent decision, the SCC held that the trial judge erred in not applying the principles of the *Gladue* decision in sentencing Ipeelee for the new offence and the violation of the LTSO. More specifically, the SCC majority held that the sentencing judge failed to consider the potential for rehabilitation or to give sufficient attention to Ipeelee's situation as an Aboriginal offender. In view of this, the SCC ruled that an appropriate sentence would be one year in prison. The dissenting judges expressed the view that there was evidence that Ipeelee posed a risk that could not be adequately managed in the community. An additional point made was that in cases involving long-term offenders and breaches of LTSOs, protection of the community should be paramount and that these circumstances limited the applicability of the *Gladue* principles.

QUESTIONS

Read the full SCC decision at http://scc.lexum.org/en/2012/2012scc13/2012scc13.html. Do you agree, or disagree with the decision of the SCC in this case? Which position—that of the majority of justices or of the dissenting justices—do you find most persuasive?

Source: *R. v. Ipeelee* (2012), SCC 13, [2012] 1 SCR 433.

AT ISSUE 9.2   IS SECTION 718.2(E) A VALUABLE SENTENCING OPTION OR A MISGUIDED EFFORT TO REDUCE ABORIGINAL OVER-REPRESENTATION IN PRISON POPULATIONS?

Supporters argue that section 718.2(e) represents enlightened sentencing policy and is only one component of a wider effort to address the over-representation of Aboriginal people in the criminal justice system and in correctional institutions. The section requires only that judges *consider* sanctions other than confinement when sentencing Aboriginal offenders. Critics counter that special sentencing provisions for Aboriginal people discriminate against non-Aboriginal offenders and are based on the faulty assumption that sentencing practices, rather than complex historical and contemporary factors, are the primary reason for the high rates of Aboriginal incarceration. To these observers, it is disconcerting that, despite initiatives and legislation, such as the *Gladue* decision, Aboriginal persons continue to be over-represented in the justice system and in corrections in proportion to their numbers in the general Canadian population. This representation has steadily increased over the past decade.

Research studies have found that section 718.2(e) is applied inconsistently by judges across the country and that, for a variety of reasons, judges' discretion may be limited in cases where Aboriginal men and women have been convicted of violent offences.[14] In several court decisions, judges have ruled that the circumstances of the offences (primarily involving violence) and the accused's prior record and other background factors required that the principles of deterrence and denunciation take precedence over rehabilitation[15] (*R v. L.D.W.*, [2005] 215 BCAC 64; *R. v. Kakekagamick*, [2006] 211 CCC 289).

QUESTIONS

What other arguments might be made in support of, or in opposition to, Section 718.2(e)? Which of these do you find most persuasive?

S. Haslip. 2000. "Aboriginal Sentencing Report in Canada: Prospects for Success-Standing Tall with Both Feet Planted Firmly in the Air." *Murdoch University Electronic Journal of Law* 7, no 1. http://www.murdoch.edu.au/elaw/issues/v7n1/haslip71nf .html; P. Stenning, C. LaPrairie, and J.V. Roberts. 2001. "Empty Promises: Parliament, the Supreme Court, and the Sentencing of Aboriginal Offenders." *Saskatchewan Law Review* 64, no. 1: 137–68; and M.E. Turpel-Lafond. 2000. "Sentencing Within a Restorative Justice Paradigm: Procedural Implications of *R. v. Gladue*." *Criminal Law Quarterly* 43, no. 1: 34–50.

HOW DO JUDGES DECIDE?

Sentencing is a very human process. Most attempts to describe the proper judicial approach to sentencing are as close to the actual process as a paint-by-numbers landscape is to the real thing.

—Ontario Court of Appeal Judge David Doherty in
R. v. Hamilton and Mason (2004: 17)

Sentencing is among the most difficult tasks that judges have to perform and probably the most controversial. This controversy occurs because Canada is a diverse and open society that encompasses a broad range of religious, social, cultural, and moral values and views; thus, Canadians have widely disparate opinions on what constitutes a fit penalty for a particular offence.

Canadian judges have considerable discretion in selecting a sentence. Section 718.3(1) of the *Criminal Code* states, "Where an enactment prescribes different degrees or kinds of punishment in respect of an offence, the punishment to be imposed is, subject to the limitations prescribed in the enactment, in the discretion of the court that convicts a person who commits the offence."

In making a sentencing decision, a judge may sometimes seek to impose a sentence that not only fits the crime and reflects the "going rate" for similar offences but also takes into account the offender's particular circumstances. In other cases, the sentence may reflect only the severity of the crime, with no consideration for the situation of the offender. In still other cases, judges are confronted with difficult issues that generate considerable media attention and public and political debate. Recall from Chapter 3 that there are high levels of public dissatisfaction with the criminal courts, centring primarily on what Canadians perceive as overly lenient sentences imposed on the convicted.

Judges exercise considerable discretion in making sentencing decisions, and this may result in non-legal factors playing a role in their decision making and contributing to sentencing disparity. Sentencing disparity involves "different sentences being meted out for similar offences committed by similar offenders in similar circumstances."[16]

There is evidence that the personal attributes of judges may influence their decision making. The political party that appointed the judge, the region of the country in which the judge practices, and the gender of the judge have been found to influence decisions. Justices in Ontario and in the Western regions of the country tend to be more liberal in their decision making.[17] Similarly female judges have been found to vote differently than male judges in some regions, with one study of the Alberta Court of Appeal finding that female judges tended to more often support the complainant in cases involving sexual and domestic violence.[18]

The findings from a study of Israeli judges highlight how factors unrelated to the case have an impact on decision making. The researchers observed the decisions of judges to release inmate applicants on parole or to have their period of incarceration reduced. Judges make these decisions in Israel. It was found that, all else being equal, at the beginning of the day the judges granted nearly two-thirds of the applications before them, but as the hours passed, the numbers fell sharply until a meal break, after which the approval rate shot back up, before falling again as the day progressed.[19]

There is also some evidence that outside interest groups may affect the decision making of the courts. Such groups as the Women's Legal Education and Action Fund (LEAF) and the Canadian Labour Conference submit briefs to the Supreme Court in support of their positions.[20]

Judges' discretion does have some limits. A key principle of sentencing—set out in section 718.2(b) of the *Criminal Code*—is that two similar crimes committed by two similar offenders in similar circumstances should draw similar sentences. In their deliberations,

217

judges consider the sentences handed down by other judges, and as noted, the *Criminal Code* gives some guidance by setting maximum sentence limits. The appellate courts defer to the sentencing decisions of lower court judges and are reluctant to overturn these unless the sentence is found to be "demonstrably unfit [because of] an error of principle, failure to consider a relevant factor, or overemphasis of the appropriate factors" *(R. v. McDonnell,* [1997]1 SCR 948). Legislation enacted in recent years, including an expansion of mandatory minimum sentences, is viewed by many observers as an attempt by the federal government to restrict the discretion exercised by judges in sentencing and to toughen up sentencing.

STATUTORY GUIDANCE

Increasingly, judges looking for guidance in sentencing can find direction from Parliament in some statutes. However, section 718 of the *Criminal Code,* reproduced at the beginning of the chapter, is merely a list of the sentencing rationales typically presented in textbooks. The fundamental principle of sentencing, as stated in section 718.1 of the *Criminal Code,* is that of proportionality: a sentence must be proportionate to the gravity of the offence and to the degree of responsibility of the offender.

In what may well be the beginning of a trend, Parliament has specified factors that judges should consider when sentencing drug cases under the *Controlled Drugs and Substances Act.* According to section 10(2) of that act, an offender may deserve a harsher sentence when he or she carried, used, or threatened to use a weapon; used or threatened to use violence; trafficked in one of the specified substances or possessed such a substance for the purposes of trafficking in or near a school, on or near school grounds, or in or near any other public place usually frequented by people under 18; or trafficked one of the specified substances or possessed such a substance for the purpose of trafficking to a person under 18. These provisions join the principles and purposes of sentencing set out in section 718 of the *Criminal Code* and indicate that Parliament is willing to give sentencing judges some guidance by designating certain types of crime as deserving of greater punishment.

MAXIMUM SENTENCES

Every offence has a maximum sentence that a judge cannot exceed. However, these maximums are so high as to provide little practical guidance. For example, life imprisonment is the maximum sentence for manslaughter. Life imprisonment is also a possible (but not probable) sentence for offences, such as piracy (s. 74), breaking and entering a dwelling house (s. 306), and stopping a mail truck to rob or search it (s. 345). If no maximum sentence is specified for an indictable offence, the maximum allowable is five years. A maximum sentence is rarely applied for an indictable offence.

For summary conviction offences, the maximum sentence is six months in prison or a $5000 fine or both (except for sexual assault, where the maximum sentence is 18 months). The same maximum sentence applies when the Crown prosecutor elects to proceed summarily on a hybrid offence. However, these limits do not apply when the defendant elects trial in a provincial or territorial court on an indictable offence (this is a common misunderstanding). Judges cannot exceed the statutory maximum sentence, even when they disagree with the decision to proceed summarily. Prosecutorial election for summary proceedings is one way that Crown counsel can limit the severity of the sentence. Election can, therefore, be used as a bargaining chip in sentencing negotiations (plea bargaining).

MANDATORY MINIMUM SENTENCES (MMS)

Several offences, on conviction, can carry mandatory minimum sentences. For example, use of a firearm during the commission of an offence carries a minimum sentence of one year in prison for the first conviction and three years for subsequent offences (both to be consecutive to any term of imprisonment imposed for the offence itself). Other offences with mandatory minimum sentences are a second conviction for impaired driving, and first- and second-degree murder.

The federal government has increased the number of offences subject to mandatory minimum sentences. Supports of MMS contend that these sentences serve as a general and specific deterrent, prevent crime by removing offenders from the community, serve as a symbolic denunciation for certain behaviours, and reduce sentencing disparity.

In contrast, opponents of MMS have raised concerns that MMS have little or no deterrent value, serve to limit judicial discretion with a resulting impact on individual cases, have significant cost implications, and may lead to unfair sentencing practices. MMS have a number of potentially adverse effects, including increased costs because of an increase in not guilty pleas and an increase in prison populations.[21,22] Research studies have found that MMS have only a modest effect on crime prevention, no effect on drug consumption or drug-related crime, and no effect in reducing sentencing disparity, primarily because of the increased role of prosecutorial discretion in MMS.

From a review of three decades of Canadian public attitudes toward crime and punishment, criminologists Kim Varma and Voula Marinos concluded that "not only does research show that the public is supportive of judicial discretion and individualized sentencing, but there is no evidence that increasing the number of offences eligible for mandatory minimums will lead to an increase in public confidence."[23]

In the absence of research evidence, the focus on increasing the number of MMS can best be viewed as an example of a politically driven criminal justice policy. An increase in MMS is the cornerstone of the federal government's crime policy, although there is evidence that the judiciary is pushing back against these provisions, with judges in a number of cases finding that MMS violate the *Charter of Rights and Freedoms*. In *R v. Smickle* (2013), ONCA 678, for example, the Ontario Court of Appeal ruled that a three-year mandatory minimum sentence for gun possession was "cruel and unusual punishment." In the view of the court, a "cavernous disconnect" existed between the severity of such an offence and the severity of the sentence.[24]

APPELLATE DECISIONS AND LEGAL PRECEDENTS

One limitation on the discretion of judges is that sentences can be changed by appellate courts if deemed too lenient or too severe. Appellate courts can also set guidelines to assist judges in the trial courts. The general range of acceptability can be discovered by reviewing judicial precedents (decisions of other trial court judges) and decisions of courts of appeal. Also important is the designation of factors that indicate that deviation from the norm is warranted.

SENTENCING AND CRIME VICTIMS

It was noted in Chapter 3 that efforts are increasing to involve victims in the criminal justice process and to ensure that the interests of crime victims are addressed. These efforts have included allowing victim impact statements, collecting fine surcharges from offenders for use in supporting victim services programs, and establishing mediation programs as forums for victim–offender reconciliation (see Chapter 13). While concerns continue that victims may have unrealistic expectations as to the impact of their statement on the sentence that is imposed, it is generally accepted that the benefits of having victim input at the sentencing state outweigh any potential drawbacks.[25]

219

VICTIM IMPACT STATEMENTS

Section 722.1 of the *Criminal Code* provides that at the sentencing stage, a crime victim can submit to the court a **victim impact statement** (VIS) explaining his or her personal and emotional reaction to being victimized, any physical injuries caused by the victimization, and the financial impact of the victimization. There are no limitations on the kinds of offences for which a VIS can be submitted. However, it is most commonly used for crimes against the person.

A VIS can take the form of a letter to the judge. Many provinces distribute standard forms, which typically ask the victim to itemize physical injuries and any permanent disability, as well as the dollar value of financial losses, such as property loss or damage, lost wages, or medical expenses not covered by insurance. There is also space to express personal reactions to the crime, including any need for counselling. At the discretion of the judge, victims may read their VIS aloud in court or testify about the impact of the crime; they are not allowed to request specific penalties or directly address the issue of sentencing.

> There are not enough words to express our sadness, loneliness, loss, and anger . . . . This incident has changed my life forever. He was my only son. Who's going to look after us when we're old? Who will bury us if we both die at the same time? Nothing is important anymore. I wonder why I have to wake up every day and face the situation. (Portion of a victim impact statement read to a provincial court judge by the mother of a police constable killed by a speeding car that ran a red light[26])

Opponents of VISs argue that they are emotionally charged and thus undermine the objectivity of the justice process. Advocates contend that VISs ensure that victims are involved in the justice process, make the justice system more accountable, help the victim recover from the victimization, and educate both offenders and judges about the real-life consequences of crime.

Although VISs are enshrined in the *Criminal Code*, no guidance is provided as to how the courts should use the information they contain. Rather, how the information is used is left to the discretion of individual judges, and there is no evidence that these statements affect the sentence imposed by the court.[27] This lack of effect may result in disillusionment among crime victims because of unmet expectations.

In reality, VISs are submitted in only a small percentage of cases, and in even fewer cases do crime victims present a VIS in court. Judges appear to value the information contained in victim impact statements, although the impact of this information on the sentence that is imposed is uncertain.[28] A number of provincial court decisions have held that crime victims should have no role in determining the type of sentence imposed, although appeal courts have set aside sentences in a number of cases where it was determined that important information from the victim impact statement had not been considered.[29]

VICTIM FINE SURCHARGE

Unless it would constitute undue hardship to the offender or his or her dependants, a sentencing judge in adult court must order the offender to pay a victim fine surcharge (VFS) equal to 15 percent of any fine. If there is no fine, an amount of up to $10,000 is set by the judge.

There are two common misunderstandings about the VFS. First, the surcharge is *not* a sentence in its own right and is always ordered in addition to another disposition. Second, the money is *not* paid to the victim. It goes into a provincial fund to pay for victim services. Some provinces also collect the VFS for *provincial* offences. The rate of non-payment of VFSs is unknown, although it can be anticipated that for many offenders, even a small amount may be beyond their means.

Victim impact statement (VIS)

A submission to a sentencing court explaining the emotional, physical, and financial impact of the crime.

YOU BE THE JUDGE

Even with the expansion in the number of offences that, on conviction, carry a MMS, Canadian judges exercise considerable discretion in sentencing. To gain an appreciation of the challenges judges face in making sentencing decisions, review the summaries of actual cases presented in Box 9.3 and place yourself in the position of the sentencing judge. Answers are given at the end of the chapter.

The purposes of sentencing, the various sentencing options available to judges, and the objectives of sentencing were discussed in this chapter. Note that you can mix and match options—that is, you can sentence the offender to a period of custody in a provincial correctional facility and add a period of probation of up to three years. Probation cannot be used in conjunction with a sentence of more than two years, which places the offender under the jurisdiction of federal corrections. While these case summaries do not provide all the materials that a sentencing judge would have access to (e.g., the pre-sentence report), the exercise does provide a sense of the challenges faced by sentencing judges.

BOX 9.3   YOU BE THE JUDGE

Read each of the following case summaries. Then decide on a sentence and note the purpose of your sentence.

CASE 1

A lawyer in private practice (a former Crown counsel) enters a plea of guilty for assaulting his former girlfriend. A review of his record indicates that he has twice before been convicted of assaulting former girlfriends. On both previous occasions, he was granted a conditional discharge and did not incur a criminal record. The current assault involved a violent attack on his former girlfriend, which included kicking and punching, two weeks after she broke up with him. Evidence submitted to the court indicates that the accused's long-term battle with alcoholism had been aggravated by the breakup.

The defence lawyer points out that since being charged, his client has been attending Alcoholics Anonymous regularly and that this and other efforts at rehabilitation make him a candidate for another conditional discharge. Furthermore, this lawyer continues, there is nothing to be gained by imposing a more severe sentence. Crown counsel contends that since the accused has been convicted twice before of the same offence, a conditional discharge would not deter future assaults. The maximum punishment for assault as an indictable offence is five years in prison; as a summary conviction, the maximum is 18 months. What do you decide?

CASE 2

A Montréal advertising executive appears before you and pleads guilty to 15 counts of fraud. The criminal offences involved defrauding taxpayers of $1.5 million. The executive admits that he filed false invoices, inflated costs, billed for meetings he did not attend, and billed the government for work that was done by non-existent employees. The executive before you is the first person charged in the $250 million scandal. Crown counsel is asking for a 34-month term in federal prison based on the severity of the breach of trust. Defence counsel is arguing for a conditional sentence, to include a series of speeches on ethics at Canadian business schools.

Since the amount involved is over $5000, the maximum penalty that can be imposed under section 280(1) of the *Criminal Code* is 10 years' imprisonment. As the presiding judge, what sentence do you impose?

CASE 3

Appearing before you for sentencing is a 21-year-old University of Manitoba student, whom you have found guilty of dangerous driving causing death. Two years earlier, the young man ran a stop sign on the way to Bible camp and killed three people in the ensuing crash. Evidence presented at trial indicated that speed and alcohol were not factors in the crash and that the man had no prior driving infractions. The man had just come from a church service and had become lost on his way to the Bible camp before running the stop sign. He has expressed deep remorse for the accident and for the deaths of the people in the other vehicle.

At trial, the man pleaded not guilty to the criminal charge. His defence lawyer sought to have his client found guilty of careless driving under the provincial *Highway Traffic Act,* which carries a penalty of a fine. However, you have determined that the evidence supports a conviction for dangerous driving causing death. The maximum penalty for this offence is 14 years in prison. The Crown is seeking an 18-month jail term. What is your decision?

Record your sentencing decisions and the reasons that you selected each particular sentence. Once you have completed all three cases, check at the end of this chapter to see the actual sentences imposed by the judges for these cases. Then ask yourself these questions: (1) Did my sentence match the sentence of the judge? (2) Was my sentence more lenient or harsher? (3) Did the judge in the actual case make a good decision?

For each decision, be prepared to discuss why you selected that sentencing option, what purpose it was supposed to serve, and whether you agree or disagree with the actual sentence that was imposed by the presiding judge.

THE EFFECTIVENESS OF SENTENCING

Despite the critical role of sentencing in the criminal justice system, there are questions about its effectiveness in addressing the needs of victims, offenders, and the community. Some of the research on the effectiveness of sentencing is summarized in Research File 9.1.

RESEARCH FILE 9.1   THE EFFECTIVENESS OF SENTENCING

Does increasing the severity of punishment have a deterrent effect on offenders?

Generally, no. It is the *certainty* of punishment, rather than the severity of punishment, that has the most significant deterrent effect on offenders and others. While persons with a stake in conformity may fear lost opportunities if they are criminally sanctioned, marginalized persons who perceive they have few legitimate opportunities (and in fact, may not have many) may not engage in this thought process.[30] Some research findings suggest that offenders do not perceive the severity of sanctions in the same way as judges and probation and parole officers. In one study, offenders ranked halfway houses as more severe than judges and did not view imprisonment as the most severe sanction.[31]

Is there consistency in sentencing?

Not always. With a few exceptions involving mandatory minimum sentences, most offences have only a maximum penalty, providing judges with considerable discretion in deciding both the objective of the sentence and the specific penalty. This disparity makes it difficult to predict with any accuracy what type of sentence will be imposed for offences, even though judges are guided by case precedents.

Are sentences effectively matched to individual offenders?

Often, no. Matching specific sentencing options with the needs and risks of offenders is, at best, an inexact science. Few research studies have examined which types of sentences are most effective (i.e., serve as a deterrent, address risk and needs) with specific types of offenders.

Is there continuity from the criminal court to corrections?

Not always. Once the offender leaves the courtroom, he or she becomes the responsibility of corrections. Judicial recommendations for placement and treatment programming are not binding on correctional decision makers. This continuity is increased in specialized courts, discussed in Chapter 7.

SUMMARY

The discussion in this chapter has focused on sentencing in the criminal courts. The purposes and principles of sentencing were set out, along with the various judicial sentencing options. Canadian judges also have additional authority to use judicial determination, issue judicial restraint orders, and to designate offenders as dangerous offenders and long-term offenders. The factors that judges take into account in making decisions were discussed, and it was noted that extra-legal variables may come into play. While section 718.2(e) of the *Criminal Code* and the *Gladue* decision require judges to consider alternatives to incarceration for Aboriginal offenders, they are applied unevenly across the country and may not be a consideration in cases involving violent offending. Victim impact statements and proposed federal legislation are designed to increase victim involvement in the sentencing process, although restorative justice approaches may hold more potential for ensuring that the needs of crime victims are met.

KEY POINTS REVIEW

1. Among the statutory objectives of sentencing are denunciation, deterrence, the separation of offenders from society, rehabilitation, and reparation for harm done.

2. The sentencing goals in the criminal courts fall into three main groups: utilitarian, retributive, and restorative.

3. Judges can select among a number of sentencing options, which include various alternatives to confinement and varying terms of imprisonment in correctional institutions.

4. Judges can impose a number of additional conditions on offenders, including judicial determination, judicial restraint orders, and dangerous offender and long-term offender designations.

5. Criminal court judges consider a wide range of factors in determining an offender's sentence.

6. Several offences, on conviction, carry mandatory minimum sentences.

7. Efforts have been made to reduce the over-representation of Aboriginal peoples in correctional institutions by considering alternatives to confinement in sentencing. The impact of section 718.2(e) and the *Gladue* decision is questionable.

8. Sentencing is among the most difficult and probably the most controversial tasks that judges have to perform.

9. Mandatory minimum sentences may not serve as a deterrent or make communities safer and can best be viewed as a politically driven crime policy.

10. There is evidence that the personal attributes of judges may influence their decision making.

11. Research evidence is, for the most part, inconclusive as to the effectiveness of the various sentencing options, although it appears that incarceration is not an effective general or specific deterrent.

KEY TERM QUESTIONS

1. Describe a **suspended sentence** and a **conditional sentence**.

2. Compare and contrast **concurrent, consecutive,** and **intermittent sentences**.

3. What are **judicial determination** and **judicial restraint orders**, and what role do they play in sentencing?

4. How do the designations of **dangerous offender** and **long-term offender** impact convicted persons?

5. What is meant by the **collateral consequences of sentencing**?

6. What was the **Gladue decision**, and what role does it play in the sentencing of Aboriginal offenders?

7. What is a **victim impact statement** (VIS), and what role does it play in the criminal justice process?

ANSWERS TO BOX 9.3

Actual Sentencing Decisions

Case 1. In February 2004, the Honourable Judge W.J. William Diebolt of the B.C. Provincial Court imposed a conditional discharge with a three-year probation order on Stephen Neville Suntok. In addition to the standard conditions of probation, the order contained the following requirements: Suntok was to take and complete counselling as directed by his probation officer, to have no direct or indirect contact with the victim, to complete 200 hours of community service, and to not consume alcohol.

In passing sentence, the judge indicated that the public interest would be best served if Suntok were rehabilitated, noting that he had been publicly humiliated and embarrassed. The sentence was criticized by Vancouver Rape Relief and Women's Shelter and by the victim. The Crown appealed the sentence, requesting a more substantial sentence. The sentence was subsequently overturned by a judge of the B.C. Court of Appeal, who imposed a suspended sentence (which carries a criminal record) with three years' probation. This judge stated, "In the circumstances a conditional discharge is not a fit sentence. I think that the nature of the assault, one akin to a spousal assault, the seriousness of the assault, and the fact of a previous conditional discharge for an assault, the terms of which were not taken seriously by the accused, are all aggravating factors. . . . The granting of a conditional discharge is not in the public interest given those considerations, in particular as they relate to general deterrence and denunciation."

Suntok was subsequently disciplined by the Law Society of British Columbia. This included a brief suspension from the practice of law in the province.

Case 2. In September 2005, Paul Coffin was sentenced to a two-years-less-a-day conditional sentence by Québec Superior Court Justice Jean-Guy Boilard. This sentence was to be served in the community. As part of the sentence, Coffin must abide by 9 p.m. to 7 a.m. curfew on weekdays and must deliver a series of lectures on business ethics to university students. Among the topics proposed by Coffin: "Never compromise your integrity, no matter what the perceived benefit" and "The only person who can rob you of your reputation, credibility, and good name is yourself." The presiding judge indicated that the guilty plea entered by Coffin, his repayment of nearly $1 million to the government, and his remorse were key factors in the decision to impose a conditional sentence rather than jail time. As well, the judge stated, "Denunciation and deterrence were the prime objectives of the sentence that will be meted out." In October 2005, the Québec Court of Appeal gave the Crown permission to appeal the sentence imposed on Coffin. In April 2006, the Québec Court of Appeal overturned the conditional sentence and ordered Coffin to serve 18 months in jail for his role in the sponsorship scandal.

Case 3. On April 8, 2005, Madam Justice Colleen Suche of the Court of Queen's Bench of Manitoba imposed a two-year suspended sentence on Charles Manty that required him to perform 100 hours of community service by speaking to young drivers about the importance of paying attention while driving.

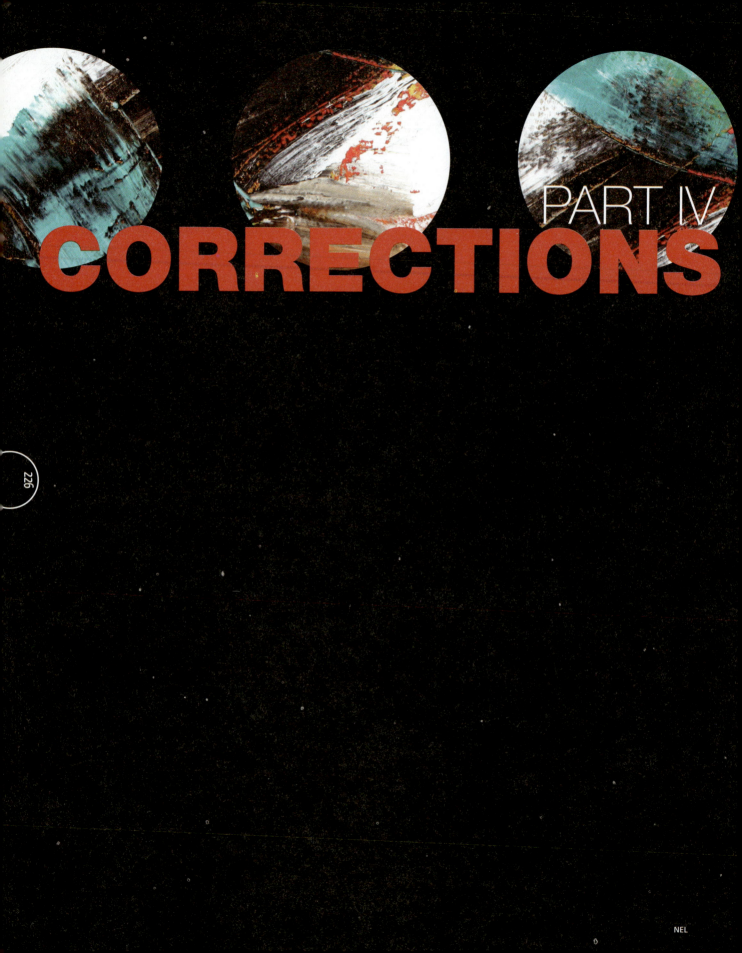

PART IV

CORRECTIONS

Chapter 10: Corrections in the Community: Alternatives to Confinement
Chapter 11: Correctional Institutions
Chapter 12: Release and Reentry

• •

Corrections

Structures, policies, and programs to sanction, punish, treat, and supervise, in the community and in correctional institutions, persons convicted of criminal offences.

Non-carceral corrections

That portion of systems of correction relating to offenders in non-institutional settings.

The chapters in this part of the text examine the corrections component of the criminal justice system. **Corrections** can be defined as the structure, policies, and programs delivered by governments, not-for-profit organizations, and members of the general public to sanction, punish, treat, and supervise, in the community and in correctional institutions, persons convicted of criminal offences.

Correctional systems and the other components of the criminal justice system have as their primary mandate the protection of society. However, there is often disagreement over how this goal can best be accomplished. Historically, the corrections pendulum has swung back and forth between policies that are more punitive and those that are more focused on the rehabilitation of offenders. In the early 21st century, a more punitive penology has emerged, although the restorative justice model is evident at various stages of the corrections process.

Note well that *community corrections* includes both alternatives to confinement (e.g., diversion, probation) and programs for offenders released from correctional institutions (e.g., parole), as well as a variety of intermediate sanctions and restorative justice initiatives (discussed in Chapter 13). Community corrections also includes criminal court judges because the correctional process really begins after the sentence is passed.

More corrections personnel, offenders, and programs are in **non-carceral corrections** because most convicted persons are not sent to a correctional institution (although most federal corrections personnel work in institutions).

Chapter 10 explores the community corrections strategies that provide alternatives to confinement and provide for the supervision and control of offenders in the community. These include diversion, probation, conditional sentences, post-release supervision and programs, and parole for offenders sentenced to a period of incarceration in a correctional institution.

The discussion in Chapter 11 centres on correctional institutions. It examines the attributes of institutions that pose challenges for inmates, correctional officers, management, and treatment staff. Chapter 12 examines the release of offenders from confinement and their reentry into the community. In recent years, there has been a precipitous drop in the rates of conditional release, a development that is largely attributed to the shift to a punitive penology.

CHAPTER 10

CORRECTIONS IN THE COMMUNITY:
ALTERNATIVES TO CONFINEMENT

LEARNING OBJECTIVES

After reading this chapter, you should be able to

- comment on the concept of community corrections
- describe the alternatives to incarceration
- discuss conditional sentences as an alternative to incarceration and the issues that surround their use
- discuss the increase in surveillance and control of offenders under supervision in the community and the impact of Bill C-10
- discuss the recruitment, training, roles, and responsibilities of probation officers, including the dual role of probation officers when supervising offenders
- discuss the obstacles to effective probation practice
- discuss the effectiveness of alternatives to confinement

Ex-offender

We should be providing offenders with more alternatives than incarceration. I think that what has to be done is that we have to work with our young offenders or our youths a lot earlier, with a lot more emphasis and a lot more money spent in the young offender area. Once a youth has entered an institution, it's going to be very, very difficult to get that person to change their ways, because once he gets in there he is going to be conditioned to the situation that is happening. It's a very negative environment. I know in my situation, I had been a youth in a training school. I was being conditioned to the adult person I would be for the longest time, and I would spend 23 years of my life in institutions. If you put that into dollars and cents, I think it could have been spent a lot better than it was on me.

Source: Personal communication with author, 2001.

Recall from the discussion of sentencing in Chapter 9 that most offenders who receive a sentence of supervision remain in the community. The passage of Bill C-10, however, has constricted the use of alternative measures and imposed mandatory minimum sentences for offenders convicted of violent offences and sexual offences.

Figure 10.1 presents a breakdown of the adult non-carceral and carceral population. Note that approximately 23 percent of offenders are in some types of custody, while 77 percent are under community supervision.

DIVERSION

Diversion

Programs that are designed to keep offenders from being processed further into the formal criminal justice system.

Diversion programs have been a feature of Canadian criminal justice for decades. Offenders can be diverted from the formal criminal justice process at several points: pre-charge, post-charge, and post-sentencing.

The objective of all diversion programs is to keep offenders from being processed further into the formal criminal justice system and, in so doing, to reduce costs and social stigmatization, and assist offenders in addressing the specific factors related to their offending. Most diversion programs require that offenders acknowledge responsibility for

FIGURE 10.1 ▶

Average Counts of Adults in Correctional Services, by Type of Supervision, 2010/2011

Source: M.Dauvergne. 2012. *Adult Correctional Statistics Canada, 2010/2011.* Ottawa: Minister of Industry. http://www.statcan.gc.ca/pub/85-002-x/2012001/article/11715-eng.pdf.

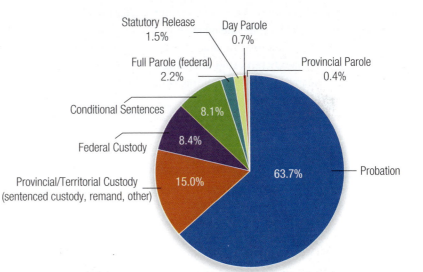

Statutory Release 1.5%
Day Parole 0.7%
Full Parole (federal) 2.2%
Provincial Parole 0.4%
Conditional Sentences 8.1%
Federal Custody 8.4%
Probation 63.7%
Provincial/Territorial Custody (sentenced custody, remand, other) 15.0%

229

their behaviour and agree to fulfill certain conditions within a specified time. These may include attending an alcohol or drug treatment program, completing a number of community service hours, or meeting other requirements. If these conditions are successfully met, the charges are withdrawn, and the person does not have a criminal record.

Traditional diversion programs focused on low-risk, first-time offenders, although in recent years, cases involving more serious offences have been referred to diversion programs. Many diversion programs are centred on the principles of restorative justice. These are discussed in Chapter 13.

A major concern with diversion program is **net-widening**—that is, involving offenders who would otherwise have been released outright by the police or not charged by Crown counsel.

There are also concerns that diversion programs can be coercive and punitive. Some ambiguity also surrounds the notion of choice in the operation of diversion programs and whether diversion programs may infringe on the rights of accused persons. A study of the John School diversion program in Toronto (a program for men apprehended for soliciting street prostitution) found that the program focused disproportionately on offenders of lower socio-economic status and that criminal charges were withdrawn if offenders waived basic procedural rights to gain admission to the program.[1]

Net-widening

A potential, unanticipated consequence of diversion programs in which persons who would otherwise have been released outright by the police or not charged by Crown counsel are involved in the justice system.

INTERMEDIATE SANCTIONS

The term **intermediate sanctions**, also often referred to as *alternative sanctions* or *community sanctions*, describes a wide variety of correctional programs that generally fall between traditional probation and incarceration, although specific initiatives may include either of these penalties. Intermediate sanctions include fines, community service, day attendance centres, home detention with or without electronic monitoring, intensive probation supervision, strict discipline camps (boot camps), conditional sentence orders, and halfway houses.

The primary objective of intermediate sanctions is to hold offenders responsible for their behaviour through restrictive and intensive intervention; treatment and rehabilitation are generally secondary, although they are usually a component of these sanctions.

Section 742 of the *Criminal Code* states that a convicted person who would otherwise be incarcerated for a period of less than two years can be sentenced to a conditional term of imprisonment to be served in the community rather than in custody. This sentence is a **conditional sentence** and the offender is required to fulfill certain conditions attached to the release. These may include abstaining from alcohol and other intoxicants, performing community service, or attending a treatment program. The offender may be required to be in their residence during certain hours of the day, often referred to as *house arrest*.

Non-compliance with the conditions of a conditional sentence can result in the offender being incarcerated. Offenders who are given a conditional sentence are often viewed as having received a slap on the wrist, although in interviews, offenders on conditional sentences mention the negative impact on their children and their interpersonal relationships and in the workplace.[2] The primary purpose of conditional sentences is to provide an alternative to imprisonment.

Considerable controversy has surrounded the use of conditional sentences since their inception in 1996. While popular with judges, concerns have been raised about high violation rates and the misuse of this sentencing option by judges, particularly in cases where offenders who committed violent offences were given a conditional sentence.

Intermediate sanctions

A term used to describe a wide range of correctional programs that generally fall between probation and incarceration, although specific initiatives may include either of these penalties as well.

Conditional sentence

A sentence for offenders receiving a sentence or sentences totalling less than two years whereby the time is served in the community (generally under house arrest) under the supervision of a probation officer.

To address these concerns, legislative provisions in Bill C-10, enacted in 2012, prevent judges from imposing a conditional sentence in cases where the offender has been convicted of an offence involving bodily harm, drug trafficking, the use of a weapon, and a variety of other cases in which the Crown had proceeded by indictment.

PROBATION

Probation

A sentence imposed on an offender by a criminal court judge that provides for the supervision of the offender in the community by a probation officer, either as an alternative to custody or in conjunction with a period of incarceration.

Section 731 of the *Criminal Code* provides that, in cases in which no minimum penalty is prescribed, the sentencing judge may place the offender on probation for up to three years. **Probation** is the most frequently used strategy for supervising offenders in the community as an alternative to incarceration, although it is used in conjunction with other sanctions as well. See Table 10.1.

The proportion of cases receiving a sentence of probation has remained stable over the years at around 45 percent, as has the average length of probation orders (around 12 months).[3] Probation is popular largely because it is so versatile: the specific conditions of a probation order can be tailored to the risk and needs of the offender.

TABLE 10.1 THE USES OF PROBATION

Adult offenders can be on probation for the following reasons:

- as part of a conditional discharge (mandatory)
- as a condition of a suspended sentence (mandatory)
- as part of an intermittent sentence (mandatory)
- a sentence on its own (the most common)
- following a prison term of two years or less
- in conjunction with a conditional sentence
- for a federal offender who received a sentence of *exactly* two years (little known)

PROBATION VERSUS PAROLE: WHAT'S THE DIFFERENCE?

Probation differs in significant ways from parole. See Table 10.2.

TABLE 10.2 PROBATION VERSUS PAROLE

Probation	Parole
imposed by a criminal court judge	granted by an administrative tribunal (a parole board)
available only for provincial or territorial offenders (except federal offenders who received a sentence or sentences totalling exactly two years)	available to federal and provincial and territorial offenders
maximum length is three years	continues until warrant expiry date (end of sentence)
may be used in conjunction with a period of confinement in a provincial or territorial institution (and following a sentence of exactly two years, in a federal correctional facility)	a form of conditional release from confinement in a provincial, territorial, or federal correctional facility
requires offender to abide by general conditions (e.g., obey the law and keep the peace) and perhaps specific conditions tailored to the offender's individual risk factors (e.g., abstain from alcohol)	requires offender to abide by general and perhaps also specific conditions that are designed to reduce risk factors (e.g., no-contact provisions)
breach of condition can be a charge under the *Criminal Code* that requires evidence for conviction of breach of probation; additional conditions may be imposed and the terms of probation extended; offenders found in breach of conditions rarely incarcerated	breach of condition may result in suspension or revocation, resulting in a return to custody; the offender may be re-released with additional conditions

ROLE AND RESPONSIBILITIES OF PROBATION OFFICERS

Probation falls under the authority of the provinces and territories. Each jurisdiction has developed its own procedures and standards for recruiting and training probation officers. Commonly, there is a pre-employment training model, wherein potential applicants must complete a number of courses (many of which are offered online), often at their own expense, before being eligible to apply for a position as a probation officer.

The myriad activities of probation officers are set out in Table 10.3.

TABLE 10.3   THE ACTIVITIES OF PROBATION OFFICERS

Officers of the Court

preparing pre-sentence reports (PSRs); attending court proceedings; applying to change conditions of probation orders; writing progress reports; consulting with Crown counsel

Investigation	**Assessment**
preparing pre-sentence reports; preparing community assessments (for provincial parole boards in Ontario and Québec); preparing case files	risk assessment and case management planning (e.g., interviewing clients and collateral contacts); making evidence-based assessments of offenders; determining appropriate interventions to address risk and need areas
Counselling	**Service Coordination**
conducting initial interviews and motivational interviewing; challenging difficult client attitudes and behaviours; supervising individuals; providing group counselling; facilitating core programs (in provinces where they play this role), such as respectful relationships, substance abuse management, violence prevention, sex offender maintenance	collaborating with police and social services; identifying educational, vocational, and employment goals; providing treatment opportunities; assisting with locating housing; addressing family, financial and other issues

Surveillance and Enforcement

monitoring compliance with conditions of probation; monitoring compliance with conditions of provincial parole (in Ontario and Québec); conducting home visits; documenting violations; preparing violation reports and recommendations; preparing violation reports for provincial parolees (in Ontario and Québec)

Source: Republished with permission of Taylor and Francis Group LLC Books from *Corrections: Foundations for the Future*, J.B. Stinchcomb © 2011; permission conveyed through Copyright Clearance Center, Inc.

THE DUAL ROLE OF PROBATION OFFICERS

Probation officers play a dual role: they provide assistance and support for offenders while they enforce the conditions of the probation order. In carrying out the assistance and support role, the probation officer may help the offender address issues that have contributed to the offence and identify resources in the community, such as alcohol and drug treatment programs, education upgrading courses, and mental health services.

However, the probation officer must at the same time ensure compliance with the general and specific conditions of the probation order. For offenders who are less cooperative, an approach based on control may be effective; for offenders who are motivated to change, the probation officer can provide encouragement, support, and assistance. Probation officers have the discretion to tailor their style of supervision to the needs and risks of the individual probationer. To be effective, probation officers must, to the greatest extent possible, balance enforcement with treatment and balance a client-centred approach with meeting organizational requirements (e.g., completing assessments and other paperwork).[4]

It is often difficult for probation officers to focus equally on both roles, and that may be a barrier to effective case management. For example, a

▼ A probation officer meets with his client.

© Mark Harvey/Alamy

probationer with a history of drug addiction who has relapsed and started using again (or who never ceased using drugs) may want to ask his or her probation officer for help finding a treatment program. However, the request could trigger a charge of breach of probation since the probationer has disclosed the illegal drug use to the probation officer. On the other hand, failing to disclose the drug relapse could result in the commission of further criminal acts to support the addiction.

Effective case management requires the identification of the risks and needs of offenders so that the appropriate level of supervision can be determined (i.e., more intensive supervision for higher risk or needs offenders and less supervision for lower risk or needs offenders) and so that the services that will address the needs of offenders can be identified.[5] Risk management and protection of the public are central features of probation supervision.[6] These features are reflected in the use of various risk assessment instruments and the classification of offenders.[7]

A core component of the probation officer's role is completing assessments, which are designed to identify the offender's needs, evaluate risk, and assist in formulating a plan of supervision. These assessments are used not only in the case management process but also by provincial or territorial parole boards in determining whether to grant conditional release to offenders in custody.

Two of the more common instruments are the Level of Service Inventory-Revised (LSI-R) and the Level of Service/Case Management Inventory (LS/CMI), which is used for both adult and young offenders. The LSI-R is a 54-item, interview-driven assessment that measures risk factors in a number of areas, including criminal history, education and employment, financial status, and drug problems, among others. The LS/CMI measures risk and need factors in a number of areas, including criminal history, alcohol or drug problems, personal problems, incarceration history, mental health concerns, among others. In Saskatchewan, probation officers use the Saskatchewan Primary Risk Assessment (SPRA) instrument for case and risk management.

In addition, other assessment instruments are used for specific groups of offenders, including sex offenders (Sex Offender Risk Assessment) and offenders convicted of spousal assault (Spousal Assault Risk Assessment).

In the new Canadian penology in the early 21st century, the focus is on the surveillance and control of offenders, and this has impacted probation practice. Over the past decade, there has been a strong shift in the role and orientation of probation officers toward control and surveillance in probation supervision.[8] This shift has been due, in large measure, to increasing caseloads, the focus on risk

233

PERSPECTIVE

Probation Officer

I think it is our responsibility to try to help individuals and to identify the issues that they have so they can begin working on themselves. For the offenders on my caseload, I try to help them with basic needs, such as food, shelter, employment training, and core programming, that will help them develop their self-confidence and address their issues. It is important to have empathy and to understand the client's needs while also having realistic expectations of them. I try to see that the conditions of the probation order are followed while at the same time respecting the person.

Source: Personal communication with author, 2012.

assessment to ensure accountability and reduce liability, and the increasing number of special, higher risk categories of offenders—such as sex offenders and assaultive male offenders—who are receiving sentences of probation.

The shifting paradigm to a focus on risk management may put pressure on probation officers to move away from developing therapeutic relationships with probationers centred on responding to risk and needs and toward a more enforcement-oriented approach centring on adherence to the conditions of probation. Research findings suggest this may be a mistake. A tough talk approach to offenders based on threats of revocation is ineffective in reducing recidivism, with one set of researchers stating, "Especially with high-risk offenders, threatening revocation and even applying punitive sanctions have minimal enduring effects. They may suppress untoward conduct in the moment, but they do not achieve lasting behavioral change—the kind of change that will contribute to public safety."[9] Rather, the focus in probation (and parole) practice should be on developing quality relationships with offenders. This skill has been determined to be one of the most important requisites for effective supervision.[10]

RISK, NEED, AND RESPONSIVITY IN PROBATION PRACTICE

A key set of concepts that have gained prominence in non-carceral and carceral corrections are the principles of risk, need, and responsivity (RNR).

The **risk principle** states that correctional interventions have a greater chance of success when they are matched with the offender's level of risk, because higher-risk offenders benefit more than medium- and low-risk offenders.

The **need principle** says that correctional interventions should target the criminogenic needs (dynamic risk factors) of offenders, including substance abuse, peer relations, and pro-criminal attitudes.

The **responsivity principle** states that correctional interventions should be matched to the learning styles and abilities of individual offenders, with particular emphasis on cognitive-behavioural interventions.

Although RNR has most frequently been associated with institutional treatment programs, it is now recognized that this model may have validity in community corrections and in providing supervision and programs for offenders who have avoided a custodial sentence and those released into the community following confinement.[11] Programs and interventions that use RNR have been proven to be more successful that those based on traditional practice.

An innovative approach that trains probation officers to use the principles of RNR in their practice is profiled in Box 10.1.

Many probation offices now have specialized supervision units composed of specially trained officers for offenders convicted of spousal assault, sex offences, and other specific types of crime. Studies suggest that specially trained probation officers are less likely to be punitive in responding to violations of a probation order, perhaps because of their more in-depth understanding of the cognitive thinking patterns and behaviours of specific groups of offenders.[12] Probation officers in many jurisdictions are also involved in facilitating programs for offenders. In B.C., for example, these include a violence prevention program, substance abuse management, respectful relationships, living skills, cognitive skills, and educational upgrading, as well as a sex offender program.

Risk principle

Correctional interventions are most effective when matched with the offender's level of risk and higher-risk offenders benefit from interventions more than medium- and low-risk offenders.

Need principle

To be effective, correctional interventions must address the criminogenic needs of offenders.

Responsivity principle

Correctional interventions should be matched to the learning styles of individual offenders.

> **BOX 10.1   THE APPLICATION OF RNR TO PROBATION PRACTICE: THE STICS INITIATIVE**
>
> In an attempt to introduce evidence-based practice into probation supervision of offender, the Strategic Training Initiative in Community Corrections (STICS) was delivered to a sample of probation officers in B.C., Saskatchewan, and PEI (the experimental group). The STICS program is centred on the principles of RNR, and it teaches probation officers ways to use these principles in supervising probationers, with particular attention to criminogenic factors, such as relationships with peers and criminal thinking patterns. A comparative group of probation officers in these provinces did not receive the STICS training (the control group), allowing for an assessment of the effectiveness of the approach.
>
> In a subsequent analysis of audio tapes recorded during client sessions conducted by probation officers from the experimental and control groups, it was found that the officers trained in STICS altered their traditional supervisory practices and incorporated the need principle into their interactions with probationers. This change included spending more time discussing criminogenic factors with their clients and less time on non-criminogenic topics, such as the conditions of probation. A review of the audiotaped sessions also revealed that the probation officers that had participated in the STICS program evidenced better skills in developing relationships with their clients and used more cognitive-behavioural intervention techniques in client sessions.[13] This approach contributed to lower rates of reoffending among probationers who were supervised by officers who had completed the STICS training.
>
> The STICS initiative demonstrated that focusing on changing the probationers' cognitive processes, including their attitudes, thinking, and perceptions of self, are as important, if not more important, than providing general assistance. On a more general level, the significance of the STICS project was that it demonstrated that it is possible to move from the conceptual level (the principles of RNR) to practice.[14]

INTENSIVE SUPERVISION PROBATION

Intensive supervision probation (ISP)

An intermediate sanction (between the minimal supervision of traditional probation and incarceration) that generally includes reduced caseloads for probation officers, increased surveillance, treatment interventions, and efforts to ensure that probationers are employed.

Intensive supervision probation (ISP) entails increased surveillance of probationers, various treatment interventions, efforts to ensure that offenders are employed, and reduced caseloads for probation officers. In Canada, ISP is used primarily with youth offenders. In ISP programs, offenders are monitored closely, and rigorous conditions are imposed on them, such as multiple weekly reporting requirements, strict enforcement of the mandatory and optional conditions on the probation order, and the requirement that offenders secure and maintain employment. ISP is more suited for offenders who are classified as posing a greater risk to reoffend in the community. An underlying premise of these programs is that they can help reduce the number of prison admissions, cut operational costs, and protect the public while providing increased supervision of more serious offenders.

THE EXPERIENCE OF PROBATIONERS

Few studies have examined the experience of persons on probation. Some evidence suggests that many probationers believe that their sentence served as a deterrent and that being on probation was beneficial.[15] A survey of offenders on probation in B.C. (N = 1121) found that probationers had a positive overall experience on probation (81 percent), a majority (90.5 percent) felt that their probation officer treated them fairly, and they did not have difficulty accessing programs (91.3 percent). Similarly, a majority of the probationers surveyed (63.5 percent) indicated that they were involved in their supervision plan. Overall client satisfaction did not vary by the gender or Aboriginal status of the probationer, nor the region of the province in which they resided.[16]

On the other hand, there is evidence that some offenders may experience **pains of probation**. Depending on the specific conditions attached to the probation order, these

Pains of probation

The emotional and economic challenges that probationers may experience while under probation supervision in the community.

pains may include deprivations of autonomy, changes to their daily life routine, the stigma associated with being on probation, and possible difficulties with employment.

In contrast to inmates in correctional institutions, who may experience physical pains, those associated with probation tend to be more economic and emotional.[17] IPS, in particular, may place restrictions on the probationer, who may view probation negatively.

Research in the United States has found that some offenders rate being on probation as more punitive than short-term prison sentences.[18,19] Offender perceptions of probation may be due, in part, to the probationers' previous experience in prison and on probation: offenders who have been previously incarcerated may not find confinement as punitive as close supervision in the community.

CHALLENGES IN PROBATION PRACTICE

In contrast to the field of policing and institutional corrections, there has been little consideration of the occupational perspectives and experiences of probation officers. Studies indicate that the most satisfying aspect of a probation officer's job is working with offenders, and the least satisfying are the ever-increasing administrative duties, including paperwork and dealing with agency management.[20,21]

Studies have found that probation officers have higher stress levels than the general population. Female probation officers, in particular, may have higher levels of stress than their male counterparts, because of the issues surrounding supervision of male probationers.[22,23]

One emerging issue is that of officer safety; some evidence shows that incidents involving probation officers are vastly under-reported. Many probation officers do not conduct visits to the homes of probationers on their caseload, often because of inadequate time or concerns with safety. Still other officers believe that home visits are intrusive on the probationer and their family.

Among the challenges that probation officers experience that may contribute to their stress level are accessing resources and services for high-need clients, including probationers who have a mental disability or an addiction; large caseloads increasingly populated by high-risk and high-needs clients; and limited time to see clients because of the increasing burden of paperwork. In Ontario, the average caseload per probation officer is 66 offenders, and in B.C., there has been a 28 percent increase in the number of offenders being supervised on probation since 2007.[24] The impact of caseload size on the quality of supervision provided and on rates of violations of probation orders and reoffending, however, is unknown. Reduced caseloads, in the absence of evidence-based treatment may not improve the effectiveness of probation. Providing probation services in remote and northern regions is also a challenge, given the lack of programs and services for offenders on probation. Probation officers may also experience challenges in supervising persons whose primary language is not English or French.

SURVEILLANCE IN THE COMMUNITY: THE USE OF ELECTRONIC MONITORING AND GPS

A key trend in community corrections is the increasing surveillance of offenders under supervision in the community. This supervision has been made possible by technology that allows authorities to track offenders via various forms of electronic monitoring and global positioning systems (GPS). While the use of these technologies may provide alternatives to confinement and allow the offender to remain in the community, there are serious issues surrounding privacy and human rights.

Electronic monitoring (EM) has been used for provincial and territorial offenders for many years. In 2012, Bill C-10 included a provision to allow Corrections Service Canada and the Parole Board of Canada to require that offenders on temporary absences (TAs), work release, parole, statutory release, or long-term supervision wear a monitoring device. This requirement will potentially result in ever-increasing numbers of offenders being under surveillance.

There are both *front-end* and *back-end* EM programs, referring to the stage of the correctional process at which the strategy is used. In some provinces, EM is imposed by the sentencing judge, while in others, EM is used as a condition of early release from incarceration. Where EM is used in support of an alternative to confinement, its primary objective is to ensure public safety while at the same time allowing the offender to remain in the community. Generally, only offenders who have been convicted of less serious, non-violent offences and who have a stable residence and a telephone are eligible to participate in EM programs.

Increasingly, GPS tracking systems are being used to monitor the location and movements of high risk offenders, including sex offenders (see Figure 10.2). GPS technology has the capacity to track an offender's movements on a continuous basis and makes it possible to determine where an offender is at any given moment. In addition, it is possible to customize the tracking, to specify the boundaries of an offender's movements, and to set out locations where the offender is not permitted (e.g., a sex offender may be prohibited from going near schools or playgrounds). A monitoring program can be designed that will alert both the offender and the agency if the offender violates certain area restrictions. (See the Media Link at the end of the chapter.)

▲ Troubled actress Lindsay Lohan wore an electronic monitoring anklet in 2011 as part of a 35-day sentence for shoplifting a necklace from a Venice, California, jewellery store.

Electronic monitoring

A correctional strategy that involves placing an offender under house arrest and then using electronic equipment to ensure that the conditions of supervision are fulfilled.

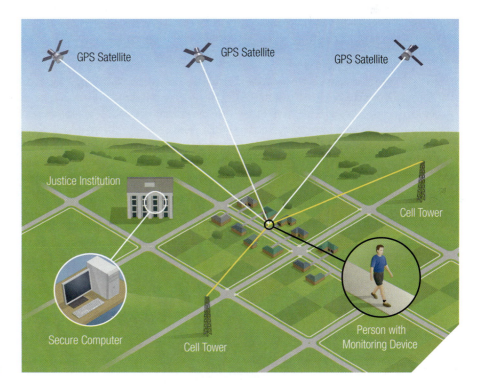

FIGURE 10.2 ►

Electronic Monitoring

It is likely that, in the coming years, advances in technology will allow authorities not only to track offenders but also to control their behaviour. This ability is certain to general considerable debate and raise concerns about privacy and other legal issues.

THE EFFECTIVENESS OF ALTERNATIVES TO CONFINEMENT

Research File 10.1 sets out what is known about the effectiveness of alternative to confinement. Note that community corrections agencies often do not gather the information required to determine the effectiveness of probation practices.[25] Few of the more

---

RESEARCH FILE 10.1   THE EFFECTIVENESS OF ALTERNATIVES TO CONFINEMENT

Does traditional diversion work?

It's hard to tell. There are few formal evaluations; it may widen the net by focusing on low-risk, first-time offenders. There is no evidence that diversion has any impact on correctional populations, but it may increase the justice system's workload and costs.[26,27] Problem-solving courts as an alternative to the justice system have shown promise. See Chapter 7.

Does EM work?

Potentially. Electronic monitoring can play a significant role in reducing rates of recidivism, even among more serious offenders, including sex offenders.[28,29] There is no evidence that EM programs reduce prison admissions, but they are less costly than incarceration. They are not generally being used as a true alternative to confinement.[30] Among probation officers and offenders in a U.S. study there was the perception that EM had a negative impact on personal and family relationships and hindered efforts to secure housing and employment.[31] These strategies may increase the workload for probation and parole officers. Net-widening, privacy issues, and the impact of surveillance on the offender and his or her family are all issues.

Are conditional sentences effective?

Potentially. Traditionally, there have been high rates of violations of conditions (up to 40 percent of cases);[32] despite new limitations under Bill C-10, there are concerns that COSs are being inappropriately used by judges. Research suggests that alternatives to custody, such as conditional sentences, may be more effective than imprisonment in reducing recidivism.[33]

Is probation effective?

Potentially. There is no evidence that traditional probation practice reduces reoffending.[34] This is due to a variety of factors, including the lack of training of probation officers in strategies that may improve probation outcomes, in particular, the absence of the principles of RNR in probation practice. Research in the United States has found that firm, fair, and caring relationships between probation officers and offenders reduce the risk of re-arrest, even after accounting for the offender's level of risk and existing personality attributes.[35] While many probationers who have committed less serious crimes successfully complete probation, less positive results are reported for offenders with lengthy criminal records and who have additional issues, such as addiction and mental illness.[36] Potential obstacles to effective probation practice are a lack of training for probation officers, the failure to identify the risk or needs of offenders and to design appropriate interventions, and low program completion rates by offenders. A study In B.C. found that only 35 percent of offenders with a condition on their probation order to complete a treatment program did so.[37] Research studies suggest that probation is most effective with those offenders who are in a stable personal relationship, are employed, have higher levels of education, and do not have an extensive criminal record. Specialized supervision units can be effective in increasing offender accountability and reducing rates of reoffending, and they have a positive impact on victim satisfaction.[38] There is growing evidence that incorporating the principles of RNR into probation practice improves the quality of supervision and case outcomes.[39]

Does intensive supervision probation work?

Yes. These programs can manage risk while providing probationers with access to treatment. ISP may be more cost-effective than incarceration and produce better outcomes.[40]

common programs for probationers, including those operated by private contractors, have been evaluated.

SUMMARY

This chapter has provided an overview of the various strategies that are used by systems of corrections as alternatives to confinement. These include traditional practices, such as diversion and probation, as well as more recent innovations, such as the electronic surveillance of offenders. The problem-solving courts, discussed in Chapter 7, are also an effort to provide an alternative to incarceration for offenders with special challenges. The effectiveness of these alternatives to confinement varies. Interventions that incorporate the principles of risk, need, and responsivity hold great promise, while others, such as traditional diversion, while widely used, have been found to be less effective.

KEY POINTS REVIEW

1. When used as an alternative to confinement, community corrections includes diversion, probation, intermediate sanctions, and restorative justice initiatives.

2. Offenders can be diverted from the criminal justice process at several points: pre-charge, post-charge, and post-sentencing.

3. There is concern that traditional diversion programs may widen the net and be coercive and punitive.

4. Probation is the most widely used strategy for supervising offenders in the community as an alternative to incarceration.

5. Intermediate sanctions, which fall between traditional probation and incarceration, have both offender-oriented objectives and system-oriented objectives.

6. There are significant differences between probation and parole.

7. Considerable controversy has surrounded the use of conditional sentences, centring on high violation rates and, before the enactment of Bill C-10, the use of conditional sentences in cases involving a violent offence.

8. Some alternatives to confinement are effective, particularly those based on the principles of risk, need, and responsivity (RNR).

KEY TERM QUESTIONS

1. Define **corrections**.

2. What are the components of **non-carceral corrections**?

3. Identify and discuss the objectives of **diversion** programs.

4. What is **net-widening**, and why is it a concern associated with diversion programs?

5. Describe the correctional strategy of **probation**.

6. Identify and discuss the objectives of **intermediate sanctions**, and provide examples of these types of sanctions, including **conditional sentences**.

7. Define and discuss the **risk principle**, the **need principle**, and the **responsivity principle**, and note their importance in correctional interventions.

8. What are the features of **intensive supervision probation**?

239

9. What is meant by the **pains of probation**, and what is their impact?

10. Describe the use of **electronic monitoring** as a corrections strategy.

MEDIA LINK

"All Sex Offenders on GPS Under California Parole Division Supervision" or go to the book's website at www.nelson.com/crimjusticeprimer 5e.com

CHAPTER 11

CORRECTIONAL INSTITUTIONS

LEARNING OBJECTIVES

After reading this chapter, you should be able to

- describe the federal and provincial and territorial systems of corrections
- discuss how prison architecture reflects philosophies of punishment and correction
- describe the types of correctional institutions and how security is maintained
- identify and discuss the challenges in correctional institutions
- describe the recruitment and training of correctional officers, their role and relationships, activities in the prison, and sources of occupational stress
- describe the dynamics of life inside prisons, including the inmate code, violence and victimization, and the experience of prison inmates
- discuss the classification of offenders, the role of risk and needs profiles, and case management
- define what is meant by throughcare
- discuss the effectiveness of correctional treatment programs

For more than 150 years in Canada, correctional institutions (as they are now called) have been a core component of the response to criminal offenders, and their use shows no sign of decline. These facilities have endured despite ongoing challenges, many of which emerged within the walls of Canada's first penitentiary in the early 1830s—overcrowding, the lack of classification of offenders, limited programming, and inadequate provisions for inmate safety, among others. Although the architecture of correctional institutions has changed over the centuries, and living conditions are greatly improved, many inmates still live in fear and have difficulty avoiding the more negative features of life inside. And, similar to their earlier counterparts, Canadian institutions in the early 21st century continue to hold a disproportionate number of persons who are marginalized in society: the poor, Aboriginal people, and persons with mental illnesses. The dynamics of life inside correctional institutions pose challenges to efforts to address the needs of inmates and to prepare them for release back into the community.

One way to track the changes in corrections philosophies is to study prison architecture. As an example, check out the three images in Box 11.1. The Kingston Penitentiary was the first prison constructed in Canada, in 1835 (and closed almost 180 years later, in 2013); the second is of Pe Sakastew Aboriginal Healing Centre, a federal correctional institution located in Hobbema, Alberta; and the third is of Central East Correctional Centre, an 1184-bed provincial correctional facility located in Lindsay, Ontario.

THE CREATION OF THE CANADIAN PENITENTIARY

The events surrounding the building of the first penitentiary in Kingston, Ontario, in the early 1800s illustrate how changes in the response to crime and criminal offenders can be influenced by social, economic, and political forces. There were influences from the United States, where between 1790 and 1830, crime came to be viewed as a consequence of community disorder and family instability rather than as a manifestation of individual afflictions. The Americans built penitentiaries in an attempt to create settings in which the criminals could be transformed into useful citizens through religious contemplation and hard work. Some of these institutions operated on a "separate and silent" system, in which prisoners were completely isolated in their cells from one another. This system came to be known as the **Pennsylvania model**.

In other penitentiaries, in what became known as the **Auburn model** (originating in New York State), prisoners worked and ate together during the day and slept in individual cells at night. A system of strict silence, which forbade prisoners from communicating or even gesturing to one another, was enforced at all times. The Auburn model was the system on which most prisons in the United States and Canada were patterned.

In Canada, the building of the first penitentiary in Kingston, Ontario, was the result of a number of influences, including developments in the United States, overcrowding in the local jails because of a lack of classification of inmates, and the view that corporal punishment was improper and degrading.[1] When completed in 1835, the Kingston Penitentiary was the largest public building in Upper Canada. It symbolized a **moral architecture**, one that reflected the themes of order and morality.

The penitentiary was to be a model for those confined in it, as well as for society, and among its goals were the eradication of the underlying causes of crime: intemperance, laziness, and a lack of moral values. Hard labour and a strong emphasis on religion were the focal points of the reformation process within the penitentiary. A strict silent system was enforced. Breaches of prison regulations brought swift and harsh punishment, including flogging, leg irons, solitary confinement, and rations of bread and water.

Pennsylvania model (for prisons)
A separate and silent system in which prisoners were completely isolated from one another; eating, working and sleeping in separate cells.

Auburn model (for prisons)
A system that allowed prisoners to work and eat together during the day and housed them in individual cells at night.

Moral architecture
The term used to describe the design of the first penitentiary in Canada, the intent of which was to reflect themes of order and morality.

BOX 11.1   THE KINGSTON PENITENTIARY, ONTARIO; PE SAKASTEW HEALING LODGE, ALBERTA; CENTRAL EAST CORRECTIONAL CENTRE, ONTARIO

An aerial view of the federal Kingston Penitentiary, constructed in 1835 and closed in 2013.

The Pe Sakastew federal minimum security correctional facility for Aboriginal offenders is located in Hobbema, Alberta, and based on a healing lodge design.

Source: © *Pe Sakastew Centre (Institutional Profiles)*, http://www.csc-scc.gc.ca/institutions/001002-4008-eng.shtml, Correctional Service Canada, 2012. Reproduced with the permission of the Minister of Public Works and Government Services Canada, 2013.

The Central East Correctional Centre, a provincial medium/maximum-security institution located in Lindsay, Ontario.

QUESTION

Compare and contrast the images of the three facilities. What does the architecture of each convey about correctional philosophy?

Brown Commission

An investigation into the operation of the Kingston Penitentiary that condemned the use of corporal punishment against inmates and emphasized the need for rehabilitation.

The conditions in Kingston lead to the creation of a Royal Commission in 1848, 13 years after it opened. The **Brown Commission** investigated charges of charges of mismanagement, theft, and mistreatment of convicts.

The commission found that the warden, Henry Smith, had indeed mismanaged the institution and that there was excessive use of corporal punishment, including the flogging of men, women, and children, some as young as 11. The warden was fired and attempts were made to reform the operation of the prison. Despite changes, corporal punishment, the silent system, and hard labour remained prominent features of prison life. In retrospect, the Brown Commission can perhaps best be viewed as a missed opportunity for Canadians to reconsider the use of imprisonment and to explore potentially more effective ways to prevent crime and reform offenders.

LOCAL JAILS AND PROVINCIAL PRISONS

Conditions in the local jails and provincial institutions at this time were generally deplorable. Prisoners were required to pay for their meals, liquor, and rent—and, on release, for the jailer's fee for his services. Those inmates unable to pay the fee were often confined for additional periods or allowed to panhandle on the streets to raise the necessary funds.[2]

Efforts were made to improve the operation of prisons in the 1880s. Federal legislation provided for the appointment of federal prison inspectors and outlined their powers and duties; addressed the need for the separate confinement of female offenders, inmates with mental disorders, and young offenders; and provided for the use of solitary confinement in federal penitentiaries. However, inmates continued to be subjected to a variety of physical disciplinary sanctions, many of which continued in use until the 1930s.[3]

Following World War II, there was a shift toward the treatment model of corrections. The federal prison system introduced vocational training, education, and therapeutic intervention techniques. These included group counselling and individual therapy. The decade of the 1960s was the height of the treatment model in Canadian corrections. However, by the late 20th and early 21st century, there was a shift toward a more conservative model of correctional practice. This change was noted as a major trend in Canadian criminal justice in Chapter 2.

TYPES OF CORRECTIONAL INSTITUTIONS

The federal government and provincial or territorial governments operate a wide variety of facilities. These include correctional institutions and correctional centres that house sentenced offenders; jails and detention centres for short-term offenders on remand, awaiting sentencing; remand centres for accused persons awaiting trial; and correctional camps, treatment centres, and community residences that house lower-risk inmates in a minimum-security setting or those on conditional release.

Federal correctional facilities are categorized in terms of security levels. **Minimum-security institutions** generally have no perimeter fencing and allow unrestricted inmate movement, except during the night. **Medium-security institutions** are surrounded by high-security perimeter fencing with some restrictions on inmate movement. **Maximum-security institutions** have highly controlled environments and high-security perimeter fencing, and inmates' movements are strictly controlled and constantly monitored by video surveillance cameras.

There is also one special handling unit (SHU) in Canada. This is a high-security institution for inmates who present such a risk to staff and other inmates that they cannot be housed even in maximum-security facilities. Correctional Service Canada (CSC) also operates a number of regional health centres. These facilities house violent offenders and offer treatment programs that focus on violence and anger management.

Minimum-security institutions
Federal correctional facilities that generally have no perimeter fencing and allow unrestricted inmate movement, except at night.

Medium-security institutions
Federal correctional facilities that have a less highly controlled institutional environment than maximum-security institutions and in which inmates have more freedom of movement.

Maximum-security institutions
Federal correctional institutions with a highly controlled institutional environment and high-security fencing. Inmates' movements are strictly controlled and monitored.

▼ Ferndale Institution, a federal minimum-security correctional facility located east of Vancouver.

Jeff Vinnick/Vancouver Sun

The provinces and territories operate facilities with different levels of security, though without uniform designations. These jurisdictions make greater use of maximum-security institutions than the federal CSC, primarily because they are responsible for housing persons who are on remand awaiting trial or sentencing. These individuals represent a broad range of security risks, and in the absence of time to assess individual offenders, all are detained in maximum security. Provincial correctional systems also operate treatment facilities for special populations, such as sex offenders. For an inside look at the New Toronto South Detention Centre, see the Media Link "Inside Toronto South's New Maximum Security Detention Centre" at the end of this chapter.

All correctional facilities have two types of security: (1) **static security** includes perimeter fencing, video surveillance, and alarms, as well as fixed security posts, such as control rooms and position posts, where officers remain in a defined area; and (2) **dynamic security** includes ongoing interaction, beyond observation, between correctional officers and inmates. It includes working with and speaking with inmates, making suggestions, providing information, and—in general—being proactive.

Static security

Fixed security apparatus in a correctional institutions, including fixed security posts wherein correctional officers are assigned to and remain in a specific area, such as a control room.

Dynamic security

A variety of ongoing, meaningful interactions between staff and inmates.

Total institutions

Correctional institutions, psychiatric hospitals, and other facilities characterized by a highly structured environment in which all movements of the inmates or patients are controlled 24 hours a day by staff.

THE CHALLENGES OF CORRECTIONAL INSTITUTIONS

Correctional institutions confront a number of challenges that may undermine their effectiveness:

*Prisons are what the sociologist Erving Goffman referred to as **total institutions**.* All aspects of life are conducted in the same place and the activities of a group of persons with similar status (inmates, in the case of prisons) are tightly scheduled and controlled by an administrative hierarchy.[4] This regimen may prevent inmates from developing the skills to function independently once released into the community.

Prisons are asked to pursue conflicting goals. While prisons protect society by housing offenders who pose a serious risk to the community, they are also charged with preparing offenders for eventual release into the community as law-abiding and contributing members of society. This balance is often referred to as the split personality of corrections.

Correctional institutions are political and public institutions. Politicians, provincial legislatures, and the federal government exercise considerable control over how correctional institutions are operated, the goals they are asked to pursue, and the resources that are available to corrections personnel. For example, it was anticipated that Bill C-10, passed in 2012, would have a significant impact on correctional institutions, including an anticipated increase in prison populations and offenders serving longer periods of time under mandatory minimum sentences.

Observers have argued that the control over inmates has been extended through the application of high technology, which allows ever-larger numbers of inmates to be housed, monitored, and controlled with fewer staff. Though institutions using high technology may be less expensive to operate, high costs may occur as a result of disturbances and riots by inmates and increased rates of recidivism when inmates are released from these facilities. Technology may improve security, but it also reduces contact between the correctional staff and inmates. All these features of new correctional institutions may heighten, rather than reduce, the pains of imprisonment, reduce staff–inmate contact and communication, and increase the stress levels and isolation of correctional officers.[5]

This lack of contact may have significant implications for the development of effective treatment interventions and for the involvement of correctional officers in positive interactions with inmates.

245

While all correctional institutions share a common identify as total institutions, some are more total than others. Correctional facilities vary in terms of their affiliation (federal, provincial, or territorial), security classification, size, management style, inmate characteristics, and other key factors that affect the dynamics of institutional life. These differences can be described as a **continuum of correctional institutions**: at one end of such a continuum would be minimum-security and community corrections facilities; at the other end would be maximum-security institutions. As one might expect, the dynamics of life inside institutions at either end of the continuum would be considerably different. Even institutions at the same security level have their own personalities—a function of history, the attitudes and behaviour of administrators and staff, the specific attributes of the inmate population, and other less tangible factors.

Continuum of correctional institutions

The differences in institutional environments among correctional institutions located at either end of the security spectrum—maximum to minimum.

PERSPECTIVE

Deputy Warden, Federal Correctional Institution

The long-term inmates are more manageable than short-term inmates. They understand they are going to have to get along with other inmates and the staff. The long-term guys are the ones who end up being on the inmate committees and taking a more balanced view of things. It's the short-term guys who are the most difficult to manage. It's this group that causes all of the problems.

Source: personal communication with author, 2007.

246

Wardens in charge of correctional institutions must address a number of challenges. These include meeting the requirements of legislation and policy, being accountable for their decisions, being aware of the requirements of the rule of law and the duty to act fairly, managing staff, and ensuring that issues that arise in the inmate population are addressed.

CONDITIONS IN CORRECTIONAL INSTITUTIONS

The first was the deplorable physical condition of the penitentiary. The cleanliness or lack of it is horrendous. There is a build up of dirt and grime throughout the Penitentiary.... Washrooms were filthy and staff often had to resort to cleaning them on their own. While some cells had been renovated, others had been plastered at some point and had gaping holes in the walls.

—Poirier[6]

A description of a Canadian prison in the 19th century? No. The findings of a committee that visited Her Majesty's Penitentiary in Newfoundland (built in 1903) and published in its report on the province's correctional institutions in 2008. The physical condition of a correctional facility can have a significant impact on the dynamics that develop among inmates and between inmates and staff and can cause higher rates of serious violence.[7,8] In a potentially precedent-setting case, a Québec judge in 2012 reduced an offender's sentence from 53 months to 44 months after calling a provincial correctional facility "unhygienic" and commenting, "There are rats and vermin (in the jail)." The judge also cited gang activity and the high rate of drug use in the prison as imposing unnecessarily severe punishment on offenders in the facility.[9]

THE GROWTH IN REMAND POPULATIONS

A pronounced trend in Canadian corrections has been the significant increase in the number of persons in remand and in the length of time served in remand. This trend has been a major contributor to overcrowding. Persons on remand outnumber those in sentenced custody,[10] which has been attributed to the lengthy delays in cases getting to trial (noted in Chapter 8) and to the rules of disclosure, which require Crown counsel to provide copies of all the evidence that is to be used at trial. In more complex cases, these documents can run thousands of pages. Offenders on remand are housed in high-security provincial or territorial institutions with minimal access to programs and services. The rapid growth in remand populations has been ascribed to an increasing focus on risk aversion in the criminal justice system and to the punitive penology described in Chapter 2.[11]

In an attempt to reduce remand populations, the federal government enacted Bill C-25, which reduced credit for time served from two days credit for every one day served to one day credit for one day served. Previously, concern was raised that defence lawyers were lengthening the justice process to secure time-served credit for their clients at sentencing. However, in *R. v. Summers* (2014, SCC 26) the Supreme Court of Canada ruled that offenders can receive extra credit for time spent in custody before they are sentenced.

THE CHANGING OFFENDER PROFILE

The number of federal offenders who are classified as maximum security at admission has increased significantly, as has the proportion of offenders serving a sentence for a violent offence. Although the majority of offenders committed to provincial or territorial institutions have been convicted of non-violent offences, these populations pose challenges as well. There are high rates of alcohol and drug problems and unstable work histories, and many inmates have been convicted of violent offences. The rates of communicable diseases are also high, including HIV/AIDS, tuberculosis, and hepatitis B and C in institutional populations.[12]

Inmates in custody are likely to be single and unmarried, and to have low levels of education. In addition, these offenders have a variety of treatment needs. More than 90 percent are assessed as requiring substance abuse treatment, and nearly 90 percent in federal custody have treatment needs in the personal or emotional domain.[13]

Four in 10 federal inmates are not Caucasian. Aboriginal peoples are over-represented, composing 4 percent of the national population but nearly 25 percent of federal prison populations. The percentages are higher for Aboriginal women inmates—34 percent of federally sentenced women. The numbers of Black inmates is growing, and this group now represents nearly 10 percent of the total federal prison population, while composing only 3 percent of the Canadian population.[14]

There are also groups of offenders who require special attention. See Table 11.1.

OVERCROWDING

Overcrowding has plagued correctional institutions since the Kingston Penitentiary was constructed in 1835. Today, many provincial or territorial and federal prisons are beyond 100 percent capacity (e.g., Saskatchewan facilities are operating at twice their capacity and nearly one-half of Ontario's institutions are overcrowded).[15,16]

Overcrowding is a result of a number of factors, including changes in judicial sentencing patterns, an increase in the number of long-term inmates, the growing reluctance

TABLE 11.1	THE CHALLENGES OF SPECIAL INMATE POPULATIONS
Senior Inmates	Offenders over age 50 are a growing segment of institution populations (20 percent of federal inmates) and offenders under community supervision (30 percent of federal offenders). They are more likely to be convicted of violent offences and sex offenses (many of which are historical); afflicted with chronic diseases and disabilities that require special attention and resources; and are vulnerable to psychological and physical victimization by younger inmates.[17]
Persons with Mental Illnesses	The number of offenders with mental health issues is growing; mental health issues are more prominent in inmate populations than in the Canadian general population: Nearly, 20 percent of provincial inmates in Ontario had a psychiatric disorder, and it is estimated that 35 percent of federal inmates have a mental illness that requires treatment intervention.[18,19] Correctional institutions have been called the "asylums of the 21st century";[20] the challenges are acute in provincial or territorial institutions because of short periods of confinement and lack of resources. The death of Ashley Smith in a federal women's correctional centre spotlighted deficiencies in the response to persons with mental illnesses who become involved in the justice and corrections systems. See Chapter 13.
Offenders with Fetal Alcohol Syndrome (FASD)	FASD is a condition of brain damage caused by alcohol consumption by a woman during pregnancy; the symptoms include impulsive violence, aggression, and learning disabilities. A study of federal inmates in Stony Mountain Institution (Manitoba) found the incidence of FASD was 10 times that found in the general population.[21]

of parole boards to release offenders into the community, and the absence of new facilities. As noted, overcrowding in provincial or territorial institutions is also related to the increase in the numbers of offenders in remand, which, in turn, is due, in part, to delays in the criminal court process. The number of incarcerated federal offenders has also been increasing.[22]

Overcrowding can affect daily prison life by heightening tensions among inmates and between inmates and correctional officers, compromising security, and overburdening treatment programs.[23] A major concern surrounding Bill C-10 and other federal legislations enacted 2010–2012 is that they will increase overcrowding in provincial or territorial and federal correctional facilities by increasing the number of mandatory minimum sentences.

INMATE GANGS

A growing challenge for prison administrators are inmate gangs that have their origins in the community and that import their affiliations and tactics into correctional institutions. It is estimated that one in six federal inmates is affiliated with a known gang or with organized crime.[24]

Aboriginal gangs are prominent in the Prairie region. The most notable of these groups are the Alberta Warriors, Indian Posse, Redd Alert, Native Syndicate, and Manitoba Warriors. Other gangs include the Asian Crazy Dragons in Alberta, the U.N. and Red Scorpion gangs in B.C., and the Hells Angels. Inside correctional institutions, gangs are involved in a variety of activities, including smuggling and dealing drugs and extortion. Gang activity may be contributing to critical incidents and, in extreme cases, to riots. For a brief look inside the culture of Aboriginal gangs, see the Media Links at the end of the chapter.

ENSURING INMATE SAFETY

The accountability of corrections officials extends to ensuring the safety of inmates in their charge—an onerous task, particularly in federal maximum-security institutions. Wardens have little say in how many inmates are sent to their facility, the types of inmates received, and when inmates will leave their institution via transfer, conditional release, or statutory release. They are, however, responsible for the safety and security of the inmates once they have arrived.

In recent years, several high-profile incidents have occurred within prisons, some of them involving inmates murdered by fellow inmates. These events have increased the pressure on the CSC to ensure that operational policies and procedures provide protection for inmates. The issues were highlighted by the murder of Denise Fayant. See Box 11.2.

BOX 11.2   THE MURDER OF DENISE FAYANT

Thirty hours after arriving at the Edmonton Institution for Women, 21-year-old Denise Fayant was strangled by her former lover with a bathrobe sash. She died two days later in hospital. An investigation into her death, which was originally ruled a suicide, found that she had been slain by two inmates, one of whom had been her former lover and against whom she was scheduled to testify. A subsequent inquiry conducted by an Alberta provincial court judge found that Fayant had repeatedly told corrections officials that she feared for her safety if they transferred her to the newly opened institution. Thirty hours after arrival, she was dead. Two inmates were later convicted and sentenced to additional federal time for her murder. The investigating judge concluded that correctional officials failed Fayant, stating, "The process failed tragically and inhumanly. Her death was avoidable."[25] In response, prison officials insisted that they had been assured by inmates in the prison that no harm would come to Fayant.

Source: From GRIFFITHS/CUNNINGHAM. *Canadian Corrections*, 2E. © 2004 Nelson Education Ltd. Reproduced by permission. www.cengage.com/permissions.

Protective custody (PC) is a section of the prison that holds inmates who are at risk in the general population. It may include inmates who have snitched or testified against other inmates, inmates who have drug debts or other outstanding

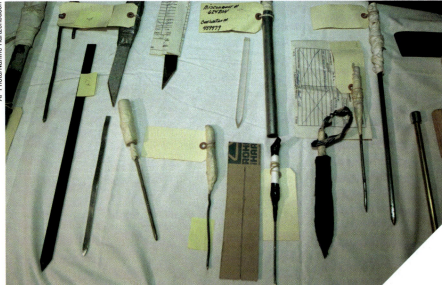

Homemade weapons confiscated from ▶
inmates

obligations, and inmates convicted of sexual crimes, such as rape and child molestation. It is also possible for an inmate who is feeling at risk to check themselves in to PC to protect themselves.

Correctional authorities must also attempt to ensure that inmates do not do self-harm. **Self-injurious behaviour (SIB)** includes head banging and skin cutting. Female offenders are at high risk of SIB, and Aboriginal offenders account for 45 percent of all self-harm incidents in federal prisons, while composing 24 percent of the prison population.[26] The suicide rate among inmates incarcerated in federal (70 per 100,000) and provincial (43 per 100,000) institutions is much higher than for the Canadian general population (10.2 per 100,000).[27]

Inmates face additional threats to their health from HIV/AIDS and other infectious diseases.[28] It is estimated that the rate of HIV/AIDS infection in federal prisons is 10 times that of the general population, and the rate for Aboriginal offenders is even higher. Though HIV can be transmitted via anal intercourse between inmates, the most frequent cause of infections is intravenous drug use and the sharing of HIV-contaminated needles and syringes. HIV and other blood-borne diseases, such as hepatitis B and C, are also transmitted by pens, pencils, and wire instruments that inmates use for body piercing and tattooing. Many offenders are already infected when they enter systems of corrections.[29] One Canadian female ex-offender recalled that 80 percent of the women in the prison were using drugs and that needle sharing was common.[30]

To reduce the risk, the CSC employs a number of prevention strategies, including providing inmates with condoms, lubricants, dental dams, and bleach kits for needles (though not needles), and it has also developed intensive support units (ISUs). These units can be accessed by inmates who have substance abuse issues and by inmates who want to reside in a drug-free environment. Preliminary evaluations indicate that the CSC ISUs have strong support from both inmates who use the units and from correctional staff, although the long-term effectiveness of these units on both drug use and recidivism is uncertain.[31,32]

Interdiction strategies include frequent searches, a urinalysis program, drug-sniffing dogs, video surveillance, and ion scanners that can detect drug residue on clothing and other objects on visitors and on inmates returning from absences in the community. The effectiveness of interdiction strategies in reducing the availability of drugs and the rates of infectious diseases is uncertain.[33]

Self-injurious behaviour (SIB)
Deliberate self-inflicted bodily harm or disfigurement.

FEMALE OFFENDERS

Female offenders present unique challenges for systems of corrections. The pathways to crime for female offenders are in many ways distinct from those of male offenders, and they require the development of gender-specific programs and interventions.

Some of the general attributes of female offenders are set out in Box 11.3.

In numerous documented instances, the human rights of women were violated, including violations of Canada's obligations under international law.[34]

THE INCIDENT AT THE KINGSTON PRISON FOR WOMEN (P4W): A WATERSHED EVENT IN WOMEN'S CORRECTIONS

On April 22, 1994, a brief but violent physical confrontation took place between six inmates and several correctional officers at the Kingston Prison for Women (which has since been closed). As a result of the incident, the women were placed

250

BOX 11.3 A PROFILE OF FEMALE OFFENDERS IN CORRECTIONS

- Female offenders represent about 1 in 10 offenders admitted to custody and, in many respects, present a different profile from male offenders.

- The number of women admitted to federal custody has increased by 40 percent in the past decade, and the number of Aboriginal women admitted to federal correctional facilities has increased 90 percent during that time.

- An increasing number of women are admitted to custody for violent crimes.

- One in 10 women are gang-affiliated, compared with one in six for male offenders.

- One in four federal female inmates have been incarcerated on drug-related charges and HIV and hepatitis C infection is generally higher among female inmates.

- In contrast to male offenders, a high percentage of female offenders have been the victims of physical and sexual abuse before incarceration, and they exhibit high rates of eating disorders, depression, and sleep disorders.

- Federal female offenders are twice as likely as male offenders to have been previously hospitalized for psychiatric reasons and to have a mental health issues.

- Female offenders generally have greater physical health and mental health needs than male inmates.

- The number of federal female offenders over the age of 50 has increased over the past decade. Compared with younger women, these offenders have lower overall risk and needs and are less likely to have substance abuse issues but have greater personal and emotional issues.

Sources: Canadian HIV/AIDS Legal Network. 2012. *Women in Prison, HIV and Hepatitis C*. Accessed March 5, 2014. http://www.aidslaw.ca/publications/publicationsdocEN.php?ref=1281; D. Calverley. 2010. "Adult Correctional Services in Canada, 2008/2009." *Juristat* 30, no. 3. Accessed March 5, 2014. http://www.statcan.gc.ca/pub/85-002-x/2010003/article/11353-eng.htm; L. Greiner and K. Allenby. 2010. "A Descriptive Profile of Older Women Offenders." Ottawa: Correctional Service of Canada. Accessed March 9, 2014. http://www.csc-scc.gc.ca/research/005008 -0229-01-eng.shtml; L. Stone. 2012. "Gangs Starting to 'Infect' Women's Prisons." *Calgary Herald*, May 25. Accessed March 9, 2014. http://www.calgaryherald.com/news/Gangs+starting+infect+women+prisons/5553864/story.html.

in segregation and criminally charged (five of the six inmates later pleaded guilty). Immediately after the incident, a high level of tension developed in the institution, compounded by the presence of a large number of overworked, overstressed, and relatively inexperienced correctional staff and correctional officers. A lack of leadership from the prison's warden contributed to the events that unfolded over the next several days.

Two days later, on April 24, three other inmates who were housed in the segregation unit caused further disruption by slashing, taking a hostage, and attempting suicide. On April 26, correctional officers from the institution demonstrated outside its walls, demanding that the inmates involved in the clash on April 22 be transferred to a higher-security institution.

On the evening of that same day, the warden sent an all-male Institutional Emergency Response Team (IERT) to extract eight inmates in the segregation unit from their cells and strip-search them. Six of the eight had been involved in the initial confrontation on April 22. The IERT did not complete the cell extractions until early the following morning, at which time the eight women were left in empty cells in the segregation unit. The women had been stripped (in the presence of male members of the IERT), dressed in paper gowns, and placed in restraints and leg irons. All the cell extractions and strip searches were recorded on videotape as per routine procedure. The following evening, seven of the eight inmates were subjected to body cavity searches. Six of the women involved in the original April 22 incident then were placed in segregation for many months.

The CSC investigated the incidents, but the report it issued left out many details. An independent judicial inquiry was demanded, and one was appointed in April 1995. It was headed by the Honourable Louise Arbour, a highly respected member of the Québec judiciary. The inquiry's final report (often called the **Arbour Report**)[35] was

Arbour Report

The report of an inquiry into events at the Kingston Prison for Women in April 1994, which documented violations of policy, the rule of law, and institutional regulations and had a significant impact on the development of women's corrections.

extremely critical of the actions taken by correctional staff, the IERT personnel, and the warden. The same report sharply criticized the response of senior CSC officials. In the end, the commissioner of corrections resigned.

The inquiry's report documented numerous violations of policy, the rule of law, and institutional regulations. For example, it criticized the use of segregation, the use of force by the IERT, and the manner in which the women had been strip-searched and subjected to body-cavity searches. The same report raised serious concerns regarding whether, without intervention and monitoring, the CSC was capable of implementing the necessary reforms to ensure adherence to justice and the rule of law. The Arbour Report made 14 key recommendations relating to cross-gender staffing in correctional institutions for women, the use of force and of IERTs, the operations of segregation units, the needs of Aboriginal women in correctional institutions, ways of ensuring accountability and adherence to the rule of law by correctional personnel, and procedures for handling inmate complaints and grievances.

The Arbour Report had a significant impact on the CSC's operations and on the development of women's corrections.[36] A deputy commissioner for women was appointed, a use-of-force policy was developed that stipulates that all-male institutional emergency response teams are never to be used as a first response in women's correctional institutions, and it is now forbidden for male staff to be present when female inmates are being strip-searched. The report also accelerated the closing of the Prison for Women in 2000 and the opening of smaller, regional facilities for federal female offenders.[37]

Despite these reforms, a number of scholars have argued that the CSC has failed to develop a correctional practice for women that is empowering and rehabilitative.[38] Although the recommendations of various commissions of inquiry, including the Arbour report, have been transformed into correctional policy, some argue that the experience of female offenders in institutions has remained largely unchanged and the focus of the system is still on punishment and control.[39,40]

In the view of feminist scholars and others, systems of corrections continue to pursue a punitive penology based on "an oppressive hierarchical structure of gender equality" in which women who resist traditional roles are viewed as a threat to male patriarchy as embodied by corrections.[41,42] Specifically, attention is called to how traditional views of femininity affect correctional policy and practice. Within this perspective, female offenders who commit crime ("misbehave") are severely punished. There have also been feminist critiques of community-based programs and services and the need for gender-responsive practices.[43]

Particular criticism has been directed toward the treatment of female offenders with mental illness. This censure was heightened by the death of Ashley Smith. See Box 11.4.

In Chapter 2, it was noted that there are ethical issues in the criminal justice system. The death of Ashley Smith illustrates how an ethical situation can be associated with a life and death situation. See At Issue 11.1.

WORKING INSIDE: THE EXPERIENCE OF CORRECTIONAL OFFICERS

Correctional officers play a pivotal role in correctional institutions. On a daily basis, it is COs who have the most contact with the inmates. Though systems of corrections make extensive use of high technology, such as video surveillance and various warning

BOX 11.4 THE DEATH OF ASHLEY SMITH

On October 19, 2007, 19-year-old Ashley Smith was found unconscious in her segregation cell at the Grand Valley Institution for Women. She died later that day. The official cause of death was self-initiated asphyxiation (suicide). However, a CSC report, made known in 2010, concluded that her death was accidental and a result of a desperate attempt for attention and interaction after having been confined in isolation for many months.[44]

At the time of her death, Ms. Smith was serving a sentence of six years and one month for a variety of weapons and assault offences that she had committed as a youth.

As a young offender, Ms. Smith was initially sent to the New Brunswick Youth Centre. During her stay in this facility, before being transferred to the Saint John Regional Correctional Centre, she accumulated more than 800 incident reports, more than 500 institutional charges, and 168 self-harm incidents.

Ms. Smith was transferred to the penitentiary at age 19 and was subsequently moved 17 times between nine different federal correctional facilities. She was in segregation during her entire confinement in the federal system.

The final report of the Office of the Correctional Investigator found that the actions of the CSC violated the law and CSC policy.[45] More specifically it found that Ms. Smith's mental health issues had not been addressed either in the youth facility or in the federal institutions in which she was confined. There had been no psychological assessment. The correctional investigator concluded that Ms. Smith's death might have been prevented had she been provided with proper care.

Among the recommendations in the correctional investigator's final report were that the CSC comply with the law and policy in its operations; improve the response to medical emergencies; review segregation policy and practices; and ensure the delivery of adequate health care, including mental health services.[46] A report on Ms. Smith's confinement in youth facilities in New Brunswick was also completed by the New Brunswick Ombudsman and Child and Youth Advocate,[47] and the Union of Canadian Correctional Officers prepared a report on the incident as well, criticizing what the union viewed as a "rush to judgment" to implicate the corrections officers (COs) involved in the incident.[48]

An investigation of the incident by the Waterloo Regional Police Services resulted in the police laying charges of criminal negligence causing death against three COs and a supervisor. Police documents filed in court alleged that the guards and supervisor were responsible for the death of Ashley Smith because of their negligence in failing to come to her aid when she was in distress in her cell. These four correctional personnel were fired, and four other COs were suspended without pay for 60 days. The acting warden and deputy warden were also fired. In 2008, an Ontario judge, on recommendation from Crown counsel, dismissed all charges of criminal negligence causing death against the COs.

The initial coroner's inquest into Ashley Smith's death collapsed in 2011 because of legal wrangling and the resignation of the coroner. In 2011, the family of Ashley Smith settled an $11 million lawsuit against the CSC. A second inquest commenced in late 2012, and it too was beset by various legal challenges and delays, concluding in late 2013. Evidence presented included the then-warden of the institution admitting that she "'probably wasn't' the best person for the job when she took on the position of acting warden" of Grand Valley Institution.[49] In his summation to the coroner's jury, the lawyer representing Ashley Smith's family urged the jury to find that her death was a homicide. In December 2013, the coroner's jury ruled that Ashley Smith's died by homicide—not suicide. Recall from Chapter 5 that the death of Robert Dziekanski was also ruled to be a homicide. As in British Columbia, the Ontario coroner's jury did not assign blame for the homicide as coroner's inquests are not adversarial hearings. The lawyer for the Smith family called on the authorities to criminally investigate senior management in the correctional institution where Ashley Smith died.[50]

For a timeline of Ashley Smith's involvement in the corrections system, related documents, and interviews, see the webpage of *The Fifth Estate*: "Out of Control" at www.cbc.ca/fifth/episodes/2009-2010/out-of-control, and "Behind the Wall: The Ashley Smith Story" at www.cbc.ca/fifth/episodes/2010-2011/behind-the-wall.

AT ISSUE 11.1 CORRECTIONAL OFFICERS AND ASHLEY SMITH: AN ETHICAL DUTY TO ACT?

The official cause of Ashley Smith's death was listed as self—initiated asphyxiation and ruled as accidental. At the time of her death she had been isolation for almost a year. She had an extensive history of "tying up"—wrapping nooses around her neck until she turned purple.

At the Coroner's inquest in 2013, it was revealed that the Acting Warden had issued an order that correctional officers were not to enter Smith's cell to cut off ligatures she had tied around her neck "as long as Smith was breathing, talking, or moving."[51] Correctional managers and COs had been reprimanded for entering her cell on previous occasions. Any instance in which the officers touched Ms. Smith required completion of a use of force report. On the day of her death, COs were right outside her cell, observing her behaviour. On one occasion, they entered briefly to determine she was still breathing, and then closed the door even though the ligature was still around her neck. She subsequently self-asphyxiated. Testimony at the inquest also revealed that several of the COs had cared deeply for her, yet were constrained by their supervisor's orders who "threatened them with criminal excessive-use-of-force sanctions for entering the cell too quickly."[52]

QUESTIONS

Should the correctional officers, who were outside of her cell observing her actions and who were aware of her pattern of behaviour, ignored the order of their supervisor and intervened to prevent her from asphyxiating herself? Did they have a moral duty to intervene and cut off the ligature regardless of the administrative consequences?

devices (static security), COs are the primary mechanism by which institutional policies and regulations are implemented and by which the inmates are managed (dynamic security). COs are also a key part of efforts to rehabilitate offenders.

RECRUITMENT AND TRAINING

At the federal level, each of the CSC's five regions (Atlantic, Québec, Ontario, Prairies, and Pacific) is responsible for recruiting, selecting, assessing, and hiring correctional officers by using national standards.

Successful applicants are required to complete the correctional training program, a combination of online and classroom training. The CSC has developed a special process for selecting and training staff to work in institutions for federally sentenced women. Specific criteria are used to identify personnel who are sensitive to women's issues, their life histories, and their unique needs. Besides the training provided to all new COs, staff selected to work in women's facilities must complete a women-centred training course. This course consists of a number of modules covering such areas as women's criminality and its links to personal history, self-injury, and suicide; same-sex relationships; cultural sensitivity; and dealing effectively with lifers.[53]

There are no nationwide standards for recruiting and training COs for provincial or territorial systems of corrections. Each province and territory has established its own procedures, standards, and training courses, and some are more complete than others. A review of training in Nova Scotia, for example, found gaps in training for front-line staff and no centralized capacity to monitor and track training requirements of personnel.[54]

THE AUTHORITY OF CORRECTIONAL OFFICERS

The authority of COs in prisons is both legal and moral. With respect to legal authority, though COs do not have the power to discipline inmates, in enforcing the policies and regulations of the institution, officers are able to initiate the punishment process. Equally important is their moral authority, which is based on establishing functional relationships with the inmates. COs have considerable discretion in carrying out their daily activities and in determining when and how they will enforce the rules and regulations of the institution. Officers are well aware that full enforcement of all institutional regulations at all times would make life unbearable for both themselves and the inmates. Studies have revealed that COs can have one of two agendas: custodial or correctional. The custodial agenda of COs centres on control and the enforcement of regulations, while the correctional agenda involves COs functioning as change agents by assisting inmates in their efforts to access programs and services and to deal with personal issues.[55]

Research studies suggest that, similar to inmates, COs have a subculture that includes a code of behaviour designed to maintain occupational solidarity and, in some instances, shield inappropriate and, in some instances, criminal behaviour.[56] In an investigation of 55 use-of-force complaints filed by inmates in Ontario provincial institutions during 2010–2012, the Ontario Ombudsman found that the allegations were substantiated in 26 cases. From the investigations, the Ombudsman concluded,

> There is a common theme in cases involving brazen acts of violence against inmates. Those responsible for assaults are emboldened in their faith in the code of silence—an unwritten social incentive to protect and show solidarity for coworkers, even if it

254

means conspiring to lie, destroy, and falsify records. Staff who breached this code become victims themselves. They are labeled "rats," ostracized, treated as pariahs, subject to direct and covert harassment and threats, and their personal safety is put in jeopardy.[57]

RELATIONSHIPS WITH INMATES

COs must learn the subtle nonverbal cues that will help them read individual inmates. They must also become familiar with the various intricacies of the inmate social system, the methods used to distribute and use contraband goods and drugs, and other activities, such as gambling, strong-arming, and debt collection. Early on, inmates will test new COs to determine how they will exercise their discretion and authority. These processes of adaptation and learning and of developing strategies to cope with the pressures and demands of everyday life in the prison are similar to those undergone by new inmates.[58]

Even though a core principle of correctional officers is "never trust an inmate," the unique features of daily life inside institutions create pressures for COs and inmates to develop accommodative relationships, which, for inmates, help reduce the pains of imprisonment and, for COs, ensure daily stability and order. The specific patterns of interaction that develop between COs and inmates depend on a variety of factors, including the individual CO, the size of the inmate population, the security level of the facility, and the policies and management style of the senior administration. Research suggests that there is variation among COs in their attitude toward and performance on the job.[59]

This diversity among officers is reflected in the comments of a former inmate who served time in Central East Correctional Centre in Ontario:

> I must say that the guards in Lindsay are one extreme to the next, you got goldie locks over on 2 pod who will shove his hand down the toilet to try to get your package and he loves the bend over and cough shit. then you got the older laid back guys that leave you alone if you are just doing your own thing that dont disrespect you like your some dog in a cage.[60]

As noted, the advent of the high-tech prison with increased surveillance and restricted inmate movement will reduce the levels of dynamic security wherein COs have frequent contact with inmates and increase static security. This reduction may exacerbate a problem that was identified in an internal CSC survey, which found that "social values around respect toward offenders have not been encouraged within the CSC to the same extent as values of respect toward the organization and co-workers—leaving this aspect to each individual's discretion."[61] This is a good example of the importance of ensuring that correctional officers are trained in ethics as well as in relationship and communication skills.

RELATIONSHIPS WITH THE ADMINISTRATION AND TREATMENT STAFF

Administrators may be viewed with a mixture of distrust and cynicism, as distant from the everyday realities of the prison, and as being more concerned with fiscal and administrative issues that have little relevance to line-level officers. Many COs hold a rather dim view of treatment programs, with many officers feeling that rehabilitation programs are a waste of time and money. The COs' view that few inmates have the ability, resources, and motivation to make significant changes in their attitudes and behaviour may limit the potential of COs to be effective change agents in the institution. They may also have a perception that many inmates become involved in treatment programs primarily to improve their chances of release on parole, rather than for self-improvement.

STRESSORS FOR CORRECTIONAL OFFICERS

Considerable evidence shows that COs experience high levels of stress and burnout.[62] These problems may have a significant impact on the COs level of support for treatment programs, the amount of sick leave and absenteeism, how the COs interaction with the inmates, and the levels of support for management.[63] Among the major causes of stress are overcrowding and understaffing and threats to personal security.[64] These can significantly affect COs' personal life.[65]

A survey of corrections employees in Saskatchewan ($N = 271$) found that nearly 80 percent of those surveyed had experienced a traumatic event in their work, and 25 percent reported symptoms of post-traumatic stress disorder, including nightmares, loss of sleep, and other forms of psychological distress.[66] Female correctional officers may experience additional stressors from working in a largely male-dominated environment that has traditionally valued toughness and physicality over communication skills and tact. This stress may extend to officers who are gay, lesbian, bisexual, or transgendered: in 2013, the Grievance Settlement Board in Québec awarded $100,000.00 to a gay correctional officer who had been subjected to taunts and homophobic slurs by his colleagues in a provincial correctional institution.[67]

DOING TIME: THE WORLD OF THE INMATE

A GENERAL PROFILE OF INMATE POPULATIONS

Offenders confined in correctional institutions tend to be, male, young, single, poorly educated, and marginally skilled. They are disproportionately Black and Aboriginal people and are likely to have a history of unstable lives. Many have grown up in dysfunctional families. Their problem-solving skills are minimal. Most are serving time in provincial or territorial institutions and more than half of the sentences are for less than one month.[68]

Many inmates are homeless or under-housed before their incarceration.[69] A large percentage have lengthy criminal histories. The treatment needs of persons incarcerated in correctional institutions are high; many suffer from alcohol or drug addiction or have a mental disorder or other affliction, such as FASD. Generally speaking, female offenders share with their male counterparts a marginalized background of poverty, alcohol or drug dependency, limited education, and minimal employment skills. In addition, female offenders may have suffered sexual and physical abuse and may be responsible for children or stepchildren.

These offenders often have few connections to mainstream Canadian society. They have needs and present risks that place significant demands on systems of corrections, in particular on provincial or territorial institutions, which tend to have fewer resources than their federal counterparts and must attempt to respond in a highly-compressed timeframe.

ENTERING THE PRISON

> I remember the day that I came in; the first time I went to the cafeteria and I could feel a hundred sets of eyes on me. I could see everybody wondering who you are, what you're in for, how long you're doing.
>
> —lifer, in Murphy and Johnsen[70]

The specific impact that entry into the prison has on the individual offender will vary, depending on many factors, including his or her personality, offence history, and previous incarcerations. First-time offenders may experience severe cultural shock, whereas offenders with extensive criminal histories and previous confinements are likely to be relatively unaffected. For these inmates, the processes and procedures related to entry into the institution and confinement are well known, as are many of the COs and inmates in the facility. Indeed, returning to the prison may be more of a homecoming than a banishment. For the uninitiated inmate, however, adjusting to the regimen of prison life can be stressful and frightening.

Regardless of background, there is a psychological and material stripping of the individual that involves a series of **status degradation ceremonies**. These rituals include the issuing of prison clothing, the assignment of an identification number, the loss of most personal possessions, and the end of unhindered communication with the outside community.[71] These procedures are the mechanism by which the offender is moved from residency in the community, with its attendant freedoms, to the world of the prison, with its rules, regulations, informal economy, and social system.

It can be argued that many of the persons entering correctional institutions have already had their status degraded, through a life of poverty, addiction, mental health issues, and growing up in dysfunctional environments. Degradation is associated with marginalization, and the profile of offenders suggests that it is persons from vulnerable groups who are most likely to end up incarcerated.

Though all incoming inmates are provided with copies of the institutional regulations and an orientation, each inmate is left to his or her own devices (and wits) to adjust to life inside and to develop strategies and techniques of coping and survival. The following is a portion of the advice given by one inmate to a second inmate who had just arrived at Millhaven, a federal correctional facility in Ontario:

> Drugs and alcohol are everywhere and I urge you to avoid that trip. Ninety percent of all killings revolve around the dope scene.... Don't accept anything from anyone, because you don't want to put yourself in a position where you'll have to repay the favor. Nothing is free. It's in your best interest to avoid cliques. You'll be spending a lot of time on your own—it's much safer that way.... Don't encourage conversation with anyone. Be brief and polite.... Don't promise anyone anything.... Stay quiet and mind your own business.[72]

Unfortunately, though systems of corrections have perfected the mechanisms for transforming citizens into inmates, there are no *status restoration ceremonies* at the end of the inmate's confinement that would function to convert the inmate back into a citizen. The consequences of this for the reentry and reintegration of offenders released from correctional institutions will be explored in Chapter 12.

LIVING INSIDE

A key concept in understanding the carceral experience is the **pains of imprisonment**. In his classic study of a maximum-security prison, presented

Status degradation ceremonies
The processing of offenders into correctional institutions whereby the offender is psychologically and materially stripped of possessions that identify him or her as a member of the free society.

Pains of imprisonment
The deprivations experienced by inmates confined in correctional institutions, including the loss of autonomy, privacy, security, and freedom of movement and association.

▼ An inmate exercises in his room.

© Andrew Aitchison/Alamy.

257

in the book *Society of Captives*, Gresham Sykes identified a number of deprivations experienced by inmates.[73] These include the loss of liberty, of access to goods and services, and of access to heterosexual relationships, as well as the loss of personal autonomy and personal security. Confinement also has collateral effects, which include the loss of personal relationships and social networks, the acquisition of self-defeating habits and attitudes, the loss of personal belongings, and a loss of the ability to maintain housing.[74]

Inmates also attempt to cope with the deprivation of heterosexual relationships and to secure sexual gratification. Masturbation and consensual sexual relations with another inmate are the two most common types of sexual activity in correctional institutions. Consensual sex, while technically homosexual, is an adaptation to a unique circumstance; inmates revert to heterosexual sexual activity when they return to the community.

The pains of imprisonment are particularly acute for inmates serving life sentences. Realistically, it is highly unlikely that most long-term offenders will be able to sustain their pre-prison relationships, especially if relations with a spouse or children were unstable.

The pains of imprisonment, combined with the challenges faced by individual inmates, may lead to self-injurious behaviour (SIB) and, in some cases, to suicide. It is only in recent years that systems of correction have given attention to these issues. As noted earlier, SIB includes any type of deliberate action that involves bodily harm or disfigurement and includes head-banging and skin cutting.[75] Female offenders are at higher risk of SIB as a way to cope with emotional pain, distress, and isolation.[76] Aboriginal offenders, as discussed, account for 45 percent of all self-harm incidents in federal prisons.[77]

THE INMATE SOCIAL SYSTEM

A universal attribute of correctional institutions is the existence of an inmate social system, often referred to as the **inmate subculture**. For decades, criminologists have attempted to determine the origins, components, and functions of the inmate social system. Explanations generally centre on the role that the subculture plays in providing inmates with illicit goods and services and the impact of pre-prison experiences and attitudes that offenders may bring into the institution.

A number of other key concepts assist in understanding the inmate social system. One is **prisonization**, which is the process by which inmates become socialized into the norms, values, and culture of the prison.[78]

Offenders are said to be **institutionalized** when they have become prisonized to such a degree that they are unable to function in the outside free community. Some offenders have spent most of their youth and adult lives confined in correctional institutions. These **state-raised offenders** have experienced only limited periods of freedom in the community and may have neither the social skills nor the ability to function outside the total institutional world of the prison. For these offenders, the prison provides security, friends, room and board, and a predictable routine, none of which is guaranteed in the outside community. The prison, not the outside community, is their home.

The longer an inmate is confined, the more difficult it may be to retain pro-social attitudes and behaviours, especially when the inmate is confined with offenders with more criminal orientations.

Inmate subculture

The patterns of interaction and the relationships that exist among inmates confined in correctional institutions.

Prisonization

The process by which inmates become socialized into the norms, values, and culture of the prison.

Institutionalized

Inmates who have become prisonized to such a degree that they are unable to function in the outside free community.

State-raised offenders

Inmates who have spent the majority of their adult (and perhaps young adult) lives confined in correctional institutions and, as a consequence, may have neither the skills nor ability to function in the outside free community; for these offenders, prison is home.

A major challenge confronting systems of correction is preventing offenders from becoming so immersed in the culture of the prison that the efforts of correctional staff to promote positive values and behaviours cannot succeed. There is also the challenge of how to "unprisonize" inmates as they move closer to their release date. This step would be part of a process of status restoration, which currently does not exist. Unfortunately, many of the attitudes and values that are embedded in the inmate social system are antithetical to those of the outside law-abiding community.

A key component of the inmate social system is the **inmate code**, a set of behavioural rules that govern interactions among the inmates and with institutional staff.[79] The rule sets include "do your own time" (i.e., mind your own business); "don't exploit other inmates"; and "don't weaken."[80] It can be anticipated that adherence to the inmate code may be more prevalent in high-security institutions, where inmates are likely to be prison veterans with more entrenched criminal attitudes and behaviours.

A number of **social (or argot) roles** are associated with the inmate social system. These roles are based on the inmate's friendship networks, sentence length, current and previous offences, degree of at least verbal support for the inmate code, and participation in illegal activities, such as gambling and drug distribution.

For example, *square johns* exhibit pro-social attitudes and behaviour and are positive toward staff and administration. *Right guys*, on the other hand, are antisocial and have negative attitudes toward authority. *Snitches* (*rats* or *squealers*) play a risky game of providing information about inmates and their activities to correctional staff.[81] A related feature of inmate society is a specialized vocabulary: a *bit* is the inmate's sentence (e.g., a five-year bit); a *beef* is the type of crime; a *fish* is a new inmate; while a *goof* is an inmate who behaves inappropriately in the institution (e.g., whistles; for some unknown reason, whistling is not permitted among inmates).

While most inmates pay at least lip service to the code, an inmate's greatest source of danger is other inmates. Prison assaults are disproportionately committed by younger inmates and in institutions that are overcrowded.[82] Inmates convicted of sex offences are at a high risk of being verbally and physically abused and victimized.[83]

Contributing to the lack of loyalty and solidarity among inmates is the rat (or snitch) system, by which inmates may improve their own position and prospects with COs and the administration at the expense of fellow inmates.

One inmate described doing your own time as follows:

> It means keep yourself separate from everything and everybody. Don't comment, interfere, or accept favours. Understand that you are "fresh meat" and need to learn the way of the joint. You have to deal with the "Vikings" (slobs, applied to both guards and cons), "booty bandits" (someone looking for ass to fuck), and the "boss," "hook," "grey suit" or "cookie" (all terms for prisons officials of various ranks) without "jeffing" (sucking up) to the staff. You have to deal with other cons who want you as a "punk" or a "fuck boy." Anybody can be carrying a "shank" (home-made knife) made out of a toothbrush and a razor blade or a piece of sharpened steel. Probably the more innocent someone looks, the more you have to worry.[84]

A defining feature of life in contemporary correctional institutions is that inmates tend to group themselves into niches or friendship networks. These networks may be based on associations formed during previous incarcerations or in the outside community; on shared ethnicity or culture; or on length of sentence (e.g., lifers

---

Inmate code

A set of behavioural rules that govern interactions among inmates and with institutional staff.

Social (or argot) roles

Roles that inmates assume based on their friendship networks, sentence length, and other factors related to their criminal history and activities in the institution.

may group together). It is this friendship group, rather than the inmate population as a whole, that provides the individual inmate with security and support and that is the recipient of the inmate's loyalty. Inmates and correctional staff distinguish between *convicts* and *inmates* (or "new school kids"), and perceive the latter as not respecting the traditional inmate social system. Although certain inmates, including those convicted of sex crimes and crimes against children, may be vulnerable to exploitation, a defining factor in establishing an inmate's status appears to be access to drugs and tobacco.

While research studies indicate that most inmates seem to ultimately adjust to life in prison, that may make it more difficult for them to survive in the outside free community on release. Ironically, it could be argued that those inmates who adjust well in the highly structured environment of correctional institutions may encounter the most difficulties on release. And there is the larger issue as to whether lengthy sentences serve as a general and specific deterrent to further criminality.

INMATE FAMILIES

Systems of correction are not designed to consider the needs of inmate families, and family members may feel isolated and neglected by correctional authorities.[85] The families of inmates may also be stigmatized and marginalized in the community.[86] Other concerns relate to finances, housing, isolation from the community, and fears related to the offender's return to the community.[87] The partners of offenders may experience trauma, shame, isolation, and depression.[88,89] Children whose parents are incarcerated can suffer from emotional, behavioural, and academic problems, the type and severity of which vary with the child's age, gender, and length of separation from parents.[90,91] For the inmate, the loss of regular family contact is one of the pains of imprisonment. Research suggests that inmate participation in family visitation programs has a positive impact on the inmate's family life, reduces institutional misconduct, and lowers the rates of reoffending.[92]

INMATE GRIEVANCES AND COMPLAINTS

Thousands of complaints and grievances are filed every year by inmates in federal and provincial or territorial correctional facilities. A very small number (as little as 5 percent) of the inmate population is responsible for nearly 70 percent of the complaints and grievances that are filed. The most frequent complaints received by the federal correctional investigator relate to health care, institutional transfers, and the use of administrative segregation.[93] A federal court judge ruled in 2012 that the CSC was not responding to official inmate grievances in a timely manner and ordered a high-level review of the grievance system. This investigation may result in significant changes in the grievance process.

CLASSIFICATION AND TREATMENT

There are three major trends in offender classification and treatment: (1) the increasing use of sophisticated risk and needs assessment instruments; (2) the increasing domination of treatment research, policy, and programs from a psychological perspective—in particular, a cognitive behavioural

▼ Inmate family visit

John Moore/Getty Images

approach; and (3) a differentiated treatment approach for women, Aboriginal peoples, and specific categories of offenders, such as sex offenders.

Classification is the process by which inmates are subdivided into groups based on a variety of factors, such as risk and needs, and is used to determine institutional placement and programming. It is a core component of correctional treatment. While the classification process in federal corrections is well established, there are major challenges in provincial and territorial facilities.[94]

The assessment process continues throughout the offender's sentence, from intake to incarceration to release from custody and up to sentence expiry. Offenders have a variety of criminogenic needs that must be addressed both within the institution and later in the community. These include education, mental health, social networks, employment, accommodation, drugs and alcohol, attitudes, and cognitive skills. All these criminogenic needs are *dynamic* risk factors—that is, they are amenable to change and have been found to be important factors to address to reduce the likelihood of reoffending.[95] (See below.)

As an example, Figure 11.1 presents data on the type of rehabilitative need of offenders admitted to correctional facilities in Saskatchewan in 2010–2011. The majority of offenders had four of the six rehabilitative needs. Note the high percentage of offenders with substance issues and social interaction issues (criminal peers and companions) among this population.[96]

The classification systems used by federal and provincial or territorial corrections generally include psychological, personality, and behavioural inventories that attempt to categorize offenders.

Risk assessment and risk management are the mantras of contemporary corrections and the assessment of risk is a key component of classification and case management. Risk assessments are designed to identify those offenders who are most likely to reoffend on release from the institution if no treatment intervention occurs.[97] In assessing the degree of risk posed by an offender, corrections personnel generally consider **static risk factors** and **dynamic risk factors**. Static risk factors include the offender's criminal history, including prior convictions, the seriousness of prior offences, and whether the offender successfully completed previous periods of supervision in the community. Dynamic risk factors are those attributes of the offender that can be altered through intervention and include vocational training and education, addiction issues, attitude and motivation, and cognitive thinking abilities, among others.

Classification

The process by which inmates are categorized through the use of various assessment instruments to determine the appropriate security level of the inmate and program placement.

Static risk factors

Attributes of the offender that predict the likelihood of recidivism but are not amenable to change, including criminal history, prior convictions, the seriousness of prior offences, and performance on previous conditional releases.

Dynamic risk factors

Attributes of the offender that can be altered through intervention, including level of education, employment skills, addiction issues, and cognitive thinking abilities, among others.

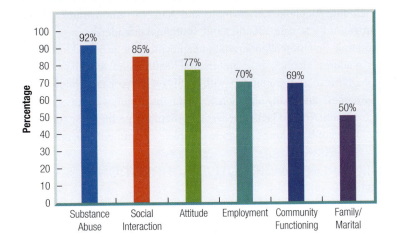

FIGURE 11.1 ▶

Adults in Sentenced Custody, by Type of Rehabilitative Need, Saskatchewan, 2010–2011

Source: M. Dauvergne. 2012. *Adult Correctional Statistics in Canada, 2010/2011*, p. 13. Ottawa: Minister of Industry. http://www.statcan.gc.ca/pub/85-002-x/2012001.article/11715-eng.pdf

Research studies have identified eight factors that reliably predict involvement in criminality: (1) lack of attachment to family or marital supports, (2) school or employment problems, (3) lack of pro-social leisure or recreational activities, (4) antisocial peers, (5) antisocial attitudes, (6) antisocial personality, (7) substance abuse, and (8) history of antisocial behaviour.[98] It is the challenge of correctional treatment staff to address these issues although some, such as family issued, are generally beyond reach.

CASE MANAGEMENT

Correctional **case management** is the process by which the needs and abilities of offenders are matched with correctional programs and services.

At the core of the case management process is the **correctional plan**, which is developed for most inmates, the exception being those serving short sentences. This plan determines the offender's initial institution placement, specific training or work opportunities, and release plan.

A major challenge for treatment staff is that most adult custodial sentences ordered by the court are short: just over 50 percent are one month or less.[99]

Case management

The process by which the needs and abilities of offenders are matched with correctional programs and services.

Correctional plan

A key component of the case management process that determines the offender's initial institution placement, specific training or work opportunities, and preparation for release.

INSTITUTIONAL TREATMENT PROGRAMS

> The emphasis should be put on programming and rehabilitation.... Here for the most part it is warehousing. It's like you are put on a shelf.
>
> —provincial inmate in Newfoundland, Carlson[100]

There is a question as to whether treatment is a priority for correctional authorities. The CSC, for example, spends less on correctional programming than on staff overtime — about 2 percent of its multibillion-dollar budget. Programs for inmates in provincial or territorial facilities are often limited and the first to be reduced in times of fiscal restraint.[101] This despite the fact that offenders in custody are generally higher risk and have more needs that those under supervision in the community.

The programs most frequently offered in correctional institutions include substance abuse management, family violence prevention, sex offender programming, violence prevention, anger management, GED (high school equivalency) courses, and various vocational programs. There may also be programs that target specific groups of offenders, such as sex offenders. In addition, there are programs facilitated by outside groups, including Alcoholics Anonymous and Narcotics Anonymous. There are also specific programs for female offenders and Aboriginal offenders.

The short time that most offenders spend in provincial or territorial institutions makes it difficult to address alcohol, drug, and mental health issues, as well as to develop specialized programs (e.g., for offenders with FASD). Overcrowding often limits inmate access to programs, and many offenders leave the institution without completing a full course of treatment.[102] This lack of access is particularly problematic for sex offenders, who may not be confined long enough to complete a treatment program.

THE PRINCIPLES OF EFFECTIVE CORRECTIONAL TREATMENT

To be effective, correctional treatment programs must be (1) based on empirically supported models of correctional change; (2) incorporate the principles of risk, needs, and responsivity (RNR); (3) be focused on the dynamic risk factors associated with the offender's criminal behaviour; (4) be monitored, evaluated, and accredited; and (5) be implemented by well-trained, dedicated program staff [103–105]

Recall that the risk principle holds that treatment interventions have a greater chance of success when they are matched with the risk level of the offender. Higher levels of service are reserved for higher-risk inmates; lower-risk inmates do not require the same level of service to benefit from treatment interventions and may, in fact, be negatively affected by intensive service delivery. Treatment programs have little impact on reoffending among low-risk offenders, and higher-risk inmates benefit from treatment programs that focus on criminogenic factors. [106]

The need principle holds that to be effective, treatment interventions must address the criminogenic needs of inmates, including alcohol or substance abuse, relations with peers, and attitudes toward and experiences with employment. The responsivity principle states that treatment interventions must be matched to the learning styles and abilities of individual inmates. This goal presents challenges to correctional systems, as many offenders have disabilities that may present obstacles to learning. Unfortunately, for a variety of reasons, including mental challenges or learning disabilities, a deeply rooted attitudinal and behavioural pattern centred on a criminal lifestyle, an extensive history of confinement in institutions, or a general lack of interest in making the effort to change, not all inmates are receptive to treatment.

MEASURING THE EFFECTIVENESS OF CORRECTIONAL TREATMENT

Recidivism rates

The number of offenders released from confinement who are subsequently returned to prison.

The traditional method used to determine success is **recidivism rates**—that is, the number of offenders who, once released from confinement, are returned to prison either for a technical violation of their parole or statutory release or for the commission of a new offence.

Using recidivism rates as a measure of success is problematic for a number of reasons. For one, it prevents an assessment of the relative improvement of the offender. For example, an offender who previously committed serious crimes and are subsequently returned to confinement for a relatively minor offence might be viewed as a relative success rather than as a failure.

It is also very difficult to directly connect an inmate's participation in treatment programs with how they do once released back into the community. There are many reasons that an individual may cease violating the law, including the efforts of a supportive family or spouse, success in securing stable employment, maturation, and the availability of programs and services in the community. On the other hand, the offender may have returned to criminal activity and not have been detected. In addition, the success or failure of an offender on release may also turn on the level and type of supervision he or she receives. Parole officers have a variety of supervision styles, ranging from officers who have a more punitive orientation to those who focus on providing services and assistance (see Chapter 12).

Rehabilitation is a value-laden process. [107] A key issue is what correctional intervention is attempting to accomplish: the bottom line is not to reoffend. The ethical issues surrounding treatment must also be addressed. See At Issue 11.2.

AT ISSUE 11.2   THE ETHICS OF CORRECTIONAL TREATMENT:
SHOULD PRISON INMATES HAVE THE RIGHT TO
REFUSE TREATMENT?

Consider the following scenario: An inmate convicted of a sex offence is sentenced to 15 years in prison. During confinement, he refuses to participate in treatment programs. As a consequence, he does not receive any form of conditional release, is denied statutory release after having served two-thirds of the sentence, and serves his entire sentence in prison. On his warrant expiry date, he is released, untreated, from the correctional institution, at high risk of reoffending.

The *Canadian Charter* of Rights and Freedoms guarantees that all persons have the right to life, liberty, and security of the person, rights that would most likely be violated by any provision of mandatory treatment.[108] A provision in the *Charter* states that inmates must provide informed consent, both at the outset and during treatment, and that the inmate has the right to refuse treatment or to withdraw from a treatment program at any time. Research suggests that mandated (coerced) participation in treatment programs is ineffective in reducing reoffending as compared with voluntary participation in treatment.[109]

QUESTIONS

What is your position on the right of inmates to refuse treatment? Would you, for example, support an attempt to impose mandatory treatment on certain categories of offenders, such as sex offenders and violent offenders?

THROUGHCARE

A long-standing challenge for correctional systems has been to ensure continuity between treatment interventions in institutional settings and those in the community following release. This is the concept of **throughcare**. Studies have found that the effectiveness of institution-based treatment programs is enhanced when there is a seamless transition to community-based treatment when the offender is released from confinement.[110]

Throughcare

The notion that there should be continuity between institutional treatment and programs and community-based services for offenders.

DOES CORRECTIONAL TREATMENT WORK?

Since the introduction of treatment programs into correctional institutions in the 1950s, there has been an ongoing debate over their effectiveness. The debate has involved politicians, community interest groups, correctional scholars, and senior and line-level corrections personnel. The debate was originally sparked by the pronouncement of the scholar Robert Martinson 40 years ago that "nothing works"—that treatment programs did not reduce reoffending.[111] Even though, on reanalysis of the data, Martinson recanted his original conclusion, the "nothing works" mantra has long been used as a political tool to justify cutting treatment programs and services for inmates and other offenders.[112]

With the usual caveats that studies vary widely in their design and analytics and that there are relatively few Canadian studies, some of what we know about the effectiveness of correctional treatment interventions are set out in Research File 11.1.

Do correctional treatment programs work?

Some do. The general consensus among researchers is that some programs work to reduce reoffending of some offenders; that treatment programs that adhere to the RNR principles can reduce rates of reoffending between 10 percent and 40 percent.[113–115]

Do correctional programs successfully address the risk and needs of offenders?

Perhaps not. A large study of federal offenders ($N = 24,315$) released on conditional release between 2005 and 2010 found no change in the offender's risk level (93.5 percent) or in needs (88.2 percent). These results suggest that whatever programming these offenders received while incarcerated did not alter their risk or needs ratings change between their entry into a correctional institution and their release.[116]

Do adult basic education and vocational or work programs reduce reoffending?

They can. Participation in prison education programs can reduce the levels of misconduct in institutions and reduce rates of reoffending.[117,118] A key requirement is throughcare—continuity between the institutional program and programs and services in the community.

Do programs for offenders with mental health issues work?

Potentially. An evaluation of the CSC Mental Health Strategy, designed to provide a continuum of care from the institution to the community, found that offenders who had access to mental health specialists were less likely to have their conditional release revoked or suspended.[119] Challenges to providing effective interventions for this population include a lack of institutional resources and the fact that inmates with mental health issues may be more likely to be held in segregation, limiting their access to programs.[120]

Do drug treatment programs for federal offenders work?

Some appear to. There is evidence that the programs for violent offenders, sex offenders, and inmates with substance abuse issues can be successful in reducing reoffending.[121] Federal inmates who reside in drug-free intensive supervision unit (ISU) programs are less likely to be returned to custody than other offenders and less likely to be returned to custody for a new offence.[122] Multistage residential programs that provide a bridge between the prison and the community can also reduce reoffending.[123] The CSC ISUs have strong support from inmates and correctional staff but their long-term impact on drug use and recidivism is uncertain.[124]

Do treatment programs in provincial or territorial institutions work?

Unknown. Despite the fact that most offenders in confinement are in these facilities, program evaluations are virtually non-existent.

Do sex offender treatment programs work?

Difficult to determine, in part because of the wide variety of offenders who are classified as sex offenders. Some interventions appear to work to reduce reoffending among certain groups of sex offenders. Offenders who participate in treatment programs generally have lower rates of reoffending than comparison groups that received no intervention; in one meta-analysis of 23 studies ($N = 6746$ offenders), it was 11 percent versus 19 percent.[125,126] Programs for sex offenders based on the principles of RNR are the most effective in reducing reoffending, as are cognitive behavioural interventions that focus on dysfunctional thoughts and feelings.[127,128]

Does effective correctional treatment save money?

Yes. An evaluation of programs in federal institutions found the following returns on a per dollar of investment:

$1 of correctional programming = return of $1–$8

$1 of sex offender programming = return of $6.59

$1 of substance abuse programs = return of $2.69

"Returns" are the cost savings associated with achieved correctional outcomes (i.e., offenders are supervised in the community and do not reoffend).

In addition, the cost of participating in institutional employment programs is = $779 in terms of good correctional outcomes, versus offenders not participating in institutional employment programs in terms of poor correctional outcomes = $15,662.[129]

SUMMARY

This discussion in this chapter has focused on the dynamics of correctional institutions. It was noted that correctional institutions are total institutions, and this has a strong impact on the relationships between and among the inmates, correctional officers, and administration, as well as the challenges encountered by treatment programs.

Among the challenges of correctional institutions are living conditions, the growth in remand populations, the changing offender profile, special inmate populations, overcrowding, inmate gangs, and inmate safety. Correctional officers play a pivotal role in institutions and must develop accommodative relationships with inmates, although there is evidence that officers may abuse their considerable powers and authority. The experiences of inmates were examined and focused on entering and living in the prison. The classification and treatment of offenders were discussed, with a particular focus on the principles of effective correctional treatment and the effectiveness of correctional programs in reducing reoffending.

KEY POINTS REVIEW

1. The events surrounding the building of the first Canadian penitentiary in the early 1800s illustrate how changes in the response to crime and criminal offenders can be influenced by social, economic, and political forces.

2. One way to trace the changing philosophy of corrections and punishment is by examining the architecture of correctional institutions over the past 200 years.

3. Among the challenges of correctional institutions are that of being a total institution, having a split personality of punishment and treatment, and being a public and political institution.

4. There has been a growth in remand populations, and the profile of offenders has changed, with an increase in special needs populations.

5. Overcrowding and inmate gangs contribute to unsafe environments for correctional staff and inmates.

6. A pivotal role in correctional institutions is played by correctional officers, who have both legal and moral authority.

7. Correctional officers must develop accommodative relationships with inmates to ensure daily stability and order.

8. Correctional officer relationships with treatment staff and the administration may be characterized by distrust and cynicism.

9. Persons confined in correctional institutions tend have low levels of education, limited employment skills, and addiction issues, and to be disproportionately Aboriginal and Black people.

10. Many inmates have lengthy criminal histories and multiple challenges, including addiction and mental illness.

11. Inmates experience many challenges, including adjusting to life inside, coping with the pains of imprisonment, navigating the inmate social system, staying safe, and maintaining personal relationships.

12. Classification is a core component of correctional treatment, and risk assessments are used to identify the degree of risk posed by the offender on release from the institution.

13. The core principles of effective correctional treatment centre on the risk-needs-responsivity (RNR) model.

14. The use of recidivism rates to measure the success of correctional treatment programs is problematic.

15. Research studies indicate that correctional treatment programs can be effective in reducing reoffending.

KEY TERM QUESTIONS

1. Compare and contrast the **Pennsylvania model** and the **Auburn model** of prisons.

2. What is **moral architecture**, and how does it help us understand the goals of the first penitentiaries that were built in Canada and how architecture can reflect correctional philosophies?

3. What was the **Brown Commission**, and why is it important in the study of Canadian corrections? What was the **Arbour Report**, and what was its significance in Canadian corrections?

4. Describe the attributes of the **minimum-, medium-,** and **maximum-security** facilities and the multilevel institutions and the special handling unit, operated by the federal Correctional Service Canada.

5. Compare and contrast **static security** and **dynamic security**.

6. Why are prisons viewed as **total institutions?**

7. What is the **continuum of correctional institutions**, and how does this concept assist our understanding of life inside prisons?

8. Define and discuss the importance of the following concepts for the study of corrections and life inside correctional institutions: (1) **status degradation ceremonies,** (2) **pains of imprisonment,** and (3) **state-raised offenders.**

9. Discuss the attributes of the **inmate subculture**, and then discuss what is known about its existence in correctional institutions.

10. Discuss the concept of **prisonization** and describe what is meant when it is said that an inmate has become **institutionalized**.

11. Identify the basic tenets of the **inmate code**, and discuss whether the code still exists among inmates in correctional institutions.

12. What are **social (or argot) roles** and how do they affect the dynamics of life inside correctional institutions?

13. Discuss **self-injurious behaviour (SIB)** among inmates.

14. Define **classification** and its role in corrections.

15. Compare and contrast **static risk factors** and **dynamic risk factors**, and note the role of each type of factor in the classification process.

16. Discuss the role of **case management** and the **correctional plan** in correctional treatment.

17. What are the issues that surround the use of **recidivism rates** as a measure of the success of correctional treatment programs?

18. Describe **throughcare** and its importance in correctional treatment.

MEDIA LINKS

 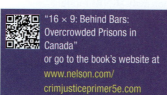 "The Devil You Know," *CBC Fifth Estate*
or go to the book's website at
www.nelson.com/
crimjusticeprimer5e.com

"16 × 9: Behind Bars:
Overcrowded Prisons in
Canada"
or go to the book's website at
www.nelson.com/
crimjusticeprimer5e.com

 "code red diss"
or go to the book's website at
www.nelson.com/
crimjusticeprimer5e.com

"Indian Posse"
or go to the book's website at
www.nelson.com/
crimjusticeprimer5e.com

 "Manitoba Warriors"
or go to the book's website at
www.nelson.com/
crimjusticeprimer5e.com

"Inside Toronto South's New
Maximum Security Detention
Centre",
or go to the book's website at
www.nelson.com/
crimjusticeprimer5e.com

CHAPTER 12

RELEASE AND REENTRY

After reading this chapter, you should be able to

- discuss the purpose and principles of conditional release
- discuss the release options for provincial, territorial, and federal inmates
- describe the issues surrounding crime victims and conditional release
- describe the dynamics of parole board decision making and the issues surrounding parole board decision making
- discuss the effectiveness of conditional release options
- describe the reintegration process and the challenges that offenders have reentering the community
- discuss the role of parole officers
- describe the challenges of special offender populations on parole
- discuss the factors influencing the success and failure of offenders on conditional release
- discuss the effectiveness of community supervision and control strategies

COMMON

"Parolee Back in Prison after Pleading Guilty to Mail Theft"—*The Province**
"Mothers Fear Addicted Parolees"—*Edmonton Journal,* July 26, 1993*
"Parolee Turns Self In"—*Brampton Guardian***

NOT SO COMMON

"20 Parolees Successfully Completed Parole This Week!"—*The Daily Planet*

QUESTIONS

In your view, what percentage of offenders successfully complete their conditional release, be it a temporary absence, a day parole, or full parole? (The answer is on page 283.) Why do you think that the media selectively reports about offenders on conditional release? Why do you think that systems of corrections do not counter the impressions of offenders on conditional release that are presented in the media?

*Material reprinted with the express permission of Postmedia News, a division of Postmedia Network Inc.
**Reprinted by permission of The Brampton Guardian.

The vast majority of offenders confined in correctional institutions are ultimately released back into the community. Federal offenders are more likely to apply for a **conditional release** because their sentences are longer.

Provincial and territorial inmates, on the other hand, are often serving such short sentences that they do not qualify for conditional release. Many of those who do qualify waive their right to a hearing and are released **cold turkey**, that is, without any supervision until their **warrant expiry date**, which marks the end of the sentence imposed by the court. For many of these offenders, conditional release is viewed by many offenders as being "set up to fail" and a form of "custody without walls."[1]

The underlying premise of conditional release programs is that the likelihood of recidivism is reduced because the offender is reintegrated back into the community under supervision. Release on parole is not a statutory right—it is a privilege. Though inmates have the right to apply for parole when eligible, there are no guarantees of a positive outcome.

Recall from Chapter 3 that the public has a dim view of the criminal justice system, and only 4 percent of respondents to national surveys have confidence in the parole board. Canadians often hear about parole in the media and in sensational headlines, particularly in cases where a violent crime has been committed by an offender on conditional release. See Box 12.1.

THE PURPOSE AND PRINCIPLES OF CONDITIONAL RELEASE

Section 100 of the *Corrections and Conditional Release Act* states,

> The purpose of conditional release is to contribute to the maintenance of a just, peaceful and safe society by means of decisions on the timing and conditions of release that will best facilitate the rehabilitation of offenders and their reintegration into the community as law-abiding citizens.

The process of determining which inmates qualify for conditional release is forward looking and predictive. It asks two basic questions that are set out in section 102 of the *Corrections and Conditional Release Act*, which states that the Parole Board of Canada (PBC) or a provincial parole board may grant parole to an offender if, in the board's opinion (1) the offender will not, by reoffending, present an undue risk to society before

Conditional release

A generic term for the various means of leaving a correctional institution before warrant expiry whereby an offender is subject to conditions that, if breached, could trigger revocation of the release and return to prison; parole is one type of conditional release.

Cold turkey release

Discharge of an offender at the end of the sentence when no conditional release or supervision is possible, such as when federal or provincial or territorial offenders serve their entire sentence in custody or provincial or territorial offenders are released at the two-thirds point of their sentence.

Warrant expiry date

The end of an offender's sentence.

the expiration, according to law, of the sentence the offender is serving; and (2) the release of the offender will contribute to the protection of society by facilitating the reintegration of the offender into society as a law-abiding citizen.

THE RELEASE OPTIONS FOR FEDERAL AND PROVINCIAL AND TERRITORIAL INMATES

The release of an offender from custody can occur at one of three points in the sentence: (1) the parole eligibility date, for either day parole or full parole; (2) the statutory release date, which generally occurs at the two-thirds point in a sentence; or (3) the warrant expiry date. The specific conditional release options available to inmates depend on the length of the offender's sentence and on whether he or she is under the supervision and control of provincial and territorial or federal systems of corrections. The release options for federal and provincial or territorial inmates are set out in Box 12.2.

Federal offenders may also be released under **one-chance statutory release**. If the conditions of the release are violated, the offender is returned to custody to serve the remainder of their sentence.

Figure 12.1 illustrates the sentencing milestones for federal offenders.

THE PAROLE PROCESS

The different stages of the parole process are depicted in Figure 12.2.

The staff in correctional institutions participate in the parole process by helping inmates to develop a **release plan**.

In provincial and territorial facilities, this function is performed by staff variously called inmate liaison officers, parole coordinators, or conditional release coordinators. In federal institutions, case management officers and institutional parole officers prepare release plans and other materials that will be used by parole boards in their deliberations. The release plan contains information about where the prospective parolee will live, employment prospects, and any arrangements for community-based support (such as residence in a halfway house or residential drug treatment facility). Release plans must be vetted by probation or parole officers in the community into which the offender will be released.

A key component of the release plan is the **community assessment**. Prepared by the probation or parole officer, this report evaluates the feasibility of the offender's proposed

One-chance statutory release

A release option whereby offenders who violate the conditions of a statutory release are required to serve the remainder of their sentence in confinement.

Release plan

A plan setting out the residential, educational, and treatment arrangements made for an inmate who is applying for conditional release.

Community assessment

An evaluation of the feasibility of the release plan, the level of supervision required, and the availability of community resources.

FIGURE 12.1 ▼

Sentencing Milestones for Federal Offenders with Fixed Sentences

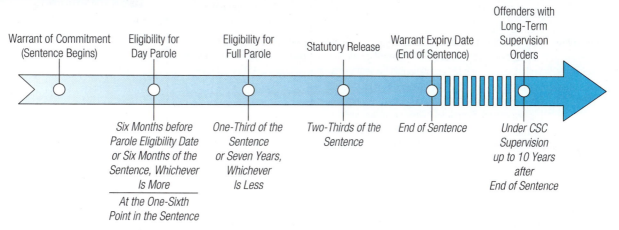

Source: © *Sentencing Milestones (A Roadmap to Strengthening Public Safety)*, http://www.publicsafety.gc.ca/cnt/cntrng-crm/csc-scc-rvw-pnl/report-rapport/trnstn-comm-eng.aspx, Correctional Service Canada, 2007. Reproduced with the permission of the Minister of Public Works and Government Services Canada, 2014.

BOX 12.2 RELEASE OPTIONS FOR FEDERAL AND PROVINCIAL AND TERRITORIAL INMATES

Type of Release	Federal	Provincial or Territorial
Temporary absences	Usually the first type of release granted; escorted (ETA) or unescorted (UTA); for medical, family, employment, education purposes.	Most common type of release.
Eligibility	ETA anytime; UTA varies with length and type of sentence; maximum-security inmates not eligible for UTAs; sentences of three years or more: may apply for UTA after serving one-sixth of sentence; sentences of two–three years: may apply for UTA six months into sentence; life sentences: may apply for UTA three years before full parole eligibility date.	Varies; in some jurisdictions inmate can apply immediately; others require waiting period; may require electronic monitoring (EM).
Day parole	Prepares offender for release on full parole by allowing participation in community-based activities; offender must return nightly to an institution or halfway house unless otherwise authorized by the PBC or a provincial parole board.	
Eligibility	Sentences of two–three years: may apply after serving six months of sentence; sentences of three years or more: may apply for day parole six months before full parole eligibility; life sentences: eligible to apply three years before full parole eligibility date.	Inmates may apply after serving one-sixth of their sentence.
Full parole	Provides an opportunity for offenders to serve remainder of the sentence under supervision in the community; parolee must report to a parole supervisor on a regular basis and abide by conditions.	
Eligibility	After serving one-third of sentence (except for offenders serving life sentences for murder); after 25 years if serving a life sentence for first-degree murder; between 10 and 25 years (set by judge at sentencing) for offenders serving life sentences for second-degree murder.	Inmates may apply after serving one-third of their sentence.
Statutory release	Provides for offenders who have not been granted parole or not applied for parole to be released to serve the remainder of their sentence under the supervision of a parole officer; a decision of Correctional Service Canada (CSC), not the PBC;[a] not available to offenders designated as Dangerous Offenders.	Not available for provincial or territorial inmates who may serve their entire sentence in custody, minus remission that is earned at a rate of one day for every two days served and allows for discharge from the institution.
Eligibility	By law, for most federal offenders after serving two-thirds of their sentence (if not released on parole); offenders serving life or indeterminate sentences not eligible; CSC may recommend that an offender be denied statutory release if it believes the offender is likely to (a) commit an offence causing death or serious harm to another person, (b) commit a sexual offence against a child, or (c) commit a serious drug offence before the end of the sentence.[b]	Unless the offender has a probation order, there will be no supervision on release.

[a] PBC may attach residency requirements if the offender poses a risk to reoffend.

[b] PBC may detain the offender, which is called **detention during the period of statutory release**; inmates detained in this manner will have their case reviewed on an annual basis.

Source: National Parole Board. 2010. *Fact Sheet: Types of Release*. http://pbc-clcc.gc.ca/infocntr/factsh/rls-eng.shtml. Reprinted by permission of the Parole Board of Canada.

Temporary absence

A type of conditional release that allows an inmate to participate in community activities, including employment and education, while residing in a minimum-security facility or halfway house.

Day parole

The authority granted by a parole board that provides an opportunity for inmates to be at large to prepare for full release (e.g., for job search) while returning at night to an institution or, more typically, to a community residential facility.

Full parole

The authority granted by a parole board for an inmate to be at large under supervision in the community for the remainder of his or her sentence.

Statutory release

A type of conditional release (made by the CSC and not the PBC) that allows incarcerated federal offenders to be released at the two-thirds point in their sentence and to serve the remaining one-third of their sentence under supervision in the community.

Detention during the period of statutory release

A decision by the PBC (after an application by the CSC) that a federal inmate be denied statutory release and be detained in the institution until warrant expiry date.

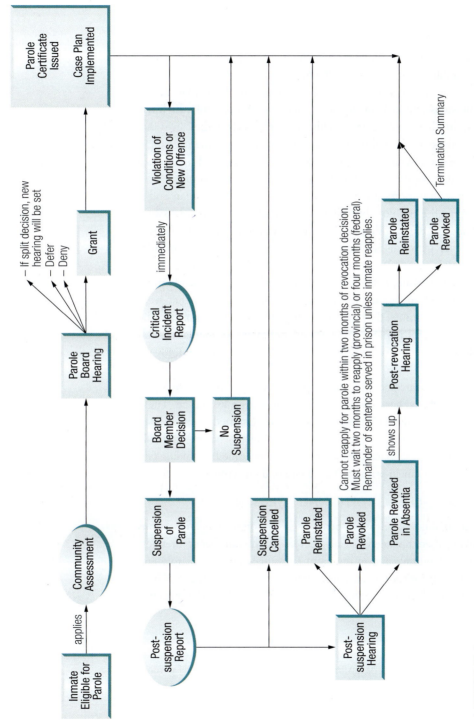

▲ FIGURE 12.2

Parole Flow Chart

Source: Justice Institute of BC, Corrections and
Community Justice Division. 1998. Reprinted with
permission.

community plan in terms of the level of supervision required and the availability of community resources. Among the areas examined in the assessment are the proposed residence; education, employment, or treatment plans; family and other support networks in the community; the extent to which the offender accepts responsibility for and understands the offending behaviour; information supplied by the victims; and any recommended special conditions the parole board may attach to the parole. Parole board members use the information contained both in the release plan and in the community assessment to determine whether an inmate should be granted a conditional release and, if so, the special conditions that should be attached to it.

An offender who presents little risk of reoffending would typically have a favourable background and no previous criminal convictions. Offenders who present a high risk must demonstrate that they have taken steps to address those aspects of their lives that would increase the likelihood of reoffending. However, as discussed later in the chapter, the general nature of the conditional release provisions gives parole board members a considerable amount of discretion in deciding whether to grant or deny parole.

Pre-release planning is an important part of the inmate's correctional plan and is directed toward managing the risk posed by offenders and, ideally, to provide access to programs and services in the community. Despite its importance in the correctional process, pre-release planning is often minimal in provincial and territorial institutions. A small sample (N = 12) of provincial inmates in Nova Scotia, some of whom had also served federal time, indicated that there was no pre-release planning and no information provided on support services in the community, and they were not generally aware of the assistance that was available to them.[2] There may also be a lack of pre-release planning for inmates with particular challenges, such as mental illness. This failure to plan hinders successful reintegration into the community on release.[3]

Federal inmates, who are incarcerated for longer periods compared with their provincial or territorial counterparts, have greater access to pre-release assistance. These inmates tend to be released in gradual stages, beginning with escorted or unescorted temporary absences. Long-term studies have shown that offenders who are gradually released from prison on conditional release are more likely to become law-abiding citizens than those offenders who stay in prison until the end of their sentence.

THE CHANGING FACE OF CONDITIONAL RELEASE

Statistics indicate that conditional release is being used less often than in previous years. Generally speaking, there has been a steady decrease in the number of offenders granted temporary absence permits and in the grant rates for federal day parole and full parole (although a slight increase occurred in both during 2011–2012).[4,5] These changes could be interpreted as being reflective of a shift toward a more punitive penology.

PAROLE BOARD GRANT RATES

The grant rates for federal and provincial or territorial day parole declined from 64 percent in 2007 to 41 percent in 2012.[6] See Figure 12.3.

The grant rates for provincial or territorial full parole steadily declined during from 2007 to 2012, as well to a low of 30 percent of cases heard. The PBC granted full parole in 23 percent of cases in 2011–2012, an increase from previous years.[7] See Figure 12.4.

It is likely that the parole grant rates are in part a reflection of the shift to a punitive penology. As concerns with risk management and negative publicity surrounding

FIGURE 12.3 ►

Grant Rates for Federal and Provincial Day Parole, 2007–2008 to 2011–2012

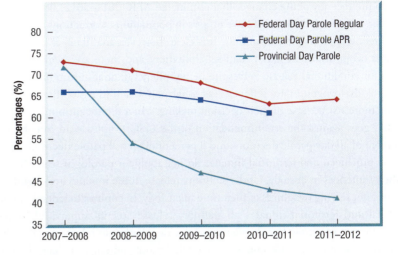

Note: APR stands for accelerated parole review.

Source: Parole Board of Canada. 2012. *Performance Monitoring Reports*, Ottawa, p. 28. Available at http://pbc-clcc.gc.ca/rprts/pmr/pmr_2011_2012/pmr_2011_2012-eng.pdf. Reprinted by permission of the Parole Board of Canada.

FIGURE 12.4 ►

Grant Rates for Federal and Provincial Full Parole, 2006–2007 to 2010–2011

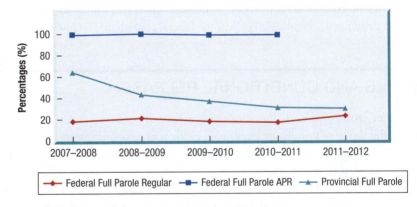

Note: Accelerated parole review (APR) for federal offenders has been abolished.

Source: Parole Board of Canada. 2012. *Performance Monitoring Reports Ottawa*, p. 31. Available at http://pbc-clcc.gc.ca/rprts/pmr/pmr_2011_2012/pmr_2011_2012-eng.pdf. Reprinted by permission of the Parole Board of Canada.

high-visibility crimes (rare as these offences are) committed by offenders on conditional release increase, this is likely to have an impact on parole board decision making.[8] This influence is reflected in statistics, which indicate that the average proportion of a sentence served before first release on parole for federal offenders is at a 10-year high: 38 percent for day parole and 42 percent for full parole. These statistics have been impacted by the elimination of accelerated parole review, which placed parole eligibility for first-time, non-violent offenders at one-sixth of sentence rather than the standard one-third.

In 2012, the full parole grant rate was the lowest in 30 years.[9] Female offenders are more likely to be successful in day parole applications, while Black offenders are the least successful.[10] Federal Aboriginal offenders are the least successful in obtaining full parole, while Black offenders have the lowest grant rate for provincial or territorial full parole. The reasons for these disparities in grant rates has yet to be explored. The proportion of sentence being served by inmates before being released on parole is the highest in a decade.[11]

Given the recency of the changes that eliminated APR (2011–2012), it is difficult to determine what impact they will have on prison populations, corrections costs, and on rates of reoffending in the community. It is clear, however, that there is an increasing emphasis on punishment rather than rehabilitation, and there are ever-fewer opportunities for conditional release.[12] Despite being independent administrative tribunals, parole boards' low grant rates reflect a "get tough" approach in which the boards have become more risk adverse in their decision making.[13] In a significant number of cases, the PBC goes against the recommendation of the CSC to release an inmate: nearly 15 percent of all day parole decisions and 8 percent of all full parole decisions.[14]

Many provincial and territorial inmates do not apply for parole; instead, they serve out their sentences in custody. Under statutory release, these inmates are eligible to be released after serving two-thirds of their time in custody. In contrast to federal offenders, provincial and territorial inmates on statutory release are not supervised by parole officers. Provincial parole boards often must decide whether to release an offender on parole who may present a risk, and with a plan that is not optimal, or to have the inmate serve until the statutory date and then leave custody with no supervision or plan.

Figure 12.5 provides a breakdown of the federal conditional release population in 2012. Note that nearly as many offenders are on statutory release as are on full parole. This statistic reflects both the decline in the full parole grant rate and the increasing levels of risk posed by federal offenders who are incarcerated and who may be less likely to receive parole. Figure 12.6 depicts the federal correctional release populations in 2012.

VICTIMS AND CONDITIONAL RELEASE

The role of crime victims in the conditional release process is sporadic. Except in Québec, the victim of the offence committed by the inmate-applicant may observe the hearing and can make a statement either in person, in writing, or via pre-recorded video.

The submission of victim statements to parole boards and attendance at hearings is rare. Of the 1063 cases heard by the Ontario Parole Board during 2011–2012, victim impact statements were submitted to the board in 53 cases. Only 16 victims attended

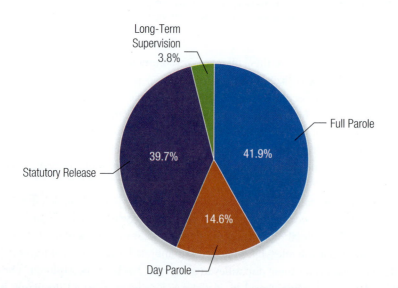

◀ FIGURE 12.5

Federal Conditional Release Population as of April 2012

Long-Term Supervision 3.8%

Full Parole

39.7%   41.9%

Statutory Release

14.6%

Day Parole

Source: Parole Board of Canada. 2012. *Performance Monitoring Report*, Ottawa, p.9. Available at http://pbc-clcc.gc.ca/rprts/pmr/pmr_2011_2012/pmr_2011_2012-eng.pdf. Reprinted by permission of the Parole Board of Canada.

FIGURE 12.6 ▶

FIGURE 12.6 ▶

Federal Conditional Release
Population by Group as of April 15,
2012

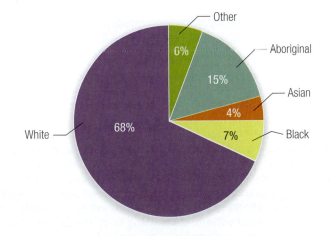

Source: Parole Board of Canada. 2012. *Performance Monitoring Report*, Ottawa, p.10. Available at http://pbc-clcc.gc.ca/rprts/pmr/
pmr_2011_2012/pmr_2011_2012-eng.pdf. Reprinted by permission of the Parole Board of Canada.

parole hearings.[15] This process is quite dissimilar to restorative justice approaches, where the victim is a key player in the discussions (see Chapter 13).

The institution where the parole hearing is held may be a considerable distance from the victim's home or the victim may not have access to a victim support person. In addition, most victims have little knowledge of the parole process; of how hearings are conducted; that the decision of the board is forward-looking and predictive; that the focus is on whether the offender, if released will reoffend before the warrant expiry date (end of sentence); and that the parole hearing is not a retrial of the case. For victims or their families, the parole hearing is the first public forum since the court where they have an opportunity to speak about the impact of the crime and to confront the offender.

It can also be very intimidating for the victim to sit in a parole hearing room with the offender present and to speak candidly about the offender's potential release. The victim may fear reprisals when the offender is released. For these and a variety of other reasons, some victims choose to make a written submission to the parole board to be considered during the hearing, while a smaller number submit video statements for parole board members to view. There are no guidelines as to how much weight victim submissions or presentations in parole hearings should be given in making the conditional release decision.

An excerpts from a victim's written submission to a parole board are presented in Box 12.3.

Most crime victims are not harassed or threatened by offenders on conditional release; however, some victims are at great risk. It is in these cases that victim notification is most crucial, for both officially sanctioned releases and unauthorized absences from community supervision.

To facilitate the sharing of information with crime victims on the movement and release of their perpetrator, the CSC operates a National Victim Services program. This program provides registered crime victims with updated information on the offender's status, notifications of parole board hearings, and release dates and conditions. The information most frequently requested by registered victims from the CSC are the release dates, release destination, and release conditions of the offender.[16] An evaluation of the program found that it was successfully achieving these objectives.[17] Similar programs are operated by provincial and territorial systems of corrections, although the effectiveness of these initiatives is unknown.

> ## BOX 12.3 EXCERPTS FROM A VICTIM'S WRITTEN SUBMISSION TO A PAROLE BOARD
>
> I have just received notification that [name removed], if granted parole, will be released as soon as [date removed]. I am writing this letter to express my opposition to his parole. I am the victim of the crimes for which Mr. [ ] was convicted. I was in an on-off relationship with Mr. [ ] that spanned for six months. During that time he was severely emotionally abusive and increasingly physically abusive. My last encounter with him resulted in a serious concussion, multiple bruises and lacerations and my fleeing the province. Several incidents prior to that last one also resulted in physical injury of varying severity. The emotional wounds were far more severe and it took along time for me to recover from them.
>
> If Mr. [ ] claims that he must be released from the correctional facility to receive treatment he is merely being manipulative. I am absolutely certain that Mr. [ ] will re-offend. I believe that he should, at least, fulfill his entire sentence. I believe that the more time he is kept from society, then the safer it will be. It is only a matter of time before he will appear before the courts again. If Mr. [ ] is released early, then it will re-affirm to him that he is able to act inappropriately without any significant fear of punishment.
>
> Source: Anonymous. Provided to the author.

PAROLE BOARD DECISION MAKING

Parole hearings are usually presided over by two board members and are generally conducted in the institution where the inmate is being held. In federal parole hearings the inmate-applicant is accompanied by his or her case manager, who serves as an assistant. Lawyers also may attend, although the parole board is an administrative tribunal and not a court of law. Different rules apply. Federal Aboriginal offenders may have an Elder or cultural adviser present at the hearing, although the number of hearings at which an Elder or cultural adviser is present has declined in recent years to around 35 percent of the hearings. Interestingly, 12 percent of federal parole hearings with an Aboriginal cultural adviser involved offenders who were not Aboriginal.[18] This fact has stirred some controversy, critics arguing that this practice undermines the integrity of Aboriginal-centred corrections.

In its deliberations, the parole board considers a number of documents contained in the inmate-applicant's parole file. These generally include, but are not limited to, police reports, reports from institutional staff on the inmate's behaviour and performance, victim impact statements, pre-sentence reports, official record of convictions, letters of support, and a community assessment prepared by a probation or parole officer.

During the hearing, the board members ask the inmate about the release plan and other questions to ascertain suitability of release. Board members are interested in the insights the offender has gained about the offence, the decisions that led to the criminal behaviour, and the steps the offender has taken to address the issues that were associated with the criminal activity. Often, this involves addressing issues related to alcohol or drug abuse, anger management, or life skills. Indications of remorse and of empathy for the victim are considered important by board members. The file review and the interview are meant to determine whether the offender can be managed at an acceptable level of risk in the community.

If the parole board determines that the level of risk the inmate-applicant presents is not manageable in the community, the application for release on day parole or full parole will be denied. If parole is granted, a certificate of parole is prepared. The parole certificate contains both mandatory conditions, such as obeying the law and keeping the peace, and additional conditions, such as abstaining from intoxicants.

▼ A parole board hearing.

AP Photo/Jessica Hill, Pool

The decision of a parole board to release an inmate back into the community is, along with the verdict of the criminal court, perhaps the most important decision that is made in the correctional process. Despite this, little attention has been given to the composition of parole boards, the relationship between member characteristics and conditional release decisions, how board members use the information contained in offender case files, and the consequences of decisions for the offender, the victims, and the community.

INMATE-APPLICANTS AND THE PAROLE HEARING

For inmates applying for conditional release, the appearance before the parole board can be stressful, intimidating, and anxiety provoking. Inmate-applicants may have little or no understanding of the role of the parole board and may be intimidated by the more sophisticated language skills of board members. Other inmate-applicants may be veterans of parole hearings. A lifer on parole who had appeared before the parole board on numerous occasions offered the following observation on parole hearings:

> Parole hearings for me now are old hat. I know how to present myself, what to do, what they want to hear, why they want to hear it. I have a good understanding of what their role is, and what they think their role is and how to approach that.[19]

Parole board members, for their part, may not realize if the inmate-applicant has a mental disorder or is still in withdrawal following a relapse into drug use while on conditional release. Board members can ask the inmate-applicant literally anything. For most inmates who pled guilty in criminal court, this is the first time they have been asked detailed questions about their crimes, their personal history, and their future intentions. The severe time constraints under which many parole boards operate place an added burden on both board members and the inmate-applicant, and that may lead to superficial coverage of some topics.

In jurisdictions where the PBC is responsible for provincial and territorial parole hearings (all except Ontario and Québec, which operate their own provincial parole boards), *paper decisions* are common, and no hearing is held. This method denies inmate-applicants the opportunity to meet face to face with the board and discuss their application. It also denies the victims of crime the chance to appear before the parole board, discuss the impact of the crime, and offer their opinion on the application.

THE DYNAMICS OF PAROLE BOARD DECISION MAKING

Despite the important role that parole boards play in the correctional process, little is known about the interactions that occur in hearing rooms between inmate-applicants and parole board members. A journalist's account, presented in Box 12.4 provides some insights.

Section 147 of the *Corrections and Conditional Release Act* sets out grounds for appeal by the inmate-applicant. As parole boards are not courts of law, appeals are generally made on the grounds that proper procedures were not followed by the board.

ISSUES IN PAROLE BOARD DECISION MAKING

A number of issues surround parole board decision making.

BOARDS MAY BE SUBJECT TO PUBLIC AND POLITICAL INFLUENCE

Parole board members are appointed by governments and positions on parole boards have long been patronage appointments—that is, rewards for supporters of the government. Members are not required by legislation to have any special training or expertise in law, criminology, psychology, or corrections. As concerns with risk management and

BOX 12.4 A JOURNALIST'S OBSERVATIONS OF THE NATIONAL PAROLE BOARD (NOW THE PAROLE BOARD OF CANADA), ONTARIO REGION

Like Santa, a parole board is supposed to know who's been good or bad, and so by the time the hearing arrives parole panelists (called directors) already know more about the prisoner than they perhaps care to—and a lot of it is not very nice.

On this particular day, three board directors—former prison warden Kenneth Payne, career correctional-service employee Sheila Henriksen and social worker John Brothers—have the final say.

Armed with documents describing the parole-seeker's criminal history, psychological assessments, education, family situation, other relationships, behaviour while in prison and the recommendation from Correctional Service Canada, the members try to evaluate what risk these individuals pose to society and determine if that risk is manageable in the community.

The first up to bat on this day is a 36-year-old Kingston man who was sentenced to life on a charge of second-degree murder for killing a friend in a dispute over a woman.

At 8:30 a.m., the slight, frail-looking man is waiting outside the hearing with his case management officer and a university law student as the morning announcements play over the intercom. The atmosphere is weirdly like high school.

When the door to the hearing room opens, the brief window of opportunity has arrived that the convict has been waiting for—make-or-break time. The parole panel will soon begin its grueling interview. No holds are barred, and no part of a convict's life is off limits.

Sitting a couple of metres from the convicts, looking them in the face, panel members have to sift through what they're hearing and judge what is sincere and what is contrived, remembering that people seldom get to this point in their lives by being totally honest.

The members take in the convict's appearance and mannerisms, dissect his answers, ask questions in different ways to get a better read and compare the answers to facts provided by the professions.

They often caution the convicts against lying because their replies must be consistent with what's in their files.

This morning, the murderer from Kingston slouches, his hair slicked back tightly like people wore in the 1950s. He is wearing dark clothes, a tweed sports jacket and unmatching light-coloured socks.

The case management officer sits at a table to his left. Right as the hearing starts, the convict withdraws his application for full parole. He says day parole will suffice.

The man has spent time in a number of jails and prisons since the murder. He stares straight ahead as the case management officer outlines his criminal record, all of it minor and non-violent up to the killing. He also relates how the convict was granted full parole twice, in 1992 and again in 1995, and violated it both times.

A doctor's report rates the probability he will reoffend within a year of release at 40 per cent, saying he suffers from an anti-social personality disorder.

A panel member asks why he withdrew his application for full parole. In a low, frail voice, the convict states the obvious: "In a realistic view, I don't think you guys would send me to full parole."

A member jokes, "You have already done some of our work for us." Mr. Payne asks the convict about the bad choices he has made through his life, and there are many. The convict says his worst was

getting involved in a relationship with the woman he killed for and, as he puts it, his "negative thinking."

The focus shifts to what he might have learned from his failures. "I needed to change the way I view things," the convict says. "I used to go through distorted thinking patterns. I have a problem over-complicating things. I used to take on other people's problems and make them my own."

In discussing an anger-management course he has just repeated, he is asked: "When was the last time you felt really angry?" "When I got the letter from the parole board that media would be at my hearing," he answers. He adds, "Nothing personal," as he turns toward the observers behind him.

Asked about the killing, the convict says he doesn't recognize the man who did it, that there are "some pretty blank spots surrounding that time."

Ms. Henriksen questions his integrity. "I have got a sense you have an ability to fool people," she says. He replies: "Sitting in the position I am in, it doesn't seem right for me to say, 'Trust me.'"

But the board chooses to trust him anyway. Following brief deliberations it grants the man once-a-month [unescorted temporary absences]. If he does well on those, the next step will be day parole and then full parole without any further hearing.

"The board is satisfied you have benefited from our programs," says Mr. Payne.

The convict thanks the directors and, as he leaves, passes the bank robber waiting outside. And the process repeats itself.

The day ends with the case of the Stratford father, a 29-year-old first time offender who smashed up his truck after a night of partying and nearly killed his passenger. His sentence was two years for criminal negligence causing bodily harm. He has served about a year.

If there is a common thread among these convicts it is the way they handle stress: Drugs and alcohol are their mainstays.

Oddly enough, the convict doesn't do a very good job of selling his case. Lucky for him it sells itself.

The case management officer gives an exemplary report on his prison behaviour, noting he attends night school and wants to pursue a trade in college.

The convict shakes as he appears before the panel members, who at times try to relax him.

One thing that works against him is a compelling victim impact statement. The victim is suing the convict. "I know he's mad but I have gone and tried to talk with him and all he does is yell at me or make rude gestures when he drives by," the convict explains. "I just wish it was me who got injured that night."

"All I know is I have two young kids I haven't seen in a month and I want to get back to them," says the man. "I can't wait."

Another quick verdict: immediate full parole. The directors deliver their judgment. And then they just hope.

Source: D. Campbell. 1997. "A Journalist Goes to Prison to See for Himself how Parole Boards Decide Which Convicts Are Good Risks and Which Ones are Not," *Ottawa Citizen*, November 3, A3. Material reprinted with the express permission of Ottawa Citizen, a division of Postmedia Network Inc.

negative publicity surrounding high-visibility crimes committed by offenders on conditional release increase, they are likely to affect the decision making of the PBC.[21] There is a concern that too much discretion has been vested in non-judicial personnel whose decisions are subjected to very little oversight. Proponents of parole have argued that there is a need to staff parole boards with persons with specialized professional competence.[22] See At Issue 12.1.

A notable trend is the appointment of retired police officers to the PBC. In the view of some observers, this selection is an effort by the federal government to interject a more conservative bias into the board's decision making. Critics argue that this represents a continuation of the federal government's get tough approach to crime.

THE ABSENCE OF CASE INFORMATION FEEDBACK TO PAROLE BOARD MEMBERS

Few if any mechanisms are in place for parole board members to receive feedback on the outcomes of their decisions—that is, to learn what happens to offenders while they are under supervision in the community and after warrant expiry and the end of supervision. Generally, parole board members learn of an inmate's behaviour on conditional release only when that person commits a high-profile crime or, by happenstance, reappears during a parole suspension hearing before one of the board members involved in the original decision.

THE ABSENCE OF CLEARLY DEFINED RELEASE CRITERIA

As noted, one criticism often levelled against parole boards is that too much discretion has been vested in non-judicial, unscrutinized decision makers. The two general criteria that are supposed to guide release decisions, as set out in the *Corrections and Conditional Release Act* (see above) have long been a source of difficulty for correctional staff, for inmates, and for parole board members themselves. Board members have access to a great deal of information on each inmate-applicant—including police reports, pre-sentence reports, the presiding judge's reasons for the sentence, materials produced by case managers (including risk and needs assessments), and parole officers' community assessments—yet it is often difficult for them to prioritize this information and make a predictive decision.

This lack of guidance, combined with the discretion exercised by board members, can result in individual styles of decision making that may, in turn, lead to disparity in decisions on applications for conditional release between boards, as well as among board members, even within the same jurisdiction. Whether a particular inmate-applicant is successful may depend on which board members happen to sit at the hearing. As well, in certain high-profile cases, the board may be presented with petitions signed by community residents opposing the release of the offender. See At Issue 12.2.

281

AT ISSUE 12.2 SHOULD THE PAROLE BOARD CONSIDER PETITIONS AGAINST THE RELEASE OF AN OFFENDER IN ITS DELIBERATIONS?

The relative of a man who was killed in an accident caused by a truck driver began an online petition in an attempt to prevent the driver from being released back into the community. Daniel Tschetter was sentenced by an Alberta court in October 2009 to a 5½-year sentence for manslaughter and obstruction of justice for an accident that killed Chris Gautreau; his girlfriend, Melaina Hovdebo; and their three children, ages 16 months and 6 and 9 years. Tschetter had been spotted driving his cement truck dangerously prior to the accident. All of the victims were killed on impact.

The woman, whose uncle died in the crash stated, "If he does get parole, he would serve less than 3½ years in jail. He killed five people; he doesn't deserve to be out." A spokesperson for the PBC stated that the board can take a petition into account in making its decision on Tschetter's application for day or full parole (he was eligible for both, having served one-third of his sentence), and also noted that the primary consideration was the risk he posed to the community should he be released.

Tschetter was denied full parole but granted day parole on September 12, 2012, and moved to a halfway house, working during the day and returning to the facility at night. In May 2013, he was denied full parole and was released on Statutory Release in June 2013, having served two-thirds of his sentence.

QUESTION

Should the parole board take into account a victim's or citizen's petition opposing the release of an offender when making its decision? If so, how much weight should it be given?

Source: Adapted from Graveland, B. 2013. "Daniel Tschetter Denied Full Parole." *Huffington Post,* May 16. Accessed March 10, 2014. http://www.huffingtonpost.ca/2013/05/16/daniel-tschetter-full-parole_n_3284284.html.

THE EFFECTIVENESS OF CONDITIONAL RELEASE

Research on the effectiveness of conditional release is presented in Research File 12.1.

THE REINTEGRATION PROCESS

Reintegration is a process, not an event. It has been defined as "all activity and programming conducted to prepare an offender to return safely to the community as a law-abiding citizen."[23]

The term should not be used too literally, as it suggests that before their incarceration, offenders had been successfully integrated into the community. Many inmates come from marginalized backgrounds and have not acquired the resources or skill sets to participate in mainstream society.[24] While offenders sent to custody experience a variety of status degradation ceremonies as they move from citizen in the community to inmate, there are no status restoration ceremonies and "rituals of reintegration" that would build on the offender's accomplishments rather than being focused solely on risk.[25] As a consequence, many newly released offenders are left to their own devices to adapt and survive.

The reintegration process for federal offenders is illustrated in Figure 12.7.

Figure 12.7 indicates that reintegration begins when the offender is first assessed and continues with institutional programming and preparation for applying for conditional

Reintegration

The process whereby an inmate is prepared for and released into the community after serving time in prison.

RESEARCH FILE 12.1   THE EFFECTIVENESS OF CONDITIONAL RELEASE

Do TAs work?

Yes. The rates of successful completion of UTAs have consistently been near the 95+ percent range.[26,27]

Is day parole an effective conditional release option?

Yes. Day parole is an important part of the graduated release of offenders from confinement. It provides inmates with access to community services, employment, and educational opportunities. The successful completion rates for provincial or territorial and federal day parole are around 90 percent.[28] Offenders on day parole accounted for 9 percent of the convictions for violent offences committed by offenders on conditional release in 2011–2012.[29]

Is parole an effective conditional release option?

Yes. Despite the fact that grant rates have declined, supervision in the community provides offenders with the best chance to address their needs while managing the risk posed to the community. Statistics indicate that those who are released on some form of conditional release do quite well. Rates of successful completion for full parole are around 80.[30] A caveat: these high rates may be due to the more restrictive release practices of parole boards. Offenders on full parole accounted for 11 percent of the convictions for violent offenders committed by offenders on conditional release in 2011–2012.[31]

However, there is little information on whether the needs of offenders have been addressed and whether their quality of life (e.g., addiction issues, housing, family stability, employment) has been addressed. Ex-offenders may remain marginalized and vulnerable. U.S. research suggests that parole supervision has little effect on re-arrest rates of offenders.[32] The level of assistance provided by parole officers may be affected by high caseloads and an emphasis on control and surveillance.

Which offenders benefit most from parole?

Low risk offenders. Success rates are generally higher for low-risk offenders without lengthy criminal histories and those who have not committed a sexual offence or another crime of violence. There is evidence from U.S. studies that female and low-risk offenders benefit most from parole supervision and community programs, while those offenders with lengthy criminal histories and who had committed crimes of violence were the least impacted by parole.[33,34]

Is statutory release (SR) a useful strategy?

Yes. Although the PBC is generally not involved in this decision, SR does provide for supervision of the highest-risk offenders. Without SR, these offenders would serve their entire sentence in custody and be released without any supervision (except if they are subject to a long-term supervision order). The successful completion rates of offenders on SR is around 60 percent.[35] The success rates of SR releases who had a period of day parole or full parole supervision before SR is up to 12 percent higher, around 72 percent. This statistic indicates the value of providing offenders, even those who are high risk, the opportunity for community supervision even though they may have not succeeded.[36]

Are parole boards effective in their decision making?

Hard to tell. The effectiveness of parole boards should be measured by more than rates of success or reoffending of offenders. The lack of standardized criteria for board membership, the potential impact of public and political influences, the absence of feedback, and broad decision making guidelines all potentially undermine the effectiveness of parole boards. As well, offenders with fetal alcohol spectrum disorders (FASD) or mental illnesses, those who are members of visible minority groups, or those who are Aboriginal peoples may be at a disadvantage in parole hearings. Many offenders, particularly in provincial and territorial institutions, do not apply for parole but rather serve their time to their **remission or discharge** date (two-thirds of their sentence) and leave the institution with no supervision or access to community-based programs and services for the balance of their sentence.

Remission or discharge

Available to provincial or territorial inmates who have served two-thirds of their sentence (often referred to as *cold turkey release* as there is no supervision by a parole officer).

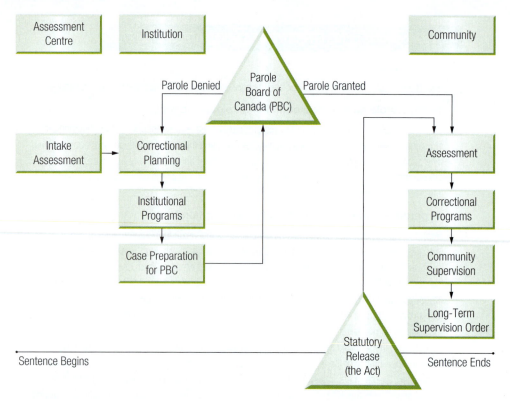

Assessment Centre

Institution

Community

Parole Board of Canada (PBC)

Parole Denied

Parole Granted

Intake Assessment → Correctional Planning

Assessment

Institutional Programs

Correctional Programs

Case Preparation for PBC

Community Supervision

Long-Term Supervision Order

Statutory Release (the Act)

Sentence Begins

Sentence Ends

Source: *Report of the Auditor General of Canada - November 1996*, Office of the Auditor General of Canada. Reproduced with the permission of the Minister of Public Works and Government Services, 2014.

release. The goal of reintegration is to avoid recidivism in the short term (i.e., until the warrant expiry date) and afterward. When required, yet another goal is to address the interests of crime victims.

Most inmates who reoffend do so within the first two years following release from a correctional institution, and this fact highlights the importance of providing support in the community.

For integration to succeed, continuity is required between the programs and services in the institution and those in the community.[37,38] This is the notion of throughcare discussed in Chapter 11. A seamless transition in treatment from the institution to the community is particularly important for offenders with special needs, such as substance abuse issues.[39]

COMING BACK: THE PAINS OF REENTRY

In Chapter 11, the various pains of imprisonment experienced by offenders who are confined in correctional institutions were discussed. On their release from confinement, some offenders may also experience **pains of reentry**.[40]

Imagine the difficulty you would have adjusting to a law-abiding lifestyle in the community if you were a parolee with a Grade 9 education, a poor record of employment, tenuous or non-existent family support, a substance abuse problem, or few or no non-criminal friends (not to mention a criminal record). Unfortunately, earning a record of positive conduct inside the correctional institution (including completion of various treatment programs) may not adequately prepare you for the challenges of adapting to

Pains of reentry

The difficulties that inmates released from prison encounter as they try to adjust to life in the community.

"Actually, there were a number of messages while you were in prison."

© Leo Cullum/The New Yorker Collection/The Cartoon Bank

life in the community. Planning a day without the rigid timetable of prison routine can be a daunting task.

A newly released offender can feel like a stranger—inadequate, acutely self-conscious, and convinced that every person on the street can tell from appearance alone that he or she has been in prison. As one woman ex-offender recounted,

> It's like you're on the bus and you think it's written on your forehead that you just came out of prison. It's terrible, it is. You got no one around. It's much easier in prison because all of the guards were around. They cared about you somewhat. Out here it just seems like you are by yourself. Just thrown out. And you are always being judged.[41]

For a released inmate who has no friends on the outside to rely on for assistance, protection, and security, the institution may exert a stronger pull than freedom itself. As one ex-offender who had served more than 20 years in prison stated to the author (in 2000): "I have never had the intensity of friendships, the trust, the companionship, in the outside community that I had when I was incarcerated."

A transition this dramatic would challenge even the most gifted individual, and it is especially difficult for marginalized and socially isolated offenders who have been incarcerated for long periods.

The pressures on released offenders may place them at risk of suicide. In a Canadian study (N = 1025) of inmates from 1995 to 2006, 47 released offenders died from all causes among the sample: 26 (2.54 percent) died by suicide. Of these, 77 percent of the deaths occurred outside the prison. These numbers suggests that offenders are more at risk of suicide in the community than in correctional institutions, a finding that should inform correctional policy and practice.[42]

THE CHALLENGES OF NEWLY RELEASED OFFENDERS

A sentence of imprisonment triggers a process whereby individuals are extracted from society and forced to adjust to a closed, structured, and artificial environment, one in which an antisocial value system predominates and inmates have little responsibility. Then, upon release, these same inmates are expected to resume or assume a law-abiding life in the community and to hold pro-social values, exercise independence of thought and decision making, and display life skills that enable them to cope with the complexities of daily life in a fast-paced society. One long-term offender commented to the author (in 2000): "The values, attitudes and behaviours that I learned inside were just the opposite of what I needed to make it in the free world." Complicating this adjustment is the fact that many offenders have few, if any, non-criminal friends or access to legitimate opportunities. All the plans to "go straight" can crumble like a New Year's resolution in February. The newly released offender may face social, economic, and personal challenges that make it difficult to avoid returning to criminal activity.

The majority of federal offenders released on conditional release have difficulties associated with the seven dynamic need domains: attitudes, community functioning, employment, marital or family, personal and emotional, associates, and substance abuse.[43]

The most frequently mentioned problems facing offenders on reentry are a lack of education and job skills; the lack of suitable housing; the absence of family support; poverty; drug and alcohol problems; and low self-esteem.[44] Criminal records preclude entry into some professions, including those requiring the employee to be bonded (insured). Some employers may have less stringent requirements but still be reluctant to hire someone with a criminal record. The job-seeking parolee may not have suitable clothes for interviews or may not possess job-specific gear, such as steel-toe boots and tools. Family reunification can be another source of stress. The longer the term of confinement, the less prepared the parolee is to resume family relations.

Awareness is emerging about homelessness and the challenges it poses to offenders released from institutions. There is evidence that homelessness is related to reoffending; 4 out of 10 admissions of homeless persons to one Toronto-area jail during one year were returnees.[45] It is estimated that 30 percent of released offenders are homeless and have no stable residence to go to when they are released.[46] Compounding the problem are provincial laws that allow landlords to deny accommodation to persons with a criminal record.[47]

Offenders often find themselves in catch-22 situations, illustrated by one released offender: "You need to meet with a worker first to get money, you need to get out of jail to meet with a worker ... you need an address to get a cheque, and a cheque to get an address."[48] There is often a lack of continuity between programs in the institution and in the community. Offenders who were in a methadone maintenance program in the institution, for example, may not have access to this program in the community, particularly those offenders from rural and remote communities.[49] Additional challenges may exist owing to mental illness, the presence of FASD, and substance abuse issues.[50]

Interviews with offenders and service providers ($N = 35$) involved in community corrections in Hamilton, Ontario, identified housing, employment opportunities, mental health counselling and addiction services as major challenges for offenders on conditional release. Speaking to the difficulties experienced upon release, one client stated, "I didn't overcome these challenges. I went back to sex trade work. Most girls, that's what they do."[51] Another commented on what happens when the ex-offender's needs are not met: "They wander the streets. They don't know how to address their needs."[52] Particular challenges were faced in staying away from old friendship networks, as were the consequences of not having timely access to treatment programs. Comments on this from the clients included the following:

- "People have big plans coming out of jail but they don't happen because of the time lag between being released from jail and arriving at the first service provider."[53]
- "A girl gets out of jail, she want to get into rehab right away. She can't go so she gets frustrated and decides, 'Well, if I can't get clean now I might as well still do drugs'."[54]

In an attempt to cope with the pains of reentry, a parolee may revert to such high-risk behaviour as heavy drinking, drug use, fighting, and spending time with old friends from prison. See the Media Links at the end of the chapter to watch the videos prepared by an ex-offender, Eddie B. Ellis, Jr., who shares his experiences.

In addition, there is concern that offenders who have been incarcerated for lengthy periods may suffer from **post-incarceration syndrome (PICS)**, the symptoms of which may include depression or anxiety. This syndrome may comprise a number of disorders that may hinder an offender's adjustment in the community.

The stress of reentry may be especially acute for the state-raised offender (see Chapter 11). These individuals have very little experience living in the outside community, have few or no family ties, and—a key point—have no stake in the community. Their friends, identity, status, and power are all inside the correctional institution. Outside in the free community, there are no guarantees of status, of security, or of a routine that provides

Post-incarceration syndrome (PICS)
A condition of offenders in custody and in the community that is caused by prolonged exposure to the dynamics of life inside correctional institutions.

for one's basic needs. In such cases, the pull of the institution may be greater than that of freedom on the streets.

Close friendships are in danger of being lost, and the inmate may feel that he or she is abandoning close friends, confidants, or lovers inside. These feelings may be especially acute when the soon-to-be-released inmate realizes that he or she has no friends on the outside who can be relied on for assistance, protection, and security.

Even offenders who, before confinement, had relatively conventional lifestyles (with the exception of their lawbreaking) can find it hard to unlearn the automatic responses acquired in an environment where physical aggression is a survival skill.

In an attempt to cope with the pains of reentry, the parolee may revert to high-risk behaviour, including heavy drinking, drug use, and resumption of friendships with former criminal associates or old friends from prison. Though most will complete their period of conditional release without committing a new offence, many will be reconvicted of a criminal offence within three years of release.

PAROLE OFFICERS AND THE SUPERVISION OF OFFENDERS

Offenders on parole are generally required to report regularly to a correctional agent, such as a parole officer. Parole officers are also involved in supervising offenders who are placed on long-term supervision orders by the court. Not all offenders who are released into the community require the same level of supervision. Assessments are made to determine the need and risk level of the offender—low, medium, or high—and these are used to determine the level and intensity of supervision. Supervision by parole officers may range from periodic telephone calls to the offender's residence to the requirement that the parolee reside in a community-based residential facility with 24-hour monitoring and attend frequent face-to-face meetings with a parole officer.[55]

The activities and responsibilities of parole officers include conducting assessments of offenders to determine their risk and needs; preparing materials for the parole board, including the community assessment; monitoring the offender's behaviour and enforcing the conditions of the parole certificate; counselling; and serving as an officer of the court, which includes giving testimony in court in cases where the parolee has been charged with a new offence.

THE DUAL FUNCTION OF PAROLE SUPERVISION

Like probation officers, parole officers have a dual role in their relations with clients. The first involves being a resource person and confidant to counter the pains of reentry. In this regard, the supportive activities of parole officers can include offering job search advice, referring clients for counselling, and advocating with welfare authorities on their behalf. The second role involves monitoring and enforcing parole conditions. To be effective, parole officers must have the capacity to understand their clients. A federal woman offender stated, "You also need counsellors who understand. Not just professionals. A degree is no good without [lived experience]. A degree is only a piece of paper. You need to understand to be able to help them, to walk in their shoes. Some of them haven't got a clue where I'm coming from. I don't want to talk to someone like that. It's very frustrating."[56] As well, high-risk offenders, such as sex offenders, may be unlikely to disclose their urges to reoffend to their parole supervisor for fear of being returned to custody.

Each parole officer has his or her own style of supervision. Some are more lenient and give the parolees assigned to them more freedom; others are much stricter. The style of supervision also depends on the level of risk the parolee poses to the community. Ideally, a balance between the two roles is achieved, with more control and surveillance during the early phases of release and more assistance as the supervision period draws to an end. The intensity of supervision will depend on the risk and needs of the parolee.

Not surprisingly, research studies have found that parole officers with more authoritarian attitudes are more inclined to enforce the conditions of parole and to send an offender to a parole board revocation hearing.[57] In recent years, there has been a marked shift toward the surveillance approach in supervising offenders on release.

To be effective, parole officers must adapt their supervision style to the risk and needs of the offender. A number of factors may hinder the efforts of parole officers, including the perceptions that each brings to the relationship. Parole officers may believe, for example, that offenders make a rationale choice as to whether to abide by the conditions of their release. The attitude of the parole officer may also hinder the efforts of offenders, particularly when the offender is treated with disrespect.[58] Offenders, on the other hand, may perceive that parole officers have little understanding of their social background and are unable to appreciate the pressures and challenges they face.[59]

The increasing emphasis on risk management in corrections and the rise of a punitive penology may transform the role of parole officers into one of monitoring and enforcing compliance with release conditions and periodically reassessing changes in risk and need.[60] The paperwork burden of conducting these assessments and recording them in computerized, centralized databases has had a strong impact on the amount of time parole supervisors can spend in face-to-face contact with clients.

Using high technology for surveillance of offenders in the community has promises and pitfalls. In corrections, the use of surveillance technology has the potential to significantly reduce costs of supervising offenders in the community and in institutions, and provides a measure of safety for crime victims and potential victims. Research in California, for example, has found that parolees who were on GPS monitoring had higher compliance rates with the conditions of their release than offenders on traditional parole, and monitored parolees committed fewer criminal offences.[61]

On the other hand, no national discussion has taken place to date that would define the limits of the deployment of technology. This lack of limits raises issues about citizen and offender rights, as well as larger issues surrounding the need to balance safety and security with the protection of citizen rights, including the right to privacy.

ADDITIONAL PROVISIONS FOR SUPERVISION

The *Criminal Code* contains a number of provisions that can be used to impose conditions and supervision on offenders once they have completed their custodial sentence and parole. One is the long-term offender designation (section 753 of the *Criminal Code*; and see Chapter 9). If certain criteria are met, indicating that the offender will present a substantial risk of committing a serious personal offence following release from custody, the sentencing judge can impose the designation of long-term offender and require the offender to be under the supervision of a parole officer for up to 10 years.

The other provision is found in section 810 of the *Criminal Code*, which can be used for offenders who have not been granted parole and who have served their entire sentence in custody. Section 810.1 may be used in situations where there is fear that the offender poses a risk to persons under 14. Under section 810.2, prosecutors may ask the court to impose restrictions on persons who are considered a high risk to commit a violent offence in the community.

PROGRAMS AND SERVICES FOR OFFENDERS

The conditional release may include a requirement that the parolee reside in a community-based residential facility with 24-hour monitoring and frequent face-to-face meetings with a parole officer. The Correctional Service of Canada operates a number of community correctional centres (CCCs) across the country and also contracts private operators (including not-for-profit organizations, such as the 7th Step Society) to provide beds in community residential facilities (CRFs). In each province and territory are parallel systems of residences that the government operates either directly or under contract with private operators. These CRFs are often called halfway houses. Most released offenders do not reside in halfway houses but rather live on their own or with their families. There are also residential treatment centres and recovery houses that specialize in alcohol and substance abuse intervention.

The CSC also operates an intensive supervision program for offenders on conditional release who have a history of violence and confinement in correctional institutions, who exhibit little motivation to change, who may have psychological disorders, and who present a high risk of reoffending. A typical candidate for the program is the high-risk offender who was denied parole and is subsequently granted statutory release. The objectives of the program are to ensure the safety of the community through a regimen of intensive supervision, to help offenders access resources and services in the community, and to manage the risk presented by the offender.

A variety of other programs across the country are designed to increase community involvement in providing assistance to released offenders. These programs are generally staffed by trained volunteers who assist with many activities, including assisting parole officers and offenders and participating in Circles of Support and Accountability (CoSAs, a restorative justice-based program discussed in Chapter 13) The London, Ontario, Community Parole Project and the Community Adult Mentoring and Support (CAMS) program in Victoria, B.C., are two examples. A number of programs are based on the principles of restorative justice. These are discussed in Chapter 13.

To assist offenders in transitioning from the correctional institution to the community, some U.S. states have developed **reentry courts**. These specialized courts operate much the same as the problem-solving courts discussed in Chapter 7. A collaborative effort is made between justice and social service personnel to assist offenders in managing the challenges of reentry. The judges are actively involved in the offender's transition from prison to the community, either by retaining jurisdiction over the offender from sentencing to warrant expiry or by assuming jurisdiction once the offender is released. Key activities of reentry courts centre on designing a reintegration plan for offenders based on their assessed needs and active oversight by the court, as well as on coordinating services and community support. The courts can be particularly helpful for female offenders who are attempting to reunite with their children following a period of incarceration.[62]

Reentry court

A problem-solving court that assists offenders in managing the challenge of reentry.

SPECIAL OFFENDER POPULATIONS ON PAROLE

As noted earlier in the chapter, offenders vary in the specific types of problems they encounter on reentry. This disparity requires that correctional systems adapt policies and programs to meet the needs of special offender populations and to manage the risks they present.

WOMEN OFFENDERS

> The system doesn't support reintegration. . . . You see them being released into the community with nothing. And how surprised should we be that they reoffend?
>
> — executive director, Elizabeth Fry Society, Ottawa[63]

Similar to their male counterparts, female offenders reentering the community must attempt to find stability in their lives. This goal requires supportive family and friendship networks, as well as access to programs and services. Finding employment may be even more challenging for women than it is for men, because women are less likely to have completed their education, often have little job experience, and may have to find and pay for daycare.[64,65] Women released from confinement may also have to address difficult issues with respect to their partners or spouses, who may also have been involved in criminal activity. This problem may place additional strains on women and increase the pains of reentry. Female offenders may be more likely to experience gender discrimination and more stigma as ex-offenders than their male counterparts, in some measure because of societal prescriptions against "misbehaving women."[66]

Among the factors that appear to be associated with reoffending among female offenders are a high-risk rating, unemployment, substance abuse, and failure to complete community-based programs.[67] Successful reintegration is facilitated by a conscious decision on the part of the female offender to live a crime-free and drug-free life, support from families, partner or spouse, and children, and a positive relationship with her parole officer.[68]

For inmate-mothers, the challenges may include reestablishing contact with their children, finding suitable accommodation with sufficient space, and attempting to regain custody if the children have been placed in care during the mother's confinement. Especially when the inmate-mother is the sole caregiver, child protection authorities may require that she obtain stable employment and suitable accommodation before being allowed to reapply for custody. The frustrations that mothers may encounter on release are reflected in the following comments of an ex-offender on parole in Ontario:

> I took parole to get my kids back. Parole agreed to my present location, but now the Children's Aid Society is saying it's not suitable for the kids. I can't rent before I know whether I am going to get my kids, and I can't get them back until I rent. I can't get mother's allowance until I have my kids, and without it I can't rent. I never know what I have to do for who. There are just so many hoops to jump through.[69]

It can be assumed that the challenges are even greater for women released from provincial and territorial institutions. These women, who may have extensive histories of abuse, addiction, or mental illness, may not have access to programs and services either while incarcerated or when released from confinement. This area is vastly underresearched in Canadian corrections.

It is estimated that approximately 40 percent of federal female offenders will return to custody, either for a violation of release conditions or having committed a new offence.[70]

HIGH-RISK OFFENDERS

To manage the risk posed by high-risk offenders, the CSC collaborates with several police departments across the country (including the Regina Police Service and the Hamilton Police Service). It involves police officers being hired to work as community corrections liaison officers (CCLOs). These officers monitor the activities of high-risk and high-needs offenders in the community and liaise between police officers and parole officers.[71] Larger police services across the country also have specialized teams that focus on chronic and high-risk offenders. Programs and services for special-needs populations are less developed in provincial and territorial corrections systems, and offenders with specific needs who reside in northern and remote areas of the country have limited access to assistance.

PERSONS WITH MENTAL ILLNESSES

Federal and provincial and territorial systems of corrections have been slow to address the challenges faced by persons with mental health issues on reentry into the community. This often leads to a cycle of release, reoffending, and reincarceration.[72] Offenders with mental health issues may be more likely to commit technical violations of their parole.[73]

Offenders with mental illnesses face special challenges on returning to the community, including social isolation, co-occurring substance abuse disorder, and lack of suitable employment and housing. A study of offenders with mental illnesses in detention in Québec found that these individual were poorly prepared to reenter the community, had difficulty accessing services, and enjoyed little continuity between programs in the institution and in the community.[74]

SEX OFFENDERS

Sex offenders on conditional release are often high profile in the media and present governments and corrections with unique challenges. Their release from prison is often front-page news in the local press or even announced over the Internet. Correctional systems use a variety of techniques to manage the risks of this offender group. Treatment interventions include the use of drugs, such as anti-androgens, to reduce sex drive and the CSC high-risk offender program, which includes a maintenance program for managing sex offenders who are on conditional release. This program is cognitive-behaviour oriented and includes individual and group counselling. It is designed to provide continuity to programs for sex offenders in correctional institutions.

Governments and systems of corrections also employ a variety of strategies to monitor and control high-risk sex offenders in the community. The monitoring of sex offenders by means of GPS systems is commonplace in the United States and will likely be adopted in Canada. Several provinces, including B.C. and Ontario, have established sex offender registries that require these offenders to register 15 days before release into the community (or on conviction if they receive a non-custodial sentence) and to reregister annually, as well as 15 days before any change of address. The centralized register database includes information on offenders, such as their names, date of birth, current address, and identifying marks, as well as photographs. Offenders remain on the registry indefinitely unless they are acquitted on appeal or receive a pardon.

Community notification (CN) is a widely used strategy designed to manage risk and protect the community from high-risk sex offenders. Decisions about CN are most often made by a committee that may be composed of a police representative, a private citizen, a specialist in medical and therapeutic interventions, and representatives from provincial or territorial and federal corrections. The practice of CN generally involves the police making a public announcement that a high-risk sex offenders has taken up residence in an area (Figure 12.8 shows the process). The premise of CN policies is that by warning potential victims and the community at large, the ability

Community notification

The practice, usually carried out by police agencies, of making a public announcement that a high-risk offender has taken up residence in an area.

of the community to protect itself is strengthened, and offenders who know they are being watched will be deterred from reoffending.[75] This strategy may also be viewed as a hardening of attitudes against certain categories of offenders and reflective of a punitive penology. The negative aspects of CN are that it may prevent the offender from reestablishing a stable residence and relationships in the community, thereby increasing the possibility of reoffending.

▲ Attempts to restrict the movements of convicted sex offenders.

▲ Community notification in Florida. Would you support using this strategy in Canada? Why? Why not?

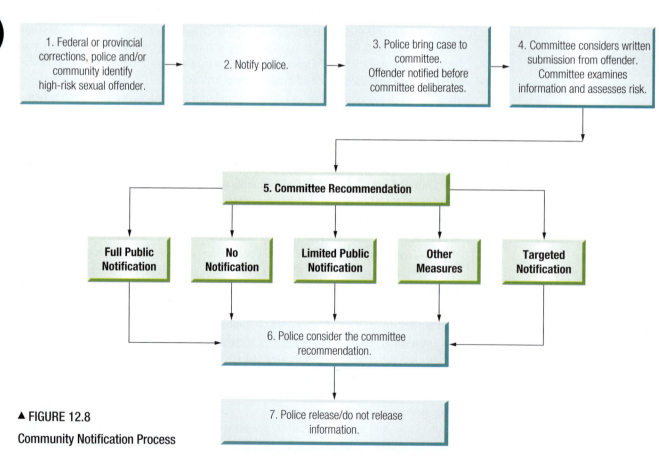

▲ **FIGURE 12.8**

Community Notification Process

Source: "Community Notification Process," Government of Manitoba, http://www.gov.mb.ca/justice/images/charteng.jpg. Copyright © 2014, Province of Manitoba

AT ISSUE 12.3 **SHOULD THE PRACTICE OF COMMUNITY NOTIFICATION BE DISCONTINUED?**

Proponents of CN contend that it alerts the neighbourhood to a potential risk, thereby reducing the likelihood of another offence; that public safety overrides any expectation the offender has for privacy; and that it serves to protect victims. Opponents of CN counter that CN is not an innovative correctional practice but rather reflective of penal populism; that there is no evidence that it is effective in reducing reoffending; that it increases public fear and paranoia; and that it makes it difficult for offenders to reintegrate into the community and, in so doing, raises the risk of reoffending.

QUESTIONS

Which arguments do you find most persuasive? Would you want to be notified of the presence of a sex offender in your neighbourhood? Explain. If so, what would the knowledge cause you to do differently? Does your province or territory have a community notification law? Check the statute books, because several do and more are planned. Check out the website of your local police. Many now have community notification pages.

Sources: A. Bain. 2011. "Please Recycle: Continuities in Punishment." *International Journal of Law, Crime, and Justice* 39, no. 2: 121–35; Y.N. Brannon, J.S. Levenson, T. Fortney, and J.N. Baker. 2007. "Attitudes about Community Notification: A Comparison of Sexual Offenders and the Non-offending Public." *Sexual Abuse: A Journal of Research and Treatment* 19, no. 4: 369–79; G. Duwe and W. Donnay. 2008. "Impact of Megan's Law on Sex Offender Recidivism: The Minnesota Experience." *Criminology* 46, no. 2: 411–46.

CN can involve proactive measures, such as distributing leaflets door to door and placing signage on the sex offender's property; or it can be passive, involving the posting of the information on the Internet to be accessed by interested parties, including persons in the market to purchase real estate. Several U.S. states post the names and home address of all sex offenders on the Internet. Information can be accessed to determine if, and how many, sex offenders live in proximity to a specific piece of property. In Canada, police departments periodically place public warnings on their websites.

CN continues to be surrounded by controversy. See At Issue 12.3.

The use of CN raises the issue of how to balance the rights of the community with the privacy rights of the offender and ethical questions as to how intrusive the state can be in a person's private life. These challenges were highlighted in a case in British Columbia. A sex offender with 42 prior offences, including sexual and violent attacks against victims as young as nine, was forced out of a community after being released from custody. He had refused to participate in treatment programs during his time in prison. The RCMP had issued a CN, releasing his photo and warning that he was a high risk to reoffend. In the words of the town's mayor: "Basically, our community did what the judicial system wouldn't. . . . We said, 'You have no rights. Get out of town.'" As the threats against him mounted, the offender decided to move to another community 70 kilometres away. "I'm in a small town right now," he commented, "and I've had the support of [the town] for long time here and I'm going to lose it over the media [coverage]. . . . Then what do I do from here, go to someone else's community?"[76]

MAKING IT OR GOING BACK: FACTORS IN THE SUCCESS OR FAILURE OF OFFENDERS ON RELEASE

It took me 34 years to get lucky, a lot of people don't get that opportunity, and they get really frustrated and they get really angry and down on themselves. They resort to alcohol and drugs, and that is sometimes why they are there in the first place, and then they just get out of control, they don't care about their life. They don't care if they get into trouble. When I look back in my life, going out on those mandatory supervision releases, I would be doing things like getting really drugged and getting high, and then hurting somebody. I think people, a lot of people, are doing that just because they don't have any positive things happening in their life, and they can't see a positive future.

—ex-offender, personal communication with author, 2000.

Even the most institutionalized state-raised inmate does not leave a correctional institution with the intent of returning. And correctional systems have as a primary objective the reduction of recidivism among offenders released into the community. Statistics indicate that most federal offenders successfully complete conditional release and do not reoffend before warrant expiry.

Among the factors that increase the likelihood of success on parole are a supportive network of family and friends, stable housing and employment, participation in treatment programs, and a conscious decision to move out of a criminal lifestyle.[77-79] There is some evidence that the ethnicity, age, and gender of the parolee may influence the decisions of supervising parole officers.[80] Research studies have also found that inmates who have a sustained pattern of visitation while incarcerated are less likely to recidivate.[81] This fact highlights the importance of offenders maintaining social networks with persons outside the institution. Unfortunately, many male and female offenders have no visitors during their period of incarceration.

▲ The choices parolees make.

Statistics indicate that over the past decade, the rate of conviction for violent offences for offenders under supervision in the community has declined. This statistic includes offenders on day parole, full parole, and statutory release.[82] Unfortunately it is the handful of offenders who commit heinous crimes again who receive the attention of the media. They often have a significant impact not only on victims but also on corrections policies and practices—which encourage tougher sentencing laws and tighten the decision making of parole boards. The silent majority of offenders who successfully complete conditional release is invisible to the community. Contrary to the images portrayed in the media, the majority of sex offenders are not rearrested for new sex crimes.

When asked about the connotations attached to the word *parolee*, community residents tend to respond in one of two ways: "got out too soon," or "dangerous to the public." These responses reflect the fact, noted in Chapter 3, that most citizens get their information on crime, criminal justice, and corrections from the media.

SUSPENSION AND REVOCATION OF CONDITIONAL RELEASE

Failing to abide by any of the set conditions, including committing a new criminal offence or failing to adhere to the conditions of the parole certificate, may result in a **suspension of conditional release**.

When a parolee is suspended, two outcomes are possible: (1) the parole supervisor cancels the suspension and releases the person from custody, or (2) the case is referred back to the provincial parole board or the PBC for a hearing to determine whether there should be a **revocation of conditional release** (which usually means a transfer back to a correctional facility).

Suspension of conditional release

A process initiated by the supervising parole officer (or in some instances by the parole board) in cases where the parolee has allegedly failed to abide by the conditions of release.

Revocation of conditional release

A decision by a releasing authority, such as a parole board, made in connection with an offender whose release has been suspended.

294

Parole officers have considerable discretion in the use of suspensions. The law states that officers *may* suspend a parolee for violating a parole condition or when new offences are alleged. The number of cases in which technical violations occur or new offences are alleged but a suspension is not imposed is unknown.

Offenders who have had their conditional release suspended are returned to the correctional facility to await a post-suspension hearing before the parole board. The board will review the report on the incident that triggered the suspension and the post-suspension report prepared by the supervising parole officer. The parole board has a number of options, including cancelling the suspension and reinstating the parole (with additional conditions if required) or ending the parole, which means that the offender remains in confinement.

Most offenders whose releases are revoked have committed *technical* violations—that is, they have violated the general or specific conditions attached to their conditional release. These include having a positive urinalysis test, being in an unauthorized area, or making contact with prohibited persons. About 10 percent of cases involve a revocation for a new offence. This statistic does not mean that only 10 percent of offenders on conditional release commit new offences. It is not known how many offences are committed but not discovered by the police or corrections authorities; how many offences are discovered but classified as technical violations because such charges are more easily proven; or how many suspensions are cancelled for other reasons when, in fact, an offence has been committed.

Statistics also indicate that 10 to 15 years after sentence completion (up to 2011–2012) 27 percent of offenders had be re-admitted to correctional institutions on a federal sentence (two years or more).[83] This figure is somewhat misleading, however, as it is unknown how many of these offenders had been incarcerated in provincial and territorial institutions during the 10- to 15-year period. These records are often not cross-referenced, making it difficult to get an accurate idea on the rates of reinvolvement in institutional corrections, much less in alternatives to confinement, such as probation or conditional sentences.

THE EFFECTIVENESS OF COMMUNITY SUPERVISION STRATEGIES

The importance of conditional release for the community and the offender requires effective supervision and control strategies. It was previously noted that recidivism rates are the primary measure of effectiveness in corrections, and this is no less true for assessing conditional release strategies. Research File 12.2 sets out what is known about the effectiveness of selected community supervision strategies. The file indicates that there are successful strategies and also that some of the more highly publicized strategies, such as community notification, are generally not effective in reducing reoffending.

REVISITING ACCOUNTABILITY FOR MANAGING OFFENDERS

A synopsis of one offender's journey through the criminal justice system illustrates the issues that surround the decision making of criminal justice professionals and accountability for these decisions. See Box 12.5.

RESEARCH FILE 12.2 THE EFFECTIVENESS OF SELECTED SUPERVISION OR CONTROL STRATEGIES

Do reentry courts work?

Potentially. There is some evidence that these courts can be effective if sufficient resources are provided, although further research remains to be completed.[84,85]

Do EM and GPS tracking reduce reoffending among parolees?

One (EM) doesn't; the other (GPS tracking) appears to. A pilot project sponsored by the Correctional Service of Canada found that the use of EM for federal offenders on parole had no impact on the rates of re-offending.[86] However, since this study, the federal government has created legislative provisions for the use of EM for federal offenders on parole. The use of GPS to track offenders on parole seems to hold considerable potential. A California study (N = 516) found that sex offenders on parole monitored by GPS had their parole revoked less often and committed fewer crimes than a matched set of sex offenders who were not monitored by GPS.[87] Studies have found that GPS programs are very time consuming for parole officers.

Do community-based programs for offenders work?

Research studies indicate that community-based programs for parolees are most effective when premised on the principles of effective correctional treatment: identifying the attributes of the offender that place them at risk for future reoffending (the risk principle); focusing on the criminogenic needs of the offender that are related to their criminal offending (the need principle); and providing programs that are matched with the abilities of the offender (the responsivity principle).[88]

Does community notification work?

No. Although CN appears to have strong support from the public, there have been few studies (none of them Canadian) about the impact of CN on reoffending among high-risk offenders. Nor have there been any about whether CN improved feelings of personal safety in the community. A U.S. study found no differences in the recidivism rates (commission of new offences or violations of release conditions) of male sex offenders.[89]

In one study (N = 318), sex offenders stated that they had experienced more vigilantism than was publicly known and that notification had had a negative impact on their efforts to reintegrate into the community.[90] In another study (N = 121), sex offenders who were required to register with the police in the community felt stigmatized and experienced difficulties in social relationships and in finding housing and employment.[91] These challenges are not conductive to successful readjustment in the community. Given the research findings regarding community notification, there is a question as to whether this practice should be continued.

Do sex offender registries work?

Not likely. While there are no Canadian studies, research in other jurisdictions has not produced any evidence that sex offender registries reduce reoffending.[92,93]

Do reentry courts reduce rates of recidivism?

Potentially. An evaluation of the Harlem (NYC) Parole Reentry Court was that reentry court parolees were in some instances less likely to be re-arrested and to be reconvicted. Parolees who completed the program were less likely to rearrested, revoked, and returned to prison than those who did not complete the program.[94] At present, not enough research has been done to determine the effectiveness of reentry courts in reducing rates of recidivism.[95,96]

BOX 12.5 THE CLINTON SUZACK CASE

THE OFFENDER

In September 1992, 27-year-old Clinton Suzack pleaded guilty to 17 charges in Sault Ste. Marie, Ontario. His record to that point dated back to 1981 and included robbery with violence, unlawful confinement, and assault. There was an Alberta-wide arrest warrant (not valid outside of Alberta) on charges of breach of probation and assault. He had a serious, long-standing alcohol problem and an explosive temper, but was bright and articulate.

The 17 charges stemmed from five incidents, involving nine victims, that had been committed between 1987 and 1992. In December 1987, Suzack assaulted a bar employee who refused to serve him. He failed to attend court and did not comply with the conditions of his bail. In June 1991, he punched a man three times in the face at a house party and viciously assaulted another partygoer with a broken bottle. The injuries to the second man's neck required surgery and a stay in the hospital's intensive care unit. Later in the evening, after the ambulance left, Suzack attacked a woman in the bathroom, punched her several times, and broke her nose. Two men who intervened were also assaulted, but they managed to subdue Suzack, who was subsequently arrested.

Another assault occurred in October 1991. Then in January 1992, Suzack assaulted and threatened a cocktail waitress and a female bar patron. In April, he assaulted a female acquaintance following an argument.

THE CROWN ATTORNEY

In September 1992, Suzack's lawyer negotiated an arrangement whereby the Crown would recommend a prison sentence of two years less a day in exchange for a guilty plea.

THE JUDGE

The plea bargain was not binding on the sentencing judge. The judge said he was inclined to hand down a sentence of four and a half years but conceded to the joint submission of the Crown and the defence attorney. He called Suzack a "vicious, violent person" but saw the guilty plea as a mitigating factor and handed down a 729-day sentence. He also ordered three years' probation—the maximum available—to follow the prison term. In addition, the judge recommended that Suzack attend the Northern Treatment Centre in Sault Ste. Marie, although with the acknowledgment that the recommendation was not binding on the provincial correctional system.

THE CORRECTIONAL SYSTEM

Suzack began his sentence in September 1992. He was classified as a high-risk inmate and sent to Millbrook, the most secure provincial institution. He repeatedly requested a transfer to a lower-security facility, but none were willing to take him. His institutional misconduct record was one obstacle. He played tackle football when only touch football was permitted, refused an assigned job as a cleaner, was rude to a guard, and was found in his cell with two other inmates after being warned this was against the rules. For these infractions, he lost seven days of recreational privileges and three days of earned remission and was reprimanded twice.

While at Millbrook, Suzack took computer and woodworking courses. He attended Alcoholics Anonymous (AA) meetings, participated in an anger management group, and engaged in educational upgrading. A report from the institution's psychologist noted the pattern of alcohol-related violence, but concluded that Suzack was "a bright, articulate individual with considerable potential [who] has demonstrated to staff that he has insights into many of his problem areas and motivation to make some changes." The release plan Suzack devised for presentation to the parole board included an intention to live with three friends in Sudbury, one of whom would employ him in his computer equipment company.

THE PROBATION AND PAROLE SYSTEM

A Sudbury probation and parole officer, in a pre-parole investigation, confirmed the release plan by contacting the people with whom Suzack intended to live. The opposition of one of his crime victims to the release was noted in the report, as was the alcohol problem and outstanding warrant. As is typically the case, the officer had never met Suzack. He recommended that parole be denied.

THE PAROLE BOARD

With a 729-day sentence, Suzack would be eligible for parole on June 2, 1993, having served one-third of the sentence (or eight months). If denied parole, he would be automatically released at the two-thirds point in his sentence (February 1994). Three members of the Ontario Board of Parole interviewed him on May 5, 1993. Before the hearing, they reviewed the pre-parole report, his prior record, and the institution's file, including the psychiatrist's report, training reports, and the reports on institutional misconducts. The Sault Ste. Marie police sent descriptions of most but not all of the offences for which Suzack had been convicted. The police "strongly opposed" parole, calling Suzack a "menace to society and a threat to the safety of the public."

The board denied Suzack parole, primarily because the proposed living arrangement would not meet his needs for community-based treatment for anger management and alcohol abuse. Also weighing against Suzack were his prior record, the severity of the current offences, his minimization of the role of alcohol in his offences, and his previous failures under community supervision (for example, his failure to comply with conditions of bail).

THE CORRECTIONAL SYSTEM

One month later, Suzack lost 14 days' recreational privileges for fighting. He then reapplied for a transfer to the Sudbury jail, which offered a temporary absence program.

The psychiatrist updated the first report by noting that since being denied parole, Suzack had completed an alcohol awareness program, a woodworking course, and an anger management program (reenrolling in the latter). Moreover, he was chairman of both the Native Sons Program and the institutional AA group, was doing schoolwork, and had volunteered in the prison chapel. While noting the seriousness of Suzack's offences, the report concluded: "He will gain little else by remaining at this facility. . . . He has exhausted the relevant treatment services here and the positive structured plan he currently has in place may not be there on discharge [in February]."

Despite the positive report, Suzack was denied admittance on the grounds of institutional misconduct.

SALVATION ARMY REHABILITATION CENTRE

To have any chance of parole, Suzack had to devise a better release plan. He applied to the Salvation Army program in nearby Hamilton. When interviewed by a staff member at the centre, Suzack indicated that all his offences stemmed from the one house party. The centre agreed to admit him into a 90-day program once he was released on parole.

THE PROBATION AND PAROLE SYSTEM

Suzack's new release plan had to be confirmed. The Sudbury probation and parole officer conducted another investigation and again recommended that parole be denied. A Hamilton probation ad parole officer confirmed the availability of the Salvation Army program. He had never met Suzack and had little information about him (because of a computer error), and therefore he was not able to offer an opinion on the suitability of parole.

THE PAROLE BOARD

Suzack got a second hearing, at the discretion of the board, because of his new release plan and recent program participation. All the above-mentioned documents were available to the board, along with a social work report and a letter from a Hamilton-based Aboriginal centre that offered Suzack the opportunity to explore Aboriginal culture. At the August 17 hearing, he was seen by three other board members (one of whom was Aboriginal). He described the programs he had taken, expressed a willingness to learn about Aboriginal culture, and articulated some insights into his past behaviour.

Board members asked Suzack about his alcohol problem, past treatment, misconducts, and outstanding charges, but little about the offences. Again, he implied that all the charges stemmed from one incident. The board granted him parole, citing his participation in all available institutional programs and the offer of admittance into the 90-day treatment program operated by the Salvation Army in Hamilton, far away from his victims.

PROBATION AND PAROLE SYSTEM

On August 26, Suzack was released from Millbrook and took up residence at the Salvation Army Rehabilitation Centre in Hamilton. He was on the caseload of the Hamilton probation and parole officer who had written the pre-parole report. This officer met Suzack for the first time five days after his release on parole. By then, the officer had gathered background information about Suzack and had begun to question whether the Salvation Army program was an appropriate placement for him. It was not a secure facility and was designed for motivated parolees who did not require close supervision.

SALVATION ARMY REHABILITATION CENTRE

The Salvation Army Rehabilitation Centre in Hamilton is one of many centres contracted by the Ontario government to provide services to released offenders. Upon Suzack's admission, the director assumed case management responsibility, instead of delegating the case to a staff member. The following day, the director and the parole officer discussed their mutual concerns. A program involving AA and attendance at the Aboriginal centre was established.

On September 9, Suzack asked to be excused from an AA meeting. The request was denied. Suzack left the Salvation Army centre later that day. The director learned of, and reported, the parole violation on the following day. An arrest warrant was issued, and his previous victims were notified.

THE OFFENDER

Suzack eluded arrest until October 7, 1993, when he and an accomplice, Peter Pennett, fatally shot a Sudbury Regional Police Constable Joe MacDonald in the back of the head after an altercation during a routine traffic stop. Convicted of first-degree murder, Suzack was sentenced to life with no eligibility for parole for 25 years. At sentencing, the judge indicated that Suzack should serve his entire sentence in maximum security. Suzack was initially housed in a maximum-security

facility in Ontario and was later moved to Joyceville, a medium-security correctional facility. He was transferred back to maximum security after being suspected in an escape plot. He was then moved back to Joyceville.

In the fall of 2001, after serving six years of his life sentence, Suzack was moved to William Head Institution, a medium-security correctional facility at the southern tip of Vancouver Island. This transfer was criticized by several police groups in Ontario, including the Ontario Association of Police Chiefs, as well as by municipal councils throughout the province. All called on the federal solicitor general to return Suzack to maximum security to serve his life sentence. As of early 2014, Suzack was still incarcerated.

THE VICTIM

The estate of the police constable filed a civil suit against the various justice agencies that had been involved in making decisions about Suzack, including the provincial parole board and probation and parole service. The case was settled out of court for an undisclosed sum.

QUESTIONS

Identify the key decisions that were made in this case. Are there decisions that could have been made that would have prevented what happened? If you were a member of a panel reviewing the civil case, would you recommend that any of the justice personnel and agencies involved in making decisions about Suzack be held civilly liable for their decisions? Explain. If you believe that the decision-making process in the Suzack case was flawed, which decision makers were most responsible?

SUMMARY

The discussion in this chapter has focused on the release of offenders from confinement and their reentry into the community. The purpose and principles of conditional release are set out in the *Corrections and Conditional Release Act* but provide only a broad framework within which release decisions are made. Conditional release is now being granted to inmates less often, reflecting the emergence of a punitive penology. There are a variety of types of release that are designed to reintegrate offenders back into the community. This plan presumes that offenders were integrated into the community before to their incarceration, a questionable assumption for many offenders who are sent to correctional institutions. For inmate-applicants, the parole hearing process can be intimidating, and there are often socio-economic and cultural disparities between board members and inmate-applicants. A number of issues surround parole board decision making, which makes it, at best, an inexact science.

The reintegration process for offenders was explored, and it was noted that offenders often experience pains of reentry that are associated with the challenges of adjusting to community life. The dual role of parole officers was noted, and the strategies used to control and manage high risk offenders were examined. The effectiveness of selected supervision and control strategies was discussed. A case study was presented to illustrate the journey of one offender through the justice and corrections system, highlighting the decisions that were made and the consequences of these decisions.

KEY POINTS REVIEW

1. The purpose and principles of conditional release are set out in the *Corrections and Conditional Release Act*.

2. The specific conditional release options that are available to inmates depend on the length of the offender's sentence and whether he or she is under the supervision and control of provincial and territorial or federal systems of corrections.

3. Often, little pre-release planning is done for provincial and territorial offenders.

4. Statistics indicate that conditional release is being used less often than in previous years.

5. The role of crime victims in the conditional release is sporadic and is most often limited to providing written impact statements to the board.

6. In making release decisions, the parole board is interested in whether the offender can be managed at an acceptable level of risk in the community.

7. For inmate-applicants, appearing before a parole board can be stressful.

8. The issues surrounding parole board decision making include these: boards may be subject to public and political influence; there is an absence of clearly defined release criteria; and feedback on case decisions to parole board members is lacking.

9. Research suggests that some conditional release options are more successful than others in reducing the likelihood of reoffending.

10. Reintegration is best understood as a process rather than as an event.

11. Many inmates experience challenges in reentering the community.

12. Female offenders experience unique challenges on reentry, including, for many women, attempting to reestablish contact and relationships with their children.

13. Parole officers play a dual role in providing assistance and monitoring offenders, although there is an increasing focus on control.

14. Offenders with mentally illnesses and sex offenders on conditional release present unique challenges for parole supervisors and community-based service providers.

15. A number of factors are related to the success of offenders on conditional release.

16. There is some question as to the effectiveness of supervision and control strategies used for offenders on conditional release.

KEY TERM QUESTIONS

1. Define the following types of **conditional release: temporary absence, day parole, full parole, remission or discharge,** and **statutory release**.

2. What is **cold turkey release**, and what issues does it raise?

3. Describe the procedures and objectives of **detention during the period of statutory release**, and then define **one-chance statutory release**.

4. What is the **warrant expiry date**?

5. Discuss the role of the **release plan** and the **community assessment** in conditional release.

6. Define **reintegration** and its objectives.

7. How do the **pains of reentry** and **post-incarceration syndrome (PICS)** affect offenders returning to the community?

8. What are **reentry courts**, and how do they work?

9. Describe **community notification**, and discuss the issues surrounding its use.

10. Define **suspension of conditional release** and **revocation of conditional release** and explain how these affect the status of an offender on conditional release.

MEDIA LINKS

 A description of a day in the life of a parole board member or go to the book's website at www.nelson.com/ crimjusticeprimer5e.com

"Virtual Hearing. A Parole Board of Canada (PBC) Hearing Room" or go to the book's website at www.nelson.com/ crimjusticeprimer5e.com

"Exclusive video from Cinellli's Parole Board Hearing" or go to the book's website at www.nelson.com/ crimjusticeprimer5e.com

"The Probation Process" or go to the book's website at www.nelson.com/ crimjusticeprimer5e.com

"A Homecomer on the Rebound" or go to the book's website at www.nelson.com/ crimjusticeprimer5e.com

"A Homecomer's Confession— Eddie B. Ellis, Jr." or go to the book's website at www.nelson.com/ crimjusticeprimer5e.com

PART V

RECONSIDERING CRIMINAL JUSTICE

Chapter 13: Restorative Justice: An Alternative Approach to Crime, Victims, and Offenders
Chapter 14: Going Forward: Challenges to and Opportunities for Criminal Justice Reform

• •

The discussion in the preceding chapters has examined the structure and operation of the Canadian criminal justice system. The chapters in this part provide the foundation for exploring how the criminal justice system can be made more effective and efficient. Chapter 13 examines restorative justice, which provides an alternative to the adversarial system of justice. In this model, equal importance is given to the victims of crime, the offender, and the community. Restorative justice holds the potential to deliver what the traditional criminal justice system has heretofore failed to: holding offenders accountable for their behaviour while at the same time meeting the needs of crime victims and the community. We'll take a close look at the principles and practice of restorative justice, as well as its limitations.

In Chapter 14, the final chapter of the book, a number of challenges confronting the criminal justice system are discussed, as are the opportunities for creating more positive outcomes.

303

CHAPTER 13

RESTORATIVE JUSTICE: AN ALTERNATIVE APPROACH TO CRIME, VICTIMS, AND OFFENDERS

LEARNING OBJECTIVES

After reading this chapter, you should be able to

- describe the basic principles of restorative justice
- compare and contrast restorative justice with adversarial justice
- understand the various restorative justice approaches
- discuss Aboriginal restorative justice initiatives
- describe the challenges surrounding restorative justice
- discuss the effectiveness of restorative justice approaches

On Saturday June 23, 2012, the Chatham-Kent (Ontario) police were dispatched to a break and enter call at a family residence.* The two complainants, who were sisters, advised the officers the home had been their mother's residence. After she died, they began looking after the property. To ensure her safety, their mother had previously installed security cameras in the home. The house was now completely empty of any contents and was not occupied. On checking the property, the sisters noticed the rear door of the home had been pried open. The cameras were motion activated and provided still pictures of several young people who had spent approximately two and half hours in the residence.

The suspects had forced their way in the back door. Once inside the suspects caused damage to the dining room chandelier, likely by swinging on it. The suspects also broke the glass shower doors, and an interior window was broken in the bathroom. Total estimated damage to the property was approximately $500. It appeared that the youth were looking for a place to party that night or in the future. Pictures of all six youth were provided by the complainants and given to the CK Police on arrival at the scene.

The six youth were subsequently identified and, following an investigation, were asked if they would be willing to participate in the Alternative Measures Program (Youth Pre-Charge Diversion) at Restorative Justice Chatham-Kent, rather than having formal charges laid against them. Most of the six young people confessed to having been in the residence. One female in the group admitted that they had been smoking marijuana.

All the youth were very remorseful and welcomed the opportunity to rid themselves of pending charges of break and enter—they agreed to attend Restorative Justice Chatham-Kent (RJCK). Following a face-to-face intake assessment with each youth and his or her parents or guardians, a plan was developed, and the program coordinator at RJCK met the six youth separately, and they received educational programming in various topics. Each youth learned about the *Youth Criminal Justice Act*, received programming in the areas of vandalism and marijuana, and also viewed the DVD *Burning Bridges*, which shows several teens who burned a historical bridge in their small hometown. All six of the youth met with the program coordinator for five sessions before the restorative justice (RJ) conference took place.

The RJ conference was held, and the six youth accused were present, along with their parents or guardians, two trained community volunteers, and the four victim participants (the two sisters, one of their husbands, and a daughter). During the RJ conference, the youth were able to tell their stories. They told what happened the day of break and enter, what they were thinking, and how they were feeling, and then what they were thinking after the incident when the police got in contact with them.

What had an enormous impact on the six youth were the *victims of their crime*. These young people truly believed that no one owned this home and that they were not trespassing or hurting anyone. When real people—faces—and their heartbreaking story came to light, all of these youth felt differently about what they had done. The six youth were very apologetic to the owners of this property and showed great remorse. These emotions brought satisfaction to both parties involved in this matter—it brought closure to all who were involved in this case and helped repair the harms that were done.

---

* This case is provided, with permission, by Chatham-Kent Restorative Justice program.

Each youth was given 10 community service hours to complete and were each requested to write letters of apology to their victims. All six successfully completed the Youth Pre-Charge Diversion program. ˙

The Youth Pre-Charge Diversion program is one initiative of RJCK, which also operates a Restorative Justice Community Conference program, and the Positive Strides program for at-risk youth. This program contains a number of modules focusing on youth and drugs or alcohol, anti-bullying and harassment, and anger management or violence prevention, among others (www.rjck.org). The success rate of the pre-charge diversion program is 92 to 100 percent after one year.

WHAT IS RESTORATIVE JUSTICE?

Concern with the effectiveness of the traditional adversarial system of criminal justice and a variety of other influences has led to the search for alternative ways to respond to persons in conflict with the law. One of these alternatives is restorative justice. **Restorative justice** is a problem-solving approach to responding to offenders based on the principle that criminal behaviour injures victims, communities, and offenders, and that all these parties should be involved in efforts to address the causes of the behaviour and its consequences.

Restorative justice is *not* a specific practice but rather a set of principles that provides the basis for a community and the justice system to respond to crime and social disorder. Key notions in restorative justice are healing, reparation, reintegration, and the prevention of future harm.[1] The use of restorative justice is not confined to the criminal justice system. It is used in schools, workplaces, and a variety of other settings.

Restorative justice

A problem-solving approach to responding to offenders based on the principle that criminal behaviour injures victims, communities, and offenders, and that all these parties should be involved in efforts to address the causes of the behaviour and its consequences.

THE PRINCIPLES OF RESTORATIVE JUSTICE

Restorative justice approaches focus on the following:[2]

- addressing the harms and needs of victims, communities, and offenders
- confirming the obligations of offenders, families, community, and society that result from these harms
- being an inclusive, collaborative process
- involving all those with a stake in the situation
- righting wrongs

See Box 13.1.

BOX 13.1   THE QUESTIONS ASKED BY TRADITIONAL CRIMINAL JUSTICE AND BY RESTORATIVE JUSTICE

THREE DIFFERENT QUESTIONS

Traditional Criminal Justice	Restorative Justice
What laws have been broken?	Who has been hurt?
Who did it?	What are their needs?
What do they deserve?	Whose obligations are these?

FIGURE 13.1 ▶

The Relationships of Restorative Justice

Source: T. F. Marshall. 1999. Restorative Justice: An Overview. *Home Office Occasional Paper 48*. (London: Home Office). Reprinted by permission of the Home Office under the terms of the Open Government Licence (OGL), http://www.nationalarchives.gov.uk/doc/open-government-licence/version/2/.

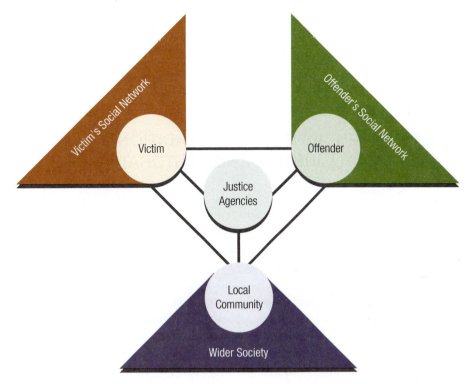

THE RELATIONSHIPS OF RESTORATIVE JUSTICE

Figure 13.1 depicts the relationships among the various parties that may be involved in a restorative justice approach.

THE DIMENSIONS OF RESTORATIVE JUSTICE

Among the more common restorative justice initiatives are victim–offender mediation, circle sentencing, community holistic healing programs, and family group conferences. Critical differences exist among the various models of restorative or community justice, including their mandate and relationship to the formal adversarial system, the role of the crime victim and other participants, and the procedures

At Aboriginal Ganootamaage Justice ▶ Services of Winnipeg, Manitoba, participants take part in a healing circle for a 20-year-old shoplifter (not shown in photo).

Winnipeg Free Press–Joe Bryksa

307

for preparation for the event and for monitoring and enforcing the agreement.[3,4] The models also differ in terms of their objectives, the degree to which the model requires that the justice system share power with community residents, and the extent to which the model is designed to empower the community and address a specific incident and behaviour.[5,6]

THE DIFFERENCES BETWEEN TRADITIONAL (ADVERSARIAL) JUSTICE AND RESTORATIVE JUSTICE

Restorative justice differs in significant ways from the traditional adversarial justice process. A comparison of the two models is presented in Table 13.1.

The primary objectives of restorative justice are to fully address the needs of victims of crime and to prevent reoffending by reintegrating offenders back into the community. Offenders are required to acknowledge and assume responsibility for their behaviour, and there is an effort to create a community of support and assistance for the victim and the offender, as well as for the long-term interests of the community.

Regardless of the specific restorative justice approach, the process ends with an agreement on how the offender will address the harm caused by the crime. These amends may include a written or verbal apology, the payment of restitution to the victim, provisions to assist the offender in changing his or her behaviour (e.g., attending a drug treatment program), or performing service to the community.[7]

Figure 13.2 provides a comparison of criminal justice and restorative justice participants and processes.

TABLE 13.1 THE PRINCIPLES OF RETRIBUTIVE AND RESTORATIVE JUSTICE

	Retributive Justice	**Restorative Justice**
Focus	focus on establishing blame and guilt	focus on problem solving, obligations, and the future
Stigma	stigma of crime permanent	stigma of crime removable
	no encouragement for repentance and forgiveness	possibilities for repentance and forgiveness
People	dependence on professionals and experts; non-residents	direct involvement by participants; local participants
Process	adversarial; state versus offender; victim ignored—offender passive	consensus; community versus problem; victim and offender's roles recognized in both problem and solution: victim rights and needs recognized; offender encouraged to take responsibility
Issues	laws broken	relationships broken
Accountability	offender accountability defined as taking punishment	offender accountability defined as understanding impact of action and helping decide how to make things right
Community	community represented abstractly by the state	community as facilitator
Tools	punishment and control	healing and support
Procedure	fixed rules	flexible

Source: Adapted from Canadian Resource Centre for Victims of Crime. 2011. "Restorative Justice in Canada: What Victims Should Know." http://www.rjlillooet.ca/documents/restjust.pdf p. 3. Reprinted with permission from the Canadian Resource Centre for Victims of Crime.

FIGURE 13.2 ►

Comparison of Criminal Justice and Restorative Justice Participants and Processes

Source: C.G. Nicholl, *Community Policing, Community Justice, and Restorative Justice: Exploring the Links for the Delivery of a Balanced Approach to Public Safety* (Washington, DC: Office of Community-Oriented Policing Programs, U.S. Department of Justice, 1999). 113 9

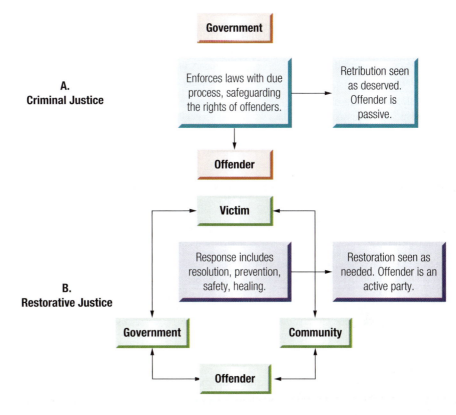

ENTRY POINTS FOR RESTORATIVE JUSTICE IN THE CRIMINAL JUSTICE SYSTEM

There are a number of entry points in the criminal justice system where restorative justice approaches can be used: police (pre-charge), Crown (post-charge and pre-conviction), court (post-conviction and pre-sentence), corrections (post-sentence), and following sentence expiry. Circles of support and accountability (CoSAs), for example, involve community residents and justice and social service personnel working with high-risk sex offenders who have completed their sentence but are still in need of assistance. See Figure 13.3.

Victim–offender mediation (VOM)

A restorative justice approach that provides an opportunity for a crime victim and the offender to communicate and address the impact of the offence, and for the offender to take responsibility for the offence and its consequences.

VICTIM–OFFENDER MEDIATION

Victim–offender mediation (VOM) programs (also often referred to as victim–offender reconciliation programs) takes a restorative approach, in which the victim and the offender have the opportunity to express their feelings and concerns. With the

FIGURE 13.3 ►

Restorative Justice: Entry Points in the Criminal Justice System

Source: *The Effect of Restorative Justice Programming: A Review of the Empirical Research Literature*, Figure 2.1, page 7, http://www.justice.gc.ca/eng/rp-pr/csj-sjc/jsp-sjp/rr00_16/rr00_16.pdf, Department of Justice Canada, 2000. Reproduced with the permission of the Department of Justice Canada, 2013.

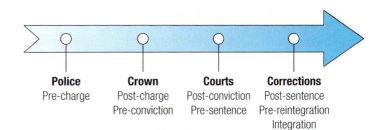

TABLE 13.2 CHANGING THE DYNAMIC: VICTIMS AND OFFENDERS	
Crime victims are provided with an opportunity to	**Offenders are provided with an opportunity to**
be directly involved in resolving the situation and addressing the consequences of the offence	acknowledge responsibility for the offence and understand the effects of the offence on the victim
receive answers to their questions about the crime and the offender	express emotions (even remorse) about the offence
express themselves about the impact of the offence	receive support to repair harm caused to the victim or oneself and family
receive restitution or reparation	make amends or restitution and reparation
receive an apology	apologize to victims
restore, when appropriate, a relationship with the offender	restore their relationship with the victim, when appropriate
reach closure	reach closure

Source: Dandurand, Y. and Griffiths, C.T. 2006). *Handbook on Restorative Justice Programmes.* Vienna: United Nations Office on Drugs and Crime, http://www.unodc.org/pdf/criminal_justice/06-56290_Ebook.pdf. Reprinted with permission.

assistance of a mediator, who is a neutral third party, the offender and the victim are able to resolve the conflict and consequences caused by the offence and, ultimately, to understand each other. See Table 13.2.

Referrals come from the police, the courts, and probation offices. For a VOM program to be used, the offender must accept responsibility for the crime, both the victim and the offender must be willing to participate, and both the victim and the offender must consider it safe to be involved in the process. The mediator assists the victim and the offender in arriving at a settlement that addresses the needs of both parties and that provides a resolution to the conflict. The mediation process has the following several steps:

1. intake of the case from a referral source

2. preparation for the mediation, which involves the mediator meeting separately with the victim and the offender

3. the mediation session

4. post-session activities, including ensuring that any agreement reached during the mediation session is fulfilled

In recent years, VOM have been extended to cases involving crimes of violence and have included incarcerated offenders. In such cases, the offender has already been sentenced and the mediation generally involves the victim or the victim's family wanting to understand why the offence occurred and whether the offender grasps the impact of the offence and the harm done. In some cases, VOM has been used when the offender is incarcerated and the family members of their victim have met. See At Issue 13.1

Restorative Resolutions is an intensive supervision program in Winnipeg that uses victim–offender mediation to achieve restorative justice. The program is operated by the John Howard Society of Manitoba and staffed by workers trained in probation practices and restorative justice. The program is an alternative to incarceration for offenders who are willing to take responsibility for their behaviour and to compensate their victims. Among the services provided are counselling, anger management, and intensive supervision. A case from the Restorative Resolutions program is presented in Box 13.2.

AT ISSUE 13.1 SHOULD VICTIM–OFFENDER MEDIATION BE USED IN CASES OF VIOLENCE?

Watch the two cases presented in the links below. Then ask yourself the following questions and discuss them with your classmates:

1. If you or a member of your family had been the victim of a violent crime, would you want to meet the offender?

2. For each of the cases, do you think that the mediation was productive?

3. Did the mediation provide closure for the victim's family? Did it assist the offender in understanding the harm done?

"Victim/Offender Mediation"
www.youtube.com/watch?v=SCiXbgUiA6U

"Meeting with a Killer" (Part 1 of 4)
www.youtube.com/watch?v=dZA88a0hYRk

BOX 13.2 A CASE STUDY FROM THE RESTORATIVE RESOLUTIONS PROGRAM, WINNIPEG

A 32-year-old man with a lengthy youth and adult record of assault and break and enter was charged with four new counts of break and enter and theft. The Crown attorney wanted a period of incarceration. Restorative Resolutions staff prepared an alternative plan recommending that the judge issue a suspended sentence, with supervision of the offender to be carried out by Restorative Resolutions; and that the offender complete the Interpersonal Communication Skills Course; complete the Addictions Foundation of Manitoba assessment; attend AA regularly; complete the conditions outlined in the mediation agreement; and receive literacy training. The judge accepted the plan.

Source: *Satisfying Justice: Safe Community Options That Attempt to Repair Harm from Crime and Reduce the Use or Length of Imprisonment* (Ottawa 2006), 5. Church Council on Justice and Corrections. Reprinted with permission.

CIRCLE SENTENCING

Circle sentencing
A restorative justice strategy that involves collaboration and consensual decision making by community residents, the victim, the offender, and justice system personnel to resolve conflicts and sanction offenders.

Circle sentencing is a restorative justice strategy that involves collaboration and consensual decision making by community residents, the victim, the offender, and justice system personnel to resolve conflicts and sanction offenders. The process for circle sentencing was established in two court cases: *R. v. Gingell* (1996), 50 CR (4th) 326 (QL) (Y Terr Ct) and *R. v. Moses*, 71 CCC (3rd) 347, [1992]3 CNLR 116 (QL)(Y Terr Ct).

Circle sentencing originally developed in several Yukon communities as a collaboration between community residents and territorial justice personnel, primarily RCMP officers and judges from the Territorial Court of Yukon. Circle sentencing is premised on traditional Aboriginal healing practices and has multifaceted objectives, including addressing the needs of communities, victims, the families of victims, and offenders through a process of reconciliation, restitution, and reparation. A fundamental principle of circle sentencing is that the sentence is less important than the process used to select it.

In circle sentencing, all the participants, including defence lawyer, prosecutor, police officer, victim and family, offender and family, and community residents, sit facing one another in a circle. The presiding judge may or may not be present. Through

TABLE 13.3	DIFFERENCES BETWEEN CRIMINAL COURT AND CIRCLE SENTENCING PRINCIPLES	

Criminal Court	Circle Sentencing
The sole focus is on the crime.	The focus includes the crime and the larger conflict that surrounded it.
The sentence is the solution to the problem.	The sentence is only one part of the solution.
The focus is on past and present conduct.	The focus is on present and future conduct.
The offender's behaviour is judged within a strict legal framework.	The offender's behaviour is judged within a holistic framework that takes into account legal and other factors, including community and family.
The sentence is focused on the offender.	The sentence considers the offender, the victim, and the community.

discussions, those in the circle reach a consensus about the best way to dispose of the case, taking into account both the need to protect the community and the rehabilitation and punishment of the offender. Note that judges are not bound by the recommendations of a sentencing circle and maintain control over sentencing at all times.

Circle sentencing has spawned a number of variations, including community sentence advisory committees, healing circles, sentencing panels, and community mediation panels.

There are significant differences between the principles of sentencing in the criminal courts and those of circle sentencing. These are highlighted in Table 13.3, and the differences in setting for the two as shown in Figure 13.4.

In contrast with the adversarial approach to justice, circle sentencing has the potential to reacquaint individuals, families, and communities with problem-solving skills; rebuild relationships within communities; and to focus on the causes, not just the symptoms of problems.

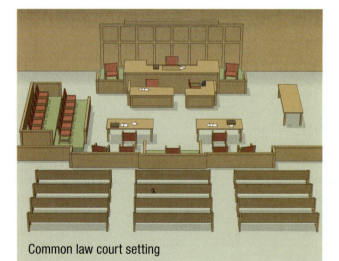

Common law court setting

Circle sentencing setting

▲ **FIGURE 13.4**

Differences between Criminal Court and Circle Sentencing Settings

Circle sentencing is generally only available to offenders who plead guilty. The operation of the circle sentencing process is specific to communities, meaning that it may (and should) vary between communities, and the circle-sentencing process relies heavily on community volunteers for its success. Both Aboriginal and non-Aboriginal victims, offenders, and community residents participate in sentencing circles.

A circle sentencing case from Yukon is presented in Box 13.3.

BOX 13.3 A CIRCLE SENTENCING IN YUKON

The victim—the wife of the offender, who had admitted to physically abusing her during two recent drunken episodes—spoke about the pain and embarrassment her husband had caused her and her family. After she had finished, she passed the ceremonial feather (used to signify who would be allowed to speak next) to the next person in the circle, a young man who spoke about the contributions the offender had made to the community, the kindness he had shown toward the Elders by sharing fish and game with them, and his willingness to help others with home repairs. An Elder then took the feather and spoke about the shame the offender's behaviour had caused to his clan, noting that in the old days, the offender would have been required to pay the woman's family substantial compensation.

After hearing this discussion, the judge confirmed that the victim still wanted to try to work it out with her estranged husband and that she was receiving help from her own support group (including a victim's advocate). Summarizing the case by again stressing the seriousness of the offence and repeating the Crown counsel's opening remarks that a jail sentence was required, the judge then proposed that sentencing be delayed for six weeks until the time of the next circuit court hearing. The judge would not impose the jail sentence if, during that time, the offender (1) met the requirements presented earlier by a friend of the offender who had agreed to lead a support group, (2) met with the community justice committee to work out an alcohol and anger management treatment plan, (3) fulfilled the expectations of the victim and her support group, and (4) completed 40 hours of service under the group's supervision. After a prayer, in which the entire group held hands, the circle disbanded, and everyone retreated to the kitchen area of the community centre for refreshments.

Source: Bazemore and Griffiths, 1997. Reprinted by permission.

Presiding judges are not obligated to follow the recommendations of sentencing circles. This occurred in the case of Christopher Pauchay, profiled in Box 13.4.

It should be pointed out that circle sentencing is not appropriate for all offenders or for all crimes. Moreover, the success of a given circle will depend on the extent to which all of its participants are committed to the principles of restorative justice.[8] Concerns have been raised, for example, as to whether crime victims—especially Aboriginal women who have been the victims of sexual assault and domestic abuse—may be pressured into participating in circle sentencing.[9]

RESTORATIVE AND COMMUNITY JUSTICE IN URBAN CENTRES: THE COLLABORATIVE JUSTICE PROJECT, OTTAWA-CARLETON JUDICIAL DISTRICT

In discussions of the potential for developing restorative justice initiatives, it is often assumed that such programs as circle sentencing, which involve substantial community participation, are suited only to rural and remote communities with a strong cultural identity and foundation. This assertion is often used to deflect suggestions that justice personnel in suburban and urban areas should explore the potential for restorative

313

BOX 13.4   THE LIMITS OF RESTORATIVE JUSTICE: THE CASE OF CHRISTOPHER PAUCHAY

Christopher Pauchay was a resident of the Yellow Quill First Nation reserve in Saskatchewan. In 2008, while severely intoxicated, he led his two daughters—aged three and one—into a blizzard and blacked out. The two girls perished in the −30°C weather. Pauchay subsequently pled guilty to criminal negligence causing death. He had a prior record and Crown counsel suggested a sentence of two and a half to five years in prison, while defence counsel argued that the judge should consider a conditional sentence, to be served at home in the community.

The presiding judge directed that a sentencing circle be formed. It was composed of police, Crown counsel, defence lawyers, elders, and others from the community, including family members. After five hours of discussions, including a lengthy conversation with Pauchay, the group recommended to the judge that that he not be sent to prison but rather remain in the community to heal under the guidance of Elders and participate in alcohol and drug treatment.

Christopher Pauchay

THE CANADIAN PRESS/Troy Fleece

Critics pointed out that, following the deaths of his two children and before the sentencing circle, Pauchay had violated his bail conditions by drinking and was, as well, charged with assaulting his common law wife. He also had a lengthy record of offences, with 52 convictions primarily related to failing to follow court orders.

The presiding provincial court judge did not follow the recommendations of the sentencing circle and sentenced Pauchay to three years in prison. The judge noted that Pauchay lacked insight into his behaviour and didn't accept responsibility for the deaths.[10–13] Pauchay subsequently served two-thirds of his sentence in confinement and was released in 2011. His sentence expired in January 2012.

314

justice approaches that would better serve the needs of offenders, their victims, and the community. But there are examples of restorative justice programs operating in rural, suburban, and urban communities.

A high-profile program that is premised on restorative justice principles is the Collaborative Justice Project. The program operates in the Ottawa-Carleton judicial district and is a post-plea, pre-sentence approach designed to provide an alternative to the traditional criminal justice process. The program is unique in the sense it takes cases involving serious criminal offences. The objective is to facilitate a dialogue between the victim and the offender that can be presented to the court at sentencing. The Collaborative Justice Project illustrates that restorative justice programs can be successfully developed and operated in urban centres. It also indicates that the use of restorative justice approaches is not restricted to minor offences but can be successfully applied to serious crimes, including crimes of violence, and may be used in conjunction with a period of incarceration.

The Project considers cases of serious offending, including robbery, break and enter, assault causing bodily harm, weapons offences, and driving offences that involve death or bodily harm and in which a conviction would normally result in incarceration. Cases are referred to the Project by a variety of sources, including the judiciary, judicial pre-trials, the Crown or defence counsel, police, probation, and victim services. The accused person must be willing to take responsibility for and work to repair the harm done by the crime.

> **BOX 13.5   IMPAIRED DRIVING CAUSING DEATH: A CASE STUDY FROM THE COLLABORATIVE JUSTICE PROJECT**
>
> **The Facts:** The accused, Robert, was driving the wrong way on a multi-lane, divided highway, entering by the off-ramp. After traveling 2 km in the wrong direction, narrowly missing several vehicles, he collided with the victim's car, killing a 60-year-old man and slightly injuring his wife. Robert had close to three times the legal limit of alcohol in his blood and was charged with impaired driving causing death and criminal negligence causing death.
>
> **Work Done:** The case worker first met with Robert to assess his interest and appropriateness for the Collaborative Justice Project. Robert was willing to take responsibility for his offence and to work toward some form of reparation, without knowing in advance what that might look like. Robert was prepared to meet with the victim's family if it would help them. He was extremely emotional.
>
> Satisfied that Robert met the criteria, the caseworker then met with Phillip, the adult son of the victim, and his mother, Claire. Phillip wanted something good to come out of the tragedy. He felt that Robert might speak to people about drinking and driving, or even go with Robert to speak to groups. However, Phillip believed that Robert would not be willing or able to speak publicly, so he didn't expect his hope could be realized. Phillip wanted to meet with Robert to learn who Robert was and whether he would drink and drive in the future. His mother didn't wish to meet Robert but needed more information about the accident from the police so that she could move on with her own grieving process.
>
> The caseworker obtained and forwarded the information to Claire. The caseworker met with Robert regularly over the next six months to discuss how he had ended up in this situation, his alcohol problem, who had harmed, and what he might do to assist the healing process. He was receiving ongoing psychological and addiction counselling. Similarly, the caseworker was meeting with Phillip to support him and his family, to explore what he needed from the process, and prepare for a possible meeting with Robert. The caseworker conveyed information between Robert and Phillip so that each had a better understanding of the other's situation and needs.
>
> Six months later, Robert and Phillip met in a mediation. They talked to each other in a supportive manner about the impact of the incident on them and their families, and about what they would like to see happen. While Robert had previously indicated that he felt unable to speak publicly about what had occurred, after meeting with Phillip, he agreed to do so with him. Robert and Phillip met on four further occasions and together addressed a high school class where students were deeply moved by the presentation.
>
> **Sentence and Follow-up:** Robert received a sentence of two years less a day in provincial JAIL. The Crown attorney's original position of three to five years was mitigated in light of the work done by the accused and the victim's son and their interest in continuing such work. During the following year, there was continuing periodic contact with Robert and Phillip. Arrangements were made for Robert to be released on temporary absence passes from time to time to speak publicly with Phillip about impaired driving and their personal experiences.
>
> Note: The names of the participants have been changed.
>
> Source: © Church Council on Justice and Corrections. Reprinted with permission.

Three criteria must be met before a case is accepted by the Project: (1) the crime is serious and the Crown is seeking a period of custody; (2) the accused person displays remorse and is willing to take responsibility for and work to repair the harm done; and (3) there is an identifiable victim who is interested in participating.

A summary of one case is presented in Box 13.5.

RESTORATIVE JUSTICE INITIATIVES IN ABORIGINAL COMMUNITIES

Aboriginal communities have become increasingly involved in developing restorative justice services and programs that are designed to address the specific needs of community residents, victims, and offenders. These initiatives have been developed as part of a process of cultural and community revitalization and in conjunction with the increasing movement to reassert their authority over all facets of community life.[14] Communities have also begun to explore alternatives to confinement to decrease the large numbers of Aboriginal people incarcerated in provincial and territorial correctional institutions.

These initiatives vary widely in the types of offences and offenders processed; in the procedures for hearing cases, reaching dispositions, and imposing sanctions; and in the extent to which they involve justice system professionals. Restorative and community justice initiatives in Aboriginal communities may be, but are not necessarily, premised on customary law and traditional practices. Many involve Elders and emphasize healing the victims, offenders, and, when required, the community. Rather than focusing only on the offender and the offence, the response to criminal behaviour occurs within a broader, holistic framework. This holistic approach facilitates the inclusion of crime victims and their families, the offender's family, and community residents in responding to the behaviour and formulating a sanction that will address the needs of all parties.[15,16]

Another attribute of these initiatives is that the Aboriginal band or community maintains a high degree of control over the disposition and sanctioning processes, which are controlled by the community or shared, on a partnership basis, with justice system personnel, as in the case of circle sentencing. Other programs are more autonomous and are controlled by the community.

Several First Nations communities have established peacemaking circles that operate under the auspices of the provincial courts. The Tsuu T'ina First Nations Court is a provincial court in Alberta that includes a peacekeeping program centred on peacemaking circles.[17] This provincial court is composed of an Aboriginal judge, Crown prosecutor, and court clerks. It includes a peacemaking program that is focused on restorative justice principles. Adult and youth cases (except those involving homicide and sexual assault) can be referred to peacemaking by the court. To be eligible for referral, the offender must admit responsibility for his or her actions, and the victim must agree to participate in the peacekeeping process.

Eligible cases are assigned to a peacemaker who facilitates a circle healing process involving Elders, the victim, the offenders, and others. In the circle, the participants discuss what happened, the impact of the offender's actions, and what should be done. Final agreements may require the offender to provide restitution, attend counselling, or complete a number of community service hours, among other things. A final ceremony is held when the offender completes the provisions in the agreement. A report is sent to the Tsuu T'ina court where the Crown counsel will review the case and, if satisfied, will drop the charges against the offender. If the charge is not dropped, the report from the peacemaking circle will be submitted to the judge at sentencing.[18]

A case heard in a Tsuu T'ina peacekeeping circle is presented in Box 13.6.

Perhaps the longest running and most successful Aboriginal community-controlled restorative justice program is the Community Holistic Circle Healing Program on Hollow Water First Nation in Manitoba. The program was designed as a community-based response to the high rates of sexual and family abuse that affected the community. It includes a 13-phase circle healing process illustrated in Figure 13.5.

The Special Gathering in the Hollow Water program is a public event that shares many similarities with the traditional justice ceremony. Traditional healing practices are used in an attempt to restore the community, the family, and individual peace and harmony. The offender signs a healing contract and apologizes publicly to the victims

FIGURE 13.5 ▶

The 13 Phases of the Hollow Water Community Holistic Circle Healing Process

Source: "Evaluation of Community Holistic Circle Healing: Hollow Water First Nation, Vol. 1 Final Report." Copyright © 2014, Province of Manitoba.

BOX 13.6   A CASE IN THE TSUU T'INA COURT

A woman attempted to steal some pills and was charged with shoplifting. She was very depressed. When asked in the peacemaking circle what skills she had, she answered that she had no skills, she had nothing. The pills were to help her cope with her depression. She had been relying on pills for a long time and she was addicted to them. Her life was going nowhere. She hadn't finished high school. In the peacemaking circle, the participants asked her if she could cook and keep house. She said yes. They asked if she could make camp. She said yes. They asked if she could make traditional garments. She said yes. Through their question she came to realize she did have skills. They asked what were her dreams. She said she wanted to go to college. The circle decided she must take counseling for drug dependency, complete high school, and then she was to go to college. She took counseling for addiction to pills. She finished her high school equivalency and registered in Mount Royal College [in Calgary].

Source: From L.S. Tony Mandamin. 2003. "Peacemaking and the Tsuu T'ina Court," *Justice as Healing: A Newsletter on Aboriginal Concepts of Justice.* Spring 8(1): 1-4. Reprinted by permission of the Native Law Centre of Canada.

---

and to the community for the harm done. The circle healing process is designed to consider the needs of all the parties to the abuse—the victim, the offender, and the community—and is directed beyond merely punishing the offender for a specific behaviour.

CHALLENGES IN RESTORATIVE JUSTICE

A number of challenges surround the use of restorative justice approaches in the criminal justice system:

- *Conquering resistance by criminal justice and correctional personnel.* Many of the key principles of restorative justice are unfamiliar to politicians, policymakers, and criminal justice personnel, including judges. Such terms as *forgiveness, community, empowerment, healing,* and *spirituality* are not found in the *Criminal Code of Canada* and are foreign to many criminal justice practitioners.

- *Overcoming limited community interest or capacity to participate in restorative justice initiatives.* While restorative justice provides an *opportunity* for communities to become actively involved in addressing crime and responding to offenders, there is no guarantee that residents will want to be involved.

- *Changing the perception that RJ approaches are soft on offenders.* In fact, restorative justice approaches require the offender to an active participant in discussions of the offence and the harm done, a role that can often be avoided in the adversarial justice process.

- *Reducing the lack of public awareness.* A survey in Alberta, for example, revealed that only 11 percent of those polled were aware of any places or people in the community that were involved in restorative justice.[19]

- *Ensuring that the victims of crime are not revictimized by being involved in circle sentencing.* Concerns have been voiced as to whether restorative or community justice provides adequate protection for victims of violence and abuse and whether the sanctions imposed are appropriate.[20] In 2000, the Government of Nova Scotia imposed a moratorium on the referral of cases of sexual assault and spousal or partner violence. Critics contend that female victims may be revictimized by participation in sentencing circles and that the needs of women victims are often not addressed.[21] See At Issue 13.2.

- *Ensuring that offenders and victims understand the objectives of the restorative justice process and are equal participants.* A key component of restorative justice approaches is participation by victims and offenders, which is viewed as empowering the two parties to have their concerns voiced and the harm done addressed. Critics, however, have expressed concern about the power dynamics that may develop and undermine the effectiveness of restorative justice practices. See Box 13.7.

AT ISSUE 13.2   SHOULD RESTORATIVE JUSTICE BE USED IN CASES OF DOMESTIC VIOLENCE?

Concerns have been expressed, particularly by women's groups, that female victims of violence may be revictimized by a restorative process. Some Aboriginal women, for example, are concerned about the high rates of sexual and physical abuse in their communities but have questioned whether restorative justice provides adequate protection for victims of violence and whether the sanctions imposed are appropriate.[22,23] A counterpoint is that restorative justice approaches may be more effective in identifying and addressing the underlying causes of the abuse and empowering female victims, and are more likely to hold the offender accountable than the adversarial court process.

QUESTION

Should cases involving sexual and physical abuse be excluded from restorative justice programs?

BOX 13.7   RESTORATIVE JUSTICE DYNAMICS: A STUDY OF VICTIM–OFFENDER MEDIATION SESSIONS

To understand the dynamics of victim–offender mediation, researchers studied 14 mediation sessions involving property and violent personal crimes. The study was designed to observe the dynamics of victim–offender mediation. Fourteen mediations were observed involving 20 offenders and 16 victims. Among the findings were that many of the victims and offenders were unclear about the purpose and goals of mediation and how it differed from the traditional criminal justice process. relied heavily on the mediator to find a "solution," and did not participate fully in the mediation process. Victims were more likely to dictate the terms of the final agreements and offenders needs were often not addressed. These findings suggest that more research should be conducted on the power dynamics of restorative justice approaches and the effect on these dynamics of the experiences of victims and offenders, and on the effectiveness of the approach.

Source: P.M. Gerkin. 2009. "Participation in Victim-Offender Mediation. Lessons Learned from Observations." *Criminal Justice Review* 34, no. 2: 226–47.

CIRCLES OF SUPPORT AND ACCOUNTABILITY (CoSAs): A RESTORATIVE, REINTEGRATIVE PRACTICE FOR HIGH-RISK OFFENDERS

Circles of Support and Accountability (CoSAs)

Community-based committees composed of criminal justice personnel and community members that provide mentoring for high-risk sex offenders whose sentences have expired.

Circles of Support and Accountability (CoSAs) were first developed by the Canadian Mennonite Community in the early 1990s and were based on the traditional Indigenous practice of healing circles. They provide support for sex offenders who are released from federal institutions at warrant expiry or whose period of supervision on conditional release has ended through warrant expiry (see Figure 13.6). CoSAs represent a counterweight to the professionalization of corrections and penal populism.[24,25]

These offenders are the most likely targets of judicial recognizances and community notification (CN). Any offender who participates in the program does so on a voluntary basis; no legal mechanism can compel an offender to be subject to monitoring.

CoSAs are centred on the principles of restorative justice, including the importance of positive relationships that can facilitate positive change in the offender while at the same time addressing the injury caused to the victim and the community.[26] The efforts of CoSAs are designed to extend contact with the offender beyond the warrant expiry date (end of sentence and parole supervision) and to engage the community in efforts to reintegrate high-risk offenders.[27]

A circle of support is a team of five or six volunteers assigned to an offender to assist him as he takes up residence in their community. Volunteers can include teachers, social workers, police officers, businesspeople, and other community residents. They help with all facets of reintegration, including housing, employment, budgeting and financial management, spiritual development, and moral support. The offender may call only in times of stress or may have daily contact with the circle members. Circle members can also mediate between the offender and the community. Mediation took place in the case of Joe, whose arrival in the community was the subject of a CN (see Box 13.8).

In Ontario, the Mennonite Central Committee operates the Community Reintegration Project (CRP), which provides the CoSA program offering support for sex offenders who are released from federal institutions at warrant expiry.

FIGURE 13.6 ▶

Circles of Support and Accountability

Source: *Circles of Support & Accountability: An Evaluation of the Pilot Project in South-Central Ontario.* Reproduced with the permission of the Minister of Public Works and Government Services Canada, 2013.

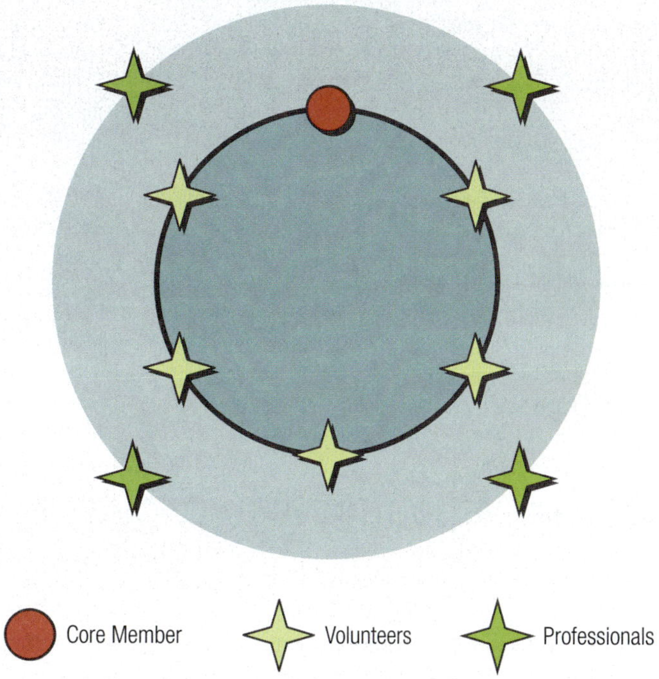

● Core Member ✦ Volunteers ✦ Professionals

BOX 13.8 JOE AND HIS CIRCLE OF SUPPORT

It began with a telephone call. "Can you help me?" the caller asked. "I'm just out of prison, and the police have already been warning everyone that I am in town. Where am I going to find a quiet place to live?" Joe, 54, had been released at Warrant Expiry from prison after serving a 6-year sentence for sexual assault against a child. It was his 8th conviction.

Joe wanted to come to our city for several reasons. He knew us, he had met public resistance in another town when he attempted to settle there before his parole was [revoked], and he suspected that he could get help in relapse prevention. We agreed to help him find accommodation, help him find a job, and try to build a Circle of friendship and support in his new city. We thought of people that we knew who could help him in each of these areas and who would be willing to work with us. We also agreed to make contact with the police.

The detectives, when we met with them, candidly said, "We don't want him here." Based on institutional reports, the police felt that Joe was likely to re-offend. There had been a lot of negative publicity recently about released prisoners re-offending, and they didn't want any of that kind of publicity for their department.

When Joe came to stay with us for the weekend while beginning the apartment search, the police quickly made his picture available to the media and warned the community of his presence among us.

The media descended upon us because we had been identified as providing support for Joe. Pickets of irate and concerned parents arrived in front of our home. After a number of angry and threatening phone calls, we finally bought a telephone answering machine.

The police mounted a plan of surveillance. They felt sure he would re-offend within a short period. They were concerned about the safety of the children in the neighbourhood, but they also wanted to ensure Joe's safety.

One of the neighbours had called the police and had a lengthy discussion with the detective. She later called to talk with me. Ann had small children and was very concerned for their safety and that of the many other children living in the area. After a discussion with her, and later with Joe, we agreed that he would meet with her to discuss her concerns. Lengthy negotiations ensued, finally resulting in a meeting proposed in a neutral site, and several other neighbours were invited to participate. The police detectives would also be present. They would be there not only as a resource, but also as people who could add to the participants' feelings of security.

Joe, accompanied by two of his friends, was the first to arrive at the meeting and take a seat on the far side of the room. Soon the neighbours began to arrive. Then the detectives entered. The ground rules of the meeting were outlined. We would go around the circle to allow everyone an opportunity to share their first name and a particular concern they brought with them. We would have a statement from the neighbourhood group, followed by an opportunity for Joe to share, and from there we would move to addressing the issues presented. Only one person at a time would speak, and they would follow our direction and instructions for the orderly addressing of the issues. Before the end of the meeting, we would decide together what of this meeting would be appropriate to share with other people, outside of this meeting.

As we began to go around the circle, the first person began by saying how much she appreciated the willingness of Joe and his friends to attend such a meeting. Ann outlined the questions she had heard the others discussing with her. There was a long list of questions: they wanted to know what had happened, what the sentence was, what treatment he had obtained, and what treatment he planned to receive now that he was released. "From your experience, what is the best way to avoid the behaviour you were charged with?" "How do you plan to deal with the negative reactions and anger of some individuals in the community?"

Joe responded, outlining in general terms his offences. Appreciation was expressed for the constructive method the residents had chosen to address their concerns, which he acknowledged were understandable. He indicated that he had received some treatment while in the institution and was planning to arrange suitable community-based therapy and had indeed made arrangements for that already. He had also set up an accountability system through his Circle of Support, by which he had daily contact with us, and we were able to make inquiry as to his faithfulness to his commitments in specific relevant areas.

We talked, and the earlier tension in the room eased as we got on with the task of problem-solving around the various issues at hand. Though all the questions were not answered, by the end of the 2½ hour meeting, there was a feeling of accomplishment and a readiness to move on.

Out of that meeting and others we had, some bridges were built. Neighbourhood residents, some of whom were vocally angry, began to see Joe as a person and recognized the difficulties with which he coped.

Throughout this time, Joe's Circle of Support met regularly with him. At least one of the Circle Members contacted him every day. After a year, we still talk to him daily. We took him to do his laundry, to shop for groceries and furnishings for his apartment.

The police have been partners with us in Joe's Circle of Support. Without the patient, humorous, understanding commitment of the detectives with whom we dealt most frequently, our efforts might not have reached this point. They came to our Circle meetings. They checked in with us frequently and we trusted their openness with us. Similarly, the police served as a buffer with the community, correcting rumours and diffusing problems.

Joe's life has settled into a comfortable pattern. He maintains a clean, comfortable apartment and has developed some close relationships. He is finding ways to spend his time and is slowly developing a small network of friends, although trust takes a long time.

QUESTION

If you had been asked to become a member of Joe's CoSA, would you have agreed? Why or why not?

Source: Courtesy of the Mennonite Central Committee of Ontario.

DO RESTORATIVE JUSTICE APPROACHES WORK?

The effectiveness of traditional criminal justice sanctions and interventions is generally measured by rates of reoffending. This measure is relatively straightforward (albeit flawed; see Chapter 11). Restorative justice approaches, on the other hand,

Can RJ approaches address the needs of crime victims?

Potentially. RJ approaches that provide an opportunity for the victim to meet face to face with the offender receive high marks from crime victims and have a positive impact on the psychological and physical health of crime victims.[28],[29] A study ($N = 34$) of victims of violent crime in Canada and Belgium who participated in victim–offender mediation, family group conferencing, or victim–offender encounters found high levels of victim satisfaction. These were ascribed to the perception that the process was procedurally just and flexible, provided care, and was empowering. These views existed regardless of the outcome of the intervention.[30]

Do RJ approaches have a positive impact on offenders?

They can. Offenders are more satisfied with restorative justice than with adversarial approaches; in RJ offenders are more likely to assume responsibility for their offending behaviour and to acknowledge the harm they have caused, and they are more likely to comply with RJ agreements than with court orders.[31],[32]

Can RJ approaches reduce reoffending?

Yes. RJ approaches can result in significant reductions in repeat offending for property and violent crime, they can be more effective with serious and violent crimes than property offences, and they can be more effective than incarceration in reducing re-offending;[33],[34] circle sentencing, in particular, does not appear to reduce reoffending among offenders, although it may function to strengthen communities and address victims' needs.[35] The Restorative Resolutions program in Winnipeg, has been successful in reducing rates of reoffending and addressing the needs of victims, offenders, and communities.[36] The Restorative Justice Chatham-Kent program (Ontario) has a high success rate with youth offenders. CoSAs have proven to be effective in reducing reoffending among high-risk sex offenders.[37],[38]

Are RJ approaches successful in facilitating community involvement?

Yes. RJ provides the opportunity for community residents to become involved in responding to criminal offenders in a proactive, problem-solving context, and they can contribute to healthier communities and improved quality of life.[39]

Can RJ approaches positively impact the administration of justice?

Yes. RJ strategies have the potential to reduce the costs of justice and the time it takes to conclude a case. They are most effective in reducing costs when used as a strategy for diversion.[40]

Are RJ initiatives in Aboriginal communities and those sponsored by Aboriginal-focused organizations effective?

They can be. Evaluations of the Hollow Water program found that it had significantly reduced the prevalence of alcohol abuse in the community; improved educational standards in the community; increased services for infants, children, and youth; increased community awareness of sexual abuse and family violence; and increased the rates of disclosure by offenders. The program is also more cost effective than the traditional criminal justice process.[41],[42] An evaluation of the Tsuu T'ina peacemaking program found that this initiative produced a number of positive outcomes.

Is circle sentencing successful in preventing reoffending?

Unknown. Few controlled evaluations of circle sentencing have been conducted. Most literature is anecdotal.

attempt to facilitate consensus, healing, and forgiveness. These concepts are difficult to quantify.

Research File 13.1 summarizes what is known about the overall effectiveness of selected aspects of restorative justice. Note that there have been few evaluations of restorative justice programs operating in Canada.

The research findings raise a number of interesting issues. See At Issue 13.3.

SUMMARY

Dissatisfaction with the traditional criminal justice process has led to the creation of a variety of restorative justice approaches that are designed to better address the needs of victims, offenders, and the community. The principles of restorative justice are quite dissimilar to those of retributive justice and focus on repairing the harm done and addressing the underlying causes of criminal behaviour. Restorative justice programs operate at all stages of the criminal justice system and in a variety of settings, including Aboriginal communities. Research studies suggest that these approaches have the potential to be more effective than the traditional criminal justice system, although numerous challenges surround the application of restorative justice principles.

KEY POINTS REVIEW

1. Concerns with the effectiveness of the traditional adversarial system of criminal justice have contributed to the creation of various restorative justice approaches.

2. Restorative justice is not a specific practice but a set of principles that guide the response to crime and social disorder.

3. The principles and practice of restorative justice are considerably different from those of retributive justice.

4. Restorative justice approaches can be used at all stages of the criminal justice process and in a variety of settings.

5. Victim–offender mediation programs are designed to allow the offender and the victim to meet with a third party and resolve the conflict and consequences caused by the offence and to understand each other.

6. There are key differences between the principles of the criminal court and those of circle sentencing.

7. Presiding judges are not bound by the recommendation of sentencing circles.

8. Restorative justice can be successfully used in cases involving serious offences and high-risk offenders.

9. Research studies suggest that restorative justice approaches can be successful alternatives to the traditional criminal justice system.

10. Among the challenges surrounding restorative justice are conquering resistance by criminal justice personnel, overcoming limited community interest or capacity to participate, changing the perception that restorative justice approaches are soft on offenders, reducing the lack of public awareness, ensuring that victims are not revictimized by participating in a restorative program, and ensuring that victims and offenders understand the objectives and process of restorative justice.

KEY TERM QUESTIONS

1. Discuss the key principles of **restorative justice**, and then compare and contrast this approach to the traditional criminal justice process.

2. What are the objectives and process of **victim–offender mediation**?

3. Compare and contrast the principles and process of **circle sentencing** with the traditional criminal court process.

4. Describe the process and objectives of **Circles of Support and Accountability (CoSAs)**.

MEDIA LINKS

"Restorative Resources—Restorative Justice in Schools." or go to the book's website at
www.nelson.com/crimjusticeprimer5e.com

"Restorative Justice in the Criminal Justice System": A police officer speaks about restorative justice
or go to the book's website at
www.nelson.com/crimjusticeprimer5e.com

"Restorative Justice Is the Law" or go to the book's website at
www.nelson.com/crimjusticeprimer5e.com

CHAPTER 14

GOING FORWARD:
CHALLENGES TO
AND OPPORTUNITIES
FOR CRIMINAL
JUSTICE REFORM

**LEARNING
OBJECTIVES**

After reading this chapter, you should be able to

- identify and discuss some of the challenges that confront the criminal justice system, including the obstacles to change

- identify and discuss some of the opportunities that exist to improve the criminal justice system

- provide examples of questions that should be asked by informed observers of the criminal justice system

In this, the final chapter, we take a step back and consider the challenges and opportunities for Canadian criminal justice. Addressing these areas will strengthen the foundations of criminal justice, increase the effectiveness of the responses to criminal offenders, and provide protection for crime victims and the community.

CHALLENGES FOR THE CRIMINAL JUSTICE SYSTEM

> In its present state, by every measure that matters, the criminal justice system is failing to deliver what can fairly be expected of it.
>
> —Klingele, Scott, and Dickey[1]

To alter the current state of the criminal justice system, it will require addressing a number of challenges, including the following:

DEVELOPING AND IMPLEMENTING EVIDENCE-BASED LEGISLATION, POLICIES, AND PROGRAMS

> It is apparent…that empirical evidence does not always inform criminal justice policy.
>
> —Vess, Day, Powell, and Graffam[2]

Historically, governments, legislators, and policymakers have not had access to a well-developed body of empirical knowledge that could inform their decisions. As a consequence, a disconnect often exists between criminal justice policy and practice and scholarly research. Too often, legislation and policy are directed by political considerations and penal populism. Bill C-10, for example, perhaps the most significant piece of criminal justice legislation in years, will have a significant impact on the criminal justice system yet was not informed by research or by the experience of other jurisdictions, such as the United States, that have found punitive penology to be both expensive and largely ineffective.

Recall that throughout the text, the term *evidence-based practice* was used in discussions of criminal justice policies and programs. An ongoing challenge in the criminal justice system is ensuring that policies and practice are informed by the findings of evaluation research. This evidence-based practice includes conducting cost–benefit analyses that examine whether the investment of resources produces effective outcomes and improves the efficiency of the justice system.[3]

Unfortunately, these practices are currently not in use. Most initiatives do not include an evaluation component and, in those relatively few instances in which programs are evaluated, the impact on operational practice may be minimal. As Pawson noted, "Evaluation research…has reached industrial proportions but remains feudal in its capacity to create change."[4] It has been argued that the criminal justice system can learn from the business sector that research is strongly related to innovative practices.[5]

The challenges to developing evidence-based practices in the criminal justice system are numerous and include the resistance of policymakers to new strategies, concerns among politicians that research findings may compromise political agendas, concerns about the costs of new initiatives, and a general fear of the unknown. Even policies and programs whose effectiveness is suspect may be preferable purely because

325

they are known. Changing the status quo may have a significant impact on agencies and their personnel as new priorities and performance measures are established and policies and programs become evidence driven.

The criminal justice system has been slow to adopt evidence-based strategies and to discard policies and programs that are not effective. The challenge, for Canadians, their governments, and their criminal justice agencies, is to undertake the fundamental structural changes that are required so that the next 50 years of criminal justice do not produce the same outcomes as the present and so that criminal justice policy and practice do not continue to reel from crisis to crisis.

Even with an increasing body of knowledge as to what works, the adoption of evidence-based practices faces numerous obstacles. A number of these are set out in Table 14.1.

There are additional challenges in promoting evidence-based practices in the criminal justice system, including the wide discretion exercised by criminal justice professionals and the diverse environments in which they carry out their tasks.[6,7] Attempts to implement evidence-based practices in the criminal justice system have been uneven but are more prevalent in policing and in federal corrections.

TABLE 14.1   CHALLENGES TO DEVELOPING EVIDENCE-BASED PRACTICES

Challenge	Why the Challenge Exists	How to Overcome the Barrier
Policymakers resistance to new strategies	Policymakers are responsive to public opinion and may be unwilling to try new things.	Engage in an awareness campaign informing policymakers of the utility of evidence-based strategies.
Concerns about cost	Because many evidence-based practices are new, start-up costs may generate resistance among the public and policymakers.	Cost–benefit analyses can demonstrate whether the start-up costs are less than the continued costs for ineffective practices.
Public desire for retribution	The public demands that offenders be punished; many evidence-based policies appear to be slaps on the wrist.	Even less severe sanctions are experienced as punitive by offenders. Those developing evidence-based practices should demonstrate the punitive nature of those practices to the public.
Complacency among line staff	Some workers implementing policies may be accustomed to old practices and resistant to change.	Leaders must demonstrate how and why new practices will make the line officers' job more practical, without adding unnecessary work.
Defining success	It is sometimes difficult to develop measures of success for evidence-based practices when individuals are focused on punishment as the definition of success.	Indicators of success should be broadly defined so that all advantages of evidence-based practices are recognized and evaluated thoroughly.
Lack of awareness about evidence-based practices	Criminal justice officials may not be aware of practices that are deemed most effective.	Through collaborative efforts, practitioners can share information about effective and promising strategies.
Cooperating with researchers	In some places a gap exists between researchers and practitioners.	Partnerships and relationships can be developed with research agencies and college or university researchers.
Fear of the unknown	Because evidence-based practices are new, leaders and practitioners may see untested practices as risky.	Pilot-test the program and demonstrate to leaders and practitioners that the principles of the new practice are based on evidence that suggest the new practice should be effective.

Source: Adapted from M. DeMichele and B. Payne. 2009. *Offender Supervision with Electronic Technology. Community Corrections Resource.* Washington, D.C.: U.S. Department of Justice. p. 62. http://www.appa-net.org/eweb/docs/APPA/pubs/OSET_2.pdf.

The development of evidence-based practice in Canadian criminal justice has also been hindered by the absence of research funding. Canada lags far behind the United States, the United Kingdom, and Australia in providing research funds for university-based scholars. In these jurisdictions, the federal government plays a significant role as a sponsor of research. Not so in Canada.

The consequences of this lack of funding are significant and include the fact that much of the research cited in this text is not Canadian. On more than one occasion in the preceding chapters, the author had to offer the caveat that the research findings on a specific topic might not apply to Canada as the projects were carried out in other countries, most notably the United States.

ENSURING ACCOUNTABILITY IN THE CRIMINAL JUSTICE SYSTEM

A recurring theme throughout the text has been the importance of accountability in the criminal justice system. Throughout the book, the discussion has highlighted the various accountability issues that exist at each stage of the criminal justice process and the presence (or not) of structures of oversight.

When criminal justice decision makers are accountable, it increases the legitimacy of their actions, raises public confidence, and can result in professional commitment to evidence-based policies and practice. Accountability also ensures that accused persons and offenders are accorded their rights and reduces the likelihood of arbitrary and abusive behaviour toward them.

When accused persons and offenders are abused or dealt with in an arbitrary fashion, or, in extreme cases, wrongfully convicted, it undermines the legitimacy of the entire criminal justice process and reduces the likelihood that intervention efforts will be successful. Recall the finding in Chapter 7 that the judges in problem-solving courts had a high degree of legitimacy in the view offenders who appeared before them and that this assisted in reducing the rates of reoffending. This result suggests that helping and human relationships can be equally, if not more, effective than "get tough" approaches to offenders.

A major challenge is that the majority of civil suits that are brought against the criminal justice system are settled out of court, with no fixing of responsibility or documentation that might provide insights into how such incidents might be avoided in the future.

THE ABSENCE OF CANADIAN RESEARCH

A key feature of the criminal justice system in Canada is the absence of evaluations of programs and strategies. There may be reluctance on the part of governments to support independent evaluations that may produce findings that call into question the effectiveness of criminal justice policy. Certainly, it can be argued that the federal Conservative government's adoption of a punitive penology and the associated legislation was not informed by independent empirical research studies and, in many instances (e.g., the effectiveness of mandatory minimum sentences), run counter to research findings. See At issue 14.1.

PROACTIVE PROBLEM-SOLVING VERSUS REACTIVE SANCTIONING

It is generally agreed that criminal justice agencies and professionals alone cannot prevent and reduce crime, address the needs of crime victims, and ensure effective interventions for offenders. As currently structured, the justice system has a very difficult

327

AT ISSUE 14.1   SHOULD THERE BE LEGISLATION THAT REQUIRES THE CRIMINAL JUSTICE SYSTEM TO ADOPT EVIDENCE-BASED PRACTICES AND TO DISCONTINUE POLICIES AND PRACTICES THAT HAVE BEEN SHOWN BY RESEARCH NOT TO BE EFFECTIVE?

A body of literature is emerging on what works and what does not work in criminal justice. Proponents of a legislative requirement argue that this is the only way in which to ensure that the justice system is effective and accountable. Those opposing this approach counter that criminal justice professionals are in the best position to determine what policies and programs are most appropriate for their particular jurisdiction and circumstance.

QUESTION
What is your view on this issue?

time providing safety and security for community residents and providing assistance to those persons who are at-risk of committing or recommitting criminal offences.

The levels of crime generally fluctuate independently of the efforts of the criminal justice system, and it is difficult to determine whether an increase in the rates of crime are due to ineffectiveness of the justice system or, conversely, whether a decrease in crime rates is due to effective criminal justice practice.

Of particular concern is the limited ability of the criminal justice system to solve problems rather than simply react to them. Generally, the criminal justice system defines problems according to the law rather than on the basis of how they are experienced by people. This tendency is reflected in the comments of a jury member following a trial in which the accused had been charged with unlawful possession of a firearm and discharging a firearm in a public place:

> At the end of the case, although we found him guilty, we felt we were no nearer to understanding why the man did what he did. He might have been mentally deranged, a drug dealer, an upset father, or high on drugs. We will never know because the case gave us less than 10% of the information that we needed to make a sensible judgment.[8]

Problem-solving courts and various restorative justice approaches offer the potential to address more than criminal behaviour, which may be only a symptom of much deeper issues.

REDUCING THE MARGINALITY OF OFFENDERS

Recall that a large number of persons who come into conflict with the law are marginalized with respect to their employment skills, education, and other capacities; may have addictions or mental illnesses; and may have few community supports.

Conflict with the law is often a symptom of much deeper social, economic, and community disorder. Of particular concern is the plight of marginalized women and the large number of missing and murdered women.

One question is whether the traditional adversarial systems of criminal justice functions to reduce this marginality? The answer is generally, no. While specific interventions may reduce *reoffending*, there is no conclusive evidence that the *marginality* of offenders (e.g., addiction, poverty, homelessness, mental illness), which may be closely related to their conflict with the law, are successfully addressed long term.

Criminal justice agencies rarely gather data that would allow a determination of the long-term impacts of interventions on persons who come into conflict with the law. There is concern that, for some persons, contact with the criminal justice system may exacerbate their marginality and the likelihood of reoffending.

Expecting that the criminal justice system alone can address these factors is unrealistic. The system can, however, be a partner, and there are numerous examples where collaborative initiatives involving justice professionals working with their counterparts in other agencies and organizations, along with the community, have had success.

ADDRESSING THE NEEDS OF VICTIMS

The criminal justice system has made some progress in recognizing and addressing the needs of crime victims, although the case of Judge Robert Dewar, discussed in Chapter 3, suggests that the "blaming the victim" mentality may be alive and well among some criminal justice professionals. General agreement exists that the marginalization and revictimization of crime victims must be addressed; key questions are how to do this and whether the federal government's Victims Bill of Rights, proposed in April 2014, including a provision that victims be allowed to participate in plea bargaining, may compromise the administration of justice.

MANAGING TECHNOLOGY

Systems of corrections are making increasing use of technology, not only for gathering and managing information but also for control and surveillance. The introduction of police drones in the absence of any use guidelines (other than those of the aviation authorities) indicates that legislation and policy have not kept pace with the rapid technological changes that are occurring, and this gap may have significant implications for the rights of offenders and citizens.

The challenge is to ensure that the criminal justice system does not come to over-rely on technology and assume that these types of strategies, in themselves, will ensure public safety. The danger is that the increasing use of technology will come at the expense of developing human and helping relationships that have been demonstrated to be a core component of successful criminal justice interventions.

ADHERING TO THE RULE OF LAW AND RESPECTING THE RIGHTS OF THE ACCUSED AND OFFENDERS

The first sentence in Chapter 1 of this text states that "A fundamental component of the criminal justice system is the rule of law." The key principles are that the government and its officials and agents, as well as individuals and private entities, are accountable under the law; laws are clear, publicized, stable, and just; laws are applied evenly and protect fundamental rights, including the security of persons and property; and the process by which the laws are enacted, administered, and enforced is accessible, fair, and efficient.

A continuing challenge for the criminal justice system is to ensure that enforcement of the law and the responses to law breaking adhere to the rule of law and that the rights of accused and convicted persons are protected. These goals are crucial to ensuring the legitimacy of the justice system and are fundamental requirements in a democratic society. The materials in this text have revealed that the criminal justice system has often come up short. A common thread in many inquiries is that criminal justice personnel, be they police, judges, or corrections personnel, did not abide by the rule of law.

CONSIDERING ETHICS IN CRIMINAL JUSTICE

Ethics remains an under-studied area of Canadian criminal justice. Ethics training for criminal justice professionals is sparse. Yet it is likely that these issues will assume even greater importance in the coming years.

Ethical questions abound at all stages of the criminal justice system. Some examples follow:

In policing

- What are the ethics of using deception to secure a confession from a criminal suspect?
- What role do the ethics of individual officers and of their police service play in biased policing?
- How are ethics related to the exercise of discretion by police officers?

In the courts

- How might ethics be undermined by the practice of plea bargaining?
- How do ethical considerations factor into determinations of punishment for convicted offenders?
- Can an adversarial justice system be an ethical system?

In corrections

- Should incarcerated persons be required to participate in treatment programs?
- Are correctional staff obligated to follow their own ethical code of conduct in making decisions about inmates, regardless of directives from management?
- Should inmate mothers be permitted to have their prison-born babies with them, regardless of whether this reduces the likelihood of their reoffending?

A challenge for the criminal justice system is to ensure that personnel receive ethics training not only at the outset of their careers but on an ongoing basis.

CRIMINAL JUSTICE IN A DIVERSE SOCIETY

Diversity is a defining characteristic of Canada. Cultural diversity poses challenges to the criminal law and to the criminal justice system. Such issues as polygamy and the proposed Québec Charter of Values highlight the very dynamic ways in which the diversity may be manifested. A key provision of the *Charter of Rights and Freedoms* is section 15(1), which states that "Every individual is equal before and under the law and has the right to the equal protection and benefit of the law without discrimination." Many of the examples presented throughout this text suggest that the criminal justice system struggles to meet the objectives of this provision.

Little attention has been given to how professionals in the criminal justice system manage when confronted by diversity. Few studies exist on the challenges experienced by Crown counsel, defence lawyers, and the judiciary in processing cases involving visible and cultural minority groups, nor do we know how effective probation officers and parole officers are in supervising persons who do not speak French or English as a first language. The potential for visible and minority communities to become involved as active partners in creating community-based programs and services to address the needs of victims and offenders has remained unexplored.

THE NEED TO REIMAGINE CRIMINAL JUSTICE

A constant refrain from criminal justice agencies and policymakers is that more resources are required to improve the effectiveness and efficiency of the criminal justice system. This exhortation is often framed in requests for more patrol officers, more prosecutors, more corrections personnel. There is no clear evidence, however, that merely adding more resources will improve outcomes for crime victims, offenders, and communities. Much more fundamental changes are required, referred to by scholars as "reimagining criminal justice."[9]

> The volume of offending in society exceeds the capacity of the institutions comprising the criminal justice system by so great an amount that even significant increases in system capacity would have only a marginal impact on the certainty and swiftness of punishment.[10]

These observers cite the massive under-reporting of crime and the amount of crime that goes undetected because of limited criminal justice resources.

OPPORTUNITIES FOR CRIMINAL JUSTICE REFORM

Where there are challenges, there are also opportunities, and this is no less so in the criminal justice system.

THE FISCAL CRISES OF GOVERNMENTS

While the cutbacks in funding for the criminal justice system are often lamented as undermining its efforts, ironically, they may provide the catalyst for reforms that have long been resisted by governments. There is an increasing movement in the United States, for example, to "put science before politics."[11]

Several scholars have noted that budget reductions have led to a new approach by policymakers to criminal justice reform called **smart on crime**, which

> emphasizes fairness and accuracy in the administration of criminal justice; alternatives to incarceration and traditional sanctions; effective preemptive mechanisms for preventing criminal behavior; the transition of formerly incarcerated individuals to law-abiding and productive lives; and evidence-based assessments of costliness, efficiency, and effectiveness of criminal justice policies.[12]

One component of this approach is addressing the issue of **over-criminalization**, which refers to "imposing penalties that have no relation to the gravity of the offence committed or the culpability of the wrong doer" and are therefore excessive and without justification.[13] Over-criminalization also involves the excessive use of the criminal law to address social problems.[14]

Initiatives, such as the problem-solving courts and various restorative justice approaches, have emerged out of an effort to reduce the over-criminalization of persons, including those from vulnerable groups.

Reduced resources can also force criminal justice agencies to develop the capacity to monitor how the resources they do have are being used and to assess the impact of their policies and strategies. This change has occurred in many police services where attention is being given to the deployment of patrol and investigative resources.

Smart on crime
An alternative approach to criminal justice reform.

Over-criminalization
The imposition of penalties, often to address social problems, "that have no relation to the gravity of the offence committed" and are therefore excessive and without justification.

EXPANDING EFFECTIVE CRIMINAL JUSTICE INTERVENTIONS AND LEARNING FROM FAILURE

The materials presented in this text reveal that some criminal justice interventions do produce positive outcomes. Specific police strategies have been shown to reduce crime and increase public safety; the work of specialized courts show promise; and correctional programs and interventions based on the principles of risks, need, and responsivity (RNR) can reduce reoffending. A key component of many successful initiatives is community engagement and the involvement of citizens in addressing crime and social disorder.

In addition to focusing on what works in criminal justice, one observer has called for the criminal justice to create a clearinghouse "to collect and disseminate detailed, reliable, factual accounts of helpful errors."[15] Criminal justice agencies and personnel would be encouraged to routinely report errors in practice to begin the process of compiling "lessons learned."[16,17]

While the research findings presented throughout the text suggest that many of the justice policy and programs are not effective, lack of receptivity continues to innovative practices that may prove to be more effective and efficient. Many of the difficulties that afflict the justice system, such as lengthy delays in resolving cases in the criminal courts, are endemic and long-standing yet remain unaddressed.

MOBILIZING THE COMMUNITY: MAINTAINING HUMAN AND HELPING RELATIONSHIPS

It was noted in Chapter 2 that a core component of the new punitive penology is penal populism, wherein politicians justify legislation and correctional policy on the basis of public pressure. This reliance continues despite the fact that the criminal justice system historically has done little to educate the public about the system and offenders. Too often, the public has been placed in the role of bystander in the criminal justice system.

In corrections, the success of Circles of Support and Accountability (CoSAs), which target high-risk offenders, illustrates the potential for criminal justice professionals, working with community residents, to be involved in reducing reoffending among high-risk offenders. There is a vast, untapped reservoir in the community that, if mobilized and supported, can play a significant role in the criminal justice system. Unfortunately, the federal government announced in early 2014 that there would be drastic cuts in federal funding for CoSA programs. There are suggestions that federal funding will be completely eliminated by September 2014, despite evaluations that have shown that CoSAs reduce sexual reoffending. This decision is reflective of the punitive penology discussed in Chapter 2. It also illustrates the challenges of implementing and sustaining evidence-based justice initiatives within the context of a larger government political agenda.

QUESTIONS TO BE ASKED ABOUT THE CRIMINAL JUSTICE SYSTEM

There is no shortage of media coverage of the criminal justice system, nor of pundits and politicians weighing in on the issue of the day. Unfortunately, most of the discussion on criminal justice policy and practice is not centred on core questions that need to be asked. Among those are the following:

- Are criminal justice policies and programs evidence-based and informed by best practices?
- What is the cost-effectiveness of criminal justice policies and practices?

- What are the costs of the "get tough" approach to criminals, including the fiscal costs of building more prison cells and the impact on the ability of offenders to successfully reintegrate back into the community?

- For any one stage of the criminal justice system, would a restorative justice approach be more appropriate or more effective?

- How do politics and ideology affect the response to criminal offenders?

- What would cause the federal government to cancel funding for a program (i.e., CoSAs) that has been shown by evaluation studies to be effective in reducing reoffending among high-risk offenders? Conversely, why would the federal government create provisions for a correctional strategy (i.e., electronic monitoring of offenders on parole) when the evaluation of a pilot project found that the correctional strategy was not effective?

- Are the current structures of accountability for personnel in the criminal justice system sufficient to ensure that discretion is being properly exercised and that personnel are held accountable for their actions?

- With respect to corrections, is the specific program or intervention being considered or used based on the principles of RNR? If not, why not?

- For female offenders in corrections, why has there not been an equivalent of the Ashley Smith case in a men's institution?

- For Aboriginal offenders, why haven't initiatives, such as the *Gladue* courts, Aboriginal corrections programs, healing lodges, and Aboriginal policing programs, reduced the levels of Aboriginal conflict with the law and the over-representation of Aboriginal offenders in the criminal justice system?

- It has long been established that offenders returning to the community from prison have a greater chance of success if provided with adequate housing, employment, and social supports. Why are these still absent for most offenders released from confinement?

- What are the implications for personal privacy when almost everyone has a cellphone camera?

- To what extent can religious and cultural practices of newcomers to Canada be accommodated by the law and the justice system?

Can you think of other questions that should be asked?

The discussion in this text has been designed to give you the information required to look critically at the criminal justice system, to ask informed questions, and to pique your curiosity about exploring further this most dynamic dimension of Canadian society. The success of this text will be measured by the extent to which it assisted you, the reader, in achieving some or all of these objectives.

SUMMARY

This chapter has identified and discussed several of the challenges and opportunities faced by the Canadian criminal justice system. A key requirement is that the justice system move toward the use of evidence-based practices, although a number of obstacles will be encountered. Throughout history, for example, systems of corrections have struggled to adhere to the rule of law and to abide by the duty to act fairly in the response to offenders. Another challenge will be maintaining the balance between the rights of the accused and the requirement to ensure the safety and security of crime victims and the community.

Despite the multicultural composition of Canadian society, little is known about the experiences of offenders from visible and cultural minority groups, their families, or

333

of the potential role their communities could play at the various stages of the criminal justice process.

The criminal justice system must discard ineffective strategies and expand effective interventions, explore the potential for integrating restorative justice approaches into the corrections process, and develop strategies to mobilize community residents as pro-active agents of change.

KEY POINTS REVIEW

1. The criminal justice system experiences numerous challenges in fulfilling its mandate to protect the community, meet the needs of crime victims, and respond effectively to criminal offenders.

2. The criminal justice system has been slow to adopt evidence-based strategies and to discard policies and programs that are not effective.

3. There are numerous obstacles to the adoption of evidence-based practices in the criminal justice system.

4. The criminal justice system experiences difficulties in problem solving and does not effectively address the marginality of persons who come into conflict with the law.

5. Ethical issues and dilemmas are endemic to the criminal justice system and require more attention from criminal justice professionals and academic researchers.

6. There are many opportunities for reforming the criminal justice system, including being smart on crime, expanding effective criminal justice interventions, learning from failures, expanding restorative justice approaches, and engaging the community.

7. There are many questions that an informed observer of the criminal justice system can ask about issues that appear to be systemic and that have, until today, resisted reforms.

KEY TERM QUESTION

1. What is meant by **smart on crime** and **over-criminalization**, and how are these notions elated to discussion of criminal justice reforms?

MEDIA LINK

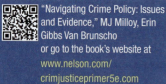

"Navigating Crime Policy: Issues and Evidence," MJ Milloy, Erin Gibbs Van Brunscho or go to the book's website at www.nelson.com/ crimjusticeprimer5e.com

Glossary

Adversarial system   A system of justice that is based on two opposing sides–the prosecution and the defence–arguing the guilt or innocence of a person before a judge or jury. (p. 28)

Arbour Report   The report of an inquiry into events at the Kingston Prison for Women in April 1994, which documented violations of policy, the rule of law, and institutional regulations and had a significant impact on the development of women's corrections. (p. 251)

Arrest warrant   A document that permits a police officer to arrest a specific person for a specified reason. (p. 95)

Auburn model (for prisons)   A system that allowed prisoners to work and eat together during the day and housed them in individual cells at night. (p. 242)

Basic qualifications (for police candidates) The minimum requirements for candidates applying for employment in policing. (p. 84)

Beyond a reasonable doubt   The standard that must be met to convict a defendant in a criminal case, which requires that the facts presented provide the only logical explanation for the crime. (p. 28)

Bias-free policing   The requirement that police officers make decisions "based on reasonable suspicion or probable grounds rather than stereotypes about race, religion, ethnicity, gender or other prohibited grounds." (p. 113)

Brown Commission   An investigation into the operation of the Kingston Penitentiary that condemned the use of corporal punishment

against inmates and emphasized the need for rehabilitation. (p. 243)

Canadian Charter of Rights and Freedoms   The primary law of the land and guarantees fundamental freedoms, legal rights, and quality rights for all citizens of Canada, including those accused of crimes. (p. 6)

Case law   Law that is established by previous court decisions and based on the rule of precedent. (p. 9)

Case management   The process by which the needs and abilities of offenders are matched with correctional programs and services. (p. 262)

Circle sentencing   A restorative justice strategy that involves collaboration and consensual decision making by community residents, the victim, the offender, and justice system personnel to resolve conflicts and sanction offenders. (p. 311)

Circles of Support and Accountability (CoSAs)   Community-based committees composed of criminal justice personnel and community members that provide mentoring for high-risk sex offenders whose sentences have expired. (p. 319)

Classification   The process by which inmates are categorized through the use of various assessment instruments to determine the appropriate security level of the inmate and program placement. (p. 261)

Clearance rates   The proportion of the actual incidents known to the police that result in the identification of a suspect, whether or not that

suspect is ultimately charged and convicted. (p. 137)

Cold turkey release   Discharge of an offender at the end of the sentence when no conditional release or supervision is possible, such as when federal or provincial or territorial offenders serve their entire sentence in custody or provincial or territorial offenders are released at the two-thirds point of their sentence. (p. 270)

Collateral consequences (of sentencing)   The sanctions and prohibitions that are placed on persons convicted of criminal offences (and their families), particularly those offenders who have been incarcerated. (p. 215)

Common law   Law that is based on custom, tradition, and practice and is generally unwritten. (p. 9)

Community assessment   An evaluation of the feasibility of the release plan, the level of supervision required, and the availability of community resources. (p. 271)

Community notification   The practice, usually carried out by police agencies, of making a public announcement that a high-risk offender has taken up residence in an area. (p. 291)

Community policing   A philosophy of policing centred on police-community partnerships and problem solving. (p. 122)

Community-based strategic policing   A model of police work that incorporates the key principles of community policing with crime prevention, crime response, and crime attack approaches. (p. 123)

Compstat   A strategy designed to increase the effectiveness and efficiency of police services while holding police personnel accountable for achieving crime reduction objectives. (p. 123)

Concurrent sentences   Sentences that are amalgamated and served simultaneously. (p. 210)

Conditional release   A generic term for the various means of leaving a correctional institution before warrant expiry whereby an offender is subject to conditions that, if breached, could trigger revocation of the release and return to prison; parole is one type of conditional release. (p. 270)

Conditional sentence   A sentence for offenders receiving a sentence or sentences totalling less than two years whereby the time is served in the community (generally under house arrest) under the supervision of a probation officer. (p. 230)

Conditional sentence of imprisonment   Offenders who receive a sentence or sentences totalling less than two years serve their time in the community under the supervision of a probation officer. (p. 209)

Conflict model   The view that crime and punishment reflect the power some groups have to influence the formulation and application of criminal law. (p. 10)

Consecutive sentences   Sentences that run separately and are completed one after the other. (p. 210)

Constitution Act, 1867   The legislation setting out the division of responsibilities between the federal and provincial or territorial governments. (p. 24)

Continuum of correctional institutions   The differences in institutional environments among correctional institutions located at either end of the security spectrum-maximum to minimum. (p. 246)

Contract policing   An arrangement whereby the RCMP and provincial or territorial police forces provide provincial and municipal policing services. (p. 70)

Correctional plan   A key component of the case management process that determines the offender's initial institution placement, specific training or work opportunities, and preparation for release. (p. 262)

Corrections   Structures, policies, and programs to sanction, punish, treat, and supervise, in the community and in correctional institutions, persons convicted of criminal offences. (p. 227)

Courtroom workgroup   The criminal justice professionals, including the judge, Crown counsel, and defence lawyer, who are present in the criminal courtroom. (p. 158)

Crime   An act or omission that is prohibited by criminal law. (p. 9)

Crime attack strategies   Proactive operations by the police to target and apprehend criminal offenders. (p. 132)

Crime control (model of criminal justice)   An orientation to criminal justice in which the protection of the community and the apprehension of offenders are paramount. (p. 21)

Crime displacement   The relocation-because of effective crime prevention and crime response initiatives-of criminal activity from one locale to another. (p. 137)

Crime rate   The number of incidents known to the police expressed in terms of the number of people in the population. (p. 45)

Criminal Code   Federal legislation that sets out criminal laws, procedures for prosecuting federal offences, and sentences and procedures for the administration of justice. (p. 24)

Criminal injury compensation   Financial remuneration paid to crime victims. (p. 52)

Criminal justice   The study of social control and the agencies that are involved in the apprehension, prosecution, defence, sentencing, incarceration, and supervision of those suspected or charged with or convicted of criminal offences. (p. 20)

Criminal justice system   All the agencies, organizations, and personnel that are involved in the prevention of, and response to, crime and to persons charged with criminal offences and persons convicted of crimes. (p. 21)

Criminal law   That body of law that deals with conduct considered so harmful to society as a whole that it is prohibited by statute and prosecuted and punished by the government. (p. 6)

Criminology   The scientific study of crime and criminal behaviour. (p. 20)

Dangerous offender   A designation made by the judge after conviction that results in an indeterminate term of imprisonment in a federal correctional institution. (p. 212)

Dark figure of crime   The difference between how much crime occurs and how much crime is reported to or discovered by the police. (p. 45)

Day parole   The authority granted by a parole board that provides an opportunity for inmates to be at large to prepare for full release (e.g., for job search) while returning at night to an institution or, more typically, to a community residential facility. (p. 272)

Detention during the period of statutory release   A decision by the PBC (after an application by the CSC) that a federal inmate be denied statutory release and be detained in the institution until warrant expiry date. (p. 272)

Discretion   The freedom to choose among different options when confronted with the need to make a decision. (p. 29, 110)

Discrimination   "Making a distinction in favour of or against a person or thing based on the group, class or category to which that person or thing belongs rather than on individual merit." (p. 113)

Diversion   Programs that are designed to keep offenders from being processed further into the formal criminal justice system. (p. 229)

Due process model (of criminal justice)   An orientation to criminal justice in which the legal rights of individual citizens, including crime suspects, are paramount. (p. 21)

Duty to act fairly   The obligation of corrections to ensure that that offenders are treated fairly by corrections personnel. (p. 32)

Dynamic risk factors   Attributes of the offender that can be altered through intervention, including level of education, employment skills, addiction issues, and cognitive thinking abilities, among others. (p. 261)

Dynamic security   A variety of ongoing, meaningful interactions between staff and inmates. (p. 245)

Electronic monitoring   A correctional strategy that involves placing an offender under house arrest and then using electronic equipment to ensure that the conditions of supervision are fulfilled. (p. 237)

Ethical dilemmas   Situations in which criminal justice personnel must decide what do to. (p. 30)

Ethical issues "Broad social questions, often concerning the government's social control mechanisms and the impact on those governed, for example, what laws to pass, what sentences to attach to certain crimes." (p. 29)

Ethics "The foundation of knowledge that describes right/wrong or better/worse … and applies to harm/care and fairness/reciprocity." (p. 29)

Evidence-based practice Policies, strategies, and programs that have been shown by evaluation research to be effective in achieving specified objectives. (p. 34)

Full parole The authority granted by a parole board for an inmate to be at large under supervision in the community for the remainder of his or her sentence. (p. 272)

Hybrid (elective) offences Offences that can be proceeded summarily or by indictment, a decision that is always made by the Crown. (p. 9, 165)

Indictable offences Generally more serious criminal offences that may carry maximum prison sentences of 14 years to life; examples include murder, robbery, and aggravated sexual assault. (p. 9)

Information A written statement sworn by an informant alleging that a person has committed a specific criminal offence. (p. 95)

Inmate code A set of behavioural rules that govern interactions among inmates and with institutional staff. (p. 259)

Inmate subculture The patterns of interaction and the relationships that exist among inmates confined in correctional institutions. (p. 258)

Institutionalized Inmates who have become prisonized to such a degree that they are unable to function in the outside free community. (p. 258)

Intelligence-led policing Policing that is guided by the collection and analysis of information that is used to inform police decision making at both the tactical and the strategic level. (p. 124)

Intensive supervision probation (ISP) An intermediate sanction (between the minimal supervision of traditional probation and incarceration) that generally includes reduced caseloads for probation officers, increased surveillance, treatment interventions, and

efforts to ensure that probationers are employed. (p. 235)

Intermediate sanctions A term used to describe a wide range of correctional programs that generally fall between probation and incarceration, although specific initiatives may include either of these penalties as well. (p. 230)

Intermittent sentence A sentence that is served on a part-time basis, generally on weekends. (p. 210)

Judicial determination An order by the sentencing judge that the offender serve one-half of the sentence before being eligible to apply for parole. (p. 211)

Judicial independence The notion that "judges are not subject to pressure and influence, and are free to make impartial decisions based solely on fact and law." (p. 168)

Judicial interim release (or bail) The release by a judge or JP of a person who has been charged with a criminal offence pending a court appearance. (p. 177)

Long-term offender A designation under section 752 or 753 of the *Criminal Code* that requires the offender to spend up to 10 years under supervision following the expiry of his or her sentence. (p. 213)

Maximum-security institutions Federal correctional institutions with a highly controlled institutional environment and high-security fencing. Inmates' movements are strictly controlled and monitored. (p. 244)

Medium-security institutions Federal correctional facilities that have a less highly controlled institutional environment than maximum-security institutions and in which inmates have more freedom of movement. (p. 244)

Minimum-security institutions Federal correctional facilities that generally have no perimeter fencing and allow unrestricted inmate movement, except at night. (p. 244)

Moral architecture The term used to describe the design of the first penitentiary in Canada, the intent of which was to reflect themes of order and morality. (p. 242)

Moral entrepreneurs Individuals, groups, or organizations that seek action against certain groups of people or certain behaviours and bring pressure on legislators to enact criminal statutes. (p. 15)

Need principle To be effective, correctional interventions must address the criminogenic needs of offenders. (p. 234)

Net-widening A potential, unanticipated consequence of diversion programs in which persons who would otherwise have been released outright by the police or not charged by Crown counsel are involved in the justice system. (p. 230)

NIMBY (not in my backyard) The resistance that communities display in response to correctional systems' efforts to locate programs and residences for offenders in a specific area. (p. 55)

Non-carceral corrections That portion of systems of correction relating to offenders in non-institutional settings. (p. 227)

Not criminally responsible on account of mental disorder (NCRMD) A defence that the accused person is not responsible for an act because of his or her mental state at the time. (p. 189)

One plus one (use of force) The generally accepted use-of-force standard that police officers have the authority to use one higher level of force than that with which they are confronted. (p. 104)

One-chance statutory release A release option whereby offenders who violate the conditions of a statutory release are required to serve the remainder of their sentence in confinement. (p. 271)

Operational field training Instructing the recruit in how to apply principles from the training academy in the community. (p. 86)

Over-criminalization The imposition of penalties, often to address social problems, "that have no relation to the gravity of the offence committed" and are therefore excessive and without justification. (p. 331)

Pains of imprisonment The deprivations experienced by inmates confined in correctional institutions, including the loss of autonomy, privacy, security, and freedom of movement and association. (p. 257)

Pains of probation The emotional and economic challenges that probationers may experience while under probation supervision in the community. (p. 235)

Pains of reentry The difficulties that inmates released from prison encounter as they try to adjust to life in the community. (p. 284)

337

Penal populism Corrections policies that are formulated in pursuit of political objectives, often in the absence of an informed public or in spite of public opinion. (p. 37)

Pennsylvania model (for prisons) A separate and silent system in which prisoners were completely isolated from one another; eating, working and sleeping in separate cells. (p. 242)

Plea bargaining An agreement whereby an accused pleads guilty in exchange for the promise of a benefit. (p. 183)

Pluralization of policing The sharing of responsibility for safety and security in the community between public and private police. (p. 73)

Police acts The legislative framework for police service. (p. 74)

Police boards and police commissions Bodies that provide oversight of police. (p. 74)

Policing "The activities of any individual or organization acting legally on behalf of public or private organizations or persons to maintain security or social order." (p. 73)

Policing standards Provisions that set out how police services are to maintained and delivered. (p. 74)

Political policing The use of the police by governments as an instrument of surveillance and control. (p. 81)

Post-incarceration syndrome (PICS) A condition of offenders in custody and in the community that is caused by prolonged exposure to the dynamics of life inside correctional institutions. (p. 286)

Post-traumatic stress disorder (PTSD) An extreme form of critical-incident stress that includes nightmares, hypervigilance, intrusive thoughts, and other forms of psychological distress. (p. 88)

Precedent A judicial decision that may be used as a standard in subsequent similar cases. (p. 8)

Preferred qualifications (for police candidates) Requirements that increase the competitiveness of applicants seeking employment in policing. (p. 84)

Preliminary hearing A hearing to determine if there is sufficient evidence to warrant a criminal trial. (p. 165)

Primary crime prevention programs Programs that identify opportunities for criminal offences and alter those conditions to reduce the likelihood that a crime will be committed. (p. 127)

Principle of accountability "The actions of police officers and police services are subject to review [and] there are formal channels that individuals can use to lodge complaints against the police." (p. 115)

Prisonization The process by which inmates become socialized into the norms, values, and culture of the prison. (p. 258)

Probation A sentence imposed on an offender by a criminal court judge that provides for the supervision of the offender in the community by a probation officer, either as an alternative to custody or in conjunction with a period of incarceration. (p. 231)

Problem-oriented policing (POP) A tactical strategy based on the idea that the police should address the causes of recurrent crime and disorder. (p. 132)

Problem-solving courts Specialized courts that are designed to divert offenders with special needs from the criminal justice system. (p. 149)

Professional model of policing A model of police work that is reactive, incident driven, and centred on random patrol. (p. 122)

Quality-of-life policing Police efforts to improve conditions in an area by targeting disruptive and annoying behaviour. (p. 132)

Racial profiling "The targeting of individual members of a particular racial group, on the basis of the supposed criminal propensity of the entire group" (*R. v. Brown*, [2003] OJ No. 1251). (p. 113)

Recidivism rates The number of offenders released from confinement who are subsequently returned to prison. (p. 263)

Recipes for action The actions typically taken by patrol officers in various kinds of encounter situations. (p. 110)

Reentry court A problem-solving court that assists offenders in managing the challenge of reentry. (p. 289)

Reintegration The process whereby an inmate is prepared for and released into the community after serving time in prison. (p. 282)

Release plan A plan setting out the residential, educational, and treatment arrangements made for an inmate who is applying for conditional release. (p. 271)

Remand The status of accused persons in custody awaiting trial or sentencing. (p. 179)

Remission or discharge Available to provincial or territorial inmates who have served two-thirds of their sentence (often referred to as cold turkey release as there is no supervision by a parole officer). (p. 283)

Responsivity principle Correctional interventions should be matched to the learning styles of individual offenders. (p. 234)

Restitution A court-ordered payment that the offender makes to the victim to compensate for loss of or damage to property. (p. 52)

Restorative justice A problem-solving approach to responding to offenders based on the principle that criminal behaviour injures victims, communities, and offenders, and that all these parties should be involved in efforts to address the causes of the behaviour and its consequences. (p. 306)

Revictimization The negative impact on victims of crime caused by the decisions and actions of criminal justice personnel. (p. 50)

Revocation of conditional release A decision by a releasing authority, such as a parole board, made in connection with an offender whose release has been suspended. (p. 294)

Risk principle Correctional interventions are most effective when matched with the offender's level of risk and higher-risk offenders benefit from interventions more than medium- and low-risk offenders. (p. 234)

Royal Canadian Mounted Police Act Federal legislation that provides the framework for the operation of the RCMP. (p. 70)

Rule of law The requirement that governments, as well as individuals, be subjected to and abide by the law. (p. 5)

Search warrant A document that permits the police to search a specific location and take items that might be evidence of a crime. (p. 98)

Secondary crime prevention programs Programs that focus on areas that produce crime and disorder. (p. 128)

338

Security certificates A process whereby non-Canadian citizens who are deemed to be a threat to the security of the country can be held without charge for an indefinite time. (p. 179)

Self-injurious behaviour (SIB) Deliberate self-inflicted bodily harm or disfigurement. (p. 250)

Smart on crime An alternative approach to criminal justice reform. (p. 331)

Social (or argot) roles Roles that inmates assume based on their friendship networks, sentence length, and other factors related to their criminal history and activities in the institution. (p. 259)

Social media Forms of electronic communication that allow users to post and share ideas, information, videos, and photographs. (p. 56)

Stare decisis The principle by which the higher courts set precedents that the lower courts must follow. (p. 9)

State-raised offenders Inmates who have spent the majority of their adult (and perhaps young adult) lives confined in correctional institutions and, as a consequence, may have neither the skills nor ability to function in the outside free community; for these offenders, prison is home. (p. 258)

Static risk factors Attributes of the offender that predict the likelihood of recidivism but are not amenable to change, including criminal history, prior convictions, the seriousness of prior offences, and performance on previous conditional releases. (p. 261)

Static security Fixed security apparatus in a correctional institutions, including fixed security posts wherein correctional officers are assigned to and remain in a specific area, such as a control room. (p. 245)

Status degradation ceremonies The processing of offenders into correctional institutions whereby the offender is psychologically and materially stripped of possessions that identify him or her as a member of the free society. (p. 257)

Statute law Written laws that have been enacted by a legislative body, such as the Parliament of Canada. (p. 9)

Statutory release A type of conditional release (made by the CSC and not the PBC) that allows incarcerated federal offenders to be released at the two-thirds point in their sentence and to serve the remaining one-third of their sentence under supervision in the community. (p. 272)

Stay of proceedings An act by the Crown to terminate or suspend court proceedings after they have commenced. (p. 186)

Suicide by cop Instances in which despondent individuals act in a manner calculated to force police to use lethal force. (p. 107)

Summary conviction offences Generally less serious offences that are triable before a magistrate or judge and, on conviction, carry a maximum penalty of a fine (not to exceed $5000) or six months in a provincial correctional facility or both. (p. 9)

Suspended sentence A sentencing option whereby the judge convicts the accused but places the offender on probation; successful completion results in no sentence being given. (p. 209)

Suspension of conditional release A process initiated by the supervising parole officer (or in some instances by the parole board) in cases where the parolee has allegedly failed to abide by the conditions of release. (p. 294)

Task environment The cultural, geographic, and community setting in which the criminal justice system operates and justice personnel make decisions. (p. 23)

Temporary absence A type of conditional release that allows an inmate to participate in community activities, including employment and education, while residing in a minimum-security facility or halfway house. (p. 272)

Tertiary crime prevention Programs that focus on intervening in the lives of known offenders to reduce the likelihood of reoffending. (p. 134)

The *Gladue* decision A decision by the SCC that held that when a term of incarceration would normally be imposed, judges must consider the unique circumstances of Aboriginal people. (p. 215)

Therapeutic justice The use of the law and the authority of the court as change agents in promoting the health and well-being of offenders while ensuring that their legal rights are protected and that justice is done. (p. 150)

Throughcare The notion that there should be continuity between institutional treatment and programs and community-based services for offenders. (p. 264)

Total institutions Correctional institutions, psychiatric hospitals, and other facilities characterized by a highly structured environment in which all movements of the inmates or patients are controlled 24 hours a day by staff. (p. 245)

Typifications Constructs based on a patrol officer's experience that denote what is typical about people and events routinely encountered. (p. 110)

Value consensus model The view that the behaviours are defined as criminal and the punishment imposed on offenders reflects commonly held opinions and limits of tolerance. (p. 10)

Victim impact statement (VIS) A submission to a sentencing court explaining the emotional, physical, and financial impact of the crime. (p. 220)

Victim-offender mediation (VOM) A restorative justice approach that provides an opportunity for a crime victim and the offender to communicate and address the impact of the offence, and for the offender to take responsibility for the offence and its consequences. (p. 309)

Warrant expiry date The end of an offender's sentence. (p. 270)

Working personality of the police A set of attitudinal and behavioural attributes that develops as a consequence of the unique role and activities of police officers. (p. 87)

Zero tolerance policing A police strategy that focuses on disorder and minor infractions; most often associated with the broken windows approach to policing a community. (p. 131)

Notes

CHAPTER 1

1. J.R. Stoner. 2009. "The Timeliness and Timelessness of Magna Carta." *First Principles*. Accessed February 15, 2014. http://www.firstprinciplesjournal.com/articles.aspx?article=1307&loc=qs.

2. L. Duhaime. 2014. "Legal Dictionary." Accessed February 15. http://www.duhaime.org/LegalDictionary/C-Page5.aspx.

3. C.T. Chesnay, C. Bellot, and M.-E. Sylvestre. 2013. "Taming Disorderly People One Ticket at a Time: The Penalization of Homelessness in Ontario and British Columbia." *Canadian Journal of Criminology and Criminal Justice* 55, no. 2: 161–85.

4. Department of Justice Canada. 2008. "Canada's System of Justice." Accessed February 15, 2014. http://www.justice.gc.ca/eng/dept-min/pub/just/03.html.

5. N. Boyd. 2007. *Canadian Law: An Introduction*. 4th ed. Toronto: Nelson Education, 49.

6. K. MacQueen. 2013. "Why It's Time to Legalize Marijuana." *MacLean's*, June 10, 3. Accessed February 16, 2014. http://www2.macleans.ca/2013/06/10/why-its-time-to-legalize-marijuana/.

7. Canadian Centre on Substance Abuse. 2013. *Clearing the Smoke on Cannabis Series: Highlights*. Ottawa: Author. http://www.ccsa.ca/2013%20CCSA%20Documents/CCSA-Clearing-Smoke-on-Cannabis-Highlights-2013-en.pdf.

8. "Canada Tokes at 4 Times World Average: UN." 2007. *CBC News,* July 9. Accessed February 16, 2014. http://www.cbc.ca/news/health/story/2007/07/09/canada-cannabis.html.

9. Sensible BC. 2014. "Welcome to the Sensible BC Campaign for a Marijuana Referendum!" Accessed February 16. http://www.sensiblebc.ca.

10. "Justin Trudeau: Marijuana Decriminalization The Way To Go." 2012. *Huffington Post,* November 14. Accessed February 16, 2014. http://www.huffingtonpost.ca/2012/11/14/justin-trudeau-marijuana-decriminalization_n_2129476.html.

11. J. Van Rassel. 2013. "Police Oppose Call to Legalize Drugs in Canada." *Calgary Herald*, May 24. Accessed February 16, 2014. http://www2.canada.com/calgaryherald/news/city/story.html?id=a10f94dc-ec82-413a-9814-6288f07ed5e5.

12. "Canadian Police Chiefs Propose Ticket System for Pot." 2013. *CBC News,* August 21. Accessed February 16, 2014. http://www.cbc.ca/news/canada/manitoba/canadian-police-chiefs-propose-ticket-system-for-pot-1.1335493.

13. E. Fowler. 2012. "A Queer Critique on the Polygamy Debate in Canada: Law, Culture, and Diversity." *Dalhousie Journal of Legal Studies* 21: 93–125.

14. N. Bala. 2009. "Why Canada's Prohibition of Polygamy is Constitutionally Valid and Sound Social Policy." *Canadian Journal of Family Law* 25, no. 2: 165–221.

15. P. Loriggio. 2012. "Ontario Court Declares HIV-Positive Killer a Dangerous Offender." *The Globe and Mail*, September 6. Accessed February 16, 2014. http://www.theglobeandmail.com/news/national/ontario-court-declares-hiv-positive-killer-a-dangerous-offender/article593402/.

16. Zvulony & Co. 2010. "Assault and Battery on the Hockey Rink." Accessed February 16, 2014. http://zvulony.ca/2010/articles/criminal-law/assault-battery-lawyer/.

17. "Teen Rugby Player Found Guilty of Manslaughter in the Death of Opponent." 2009. *CBC News,* May 28. Accessed February 16, 2014. http://www.cbc.ca/news/canada/toronto/story/2009/05/28/castillo-guilty.html.

18. Ibid.

19. Zvulony & Co. 2010. "Assault and Battery on the Hockey Rink," 12. Accessed February 16, 2014. http://zvulony.ca/2010/articles/criminal-law/assault-battery-lawyer/.

20. M.P. Robert. 2011. "Les Crimes d'Honneur ou le Deshonneur du Crime: Etude des Cas Canadiens." *Canadian Criminal Law Review* 16, no. 1: 49–87.

21. Ibid.

CHAPTER 2

1. D.E. Duffee, and E.R. Maguire. 2007. *Criminal Justice Theory: Explaining the Nature and Behavior of Criminal Justice.* New York: Routledge, 6.

2. J.B. Snipes and E.R. Maguire. 2007. "Foundations of Criminal Justice Theory." In *Criminal Justice Theory: Explaining the Nature and Behavior of Criminal Justice,* edited by D.E. Duffee and E.R. Maguire, 27–49. New York: Routledge.

3. J.B. Snipes and E.R. Maguire. 2007. "Foundations of Criminal Justice Theory." In *Criminal Justice Theory: Explaining the Nature and Behavior of Criminal Justice,* edited by D.E. Duffee and E.R. Maguire, 29. New York: Routledge.

4. H. Packer. 1964. "Two Models of the Criminal Process." *University of Pennsylvania Law Review* 113: 1–68.

5. T.J. Bernard and R.S. Engel. 2001. "Conceptualizing Criminal Justice Theory." *Justice Quarterly* 18, no. 1: 1–30.

6. T.J. Bernard and R.S. Engel. 2001. "Conceptualizing Criminal Justice Theory." *Justice Quarterly* 18, no. 1: 5, 18.

7. C.T. Griffiths. 2013. *Canadian Police Work.* 3rd ed. Toronto: Nelson.

8. *Anti-terrorism Act.* 2001. Last modified January 30, 2014. http://laws.justice .gc.ca/en/A-11.7.

9. *Sex Offender Information Registration Act.* 2004. Accessed on February 16, 2014. http://www.canlii.org/en/ca/laws/stat/ sc-2004-c-10/latest/sc-2004-c-10.html.

10. "Beyond a Reasonable Doubt." 2014. *Free Dictionary.* Accessed February 16, 2014. http://legal-dictionary.thefreedictionary .com/Beyond+a+Reasonable+Doubt.

11. C.T. Griffiths and D. Murdoch. 2014. *Canadian Corrections.* 4th ed. Toronto: Nelson.

12. "What Is Ethics?" 2014. *Ethics Defined,* February 16. Accessed March 6, 2014. http://www.ethicsdefined.org/ what-is-ethics/.

13. Ibid.

14. C. Banks. 2013. *Criminal Justice Ethics: Theory and Practice.* 3rd ed. Los Angeles: Sage, 3.

15. J.M. Pollock. 2012. *Ethical Dilemmas and Decisions in Criminal Justice.* 8th ed. Belmont, CA: Wadsworth, 14–15.

16. J.M. Pollock. 2012. *Ethical Dilemmas and Decisions in Criminal Justice.* 8th ed. Belmont, CA: Wadsworth, 5.

17. M.C. Braswell, B.R. McCarthy, and B.J. McCarthy. 2012. *Justice, Crime, and Ethics.* Burlington, MA: Elsevier.

18. C. Harfield. 2012. "Police Informers and Professional Ethics." *Criminal Justice Ethics* 31, no. 2: 73–95.

19. C. Banks. 2013. *Criminal Justice Ethics: Theory and Practice.* 3rd ed. Los Angeles: Sage, 3.

20. I. Mulgrew. 2011. "Clifford Olson—Canada's National Monster—Dead at 71." *Vancouver Sun,* October 3. Accessed February 16, 2014. http://www.vancouversun.com/news/ Clifford+Olson+Canada+national +monster+dead/5484826/story.html.

21. M. McIntyre. 2013. "Cops Pay Serial Killer Lamb $1,500 for Information on Killings." *Winnipeg Free Press,* November 15. Accessed February 16, 2014. http://www .winnipegfreepress.com/local/Police-admit -paying-serial-killer-Lamb-for-information -on-killings-232090561.html.

22. M.A. Jackson and C.T. Griffiths. 1995. *Canadian Criminology.* Toronto: Harcourt, Brace, Jovanovich.

23. R. Paternoster. 2010. "How Much Do We Really Know About Criminal Deterrence?" *Journal of Criminal Law & Criminology* 100, no. 3: 765.

24. Native Women's Association of Canada. 2007. *Aboriginal Women and Gangs: An Issue Paper.* Cornerbrook, NL: Author. http://www.laa.gov.nl.ca/laa/naws/pdf/ nwac-gangs.pdf.

25. A. Webster. 2007. *Sheltering Urban Aboriginal Homeless People: Assessment of Situation and Needs.* Ottawa: Human Resources and Social Development Canada. http://pathprogram.samhsa.gov/ ResourceFiles/NAFC-Homeless-Final-12 -02-08%5B1%5D.pdf.

26. M.B. Castellano, L. Archibald, and M. DeGagne. 2008. *From Truth to Reconciliation: Transforming the Legacy of Residential Schools.* Ottawa: Aboriginal Healing Foundation. http://www.ahf.ca/ downloads/from-truth-to-reconciliation -transforming-the-legacy-of-residential -schools.pdf.

27. F. Iacobucci. 2013. *First Nations Representation on Ontario Juries.* Toronto: Attorney General of Ontario. http://www .attorneygeneral.jus.gov.on.ca/english/ about/pubs/iacobucci/pdf/First_Nations _Representation_Ontario_Juries.pdf.

28. M. Rempel, K. Burke, and T. Kunkel. 2009. *Seven Program Design Features: Adult Drug Court Principles, Research, and Practice.* Washington, D.C.: American University. http://www1.spa.american.edu/ justice/documents/4111.pdf.

29. D. Quan. 2012. "Inmate Complaints Not Addressed Speedily, Judge Ruled." *Ottawa Citizen,* August 8. Accessed February 16, 2014. http://o.canada.com/news/inmate -complaints-not-addressed-speedily-judge -ruled/.

30. "Canada's Police among the Best Paid in the World." 2012. *The Globe and Mail,* March 21. Accessed February 16, 2014. http://www.theglobeandmail.com/ commentary/editorials/canadas-police -among-the-best-paid-in-the-world/ article535381/.

31. Public Safety Canada Portfolio Corrections Statistics Committee. 2012, 21. *2012 Annual Report: Corrections and Conditional Release Statistical Overview.* Ottawa: Ottawa: Public Works and Government Services Canada. http://www.publicsafety .gc.ca/cnt/rsrcs/pblctns/2012-ccrs/ index-eng.aspx.

32. M. Olotu, D. Luong, C. MacDonald, M. McKay, S. Heath, N. Allegri, and E. Loree. 2011, 106. *Chapter 1: Correctional Interventions. Report of the Evaluation of CSC's Community Corrections.* Ottawa: Correctional Service Canada. http://www .csc-scc.gc.ca/text/pa/ev-cci-fin/ev-cci -fin-eng.pdf.

33. A. Rajekar and R. Mathilakath. 2010. *The Funding Requirement and Impact of the "Truth in Sentencing Act" on the Correctional System in Canada.* Ottawa: Government of Canada. http://www.parl .gc.ca/PBO-DPB/documents/TISA_C-25 .pdf.

34. Ibid.

341

35. Public Safety Canada Portfolio Corrections Statistics Committee. 2012. *2012 Annual Report: Corrections and Conditional Release Statistical Overview*. Ottawa: Ottawa: Public Works and Government Services Canada. http://www.publicsafety .gc.ca/cnt/rsrcs/pblctns/2012-ccrs/ index-eng.aspx.

36. J.V. Roberts, L.J. Stalans, D. Indermaur, and M. Hough. 2003. *Penal Populism and Public Opinion: Lessons from Five Countries*. New York: Oxford University Press.

37. C.T. Griffiths and D. Murdoch. 2014. *Canadian Corrections*. 4th ed. Toronto: Nelson.

38. J. Forman. 2011. "The Black Poor, the Black Elites, and America's Prisons." *Cardozo Law Review* 32, no. 3: 793.

39. M. Lagos and R. Gabrielson. 2012. "Drug Rehab Called Key to Avoid Third Strike." *San Francisco Chronicle*, September 29. Accessed February 16, 2014. http://www .sfgate.com/crime/article/Drug-rehab-called -a-key-to-avoid-3rd-strike-3906024.php.

40. E. Slater. 2005. "Pizza Thief Gets 25 Years to Life: Crime: Judge Cites Five Prior Felony Convictions in Sentencing Jerry Dewayne Williams Under 'Three Strikes' Law. Defense Attorney Says He Will Appeal 'Excessive Punishment.'" *Los Angeles Times*, March 3. Accessed February 16, 2014. http://articles .latimes.com/1995-03-03/local/ me-38258_1_jerry-dewayne-williams.

41. "US Plans Lower Sentences for Drug Users." 2013. *Daily Nation*. August 12. Accessed February 16, 2014. http:// www.nation.co.ke/News/world/US-plans -lower-sentences-for-drug-users/-/ 1068/1945674/-/13er4o/-/index.html.

42. J. Petersilia. "Beyond the Prison Bubble," *Federal Probation* 75, no. 1: 2–4.

43. Canadian Civil Liberties Association. 2012. "Omnibus Crime Bill C-10." Accessed February 16, 2014. http://www.ccla.org/ omnibus-crime-bill-c-10.

44. "Mandatory Sentencing for Gun Possession Struck Down." 2013. *The Globe and Mail*, November 14. Accessed February 16, 2014. http://www.theglobeandmail.com.

45. K. O'Malley. 2013. "Government Can't Provide Full Cost of RCMP, Prison-Related Legal Fees." *Inside Politics Blog*, March 19. http://www.cbc.ca/newsblogs/politics/ inside-politics-blog/2013/03/government -cant-provide-full-cost-of-rcmp-prison -related-legal-fees.html.

46. Ibid.

47. C.T. Griffiths and D. Murdoch. 2014. *Canadian Corrections*. 4th ed. Toronto: Nelson.

48. R. Nakhaie and W. de Lint. 2013. "Trust and Support for Surveillance Policies in Canadian and American Opinion." *International Journal of Criminal Justice* 23, no. 2: 149–169.

49. P. Bulman. 2013. "Sex Offenders Monitored by GPS Found to Commit Fewer Crimes." *NIJ Journal* 271. February. 22–25. Accessed February 16, 2014. http://www.nij.gov/ journals/271/gps-monitoring.htm.

50. "Stanley Cup Riot Charges Laid Against Another 29 People." 2013. *Huffpost British Columbia,* August 1. Accessed February 16, 2014. http://www.huffingtonpost .ca/2013/08/01/stanley-cup-riot-charges _n_3691048.html.

51. J. O'Brien. 2013. "Mental Illness Calls Cost London Force $12 Million in 2012, Says Chief Brad Duncan." *London Free Press*, January 23. Accessed February 16, 2014. http://www.lfpress.com/2013/01/23/ mental-illness-calls-cost-london-force-12 -million-in-2012-says-chief-brad-duncan.

52. L. Perreaux. 2013. "Proposed Quebec Values Charter Violates Rights, Commission Says." *The Globe and Mail*, October 17. Accessed March 6, 2014. http://www.theglobeandmail.com/ news/politics/proposed-quebec-values -charter-violates-rights-commission-says/ article14905706/.

53. N. Sharma. 2013. "The Moral Case Against the Quebec Charter of Values." *Huffington Post*, November 17. Accessed March 6, 2014. http://www.huffingtonpost .ca/nishaan-sharma/quebec-charter-of -values_b_4289021.html.

54. S. Fatima. 2013. "Most Canadians Oppose Firings Based on Quebec's Secular Charter." *The Globe and Mail*, October 4. Accessed March 6, 2014. http://www.theglobeandmail.com/news/ politics/most-canadians-oppose-firings -based-on-quebecs-secular-charter-poll/ article14651367.

CHAPTER 3

1. S. Newark. 2011. *Why Canadian Crime Statistics Don't Add Up*. Ottawa: Macdonald-Laurier Institute for Public Policy. http://macdonaldlaurier.ca/files/pdf/ MLI-Crime_Statistics_Review-Web.pdf.

2. C. LaPrairie. 1994. *Seen but Not Heard: Native People in the Inner City*. Ottawa: Department of Justice, 34.

3. S. Perreault and S. Brennan. 2010. "Criminal Victimization in Canada, 2009." *Juristat*. Accessed March 8, 2014. http:// www.statcan.gc.ca/pub/85-002-x/ 2010002/article/11340-eng.htm.

4. S. Perreault. 2013. "Police-Reported Crime Statistics in Canada, 2012." *Juristat*. Accessed March 8, 2014. http://www .statcan.gc.ca/pub/85-002-x/2013001/ article/11854-eng.pdf.

5. K. Stastna. 2013. "What's Behind Canada's Improving Crime Stats?" *CBC News*, July 26. Accessed February 21, 2014. http:// www.cbc.ca/news/cnaada/calgary/ story/2013/07/25/crime-stats-follow.html.

6. I. Mulgrew. 2011. "Crime Exacts Massive Social, Economic, and Emotional Toll." *Vancouver Sun,* May 2. Accessed February 21, 2014. http://www.canada.com/ vancouversun/news/westcoastnews/story .html?id=41cceadc-eceb-46c6-bfe9-abc 92c6aed65.

7. T. Zhang, J. Hoddenbagh, S. McDonald, and K. Scrim. 2012. *An Estimation of the Economic Impact of Spousal Violence in Canada, 2009*. Ottawa: Department of Justice. http://www.justice.gc.ca/eng/ rp-pr/cj-jp/fv-vf/rr12_7/index.html.

8. MedicalMarijuana.ca. 2013. "$8,750 Cost to B.C. Taxpayers for Each Pot Conviction, Most for Simple Possession." Accessed February 21, 2014. http:// medicalmarijuana.ca/news/0/71.

9. NORML Women's Alliance of Canada. 2013. "Cannabis Facts." Accessed February 21, 2014. http://normlwomen.ca/ cannabis_facts.

10. J. Latimer and N. Desjardins. 2007. *The 2007 National Justice Survey: Tackling Crime and Public Confidence*. Ottawa: Department of Justice. http://www.justice .gc.ca/eng/rp-pr/csj-sjc/jsp-sjp/rr07_4/ rr07_4.pdf.

11. Parole Board of Canada. 2012. *Performance Monitoring Report 2011/2012*. Ottawa: Author. http://pbc-clcc.gc.ca/rprts/pmr/pmr_2011_2012/pmr_2011_2012-eng.pdf.

12. S. Perreault and S. Brennan. 2010. "Criminal Victimization in Canada, 2009." *Juristat*. Accessed March 8, 2014. http://www.statcan.gc.ca/pub/85-002-x/2010002/article/11340-eng.htm.

13. Public Safety Canada. 2012. *Corrections and Conditional Release Statistical Overview*. Ottawa: Public Works and Government Services Canada. http://www.publicsafety.gc.ca/cnt/rsrcs/pblctns/2012-ccrs/2012-ccrs-eng.pdf.

14. S. Perreault and S. Brennan. 2010. "Criminal Victimization in Canada, 2009." *Juristat*. Accessed March 8, 2014. http://www.statcan.gc.ca/pub/85-002-x/2010002/article/11340-eng.htm.

15. R. Fitzgerald. 2008. "Fear of Crime and the Neighbourhood Context in Canadian Cities." *Crime and Justice Research Paper Series*. Ottawa: Minster of Industry. http://www.statcan.gc.ca/pub/85-561-m/85-561-m2008013-eng.pdf.

16. J.V. Roberts and K. Roach. 2004. *Community-Based Sentencing: The Perspectives of Crime Victims*. Ottawa: Research and Statistics, Department of Justice. http://canada.justice.gc.ca/eng/rp-pr/cj-jp/victim/rr04_vic1/rr04_vic1.pdf.

17. J.V. Roberts. 2008. "Victim Impact Statements: Lessons Learned and Future Priorities." *Victims of Crime Research Digest* 1:3–16. http://www.justice.gc.ca/eng/rp-pr/cj-jp/victim/rr07_vic4/p1.html?pedisable=true.

18. Regina Police Service. 2013. "Family Services." Accessed March 7, 2014. http://www.reginapolice.ca/about-us/criminal-investigation-division/family-services/.

19. Alberta Solicitor General and Public Security. 2011. *Survey of Albertans*. Edmonton: Author. http://www.solgps.alberta.ca/Publications1/Survey%20of%20Albertans/2011%20Survey%20of%20Albertans.pdf.

20. E. Smith. 2004. *Nowhere to Turn? Responding to Partner Violence against Immigrant and Visible Minority Women*. Ottawa: Canadian Council on Social Development.

21. SGM Law. 2014. "Notable Cases, Civil Litigation: Jane Doe v. Metropolitan Toronto (Municipality) Commissioners of Police." Accessed February 21. http://www.sgmlaw.com/en/about/JaneDoev.MetropolitanTorontoMunicipalityCommissionersofPolice.cfm.

22. A. Macklin. 2013. "Community Management of Offenders: The Interaction of Social Support and Risk." *Federal Probation* 77, no. 1: 1–6.

23. S. Perreault and S. Brennan. 2010. "Criminal Victimization in Canada, 2009." *Juristat*. Accessed March 8, 2014. http://www.statcan.gc.ca/pub/85-002-x/2010002/article/11340-eng.htm.

24. J.V. Roberts. 2007. "Public Confidence in Criminal Justice in Canada: A Comparative and Contextual Analysis." *Canadian Journal of Criminology and Criminal Justice* 49, no. 2: 153–84.

25. Ipsos Reid, 2011. "A Matter of Trust." Accessed February 21, 2014. http://www.ipsos-na.com/news/client/act_dsp_internal_pdf.cfm?pdf=5100.pdf.

26. M. Kennedy. 2012. "Despite Falling Crime Rates, Many Canadians Believe Justice System is Too Lax: Pollster." *Postmedia News*, July 24. Accessed February 21, 2014. http://o.canada.com/news/despite-falling-crime-rates-many-canadians-believe-justice-system-too-lax-pollster/.

27. J.V. Roberts, N. Crutcher, and P. Verbrugge. 2007. "Public Attitudes to Sentencing in Canada: Exploring Recent Findings." *Canadian Journal of Criminology & Criminal Justice* 49, no. 1: 75–107.

28. J.V. Roberts. 2007. "Public Confidence in Criminal Justice in Canada: A Comparative and Contextual Analysis." *Canadian Journal of Criminology and Criminal Justice* 49, no. 2: 153–84.

29. Canadian Bar Association. 2013, 6. *Reaching Equal Justice: An Invitation to Envision and Act*. Ottawa: Author. http://www.cba.org/CBA/equaljustice/main/.

30. C.G. Nicholl. 1999. *Community Policing, Community Justice, and Restorative Justice: Exploring the Links for the Delivery of a Balanced Approach to Public Safety*, Washington, D.C.: U.S. Department of Justice, Office of Community-Oriented Policing, 57–58. http://www.cops.usdoj.gov/Publications/e09990014_web.pdf.

31. C. Silva. 2013. "Armed Citizen Project Pushes Free Guns on U.S. Cities to Help with Crime," *The Globe and Mail*, March 29. Accessed February 21, 2014. http://news.yahoo.com/arizona-gun-proponents-launch-free-gun-program-073229701.html.

32. J.B. Sprott, C.M. Webster, and A.N. Doob. 2013. "Punishment Severity and Confidence in the Criminal Justice System." *Canadian Journal of Criminology and Criminal Justice* 55, no. 2: 279–92.

33. K. Dowler, T. Fleming, and S.L. Muzzatti. 2007. "Constructing Crime: Media, Crime, and Popular Culture." *Canadian Journal of Criminology & Criminal Justice* 48, no. 6: 837–50.

34. Parole Board of Canada. 2012. *Performance Monitoring Report 2011/2012*. Ottawa: Author. http://pbc-clcc.gc.ca/rprts/pmr/pmr_2011_2012/pmr_2011_2012-eng.pdf.

35. J.S. Rosenberger and V.J. Callanan. 2011. "The Influence of Media on Penal Attitudes," *Criminal Justice Review* 36, no. 4: 435–55.

36. J.B. Sprott and A.N. Doob. 2009. "The Effect of Urban Neighborhood Disorder on Evaluations of the Police and Courts." *Crime and Delinquency* 55, no. 3: 339–62.

37. Public Safety Canada. 2013. *Public Safety Canada 2010–2011 Evaluation of the Effective Corrections and Citizen Engagement Initiatives*. Ottawa: Author. http://www.publicsafety.gc.ca/cnt/rsrcs/pblctns/vltn-ffctv-crrctns-2010-11/index-eng.aspx.

38. N. Boyd. 2012. *The Rule of Law, the Charter of Rights and Confidence in the Legal System: Lessons from Canada*. Vancouver: International Centre for Criminal Law Reform and Criminal Justice Policy.

39. D. Ryan. 2012. "Rioting Teen Nathan Kotylak and Family Face Backlash, Forced to Leave Home." *Vancouver Sun*, June 11. Accessed February 21, 2014. http://www.vancouversun.com/technology/Rioting+teen+Nathan+Kotylak+family+face+backlash+forced+leave+home/4972283/story.html.

343

40. J. Uechi. 2011. "Judged in the Court of Facebook." *The Tyee,* July 19. http://thetyee.ca/Mediacheck/2011/06/19/CourtofFacebook/.

41. B. Bouw. 2011. "Faces in the Mob wSeek Forgiveness After Vancouver's Stanley Cup Riots." *The Globe and Mail*, June 19. Accessed February 21, 2014. whttp://www.theglobeandmail.com/news/british-columbia/faces-in-the-mob-seek-forgiveness-after-vancouvers-stanley-cup-riots/article1357876/.

42. J. Williams. 2011a. Group Calls for Olympic Ban of Rioting Canadian Water Polo Star Nathan Kotylak." *examiner.com*, June 20. Accessed February 21, 2014. http://www.examiner.com/article/group-calls-for-olympic-ban-of-rioting-canadian-water-polo-star-nathan-kotylak.

43. J. Williams. 2011b. "Nathan Kotylak 'Pathological Narcissistic' Says Alleged Ex Girlfriend." *examiner.com*, June 25. Accessed February 21, 2014. http://www.examiner.com/article/nathan-kotylak-pathological-narcissistic-says-alleged-ex-girlfriend.

44. J. Davison. 2012. "Online Vigilantes: Is 'Doxing' a Neighbourhood Watch or Dangerous Witch Hunt?" *CBC News*, October 22. Accessed February 21, 2014. http://www.cbc.ca/news/technology/story/2012/10/19/f-doxing-tracking-online-identity-anonymity.html.

45. T. Alamenciak and P. Fong. 2012. "Amanda Todd: Online Group Anonymous Now Accuses U.S. Man of Tormenting Amanda Todd." *Toronto Star*, October 17. Accessed February 21, 2014. http://www.thestar.com/news/canada/2012/10/17/amanda_todd_online_group_anonymous_now_accuses_us_man_of_tormenting_amanda_todd.html.

46. P. Wright. 2013. "Anonymous: We Will Name 'Rapists' of Suicide Victim Rehtaeh Parsons." *Telegraph*, April 11. Accessed February 21, 2014. http://www.telegraph.co.uk/news/worldnews/northamerica/canada/9987383/Anonymous-we-will-name-rapists-of-suicide-victim-Rehtaeh-Parsons.html.

47. http://www.cnn.com/2013/03/17/justice/ohio-steubenville-case.Anonymous.

48. S. Almasy. 2013. "Two Teens Found Guilty in Steubenville Rape Case." *CNN Justice,* March 17. Accessed February 21, 2014. http://www.cnn.com/2013/03/17/justice/ohio-steubenville-case.Anonymous .2013. "#OpJustice4Rehtaeh 4/13 Press Release." *Pastebin.com,* April 13. http://pastebin.com/a8GtD7eg.

49. Ibid.

50. R. Freeman. 2012. "Abbotsford Man Among Three Charged after 'Super Hero' Stings." *Abbotsford News*, June 8. Accessed February 21, 2014. http://www.abbynews.com/news/158173125.html?mobile=true.

51. G. Ivanov. 2013. "What Is Anonymous? Everything You Ever Wanted to Know about the Shadowy Internet Group." *PolicyMic,* January 26. http://www.policymic.com/articles/23922/what-is-anonymous-everything-you-ever-wanted-to-know-about-the-shadowy-internet-group.

CHAPTER 4

1. A. Goldsmith. 2010. "Policing's New Visibility." *British Journal of Criminology* 50, no. 5: 914–34.

2. C. Reith. 1956. *A New Study of Police History*. London: Oliver and Boyd.

3. T.J. Juliani, C.K. Talbot, and C.H.S. Jayewardene. 1984. "Municipal Policing in Canada: A Developmental Perspective." *Canadian Police College Journal* 8, no. 3: 315–85.

4. C.T. Griffiths. 2013. *Canadian Police Work*. 3rd ed. Toronto: Nelson.

5. M. Burczycka. 2013. *Police Resources in Canada 2012*. Ottawa: Statistics Canada. http://www.statcan.gc.ca/pub/85-225-x/85-225-x2012000-eng.pdf.

6. P. Palango. 1998. *The Last Guardians: The Crisis in the RCMP—and in Canada*. Toronto: McClelland and Stewart.

7. T. Donais. 2004. "Peacekeeping's Poor Cousin: Canada and the Challenge of Post-conflict Policing." *International Journal* 59, no. 4: 943–963.

8. B. Dupont and S. Tanner. 2009. "Not Always a Happy Ending: The Organisational Challenges of Deploying and Integrating Civilian Peacekeepers (A Canadian Perspective)." *Policing & Society* 19, no. 2: 134–46.

9. J.E. Salahub. 2013. "Forget Peacekeeping: Canada Should Focus on Policing." *Vancouver Sun*, January 14. Accessed February 23, 2014. http://www.nsi-ins.ca/fr/nouvelles/forget-peacekeeping-canada-should-focus-on-policing/.

10. R. McLeod. 2002. *Parapolice: A Revolution in the Business of Law Enforcement*. Toronto: Boheme Press.

11. G.S. Rigakos. 2003. *The New Parapolice*: *Risk Markets and Commodified Social Control*. Toronto: University of Toronto Press.

12. S. Burbidge. 2005. "The Governance Deficit: Reflections on the Future of Public and Private Policing in Canada." *Canadian Journal of Criminology and Criminal Justice* 47, no. 1: 63–87.

13. C. Clarke and C. Murphy. 2002. *In Search of Security: The Roles of Public Police and Private Agencies—Discussion Paper*. Ottawa: Law Reform Commission of Canada. http://dalspace.library.dal.ca:8080/bitstream/handle/10222/10292/In%20Search%20of%20Security%20Discussion%20Paper%20EN.pdf?sequence=1.

14. D.H. Bayley and C.D. Shearing. 1996. "The Future of Policing." *Law and Society Review* 33, no. 3: 585–606.

15. P.F. McKenna. 2002. *Police Powers I*. Toronto: Prentice-Hall.

16. Law Reform Commission of Canada. 2006. *In Search of Security: The Future of Policing in Canada*. Ottawa: Minister of Public Works and Government Services, 120–121.

17. S. Miller and J. Blackler. 2005. *Ethical Issues in Policing*. Aldershot, UK: Ashgate Publishing.

18. J.M. Pollock. 2010. *Ethical Dilemmas and Decisions in Criminal Justice*. Belmont, CA: Wadsworth/Cengage Learning, 182.

19. S. Miller and J. Blackler. 2005. *Ethical Issues in Policing*. Aldershot, UK: Ashgate Publishing.

20. P.K. Manning. 2005. "The Police: Mandate, Strategies, and Appearances." In *Policing: Key Readings,* edited by T. Newburn, 191–214. Portland: Willan Publishing.

344

21. Toronto Police Service. 2011. *Planning for the Future ... Scanning the Toronto Environment*. Toronto: Author, 169. http://www.torontopolice.on.ca/publications/files/reports/2011envscan.pdf.

22. D.H. Bayley. 2005. "What Do the Police Do?" In *Policing: Key Readings,* edited by T. Newburn, 141–49. Portland: Willan Publishing.

23. C.T. Griffiths. 2013. *Canadian Police Work.* 3rd ed. Toronto: Nelson.

24. A. Malm, N. Pollard, P. Brantingham, T. Tinsley, D. Plecas, P. Brantingham, I. Cohen, and B. Kinney. 2005. *A 30-Year Analysis of Police Service Delivery and Costing: "E" Division. Research Summary.* Ottawa: Royal Canadian Mounted Police. http://www.ufv.ca/media/assets/ccjr/ccjr-resources/ccjr-publications/30_Year_Analysis_(English).pdf.

25. Toronto Police Service. 2011. *Planning for the Future ... Scanning the Toronto Environment*. Toronto: Author, 14. http://www.torontopolice.on.ca/publications/files/reports/2011envscan.pdf.

26. Department of Justice Canada. 1985, 1. *Canadian Human Rights Act.* http://laws-lois.justice.gc.ca/eng/acts/h-6/.

27. Toronto Police Service. 2011. *Planning for the Future ... Scanning the Toronto Environment*. Toronto: Author, 175. http://www.torontopolice.on.ca/publications/files/reports/2011envscan.pdf.

28. A. Morrow. 2011. "What Price for Law and Order?" *The Globe and Mail*, January 8, A4.

29. P.K. Manning. 2005. "The Police: Mandate, Strategies, and Appearances." In *Policing: Key Readings,* edited by T. Newburn, 191–214. Portland: Willan Publishing.

30. R. Whitaker, G.S. Kealy, and A. Parnaby. 2012. *Secret Service: Political Policing in Canada from the Fenians to Fortress America.* Toronto: University of Toronto Press, 7.

31. R. Whitaker, G.S. Kealy, and A. Parnaby. 2012. *Secret Service: Political Policing in Canada from the Fenians to Fortress America.* Toronto: University of Toronto Press.

32. S. Hewitt. 2000. "'Information Believed True': RCMP Security Intelligence Activities on Canadian University Campuses and the Controversy Surrounding Them, 1961–1971." *Canadian Historical Review* 81, no. 2: 191–228.

33. S. Hewitt. 2002. *Spying 101: The RCMP's Secret Activities at Canadian Universities, 1917–1997.* Toronto: University of Toronto Press.

34. R. Whitaker, G.S. Kealy, and A. Parnaby. 2012. *Secret Service: Political Policing in Canada from the Fenians to Fortress America.* Toronto: University of Toronto Press.

35. C. Murphy. 2012. "Canadian Police and Policing Policy, Post-9/11." In *Canadian Criminal Justice Policy: Contemporary Perspectives*, edited by K. Ismaili, U.J. Sprott, and K. Varma, 1–20. Toronto: Oxford University Press, 13.

36. Ibid.

37. F. Wilson-Bates. 2008. *Lost in Transition: How a Lack of Capacity in the Mental Health System Is Failing Vancouver's Mentally Ill and Draining Police Resources*, Vancouver: Vancouver Police Department. https://vancouver.ca/police/assets/pdf/reports-policies/vpd-lost-in-transition.pdf

38. B. Henson, B.W. Reyns, C.F. Klahm, and J. Frank. 2010. "Do Good Recruits Make Good Cops? Problems Predicting and Measuring Academy and Street-Level Success." *Police Quarterly* 13, no. 1: 5–26.

39. D.P. Rosenbaum, A.M. Schuck, and G. Cordner. 2011. *The National Police Research Platform: The Life Course of New Officers. Research Review*. Washington, D.C.: National Institute of Justice. http://www.nationalpoliceresearch.org/storage/Recruits%20Life%20Course.pdf.

40. Montréal Police Service. 2013. *Annual Review 2012*. Montréal: Author. http://www.spvm.qc.ca/upload/documentations/264812089.pdf.

41. J.B.L. Chan. 2003. *Fair Cop: Learning the Art of Policing*. Toronto: University of Toronto Press.

42. A.T. Chappell and L. Lanza-Kaduce. 2010. "Police-Academy Socialization: Understanding the Lessons Learned in a Paramilitary-Bureaucratic Organization." *Journal of Contemporary Ethnography* 39, no. 2: 187–214.

43. S.D. Mastrofski and R.R. Riti. 1996. "Police Training and the Effects of Organizations on Drunk Driving Enforcement." *Justice Quarterly* 3, no. 2, 291–320.

44. R. Haarr. 2001. "The Making of a Community Policing Officer: The Impact of Basic Training and Occupational Socialisation of Police Recruits. *Police Quarterly* 4, no. 4: 402–33.

45. J.K. Skolnick. 1966. *Justice without Trial: Law Enforcement in a Democratic Society*. New York: John Wiley and Sons, 4.

46. A. Goldsmith. 1990. "Taking Police Culture Seriously: Discretion and the Limits of the Law." *Policing and Society* 1, no. 1: 91–114.

47. S. Herbert. 1998. "Police Subculture Revisited." *Criminology* 36, no. 2: 343–69.

48. E.A. Paoline. 2004. "Shedding Light on Police Culture: An Examination of Officers' Occupational Attitudes." *Police Quarterly* 7, no. 2: 205–37.

49. M. Morash, R. Haarr, and D.-H. Kwak. 2006. "Multilevel Influences on Police Stress." *Journal of Contemporary Criminal Justice* 22, no. 1: 26–43.

50. J.R.L. Parsons. 2004. "Occupational Health and Safety Issue of Police Officers in Canada, the United States, and Europe: A Review Essay." Accessed February 23, 2014. http://wenku.baidu.com/view/bcf00ef9941ea76e58fa040f.html.

51. D.P. Rosenbaum, A.M. Schuck, and G. Cordner. 2011. *The National Police Research Platform: The Life Course of New Officers. Research Review*. Washington, D.C.: National Institute of Justice, 13. http://www.nationalpoliceresearch.org/storage/Recruits%20Life%20Course.pdf.

52. L. Duxbury and C. Higgins. 2012. "Summary of Key Findings: Caring for and About Those Who Serve: Work-life and Employee Well Being Within Canada's Police Departments." Accessed February 23, 2014. http://sprott.carleton.co/wp-content/files/Duxbury-Higgins-Police2012_keyfindings.pdf.

53. W.P. McCarty, A. Schuck, W. Skogan, and D. Rosenbaum. 2011. *Stress, Burnout, and Health. Topical Report*. Washington, D.C.: National Institute of Justice. http://www.nationalpoliceresearch.org/storage/updated-papers/Stress%20Burnout%20%20and%20Health%20FINAL.pdf.

54. W.P. McCarty and W.G. Skogan. 2013. "Job-Related Burnout Among Civilian and Sworn Police Personnel." *Police Quarterly* 16, no. 1: 66–84.

55. K.M. Gilmartin. 2002. *Emotional Survival for Law Enforcement: A Guide for Officers and Their Families*. Tucson: E-S Press.

56. B. Pearsall. 2012. "Sleep Disorders, Work Shifts, and Offer Wellness." *NIJ Journal* June, no. 270. Accessed February 23, 2014. http://www.nij.gov/nij/journals/270/officer-wellness.htm.

57. J.M. Shane. 2010. "Organizational Stressors and Police Performance." *Journal of Criminal Justice* 38, no. 4: 807–18.

58. K. Dowler and B. Arai. 2008. "Stress, Gender and Policing: The Impact of Perceived Gender Discrimination on Symptoms of Stress." *International Journal of Police Science & Management* 10, no. 2: 123–35.

59. Royal Canadian Mounted Police. 2009. *Results—RCMP Employee Opinion Survey 2009*. Ottawa: Author. http://www.rcmp-grc.gc.ca/surveys-sondages/2009/emp/empl2009_result-eng.htm.

60. Commission for Complaints Against the RCMP. 2013. *Public Interest Investigation into Issues of Workplace Harassment within the Royal Canadian Mounted Police: Final Report*. Ottawa: Author. http://www.cpc-cpp.gc.ca/cnt/decision/pii-eip/wHarass-harceT/rep-rap2013-eng.aspx.

61. D. LeBlanc. 2012. "Female Mounties Fear Backlash Over Reporting Harassment, Report Shows," *The Globe and Mail*, September 18. Accessed February 23, 2014. http://www.theglobeandmail.com/news/national/female-mounties-fear-backlash-over-report-shows/article4550565/.

62. K. Drews. 2013. "RCMP Sexual Harassment Lawsuit Gains Toronto Professor's Support." *Huffington Post*, June 11. Accessed February 23, 2014. http://www.huffingtonpost.ca/2013/06/11/rcmp-sexual-harassment-lawsuit_n_3424321.html.

63. V. Lindsay, W.B. Taylor, and K. Shelley. 2008. "Alcohol and the Police: An Empirical Examination of a Widely Held Assumption." *Policing: An International Journal of Police Strategies and Management* 31, no. 4: 596–609.

64. R. Loo. 2003. "A Meta-Analysis of Police Suicide Rates: Findings and Issues." *Suicide and Life-Threatening Behavior* 33, no. 3: 313–25.

65. S.P. McCoy and M.G. Aamodt. 2010. "A Comparison of Law Enforcement Divorse Rates with Those of Other Occupations." *Journal of Police and Criminal Psychology*, 25 no. 1: 1–16.

66. M.L. Arter. 2008. "Stress and Deviance in Policing." *Deviant Behavior* 29, no. 1: 43–69.

67. C. Regehr, D. Johanis, G. Dimitropoulos, C. Bartram, and G. Hope. 2003. "The Police Officer and the Public Inquiry: A Qualitative Inquiry into the Aftermath of Workplace Trauma." *Brief Treatment and Crisis Intervention* 3, no. 4: 383–96.

CHAPTER 5

1. B. Van Allen. 2009. *Police Powers: Law, Order and Accountability*. Toronto: Pearson Prentice-Hall.

2. J. Cameron and J. Stribopolous. 2008. *The Charter and Criminal Justice Twenty-Five Years Later*. Markham: LexisNexis.

3. P.M. Bolton. 1991. *Criminal Procedure in Canada*. 10th ed. North Vancouver: Self-Counsel Press, 24.

4. "Supreme Court Muzzles Sniffer Dogs." 2008. *CanWest News Service,* April 25. http://www.canada.com/globaltv/national/story.html?id=7cef5f97-7bfa-48bb-97db-05e8754897eb.

5. S. Fine. 2013. "Supreme Court Allows Wider Use of 'Sniffer Dogs.'" *The Globe and Mail*, September 27. Accessed February 25, 2014. http://www.theglobeandmail.com/news/national/police-within-their-rights-to-use-sniffer-dogs-supreme-court-rules/article14564884/.

6. Ibid.

7. J. Tibbetts. 2007. "Top Court Gives Police Ammo to Fight Gun Crimes." *Vancouver Sun,* July 7, A4.

8. Canadian Civil Liberties Association. 2013. "*R v Vu*: Privacy Rights Protected in Recent SCC Ruling." *CCLA Rights Watch*, November 8. Accessed February 25, 2014. http://www.ccla.org/rightswatch/2013/11/08/r-v-vu-privacy-rights-protected-in-recent-scc-ruling/.

9. D. Bell. 2013. "Ottawa Police Chief Supports Taking DNA from Anyone Arrested." *Ottawa Sun*, October 4, 1. Accessed February 25, 2014. http://www.ottawasun.com/2013/10/04/ottawa-police-chief-supports-taking-dna-records-from-anyone-arrested.

10. "Chief Rich Hanson's Call for DNA Sample Collection at Arrests Gains Traction in Ottawa." 2013, 1. *Huffington Post Alberta,* October 4. Accessed February 25, 2014. http://www.huffingtonpost.ca/2013/10/04/dna-sample-police-chief-rick-hanson_n_4045157.html.

11. C. Sherrin 2005. "False Confessions and Admissions in Canadian Law." *Queen's Law Journal* 30: 601–59.

12. K.T. Keenan and J. Brockman. 2011. *Mr. Big: Exposing Undercover Investigations in Canada*. Halifax: Fernwood Press.

13. C.G. Mentuck. 2008. "When 'Mr. Big' Stings Go Wrong." *Canada.com,* November 3. http://www.canada.com/theprovince/news/story.html?id=433130bc-f5ea-4393-b186-287812f1d96c.

14. T.E. Moore. 2009. "Eliciting Wrongful Convictions by Mr. Big Lies—The Unger Case." *LEAP Blog*, November 21. Accessed March 7, 2014. http://windsorlaw-leap.blogspot.ca/2009/11/eliciting-wrongful-convictions-by-mr.html.

15. G. Lang. 2013. "Highest Court to Hear Mr. Big Case." *Lawdiva's Blog,* December 4. http://lawdiva.wordpress.com/2013/12/04/highest-court-to-hear-mr-big-case/.

16. J. Brean. 2013. "Juries Rarely Convict Police." *National Post*, August 20, A1.

17. P. Bulman. 2010. "Police Use of Force: The Impact of Less-Lethal Weapons and Tactics," *NIJ Journal* 267:4–10. Accessed February 25, 2014. https://ncjrs.gov/pdffiles1/nij/233280.pdf.

18. Expert Panel on the Medical and Physiological Impacts of Conducted Energy Weapons. 2013. *The Health Effects of Conducted Energy Weapons*. Ottawa: Council of Canadian Academies and Canadian Academy of Health Sciences. http://www.scienceadvice.ca/uploads/eng/assessments%20and%20publications%20and%20news%20releases/CEW/CEW_fullreportEN.pdf.

19. "Mountie in Dziekanski Taser Death Not Guilty of Lying." 2013. *CBC News,* July 29. Accessed March 7, 2014. http://www.cbc.ca/news/canada/british-columbia/mountie-in-dziekanski-taser-death-not-guilty-of-lying-1.1302503.

20. D. Meissner. 2012. "BC Police Taser use Down 87 Per Cent Since Robert Dziekanski's Death." *Canadian Press*, October 9. Accessed March 7, 2014. http://www.huffingtonpost.ca/2012/10/09/bc-taser-use-police-down-87-per-cent_n_1952239.html.

21. G.P. Alpert. 2009. "Interpreting Police Use of Force and the Construction of Reality." *Criminology and Public Policy* 8, no. 1: 111–115.

22. R.B. Parent. 2006. "The Police Use of Deadly Force: International Comparisons." *Police Journal* 79: 230–37.

23. V.B. Lord. 2012. "Factors Influencing Subjects' Observed Level of Suicide by Cop Intent," *Criminal Justice and Behavior* 39, no. 12: 1633–46.

24. R.B. Parent. 2004. "Aspects of Police Use of Deadly Force in North America: The Phenomenon of Victim-Precipitated Homicide." PhD diss., Simon Fraser University, Vancouver.

25. N. Addis and C. Stephens. 2008. "An Evaluation of a Police Debriefing Programme: Outcomes for Police Officers Five Years After a Police Shooting." *International Journal of Police Science & Management* 10, no. 4: 361–73.

26. C.J. Harris. 2009. "Police Use of Improper Force: A Systematic Review of the Literature." *Victims and Offenders* 4:25–41.

27. E.A. Paoline and W. Terrill. 2007. "Police Education, Experience, and the Use of Force." *Criminal Justice and Behavior* 34, no. 2: 179–96.

28. J.P. McElvain and A.J. Kposowa. 2008. "Police Officers Characteristics and the Likelihood of Using Deadly Force." *Criminal Justice and Behavior* 35, no. 4: 505–21.

29. R.R. Johnson. 2011. "Suspect Mental Disorder and Police Use of Force." *Criminal Justice and Behavior* 38, no. 2: 127–45.

30. K.B. Carlson. 2013. "Toronto Police Officer Charged in Sammy Yatim Shooting to Turn Himself in Tuesday." *The Globe and Mail*, August 19. Access February 25, 2014. http://www.theglobeandmail.com/news/toronto/ontario-police-watchdog-lays-second-degree-murder-chage-in-sammy-yatim-shooting/article13837354/.

31. Danville Police Department. 2012. *Officer-Worn Camera Program*. Danville, Virginia. http://www.theiacp.org/Portals/0/pdfs/LEIM/2012Presentations/OPS-Officer-WornCameras.pdf.

32. National Institute of Justice. 2012. *A Primer on Body-Worn Cameras for Law Enforcement*, Washington, D.C.: U.S. Department of Justice. http://www.justnet.org/pdf/00-body-Worn-Cameras-508.pdf.

33. R.J. Lundman. 1980. *Police and Policing—An Introduction*. New York: Holt, Rinehard, and Winston, 110–111.

34. L. Westmarland. 2013. "'Snitches Get Stitches': US Homicide Detectives' Ethics and Morals in Action," *Policing & Society* 23, no. 3: 312.

35. W.J. Closs and P.F. McKenna. 2006. "Profiling a Problem in Canadian Police Leadership: The Kingston Police Data Collection Project," *Canadian Public Administration* 49, no. 2, 143–60.

36. A.G. Crocker, K. Hartford and L. Heslop. 2009. "Gender Differences in Police Encounters Among Persons With and Without Serious Mental Illness." *Psychiatric Services* 60, no. 1: 86–93.

37. A.T. Chappell, J.M. MacDonald, and P.W. Manz. 2006. "The Organizational Determinants of Police Arrest Decisions." *Crime and Delinquency* 52, no. 2: 287–306.

38. Department of Justice Canada. 1985, 1. *Canadian Human Rights Act.* http://laws-lois.justice.gc.ca/eng/acts/h-6/.

39. "Discrimination." 2014. *Dictionary.com*. Accessed February 26, 2014. http://dictionary.reference.com/browse/discrimination.

40. Canadian Association of Chiefs of Police. 2004. "Bias-Free Policing." In *Resolutions Adopted at the 99th Annual Conference*. August. Vancouver: Author, 7.

41. R. Bahdi. 2003. "No Exit: Racial Profiling and Canada's War Against Terrorism." *Osgoode Hall Law Journal* 41, no. 2&3: 293–316.

42. D.M. Tanovich. 2008. "A Powerful Blow Against Police Use of Drug Courier Profiles." *Criminal Reports* 55, 6th Series: 379–93.

43. A. Leclair. 2013. "Racial Profiling Complaints in Quebec Up Over 50 Per Cent." *Global BC,* October 24. http://globalnews.ca/news/922013/racial-profiling-complaints-against-montreal-police-up-over-50-per-cent/.

44. V. Satzewich and W. Shaffir. 2009. "Racism versus Professionalism: Claims and Counter-Claims About Racial Profiling." *Canadian Journal of Criminology* 51, no. 2: 199–226.

45. V. Satzewich and W. Shaffir. 2009. "Racism versus Professionalism: Claims and Counter-Claims About Racial Profiling." *Canadian Journal of Criminology* 51, no. 2: 210.

46. L. Peoples. 2009. "Last Name Searches in Marijuana Grow-Operations Investigations in *R. v. Li* and *R. v. Nguyen*: Is the Racial Profiling Analysis Sufficient?" Accessed February 25, 2014. https://web4.uwindsor.ca/units/law/LEAP.nsf/a1b249f15dfa39be8525730600490eda/05703ae2c47ce7e68525767b006e9e78/$FILE/LastNameSearchesGrowOps.pdf.

47. Hon. Mr. Justice D.H. Wright (Commissioner). 2004. *Commission of Inquiry into Matters Relating to the Death of Neil Stonechild*. Regina: Saskatchewan Department of Justice. http://www.stonechildinquiry.ca/finalreport/default.shtml.

48. S. Reber and R. Renaud. 2005. *Starlight Tour: The Last, Lonely Night of Neil Stonechild*. Toronto: Random House Canada.

49. C. Clarke and C. Murphy. 2002. *In Search of Security: The Roles of Public Police and Private Agencies—Discussion Paper*. Ottawa: Law Reform Commission of Canada. Accessed February 25, 2014. http://dalspace.library.dal.ca:8080/bitstream/handle/10222/10292/In%20Search%20of%20Security%20Discussion%20Paper%20EN.pdf?sequence=1.

347

50. Law Reform Commission of Canada. 2006. *In Search of Security: The Future of Policing in Canada*. Ottawa: Minister of Public Works and Government Services, 88–89. http://www.policingsecurity.ca/wp-content/uploads/2013/05/In-Search-of-Security.pdf.

51. C. Murphy and P.F. McKenna. 2010. *Police Investigating Police: A Critical Analysis of the Literature*. Ottawa: Commission for Public Complaints Against the RCMP. Accessed March 7, 2014. http://www.cpc-cpp.gc.ca/cnt/tpsp-tmrs/police/projet-pip-pep-eng.aspx.

52. Ontario Office of the Chief Coroner. 2011. *Report for 2009–2011 (Ontario)*. Toronto: Author. http://www.mcscs.jus.gov.on.ca/stellent/groups/public/@mcscs/@www/@com/documents/webasset/ec161620.pdf.

53. Justice Institute of British Columbia. 2005. "British Columbia Police Code of Ethics." Accessed February 25, 2014. http://www.jibc.ca/programs-courses/schools-departments/school-public-safety-security/police-academy/resources/code-ethics/british-columbia-police-code-ethics.

54. Royal Canadian Mounted Police. 2012. "Core Surveys 2012: National Level Results." Accessed February 25, 2014. http://www.rcmp-grc.gc.ca/surveys-sondages/2012/result-nat12-eng.htm.

CHAPTER 6

1. C.T. Griffiths. 2013. *Canadian Police Work*. 3rd ed. Toronto: Nelson.

2. N.M. Connell, K. Miggans, and J.M. McGloin. 2008. "Can a Community Policing Initiative Reduce Serious Crime?" *Police Quarterly* 11, no. 2: 127–50.

3. B. Whitelaw and R.B. Parent. 2013. *Community-Based Strategic Policing in Canada*. 4th ed. Toronto: Nelson.

4. P. Parshall-McDonald. 2002. *Managing Police Operations—Implementing the New York Crime Control Model—CompStat*. Belmont: Wadsworth/Thomson Learning.

5. J.J. Willis, S.D. Mastrofski, and T. Kochel. 2010. "The Co-implementation of CompStat and Community Policing." *Journal of Criminal Justice* 38, no. 5: 969–80.

6. N. Cope. 2004. "Intelligence Led Policing or Policing Led Intelligence? Integrating Volume Crime Analysis into Policing." *British Journal of Criminology* 44, no. 2: 188–203.

7. B. Pearsall. 2010. "Predictive Policing: The Future of Law Enforcement?" *NIJ Journal* 266: 16–19. Accessed February 27, 2014. https://www.ncjrs.gov/pdffiles1/nij/230414.pdf.

8. B. Pearsall. 2010. "Predictive Policing: The Future of Law Enforcement?" *NIJ Journal* 266: 17. Accessed February 27, 2014. https://www.ncjrs.gov/pdffiles1/nij/230414.pdf.

9. L. Cao. 2011. "Visible Minorities and Confidence in the Police." *Canadian Journal of Criminology and Criminal Justice* 53, no. 1: 1–26.

10. J. Sprott and A.N. Doob. 2009. "The Effect of Urban Neighborhood Disorder on Evaluations of the Police and Courts," *Crime and Delinquency* 55, no. 3: 339–62.

11. A. Rix, F. Joshua, M. Maguire, and S. Morton. 2009. *Improving Public Confidence in the Police: A Review of the Evidence. Research Report 28*. London, UK: Home Office. https://www.gov.uk/government/uploads/system/uploads/attachment_data/file/115848/horr50-report.pdf.

12. M. Pauls. 2005. "An Evaluation of the Neighbourhood Empowerment Team (NET): Edmonton Police Service." *Canadian Review of Police Research* 1. Accessed February 27, 2014. http://crpr.icaap.org/index.php/crpr/article/view/42/38.

13. M. Barkley. 2009. *CCTV Pilot Project Evaluation Report*. Toronto: Toronto Police Service. http://geeksandglobaljustice.com/wp-content/TPS-CCTV-report.pdf.

14. J.H. Ratcliffe, T. Taniguchi, and R.B. Taylor. 2009. "The Crime Reduction Effects of Public CCTV Cameras: A Multi-Method Spatial Approach." *Justice Quarterly* 26, no. 3: 746–70.

15. B.C. Welsh and D.P. Farrington. 2009. "Public Area CCTV and Crime Prevention: An Updated Systematic Review and Meta-Analysis." *Justice Quarterly* 26, no. 4: 716–45.

16. S.J. McLean, R.E. Worden, and M. Kim. 2013. "Here's Looking at You: An Evaluation of Public CCTV Cameras and Their Effects on Crime and Disorder." *Criminal Justice Review* 38, no. 3: 303–34.

17. J. Ratcliffe. 2009. *Video Surveillance of Public Places*. Washington, D.C.: U.S. Department of Justice, Center for Problem-Oriented Policing. http://www.popcenter.org/responses/video_surveillance/.

18. T. Bennett, K. Holloway, and D.P. Farrington. 2006. "Does Neighborhood Watch Reduce Crime? A Systematic Review and Meta-Analysis." *Journal of Experimental Criminology* 2, no. 4: 437–58.

19. D. Challinger. 2004. *Crime Stoppers Victoria: An Evaluation*. Canberra: Australian Institute of Criminology. http://www.popcenter.org/library/scp/pdf/198-Challinger.pdf.

20. D. Horn. 2013. "Gun Buy-Backs Popular But Ineffective, Experts Say." *Cincinnati Enquirer*, January 13. Accessed February 27, 2014. http://www.usatoday.com/story/news/nation/2013/01/12/gun-buybacks-popular-but-ineffective/1829165/.

21. D.P. Rosenbaum. 2007. "Just Say No to D.A.R.E." *Criminology and Public Policy* 6, no. 4: 815–24.

22. A.M. Schuck. 2013. "A Life-Course Perspective on Adolescents' Attitudes to Police." *Journal of Research in Crime and Delinquency* 50, no. 4: 579–607.

23. C. Corter and R.D. Peters. 2011. "Integrated Early Childhood Services in Canada: Evidence from the Better Beginnings, Better Futures (BBBF) and Toronto First Duty (TFD) Projects." *Encyclopedia of Early Childhood Development*. Accessed February 27, 2014. http://www.child-encyclopedia.com/pages/PDF/Corter-PetersANGxp1.pdf.

24. L. MacRae, J.J. Paetsch, L.D. Bertrand, and J.P. Hornick. 2005. *National Police Leadership Survey on Crime Prevention Through Social Development*. Ottawa: Public Safety Canada. http://www.publicsafety.gc.ca/lbrr/archives/hv%207431%20m29%202005-eng.pdf.

25. C. Na and D.C. Gottfredson. 2013. "Police Officers in Schools: Effects on School Crime and the Processing of Offending Behaviors." *Justice Quarterly* 30, no. 4: 619–50.

26. S.A. Anderson, R.M. Sabatelli, and J. Trachtenberg. 2007. "Community Police and Youth Programs for Positive Youth Development." *Police Quarterly* 10, no. 1: 23–40.

27. Public Safety Canada. 2013. "Community Mobilization Prince Albert (Synopsis)." http://www.publicsafety.gc.ca/cnt/cntrng-crm/plcng/cnmcs-plcng/ndx/snpss-eng.aspx?n=152.

28. D.P. Rosenbaum. 2007. "Just Say No to D.A.R.E." *Criminology and Public Policy* 6, no. 4: 815–24.

29. B.C. Welsh and D.P. Farrington. 2005. "Evidence-Based Crime Prevention: Conclusions and Directions for a Safer Society." *Canadian Journal of Criminology and Criminal Justice* 47, no. 2: 337–54.

30. Ottawa Police Service. 2012. *Environmental Scan: 2012*. Ottawa: Author. http://www.ottawapolice.ca/Libraries/Corporate_Speeches_FR/OPS_Environmental_Scan_2012_-_Eng.sflb.ashx.

31. J.Q. Wilson and G.L. Kelling. 1982. "Broken Windows: The Police and Neighborhood Safety." *Atlantic Monthly*, March, 29–38.

32. R.H. Burke. 1998. "The Socio-Political Context of Zero Tolerance Policing Strategies." *Policing* 21, no. 4: 667.

33. B.E. Harcourt. 2001. *Illusions of Order—The False Promise of Broken Windows*. Cambridge: Harvard University Press.

34. J.C. Hinkle and D. Weisburd. 2008. "The Irony of Broken Windows: A Micro-Place Study of the Relationship Between Disorder, Focused Police Crackdowns, and Fear of Crime." *Journal of Criminal Justice* 36, no. 6: 503–12.

35. P.K.B. St. Jean. 2007. *Pockets of Crime: Broken Windows, Collective Efficacy, and the Criminal Point of View*. Chicago: University of Chicago Press.

36. M.S. Scott. 2003. *The Benefits and Consequences of Police Crackdowns*. Washington, D.C.: Office of Community Oriented Policing Services, U.S. Department of Justice. http://www.popcenter.org/Responses/police_crackdowns/print/.

37. A. Gabbat. 2013. "Stop and Frisk: Only 3% of 2.4 million Stops Result in Conviction, Report Finds." *Guardian*, November 14. Accessed February 27, 2014. http://www.theguardian.com/world/2013/nov/14/stop-and-frisk-new-york-conviction-rate.

38. J. Goldstein. 2013. "Judge Rejects New York's Stop and Frisk Policy." *The New York Times*, August 12. Accessed February 27, 2014. http://www.nytimes.com/2013/08/13/nyregion/stop-and-frisk-practice-violated-rights-judge-rules.html?_r=0.

39. J. Rankin. 2013. "As Criticism Piles Up, So Do the Police Cards." *Toronto Star*, September 27. Accessed February 27, 2014. http://www.thestar.com/news/gta/knowntopolice2013/2013/09/27/as_criticism_piles_up_so_do_the_police_cards.html.

40. J. Keating. 2010. "City Rooming House Costs a Whopping $25,000 for Police." *Province*, July 20, A4. Accessed February 27, 2014. http://www2.canada.com/theprovince/news/story.html?id=356d1e4d-5c18-4ae2-bf5c-d09fa1fa7ebc.

41. J.E. Eck. 2004. "Why Don't Problems Get Solved?" In *Community Policing: Can It Work?*, edited by W.G. Skogan, 185–206. Belmont: Wadsworth/Thomson Learning.

42. R.H. Burke. 1998. "The Socio-political Context of Zero Tolerance Policing Strategies." *Policing* 21, no. 4: 666–82.

43. S.N. Durlauf and D.S. Nagin. 2011. The Deterrent Effect of Imprisonment." In *Controlling Crime: Strategies and Tradeoffs*, edited by P.J. Cook, J. Ludwig, and J. McCrary, 43–94. Chicago: University of Chicago Press.

44. B.E. Harcourt and J. Ludwig. 2006. "Broken Windows: New Evidence from New York City and a Five-City Social Experiment." *University of Chicago Law Review* 73, no. 1: 271–320.

45. J. Hyunseok, L.T. Hoover, and B.A. Lawton. 2008. "Effect of Broken Windows Enforcement on Crime Rates." *Journal of Criminal Justice* 36, no. 6: 529–38.

46. J.C. Hinkle and D. Weisburd. 2008. "The Irony of Broken Windows: A Micro-Place Study of the Relationship Between Disorder, Focused Police Crackdowns, and Fear of Crime." *Journal of Criminal Justice* 36, no. 6: 503–12.

47. M.S. Scott. 2003. *The Benefits and Consequences of Police Crackdowns*. Washington, D.C.: Office of Community Oriented Policing Services, U.S. Department of Justice. http://www.popcenter.org/Responses/police_crackdowns/print/.

48. M. Axford and R. Ruddell. 2010. "Police-Parole Partnerships in Canada: A Review of a Promising Programme." *International Journal of Police Science and Management* 12, no. 2: 274–86.

49. J. Armstrong and S. Mallen. 2013. "TAVIS: Police Unit Faces Criticism as It Tries to Bridge Gaps in Toronto Neighbourhoods." *Global News*, October 23. Accessed February 27, 2014. http://globalnews.ca/news/920979/following-tavis-officers-on-walkabout-of-jamestown-neighbourhood/.

50. J.E. Eck, S. Chainey, J.G. Cameron, M. Leitner, and R.E. Wilson. 2005. *Mapping Crime: Understanding Hot Spots*. Washington, D.C.: National Institute of Justice. http://discovery.ucl.ac.uk/11291/1/11291.pdf.

51. J.M. Gau and R.K. Brunson. 2010. "Procedural Justice and Order Maintenance Policing: A Study of Inner-City Young Men's Perceptions of Police Legitimacy." *Justice Quarterly* 27, no. 2: 255–79.

52. S.N. Durlauf and D.S. Nagin. 2011. The Deterrent Effect of Imprisonment." In *Controlling Crime: Strategies and Tradeoffs*, edited by P.J. Cook, J. Ludwig, and J. McCrary, 43–94. Chicago: University of Chicago Press.

53. C. Menton. 2008. "Bicycle Patrols: An Underutilized Resource." *Policing: An International Journal of Police Strategies & Management* 31, no. 1: 93–108.

54. Ratcliffe, J.H., T. Taniguchi, E.R. Goff, and J. Wood. 2011. "The Philadelphia Foot Patrol Experiment: A Randomized Controlled Trial of Police Patrol Effectiveness in Violent Crime Hotspots." *Criminology* 49, no. 3: 795–831.

55. D. Lilley and S. Hindjua. 2006. "Officer Evaluation in the Community Policing Context." *Policing* 29, no. 1: 19–37.

56. S. Mertl. 2013. "Privacy, Intrusion Issues Dog Rollout of Unmanned Drones by Police." *Dailey Brew*, November 12.

349

Accessed February 27, 2014. http://ca.news.yahoo.com/blogs/dailybrew/privacy-intrusion-issues-dog-rollout-unmanned-drones-police-215353890.html.

57. G. Guma. 2013. "Drones and Law Enforcement in America: The Unmanned Police Surveillance State." Global Research, April 12. Accessed February 27, 2014. http://www.globalresearch.ca/drones-and-law-enforcement-in-america-the-unmanned-police-surveillance-state/5330984.

58. J. Bronskill. 2013. "Study Urges Privacy Policy before Widespread Use of Drones." *Canadian Press*, November 12. Accessed February 27, 2014. http://www.metronews.ca/news/canada/851618/study-urges-privacy-policy-before-widespread-use-of-drones/.

59. A. Cavoukian. 2012. *Privacy and Drones: Unmanned Aerial Vehicles*. Ottawa: Information and Privacy Commissioner. http://www.ipc.on.ca/images/Resources/pbd-drones.pdf.

60. C. Parsons and A. Molnar. 2013. *Watching Below: Dimensions of Surveillance by UAVs*. Toronto: Block G Privacy and Security Consulting.

61. P. Henningsen. 2013. "Police State USA. Glimmer of Hope: Citizens Force Seattle to Scrap Police Drones." Global Research, February 10. Accessed February 27, 2014. http://www.globalresearch.ca/police-state-usa-glimmer-of-hope-citizens-force-seattle-to-scrap-police-drones/5322552?print=1.

62. N. Robertson. 2012. "Policing: Fundamental Principles in a Canadian Context," *Canadian Public Administration* 55, no. 3: 343–63.

63. P.-P. Pare, R. Felson, and M. Ouimet. 2007. "Community Variation in Crime Clearance: A Multilevel Analysis with Comments on Assessing Police Performance." *Journal of Quantitative Criminology* 23, no. 3: 243–58.

64. T.I. Gabor. 2003. *Assessing the Effectiveness of Organized Crime Control Strategies: A Review of the Literature*. Ottawa: Department of Justice Canada, 6. http://www.justice.gc.ca/eng/rp-pr/csj-sjc/jsp-sjp/rr05_5/rr05_5.pdf.

65. R.T. Guerette. 2009. *Analyzing Crime Displacement and Diffusion*. Washington, D.C.: U.S. Department of Justice, Office of Community Oriented Policing Services. http://www.popcenter.org/tools//displacement/print/.

66. J. Austin and M.P. Jacobson. 2013. *How New York City Reduced Mass Incarceration: A Model for Change?* New York: Brennan Center for Justice and the Vera Institute of Justice. http://www.brennancenter.org/sites/default/files/publications/How_NYC_Reduced_Mass_Incarceration.pdf.

67. J. Tierney. 2013. "Prison Population Can Shrink When Police Crowd Streets." *The New York Times*, January 25, 3. Accessed February 27, 2014. http://www.nytimes.com/2013/01/26/nyregion/police-have-done-more-than-prisons-to-cut-crime-in-new-york.html?pagewanted=all.

68. Ibid.

69. P. Heaton and B.A. Jackson. 2012. "Short-Term Savings, Long-Term Losses: When Police Departments Respond to Economic Pressure by Cutting Their Forces." Rand Corporation, November 12. Accessed February 27, 2014. http://www.rand.org/blog/2012/11/short-term-savings-long-term-losses-when-police-departments.html.

70. C.T. Griffiths and D. Murdoch. 2014. *Canadian Corrections*. 4th ed. Toronto: Nelson.

71. F. Wilson-Bates. 2008. *Lost in Transition: How a Lack of Capacity in the Mental Health System Is Failing Vancouver's Mentally Ill and Draining Police Resources*. Vancouver: Vancouver Police Department. https://vancouver.ca/police/assets/pdf/reports-policies/vpd-lost-in-transition.pdf.

72. M. Ibrahim. 2013. "Police Stuck 'Babysitting' in Hospitals, Chief Says." *Edmonton Journal*, August 21. Accessed February 27, 2014. http://www2.canada.com/edmontonjournal/news/story.html?id=91c06643-2f41-4735-bf75-9fb8e42893f6.

73. Vancouver Police Department. 2013. *Vancouver's Mental Health Crisis: An Update Report*. Vancouver: Author. http://vancouver.ca/police/assets/pdf/reports-policies/mental-health-crisis.pdf.

74. R.S. Engel and E. Silver. 2001. "Policing Mentally Disordered Suspects: A Reexamination of the Criminalization Hypothesis." *Criminology* 39, no. 2: 225–52.

75. D. Cotton. 2004. "The Attitudes of Canadian Police Officers toward the Mentally Ill." *International Journal of Law and Psychiatry* 27, no. 2: 135–46.

76. D. Cotton and T.G. Coleman. 2010. "Canadian Police Agencies and Their Interactions with Persons with a Mental Illness: A Systems Approach." *Police Practice and Research* 11, no. 4: 301–14.

77. J.D. Livingston, C. Weaver, N. Hall, and S. Verdun-Jones. 2008. *Criminal Justice Diversion for Persons for Mental Disorders. A Review of Best Practices*. Vancouver: The Law Foundation of British Columbia, B.C. Mental Health &. Addiction Services, Canadian Mental Health. Association BC Division. http://www.cmha.bc.ca/files/DiversionBestPractices.pdf.

78. S. Franz and R. Borum. 2010. "Crisis Intervention Teams May Prevent Arrests of People with Mental Illness." *Police Practice and Research* 12, no. 3: 265–72.

79. P. Roth. 2013. "Edmonton Police Using Less Force with the Mentally Ill After University of Alberta Course." *Edmonton Sun*, March 18. Accessed February 27, 2014. http://www.edmontonsun.com/2013/03/18/edmonton-police-using-less-force-with-the-mentally-ill-after-university-of-alberta-course.

80. S. Kisely, L.A. Campbell, S. Peddle, S. Hare, M. Psyche, D. Spicer, and B. Moore. 2010. "A Controlled Before-and-After Evaluation of a Mobile Crisis Partnership Between Mental Health and Police Services in Nova Scotia." *Canadian Journal of Psychiatry* 55, no. 10: 662–68.

81. Vancouver Police Department. 2011. *The Tragedy of Missing and Murdered Aboriginal Women in Canada. We Can Do Better. A Position Paper by the Sisterwatch Project of the Vancouver Police Department and the Women's Memorial March Committee*. Vancouver: Author. https://vancouver.ca/police/assets/pdf/reports-policies/missing-murdered-aboriginal-women-canada-report.pdf.

82. Human Rights Watch. 2013, 7. "Those Who Take Us Away. Abusive Policing and Failures in Protection of Indigenous Women and Girls in Northern British Columbia, Canada." http://www.hrw.org/reports/2013/02/13/those-who-take-us-away.

83. Ibid.

84. D. LePard. 2010. *Missing Women Investigation Review. Summary Report.* Vancouver: Vancouver Police Department. http://vancouver.ca/police/media/2010/mw-summary-report.pdf.

85. The Honourable W.T. Oppal (Commissioner). 2012. "Executive Summary." *Forsaken: The Report of the Missing Women Commission of Inquiry.* Victoria: Minister of Justice and Attorney. Gen. of British Columbia. http://www.ag.gov.bc.ca/public_inquiries/docs/Forsaken-ES.pdf.

CHAPTER 7

1. J. Boyce. 2013. "Adult Criminal Court Statistics in Canada, 2011/2012." *Juristat.* Accessed March 1, 2014. http://www.statcan.gc.ca/pub/85-002-x/2013001/article/11804-eng.pdf.

2. J. Boyce. 2013. "Adult Criminal Court Statistics in Canada, 2011/2012." *Juristat,* 5. Accessed March 1, 2014. http://www.statcan.gc.ca/pub/85-002-x/2013001/article/11804-eng.pdf.

3. J. Boyce. 2013. "Adult Criminal Court Statistics in Canada, 2011/2012." *Juristat,* 8. Accessed March 1, 2014. http://www.statcan.gc.ca/pub/85-002-x/2013001/article/11804-eng.pdf.

4. C.M. Webster and A.N. Doob. 2003. "The Superior/Provincial Court Distinction: Historical Anachronism or Empirical Reality?" *Criminal Law Quarterly* 48, no. 1: 77–109.

5. J. Weekes, R. Mugford, G. Bourgon, and S. Price. 2007. *Drug Treatment Courts: FAQs.* Ottawa: Canadian Centre on Substance Abuse. Accessed March 1, 2014. http://sentencing.nj.gov/downloads/pdf/articles/2007/Feb2007/document01.pdf.

6. R. Porter, M. Rempel, and A. Mansky. 2010. *What Makes a Court Problem-Solving?: Universal Performance Indicators for Problem-Solving Justice.* Washington, D.C.: Center for Court Innovation. http://www.courtinnovation.org/sites/default/files/What_Makes_A_Court_P_S.pdf.

7. R. Saner. 2010. *Community Perceptions of Red Hook, Brooklyn: Views of Quality of Life, Safety, and Services.* New York: Center for Court Innovation. http://www.courtinnovation.org/sites/default/files/Community_Perceptions.pdf.

8. A.J. Lurigio and J. Snowden. 2009. "Putting Therapeutic Jurisprudence into Practice: The Growth, Operations, and Effectiveness of Mental Health Court." *Justice System Journal* 30, no. 2: 196–218.

9. F. Sirotich. 2009. "The Criminal Justice Outcomes of Jail Diversion Programs for Persons with Mental Illness: A Review of the Evidence." *Journal of the American Academy of Psychiatry and Law* 37, no. 4: 461–72.

10. E. Slinger and R. Roesch. 2010. "Problem-Solving Courts in Canada: A Review and a Call for Empirically Based Evaluation Methods." *International Journal of Law and Psychiatry* 33, no. 4: 260.

11. P. Allard, T. Lyons, and R. Elliott. 2011. *Impaired Judgment: Assessing the Appropriateness of Drug Treatment Courts as a Response to Drug Use in Canada,* Toronto: Canadian HIV/AIDS Legal Network. http://www.aidslaw.ca/publications/interfaces/downloadFile.php?ref=2034.

12. N. Bakht. 2005. "Problem Solving Courts as Agents of Change." *Criminal Law Quarterly* 50, no. 3: 12–38.

13. Edmonton Drug Treatment and Community Restoration Court. 2014. "The Court Team." Accessed March 1. http://www.edtcrc.ca/pages/The_Program/The_Court_Team.aspx.

14. J.P. Hornick, K. Kluz, and L.D. Bertrand. 2011. *An Evaluation of Yukon's Community Wellness Court.* Whitehorse: Yukon Justice. http://www.yukoncourts.ca/pdf/cwc_final_report_05-10-11.pdf.

15. A.J. Lurigio and J. Snowden. 2009. "Putting Therapeutic Jurisprudence into Practice: The Growth, Operations, and Effectiveness of Mental Health Court." *Justice System Journal* 30, no. 2: 207.

16. B. Newton-Taylor, L. Gliksman, and J. Patra. 2009. "Toronto Drug Treatment Court: Participant Intake Characteristics as Predictors of 'Successful' Program Completion." *Journal of Drug Issues* 39, no. 4: 965–88.

17. Department of Justice Canada. 2009. "Drug Treatment Court Funding Program Summative Evaluation. Final Report." Accessed March 1, 2014. http://www.justice.gc.ca/eng/rp-pr/cp-pm/eval/rep-rap/09/dtcfp-pfttt/P2.html.

18. A. Verhaaff. 2011. "Individual Factors Predicting Mental Health Court Diversion Outcome." MA thesis, University of Ontario Institute of Technology. Accessed March 1, 2014. https://ir.library.dc-uoit.ca/bitstream/10155/164/1/Verhaaff_Ashley.pdf.

19. L. Gutierrez and G. Bourgon. 2009. "Drug Treatment Courts: A Quantitative Review of Study and Treatment Quality." Accessed March 1, 2014. http://www.publicsafety.gc.ca/cnt/rsrcs/pblctns/2009-04-dtc/.

20. C.T. Lowenkamp, J. Pealer, P. Smith, and E.J. Latessa. 2006. "Adhering to the Risk and Needs Principles: Does It Matter for Supervision-Based Programs?" *Federal Probation* 70, no. 3: 3–8.

21. British Columbia Ministry of Attorney General and Ministry of Public Safety and Solicitor General. 2010. *Downtown Community Court in Vancouver. Interim Evaluation Report.* Victoria: Author. http://www.criminaljusticereform.gov.bc.ca/en/reports/pdf/interimevaluation.pdf.

22. S. Lange, J. Rehm, and S. Popova. 2011. "The Effectiveness of Criminal Justice Diversion Initiatives in North America: A Systematic Literature Review," *International Journal of Forensic Mental Health* 10, no. 3: 2–14.

23. C.M. Sarteschi, M.G. Vaughn, and K. Kim. 2011. "Assessing the Effectiveness of Mental Health Courts: A Quantitative Review." *Journal of Criminal Justice* 39, no. 1, 12–20.

24. D.E. McNiel and R.L. Binder. 2010. "Stakeholder Views of a Mental Health Court." *International Journal of Law and Psychiatry* 33, no. 4: 227–35.

25. C. Mitton, L. Simpson, L. Gardner, F. Barnes, and G. McDougall. 2007. "Calgary Diversion Program: A Community-Based

351

Alternative to Incarceration for Mentally Ill Offenders." *Journal of Mental Health Policy Economics* 10, no. 3: 145–51. http://www.ncbi.nlm.nih.gov/pubmed/17890831.

26. Public Safety Canada. 2007. "Toronto Drug Treatment Court Project." Accessed March 1, 2014. http://www.publicsafety.gc.ca/cnt/rsrcs/pblctns/drgtrtmnt-trnt/index-eng.aspx.

27. B. Newton-Taylor, L. Gliksman, and J. Patra. 2009. "Toronto Drug Treatment Court: Participant Intake Characteristics as Predictors of 'Successful' Program Completion." *Journal of Drug Issues* 39, no. 4: 965–88.

28. M.W. Finigan, S.M. Carey, and A. Cox. 2007. *Impact of a Mature Drug Court Over 10 Years of Operation: Recidivism and Costs*. Washington, D.C.: U.S. Department of Justice, National Institute of Justice. http://www.ncjrs.gov/pdffiles1/nij/grants/219224.pdf.

29. P. Allard, T. Lyons, and R. Elliott. 2011. *Impaired Judgment: Assessing the Appropriateness of Drug Treatment Courts as a Response to Drug Use in Canada*, Toronto: Canadian HIV/AIDS Legal Network. http://www.aidslaw.ca/publications/interfaces/downloadFile.php?ref=2034.

30. British Columbia Ministry of Attorney General and Ministry of Public Safety and Solicitor General. 2010. *Downtown Community Court in Vancouver. Interim Evaluation Report*. Victoria: Author. http://www.criminaljusticereform.gov.bc.ca/en/reports/pdf/interimevaluation.pdf.

31. J.M. Somers, A. Moniruzzaman, S.N. Rezansoff, and M. Patterson. 2014. "Examining the Impact of Case Management in Vancouver's Downtown Community Court: A Quasi-Experimental Design." *PLoS ONE* 9(3): e90708. doi:10.1371/journal.pone.0090708.

32. British Columbia Ministry of Justice. 2013. *Downtown Community Court in Vancouver: Efficiency Evaluation*. Victoria: Author. Accessed March 21, 2014. http://www.criminaljusticereform.gov.bc.ca/en/reports/pdf/DCCEfficiency_Evaluation.pdf.

33. Campbell Research Associates. 2008. *Evaluation of the Aboriginal Legal Services of Toronto Gladue Caseworker Program. Year Three October 2006–September 2007*. Mississauga: Author. http://www.aboriginallegal.ca/docs/Year_3.pdf.

34. P. de Jong. 2003. *Legal Service Provision in Northern Canada: Summary of Research in the Northwest Territories, Nunavut, and the Yukon*. Ottawa: Department of Justice Canada. http://www.justice.gc.ca/eng/rp-pr/aj-ja/rr03_la15-rr03_aj15/rr03_la15.pdf.

35. L. Hausegger, M. Hennigar, and T. Riddell. 2009. *Canadian Courts: Law, Politics, and Process*. Toronto: Oxford University Press, 104.

36. L. Hausegger, M. Hennigar, and T. Riddell. 2009. *Canadian Courts: Law, Politics, and Process*. Toronto: Oxford University Press, 105.

37. K. Makin. 2009. "Two-Thirds Back Electing Judges." *The Globe and Mail*, March 31. Accessed March 2, 2014. http://www.theglobeandmail.com/news/national/two-thirds-back-electing-judges/article1073476/.

38. J. Tibbetts. 2009. "Federal Court Quashes Security Certificate Against Hassan Almrei." *Vancouver Sun*, December 14. Access March 1, 2014. http://www2.canada.com/story.html?id=2338927.

39. K. Makin. 2013. "Supreme Court Needs More Women, Departing Judge Says." *The Globe and Mail*, February 2. Accessed March 1, 2014. http://www.theglobeandmail.com/news/national/supreme+-court-needs-more-women-departing-judge-says/article8149711/.

40. D. Small. 2012. "Canada's High Court Unchains Injection Drug Users; Implications for Harm Reduction as Standard of Health Care." *Harm Reduction Journal* 9, no. 1: 34.

41. J. Eisenstein and H. Jacobs. 1991. *Felony Justice*. Lanham, MD: University Press in America.

42. K.M. Campbell. 2011. "Expert Evidence from 'Social' Scientists: The Importance of Context and the Impact on Miscarriages of Justice." *Canadian Criminal Law Review* 16, no. 1: 34.

43. Canadian Superior Court Judges Association. 2013. "The Role of the Judge." Accessed March 1, 2014. http://www.cscja-acjcs.ca/role_of_judge-en.asp?l=5.

44. Ontario Attorney General. 2005. *Role of the Crown Counsel. Preamble to the Crown Policy Manual*. Toronto: Author. http://www.attorneygeneral.jus.gov.on.ca/english/crim/cpm/2005/CPMPreamble.pdf.

45. Department of Justice Canada. 2013a. "A Crime Victim's Guide to the Criminal Justice System." Accessed March 1, 2014. http://www.justice.gc.ca/eng/rp-pr/cj-jp/victim/guide/seco.html.

46. Public Prosecution Service of Canada. 2013. "Annual Report, 2012–2013." Accessed March 1, 2014. http://www.ppsc-sppc.gc.ca/eng/pub/ar-ra/2012_2013/index.html.

47. L. Millan. 2012. "Government Lawyers Buckling under Workloads." *Lawyers Weekly*, September 28. Accessed March 1, 2014. http://www.lawyersweekly.ca/index.php?section=article&articleid=1749.

48. J. Eisenstein and H. Jacobs. 1991. *Felony Justice*. Lanham, MD: University Press in America.

49. L. Hausegger, M. Hennigar, and T. Riddell. 2009. *Canadian Courts: Law, Politics, and Process*. Toronto: Oxford University Press, 145.

50. J. Makarenko. 2007. "Supreme Court of Canada Appointment Process." *Maple Leaf Web*, February 1. Accessed March 1, 2014. http://mapleleafweb.com/features/supreme-court-canada-appointment-process.

51. S. Fine. 2013. "Harper's Nomination Continues Supreme Court's Shift to the Right," *The Globe and Mail*, September 30. Accessed March 1, 2014. http://www.theglobeandmail.com/news/national/harper-nominates-marc-random-for-supreme-court/article14602137/.

52. A. Boughner. 2012. "Mixing Justice and Politics: Cabinet Members Allowed to Be Appointed as Judges." Care2 Causes, August 14. Accessed March 1, 2014. http://www.care2.com/causes/mixing-justice-and-politics-cabinet-members-allowed-to-be-appointed-as-judges.html.

53. C. Forcese and A. Freeman. 2005. *The Laws of Government: The Legal Foundations of Canadian Democracy*. Toronto: Irwin Law.

54. J. Russell. 2013. "Appointment of Judges Politically Biased in Alberta, Critics Say." *CBC News*, July 25. Accessed March 1, 2014. http://www.cbc.ca/news/canada/edmonton/appointment-of-judges-politically-biased-in-alberta-critics-say-1.1387789.

55. Ibid.

56. K. Makin. 2012. "Of 100 New Federally Appointed Judges 98 Are White, Globe Finds," *The Globe and Mail*, September 6. Accessed March 1, 2014. http://www.theglobeandmail.com/news/politics/of-100-new-federally-appointed-judges-98-are-white-globe-finds/article4101504/.

57. K. Makin. 2013. "Supreme Court Needs More Women, Departing Judge Says." *The Globe and Mail*, February 2, 2. Accessed March 1, 2014. http://www.theglobeandmail.com/news/national/supreme+-court-needs-more-women-departing-judge-says/article8149711/.

58. K. Makin. 2012. "Of 100 New Federally Appointed Judges 98 Are White, Globe Finds," *The Globe and Mail*, September 6, 1. Accessed March 1, 2014. http://www.theglobeandmail.com/news/politics/of-100-new-federally-appointed-judges-98-are-white-globe-finds/article4101504/.

59. Ibid.

60. K. Makin. 2013. "Supreme Court Needs More Women, Departing Judge Says." *The Globe and Mail*, February 2. Accessed March 1, 2014. http://www.theglobeandmail.com/news/national/supreme+-court-needs-more-women-departing-judge-says/article8149711/.

61. S. Lange, J. Rehm, and S. Popova. 2011. "The Effectiveness of Criminal Justice Diversion Initiatives in North America: A Systematic Literature Review," *International Journal of Forensic Mental Health* 10, no. 3: 2.

62. S.J. Choi, G. Mitu Gulati, and E.A. Posner. 2007. "Professional or Politicians: The Uncertain Empirical Case for an Elected Rather than Appointed Judiciary." *Journal of Law, Economics, & Organization* 26, no. 2: 290–336.

63. M. Iaryczower, G. Lewis, and M. Shum. 2013. "To Elect or to Appoint? Bias, Information, and Responsiveness of Bureaucrats and Politicians." *Journal of Public Economics* 97, 230–44.

64. Department of Justice Canada. 2013c. "A Crime Victim's Guide to the Criminal Justice System: Publication Bans. Accessed March 7, 2014. http://www.justice.gc.ca/eng/rp-pr/cj-jp/victim/guide/secf.html#id_2.

65. Ontario Court of Justice. 2014. "Principles of Judicial Office." Accessed March 1. http://www.ontariocourts.ca/ocj/ojc/principles-of-judicial-office/.

66. Canadian Judicial Council. 1998. *Ethical Principles for Judges*. Ottawa: Author. http://www.cjc-ccm.gc.ca/cmslib/general/news_pub_judicialconduct_Principles_en.pdf.

67. Ibid., 13.

68. Ibid.

69. Ontario Judicial Council. 2011. *Sixteenth Annual Report, 2010–2011*. Toronto: Author. http://www.ontariocourts.ca/ocj/files/annualreport/ojc/2010-2011-EN.pdf.

70. Manitoba Courts. 2014. "What to Do If You Have a Complaint about a Judge of the Provincial Court of Manitoba." Accessed March 1. http://www.manitobacourts.mb.ca/complaints/complaint_judge_pr.html.

71. Canadian Judicial Council. 2011. "Canadian Judicial Council Completes Its Review of Complaints Made Against Justice Robert Dewar." *News Release*, November 9. Accessed March 1, 2014. https://www.cjc-ccm.gc.ca/english/news_en.asp?selMenu=news_2011_1109_en.asp.

72. L. Chwialkowska. 2002. "Firing of Judge Who Insulted Acadians." *National Post*, February 8, A4.

73. R.F. Devlin and P. Heffernan. 2008. "The End(s) of Self Regulation? *Alberta Law Review* 45, no. 5: 169–213.

74. L. Finch, R. Bauman, and T. Crabtree. 2012. "Judicial Independence (And What Everyone Should Know About It)." Vancouver: Chief Justices of British Columbia Courts, 1. http://www.courts.gov.bc.ca/about_the_courts/Judicial%20Independence%20Final%20Release.pdf.

75. The Hon. J.C. Bouck. 2009. "Television Cameras in Canadian Trial Courtrooms." *Boucks Law Blog*, February 16. http://bouckslawblog.typepad.com/bouckslawblog/page/4/.

76. L. Finch, R. Bauman, and T. Crabtree. 2012. "Judicial Independence (And What Everyone Should Know About It)." Vancouver: Chief Justices of British Columbia Courts, 4. http://www.courts.gov.bc.ca/about_the_courts/Judicial%20Independence%20Final%20Release.pdf.

77. "Complaint against N.S. Judge Partly Founded." 2011. *Canadian Press,* January 13, 1. Accessed March 1, 2014. http://www.cbc.ca/news/canada/nova-scotia/complaint-against-n-s-judge-partly-founded-1.991228.

78. Department of Justice Canada. 2013b. "Nova Scotia Judicial Appointments Announced." Accessed March 1, 2014. http://www.justice.gc.ca/eng/news-nouv/ja-nj/2013/doc_32968.html.

CHAPTER 8

1. Public Prosecution Service of Canada. 2013, 1. "Annual Report, 2012–2013." Accessed March 3, 2014. http://www.ppsc-sppc.gc.ca/eng/pub/ar-ra/2012_2013/index.html.

2. Public Prosecution Service of Canada. 2013, 2. "Annual Report, 2012–2013." Accessed March 3, 2014. http://www.ppsc-sppc.gc.ca/eng/pub/ar-ra/2012_2013/index.html.

3. I. Gomme and M.P. Hall. 1995. "Prosecutors at Work: Role Overload and Strain." *Journal of Criminal Justice* 23, no. 2: 194.

4. D. Layton. 2002. "The Prosecutorial Charging Decision." *Criminal Law Quarterly* 46, no. 1/2: 447–82.

5. Y. Dandurand. 2009. *Addressing Inefficiencies in the Criminal Justice Process. Vancouver: International Centre for Criminal Law Reform and Criminal Justice Policy. A Preliminary Review*. Vancouver: International Centre for Criminal Law Reform and Criminal Justice Policy. http://www.criminaljusticereform.gov.bc.ca/en/reports/pdf/InefficienciesPreliminaryReport.pdf.

6. L. Hausegger, M. Hennigar, and T. Riddell. 2009. *Canadian Courts: Law, Politics, and Process*. Toronto: Oxford University Press, 290.

7. G. Kellough and S. Wortley, 2002. "Remand for Plea: Bail Decisions and Plea Bargaining as Commensurate Decisions." *British Journal of Criminology* 42:186–210.

8. John Howard Society of Ontario. 2013. *Reasonable Bail?* Toronto: Author. http://johnhoward.on.ca/pdfs/Reasonable%20Bail%20-%20JHSO%20Report%202013%20final.pdf.

9. J.B. Sprott and N.M. Myers. 2011. "Set Up to Fail: The Unintended Consequences of Multiple Bail Conditions." *Canadian Journal of Criminology and Criminal Justice* 53, no. 4: 404–23.

10. G. Zochodne. 2013. "Free, But for How Long? The City That Never Fails to 'Fail to Comply.'" *The Oshawa Express*, August 27. Accessed March 3, 2014. http://www.oshawaexpress.ca/viewposting.php?view=5198.

11. "Bail and Violence Against Women: Michael Enright Talks to Elizabeth Sheehy and James Morton." 2013. *Sunday Edition*, January 27. Accessed March 2, 2014. http://www.cbc.ca/thesundayedition/shows/2013/01/27/violence-against-women-and-bail/.

12. M.F. McLellan. 2010. "Bail and the Diminishing Presumption of Innocence." *Canadian Criminal Law Review* 15, no. 1: 57–74.

13. N.M. Myers. 2009. "Shifting Risk: Bail and the Use of Sureties." *Current Issues in Criminal Justice* 21, no. 1: 127–47.

14. John Howard Society of Ontario. 2013. *Reasonable Bail?* Toronto: Author, 3. http://johnhoward.on.ca/pdfs/Reasonable%20Bail%20-%20JHSO%20Report%202013%20final.pdf.

15. R. Gartner, C.M. Webster, and A.N. Doob. 2009. "Trends in the Imprisonment of Women in Canada." *Canadian Journal of Criminology and Criminal Justice* 51, no. 2: 169–98.

16. P. De Jong. 2003. *Legal Service Provision in Northern Canada: Summary of Research in the Northwest Territories, Nunavut, and the Yukon*. Ottawa: Department of Justice. http://www.justice.gc.ca/eng/rp-pr/aj-ja/rr03_la15-rr03_aj15.rr03_la15.pdf.

17. S. Friedman. 2013. "Right to Know: Legal Aid Off Limits to All But the Poorest." *Ottawa Citizen*, April 20. Accessed March 3, 2014. http://www.affordabledefence.com/archives/right-to-know-legal-aid-off-limits-to-all-but-the-poorest/.

18. M.A. MacInnes. 2013. "The Crisis in Legal Aid Hurts Some Canadians More Than Others." Accessed March 3, 2014. http://www.cba.org/CBA/Advocacy/legalaid/PrintHTML.aspx?DocId=15267.

19. C. Ruby. 2011. "The Shame of Legal Aid Ontario." *Lawyers Weekly* 30, no. 39. Accessed March 3, 2014. http://www.lawyersweekly.ca/index.php?section=article&volume=30&number=39&article=3.

20. S.N. Verdun-Jones. 2011. *Criminal Law in Canada. Cases, Questions and the Code*. Toronto: Nelson, 185.

21. Law Reform Commission of Canada. 1975. *Criminal Procedure: Control of the Process, Working Paper 15*. Ottawa: Information Canada, 46, 48. http://www.lareau-law.ca/LRCWP15.pdf.

22. S. Verdun-Jones. 2012. "Plea Bargaining." In *Criminal Justice in Canada: A Reader*. 4th ed., edited by J.D. Roberts and M.G. Gorssman, 166. Toronto: Nelson.

23. K. Makin. 2003. "In the Back Halls of Justice." *The Globe and Mail*, April 26, F6.

24. S.N. Verdun-Jones and A.A. Tijerino. 2005. "Victim Participation in the Plea Negotiation Process: An Idea Whose Time Has Come?" *Criminal Law Quarterly* 50, no. 1/2: 190–212.

25. K. Makin. 2003. "In the Back Halls of Justice." *The Globe and Mail*, April 26, F6.

26. L. Hausegger, M. Hennigar, and T. Riddell. 2009. *Canadian Courts: Law, Politics, and Process*. Toronto: Oxford University Press, 293.

27. M. Sinha. 2009. "An Investigation into the Feasibility of Collecting Data on the Involvement of Adults and Youth with Mental Health Issues in the Criminal Justice System." Accessed March 3, 2014. http://www.statcan.gc.ca/pub/85-561-m/85-561-m2009016-eng.htm.

28. S.N. Verdun-Jones. 2011. *Criminal Law in Canada. Cases, Questions and the Code*. Toronto: Nelson, 185.

29. J. Turner. 2013. "Greyhound Bus Killer Vince Li Gets Freedom to Travel to Winnipeg, Beaches," *Winnipeg Sun*, May 17. Accessed March 3, 2014. http://www.winnipegsun.com/2013/05/17/greyhound-bus-killer-vince-li-gets-freedom-to-travel-to-winnipeg-beaches.

30. K. Annable. 2014. "Bus Beheader Vince Li Granted Unescorted Trips to Selkirk." *Winnipeg Sun*, February 28. Accessed March 8, 2014. http://www.winnipegsun.com/2014/02/27/bus-beheader-vince-li-granted-unescorted-trips-to-selkirk.

31. Canadian Press. 2014. "Vince Li Decision Sparks War of Words Between Manitoba, Ottawa." *CBC News*, March 1. Accessed March 8, 2014. http://www.cbc.ca/news/canada/manitoba/vince-li-decision-sparks-war-of-words-between-manitoba-ottawa-1.2556328.

32. S.N. Verdun-Jones. 2011. *Criminal Law in Canada. Cases, Questions and the Code*. Toronto: Nelson.

33. K.-L. Tang. 2003. "Battered Women Syndrome Testimony in Canada: Its Development and Lingering Issues." *International Journal of Offender Therapy and Comparative Criminology* 4, no. 6: 618–29.

34. S. Boesveld. 2011. "Unbalanced Jury Pool Stalls Trial." *National Post*, March 17, A10.

35. F. Iacobucci (The Honourable). 2013. *First Nations Representation on Ontario Juries. Report of the Independent Review Conducted by the Honourable Frank Iacobucci*. Toronto: Government of Ontario. http://www.attorneygeneral.jus.gov.on.ca/english/about/pubs/iacobucci/pdf/First_Nations_Representation_Ontario_Juries.pdf.

36. C. Perkel. 2013. "Manslaughter Conviction Tossed Over Lack of Aboriginals on Ontario Juries." *National Post*, June 13. Access March 3, 2014. http://news.nationalpost.com/2013/06/14/manslaughter-conviction-tossed-over-lack-of-aboriginals-on-ontario-juries/.

37. R.L. Wiener, D.A. Krauss, and J.D. Lieberman. 2011. "Mock Jury Research: Where Do We Go From Here?" *Behavioral Sciences and the Law* 29, no. 3: 467–79.

38. H.M. Hosch, S.E. Culhane, V.A. Tubb, and E.A. Granillo. 2011. "Town vs. Gown: A Direct Comparison of Community Residents and Student Mock Jurors." *Behavioral Sciences and the Law* 29, no. 3: 452–66.

39. S.R. Keller and R.L. Wiener. 2011. "What Are We Studying? Student Jurors, Community Jurors, and Construct Validity." *Behavioral Sciences and the Law* 29, no. 3: 376–94.

40. B.P. Hrycan. 2006. "The Myth of Trial by Jury." *Criminal Law Quarterly* 51, no. 2: 157–68.

41. S. Simon. 2011. "Limited Diagnosticity of Criminal Trials." *Vanderbilt Law Review* 64, no. 1: 214.

42. Y. Tinsley. 2001. "Juror Decision-Making: A Look Inside the Jury Room." In *The British Criminology Conference: Selected Proceedings, Volume 4—Papers from the British Society of Criminology Conference, Leicester, July 2000,* edited R. Tarling. Accessed March 3, 2014. http://britsoccrim.org/volume4/004.pdf.

43. D.E. Shelton, Y.S. Kim, and G. Barak. 2006. "A Study of Juror Expectations and Demands Concerning Scientific Evidence: Does the 'CSI Effect' Exist?" *Vanderbilt Journal of Entertainment & Technology Law* 9, no. 2: 331–68.

44. D.J. Devine, L.D. Clayton, B.B. Dunford, R. Seying, and J. Pryce. 2000. "Jury Decision Making: 45 Years of Empirical Research on Deliberating Groups." *Psychology, Public Policy, and Law* 7, no. 3: 622–727.

45. S. Mulrain. 2013. "R. v. N.S.—Redux." *Davis LLP Litigation and Dispute Resolution Blog,* May 3. Accessed March 8, 2014. http://www.davis.ca/en/dntry/litigation/r-v-ns-redux.

46. M.H. Ogilvie. 2013. "Niqabs in Canadian Courts: R v NS." *Ecclesiastical Law Journal* 15, no. 3: 334–43.

47. "Muslim Woman Will Not Testify After Being Told She Must Remove Face Veil." 2014. *Guardian,* January 27. Accessed March 8, 2014. http://www.theguardian.com/uk-news/2014/jan/27/muslim-woman-face-veil-court-trial-witness.

48. R. Camber. 2012. "Muslim Juror Who Refused to Take Veil Off Is Ordered to Stand Down by Judge Because He Wouldn't Be Able to See Her Facial Expressions. *Daily Mail,* March 19. Accessed March 8, 2014. http://www.dailymail.co.uk/news/article-2117310/Veiled-Muslim-juror-asked-stand-judge-wouldn-t-able-facial-expressions.html.

49. P.J. LeSage (The Honourable), and M. Code. 2008. *Report of the Review of Large and Complex Criminal Case Procedures.* Toronto: Attorney General of Ontario. http://www.attorneygeneral.jus.gov.on.ca/english/about/pubs/lesage_code/lesage_code_report_en.pdf.

50. J. Boyce. 2013. "Adult Criminal Court Statistics in Canada, 2011/2012." *Juristat,* 16. Accessed March 2, 2014. http://www.statcan.gc.ca/pub/85-002-x/2013001/article/11804-eng.pdf.

51. D.C. Cowper (Chair). 2012. *A Criminal Justice System for the 21st Century: Final Report to the Minister of Justice and Attorney General Honourable Shirley Bond.* Victoria: BC Justice Reform Initiative, 4. http://www.ag.gov.bc.ca//public/justice-reform/pdf/CowperFinalReport.pdf.

52. A. Humphreys. 2013. "'The System is Sick': Canada's Courts are Choking on an Increase in Evidence." *National Post,* May 3. Accessed March 3, 2014. http://news.nationalpost.com/2013/05/03/canadas-courts-are-choking-on-an-increase-in-evidence/.

53. C.M. Webster. 2009. "Out of Sight, Out of Mind: A Case Study of Bail Efficiency in an Ontario Video Remand Court." *Current Issues in Criminal Justice* 21, no. 1: 103–26.

54. "31 Hells Angels-linked Drug Cases Dropped in Quebec." 2011. *CBC News,* May 31. Accessed March 2, 2014. http://www.cbc.ca/news/canada/montreal/31-hells-angels-linked-drug-cases-dropped-in-que-1.1087912.

55. K. Bolan. 2013. "Nanaimo Hells Angel Sees Criminal Charges Stayed After Court Delays." *Vancouver Sun,* June 4. Accessed March 2, 2014. http://www.vancouversun.com/news/Nanaimo+Hells+Angel+sees+criminal+charges+stayed+after+court/8477653/story.html.

56. K.M. Campbell and M.S. Denov. 2004. "Wrongful Conviction: Perspectives, Experiences and Implications for Justice." *Canadian Journal of Criminology and Criminal Justice,* Special Issue, 46, no. 2: 101–208.

57. R. Bajer, M. Trepanier, E. Campbell, D. LePard, N. Mahaffy, J. Robinson, and D. Stewart. 2007. *Wrongful Convictions in Canada.* Vancouver: International Society for Reform of the Criminal Law. http://www.millerthomson.com/assets/files/article_attachments/Wrongful_Convictions_in_Canada.pdf.

58. S. Bindman and M. Nethery (Co-chairs). 2011. "The Path to Justice: Preventing Wrongful Convictions. Report of the Federal/Provincial/Territorial Heads of Prosecutions' Subcommittee on the Prevention of Wrongful Convictions." Accessed March 3, 2014. http://www.ppsc-sppc.gc.ca/eng/pub/ptj-spj/.

59. G.L. Wells, A. Memmon, and S.D. Penrod. 2006. "Eyewitness Evidence. Improving Its Probative Value." *Psychological Science in the Public Interest* 7, no. 2: 45–75.

60. Department of Justice Canada. 2014. "Criminal Conviction Review." Accessed March 2. http://canada.justice.gc.ca/eng/cj-jp/ccr-rc/index.html.

61. The Honourable T.A. Hickman. 1986. *Royal Commission on the Donald Marshall, Jr. Inquiry.* Halifax: Government of Nova Scotia. https://www.novascotia.ca/just/marshall_inquiry/_docs/Royal%20Commission%20on%20the%20Donald%20Marshall%20Jr%20Prosecution_findings.pdf.

62. S.M. Kassin. 2005. "On the Psychology of Confessions. *Does* Innocence *Put* Innocents at *Risk?*" *American Psychologist* 60, no. 3: 215–28.

63. C. Sherrin. 2008. "The Charter and Protection Against Wrongful Conviction: Good, Bad or Irrelevant?" In *The Charter and Criminal Justice Twenty-Five Years Later,* edited by J. Cameron and J. Stribopoulos, 377–414. Markham, ON: LexisNexis.

64. "Widely Used Police Interrogation Technique Can Result in False Confession: Disclosure." 2003. *CBC News,* January 28. Accessed March 2, 2014. http://www.cbc.ca/news/canada/widely-used-police-interrogation-technique-can-result-in-false-confession-disclosure-1.389125.

355

65. C. Sherrin. 2008. "The Charter and Protection Against Wrongful Conviction: Good, Bad or Irrelevant?" In *The Charter and Criminal Justice Twenty-Five Years Later*, edited by J. Cameron and J. Stribopoulos, 377–414. Markham, ON: LexisNexis.

66. S.M. Smith, V. Stinson, and M.W. Patry. 2010. "High-Risk Interrogation: Using the 'Mr. Big Technique' to Elicit Confessions." *Law and Human Behavior* 34, no. 1: 39–40.

67. "Exculpatory Evidence." 2014. Free Dictionary. Accessed February 16. http://www.lega-dictionary.thefreedictionary.com/Exculpatory+evidence.

68. N. Macdonald. 2009. "Wrong Man, Yet Again?" *Maclean's*, October 22. Accessed March 3, 2014. http://www2.macleans.ca/2009/10/22/wrong-man-yet-again/.

69. E. Cunliffe. 2013. "Independence, Reliability, and Expert Testimony in Criminal Trials." *Australian Journal of Forensic Sciences* 45, no. 3: 284–95.

70. K.M. Campbell. 2011. "Expert Evidence from "Social" Scientists: The Importance of Context and the Impact on Miscarriages of Justice." *Canadian Criminal Law Review* 16, no. 11: 13–35.

71. The Honourable S.T. Goudge. 2008. *Inquiry into Pediatric Forensic Pathology in Ontario. Report*. Toronto: Attorney General of Ontario. Accessed March 3, 2014. http://www.attorneygeneral.jus.gov.on.ca/inquiries/goudge/report/.

72. Ontario Office of the Chief Coroner. 2007. "Public Announcement of Review of Criminally Suspicious and Homicide Cases Where Dr. Charles Smith Conducted Autopsies or Provided Opinions." Accessed March 3, 2014. http://netk.net.au/Canada/Morin000.asp.

73. C. Blatchford. 2012. "Charles Smith's Punishment Deemed a 'Slap on the Wrist.'" *The Globe and Mail*, September 10. Accessed March 2, 2014. http://www.theglobeandmail.com/news/national/charles-smiths-punishment-deemed-a-slap-on-the-wrist/article622010/.

74. "Disgraced Pathologist Charles Smith Stripped of Licence." 2011. *CBC News*, February 1. http://www.cbc.ca/news/canada/toronto/disgraced-pathologist-smith-stripped-of-licence-1.1012791.

CHAPTER 9

1. M. Tonry. 2013. "'Nothing' Works: Sentencing 'Reform' in Canada and the United States." *Canadian Journal of Criminology and Criminal Justice* 55, no. 4: 473.

2. Jeralyn. 2010. "TX Judge Imposed Six Years of Shaming Punishment." *Talkleft.com*, October 11. Accessed March 4, 2014. http://www.talkleft.com/story/2010/10/11/05747/100/crimenews/TX-Judge-Imposes-Six-Years-of-Shaming-Punishment.

3. C. Purdy. 2013. "Armoured Car Shooter Won't Get out of Prison for at Least 40 Years." *The Globe and Mail*, September 11. Accessed March 4, 2014. http://www.theglobeandmail.com/news/national/armoured-car-shooter-wont-get-out-of-prison-for-at-least-40-years/article14255049.

4. Angus Reid Public Opinion. 2012. "Canadians Hold Conflicting Views on the Death Penalty." February 8. Accessed March 8, 2014. http://www.angusreidglobal.com/wp-content/uploads/2012/02/2012.02.08_Death_CAN.pdf.

5. S.H. Decker and C.W. Kohfeld. 1990. "The Deterrent Effect of Capital Punishment in the Five Most Active Execution States: A Time Series Analysis." *Criminal Justice Review* 15, no 2: 173–91.

6. S.P. Klein, R.A. Berk, and L.J. Hickman. 2006. *Race and the Decision to Seek the Death Penalty in Federal Cases: Executive Summary*. Washington, D.C.: U.S. Department of Justice. https://www.ncjrs.gov/pdffiles1/nij/grants/214729.pdf.

7. Public Safety Canada. 2014. "Dangerous Offender Designation." Accessed March 8, 2014. http://www.publicsafety.gc.ca/cnt/cntrng-crm/crrctns/protctn-gnst-hgh-rsk-ffndrs/dngrs-ffndr-dsgntn-eng.aspx.

8. Public Safety Canada. 2012. *Corrections and Conditional Release Statistical Overview: 2012 Annual Report*. Ottawa: Public Works and Government Services Canada, 103. http://www.publicsafety.gc.ca/cnt/rsrcs/pblctns/2012-ccrs/2012-ccrs-eng.pdf.

9. D. Slade. 2013. "Banff Rapist Denied Bid to Leave B.C. Prison to Appeal Sentence, Dangerous Offender Tag in Alberta." *Calgary Herald*, May 15. Accessed March 4, 2014. http://www.calgaryherald.com/news/Banff+rapist+denied+leave+prison+appeal+sentence+dangerous+offender+Alberta/8391034/story.html.

10. Public Safety Canada. 2008. *Corrections and Conditional Release Statistical Overview: Annual Report, 2008*. Ottawa: Public Works and Government Services Canada, 109. http://www.publicsafety.gc.ca/cnt/rsrcs/pblctns/2008-ccrs/2008-ccrs-eng.pdf.

11. L. Hausegger, M. Hennigar, and T. Riddell. 2009. *Canadian Courts: Law, Politics, and Process*. Toronto: Oxford University Press, 104.

12. J. Boyce. 2013. "Adult Criminal Court Statistics in Canada, 2011/2012." *Juristat*, 13. Accessed March 4, 2014. http://www.statcan.gc.ca/pub/85-002-x/2013001/article/11804-eng.pdf.

13. S.B. Berson. 2013. "Beyond the Sentence—Understanding Collateral Consequences." *NIJ Journal* 272: 26–28. Accessed March 4, 2014. https://ncjrs.gov/pdffiles1/nij/241927.pdf.

14. G. Balfour. 2013. "Do Law Reforms Matter? Exploring the Victimization-Criminalization Continuum in the Sentencing of Aboriginal Women in Canada." *International Review of Victimology* 19, no. 1: 85–102.

15. B.R. Pfefferle. 2006. "*Gladue* Sentencing: Uneasy Answers to the Hard Problem of Aboriginal Over-Incarceration." *Manitoba Law Journal* 32, no. 2: 113–43.

16. L. Hausegger, M. Hennigar, and T. Riddell. 2009. *Canadian Courts: Law, Politics, and Process*. Toronto: Oxford University Press, 300.

17. D.R. Songer and S.W. Johnson 2007. "Judicial Decision Making in the Supreme Court of Canada: Updating the Personal Attribute Model." *Canadian Journal of Political Science* 49, no. 4: 927.

18. J. Stribopoulos and M.A. Yahya. 2007. "Does a Judge's Party of Appointment or Gender Matter to Case Outcomes? An

Empirical Study of the Court of Appeal for Ontario." *Osgoode Hall Law Journal* 45, no. 2: 315–63.

19. S. Danziger J. Levav, and L. Avnaim-Pesso. 2011. "Extraneous Factors in Judicial Decisions." *Proceedings of the National Academy of Sciences* 108, no. 17: 6889–92.

20. C.P. Manfredi. 2004. *Feminist Activism in the Supreme Court.* Vancouver: UBC Press.

21. T. Gabor and N. Crutcher. 2002. *Mandatory Minimum Penalties: Their Effects on Crime, Sentencing Disparities, and Justice System Expenditures.* Ottawa: Research and Statistics Division, Department of Justice Canada. http://www.justice.gc.ca/eng/rp-pr/csj-sjc/ccs-ajc/rr02_1/rr02_1.pdf.

22. A.K. Malik. 2007. "Mandatory Minimum Sentences: Shackling Judicial Discretion for Justice or Political Expediency?" *Criminal Law Quarterly* 53, no. 2: 236–59.

23. K.N. Varma and V. Marinos. 2013. "Three Decades of Public Attitudes Research on Crime and Punishment in Canada." *Canadian Journal of Criminology and Criminal Justice* 55, no. 4: 555–56.

24. Canadian Press. 2013. "Mandatory Minimum Sentences for Gun Crimes Ruled Unconstitutional." *The Globe and Mail*, November 13. Accessed March 4, 2014. http://www.theglobeandmail.com/news/national/mimimun-sentencing-law-for-gun-crimes-ruled-unconstitutional/article15387142/.

25. J.V. Roberts. 2008. "Victim Impact Statements: Lessons Learned and Future Priorities," *Victims of Crime Research Digest.* Accessed March 4, 2014/ http://www.justice.gc.ca/eng/rp-pr/cj-jp/victim/rr07_vic4/p1.html?pedisable=true.

26. T. Beutel. 2004. "Guan Gets off with Just Probation." *Richmond (BC) News*, June 17.

27. J.V. Roberts. 2003. "Victim Impact Statements and the Sentencing Process: Recent Developments and Research Findings." *Criminal Law Quarterly* 47, no. 3: 365–96.

28. J.V. Roberts and A. Edgar. 2007. "Victim Impact Statements at Sentencing: Judicial Experiences and Perceptions—A Survey of Three Jurisdictions." *JustResearch* 14:14–17. Accessed March 4, 2014. http://www.justice.gc.ca/eng/rp-pr/jr/jr14/jr14.pdf.

29. S.N. Verdun-Jones and Tijerino, A.A. 2002. "The Influence of Victim Impact Statements on the Sentencing Process: The Emerging Canadian Jurisprudence." *Victim Participation in the Plea Negotiation Process in Canada: A Review of the Literature and Four Models for Law Reform.* Ottawa: Policy Centre for Victim Issues. http://canada.justice.gc.ca/eng/rp-pr/cj-jp/victim/rr02_5/rr02_5.pdf.

30. S.N. Durlauf and D.S. Nagin. 2011. "The Deterrent Effect of Imprisonment." In *Controlling Crime: Strategies and Tradeoffs*, edited by P.J. Cook, J. Ludwig, and J. McCrary, 43–94. Chicago: University of Chicago Press. http://www.nber.org/chapters/c12078.pdf.

31. D. May, N.T. Moore, and P.B. Wood. 2008. "Offenders, Judges, and Officers Rate the Relative Severity of Alternative Sanctions Compared to Prison," *Journal of Offender Rehabilitation* 46, no. 3, 49–70.

CHAPTER 10

1. B. Fischer, S. Wortley, C. Webster, and M. Kirst. 2002. "The Socio-Legal Dynamics and Implications of Diversion." *Criminology and Criminal Justice* 2, no. 4: 385–410.

2. J.V. Roberts. 2012. "Serving Time at Home: The Conditional Sentence of Imprisonment." In *Criminal Justice in Canada: A Reader.* 4th ed., edited by J.V. Roberts and M.G. Grossman, 178–86. Toronto: Nelson.

3. J. Boyce. 2013. "Adult Criminal Court Statistics in Canada, 2011/2012." *Juristat.* Accessed March 8, 2014. http://www.statcan.gc.ca/pub/85-002-x/2013001/article/11804-eng.pdf.

4. J. Matthews. 2009. "'People First: Probation Officer Perspectives on Probation Work'—A Practitioner's Response." *Probation Journal* 56, no. 1: 61–67.

5. J. Bonta, T. Rugge, B. Sedo, and R. Coles. 2004. *Case Management in Manitoba Probation.* Ottawa: Public Safety Canada. Accessed March 5, 2014. http://www.publicsafety.gc.ca/cnt/rsrcs/pblctns/cs-mngmnt-mntb/index-eng.aspx.

6. G. Robinson. 2002. "Exploring Risk Management in Probation Practice." *Punishment & Society* 4, no. 1: 5–25.

7. L.A. Gould, M. Pate, and M. Sarver. 2011. "Risk and Revocation in Community Corrections: The Role of Gender." *Journal of Community and Criminal Justice* 58, no. 3: 250–64.

8. R. Burnett and F. McNeill. 2005. "The Place of the Officer-Offender Relationship in Assisting Offenders to Desist from Crime." *Probation Journal* 52, no. 3: 221–42.

9. L. Gleicher, S.M. Manchak, and F.T. Cullen. 2013. "Creating a Supervision Tool Kit: How to Improve Probation and Parole." *Federal Probation* 77, no. 1: 2.

10. C. Trotter. 2013. "Reducing Recidivism through Probation Supervision: What We Know and Don't Know about Four Decades of Research." *Federal Probation* 77, no. 2: 43–48.

11. J. Bonta, G. Bourgon, T. Rugge, T-L. Scott, A.K. Yessine, L. Gutierrez, and J. Li. 2011. "An Experimental Demonstration of Training Probation Officers in Evidence-Based Community Supervision." *Criminal Justice and Behavior* 38, no. 11: 1127–48.

12. J. Louden, J.L. Skeem, J. Camp, and E. Christensen. 2008. "Supervising Probationers with Mental Disorder: How Do Agencies Respond to Violations?" *Criminal Justice and Behavior* 35, no. 7: 832–47.

13. J. Bonta, G. Bourgon, T. Rugge, T-L. Scott, A.K. Yessine, L. Gutierrez, and J. Li. 2011. "An Experimental Demonstration of Training Probation Officers in Evidence-Based Community Supervision." *Criminal Justice and Behavior* 38, no. 11: 1144.

14. G. Bourgon, L. Gutierrez, and J. Ashton. 2012. *From Case Management to Change Agent: The Evolution of 'What Works' in Community Supervision.* Ottawa: Public Safety Canada. Accessed March 5, 2014. http://www.publicsafety.gc.ca/cnt/rsrcs/pblctns/2012-01-cmc/index-eng.aspx.

15. B.K. Applegate, H.P. Smith, A.H. Sitren, and N.F. Springer. 2009. "From the Inside: The Meaning of Probation to Probationers." *Criminal Justice Review* 34, no. 1: 80–95.

16. R.A. Malatest & Associates Ltd. 2008. *BC Community Corrections Client Survey Research. Client Satisfaction—Community*

357

Corrections Services, Victoria: BC Ministry of Public Safety and Solicitor General.

17. I. Durnescu. 2011. "Pains of Probation: Effective Practice and Human Rights." *International Journal of Offender Therapy and Comparative Criminology* 55, no. 4: 530–45.

18. B.M. Crouch. 1993. "Is Incarceration Really Worse? Analysis of Offenders' Preferences for Prison Over Probation." *Justice Quarterly* 10, no. 1: 67–88.

19. J. Petersilia and S. Turner. 1993. "Intensive Probation and Parole." In *Crime and Justice: A Review of the Research,* edited by M. Tonry, 281–335. Chicago: University of Chicago Press.

20. J. Annison, T. Eadie, and C. Knight. 2008. "People First: Probation Officer Perspectives on Probation Work." *Probation Journal* 55, no. 3: 259–71.

21. J. Matthews. 2009. "'People First: Probation Officer Perspectives on Probation Work'—A Practitioner's Response." *Probation Journal* 56, no. 1: 61–67.

22. C. Simmons, J.K. Cochran, and W.R. Blount. 2007. "The Effects of Job-Related Stress and Job Satisfaction on Probation Officers' Inclination to Quit." *American Journal of Criminal Justice* 21, no. 2: 213–29.

23. R.N. Slate, T.L. Wells, and W.W. Johnson. 2003. "State Probation Officer Stress and Perceptions of Participation in Workplace Decision Making." *Crime and Delinquency* 49, no. 4: 519–41.

24. British Columbia Office of the Auditor General. 2011. *Effectiveness of BC Community Corrections.* Accessed March 5, 2014. http://www.bcauditor .com/pubs/2011/report10/bc-community -corrections-cccp.

25. Ibid.

26. J. Bonta. 1998. "Adult Offender Diversion Programs: Research Summary." *Corrections Research and Development* 3, no. 1. Accessed March 5, 2014. http:// www.publicsafety.gc.ca/cnt/rsrcs/pblctns/ ffndr-dvrsn/ffndr-dvrsn-eng.pdf.

27. J. Nuffield. 1997. *Diversion Programs for Adults,* Ottawa: Solicitor General Canada. Accessed March 5, 2014. http:// www.in.gov/idoc/files/Nuffield_1997 _Diversion1.pdf.

28. W. Bales, K. Mann, T. Blomberg, G. Gaes, K. Barrick, K. Dhungana, and B. McManus. 2010. *A Quantitative and Qualitative Assessment of Electronic Monitoring.* Washington, D.C.: National Institute of Justice, U.S. Department of Justice. http://www.criminologycenter.fsu.edu/p/ pdf/EM%20Evaluation%20Final%20 Report%20for%20NIJ.pdf.

29. S. Bottos. 2007. *An Overview of Electronic Monitoring in Corrections: Issues and Implications.* Ottawa: Correctional Service of Canada. http://www.csc-scc.gc.ca/ research/092/r182-eng.pdf.

30. J. Bonta, S. Wallace-Capretta, and J. Rooney. 2000. "Can Electronic Monitoring Make a Difference? An Evaluation of Three Canadian Programs." *Crime and Delinquency* 46, no. 1: 61–75.

31. W. Bales, K. Mann, T. Blomberg, G. Gaes, K. Barrick, K. Dhungana, and B. McManus. 2010. *A Quantitative and Qualitative Assessment of Electronic Monitoring.* Washington, D.C.: National Institute of Justice, U.S. Department of Justice. http://www.criminologycenter.fsu.edu/p/ pdf/EM%20Evaluation%20Final%20 Report%20for%20NIJ.pdf.

32. D. North. 2001. "The Catch-22 of Conditional Sentencing." *Criminal Law Quarterly* 44, no. 3: 342–74.

33. J. Cid. 2009. "Is Imprisonment Criminogenic? A Comparative Study of Recidivism Rates Between Prison and Suspended Prison Sanctions." *European Journal of Criminology* 6, no. 6: 459–80.

34. J. Bonta, G. Bourgon, T. Rugge, T-L. Scott, A.K. Yessine, L. Gutierrez, and J. Li. 2011. "An Experimental Demonstration of Training Probation officers in Evidence-Based Community Supervision." *Criminal Justice and Behavior* 38, no. 11: 1129.

35. P.J. Kennealy, K.L. Skeam, S.M. Manchuk, and J.E. Louden. 2012. "Firm, Fair, and Caring Officer-Offender Relationships Protect Against Supervision Failure." *Law and Human Behavior* 36, no. 6: 496–505.

36. M. DeLisi and P.J. Conis. 2013. *American Corrections: Theory, Research, Policy, and Practice.* 2nd ed. Burlington, MA: Jones & Bartlett Learning, 248.

37. British Columbia Office of the Auditor General. 2011. *Effectiveness of BC Community Corrections.* Accessed March 5, 2014. http://www.bcauditor .com/pubs/2011/report10/bc-community -corrections-cccp.

38. A.R. Klein, D. Wilson, A.H. Crowe, and M. DeMichele. 2008. *Evaluation of the Rhode Island Probation Specialized Domestic Violence Supervision Unit.* Washington: U.S. Department of Justice. http://www.ncjrs.gov/pdffiles1/nij/ grants/222912.pdf.

39. J. Bonta, G. Bourgon, T. Rugge, T-L. Scott, A.K. Yessine, L. Gutierrez, and J. Li. 2011. "An Experimental Demonstration of Training Probation officers in Evidence-Based Community Supervision." *Criminal Justice and Behavior* 38, no. 11: 1129.

40. M. DeLisi and P.J. Conis. 2013. *American Corrections: Theory, Research, Policy, and Practice.* 2nd ed. Burlington, MA: Jones & Bartlett Learning, 251.

CHAPTER 11

1. R. Baehre. 1977. "Origins of the Penitentiary System in Upper Canada." *Ontario History* 69, no. 3: 185–207.

2. D. Coles. 1979. *Nova Scotia Corrections: An Historical Perspective.* Halifax: Corrections Services Division, Province of Nova Scotia, 8.

3. M. MacGuigan. 1977. *Report to Parliament by the Sub-Committee on the Penitentiary System in Canada.* Ottawa: Supply and Services Canada, 12.

4. E. Goffman. 1961. *Asylums: Essays on the Social Situation of Mental Patients and Other Inmates.* Garden City: Doubleday, 6.

5. P. Hancock and Y. Jewkes. 2011. "Architectures of Incarceration: The Spatial Pains of Imprisonment." *Punishment & Society* 13, no. 5: 611–29.

6. S. Poirier (Chairperson). 2008. *Decades of Darkness: Moving Towards the Light. A Review of the Prison System in Newfoundland and Labrador.* St. John's: Ministry of Justice, 17. http://www.justice .gov.nl.ca/AC_Report.pdf.

7. D.M. Bierie. 2012. "Is Tougher Better? The Impact of Physical Prison Conditions

on Inmate Violence." *International Journal of Offender Therapy and Comparative Criminology* 56, no. 3: 338–55

8. W.W. Franklin, C.A. Franklin, and T.C. Pratt. 2006. "Examining the Empirical Relationship Between Prison Crowding and Inmate Misconduct: A Meta-Analysis of Conflicting Research Results." *Journal of Criminal Justice* 34, no. 4: 401–12.

9. QMI Agency. 2012. "'Unhygienic' Prison Conditions Leads to Less Time for Prisoner." *Canoe Network,* October 12. Accessed March 5, 2014. http://www.sunnewsnetwork.ca/sunnews/canada/archives/2012/10/20121013-121856.html.

10. L. Porter and D. Calverley. 2011. "Trends in the Use of Remand in Canada." *Juristat.* http://www.statcan.gc.ca/pub/85-002-x/2011001/article/11440-eng.pdf.

11. C.M. Webster, A.N. Doob, and N.M. Myers. 2009. "The Parable of Ms. Baker: Understanding Pre-Trial Detention in Canada." *Current Issues in Criminal Justice* 21, no. 1: 79–102.

12. M. Dauvergne. 2012. "Adult Correctional Statistics in Canada, 2010/2011." *Juristat,* 12. Accessed March 5, 2014. http://www.statcan.gc.ca/pub/85-002-x/2012001/article/11715-eng.pdf.

13. D. Calverley. 2010. "Adult Correctional Services in Canada, 2008/2009." *Juristat* 30, no. 3. Accessed March 5, 2014. http://www.statcan.gc.ca/pub/85-002-x/2010003/article/11353-eng.htm.

14. Office of the Correctional Investigator. 2013. *Annual Report, 2012–2013.* Ottawa: Author. http://www.oci-bec.gc.ca/cnt/rpt/pdf/annrpt/annrpt20122013-eng.pdf.

15. W. Campbell. 2013a. "Overcrowding in Ontario Jails at Six-Year High, Sparking Violence Behind Bars." *Canadian Press,* July 28. Accessed March 5, 2014. http://www.vancouversun.com/news/national/Ontario+jail+overcrowding+sixyear+high+sparking+violence/8718339/story.html.

16. K.B. Carlson. 2011. "Prison Ground Break," *National Post,* September 24, A4.

17. Office of the Correctional Investigator. 2011. *Annual Report, 2010–2011.* Ottawa: Author. http://www.oci-bec.gc.ca/cnt/rpt/pdf/annrpt/annrpt20102011-eng.pdf.

18. K. Makin. 2010. "Senator Fights for Mentally Ill in Prison." *The Globe and Mail,* November 19, A9.

19. K. Makin. 2011. "To Heal and Protect: Mental Illness and the Justice System." *The Globe and Mail,* January 21.

20. Mental Health Commission of Canada. 2012. *Changing Directions, Changing Lives: The Mental Health Strategy for Canada.* Calgary: Author, 60. http://strategy.mentalhealthcommission.ca/pdf/strategy-text-en.pdf.

21. P. MacPherson and A.E. Chudley. 2007. *FASD in a Correctional Population: Preliminary Results from an Incidence Study.* Montague, PEI: Addictions Research Centre.

22. Public Safety Canada Portfolio Corrections Statistics Committee. 2012. *Corrections and Conditional Release Statistical Overview.* Ottawa: Ottawa: Public Works and Government Services Canada, 35. http://www.publicsafety.gc.ca/cnt/rsrcs/pblctns/2012-ccrs/2012-ccrs-eng.pdf.

23. Office of the Correctional Investigator. 2010. *Annual Report, 2009–2010.* Ottawa: Author. http://www.oci-bec.gc.ca/cnt/rpt/pdf/annrpt/annrpt20092010-eng.pdf.

24. R. Sampson (Chair). 2007. *Report of the Correctional Service of Canada Review Panel: A Roadmap to Strengthening Public Safety.* Ottawa: Minister of Public Works and Government Services Canada. http://www.ccjc.ca/about/cscrpreport-eng.pdf.

25. "Report Slams Women's Prison." 2000. *CBC News,* February 8. Accessed March 8, 2014. http://www.cbc.ca/news/canada/report-slams-women-s-prison-1.210695.

26. Office of the Correctional Investigator. 2012. *Annual Report, 2011–2012.* Ottawa: Author, 36. http://www.oci-bec.gc.ca/cnt/rpt/pdf/annrpt/annrpt20112012-eng.pdf.

27. Public Safety Canada Portfolio Corrections Statistics Committee. 2012. *Corrections and Conditional Release Statistical Overview.* Ottawa: Ottawa: Public Works and Government Services Canada, 67. http://www.publicsafety.gc.ca/cnt/rsrcs/pblctns/2012-ccrs/2012-ccrs-eng.pdf.

28. R. Jurgens, M. Novak, and M. Day. 2011. "HIV and Incarceration: Prisons and Detention." *Journal of the International AIDS Society* 14, no. 1: 26–42.

29. D. Werb, T. Kerr, W. Small, K. Li, and J. Montaner. 2008. "HIV Risks Associated with the Incarceration Among Injection Drug Users: Implications for Prison-Based Public Health Strategies." *Journal of Public Health* 30, no. 2: 126–32.

30. Canadian HIV/AIDS Legal Network. 2012. *Women in Prison, HIV and Hepatitis C,* 1. Accessed March 5, 2014. http://www.aidslaw.ca/publications/publicationsdocEN.php?ref=1281.

31. R. Jurgens, A. Ball, and A. Verster. 2009. "Interventions to Reduce HIV Transmission Related to Injecting Drug Use in Prison." *Lancet Infectious Diseases* 9, no. 1: 57–66.

32. D.D. Varis. 2001. "Intensive Support Units for Federal Inmates: A Descriptive Review." *Forum on Corrections Research* 13, no. 3. Accessed March 5, 2014. http://www.csc-scc.gc.ca/publications/forum/e133/133m_e.pdf.

33. S.K.H. Chu and R. Elliott. 2009. *Clean Switch: The Case for Prison Needle and Syringe Programs in Canada.* Toronto: Canadian HIV/AIDS Legal Network. http://www.aidslaw.ca/publications/interfaces/downloadFile.php?ref=1496.

34. E. Bingham and R. Sutton. 2012. *Cruel, Inhuman, and Degrading? Canada's Treatment of Federally Sentenced Women with Mental Health Issues.* Toronto: International Human Rights Program, University of Toronto. http://www.dawncanada.net/main/wp-content/uploads/2013/12/Cruel-and-Inhuman_FINAL_Print.pdf.

35. L. Arbour (Honourable). 1996. *Report of the Commission of Inquiry into Certain Events at the Prison for Women in Kingston.* Ottawa: Public Works and Government Services Canada. Accessed March 6, 2014. http://www.justicebehindthewalls.net/resources/arbour_report/arbour_rpt.htm.

36. C. Glube (Chair). "Moving Forward with Women's Corrections." Ottawa:

359

Correctional Service of Canada. Accessed March 9, 2014. http://www.csc-scc.gc.ca/publications/fsw/wos29/wos29-eng.shtml.

37. S. Hayman. 2006. *Imprisoning Our Sisters: The New Federal Women's Prisons* in *Canada*. Kingston, ON: McGill-Queen's University Press.

38. J. Ferrari. 2011. "Federal Female Incarceration in Canada: What Happened to Empowerment?" MA thesis, Queen's University, Kingston. Accessed March 8, 2014. https://qspace.library.queensu.ca/bitstream/1974/6352/3/Ferrari_Jacqueline_201104_MA.pdf.

39. L. Arbour (Honourable). 1996. *Report of the Commission of Inquiry into Certain Events at the Prison for Women in Kingston.* Ottawa: Public Works and Government Services Canada. Accessed March 6, 2014. http://www.justicebehindthewalls.net/resources/arbour_report/arbour_rpt.htm.

40. J. Ferrari. 2011. "Federal Female Incarceration in Canada: What Happened to Empowerment?" MA thesis, Queen's University, Kingston, 115. Accessed March 8, 2014. https://qspace.library.queensu.ca/bitstream/1974/6352/3/Ferrari_Jacqueline_201104_MA.pdf.

41. C.A. Dell, C.J. Fillmore, and J.M. Kilty. 2009. "Looking Back 10 Years after the Arbour Inquiry: Ideology, Policy, Practice, and the Federal Female Prisoner." *Prison Journal* 89, no. 3: 286, 291.

42. S.T. Marcus-Mendoza. 2004. "Feminist Therapy Behind Bars." *Women Studies Quarterly* 32, no. 3&4: 49–60.

43. M. Morash. 2010. *Women on Probation and Parole: A Feminist Critique of Community Programs and Services.* Lebanon, NE: Northeastern University Press.

44. K. Makin. 2010. "Senator Fights for Mentally Ill in Prison." *The Globe and Mail,* November 19, A9.

45. Office of the Correctional Investigator. 2008. *A Preventable Death.* Ottawa: Author. Accessed March 8, 2014. http://www.oci-bec.gc.ca/cnt/rpt/oth-aut/oth-aut20080620-eng.aspx.

46. Ibid.

47. New Brunswick Ombudsman and Child and Youth Advocate. 2008. *Ashley Smith: A Report of the New Brunswick Ombudsman and Child and Youth Advocate on the Services Provided to a Youth Involved in the Youth Justice System.* Fredericton: Author. http://www.gnb.ca/0073/PDF/AshleySmith-e.pdf.

48. Union of Canadian Correctional Officers. 2008. *Rush to Judgment: A Report on the Death in Custody of Ashley Smith, an Inmate at Grand Valley Institution for Women.* Ottawa: Author. http://www.ucco-sacc.csn.qc.ca/Documents/UCCO-SACC/National/documents/Issues/GVI/Full%20Report%20-%20A%20Rush%20to%20Judgment.pdf.

49. D. Vincent. 2013. "Ashley Smith Inquest: Warden Admits Lack of Experience." *Toronto Star,* October 2. Accessed March 5, 2014. http://www.thestar.com/news/canada/2013/10/02/ashley_smith_inquest_warden_admits_lack_of_experience.html.

50. K.B. Carlson. 2013. "Mother 'Elated' as Ashley Smith's Jail Death is Ruled a Homicide." *The Globe and Mail,* December 19. Accessed March 5, 2014. http://www.theglobeandmail.com/news/national/ashley-smith-inquest/article16052548/.

51. D. Vincent. 2013. "Ashley Smith Inquest: Warden Admits Lack of Experience." *Toronto Star,* October 2. Accessed March 5, 2014. http://www.thestar.com/news/canada/2013/10/02/ashley_smith_inquest_warden_admits_lack_of_experience.html.

52. C. Perkel. 2013. "Jurors Urged to Find Segregation-Cell Death of Ashley Smith a Homicide." *The Globe and Mail,* November 25. Accessed March 9, 2014. http://www.theglobeandmail.com/news/national/jurors-ureged-to-find-segregation-cell-death-of-ashley-smith-a-momicide/article15587856/.

53. T. Lajeunesse, C. Jefferson, J. Nuffield, and D. Majury. 2000. *The Cross Gender Monitoring Project: Third and Final Report.* Ottawa: Correctional Service of Canada. Accessed March 5, 2014. http://www.csc-scc.gc.ca/publications/fsw/gender3/toc-eng.shtml.

54. Deloitte & Touche. 2008. *Report on Nova Scotia's Adult Correctional Facilities.* Halifax: Department of Justice. http://www.gov.ns.ca/just/global_docs/Deloitte%20Report%20-%20NS%20Correctional%20Facilities%20Nov08.pdf.

55. K. Kauffman. 1988. *Prison Officers and Their World.* Cambridge, MA: Harvard University Press.

56. M.A. Farkas. 1997. "The Normative Code among Correctional Officers: An Exploration of Components and Functions." *Journal of Crime and Justice* 20, no. 1: 23–36.

57. A. Marin. 2013. *The CODE: Investigation into the Ministry of Community Safety and Correctional Services Response to Allegations of Excessive Use of Force against Inmates.* Toronto: Ombudsman Ontario, 9. http://www.ombudsman.on.ca/Ombudsman/files/45/450c6aa8-3481-43d6-bce1-8141fa6bbbda.pdf.

58. M. Welch. 2011. *Corrections: A Critical Approach.* 3rd ed. New York: Routledge.

59. M.A. Farkas. 2000. "A Typology of Correctional Officers." *International Journal of Offender Therapy and Comparative Criminology* 44, no. 4: 431–49.

60. easter bunny. 2009. "Prison Stories: Ontario, Central East Correctional Centre." *Inside Prison Blog,* February 25. Accessed March 5, 2014. http://www.insideprison.com/prison_stories.asp?story_id=1130&pNum=2.

61. W. Campbell. 2013b. "Prison Guards Lack 'Common Understanding' on Basic Respect for Inmates: Survey," *The Canadian Press,* March 31. Accessed March 5, 2014. http://www.globalnews.ca/news/441900/prison-guards-lack-common-understanding-on-basic-human-respect-for-inmates/.

62. G. Keinan and A. Malach-Pines, 2007. "Stress and Burnout Among Prison Personnel: Sources, Outcomes, and Intervention Strategies." *Criminal Justice and Behavior* 34, no. 3: 380–98.

63. E. Lambert, N.L. Hogan, I. Altheimer, S. Jiang, and M.T. Stevenson. 2010. "The Relationship between Burnout and Support for Punishment and Treatment: A Preliminary Examination."

International Journal of Offender Therapy and Comparative Criminology 54, no. 6: 1004–22.

64. N. Boyd. 2011. *Abnormal Working Conditions: Correctional Officers in British Columbia, 2011*. Burnaby, BC: British Columbia Government Employees Union, i. http://www.bcgeu.ca/sites/default/files/FINAL%20Boyd-Report-2011.pdf.

65. M. Brosnahan. 2012. "Record-High Prison Numbers Sparking Violence." *CBC News*, August 27.

66. B.L. Stadnyk. 2003. "PTSD in Corrections Employees in Saskatchewan." MA thesis, University of Regina. Accessed March 5, 2014. http://rpnascom.jumpstartdev.com/sites/default/files/PTSDInCorrections.pdf.

67. J. Rankin and S. Contenta. 2013. "Gay Canadian CO Suffered Poisoned Workplace." *Toronto Star,* November 18. Accessed March 5, 2014. http://www.thestar.com/business/2013/11/18/gay_ontario_jail_guard_bob_ranger_suffered_poisoned_workplace.html.

68. Public Safety Canada Portfolio Corrections Statistics Committee. 2012. *Corrections and Conditional Release Statistical Overview*. Ottawa: Ottawa: Public Works and Government Services Canada. http://www.publicsafety.gc.ca/cnt/rsrcs/pblctns/2012-ccrs/2012-ccrs-eng.pdf.

69. John Howard Society of Toronto. 2010. *Homeless and Jailed: Jailed and Homeless*. Accessed March 5, 2014. http://www.johnhoward.ca/document/JHS-Toronto%20Report%20Homeless%20and%20Jailed.pdf.

70. P.J. Murphy and L. Johnsen. 1997. *Life 25: Interviews with Prisoners Serving Life Sentences*. Vancouver: New Star, 41.

71. R.A. Cloward. 1969. "Social Control in the Prison." In *Prison within Society: A Reader in Penology,* edited by L. Hazelrigg, 78–112. Garden City: Doubleday.

72. R. Dube. 2002. *The Haven: A True Story of Life in the Hole*. Toronto: HarperCollins, 238–39.

73. G.M. Sykes. 1958. *Society of Captives—A Study of a Maximum Security Institution*. Princeton: Princeton University Press.

74. M. Borzycki. 2005. *Interventions for Prisoners Returning to the Community*. Canberra: Australian Institute of Criminology. http://www.aic.gov.au/documents/F/6/E/%7BF6E2B190-2C21-4C7D-B45F-2C7D6FA3DE45%7D2005-03-prisoners.pdf.

75. J. Power and S.L. Brown. 2010. *Self-Injurious Behaviour: A Review of the Literature and Implications for Corrections*. Ottawa: Correctional Service of Canada, 1. http://www.csc-scc.gc.ca/005/008/092/005008-0216-01-eng.pdf.

76. C.A. Dell and T. Beauchamp. 2006. "Self-Harm among Criminalized Women." *Fact Sheet*. Canadian Centre on Substance Abuse. Accessed March 5, 2014. http://www.addictionresearchchair.ca/wp-content/uploads/Self-Harm-Among-Criminalized-Women.pdf.

77. Office of the Correctional Investigator. 2012. *Annual Report, 2011–2012*. Ottawa: Author, 36. http://www.oci-bec.gc.ca/cnt/rpt/pdf/annrpt/annrpt20112012-eng.pdf.

78. D. Clemmer. 1940. *The Prison Community*. Boston: Christopher.

79. G.M. Sykes and S.L. Messinger. 1960. "The Inmate Social System." In *Theoretical Studies in the Social Organization of the Prison,* edited by R.A. Cloward, D.R. Cressey, G.H. Grosser, R. McCleery, L.E. Ohlin, G.M. Sykes, and S.L. Messinger, 5–19. New York: Social Science Research Council.

80. M. Welch. 2011. *Corrections: A Critical Approach*. 3rd ed. New York: Routledge, 137.

81. M. Welch. 2011. *Corrections: A Critical Approach*. 3rd ed. New York: Routledge, 137–38.

82. K.F. Lahm. 2008. "Inmate-On-Inmate Assault: A Multilevel Examination of Prison Violence." *Criminal Justice and Behavior* 35, no. 1: 120–37.

83. R. Ricciardelli and M. Moir. 2013. "Stigmatized Among the Stigmatized: Sex Offenders in Canadian Penitentiaries." *Canadian Journal of Criminology and Criminal Justice* 55, no. 3: 353–85.

84. S. Thompson. 2002. *Letters from Prison: Felons Write about the Struggle for Life and Sanity behind Bars*. Toronto: HarperCollins, 15–16.

85. R. Light and B. Campbell. 2006. "Prisoners' Families: Still Forgotten Victims?" *Journal of Social Welfare & Family Law* 28, no. 3–4: 297–308.

86. S. Hannem. 2011. "Stigma and Marginality: Gendered Experiences of Families of Male Prisons in Canada." In *Critical Criminology in Canada: New Voices, New Directions,* edited by A. Doyle and D. Moore, 183–217. Vancouver: UBC Press.

87. D. Braman. 2007. *Doing Time on the Outside: Incarceration and Family Life in Urban America*. Ann Arbor: University of Michigan Press.

88. R. Light and B. Campbell. 2006. "Prisoners' Families: Still Forgotten Victims?" *Journal of Social Welfare & Family Law* 28, no. 3–4: 297–308.

89. S. Moroney. 2011. *Through the Glass*. Toronto: Doubleday Canada.

90. R.C. Johnson. 2009. "Ever-Increasing Levels of Parental Incarceration and the Consequences for Children." In *Do Prisons Make Us Safer? The Benefits and Costs of the Prison Boom,* edited by S. Raphael and M.A. Stoll, 177–206. New York: Russell Sage Foundation.

91. J. Murray. 2010. "The Cycle of Punishment: Social Exclusion of Prisoners and Their Children." *Criminology and Criminal Justice* 7, no. 1: 55–81.

92. D. Derkzen, R. Gobeil, and J. Gileno. 2009. *Visitation and Post-Release Outcome among Federally Sentenced Offenders*. Ottawa: Correctional Service of Canada. Accessed March 5, 2014. http://www.csc-scc.gc.ca/research/r205-eng.shtml.

93. Public Safety Canada Portfolio Corrections Statistics Committee. 2012. *Corrections and Conditional Release Statistical Overview*. Ottawa: Ottawa: Public Works and Government Services Canada, 31. http://www.publicsafety.gc.ca/cnt/rsrcs/pblctns/2012-ccrs/2012-ccrs-eng.pdf.

94. S. Poirier (Chairperson). 2008. *Decades of Darkness: Moving Towards the Light. A Review of the Prison System*

in *Newfoundland and Labrador*. St. John's: Ministry of Justice, 17. http://www.justice.gov.nl.ca/AC_Report .pdf.

95. G. Harper and C. Chitty. 2005. *The Impact of Corrections on Re-Offending: A Review of "What Works"* (Home Office Research Study 291). London: Development and Statistics Directorate, Home Office. http://webarchive.nationalarchives.gov .uk/20110218135832/rds.homeoffice.gov .uk/rds/pdfs04/hors291.pdf.

96. M. Dauvergne. 2012. "Adult Correctional Statistics in Canada, 2010/2011." *Juristat,* 12. Accessed March 5, 2014. http://www.statcan.gc.ca/pub/85-002-x/ 2012001/article/11715-eng.pdf.

97. G. Taylor 1997. "Implementing Risk and Needs Classification in the Correctional Service of Canada." *Forum on Corrections Research* 9, no. 1: 32–35.

98. D.A. Andrews and J. Bonta. 2010. *The Psychology of Criminal Conduct.* 5th ed. New Providence: Matthew Benders & Company.

99. Public Safety Canada Portfolio Corrections Statistics Committee. 2012. *Corrections and Conditional Release Statistical Overview.* Ottawa: Ottawa: Public Works and Government Services Canada, 11. http://www.publicsafety .gc.ca/cnt/rsrcs/pblctns/2012-ccrs/ 2012-ccrs-eng.pdf.

100. S. Poirier (Chairperson). 2008. *Decades of Darkness: Moving Towards the Light. A Review of the Prison System in Newfoundland and Labrador.* St. John's: Ministry of Justice, 149 http://www .justice.gov.nl.ca/AC_Report.pdf.

101. Office of the Correctional Investigator. 2011. *Annual Report, 2010–2011.* Ottawa: Author, 32. http://www.oci-bec. gc.ca/cnt/rpt/pdf/annrpt/ annrpt20102011-eng.pdf.

102. C.T. Lowenkamp, E.J. Latessa, and P. Smith. 2006. "Does Correctional Program Quality Really Matter? The Impact of Adhering to the Principles of Effective Intervention." *Criminology & Public Policy* 5, no. 3: 575–94.

103. D.A. Andrews and J. Bonta. 2010. *The Psychology of Criminal Conduct.* 5th ed. New Providence: Matthew Benders & Company.

104. J. Bonta and D.A., Andrews. 2010. "Viewing Offender Assessment and Treatment through the Lens of the Risk-Need-Responsivity Model." In *Offender Supervision: New Directions in Theory, Research and Practice,* edited by F. McNeil, P. Raynor, and C. Trotter, 19–40. New York: Wilan Publishing.

105. Office of the Correctional Investigator. 2011. *Annual Report, 2010–2011.* Ottawa: Author, 44. http://www.oci-bec.gc.ca/cnt/ rpt/pdf/annrpt/annrpt20102011-eng.pdf.

106. P. Smith and P. Gendreau. 2007. "The Relationship Between Program Participation, Institutional Misconduct, and Recidivism among Federally Sentenced Adult Male Offenders." *Forum on Corrections Research* 19, no: 1. Accessed March 5, 2014. http://www .csc-scc.gc.ca/text/pblct/forum/ Vol19No1/v19n1-chap2-eng.pdf.

107. A. Day and T. Ward. 2010. "Offender Rehabilitation as a Value-Laden Process." *International Journal of Offender Therapy and Comparative Criminology* 54, no. 3: 289–306.

108. C. McKinnon. 1995. "The Legal Right of Offenders to Refuse Treatment." *Forum on Corrections Research* 7, no. 3: 43–47.

109. K.K. Parhar, J.S. Wormith, D.M. Derkzen, and A.M. Beauregard. 2008. "Offender Coercion in Treatment: A Meta-Analysis of Effectiveness." *Criminal Justice and Behavior* 35, no. 9: 1109–35.

110. A.L. Solomon, K.D. Johnson, J. Travis, and E.C. McBride. 2004. *From Prison to Work: The Employment Dimensions of Prisoner Reentry.* Washington: Justice Policy Center, Urban Institute. http://www.urban .org/UploadedPDF/411097_From_Prison _to_Work.pdf.

111. R. Martinson. 1974. "What Works? Questions and Answers About Prison Reform." *Public Interest* 35:22–54.

112. R. Martinson. 1979. "New Findings, New Views: A Note of Caution Regarding Sentencing Reform." *Hofstra Law Review* 7:243–58.

113. J. Bonta. 1997. *Offender Rehabilitation: From Research to Practice.* Ottawa: Department of the Solicitor General of Canada. http://www.publicsafety.gc.ca/ cnt/rsrcs/pblctns/ffndr-rhblttn-rsrch/ffndr -rhblttn-rsrch-eng.pdf.

114. L.W. Sherman, D. Gottfredson, D. MacKenzie, J. Eck, P. Reuter, and S. Bushway. 1997. *Preventing Crime: What Works, What Doesn't, What's Promising—A Report to the United States Congress.* Accessed March 5, 2014. http://www.ncjrs.gov/works.

115. P. Smith, P. Gendreau, and K. Swartz. 2009. "Validating the Principles of Effective Intervention: A Systematic Review of the Contributions of Meta-Analysis in the Field of Corrections." *Victims and Offenders* 4, no. 2: 148–69.

116. M. Olotu, D. Luong, C. MacDonald, M. McKay, S. Heath, N. Allegri, and E. Loree. 2011. "Chapter 1: Correctional Interventions." *Report of the Evaluation of CSC's Community Corrections.* Ottawa: Correctional Service Canada, 48. http://www.csc-scc.gc.ca/text/ pa/ev-cci-fin/ev-cci-fin-eng.pdf.

117. J.H. Esperian. 2010. "The Effect of Prison Education on Recidivism." *Journal of Correctional Education* 61, no. 4: 34.

118. John Howard Society of Alberta. 2002. *Inmate Education.* Accessed March 5, 2014. http://www.johnhoward.ab.ca/pub/ respaper/educa02.htm.

119. N. Allergi, K. Deleveus, D. Loung, H. Li, T. Jensen, D. Batten, K. Barney, E. Loree, and M. Henighan. 2008. *Evaluation Report: Community Mental Health Initiative.* Ottawa: Correctional Service of Canada. http://www.csc-scc.gc .ca/text/pa/ev-cmhi-394-2-51/cmhi -eng.pdf.

120. M. Olotu, D. Luong, C. MacDonald, M. McKay, S. Heath, N. Allegri, and E. Loree. 2011. "Chapter 1: Correctional Interventions." *Report of the Evaluation of CSC's Community Corrections.* Ottawa: Correctional Service Canada, 66. http://www.csc-scc.gc.ca/text/ pa/ev-cci-fin/ev-cci-fin-eng.pdf.

121. S. Belenko, C. Foltz, M.A. Lang, and H-E. Sung. 2004. "Recidivism Among High-Risk Drug Felons: A Longitudinal Analysis Following Residential Treatment." *Journal of Rehabilitation* 40, no. 1: 105–32.

122. D.D. Varis, D. Lefebvre, and B.A. Grant. 2005. *Intensive Support Units for Federal Offenders with Substance Abuse Problems: An Impact Analysis.* Ottawa: Correctional Service of Canada. http://www.publications .gc.ca/collections/collection_2010/scc-csc/ PS83-3-151-eng.pdf.

362

123. J.A. Inciardi, S.S. Martin, and C.A. Butzin. 2004. "Five-Year Outcomes of Therapeutic Community Treatment of Drug-Involved Offenders after Release from Prison." *Crime and Delinquency* 50, no. 1: 88–108.

124. D.D. Varis. 2001. "Intensive Support Units for Federal Inmates: A Descriptive Review." *Forum on Corrections Research* 13, no. 3. Accessed March 5, 2014. http://www.csc-scc.gc.ca/publications/forum/e133/133m_e.pdf.

125. R.K. Hanson and M.T. Bussiere. 1998. "Predicting Relapse: A Meta-Analysis of Sexual Offender Recidivism Studies." *Journal of Consulting and Clinical Psychology* 66, no. 2: 348–62.

126. F. Losel and M. Schmucker. 2005. "The Effectiveness of Treatment for Sexual Offenders: A Comprehensive Meta-Analysis." *Journal of Experimental Criminology* 1, no. 1: 117–46.

127. F. Cortoni and K.L. Nunes. 2007. *Assessing the Effectiveness of the National Sexual Offender Program*, Ottawa: Correctional Service of Canada. Accessed March 5, 2014. http://www.csc-scc.gc.ca/research/r183-eng.shtml.

128. R. Hanson and K.E. Morton-Bourgon. 2009. "The Accuracy of Recidivism Risk Assessments for Sexual Offenders: A Meta-analysis of 188 Prediction Studies." *Psychological Assessment* 21, no. 1: 1–21.

129. M. Olotu, D. Luong, C. MacDonald, M. McKay, S. Heath, N. Allegri, and E. Loree. 2011. "Chapter 1: Correctional Interventions." *Report of the Evaluation of CSC's Community Corrections*. Ottawa: Correctional Service Canada, 106. http://www.csc-scc.gc.ca/text/pa/ev-cci-fin/ev-cci-fin-eng.pdf.

CHAPTER 12

1. M. Halsey. 2008. "Assembling Recidivism: The Promise and Contingencies of Post-release Life." *Journal of Criminal Law and Criminology* 97 no. 4: 1256.

2. C. Marshall. 2008. *HIV/AIDS and Hepatitis in Correctional Facilities: Reducing the Risks*. Halifax: Nova Scotia Advisory Commission on AIDS, 26. http://www.gov.ns.ca/AIDS/documents/HIV-AIDS-Hepatitis-C-Correctional%20Facilities.pdf.

3. Schizophrenia Society of Ontario. 2012. *Provincial Correctional Response to Individuals with Mental Illness in Ontario: A Review of the Literature*. Toronto: Author, 4. http://cefso.ca/wwdnews/uploads/Provincial_Corrections_Literature_Review_Final_March_2012.pdf.

4. Parole Board of Canada. 2012. *Performance Monitoring Report 2010–2011*. Ottawa: Author, vi. http://pbc-clcc.gc.ca/rprts/pmr/pmr_2010_2011/pmr_2010_2011-eng.pdf.

5. Public Safety Canada Portfolio Corrections Statistics Committee. 2012. Ottawa: Public Works and Government Services Canada. http://www.publicsafety.gc.ca/cnt/rsrcs/pblctns/2012-ccrs/2012-ccrs-eng.pdf.

6. Parole Board of Canada. 2012. *Performance Monitoring Report 2010–2011*. Ottawa: Author, 28. http://pbc-clcc.gc.ca/rprts/pmr/pmr_2010_2011/pmr_2010_2011-eng.pdf.

7. Parole Board of Canada. 2012. *Performance Monitoring Report 2010–2011*. Ottawa: Author, 31. http://pbc-clcc.gc.ca/rprts/pmr/pmr_2010_2011/pmr_2010_2011-eng.pdf.

8. I. Zinger. 2012. "Conditional Release and Human Rights in Canada: A Commentary." *Canadian Journal of Criminology and Criminal Justice* 54, no. 1: 121.

9. M. Dauvergne. 2012. "Adult Correctional Statistics in Canada, 2010/2011. *Juristat,* 15. Accessed March 10, 2014. http://www.statcan.gc.ca/pub/85-002-x/2012001/article/11715-eng.htm.

10. Parole Board of Canada. 2012. *Performance Monitoring Report 2010–2011*. Ottawa: Author, 19. http://pbc-clcc.gc.ca/rprts/pmr/pmr_2010_2011/pmr_2010_2011-eng.pdf.

11. Public Safety Canada Portfolio Corrections Statistics Committee. 2012. Ottawa: Public Works and Government Services Canada, 83. http://www.publicsafety.gc.ca/cnt/rsrcs/pblctns/2012-ccrs/2012-ccrs-eng.pdf.

12. I. Zinger. 2012. "Conditional Release and Human Rights in Canada: A Commentary." *Canadian Journal of Criminology and Criminal Justice* 54, no. 1: 120.

13. I. Zinger. 2012. "Conditional Release and Human Rights in Canada: A Commentary." *Canadian Journal of Criminology and Criminal Justice* 54, no. 1: 117–35.

14. I. Zinger. 2012. "Conditional Release and Human Rights in Canada: A Commentary." *Canadian Journal of Criminology and Criminal Justice* 54, no. 1: 122.

15. Ontario Parole Board. 2012. *2011–2012 Annual Report*. Toronto: Ministry of Community Safety and Correctional Services, 13. http://www.opb.gov.on.ca/stellent/groups/public/@abcs/@www/@operb/documents/abstract/ec161356.pdf.

16. Public Safety Canada Portfolio Corrections Statistics Committee. 2012. Ottawa: Public Works and Government Services Canada, 119. http://www.publicsafety.gc.ca/cnt/rsrcs/pblctns/2012-ccrs/2012-ccrs-eng.pdf.

17. M.K. Olotu, and M.G. Beaupre. 2010. *Evaluation Report. National Victim Services Program*. Ottawa: Correctional Service of Canada. Accessed March 10, 2014. http://csc-scc.gc.ca/text/pa/nvsp/index-eng.shtml.

18. Public Safety Canada Portfolio Corrections Statistics Committee. 2012. Ottawa: Public Works and Government Services Canada, 81. http://www.publicsafety.gc.ca/cnt/rsrcs/pblctns/2012-ccrs/2012-ccrs-eng.pdf.

19. P.J. Murphy, L. Johnsen, and J. Murphy. 2002. *Paroled for Life: Interviews with Parolees Serving Life Sentences*. Vancouver: New Star, 93.

20. J. Morton and M.M. Persaud. 2011. "Justice Shouldn't Be Political." *Ottawa Citizen*, February 23, A13.

21. I. Zinger. 2012. "Conditional Release and Human Rights in Canada: A Commentary." *Canadian Journal of Criminology and Criminal Justice* 54, no. 1: 121.

22. M.A. Paparozzi and R. Guy. 2009. "The Giant that Never Woke: Parole Authorities as the Lynchpin to Evidence-Based Practices and Prisoner Reentry." *Journal of Contemporary Justice* 25, no. 4: 397–411.

23. A. Thurber. 1998. "Understanding Offender Reintegration." *Forum on Corrections Research* 10, no. 1: 14.

363

24. C.T. Griffiths, Y. Dandurand, and D. Murdoch. 2007. *The Social Reintegration of Offenders and Crime Prevention*. Ottawa: National Crime Prevention Centre, Public Safety Canada. http://publications.gc.ca/collections/collection_2009/sp-ps/PS4-49-2007E.pdf.

25. S. Maruna. 2011. "Reentry as a Rite of Passage." *Punishment & Society* 13, no. 1: 3–28.

26. Ontario Parole Board. 2012. *2011–2012 Annual Report*. Toronto: Ministry of Community Safety and Correctional Services. http://www.opb.gov.on.ca/stellent/groups/public/@abcs/@www/@operb/documents/abstract/ec161356.pdf.

27. Public Safety Canada Portfolio Corrections Statistics Committee. 2012. Ottawa: Public Works and Government Services Canada. http://www.publicsafety.gc.ca/cnt/rsrcs/pblctns/2012-ccrs/2012-ccrs-eng.pdf.

28. Public Safety Canada Portfolio Corrections Statistics Committee. 2012. Ottawa: Public Works and Government Services Canada, 46, 49. http://www.publicsafety.gc.ca/cnt/rsrcs/pblctns/2012-ccrs/2012-ccrs-eng.pdf.

29. Public Safety Canada Portfolio Corrections Statistics Committee. 2012. Ottawa: Public Works and Government Services Canada, 43. http://www.publicsafety.gc.ca/cnt/rsrcs/pblctns/2012-ccrs/2012-ccrs-eng.pdf.

30. Public Safety Canada Portfolio Corrections Statistics Committee. 2012. Ottawa: Public Works and Government Services Canada, 46, 49. http://www.publicsafety.gc.ca/cnt/rsrcs/pblctns/2012-ccrs/2012-ccrs-eng.pdf.

31. Public Safety Canada Portfolio Corrections Statistics Committee. 2012. Ottawa: Public Works and Government Services Canada, 43. http://www.publicsafety.gc.ca/cnt/rsrcs/pblctns/2012-ccrs/2012-ccrs-eng.pdf.

32. A.L. Solomon, V. Kachnowski, and A. Bhati. 2005. *Does Parole Work? Analyzing the Impact of Postprison Supervision on Rearrest Outcomes*. Washington: Urban Institute. http://www.urban.org/UploadedPDF/311156_Does_Parole_Work.pdf.

33. B.M. Huebner and M.T. Berg. 2011. "Examining the Sources of Variation in Risks for Recidivism." *Justice Quarterly* 28, no. 1: 146–73.

34. A.L. Solomon, V. Kachnowski, and A. Bhati. 2005. *Does Parole Work? Analyzing the Impact of Postprison Supervision on Rearrest Outcomes*. Washington: Urban Institute. http://www.urban.org/UploadedPDF/311156_Does_Parole_Work.pdf.

35. Public Safety Canada Portfolio Corrections Statistics Committee. 2012. Ottawa: Public Works and Government Services Canada, 46. http://www.publicsafety.gc.ca/cnt/rsrcs/pblctns/2012-ccrs/2012-ccrs-eng.pdf.

36. Parole Board of Canada. 2012. *Performance Monitoring Report 2010–2011*. Ottawa: Author, 44. http://pbc-clcc.gc.ca/rprts/pmr/pmr_2010_2011/pmr_2010_2011-eng.pdf.

37. K. Bumby, M. Carter, S. Gibel, L. Gilligan, and R. Stroker. 2007. *Increasing Public Safety Through Successful Offender Reentry: Evidence-Based and Emerging Practices in Corrections*. Washington: Center for Effective Public Policy and Bureau of Justice Assistance. http://www.cepp.com/documents/CEPP%20SVORI_final.pdf.

38. P.B. Burke. 2008. *TPC Reentry Handbook: Implementing the NIC Transition for Prison to the Community Model*. Washington: National Institute of Corrections, U.S. Department of Justice. http://static.nicic.gov/Library/022669.pdf.

39. L. Gideon. 2009. "What Shall I Do Now?: Released Offenders' Expectations for Supervision Upon Release." *International Journal of Offender Therapy and Comparative Criminology* 53, no. 1: 43–56.

40. C.T. Griffiths and D. Murdoch. 2014. *Canadian Corrections*. 4th ed. Toronto: Nelson, 256.

41. M.R. Maidment. 2006. *Doing Time on the Outside: Deconstructing the Benevolent Community*. Toronto: University of Toronto Press, 103.

42. M.S. Daigle and H. Naud. 2012. "Risk of Dying by Suicide Inside or Outside Prison: The Shortened Lives of Male Offenders." *Canadian Journal of Criminology and Criminal Justice* 54, no. 4: 511–28.

43. M. Olotu, D. Luong, C. MacDonald, M. McKay, S. Heath, N. Allegri, and E. Loree. 2011. *Report of the Evaluation of CSC's Community Corrections. Chapter 1: Correctional Interventions*. Ottawa: Correctional Service Canada, 47. http://www.csc-scc.gc.ca/text/pa/ex-cci-fin/ev-cci-fin-eng.pdf.

44. J.B. Helfgott and E. Gunnison. 2008. "The Influence of Social Distance on Community Corrections Officer Perceptions of Offender Reentry Needs." *Federal Probation* 72, no. 1: 9–14.

45. S. Novac, J. Herner, E. Paradis, and A. Kellen. 2006. *Justice and Injustice: Homelessness, Crime, Victimization, and the Criminal Justice System* (Research Paper #207). Toronto: Centre for Urban and Community Studies, University of Toronto. http://www.urbancentre.utoronto.ca/pdfs/researchprojects/Novacet-al-207-JusticeHomeless2006.pdf.

46. R. Zorzi, S. Scott, D. Doherty, A. Engman, C. Lauzon, M. McGuire, and J. Ward. 2006. "Housing Options Upon Discharge from Correctional Facilities." Ottawa: Canada Mortgage and Housing Corporation. Accessed March 10, 2014. http://www.cmhc-schl.gc.ca/odpub/pdf/65340.pdf?fr=1343101698796.

47. H. Echenberg and J. Jensen. 2009. "Risk Factors for Homelessness." Ottawa: Social Affairs Division, Parliamentary Information and Research Service, 2. Accessed March 10, 2014. http://www.parl.gc.ca/Content/LOP/ResearchPublications/prb0851-e.pdf.

48. S. Poirier (Chairperson). 2008. *Decades of Darkness, Moving Towards the Light: A Review of the Prison System in Newfoundland and Labrador*. St. John's: Government of Newfoundland/Labrador, 27. http://www.justice.gov.nl.ca/just/publications/ac_report.pdf.

49. S. Poirier (Chairperson). 2008. *Decades of Darkness, Moving Towards the Light: A Review of the Prison System in Newfoundland and Labrador*. St. John's: Government of Newfoundland/Labrador, 30. http://www.justice.gov.nl.ca/just/publications/ac_report.pdf.

50. C.T. Griffiths, Y. Dandurand, and D. Murdoch. 2007. *The Social Reintegration of Offenders and Crime Prevention*. Ottawa: National Crime Prevention Centre,

Public Safety Canada. http://publications .gc.ca/collections/collection_2009/sp-ps/ PS4-49-2007E.pdf.

51. Social Planning and Research Council of Hamilton. 2010. *Hamilton Community Correctional Services Needs Assessment.* Hamilton: Author, 15. http://www.sprc .hamilton.on.ca/wp-content/uploads/2010/ 02/Hamilton-Community-Correctional-Services -Needs-Assessment-February-2010.pdf.

52. Social Planning and Research Council of Hamilton. 2010. *Hamilton Community Correctional Services Needs Assessment.* Hamilton: Author, 16. http://www.sprc .hamilton.on.ca/wp-content/uploads/2010/02/ Hamilton-Community-Correctional-Services -Needs-Assessment-February-2010.pdf.

53. Ibid.

54. Ibid.

55. Correctional Service of Canada. 2013. "Commissioner's Directive: Community Supervision." Accessed March 10, 2014. http://www.csc-scc.gc.ca/policy-and -legislation/715-1-cd-eng.shtml.

56. M.R. Maidment. 2006. *Doing Time on the Outside: Deconstructing the Benevolent Community.* Toronto: University of Toronto Press, 111.

57. B. Steiner, L.F. Travis, M.D. Makarios, and T. Brickley. 2011. "The Influence of Parole Officers' Attitudes on Supervision Practices." *Justice Quarterly* 28, no. 6: 903–27.

58. E. Gunnison and J.B. Helfgott. 2011. "Factors That Hinder Offender Reentry Success: A View from Community Corrections Officers." *International Journal of Offender Therapy and Comparative Criminology* 55, no. 2: 296.

59. J. Helfgott. 1997. "Ex-offender Needs versus Criminal Opportunity in Seattle, Washington." *Federal Probation* 61, no. 2: 12–24.

60. M. Lynch. 1998. "Waste Managers? The New Penology, Crime Fighting, and Parole Agent Identity." *Law and Society Review* 32:839–69.

61. P. Bulman. 2013. "Sex Offenders Monitored by GPS Found to Commit Fewer Crimes." *NIJ Journal* 271: 22–25. Accessed March 10, 2014. http://www.nij .gov/journals/271/gps-monitoring.htm.

62. E. McGrath. 2012. "Reentry Courts: Providing a Second Chance for Incarcerated Mothers and Their Children." *Family Court Review* 50, no. 1: 113–27.

63. L. Stone. 2012. "After an Inmate's Release, the Struggle Begins." *Calgary Herald*, May 25.

64. C. Glube (Chair). 2006. "Moving Forward with Women's Corrections." Ottawa: Correctional Service of Canada. Accessed March 10, 2014. http://www.csc-scc.gc.ca/ text/prgrm/fsw/wos29/wos29-eng.shtml.

65. R. Sampson (Chair). 2007. *Report of the Correctional Service of Canada Review Panel.* Ottawa: Minister of Public Works and Government Services Canada. http:// publications.gc.ca/collections/collection _2008/ps-sp/PS84-14-2007E.pdf.

66. T.P. LeBel. 2011. "'If One Doesn't Get You Another One Will': Formerly Incarcerated Persons' Perceptions of Discrimination." *Prison Journal* 92, no. 1: 63–87.

67. F.I. Matheson, S. Doherty, and B.A. Grant. 2009. *Women Offender Substance Abuse Programming & Community Reintegration.* Ottawa: Correctional Service of Canada. http://www.csc-scc.gc.ca/research/092/ r202-eng.pdf.

68. R. Gobeil. 2008. "Staying Out: Women's Perceptions of Challenges and Protective Factors in Community Reintegration." Ottawa: Correctional Service of Canada. Accessed March 10, 2014. http://www .csc-scc.gc.ca/research/r201-eng.shtml.

69. S. Wine. 1992. *A Motherhood Issue: The Impact of Criminal Justice System Involvement on Women and Their Children.* Ottawa: Solicitor General, 111.

70. L. Stone. 2012. "After an Inmate's Release, the Struggle Begins." *Calgary Herald*, May 25.

71. M. Axford and R. Ruddell. 2010. "Police-Parole Partnerships in Canada: A Review of a Promising Programme." *International Journal of Police Science and Management* 12, no. 2: 274–86.

72. C.T. Griffiths, Y. Dandurand, and D. Murdoch. 2007. *The Social Reintegration of Offenders and Crime Prevention.* Ottawa: National Crime Prevention Centre, Public Safety Canada. http://publications .gc.ca/collections/collection_2009/sp-ps/ PS4-49-2007E.pdf.

73. S. Steen, T. Opsal, P. Lovegrove, and S. McKinzey. 2012. "Putting Parolees Back in Prison: Discretion in the Parole

Revocation Process." *Criminal Justice Review* 38, no. 1: 70–93.

74. Le Protectuer du Citoyen. 2011. *Report by the Quebec Ombudsman. Toward Services That Are Better Adjusted to Detainees with Mental Disorders.* Quebec City: Author, 6. http://www .protecteurducitoyen.qc.ca/fileadmin/medias/ pdf/rapports_speciaux/10-05-11_Rapport _sante_mentale_FINAL_EN.pdf.

75. R.G. Zevitz. 2006. "Sex Offender Community Notification: Its Role in Recidivism and Offender Reintegration." *Criminal Justice Studies* 19, no. 2: 193–208.

76. "'You Have No Rights. Get Out' B.C. Town Tells Sex Offender." 2005. *CBC News,* October 19. Accessed March 10, 2014. http://www.cbc.ca/news/ canada/story/2005/10/19/merritt-sex -offender051019.html?print.

77. S.J. Bahr, L. Harris, J.K. Fisher, and A.H. Armstrong. 2010. "Successful Reentry: What Differentiates Successful and Unsuccessful Parolees?" *International Journal of Offender Therapy and Comparative Criminology* 54, no. 5: 667–92.

78. M. Makarios, B. Steiner, and L.T. Travis. 2010. "Examining the Predictors of Recidivism Among Men and Women Released from Prison in Ohio." *Criminal Justice and Behavior* 37, no. 12: 1377–91.

79. C.A. Visher, S.A. Debus-Sherrill, and J. Yahner. 2011. "Employment after Prison: A Longitudinal Study of Former Prisoners." *Justice Quarterly* 28, no. 5: 698–718.

80. S. Steen, T. Opsal, P. Lovegrove, and S. McKinzey. 2012. "Putting Parolees Back in Prison: Discretion in the Parole Revocation Process." *Criminal Justice Review* 38, no. 1: 70–93.

81. J.C. Cochran. 2014. "Breaches in the Wall: Imprisonment, Social Support, and Recidivism." *Journal of Research in Crime and Delinquency* 51, no. 2: 200–29.

82. Public Safety Canada Portfolio Corrections Statistics Committee. 2012. Ottawa: Public Works and Government Services Canada, 95. http://www.publicsafety.gc.ca/cnt/rsrcs/ pblctns/2012-ccrs/2012-ccrs-eng.pdf.

83. Public Safety Canada Portfolio Corrections Statistics Committee. 2012. Ottawa: Public Works and Government Services Canada, 58. http://www.publicsafety.gc.ca/cnt/ rsrcs/pblctns/2012-ccrs/2012-ccrs-eng.pdf.

365

84. D.J. Farole. 2003. *The Harlem Parole Reentry Court Evaluation: Implementation and Preliminary Impacts.* New York: Center for Court Innovation. http://www.courtinnovation.org/pdf/harlem_reentry_eval.pdf.

85. S. Maruna and T. LeBel. 2003. "Welcome Home? Examining the 'Reentry Court' from a Strengths-Based Perspective." *Western Criminology Review* 4, no. 2: 91–107. Accessed March 10, 2014. http://wcr.sonoma.edu/v4n2/manuscripts/marunalebel.pdf.

86. M.K. Olotu, M. Beaupre, and P. Verbrugge. 2009. "Evaluation Report: Electronic Monitoring Program Pilot." Ottawa: Correctional Service of Canada. Accessed March 10, 2014. http://www.csc-scc.gc.ca/text/pa/empp/index-eng.shtml. http://www.casomb.org/docs/CASOMB%20Report%20Jan%202010_Final%20Report.pdf.

87. P. Bulman. 2013. "Sex Offenders Monitored by GPS Found to Commit Fewer Crimes." *NIJ Journal* 271. February. 22-25. Accessed February 16, 2014. http://www.nij.gov/journals/271/gps-monitoring.htm.

88. C.T. Lowenkamp, J. Pealer, and P. Smith. 2006. "Adhering to the Risk and Need Principles: Does It Matter for Supervision-Based Programs?" *Federal Probation* 70, no. 3: 3–8.

89. R.G. Zevitz. 2006. "Sex Offender Community Notification: Its Role in Recidivism and Offender Reintegration." *Criminal Justice Studies* 19, no. 2: 193–208.

90. Y.N. Brannon, J.S. Levenson, T. Fortney, and J.N. Baker. 2007. "Attitudes about Community Notification: A Comparison of Sexual Offenders and the Non-offending Public." *Sexual Abuse: A Journal of Research and Treatment* 19, no. 4: 369–79.

91. R. Tewksbury. 2005. "Collateral Consequences of Offender Registration." *Journal of Contemporary Criminal Justice* 21, no. 1: 67–81.

92. J. Vess, B. Langskaill, A. Day, M. Powell, and J. Graffam. 2011. "A Comparative Analysis of Australian Sex Offender Legislation for Sex Offender Registries." *Australian & New Zealand Journal of Criminology* 44, no. 3: 404–24.

93. J. Vess, A. Day, M. Powell, and J. Graffam. 2013. "International Sex Offender Registration Laws: Research and Evaluation Issues Based on a Review of Current Scientific Literature." *Police Practice & Research* 14, no. 3: 205–18.

94. Z. Hamilton. 2010. *Do Reentry Courts Reduce Recidivism? Results from the Harlem Parole Reentry Court.* Washington, D.C.: Center for Court Innovation. http://www.courtinnovation.org/sites/default/files/Reentry_Evaluation.pdf.

95. D.J. Farole. 2003. *The Harlem Parole Reentry Court Evaluation: Implementation and Preliminary Impacts.* New York: Center for Court Innovation. http://www.courtinnovation.org/pdf/harlem_reentry_eval.pdf.

96. S. Maruna and T. LeBel. 2003. "Welcome Home? Examining the 'Reentry Court' from a Strengths-Based Perspective." *Western Criminology Review* 4, no. 2: 91–107. Accessed March 10, 2014. http://wcr.sonoma.edu/v4n2/manuscripts/marunalebel.pdf.

CHAPTER 13

1. R.B. Cormier. 2002. *Restorative Justice: Directions and Principles—Developments in Canada.* User Report 2002-02. Ottawa: Department of the Solicitor General Canada. http://publications.gc.ca/collections/Collection/JS42-107-2002E.pdf.

2. H. Zehr and A. Gohar. 2002. *The Little Book of Restorative Justice.* Intercourse, PA: Good Books, 33. http://www.unicef.org/tdad/littlebookrjpakaf.pdf.

3. Y. Dandurand and C.T. Griffiths. 2006. *Handbook on Restorative Justice Programmes.* Vienna, Austria: United Nations Office on Drugs and Crime. http://www.unodc.org/pdf/criminal_justice/06-56290_Ebook.pdf.

4. G. Johnstone and D.W. Van Ness. 2006. *Handbook of Restorative Justice.* Portland: Willan Publishing.

5. G. Bazemore and C.T. Griffiths. 1997. "Conferences, Circles, Boards, and Mediations: The 'New Wave' of Community Justice Decision Making." *Federal Probation* 61, no. 2: 25–37.

6. Y. Dandurand and C.T. Griffiths. 2006. *Handbook on Restorative Justice Programmes.* Vienna, Austria: United Nations Office on Drugs and Crime. http://www.unodc.org/pdf/criminal_justice/06-56290_Ebook.pdf.

7. Prison Fellowship International. 2008. "What Is Restorative Justice?" Washington, D.C.: Centre for Justice & Reconciliation. Accessed March 9, 2014. http://www.pfi.org/cjr/restorative-justice.

8. J. Dickson-Gilmore and C. LaPrairie. 2005. *Will the Circle Be Unbroken? Aboriginal Communities, Restorative Justice and the Challenges of Conflict and Change.* Toronto: University of Toronto Press.

9. A. Acorn. 2004. *Compulsory Compassion: A Critique of Restorative Justice.* Vancouver: UBC Press.

10. "Father of 2 Girls Who Froze to Death Needs Treatment, Not Jail, Judge Hears." 2009. *CBC News*, February 13. Accessed March 9, 2014. http://www.cbc.ca/news/canada/saskatchewan/story/2009/02/13/sentencing.html.

11. "Father of Girls Who Froze to Death Gets 3 Years in Prison." 2009. *CBC News*, March 6. Accessed March 9, 2014. http://www.cbc.ca/news/canada/saskatchewan/father-of-girls-who-froze-to-death-gets-3-years-in-prison-1.840881.

12. K. Libin. 2009. "Sentencing Circles: The Jury's Out." *National Post*, February 28, A10.

13. C. Purdy. 2009. "Healing Won't Happen in Jail." *The Globe and Mail*, February 14, A8.

14. C.T. Griffiths and R. Hamilton. 1996. "Sanctioning and Healing: Restorative Justice in Canadian Aboriginal Communities." In *Restorative Justice: Theory, Practice, and Research*, edited by J. Hudson and B. Galaway, 175–91. Monsey, NY: Criminal Justice Press.

15. R.G. Green. 1997. "Aboriginal Community Sentencing and Mediation: Within and Without the Circle." *Manitoba Law Journal* 25, no. 1: 77–125.

16. R.G. Green. 1998. *Justice in Aboriginal Communities: Sentencing Alternatives.* Saskatoon: Purich Publishing.

17. L.S.T. Mandamin. 2003. "Peacemaking and the Tsuu T'ina Court." *Native Law Centre* 8, no. 1: 1–4.

18. Ibid.

19. Alberta Solicitor General and Public Security. 2011. *2011 Survey of Albertans.* Edmonton: Author. http://www.solgps.alberta.ca/Publications1/Survey%20of%20Albertans/2011%20Survey%20of%20Albertans.pdf.

20. L. Presser and P. Van Voorhis. 2002. "Values and Evaluation: Assessing Process and Outcomes of Restorative Justice Programs." *Crime and Delinquency* 48, no. 1: 162–88.

21. A. Cameron. 2006. "Sentencing Circles and Intimate Violence: A Canadian Feminist Perspective." *Canadian Journal of Women and the Law* 18, no. 2: 479–512.

22. L. Presser and P. Van Voorhis. 2002. "Values and Evaluation: Assessing Process and Outcomes of Restorative Justice Programs." *Crime and Delinquency* 48, no. 1: 162–88.

23. A. Shagufta. 2010. "Should Restorative Justice Be Used for Cases of Domestic Violence?" *International Journal of Restorative Justice* 6, no. 1: 1–48.

24. A. Bates, R. Saunders, and C. Wilson. 2007. "Doing Something About It: A Follow-Up Study of Sex Offenders Participating in Thames Valley Circles of Support and Accountability." *British Journal of Community Justice* 5, no. 1: 19-42.

25. A. Bates, R. Macrae, C. Webb, and D. Williams. 2011. "Ever-Increasing Circles: A Descriptive Study of Hampshire and Thames Valley Circles of Support and Accountability 2002–2009." *Journal of Sexual Aggression* 18, no. 3: 355–73.

26. C. Wilson. 2011. "The Realities of Practice." In *A Community-Based Approach to the Reduction of Sexual Reoffending*, edited by S. Hanvey, T. Philpot, and C. Wilson, 58–71. London: Jessica Kingsley.

27. C. Wilson, T. Philpot, and S. Hanvey. 2011. *A Community-Based Approach to the Reduction of Sexual Offending.* London, England: Jessica Kingsley Publishers.

28. L.W. Sherman and H. Strang. 2007. *Restorative Justice: The Evidence.* London: The Smith Institute. http://www.smith-institute.org.uk/file/RestorativeJusticeTheEvidenceFullreport.pdf.

29. T. Rugge, J. Bonta, and S. Wallace-Capretta. 2005. *Evaluation of the Collaborative Justice Project: A Restorative Justice Program for Serious Crime.* Ottawa: Public Safety Canada. http://www.publicsafety.gc.ca/cnt/rsrcs/pblctns/cllbrtv-jstc-prjct/cllbrtv-jstc-prjct-eng.pdf.

30. T. Van Camp and J.-A. Wemmers. 2013. "Victim Satisfaction with Restorative Justice: More Than Simply Procedural Justice." *International Review of Victimology* 19, no. 2: 117–43.

31. L.W. Sherman and H. Strang. 2007. *Restorative Justice: The Evidence.* London: The Smith Institute. http://www.smith-institute.org.uk/file/RestorativeJusticeTheEvidenceFullreport.pdf.

32. T. Rugge and T.-L. Scott. 2009. "Restorative Justice's Impact on Participants' Psychological and Physical Health." Ottawa: Public Safety Canada. Accessed March 9, 2014. http://www.publicsafety.gc.ca/cnt/rsrcs/pblctns/2009-03-rjp/index-eng.aspx.

33. L.W. Sherman and H. Strang. 2007. *Restorative Justice: The Evidence.* London: The Smith Institute. http://www.smith-institute.org.uk/file/RestorativeJusticeTheEvidenceFullreport.pdf.

34. T. Rugge, J. Bonta, and S. Wallace-Capretta. 2005. *Evaluation of the Collaborative Justice Project: A Restorative Justice Program for Serious Crime.* Ottawa: Public Safety Canada. http://www.publicsafety.gc.ca/cnt/rsrcs/pblctns/cllbrtv-jstc-prjct/cllbrtv-jstc-prjct-eng.pdf.

35. J. Fitzgerald. 2008. "Does Circle Sentencing Reduce Aboriginal Offending?" *Crime and Justice Bulletin* 115. Sydney: NSW Bureau of Crime, Statistics, and Research. http://www.lawlink.nsw.gov.au/lawlink/bocsar/ll_bocsar.nsf/vwFiles/cjb115.pdf/$file/cjb115.pdf.

36. J. Bonta, S. Wallace-Capretta, J. Rooney and K. Mcanoy. 2010. "An Outcome Evaluation of a Restorative Justice Alternative to Incarceration." *Contemporary Justice Review* 5 no. 4: 319–38.

37. R.J. Wilson, J.E. Picheca, and M. Prinzo. 2007. Evaluating the Effectiveness of Professionally-Facilitated Volunteerism in the Community-Based Management of High Risk Sexual Offenders: Part One—Effects on Participants and Stakeholders. *Howard Journal of Criminal Justice* 46:289–302.

38. C. Wilson, T. Philpot, and S. Hanvey. 2011. *A Community-Based Approach to the Reduction of Sexual Offending.* London, England: Jessica Kingsley Publishers.

39. T. Rugge and T.-L. Scott. 2009. "Restorative Justice's Impact on Participants' Psychological and Physical Health." Ottawa: Public Safety Canada. Accessed March 9, 2014. http://www.publicsafety.gc.ca/cnt/rsrcs/pblctns/2009-03-rjp/index-eng.aspx.

40. Y. Dandurand and C.T. Griffiths. 2006. *Handbook on Restorative Justice Programmes.* Vienna, Austria: United Nations Office on Drugs and Crime. http://www.unodc.org/pdf/criminal_justice/06-56290_Ebook.pdf.

41. J. Couture, T. Parker, R. Couture, and P. Laboucane. 2001. "A Cost-Benefit Analysis of Hollow Water's Community Holistic Healing Process." Accessed March 9, 2014. http://www.publicsafety.gc.ca/cnt/rsrcs/pblctns/cst-bnft-hllw-wtr/index-eng.aspx.

42. T. Lajeunesse and Associates, Ltd. 1996. *Evaluation of Community Holistic Circle Healing: Hollow Water First Nation, Vol. 1. Final Report.* Winnipeg: Manitoba Department of Justice.

CHAPTER 14

1. C. Klingele, M.S. Scott, and W.J. Dickey. 2010. "Reimagining Criminal Justice." *Wisconsin Law Review* 4: 953.

2. J. Vess, A. Day, M. Powell, and J.G. Raffam. 2013. "International Sex Offender Registration Law: Research and Evaluation Issues Based on a Review of Current Scientific Literature." *Police Practice and Research* 14, no. 3: 205–18.

3. J. Roman. 2013. "Cost-Benefit Analysis of Criminal Justice Reforms." *NIJ Journal* 272. Accessed March 9, 2014. https://ncjrs.gov/pdffiles1/nij/241929.pdf.

4. R. Pawson. 2006. *Evidence-Based Policy.* London: Sage, 7.

5. A. Fox. "What Lessons Can Business Teach Criminal Justice? Invest in Research." *Huffington Post*, July 1. Accessed March 9, 2014. http://www.huffingtonpost.com/

367

aubrey-fox/what-lessons-can-business
_b_3530295.html.

6. D.P. Mears. 2007. "Toward Rational and Evidence-Based Crime Policy." *Journal of Criminal Justice* 35, no. 6: 667–82.

7. D.P. Mears and J.C. Barnes. 2010. "Toward a Systematic Foundation for Identifying Evidence-Based Criminal Justice Sanctions and Their Relative Effectiveness." *Journal of Criminal Justice* 38, no. 4: 702–10.

8. C.G. Nicholl. 1999. *Community Policing, Community Justice, and Restorative Justice: Exploring the Links for the Delivery of a Balanced Approach to Public Safety.* Washington, D.C.: Office of Community Oriented Policing Services, Department of Justice, 48. http://www.copos.usdoj.gov/Publicaions/e09990014_web.pdf.

9. C. Klingele, M.S. Scott, and W.J. Dickey. 2010. "Reimagining Criminal Justice." *Wisconsin Law Review* 4: 953.

10. C. Klingele, M.S. Scott, and W.J. Dickey. 2010. "Reimagining Criminal Justice." *Wisconsin Law Review* 4: 959.

11. J. Schoenfeld. 2012. "Evidence-based Policy and the Politics of Criminal Justice Reform." *Criminology and Public Policy* 11, no. 2: 380.

12. R.A. Fairfax. 2011. "From 'Overcriminalization' to 'Smart on Crime': American Criminal Justice Reform— Legacy and Prospects." *Journal of Law, Economics & Policy* 7, no 4: 597–98.

13. "Over-criminalization." 2014. USLegal, March 9. http://definitions.uslegal.com/o/over-criminalization/.

14. J.G. Malcolm. 2013. "Defining the Problem and Scope of Over-Criminalization and Over-Federalization: Testimony before the Committee on the Judiciary Over-criminalization Task Force, U.S. House of Representatives, June 14. Accessed March 9, 2014.

15. J.M. Doyle. 2010. "Learning from Error in American Criminal Justice." *Journal of Criminal Law and Criminology* 100, no. 1: 109–47. http://heritage.org/research/testimony/2013/06/defining-the-problem-and-scope-of-overcriminalization-and-overfederalization.

16. Ibid.

17. P. O'Hara. 2005. *Why Law Enforcement Organizations Fail.* Durham, NC: Carolina Academic Press.

Index

369

373

375

376

377

378

379